International Business–Society Management

Linking corporate responsibility and globalization

Rob van Tulder,
with Alex van der Zwart

Routledge
Taylor & Francis Group

LONDON AND NEW YORK

First published 2006
by Routledge
2 Park Square, Milton Park, Abingdon, Oxon OX14 4RN

Simultaneously published in the USA and Canada
by Routledge
270 Madison Ave, New York, NY 10016

Reprinted 2006

Routledge is an imprint of the Taylor & Francis Group

© 2006 Rob van Tulder, with Alex van der Zwart

Typeset in Perpetua and Bell Gothic by
Florence Production Ltd, Stoodleigh, Devon
Printed and bound in Great Britain by
TJ International Ltd, Padstow, Cornwall

British Library Cataloguing in Publication Data
A catalogue record for this book is available from the British Library

Library of Congress Cataloging in Publication Data
Tulder, Rob van.
 International business–society management: linking corporate
 responsibility and globalization/Rob van Tulder and Alex van der
 Zwart.
     p. cm.
 "Simultaneously published in the USA and Canada"
 Includes bibliographical references and index.
 1. International business enterprises.   2. Social responsibility of
 business.   3. Globalization.   I. Zwart, Alex van der.   II. Title.
 HD62.4.T84 2006
 658.4′08 – dc22   2005019517

ISBN10: 0–415–34241–4 (hbk)
ISBN10: 0–415–34240–6 (pbk)

ISBN13: 9–78–0–415–34241–4 (hbk)
ISBN13: 9–78–0–415–34240–7 (pbk)

International Business–Society Management

Entering the twenty-first century, the traditional divides between state, civil society and markets have become redefined. Bargaining over corporate responsibilities increasingly centres around corporate reputation and the question of whether businesses are part of society's problems or part of their solution.

International Business–Society Management discusses and contextualizes contemporary debates on international corporate social responsibility, globalization and the impact of reputation, and integrates them into a new and coherent framework: Societal Interface Management. Using this unique framework, it explores the interfaces between international corporations, governments and civil society representatives. Comprehensive and wide-ranging in international analysis and scholarship, the text applies this framework in action via in-depth case chapters including studies of:

- Nike – labour circumstances
- Shell – waste dumping
- Triumph International – dictatorship
- GlaxoSmithKline – HIV/AIDS
- ExxonMobil – global warming.

An accompanying website (www.ib-sm.org) specially designed for this book contains many other case studies applying the same framework, as well as issue dossiers containing additional information on the challenges that confront international firms.

Drawing on a wealth of experience, both in research and teaching, the authors have developed a text that will be essential reading for all those studying and teaching business ethics, international business, political economics, economic geography, reputation, public relations, corporate social responsibility or corporate accountability.

Rob van Tulder is Professor of International Business Studies at the Rotterdam School of Management.

Alex van der Zwart is a business consultant specializing in Business–Society Management, corporate social responsibility and reputation and sustainability issues.

Contents

v

CONTENTS

Figures

FIGURES

Tables

Boxes

Abbreviations and acronyms

AA1000	AccountAbility 1000 (standard of Institute of Social and Ethical Accountability)
ABP	Algemeen Burgerlijk Pensioenfonds (General Pension Fund in the Netherlands)
AEX	Amsterdam Stock Exchange
AICPA	American Institute of Certified Public Accountants
ANGO	Advocacy Oriented Non-Governmental Organization
APEC	Asia Pacific Economic Cooperation
ART	antiretroviral therapies
ARV	antiretroviral (medicines)
ASEAN	Association of South East Asian Nations
B&S	Business and Society Management
BAT	Best Available Technology; British American Tobacco
BCI	Business-Community Involvement
BCN	Burma Center Netherlands
BINGO	Business Interested Non-Governmental Organization
BiS	Business in Society
BONGO	Business Organized Non-Governmental Organization
BRONGO	Broker Oriented Non-Governmental Organization
B–SM	Business–Society Management
b2b	business-to-business
b2c	business-to-consumer
CCC	Corporate Communication Centre; Clean Clothes Campaign
CCCB	Center for Corporate Citizenship
CEFTA	Central European Free Trade Association
CEO	Chief Executive Officer
CEPAA	Council on Economic Priorities Accreditation Agency
CERES	Coalition for Environmentally Responsible Economies
CESR	Committee of European Securities Regulators
CFO	Chief Financial Officer
CFP	Corporate Financial Performance
CIIR	Catholic Institute for International Relations
CIS	Commonwealth of Independent States
CM	Common Market
CO_2	carbon dioxide
CPB	Central Planning Bureau (Dutch planning institute)
CSP	corporate social performance
CSR	corporate *self*-responsibility; corporate social responsiveness; corporate social responsibility; corporate societal responsibility
CU	customs union
DANGO	Direct Action Oriented Non-Governmental Organization

DJSGI	Dow Jones Sustainability Group Index
DNDI	Drugs for Neglected Diseases Initiative
DONGO	Discussion and Dialogue Oriented Non-Governmental Organization
DSI400	Domini 400 Social Index
EBNSC	European Business Network for social cohesion
EC	European Commission
EFQM	European Foundation for Quality Management
EFTA	European Free Trade Agreement
EITI	Extractive Industries Transparency Initiative
EMU	Economic and Monetary Union
EPU	Economic and Political Union
ERT	European Roundtable of Industrialists
ETUC	European Trade Union Confederation
ETUI	European Trade Union Institute
EU	European Union
Eurosif	European Sustainable and Responsible Investment Forum
EWC	European Works Council
FAO	Food and Agricultural Organisation (UN)
FASB	Financial Accounting Standards Board
FBC	Free Burma Coalition
FBS	Foundation for Business and Society
FCAA	Funders Concerned about Aids
FCC	Federal Communications Commission
FD	Financieele Dagblad (Dutch Financial Times)
FDA	Food and Drug Administration
FDI	Foreign Direct Investment
FERC	Federal Energy Regulatory Commission
FIFA	Fédération Internationale de Football Association
FLA	Fair Labor Association
FNV	Federatie Nederlandse Vakbeweging (Dutch Federation of Trade Unions)
FOE	Friends of the Earth
FSC	Forest Stewardship Council
FSG	Federal Sentencing Guidelines
FT	Financial Times
FTA	Free Trade Agreement
FTAA	Free Trade Area of the Americas
fte	full-time equivalent
FTSE	Financial Times Stock Exchange
GATT	General Agreement on Tariffs and Trade
GBC	Global Business Coalition on HIV/Aids
GCC	Global Climate Coalition
GDP	Gross Domestic Product
GIN	Global Issues Network
GINGO	Government Interested Non-Governmental Organization
GMO	Genetically Modified Organisms
GNP	Gross National Product
GONGO	Government Organized Non-Governmental Organization
GRI	Global Reporting Initiatives
GSE	Government Sponsored Enterprise
HDI	Human Development Index
HNGO	Hybrid Non-Governmental Organization
HRM	human resource management
HSE	Health Safety and Environment

IAS	International Accounting Standard
IB	International Business
IBE	International Business Ethics
IB–SM	International Business–Society Management
ICC	International Chamber of Commerce
ICFTU	International Confederation of Free Trade Unions
ICN	India Committee of the Netherlands (known as LIW in the Netherlands)
ICR	indifferent corporate responsibility; international corporate responsiveness; international corporate responsibility; international community responsibility
ICSID	International Centre for the Settlement of Investment Disputes
ICT	Information and Communication Technology
IFC	International Finance Corporation (World Bank)
ILO	International Labor Organization
IM	International Management
IMF	International Monetary Fund; International Metalworkers' Federation
INGO	International Non-Governmental Organization
IOC	International Olympic Committee
IPE	International Political Economy
IPR	intellectual property rights/regime
ISCT	Integrated Social Contract approach
ISO	International Standards Organisation
ITU	International Telecommunications Union
JETRO	Japan External Trade Organisation
M&As	mergers and acquisitions
MBA	Master of Business Administration
Mercosur	Southern Common Market
MFN	most-favoured nation
MITI	Ministry of International Trade and Industry
MNE	Multinational Enterprise
MSF	Médecins sans Frontières
NAFTA	North American Free Trade Agreement
NCD	Netherlands Committee of Directors
NCP	National Contact Point
NGO	Non-Governmental Organization
NRC	*NRC Handelsblad* (Dutch newspaper)
NYSE	New York Stock Exchange
ODA	Official Development Assistance
OECD	Organisation for Economic Cooperation and Development
ONGO	Operational Non-Governmental Organization
PA	Public Affairs
PCU	partial customs union
PGGM	Pensioenfonds voor de Gezondheid, Geestelijke en Maatschappelijke belangen (Dutch pension fund)
PONGO	Partnership Oriented Non-Governmental Organization
PPP	Purchasing Power Parity; Public–Private Partnership
PR	public relations
PSW	Pensioen- en Spaarfondsenwet (Dutch Pension and Savings Funds Act)
PTA	preferential trade agreement
PWBLF	Prince of Wales Business Leaders Forum
R&D	research and development
RIA	regional integration agreement
RSM	Rotterdam School of Management
SA8000	Social Accountability 8000 (standard)

SAARC	South Asian Association for Regional Cooperation
SACU	South African Customs Union
SADC	Southern African Development Community
SAFTA	South Asian Free Trade Area
S&P	Standard & Poor
SCOPE	International Business–Society Management Centre (Rotterdam School of Management)
SEC	Securities and Exchange Commission
SEPT(E)	Social, Economic, Political, Technological (and Ecological)
SER	Social-Economic Council (Netherlands)
SGO	Semi-independent/Self-Governing Organizations
SHANGO	Shareholding Non-Governmental Organization
SIF	Social Investment Forum
SINGO	Single-Issue Non-Governmental Organization
SOE	state-owned enterprise
SRI	socially responsible investment
SRO	self-regulatory organizations
STRONGO	Strategic Stakeholder Oriented Non-Governmental Organization
SUNGO	Supervisory Non-Governmental Organization
TI	Transparency International
TNC	transnational corporation
TNI	Transnationality Index
Triple-A	highest credit rating
Triple-E	Efficiency, Ethics/Equity, Effectiveness
Triple-P	People, Planet and Profit
TRIPS	Trade-Related Aspects of Intellectual Property Rights
UK	United Kingdom
UN	United Nations
UNAids	Joint United Nations Programme on HIV/Aids
UNCTAD	United Nations Conference on Trade Aid and Development
UNDP	United Nations Development Programme
UNEP	United Nations Environment Programme
UNHCR	United Nations Refugee Agency
UNICEF	United Nations Children's Fund
US	United States (of America)
Vk	*Volkskrant* (Dutch newspaper)
WBCSD	World Business Council for Sustainable Development
WEF	World Economic Forum (Davos)
WFSGI	World Federation of the Sporting Goods Industry
WHO	World Health Organisation
WHSE	Welfare, Health, Safety and Environment
WIPO	World Intellectual Property Organization
WONGO	Watchdog Oriented Non-Governmental Organization
WRM	World Rainforest Movement
WSF	World Social Forum
WTO	World Trade Organisation (previously: GATT)
WWF	World Wildlife Fund
WWW	World Wide Web

Website

International Business–Society Management is the product of an ongoing research effort on the interaction between International Business strategies, regulation and societal change. Several research projects are under way, of which only a small part has already been published. These research projects are coordinated by Professor Rob van Tulder and headed by the *SCOPE Expert Centre*, located at the department of Business–Society Management at the Rotterdam School of Management (RSM). Since its establishment in 1997, a main preoccupation of SCOPE has been to document the internationalization strategies of the largest (core) firms in the world. This book explains the main concepts and principles pioneered at RSM.

The publication of this book coincides with the launching of a website (www.ib-sm.org). The Internet offers an excellent means to keep up with research projects at the Expert Centre and perhaps even to contribute to it. It offers visitors the opportunity to comment on the book and refine its concepts and assertions. Moreover, the site is frequently updated with recent examples, research results, issue discussions and exemplary cases. The website gives tutors access to material for discussions in class or courses.

The website contains the following material:

- **Cases:** many additional cases, employing the methodology found in Part III
- **Issues:** issue dossiers of many of the issues discussed in this volume, applying the methodology of Chapter 10
- **International Business:** links to ongoing SCOPE research projects; full coverage of the latest publications and PhD dissertations
- **Codes of conduct:** information on general research on codes, and their effectiveness as regards specific issues (child labour, poverty, labour conditions, diseases)
- **Stakeholder dialogue:** information on ongoing research on dialogues and applying the principles of a strategic stakeholder dialogue
- **Reputation:** links to the Corporate Communication Centre (CCC) of the Department of Business–Society Management at RSM
- **Leaders:** up-to-date information on leadership research projects
- **Business ethics:** links to Ethicon, the International Business Ethics Centre of the Department of Business–Society Management at RSM
- **NGO strategies:** studies on collaborative or conflict strategies of NGO
- **Development:** link to ECSAD, the collaborative expert centre on sustainable business and development collaboration
- **Skills:** how to survive in the *international bargaining society*; a website with links to all the relevant skills (based on the Skill Sheets by Rob van Tulder).

Preface and acknowledgements

LINKING CORPORATE RESPONSIBILITY AND GLOBALIZATION

The original function of catchwords was to aid printers. The first word of a page was printed in the bottom right-hand corner of the preceding page in order to help the printer gather the printed sheets in the correct order before they were bound. Today catchwords have been promoted to head the pages of newspapers and journals, in the form of concepts or phrases reiterating particular messages. Catchwords are more than a summary of a particular matter; they are supposed to initiate change by binding people to the principles they embody. As Scottish writer Robert Louis Stevenson (1850–1894) once stated: 'man is a creature who lives not upon bread alone, but primarily by catchwords'.

The key catchwords of the 1990s were 'globalization', 'liberalization' and 'privatization'. In the twenty-first century, 'corporate responsibility', 'corporate citizenship', 'accountability' and 'transparency' have rapidly become the latest additions to the list of catchwords. Hardly a day goes by without some reference being made by the media to globalization and corporate responsibility. Firms are not necessarily held responsible for (global) societal problems, but they are increasingly considered to be part of 'the' solution. Consequently, managers are confronted with an ever-expanding range of societal issues that they are expected to address: from poverty, child labour, global warming, food safety, HIV/Aids to dictatorial regimes. While the catchwords of the past decade differ, the underlying messages are strongly related and show remarkable similarities. Firms that are endeavouring to be good 'global corporate citizens' are clearly trying to address two decades of trends at the same time.

Catchwords are almost always very broad analytical (container) concepts where the positive ideology associated with the term often obscures the discussion, analysis and, consequently, appropriate action. Adherents to catchwords can fall victim to their general appeal. Despite the abundance of corporate 'responsibility' instruments such as codes of conduct, sustainability reports and business–community projects most people still regard these efforts essentially as 'public relations' activities. At present, many firms lack legitimacy in a manner comparable to the legitimacy problems of governments in the 1990s. Critics argue that 'corporate citizenship' is a contradiction in terms: corporations are not citizens. Catchwords, if not supported by sophisticated concepts and translated into unambiguous action, risk becoming ideologies or belief systems and losing momentum as rapidly as they gained popularity. There are already signs that the corporate responsibility movement is faltering, as in the case of the globalization movement in the second half of the 1990s.

One of the explicit objectives of this book is to contribute to sustaining the momentum of responsible business initiatives that have an important role to fulfil in addressing the sizable problems humanity still faces today. This requires that catchwords move beyond the PR-realm to be placed in a constructive and realistic framework that enables managerial, societal and scientific progress. This study confronts various catchwords with empirical reality (as far as can be known) and advances more concise categorizations and explanations. In doing so, we hope to contribute to a more systematic and realistic approach to both globalization and corporate responsibility devoid of ideological overtones. There is a 'business case' for international corporate responsibility, but it is more complex than many managers, citizens, politicians, students – and even academic scholars – perhaps would prefer it to be. Hence the book format, rather than an article.

LINKING SCIENTIFIC DISCIPLINES AND MANAGERIAL APPROACHES

The object of study of two key scientific disciplines, International Business and Business and Society, corresponds with central notions contained in popular catchwords like 'globalization' and 'corporate responsibility' respectively.

For the past two to three decades, the two disciplines largely developed in isolation. Recently, however, many scholars in these two disciplines have come to acknowledge the limits of their methods and concepts and that the time is ripe to start learning from each other. The leading research question in International Business (IB) is 'what determines the international success and failure of firms' (Peng, 2004: 106). In practice, IB is closely related to the department of strategic management of firms. The IB research agenda, however, seems to be 'running out of steam' (ibid.: 105). An increasing number of scholars attribute this to a lack of insight into societal issues. 'Although IB scholars are arguably the prime experts on Multinational Enterprises (MNEs), they have contributed relatively little to explaining and evaluating "the role of MNEs in society"' (Meyer, 2004: 261). Examining the relationship with society is therefore vital for further progress in IB research (cf. Teegen et al., 2004).

The Business and Society Management (B&S) research agenda on IB issues is yet to pick up steam. This research area is still relatively new, and its academic community fairly diverse (ranging from business ethicists and philosophers to political economists). In practice, B&S questions are habitually addressed by the department of Public Affairs of companies. One of the leading research questions in B&S is, 'how should firms interact with society at large?' Increasingly, however, IB is considered one of the most important areas for further research on Business and Society issues (cf. Veser, 2004). But this area in particular is still in its infancy: 'international corporate responsibility theory and practice is an evolving area of inquiry still at an early stage of development' (Windsor, 2004: 47).

The implication seems relatively straightforward: the disciplines are courting each other, when will the marriage take place? Unfortunately, as in human relations, scientists do not collaborate that readily. Scientific disciplines often develop through specialization (and in isolation), and for very good reasons. In the past, IB scholars displayed an empirical orientation, largely because the macro-economic models of international trade and investment did not account for firm strategies. They also focused largely on internal company processes, due to the substantial difficulties involved in conceptualizing and researching the interaction of firms with society in a meaningful and statistically relevant manner. IB scholars have their scientific roots in macro-economics, political economy, business history and strategic management studies.

B&S scholars started off with a number of theoretical and philosophical questions for which hardly any empirical data could be collected. Consequently, they focused largely on political and ethical conceptualizations and an occasional case study in order to better understand the position of companies in society. Most B&S scholars have their scientific roots in philosophy, political science, sociology and communication sciences. An effort to synthesize insights from both (and other) disciplines thus not only requires the integration of approaches, but also necessitates the bridging of scientific 'temperaments' and well-established scientific and methodological traditions. The potential marriage will be intercultural and might therefore take some time to be concluded. This book is a serious mediation effort between the courting parties and therefore adopts a multi-level and multi-disciplinary approach.

- *Multi-level*: The integration of IB and B&S presents a classic level-of-analysis problem: where to start in analysing societal processes – at the level of managers, firms (micro), networks (meso), national economies or globally (macro). Choosing any of these levels of analysis a priori jeopardizes the sophistication of the analysis and the societal and managerial relevance of its conclusions.
- *Multi-disciplinary*: Building on the collective insights of a large number of scientific disciplines requires an eclectic approach (cf. John Dunning, 1993). This book develops a number of eclectic and interdisciplinary concepts and tools that will enable us to (1) understand the nature of global societal change, and (2) explore the opportunity for firms – given these societal changes – to become a 'good company'. The leading research question for integrative International Business–Society Management thus becomes, 'what determines the international success and failure of firms in their interaction with society?'

AN INTELLECTUAL TRIBUTE

It is not the first time a synthesis of this kind has been sought. This calls for an overview of the intellectual disciplines that inform the present inquiry. This book pays immense intellectual tribute to the insights other scholars have accumulated through multi-level and multi-disciplinary research. They come from four strongly interrelated and broadly defined academic disciplines.

1 *International Business*: The 1990s saw the publication of a growing number of increasingly sophisticated introductory books on 'the International Business environment' (e.g. Morrison, 2002; Brooks *et al.*, 2004). Particularly relevant for the approach adopted in this book are the efforts of three IB scholars and their research teams who dared to take up 'big themes' in which the relationship of firms with society was central, albeit very difficult to quantify. First, the late Ray Vernon contributed through his inspiring work on firm–government bargaining relations under almost poetic titles such as *Sovereignty at Bay* (Vernon, 1971) and *In the Hurricane's Eye* (Vernon, 1998) and his efforts in collecting large quantities of primary firm-level data (the renowned Harvard Multinational Enterprise project). Second, John Dunning's seminal (1993) book, *Multinational Enterprises and the Global Economy* has provided a true interdisciplinary basis for our approach. But the present study is also a tribute to Dunning's less often cited work on what can be called 'extrinsic' motives of internationalization (see Chapter 3) and his more personal statements on the future of globalization as discussed for instance in *Global Capitalism at Bay* (Dunning, 2001). Finally, Alan Rugman's consistently holistic approach to IB both at the introductory level (Rugman and Hodgetts, 2002) and at the conceptual and empirical level proved particularly helpful. The link Rugman established between internationalization and regulatory frameworks (Rugman and Verbeke, 2004), the idea of 'flagship firms' to conceptualize the position of companies in networks (Rugman and D'Cruz, 2000) and his provocative ideas in *The End of Globalization* (Rugman, 2002) in particular, provided a backdrop for the discussions and analyses in this book.

2 *Business–Society Management and business ethics*: The expanding B&S community has produced a number of solid textbooks that exhibit strong overlap with the 'business environment' approach of IB (Waddock, 2002; Lawrence *et al.*, 2005). The approach of this book also profited much from the latest integrative analyses in business ethics expounded in *The Balanced Company* (Kaptein and Wempe, 2002), the contributions of Henk van Luijk, in corporate communication (Fombrun and van Riel, 2004) and in Business-Community Involvement (Meijs and van der Voort, 2004). The greatest tributes should go to two sources. The first is the seminal study by Tom Donaldson, *The Ethics of International Business* (1989) which established IB ethics as a credible and separate discipline. The second is the book by Steven Wartick and Donna Wood, *International Business and Society* (1999), which represents the first sophisticated attempt to move B&S into the international realm.

3 *International political economy and economic geography*: In international political economy, the recent works of Robert (and Jean) Gilpin on global capitalism (2002) proved a solid general and macro-economic point of departure for the approach in this book. In economic geography, the various editions of Peter Dicken's seminal publication *Global Shift* (2003) showed that it is possible to link location detail and sectoral depth with global overviews. John Braithwaite and Peter Drahos's book *Global Business Regulation* (2000) offered a fascinating sociological account of the role of 'epistemic communities' in shaping international regulation. The annual UNCTAD World Investment Report that has been compiled under the direction of Karl Sauvant since the early 1990s provided a platform for some of the studies that were conducted in preparation for this book – particularly the collaboration between UNCTAD and Erasmus University since 1997 in gathering the World's largest TNCs listings.

4 *International Relations*: The pioneering work of political scientists and International Relations scholars on multinational enterprises and international regulation provided a solid foundation on which this book could build. The classic work of Robert Cox, *Production, Power and World Order* (1987), is a case in point. In addition, a large number of projects at the Berkeley Roundtable on the International Economy (BRIE) coordinated by John Zysman and Stephen Cohen, as well as the work of John Gerard Ruggie on global governance and Peter Katzenstein on business-government relations have showed that it is possible to integrate company strategy into international relations. Insights from institutional economics (Geoff Hodgson) and the regulation school (Robert Boyer) provided the vital ingredients to link institutional change with business strategies, while ideas concerning the concept of industrial diplomacy by John Stopford and Susan Strange (1991) helped shape the rival actor perspective in this book. An earlier study by van Tulder and Junne (1988) highlighted the role of multinational enterprises in technological development and built on the seminal and inspired work of Chris Freeman (such as *The Economics of Hope* (1992) next to his more mainstream work) and other 'heterodox' theorists on long-wave innovation theory. Ruigrok and van Tulder's *The Logic of International Restructuring* (1995) delineated the international bargaining framework that grounds the logic of international restructuring. The framework included a dependency scale by means of which relationships with societal stakeholders inside and outside the value chain can be assessed. The present study builds on both frameworks. Ans Kolk's recent work on codes of conduct and environmental strategies and regulation (e.g. Kolk, 2000; van Tulder and Kolk, 2001) has made a significant contribution to empirically substantiating a number of generic claims.

AIMS AND CONTENTS

The study endeavours to make a contribution in three areas. (1) *Scientific relevance*: the study seeks to *understand* what lies behind concepts such as globalization, liberalization, deregulation, accountability, corporate citizenship, (international) corporate social responsibility or transparency. Myths are debunked or put into perspective. The study integrates IB and B&S approaches (among others) through the development of eclectic theoretical constructs and the accumulation of empirical insights. (2) *Societal relevance*: the study helps to *assess* possible societal outcomes of (ir)responsible business strategies. A number of relatively new analytical concepts are introduced to enable an accurate assessment of societal challenges: the (international) bargaining society, the Triple-E (trade-off between Equity and Efficiency), rival institutions/organizations/states, societal triangle, identification of major societal issues and prime responsibilities; profiles of NGO/government–firm interaction; an overview of various types of approaches to address societal issues – conflict, cooperation, (strategic) partnerships. (3) *Managerial relevance*: the study seeks to present the 'business case' for international corporate responsibility (ICR). The study hopes to assist managers to *operationalize and implement* a sophisticated strategy to engage with relevant stakeholders. Relatively new managerial concepts introduced in this study are: Societal Interface Management, proactive ICR, proactive corporate citizenship, strategic stakeholder dialogue, Triangle management. A new *case study methodology* elaborated on in Part III should help students, managers, NGOs and public officials to understand, assess and appropriately address relevant issues.

This book consists of three parts. Part I (*Rivalry in a Changing Society*) analyses the most important societal movements since 1989 along three fundamental institutional building blocks (market, state, civil society). It examines the extent to which proclaimed trends such as 'globalization', 'liberalization', the 'emancipation of civil society' and the 'retreat of governments' can really be substantiated. The societal change these trends signify has created a large number of (institutional) voids within which firms have to operate and managers have to bargain to implement appropriate strategies. Therefore, firms face the challenge of so-called Societal Interface Management. Part II (*International Corporate Responsibility*) develops the business case for responsible firms at the local, national and international levels. To this end, key social issues are analysed in order to establish the nature of firms' primary and secondary responsibilities in the bargaining/contemporary society. Reputation often functions as a triggering mechanism for responsible firm behaviour, but it is not entirely clear how effective reputation is as a mechanism for stimulating responsible conduct. The relative success of a firm depends upon the corporate accountability regime(s) in which it operates. Managing across borders implies managing various regimes, which gives rise to a large number of dilemmas. Part III (*The International Bargaining Society in Action*) presents five notorious cases in which NGOs have sought confrontation with big, multinational enterprises (MNEs) in order to address specific issues such as labour circumstances, waste treatment, dictatorships, health and global warming. The cases make it possible to analyse the corrective effect of the reputation mechanism for MNEs. What kind of self-regulation efforts did develop and how effective have they been in addressing the issues at stake? The cases show that past (confrontation) strategies have only partially been effective. Instead, and in conclusion, Part III presents an interactive model to move beyond the manifold dilemmas that are linked to the implementation of socially responsible corporate strategies: the strategic stakeholder dialogue.

ACKNOWLEDGEMENTS

This book is the fruit of seven years' lectures, classes, exploratory research, dozens of publications and presentations before managers and policy makers around the world. These activities were organized around the formation of the department of Business–Society Management at the Faculty of Business Administration, Rotterdam School of Management. The department of Business–Society Management was founded in 1999 with the objective to develop the discipline by the same name. Since then the department has attracted a constant stream of enthusiastic graduate, postgraduate and PhD students and has produced a sizable output in articles, books and speeches. It was in this dynamic academic environment that the Dutch predecessor to this book entitled *Reputations at Stake* (2003) was produced. The book was nominated 'Best Management Book of the Year 2003' in the Netherlands and has already seen four reprints. The present study follows a similar basic structure and integrates some of the cases and builds upon the conceptual framework of the 2003 publication.

This book is still a 'work in progress' (see p. xvii) and would not have been possible without the contribution of, and interaction with, the numerous people that crossed our path and sometimes participated in our research projects – sometimes temporarily, but increasingly on a more permanent basis. These interactions with students, scholars, policy makers, citizens and managers reinforce the impression that the discipline of 'International Business–Society Management' is not only badly needed, but also feasible and viable as it is presented in this book. The publication of this book should help maintain the momentum in this area of inquiry.

The following persons should be acknowledged for their assistance and input in specific research projects, the findings of which have been integrated into this book: Carola van Lamoen (sustainability reporting), David Frans (internationalization profiles), Alfred Slager (banks), Guyong Liang and Ying Liu (competition policy and China), Alan Muller (regionalization), Arjen Mulder (public–private partnerships), Frank Appeldoorn and Robert van Raamsdonk (Corporate Governance), Bart Westdijk (poverty), Bas van Rijsbergen (HIV/Aids), Carlijn Welters and Inge Sloekers (codes of conduct), Gail Whiteman (indigenous peoples, mining, pharmaceuticals), Jeroen van Wijk (intellectual property, piracy), Eveline van Mil (NGO roles), Saskia Kersemaekers (codes), Arjen Slangen (cultural distance), Cynthia Piqué, Peter-Willem van Lindenberg, Li An Phoa and Deirdre de Graaf (leadership), Xavier van Leeuwen (newspapers), Jeannette Baljeu (OECD Guidelines), Eva Oskam and Erik-Hans Kok (internationalization database), Florence Akebe (issues), Marijn Post (illustrations), Karlijn Buis, Han van Midden and Esther Kostwinder (case studies); Sarah van Nispen, Amber Zonnenberg, Karel van Nierop, Saman Ramadhan, Michel Wijbrands, Jan-Willem de Jong, Annelien Gijzen and many others who – as the first generations of B–SM (Business–Society Management) students – contributed by writing Master's theses, case essays or other research products that have shaped our thinking and knowledge. The cases – in this book as well as on the website – are based on a large number of interviews. We are grateful for the time set aside and the depth and openness of those interviews. A special word of thanks goes to Fabienne Fortanier for her continuous support and critical engagement with the ideas presented in this study. Of course, the full responsibility of the text in this book remains with the authors.

With painstaking rigour, patience and intellectual acuity, Friedl Marincowitz went through the manuscript at various stages of its development and assisted in reformulating an innumerable number of lines that would not have been intelligible otherwise. We are grateful to Francesca Heslop, Jacqueline Curthoys and Emma Joyes at Routledge for their support and patience with the lengthy process of bringing this manuscript to completion.

Part I

Rivalry in a changing society

INTRODUCTION TO PART I

SIXTEEN YEARS AFTER THE WALL . . .

November 1989 appeared to be such a promising start. With the fall of the Berlin Wall, the most significant ideological clash of the twentieth century that had the world in a stranglehold for so long came to an end: the opposition between capitalism and communism, between the 'free' market and the 'plan economy'. Philosophers (Fukuyama, 1992) announced the end of history; economists and managers saw a vast market and considerable opportunities opening up, particularly for Western firms; political scientists declared the victory of parliamentary democracy as the decision-making model for society. With the rise of the Internet in the mid-1990s and economic globalization seeming an irrevocable fact, the notion quickly took hold that the world population was living in a 'global village' where distances would disappear and everyone would be better off. The entire global population would profit from the benefits of the new technologies and an ever-expanding market economy. The Internet held the promise of democratization and enhanced power to individual citizens and consumers. Many economies perhaps still had to undergo some transformation in order to create the conditions for continuous economic growth, but that was just a matter of time. A global round of further trade liberalization was in the making. In many countries a series of privatization and deregulation measures were in the starting blocks and launched with much enthusiasm.

More than a decade later, this vision is more nebulous than ever and the hangover for some consequently all the greater. A number of former plan economies that tried to adopt capitalism most ardently and applied the 'shock therapy' advocated by international organizations such as the International Monetary Fund slid into a state of almost total chaos. Such is their deterioration that even average life expectancy has declined (World Bank, 2003). The anti-globalist movement started using the World Wide Web specifically to protest against the excesses of globalization. It turned out that technological development does not always equal progress and that it has created a number of complex moral dilemmas, such as personal privacy in information networks and the patentability of genetic material. There is talk of a growing 'digital divide' between the 'haves' and the 'have-nots' in the Information Age. Weak international agreements are being reached to address pressing environmental problems such as global warming. Further steps in multilateral trade and investment liberalization have stalled. Countries are hauling themselves along from one financial crisis to the next. Never before has the United Nations Security Council had to debate the possibility of war as often as it has in the 1990–2000 period.[1] Interstate wars are replaced by intra-state (civil) wars.

By the end of the 1990s, the dotcom generation of Internet firms appeared to consist partly of hot air. Stock markets plummeted, plunging many small investors into a crisis – and no one knows whether this instability will persist or decline. The list is endless.

Global income inequality, on the one hand, is probably greater than ever in human history. Despite a relative decline in the number of poor people, the absolute number of poor people barely surviving on less than US$2 a day is estimated at slightly below 3 billion – still half the world's population. The income of the richest 1 per cent totals the sum of the bottom 57 per cent.[2] The earnings of the three richest men in the world (all businessmen) are almost half of the income generated by all Sub-Saharan African national economies put together.[3] On the other hand, never before have so many people enjoyed such (economic) prosperity as they do today. Thus, a world of paradoxes unfolds. A world that is embedded in a network(ed) society, characterized by multiple decision-making centres and governed by the rules of international bargaining and negotiation rather than the rule of law.

NEW ENEMIES

In the meantime, and partly as a result of this unfolding international bargaining society, capitalism has acquired two new enemies. First, an *external* enemy displayed itself in the form of international terrorism. Attacks on the World Trade Center in New York and the Pentagon in Washington on 11 September 2001, followed by a sequence of bloody attacks in a large number of places (Bali in 2002 and 2005, Istanbul in 2003, Madrid in 2004, London in 2005), represent the most explicit, recent and bloody manifestations of rising global terrorism. But, the problem had already presented itself in the first half of the 1990s. From academia, the warning of a 'clash of civilisations' (Huntington, 1993) sounded and in more managerial terms, there was talk of 'McWorld versus Jihad' (Barber, 1995). Second, an *internal* enemy in the form of the self-enriching businessman gained ground. Not only did business leaders succeed in negotiating high earnings for themselves, they also managed to re-label billions in costs as an asset or as 'growth in earnings' in order to keep share prices artificially high. This they accomplished through creative bookkeeping constructions and often with the assistance of their external accountants. The American magazine *Business Week* (13 June 2002) talked of 'evil forces from within' that are threatening capitalism.

In the US, icons of American commerce such as Xerox, WorldCom, Enron, General Motors, Merck and Arthur Andersen crumbled. President George W. Bush Jr, a former businessman himself, also came under fire on charges of insider trading. He tried to quell emotions by calling for more controls, but ultimately placed the onus on companies to act more ethically. It turned out that this state of affairs was not restricted to the US. In Europe and Asia, big companies such as Vivendi Universal, Deutsche Telekom, Lernhout&Hauspie, Parmalat, Adecco, Ahold, Daewoo, Hyundai, Sumitomo and Elf also buckled. No country was spared the embarrassment of some sort of corporate scandal. On all sides respected businessmen were accused of insider trading, fraud or reaping excessive earnings. Some ended up in jail, some even committed suicide – an outcome reminiscent of 'Black Monday' and the aftermath of the big October stock market crash in 1929. In the Netherlands, the chairman of the largest trade union called for a 'kleptocrat' tax. Government leaders around the world condemned corporate self-enrichment but generally refrained from imposing higher taxes or more stringent laws. A contributing factor might have been that some political leaders themselves were being accused of self-enrichment at the time. Evidence of conflicts of interests came to light and cast doubt on the 'independence' of accountants, consultants and stock market analysts. Confidence in the economic system and companies suffered heavy blows on all fronts.

CONFRONTING COMPLEXITIES

These developments resulted in societies and corporations being confronted with increasingly complex and 'messy' problems (cf. Ackoff, 1999). Big (internationally operating) firms are becoming 'societies' on their own. The bigger and the more entangled with societal issues firms become, the more difficult it becomes to analyse firm strategies isolated from society and vice versa. Drastic societal and economic change always spurs the quest for a 'best-practice', preferably a single recipe and benchmark for economic success. This propensity is often motivated by the desire to limit uncertainty rather than a true scientific ambition. Nevertheless, the pursuit of these yardsticks holds a magical appeal to many business people and policy makers alike. In the organizational and institutional literature, this pursuit is further reinforced by the idea of institutional isomorphism (DiMaggio and Powell, 1983) that signals a growing tendency towards convergence of institutions and organizational forms around the world, as the consequence of the network(ed) and global society.

Akin to the quest for the Holy Grail or the Golden Fleece, the search for 'best practice' is bound to remain elusive or turn out to be a disappointment even if the object of desire is found (Easterly, 2002: xi). A troubling factor for many an ambitious quest is that societies and firms can (and have been) economically successful on the basis of very divergent characteristics. Strategic thinkers consistently argue that success is achieved precisely *because* of the implementation of diverging strategies. Other authors who have analysed the main tenets of the process of change since the early 1990s have stressed various aspects of 'rivalry': rival states, rival firms (Stopford and Strange, 1991), rival organizational forms (Ingram and Clay, 2000), rival cultures (Snow and Colini, 1993), rival capitalisms (Albert, 1993; Hart, 1992) rival social movements, rival ideologies, rival institutions (van Tulder and Ruigrok, 1997).

ADDRESSING THE NATURE OF INTERACTIONS

The degree of rivalry represents the process dimension of institutional and organizational interaction, whereas the degree of convergence or divergence represents the outcome dimension of interaction.

- *Rivalry*: Rivalry entails competition. The concept of market competition, for instance, is a central notion of classical economics and is generally depicted as a process of rivalry between economic actors. Rivalry is not a priori positive or negative. It expresses a process characteristic of interaction. In Darwin's evolutionary reasoning, rivalry enacts a process of natural selection in which the fittest survive. In this case rivalry represents a 'race to the top'. In international arenas, rivalry can exist between governments, firms and NGOs. Rivalry between political, social and economic systems can also lead to exclusion – that protects the unfit from the fitter – or to unfavourable copying or herding behaviour that results in a weakening of all actors concerned. In this case rivalry represents a 'race to the bottom'.
- *Divergence/convergence*: Rivalry or competition is neither a sufficient nor a necessary condition for divergence or diversity. When systems, individuals, countries or organizations do not interact or complement each other, divergence can result in a state of non-rival co-existence or co-habitation. Convergence, on the other hand, can lead to uniformity and isomorphism, but it does not say much about the underlying process either which – even in the case of isomorphism – might still lead to sustained rivalry. Actors that operate in the same markets under harmonized rules can be bigger rivals than in cases where they operate in differing institutional settings. Consequently, four positions can be distinguished: (1) race, (2) contest, (3) co-alignment, (4) co-habitation (Table I.1).

A **race** represents foremost *regulated* rivalry. The 'track' is set and enables actors to compete, but also to identify – for the moment – 'the winner'. The process leads to a greater convergence between the actors. A race requires a certain degree of harmonization of institutions. The race can be positive (race to the top) or negative (race to the bottom). In the case where a dominant

Table I.1 Interaction dynamics

		Process	
		Intense rivalry	Limited rivalry
Outcome	Convergence	Race	Co-alignment
	Divergence	Contest	Co-habitation

(hegemonic) actor imposes its rules on other actors, this could perhaps lead to short-term unifor-mity of rules, but cannot take away the underlying feeling of rivalry that its rivals feel. The imposition of the de facto standard in computer software programs by Microsoft, for instance, triggered other forms of rivalry (litigatious) in an otherwise 'harmonized' market place. Actors that are confronted with an extrinsically imposed uniformity due to a leading (hegemonic) actor will always try to chal-lenge the latter's position. One of their means is to try changing the rules of the game to their own advantage. Company rivalry is as much about technological or market strategies, as about competing rules.

A **contest** represents a much less regulated form of interaction in which it is not always possible to distinguish a 'winner'. The stage is set, but the rules are less transparent. In case the outcome of a race is contested, actors literally enter into a divergent position. Active exclusion of other actors through discrimination or through retaliation (tit-for-tat action) are expressions of rivalry that rein-force divergence. The 'clash of civilizations' (Huntington, 1993) or contests in 'uniqueness' as can be witnessed in beauty pageant elections are concrete examples of diversity enhancing rivalry. Actors confronted with a dominant actor can challenge the latter's position by changing the rules of the game, thus creating rivalry by divergence.

Co-alignment is the interaction principle in case interaction is aimed at convergence. Co-align-ment is a term used in organizational and change management theories where it refers to the idea that firms reap competitive advantage and good performance when they are aligned with their environ-ment, or when strategy and implementation are aligned. Co-alignment as an organization principle has, for instance, been applied for IT strategies. Co-alignment involves cooperation between the actors, rather than rivalry, in achieving shared strategic goals. It supports processes that lead to (institutional and organizational) *isomorphism*.

Co-habitation exists when actors 'agree to disagree', but without expressing any ambition of becom-ing superior over the other (which would entail a measure of rivalry). Co-habitation involves neither intense cooperation nor strong rivalry between actors. The term has been practised in particular to characterize 'living arrangements' in marital and political relationships. Political co-habitation in France for instance was practised when a president and a cabinet of opposing political orientations co-governed the country. Coalition governments are another example of co-habitation; the alliance is temporary and at elections the parties contest again – preferably by stressing their own 'unique' characteristics. Co-habitation entails a process of enduring *polymorphism*.

ASSESSING THE NATURE AND THE DIRECTION OF CHANGE

Part I of this book offers an analysis of the most important societal movements of the 1990s along three fundamental institutional building blocks of societies: the market, state and civil society. Chapter 1 (rival institutions) outlines how these coordinating mechanisms of society *generally* func-tion and interact with one another. In the past, the distribution of responsibilities and the 'spheres of influence' of these three institutions have created significant stability and economic welfare in many industrialized countries – regardless of their differing social and economic foundations. Chapter 2 (rival models) delineates what constitutes economic 'success' and which major societal models compete at present.

In Chapters 3 to 5 (rival trends), the most important changes within and between the societal spheres/institutions are examined. Nothing seems more difficult to predict than the future. Only slightly less difficult, it seems, is to grasp present 'trends' or what is portrayed as such. As the future is firmly rooted in past and present trends, assessing them inaccurately arguably has greater consequences for the organization of society than not being able to forecast the future. The 1990s was, indeed, a decade of heightened expectations based upon a number of promising trends. These were perceived by many as 'certain' and embodied in five catchwords: globalization, democratization, deregulation, liberalization and privatization. At the same time, economic, political and business literature became riddled with concepts such as 'management of uncertainty', 'volatility', 'risk management', 'ambiguity' and 'dilemmas'. The combination of certainty and uncertainty seems peculiar, but the two phenomena, in fact, are strongly related: increased (perceived) ambiguity triggers a search for certainty in (perceived) trends. If proclaimed with enough gusto, a 'trend' may very well become a self-fulfilling prophecy. Chapters 3 to 5 address the various dimensions of the (perceived) trends since the early 1990s, their origins and their effects on societal institutions and organizational forms. To what extent can these trends empirically be substantiated, what rival trends have emerged, what are the trade-offs between them and which challenges still lay ahead?

The societal changes that occurred in the 1990s are often characterized by three clusters of trends: (1) an advancing business sector – advancing global markets, increased competition and rapid technological progress driven by the efforts of a multitude of small enterprises (Chapter 3); (2) a more emancipated and assertive civil society which – aided especially by new information and communication technology (ICT) – is increasingly able to represent itself internationally (Chapter 4); and (3) a receding government (state) realized through privatization and deregulation (Chapter 5). To what extent are these indeed adequate characterizations? The shifting societal institutional arrangements overlap and consequently also come into conflict with one another. The conclusion of Chapter 5 identifies the most significant trends and frictions and the geographical contexts (local/national/regional/global) in which they currently occur.

Chapters 6 and 7 (managing rivalry) finally outline the nature of the problems of legitimacy, control and effectiveness that arise from these boundary conflicts. The evolving international 'networking' or 'bargaining society' (Chapter 6) creates an uncertain environment or context in which trends and counter-trends appear that are not easy to map – let alone for business and societal groups to anticipate. In such circumstances, the relationship between International Business and society is perhaps best understood as a kind of 'Societal Interface Management' where it is more important to identify the challenges than to delineate exact best-practice strategies. Chapter 7 maps the most significant challenges for International Business at its interface with society.

Chapter 1

Rival institutions: society as triangular relationship

1.1 INTRODUCTION: RIVAL INSTITUTIONS, RIVAL ORGANIZATIONAL FORMS

A changing society triggers rivalry: between groups and social movements within society, between different societies (states) and within specific groups. This chapter aims to identify the main features of rivalry with reference to important organizational and institutional characteristics of societies. Organizations that create and distribute value in society can have many characteristics as regards size, relative importance and performance. The debate on the most appropriate organizational forms in societies is biased towards so called 'public' companies – companies that are listed on stock exchanges. The bulk of (international) business studies concentrate on documenting the profitability, the innovativeness and the continuity of big companies such as General Electric, Microsoft, Siemens, Samsung, Wal-Mart, Nokia or Toyota. But the organizational forms found in societies are much more diverse. What to think of state-owned enterprises, are they the same as public companies and how important are they still? What is to be made of 'family-owned' firms, cooperatives and the non-profit and informal sector for economic success? Often, these organizational forms are treated with disdain – or are just ignored – because they do not belong to the organizational orthodoxy. By doing this, scholars overlook the largest part of societies and miss out on most of its actual dynamism.

This chapter will show that a study on the role(s) of 'business' in society cannot abstain from taking all these organizational forms into account. They present complementary as well as rival forms for implementing business strategies. The chapter's prime aim is to disentangle the conceptual and ideological ambiguity surrounding many of these organizational forms and to put the various organizational forms into a clear institutional perspective. This (and the following) chapter signifies a quest for the relevant principles or ground rules – generally referred to as 'institutions'[1] – that govern different societies. A growing body of literature acknowledges that the adoption of 'appropriate' institutions of 'good governance' is one of the preconditions for macro-economic success (cf. World Bank, 1997). However, the very definition of 'appropriate' and 'good' institution/governance can vary from country to country, and over time. In addition, the success or failure of individual business strategies is also strongly influenced by the institutional and cultural context in which managers operate. The very definition of what constitutes a 'business' is influenced by national idiosyncracies. Institutional environments shape corporate perceptions and interpretations of the most 'appropriate' strategy. These are the 'institutional drivers' of strategy (Levy and Kolk, 2002).

In order to analyse the functioning of societies and the relative success of specific business strategies within these countries, sociologists, political scientists, economists and management scientists often depict society in the form of a triangle with three distinct, but related, 'spheres'. Each sphere of society organizes itself in a very specific manner and according to its own logic. This chapter addresses in particular two topics: first the distinguishing general characteristics of the three spheres (section 1.2), and second the characteristics of hybrid organizational forms that connect the three spheres (section 1.3). A leading question is whether any one of these forms can be considered to be economically and socially successful separate from the other organizational forms (section 1.4).

1.2 THE SOCIETAL TRIANGLE: SEPARATE INSTITUTIONAL SPHERES

To depict society as a triangle entails distinguishing relatively separate spheres that organize themselves on the basis of different 'rules of the game' or 'institutions'. Three primary institutions can be distinguished in the triangle: the state, market and civil society (Figure 1.1). The functioning of these societal 'spheres' – individually and in interaction with one another – determines the manner in which a society functions as a whole.

Each of the three spheres employs a logic, rationality and ideology of its own. They essentially also occupy a different role and position in society. Through legislation, the government (state) provides the legal framework that structures society. The market sector (market) primarily creates value and welfare for society by converting *inputs* (such as natural resources, labour and money) into *outputs* (such as products, services, economic growth, employment and income) within the bounds of the legal framework. In this way, business satisfies the needs of society by means of market transactions in pursuit of profit. Civil society represents the sum

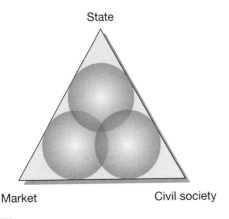

Figure 1.1 The societal triangle

of social relations among citizens that structures society outside politics and business. It includes the family, voluntary organizations, societal groupings, churches and trade unions. Being an organized network of citizens, civil society fulfils the need for relationships and socialization through the development and sharing of norms (Wartick and Wood, 1999).

Different coordination mechanisms

Societal and human relations shape a society. They do, however, require coordination and regulation. Competition (market mechanism), control and codification (government regulations), shared norms and values and structure and cooperation within communal relations (such as families and local communities) form the chief coordinating mechanisms for social conduct and interaction (CPB, 1997). The market regulates through competition, profit and rewards, the state through legislation, and civil society through participation and collective action. The sources of income of the three spheres differ fundamentally: governments levy taxes; companies generate profits; and (non-profit) civil organizations depend on donations, subsidies and other voluntary contributions. They also 'produce' different goods. The state specifically tends to supply those goods that would not readily be produced otherwise given that their (marginal) returns cannot be distributed that easily. This applies to so-called 'public goods' such as defence and infrastructure which are funded by taxes. In the case of public goods it is not always possible to distinguish who pays and who benefits. Private goods can be sold much more easily as singular (discrete) products rendering turnover and profits. Their distribution via markets is easier to organize. Then there are a large number of goods and services that are particularly important to some groups, but which are insufficiently provided for by the market and the state. This is the territory of the third building block, civil society which generally concerns the provision of so-called 'club goods'.[2] In the case of club goods it is impossible to price the discrete units of goodwill benefits they generate, whereas some of the benefits are exclusive and accessible only by club (family, city) members (cf. Prakash, 2002: 187). Through donations, sponsorship and contributions from members – and often with the assistance of unpaid volunteers – non-profit organizations make their contribution to the smooth functioning of this societal sphere.

Difference between *de jure* and de facto control

In each sphere, comparable discrepancies exist between who is pulling the strings *de jure* and de facto. This is also referred to as the principal–agent problem: in theory the agent (manager) carries out the principal's (shareholder) instructions, but in practice it often seems to function in a completely different way. The legal (or primary) control of the state in a parliamentary democracy takes place via the electorate and political parties (parliament), but the actual (informal) control is often in the hands of civil servants although they have not been elected. In the case of listed companies, the owners (shareholders) and members of the Supervisory Board are in charge, but in practice, managers and non-elected members of the Board of Directors usually take the lead. The same applies to managers of civil society organizations (also referred to as 'technocrats') who often have disproportionate power to that of members and are not controlled by voting procedures.

Weaknesses and factors of failure

The primary weaknesses of the three societal spheres are linked to some of their intrinsic characteristics: rigidity (or bureaucratization) in the case of government as a result of large and stable income flows which are minimally and infrequently (once in four years at election time)

9

properly accounted for;[3] monopoly-forming in the case of entrepreneurs who, as a result of imperfect markets, could be inclined to give preference to higher profits above competition; fragmentation in the case of civil society due to insufficient resources for financing organizations and launching campaigns and a lack of professionalism thanks to the use of large numbers of volunteers.

Table 1.1 summarises the most important characteristics of the three societal coordinating mechanisms/spheres. The manner in which these spheres develop for a large part still depends

Table 1.1 Characteristic coordination mechanisms

	State	Market	Civil society
Primary importance	Political	Economic	Social
De jure/primary control	Voters, political parties	Owners, Supervisory Board	Society, members
De facto/informal control often	Officials	Managers, Board of Directors	Managers, technocrats
Goods produced	Public goods	Private goods	Group/club goods
Core responsibilities	Enforcement of national standards and norms	Production of goods and services	Mobilization of society
Primary resources	Legislation/police/ armed forces/ monopoly on violence	Financial capital, labour, natural resources	Energy of volunteers
Primary weaknesses	Rigidity and bureaucratization	Monopoly and other forms of 'market failures'	Fragmentation
Financed by	Taxes	Profits	Donations, contributions
Ideologies	Anarchy/democracy/ liberalism/ totalitarianism	Market capitalism/ mixed economy/ socialism/utopian communism	Individualism/ collectivism
Formal consultation on economic structuring between	Government (especially ministries of economic affairs, trade, environment, transport, technology, agriculture)	Employers organizations; often distinction between large companies and MSE	Trade unions; (small) shareholder associations; NGOs regarding covenants
Prevalent liability	No liability	Limited liability	Personal liability
Parameters	Coercion; codification	Competition	Cooperation; co-optation
Dominant organizational form	Departments, ministries, local councils, provinces/ federal states	For-profit; Plc, Ltd, AG, SA	Non-profit; Voluntary organization; Foundation; Association

Source: based on Waddell (2000: 113); Wartick and Wood (1999: 26 ff.); World Bank (1997); own observations on internal processes. The three spheres are traditionally inward looking and often even display autistic streaks. The relative separation of the three spheres is illustrated, for example, by the career paths of leaders in these sectors (Box 1.1).

BOX 1.1 STRICT SEPARATION OF RECRUITMENT AND CAREER PATHS

Research conducted by the SCOPE expert centre of Erasmus University for the year 2000 shows that the leaders in the three societal spheres follow strictly separate career paths. Figure 1.2 depicts how company, government and international civil society leaders' careers have unfolded in terms of the three societal spheres.[4] Civil society leaders have spent more than two-thirds of their working lives in the same societal sphere. State leaders (heads of state) worked in exclusively government-related organizations for more than three-quarters of their careers (for example, as civil servants or politicians), while corporate leaders almost exclusively (97 per cent) pursued a career in the market sector.

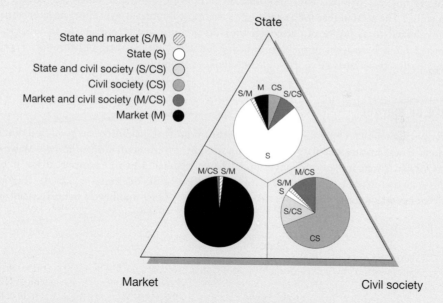

Figure 1.2 *Background of leaders*

For the moment, there is only scant evidence of crossover behaviour between the spheres: leaders from international civil society (15 per cent) more often have a corporate background than leaders of state (7 per cent). The separation of career paths already starts with education: leaders of state mostly studied law (33 per cent) and general social sciences, while more than 50 per cent of corporate leaders studied economics and business administration. Representatives of civil society have a more diffuse background. On the whole, the three building blocks of society consequently represent relatively closed networks (bulwarks?) of recruitment and career paths.

1.3 SOCIETAL COMPLEXITY: HYBRIDIZATION

The societal triangle and its institutional arrangements are complex. None of the three institutional spheres operates in isolation of the others. The market, for instance, has to take the other spheres of influence into consideration. In addition to the competition mechanism then, companies also have to deal with the two other spheres and their respective coordinating mechanisms. The practice of business always takes place at the interface of a number of coordinating mechanisms, and business is grounded in society by legislation, competition and shared values and norms (Etzioni, 1988).

The manner in which people and firms generally engage with institutions (i.e. the 'rules of the game') contributes to societal complexity. They adapt to them in part, but they also try to mould institutions to serve their own interests. From time to time, the societal need arises for organizations that bridge the different institutions. The result is a whole range of hybrid organizations that operate in between the three coordinating mechanisms. Often they do so very successfully (Figure 1.3). But the basis of their success is not easy to decipher: (1) state or market, (2) profit or non-profit, (3) public or private, (4) governmental or non-governmental? These very concepts acquire a different meaning in different societal constellations: 'state' is not always related to 'public', 'market' does not necessarily only imply 'profit', 'non-profit' is not synonymous with 'non-market', 'non-governmental' does not always imply 'non-state'. The section that follows identifies the most important hybrid organizations that are often referred to as businesses although they do not necessarily operate in an environment governed solely by market principles. In many countries, these hybrid organizations represent a large part – two-thirds or more – of the whole economy.

State or market?

Market economies can only function within institutions that guarantee the good functioning of markets. These institutions are generally supported by governmental organizations. Many regulatory organizations initiated by government have occupied a hybrid position at the interface of the state and market (see Chapter 3 for a discussion of the dilemmas involved). Regulatory agencies operate outside the production value chain. A large number of hybrid organizations

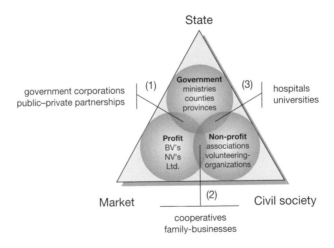

Figure 1.3 *Hybrid organizations*

at the state–market interface, however, function *within* the production value chain. They generate a considerable share of the national product and income. State-owned enterprises and so-called 'public–private partnerships' (PPPs) in particular, operate in this area.

The resilience of state-owned enterprises

The number of partly or wholly state-owned enterprises on the first 100 firms on the *Fortune* Global 500 list in 1990 was 18 (Ruigrok and van Tulder, 1995: 169 ff.). In 2003, this figure was only slightly lower: 15 of the first 100. In 2003, majority state-owned firms (50 per cent or more) represented seven per cent of the total Global 500 list. Many companies from developing countries on the *Fortune* Global 500 list are wholly or partly state owned. In these countries it is often argued that these large companies have a strong influence on the development model of the country and that it might therefore be necessary to control them. State ownership, however, is accompanied by bureaucratization and politicization (see Table 1.1). Compared to market players, many state-owned companies consequently suffer from inefficiencies. As a result, wholly state-owned enterprises are dwindling or are under heavy pressure to become more efficient in particular countries and in particular sectors. But they are not extinct. There is a sort of minimum level of state ownership in most countries – depending on other institutions and the international position of the country in question. As nineteenth- and twentieth-century history has shown, privatization exercises are often followed by (re)nationalizations and vice versa. The trends come in waves, whereby governments emulate strategies of their peer group (cf. Mulder, 2004; Megginson and Netter, 2001).

Even with the decline in the 1990s of the number of companies wholly controlled by government in many economies, at least ten per cent of the Gross National Product (GNP) of most OECD countries still originates from state-owned enterprises. World Bank estimates of the share of state-owned enterprises in the US and the UK amount to approximately 2–3 per cent, but in Continental European countries the share is considerably higher. Privatization in the 'market economies' of OECD countries occurred primarily in the telecommunications sector, financial services, transport and public utilities. But complete privatization did not always take place. The government share in these companies often decreased or changed in nature. The result is that in many European countries, state ownership or state influence is still considerable. Large companies such as Renault in France or Volkswagen in Germany are still (partly) state owned. Their continuity has been enhanced by the deep and silent pockets of their shareholders. The same holds true for many of the telecommunications firms in Europe. Despite pressure from the European Commission, European (local) governments have important minority shareholdings in utility firms (energy, water), railways and the like. French state-owned firms in particular have been very successful in their internationalization strategy – often having acquired firms that had just been privatized. By the time ten new states – all transition economies – became members of the European Union in May 2004, some of them paradoxically had gone further in their privatization efforts than many of the existing members.[5]

State ownership as a relevant organizational form in many developed countries is therefore still important. But its exact impact (let alone its performance) is difficult to assess. The functioning of most market economies remains strongly intertwined with the operations of state-owned or state-controlled firms. A good example is provided by Sweden – home of many multinationals and undoubtedly considered a market economy. In the 2000 Annual Report on government-owned companies,[6] we find that the Swedish government is the largest player in financial markets. This is partly because of Swedish Pension Insurance Fund holdings of listed shares and bonds, and partly because of direct holdings in government-owned companies. Companies with direct government influence constitute around 25 per cent of the domestic corporate sector, with 240,000 people directly employed by these companies. The Swedish government has direct ownership of five publicly listed companies. Consequently, the Swedish state is the largest shareholder on the Stockholm Stock Exchange, with 5 per cent of total value of shares listed. So, although an increasing number of state-owned companies operate according to market principles, they still remain 'state' and it is therefore difficult to imagine them going bankrupt. The liabilities of the managers of these companies are also different from what they would be in a market environment.

The introduction of a market economy in transition economies and in developing countries is mistakenly considered to signify the end of state-owned firms (Box 1.2). In many developing countries the relative share of state-owned companies is somewhere in between the European and the Anglo-Saxon model. The oil-rich countries of the Middle East started to accumulate their substantial wealth – some of them ranking among the countries with the highest per capita GDP in the world – only after nationalizing most of the oil companies active in their territories.

BOX 1.2 RIVAL TRANSITION TRAJECTORIES: EVOLUTION VERSUS SHOCK

The very definition of 'transition economies' is linked to their transition from a plan economy (with 100 per cent of the economy in the hands of state-owned enterprises) to a 'market economy'. Depending on the privatization strategies chosen, the share of state-owned enterprises (SOE) became large or small. The effectiveness of either strategy for economic growth and the competitiveness of the economy is still debated (cf. Liang, 2004; Stiglitz, 1999).

Since 1978, the Chinese government has been following a gradual trajectory towards a market economy, thereby also introducing foreign firms in the market as a lever to introduce the logic of the market to state-owned firms. Foreign firms could only acquire market share through joint ventures with local firms. The share of state-owned and state-holding enterprises – approximately 300,000 firms – in gross industrial output value in 2002 was still 41 per cent, according to data of the Economist Intelligence Unit. All 11 Chinese firms on the *Fortune Global 500* list in 2002 were state-owned enterprises.

Hungary, on the other hand, provides an example of a rapid transition strategy with quick privatizations – the so-called 'shock' therapy. When the government's privatization programme ended in 1998 – less than ten years after it commenced in 1989 – the state-owned sector was still generating 20 per cent of GDP. In Hungary, rapid privatization also involved selling ownership to foreign firms. In 1998, foreign owners controlled 70 per cent of financial institutions, 66 per cent of industry, 90 per cent of telecommunications and 50 per cent of the trading sector in Hungary (van Tulder, 2004b).

The challenge of public–private partnerships (PPPs)

The second hybrid organizational form in between state and market are *public–private partnerships*. They involve any agreement (partnership) between public and private parties. In general, 'private parties' are firms. Since the beginning of the 1990s, the number of PPPs has increased. A major reason has been budgetary problems and the poor government performance in areas such as public infrastructure – from roads, railways, water supply, city development to even social security systems and the (private) management of (public) jails. The idea of PPPs is quite old, but in its modern forms its roots can be found in the US and, later, in the UK. It was further favoured in the scientific discipline of New Public Management which supports a more managerial approach to state operations (cf. Osborne, 2000). PPPs were introduced to facilitate flexibility in the interaction between the societal spheres. PPPs often involve billions of euros/dollars and may therefore be highly rewarding, but also highly risky for most parties involved. PPPs require high initial investments and a long pay-back time – which has always been one of the reasons why governments have invested in the provision of these goods and services (see Chapter 6). PPPs account for larger transportation/infrastructure investments in Europe such as the Eurotunnel and the Oresund link, where the European Commission, in close consultation with the European Roundtable of Industrialists (ERT) (a lobby group of big European firms), played a cataclysmic role. PPPs take on a wide variety of forms. A partnership can take the form of a lease or concession contract: the government retains ownership, whereas the private sector manages and operates the services. The involvement of the private sector can be limited to design and construction contracts, but can ultimately also involve full ownership of the project.

A good example of the wide range of public–private arrangements, is the urban water sector (OECD policy brief, April 2003). In most OECD countries – as in most developing countries – the involvement of the private sector (market) is increasing. There is limited private involvement through design and construction contracts. In the UK (England and Wales) the sector is largely privatized although strictly regulated by an independent body. In other countries, such as Germany (96 per cent), the Netherlands (100 per cent) or the US (85 per cent) the management of water in 2002 is still largely in the hands of governments. In contrast, in France – the country that is associated with large state-led projects – the actual management of the water system is 80 per cent in the hands of the private sector, although the supply of water is entirely publicly owned.

In developing countries, PPPs became popular in the 1990s as well. But their effectiveness – in terms of attracting private capital, providing services to the population that otherwise would not have been produced, lowering prices for consumers – has been seriously questioned. Since 2000, public and private parties' enthusiasm for PPPs in the water sector in developing countries has decreased substantially. PPPs rarely provide an 'easy fix' for underinvestment in certain areas.

Profit or non-profit?

Two oxymorons can be found particularly at the interface between the market and civil society: (1) the non-profit and (2) the informal sector. They both represent social institutions that generally operate outside the confines of the state and the market. But rather than defining what they are, they are identified on the basis of what they are not: not for-profit, not formal. Consequently, these sectors are also rather poorly researched and their relative importance for economic and job growth in countries is not very well understood. Two formal business organizations in particular exist at the interface of the market and civil society: the family-owned/controlled firm and the cooperative. Their hybrid orientation towards either profit or non-profit provides them with particular strategic characteristics and a particular performance logic. This section also inventories their relative importance for economies and related performance claims.

The underestimated importance of the informal sector

The informal sector represents one of the most underestimated factors of societal performance. Members of the informal sector do not pay taxes, are unorganized, unregulated, have little job security, have no access to fringe benefits from institutional sources, comprise the majority of economically active women in developing countries, are local and operate individually or within the organization of the family. The alternative names given to the informal sector are telling: black economy, community of the poor, parallel economy, shadow economy, transient sector, flexible economy, urban subsistence sector.[7] The existence of an informal sector is therefore generally discussed with considerable suspicion. Nevertheless the informal sector is of great importance to the functioning of many societies, including high-income countries. It was estimated at 41 per cent of the official GDP in developing countries. The grey economy is growing. In high-income countries, the relative importance can range from around 9 per cent in the US and Switzerland to an alleged 30–48 per cent of the official labour force in Italy (Schneider, 2002). In European OECD countries, 48 million people work illegally and it is quite likely that their productivity is considerably higher than those active in the official economy (ibid.).

Mainstream economists assert that the informal economy slows down overall economic growth, by limiting productivity rises and the growth of companies (that want to stay small in order to evade the attention of tax authorities) (Farrell, 2004). Formalizing the informal sector adds to growth and could lower the taxes imposed on the firms that already operate in the formal economy. This option might be theoretically sound but proves practically unfit, in partic-ular, in countries with weakly developed governments. In practice, the informal economy proves to be a major growth sector especially in developing countries. It is responsible for 93 per cent of new jobs in Africa and 83 per cent of new jobs in Latin America and the Caribbean. Informal sector workers are responsible for nearly three-quarters of manufacturing in South East Asia (Charmes, 2000). In several African countries, the informal sector gener-ates nearly 30 per cent of the total income. The non-agricultural contribution of the informal sector to these countries' GDP ranges from 45 per cent to 60 per cent. The informal economy also serves as 'buffer' in times of crisis. In the wake of the Asia crisis (1997 onwards), formal employment in many Asian countries collapsed, which was compensated for by a strong rise in informal employment. The 'labour reserve' in many countries keep themselves occupied (and retrain themselves) in the informal economy thus providing pools of people to hire once the economy recovers.

The growth potential of non-profit

The non-profit sector differs from the informal sector in one important respect: income earned is officially registered. But in other respects, its function resembles that of the informal sector: job provider, buffer in times of economic downturn, provider of social capital. While its exact size is less difficult to assess, it is not straightforward due to the 'bewildering array of entities' (Salomon *et al.*, 2000) that can belong to this sector. It represents an approximate capital of 1.1 trillion dollars annually and employs approximately 19 million employees (Zadek, 2003). The non-profit sector (even excluding its religious sub-sector, one of the oldest and largest 'multi-nationals' in the world) would constitute the eighth largest economy in the world. The US has always been regarded as the country with the most extensive non-profit sector which is also supposed to compensate for the excesses of a highly commercialized economy. According to an assessment of the Johns Hopkins Institute (1997), the non-profit sector – as measurable com-ponent of *civil society* – provided 12 per cent of jobs in the US in 1995. The situation, however, in countries such as Australia (10 per cent) and Israel (11 per cent) appears to be similar. The non-profit sector in small European countries such as Belgium (13 per cent), Ireland (14 per cent) and the Netherlands (19 per cent) has an even greater share in the economy. A significant number (60–70 per cent) of registered staff in the non-profit sector has a paid job. In the 1990s,

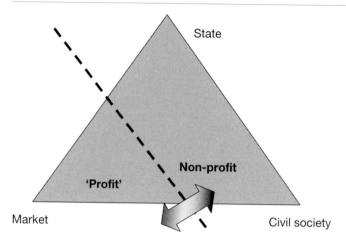

Figure 1.4 The profit–non-profit interface

employment in the non-profit sector grew even faster than it did in the economy as a whole. In most countries, therefore, the informal sector and/or the non-profit sector can be considered to be a very important 'job engine' complementary to the formal and for-profit sector.

The business of family businesses

The greatest part of economies is organized in the form of (small) family businesses. In most developing countries the overwhelming majority of firms are family run and often part of the informal sector. In most developed countries family-run businesses also constitute the best part of the formal economy. The US, for instance, has over 24 million family-run businesses, representing 95 per cent of all the companies. Because of their smaller average size than publicly owned companies they occupy a smaller – but nevertheless substantial – part of the economy. In the Netherlands, for instance, 200,000 family-owned firms produce 54 per cent of the GDP (*Vk*, 3 May 2004). The vast majority of family businesses are not publicly traded (private) firms, consisting of a single founder-owner and perhaps a number of relatives employed (*The Economist*, 6 November 2004).

But family owernership does not prevent firms from growth. Some of the largest international corporations are also (private) family firms. In 2002, *Forbes* magazine recorded 257 large private corporations in the US with annual revenues of at least US$1 billion. The list contains prominent companies in construction, food processing and food distribution, auditing and consulting and energy wholesale and retail. Combined, these giant corporations employ 3 million people and contribute more than US$700 billion per year in products and services to the US economy. By far the largest family-owned firms in the US are Cargill (with almost US$60 billion in revenues and 100,000 employees) and Koch (with US$40 billion in revenues and 17,000 employees). With sales of US$43.7 billion in 2002, Glencore International of Switzerland would be the second largest private company in the world, according to *Forbes*' estimates. Discount grocer Aldi of Germany is no. 2 and retailer ITM of France is no. 3. There is a vision behind private ownership of companies: sometimes inspired by religious principles, but in any case the conviction is held that one does not want to be dependent on capital markets, interfering and demanding investors or annoying banks. In the case of the smaller family businesses in particular, continuity is often of greater importance than profit maximization.

Some of the largest public companies are also family controlled or family owned. One-third of the Standard & Poor (S&P) 500, more than half the top 250 'public' companies in France and Germany, and most large South Korean companies are family controlled (*FT*, 30 September 2003). They include such well-known firms as News Corp (Murdoch), BMW (Quandt family) Michelin, Peugeot, Samsung (Lee family), LG group (Koh and Huh families), Philips, Wal-Mart (Walton family), Ford, Fiat (Agnelli family) or Toyota (Toyoda family). In all these companies, the founding families still have a blocking minority.

Family-controlled public companies in the S&P 500 have not only yielded higher profits but also higher share prices than non-family-owned firms – in the event a family member served as CEO (Anderson and Reeb, 2003). This phenomenon runs counter to the Anglo-Saxon orthodoxy that attributes better performance to publicly listed companies and upholds the idea that minority shareholders are adversely affected by family ownership. Family ownership is an effective organizational structure. This makes sense because the business leader has a longer-term interest in the sustained well-being of the family firm. As one group put it, 'the involved family members see themselves as the stewards of the firm'. Besides, most of these leaders have had extensive training within the company and know the company inside-out. The principal–agent problem – where investors are unable to rely on a chief executive to act on their behalf – 'is more effectively curtailed by blood ties and family ownership than incentive packages' (John Gapper in *FT*, 30 September 2003).

Family ownership, however, has disadvantages as well, for instance lack of transparency, the risk of nepotism and the ever-looming problem of 'handing over the reins' at the right time. In the *Forbes* 2003 list of richest people in the world, seven of the first ten people listed are owners of family-owned and/or family-controlled firms (including the Albrecht and Walton family and Warren Buffet).[8]

The economic function of cooperatives

Another phenomenon is the advent of the modern cooperative. Cooperatives are a global and widely underestimated phenomenon. They belong to what is called the 'social' or 'solidarity' economy. They are an important segment of many economies. Since 1975, the number of members associated with cooperatives around the world has, according to the Geneva-based International Cooperative Alliance, more than doubled. Around 725 million people in world are connected to cooperatives either as consumers, owners or occupants (*New Internationalist*, June 2004). Cooperatives occupy 20–30 per cent of the jobs in European countries such as Ireland, Germany, Denmark, Luxembourg and Austria. In Anglo-Saxon countries cooperatives hold a more modest position. In the UK, for instance, 10–20 per cent of jobs are in the cooperative sector (Demoustier, 2001). Cooperatives are not supposed to be profit-driven, but in most countries they are allowed to redistribute the surplus earned (i.e. the profit) to their members. Cooperatives are neither wholly profit nor wholly non-profit organizations, but this does not have to be a liability. Comparable mechanisms apply to Islamic (commercial) banks (Box 1.3).

Cooperatives constitute an important part of the agriculture, banking and housing industry, where that can be very competitive and profitable – provided we use a correct yardstick. In developing countries, cooperatives often present the only viable way to organize groups of small farmers. But also in developed countries, the cooperative sector is very competitive. According to management guru Michael Porter (1990), the agricultural cluster in the Netherlands, for instance, represents the most competitive part of the economy – resulting in very high export quotas. Most exports in this sector are organized as cooperatives. Financial intermediaries in the agriculture sector are also organized as cooperatives. Many of them were

BOX 1.3 ISLAMIC BANKING: THE INTEREST IN NON-INTEREST

Commercial banking involves charging interest. This, however, is prohibited by Islam and explains why considerable parts of Islamic economies are governed by barter trade and/or simple financial transactions. Nevertheless, banks that adhere to the moral rules of Islam do exist. And even to the moral rules of other cultures: according to the London-based Institute for Islamic Banking and Insurance:[9]

> interest (or 'usury') was prohibited in both the Old and New Testaments of the Bible, while Shakespeare and many other writers, particularly those writing in the nineteenth century, have attacked the barbarity of the practice. Much of the morality championed by Victorian writers such as Dickens – ranging from the equitable distribution of wealth through to man's fundamental right to work – is clearly present in modern Islamic society.

Islamic banking practices and principles date back to the early part of the seventh century. In practice, Islamic banking does not mean that these banks cannot earn a profit. It requires a form of 'participatory financing' that differs fundamentally from the practice of commercial banks.

The revival of Islamic banking coincided with the worldwide celebration of the advent of the fifteenth century of the Islamic calendar (*Hijra*) in 1976, along with the growing income of many Muslims – in particular those in oil-producing countries. Islamic banking really took off when two Muslim countries introduced it as the *only* system for banking in their countries. The governments of Iran and Pakistan took steps in 1981 to apply the principles of interest-free banking to all banks (Gafoor, 1995). Today, Islamic banking is estimated to be managing funds amounting to approximately US$200 billion. The clients of Islamic banks are not confined to Muslim countries but are spread across Europe, the US and the Far East. In these countries, Islamic banking is primarily aimed at local Muslim communities.

founded as cooperatives by the turn of the nineteenth century to address the financial needs of the farming community. It classified its farmers as 'members' rather than as 'customers'. Consequently, cooperative banks are extremely local organizations – although often coordinated by national organizations.

Housing cooperatives[10] compete on the market for (cheap) houses; agriculture cooperatives often act as suppliers to retailers and the agro-food processing industry that is largely organized as for-profit. Through their decentralized structure, financial cooperatives are well positioned in local and regional communities which, in turn, give them access to detailed information about their clients – often members and proprietors of the local bank. At the same time, cooperative banks compete directly with commercial banks in many submarkets. European cooperative banks with 38 million members, 100 million clients, 2.5 trillion euros in assets, 1.3–1.4 trillion euros in deposits and loans, rank among the leading firms in financial intermediation. They hold a 17 per cent market share in Europe in credits. In some countries, this share is even higher: France (leading bank: Crédit Agricole), Finland (Okobank), the Netherlands (Rabobank), Italy (Banche Populari) up to 30 per cent.[11] In many developing and transition economies, the position of cooperatives is even stronger.

One of the biggest problems of the cooperative construction is the lack of flexibility and the risk of underinvestment. Cooperatives cannot generate money by issuing shares. This has prevented many cooperatives in the 1990s from engaging in rapid internationalization. Instead, they sought, for example, (international) expansionary coalitions with other cooperatives. In doing so, they initially appeared to be lagging behind companies listed on the stock exchange, but they have also been less at risk of getting into acute financial troubles caused by downward pressure on share prices. Consequently, the creditworthiness of cooperative banks is often better than that of commercial actors. According to international rating agencies Moody's, S&P and IBCA, the Dutch cooperative Rabobank is the most creditworthy bank of the country. It is the only bank with a Triple-A rating.

Public or private?

The distinction between 'public' and 'private' is severely hampered by contextual ambiguity. When a company goes 'public', it means that it gets listed on the stock exchange as a public limited company (plc). This is the case in the Anglo-Saxon system. But in many other countries, companies are 'private' almost by definition and the 'public corporation' is synonymous with 'state-owned' enterprise. The public corporation was originally a Dutch invention. In early seventeenth-century Holland, the emergence of the public corporation with limited (shareholder) liability was directly linked to managing the sizable risks associated with international trade. In the past, only states were able to cover the risks of big international endeavours. According to the old system, the owners of a ship that sunk were personally liable for the damages. Liability could even be passed on, keeping families in extreme poverty for many generations. So, if governments were not prepared to invest 'public money' (retained earnings recovered by taxes) in these projects, nothing would happen. Under these circumstances, private initiatives would remain small and a system of 'guilds' and artisans prevailed. The Ltd construction made it possible to finance big operations where the risk was borne by the investors. It also made it possible to reap large profits. And because profits outpaced losses (bankruptcies), it boosted the economy as a whole.

The Netherlands not only became the breeding ground for the first stock exchange, but also for the first real multinational corporation (the East Indies Company Ltd founded in 1602). The limited liability status of big public companies has remained, but it has also increasingly become subject to debate. One of the arguments against it is that it unduly stimulates firm managers to take excessive risks. The debate intensified in the wake of the wave of corporate scandals in the 1990s which has resulted, for instance, in the US Sarbannes Oxley Act. According to this Act, CEOs of publicly quoted companies at US stock exchanges are held personally (privately) accountable to a certain extent.

The notions of 'public' and 'private' generate considerable confusion in the international arena. A public company does not necessarily act in the public interest and/or provide public goods. So it is perhaps best to draw two distinctions delineating two different kinds of interfaces: between public and private organizations, and between the provision of public and private goods. Figure 1.5 depicts the two interfaces.

Where the two lines on the figure cross, two organizational forms appear that combine potentially divergent roles: (1) 'public' organizations producing private goods, and (2) 'private' organizations producing public or semi-public goods.

Public firms, private goods

The first category is generally covered by publicly listed companies which have already been discussed. These are the companies that are covered by most of the listings in *Business Week*, *Fortune* or the *Financial Times*. Some of these listings are even constructed on the basis of their 'market

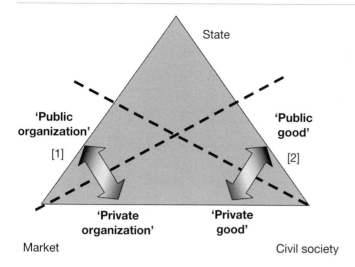

Figure 1.5 *The public–private interfaces*

capitalization' which implies that they are ranked according to the value they represent on stock exchanges. Throughout the 1990s, Microsoft, for instance, was the 'biggest' company according to these rankings. In the *Fortune* list (based on turnover) Microsoft only ranked 130 in 2003. When referring to 'public' companies, in general one refers to a private sector company with its shares listed at a stock exchange. A 'private' company, then, is a private sector company of which the ownership is maintained by a limited number of parties that are known to the company.

A typical hybrid organization operating at the grey public–private interface are so-called 'Government Sponsored Enterprises' (GSEs). GSEs are public companies with shareholders that receive government subsidies. In the US, GSEs were created by Congress to reduce the cost of capital for specific groups such as students, farmers and homeowners. GSEs have the implicit backing of the government, which gives investors in these companies the certainty that their investment is more or less guaranteed, and thus a higher yield. It makes them very competitive and profitable. In 2004, one of the biggest GSEs (Fannie Mae, the largest home mortgage corporation and the third biggest financial institution in the US) was hit by an accounting scandal (see Chapter 10).

Private organizations, public goods

The second category involves organizations that operate at the interface of the state and civil society. They are assumed to be part of the public infrastructure, but operate (semi) independently and deliver private goods and services. This includes, in particular, public universities/ schools, hospitals and legal functions represented by judges and public prosecutors, for example. These organizations are partly financed by public and partly by private funds for the benefit of those making use of the facility. Only patients make use of hospitals and only those with appropriate schooling may study at a university. Differences between countries exist specifically regarding public as opposed to private funding (often through fees) of the facilities.

Take, for example, the funding of education. According to OECD estimates, on average, public spending on education in 2000 covered around 88 per cent of all education expenses. The distribution of government spending among the categories of primary, secondary and tertiary education differs. The US – leading in absolute and relative investment in tertiary education – spent 7 per cent of GDP on tertiary education of which only a third came from government coffers. The remainder was from 'private' sources, primarily tuition fees, but also sponsoring from companies. In most continental European countries, governments fund 85 per cent of tertiary education costs. In primary and secondary education, however, the US government also funds 90 per cent of all costs.

Private spending is increasing in many countries primarily due to increased tuition fees payed by the participants (from civil society) and lowered spending by governments. In many developing countries, public funding – both in absolute and in relative terms – of primary and secondary education is substantially below that of developed countries. Poor education as a factor in impeded national development can therefore be attributed primarily to insufficient government investment in education. Asian countries such as Japan and Korea resemble the American model with a substantial part of tertiary education being funded privately.

The financing of most of these (hybrid) organizations around the world has come under pressure due to the budgetary crisis of most governments. Over the years, it has led to ever-increasing individual contributions, respectively collected via personal risk payments or tuition fees. As such, these organizations have gradually become hybrids also in their financing structure. Finally, a movement towards the market can be ascertained. Hybrid hospitals establish one ward for private patients with the objective of financing the rest of the hospital in this manner. Public services can thus in part be privately funded via 'cross-subsidies'. This is an old principle that has been used a lot in the past, for example, to finance telecom infrastructure: cross-subsidies flowed from larger to smaller customers, but also from urban agglomerations to users in the countryside. This created the preconditions for successful nationwide network economies and ultimately also for national development. With the privatization of telecommunications, the discussion on 'universal services' – especially in developing countries – has erupted once again and was prompted by the simple question: 'Who pays and who profits from a purportedly public good?' As waiting lists for health care grow longer in some countries, the discussion has also flared up about the appropriate balance between public and private, and the question as to what extent these institutions may be profit oriented. There seem to be limits though: a university cannot readily be organized purely via the market mechanism, as this would imply that students who have more money (spending power) can 'buy' higher marks.[12]

Governmental or non-governmental?

Representatives of civil society are often referred to as 'non-governmental organizations' (NGOs). In 2000 the US accounted for at least 43,958 NGOs (UIA, 2001). Since the fall of the Berlin Wall, around 100,000 NGOs were created in Central and Eastern Europe (Rischard, 2002: 48). Some NGOs have well over 1 million members. The World Wildlife Fund, for instance, has 5 million members. But the 'non-governmental' concept differentiates too little. As with so many concepts in social sciences, it only specifies what the group is not. Market organizations could also fall into this category. Entrepreneurs, after all, are also citizens (see Figure 1.6).

In practice, however, companies are not often referred to as NGOs. Companies are profit oriented. The real NGO is not only non-governmental, but also not profit oriented. The interests NGOs promote can then be divided into 'private' and 'public' interests. When the acting agents coincide with the (potential) beneficiaries of the pressure exerted, it is a matter of protection of private interests. This is the case for many business associations. But does FIFA (world football organization) only represent the private interests of the associated football clubs, or a wider public interest (such as football fans)? When the acting agents do not coincide with the

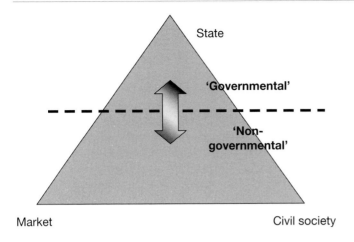

Figure 1.6 The government–non-government interface

(potential) beneficiaries, representation is geared towards the public or common interest. In this sense, non-profit-oriented NGOs generally aim at representing the public interest in one way or another. NGOs can be distinguished by (a) type of movement and (b) legal personality.

Different types of movements

A movement is a conscious, collective and organized endeavour to bring about large-scale change in the social order (Wilson, 1975: 8). A movement usually consists of a number of so-called 'Single-Issue NGOs' (SINGOs) that focus exclusively on one issue, such as child labour, genetic modification, noise nuisance, human rights or environmental degradation. There are also 'Single-Company NGOs' that exclusively follow one specific company. Examples include McSpotlight (focusing on McDonald's), Wal-Mart Watch (focusing on Wal-Mart) and NikeWatch (focusing on Nike). Organizations such as Greenpeace, Friends of the Earth and the World Wildlife Fund form part of the environmental movement. The social movement is concerned with issues such as working conditions, human rights, child labour and discrimination. Organizations such as Amnesty International, Clean Clothes Campaign, consumer organizations and trade unions fall into this category.

With/without legal personality

For individuals and groupings without corporate personality, the term 'pressure groups' is often employed. These are characterized by limited formalization and division of labour. Once they have achieved their objectives, organizations such as these often quickly cease to exist. Since it is tough to define their constituency, they have a lot of freedom of movement and can afford to take radical and aggressive action. They do not, after all, have to take the opinions of members or donors into account. The absence of a constituency that can be called to account, renders these groupings a most unpredictable counterpart of companies and governments. NGOs with legal personality can, for example, institute a civil lawsuit against someone.

Two legal forms prevail: associations and foundations. An association (or society) has members who make a financial contribution. It is compulsory for an association to hold membership meetings where the members determine the budget and elect the executive committee. An association also has donors, but in contrast to members, they cannot vote. Donors support the association with financial contributions on a regular basis. Friends of the Earth is an example of an NGO that has chosen the legal form of an association. A foundation has a board of directors that is self-appointed. Foundations obtain resources from donors who have no formal means at their disposal to influence the organization's policy. Examples of large NGOs whose legal form is a foundation include Greenpeace, Clean Clothes Campaign (CCC) and the World Wildlife Fund (WWF).

1.4 CONCLUSION: DECIPHERING SOCIETAL COMPLEXITY

The organizational outlook of societies proves rather complex and diverse. Part of the complexity is caused by the large number of hybrid forms existing and the active pursuit along the borders of these organizational forms across countries. Section 1.3 classified the various organizational forms along four dichotomies: public/private goods, public/private interests, profit/non-profit, governmental/non-governmental.

On the basis of these dichotomies it is possible to first distinguish three principal organizational forms (cf. Figure 1.7):

- (A) the ideal-type state roles: a public organization, governmental and non-profit oriented for the provision of public goods. This is the entity most people would refer to when they talk about 'states'.
- (B) the ideal-type civil society role: a private organization, non-profit oriented, oriented at the provision of public goods, non-governmental. This is the enitity most people would refer to when they talk about 'NGOs'.
- (C) the ideal-type market roles: a public organization, profit oriented for the provision of private goods and non-governmental. This is the entity most people would refer to when they talk about 'firms'.

Five additional hybrid organizations could be identified. These are listed below; the numbers refer to those on Figure 1.7. The interesting paradox exists in most societies that all these organizations – even when they have a non-profit orientation – can generate considerable funds

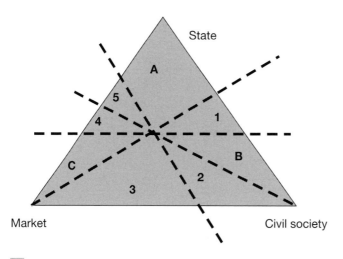

Figure 1.7 A kaleidoscope of organizational forms

and add value to the economy (accounted for as income/value added in national accounts). So they all have an important function in the economy and make up the 'fabric' that constitutes the Gross Domestic Product (GDP). The extent to which these organizations are rival and lead to more or less societal convergence (see Introduction to Part I), depends on other organizational principles that will be treated in Chapter 2:

- At the state–civil society interface: (1) non-profit, private organizations, for the provision of public goods, (predominantly) funded by governments; we find most public universities, legal institutions, public hospitals and government sponsored enterprises in this category.
- At the market–civil society interface: (2) non-profit, private organizations, providing private goods, non-governmental; we find most cooperatives in this category; (3) for-profit, private organizations for the provision of private goods, non-governmental; we find most family-owned firms in this category.
- At the market–state interface: (4) for-profit, public organizations, that are (partly or wholly) governmental and produce private goods; we find most state-owned companies in this category; (5) for-profit public organizations, that are (partly) governmental but produce a public good; we find most public–private partnerships in this category.

Hybrid organizations that operate at or across these interfaces have traditionally been the frontrunners in the area of socially responsible business practice. They often have their origins in social ideals, such as cooperatives that want to break through the might of the market (via distributive trade) in favour of the welfare of 'members'; family businesses that shun interference from the capital markets (in the form of shareholders) in favour of the longer-term interests of the family; Islamic banks that are set up according to religious principles and hospitals that have to be efficient, but at the same time look after the health of their patients. In periods of recession family-owned firms show greater stability than publicly owned firms; they also are less inclined to shun employees. This chapter has explored the existing evidence on their profitability and has shown that hybrid organizations are not necessarily less profitable than the ideal-type for-profit organizations (type C). In terms of stability, employment and growth prospects they even provide a viable alternative in many societies. Traditionally, all large hybrid organizations, given the nature of their position in society, are intrinsically more concerned with the principles of socially responsible management than non-hybrid organizations are.[13] The same applies to their communication strategy. For hybrid organizations, an annual report is always more than a reproduction of the profit-loss account – even if it is only because it is exceptionally difficult to calculate – in that it serves as a strategic tool for the organization to position itself towards its various constituencies both inside and outside the company.

25

Chapter 2

Rival models: interactions within and between societies

CHAPTER CONTENTS

2.1 INTRODUCTION: IDENTIFYING SUCCESSFUL MODELS

In the debate about the most appropriate institutions for business, sweeping claims are regularly made. In the 1990s, the institutions of the Anglo-Saxon model seemed to dominate and the (public) firm aimed at 'shareholder' value was proclaimed to be the most successful. Critics of this model often reiterated a set of drawbacks of the model, such as low trust, high transaction costs (due to litigation) and great uncertainty (particularly for small shareholders). But the strongest criticism, in practice, came from equally successful contenders from continental Europe and Asia who employed different societal models featuring different business institutions (for instance private firms) aimed at creating so-called 'stakeholder' value and in which governments played a more active role. To what extent do countries display similarities and/or divergence in their models?

There are good reasons why rival organizational forms exist (Chapter 1). It is not the characteristics of the individual spheres that determine the success or dominance of a particular society. Neither can individual organizational (business) forms be successful on their own. Economic and business success critically depends on the interaction between the institutional spheres and the way they are balanced. Henry Mintzberg explains it as follows: 'it was not "capitalism" that triumphed after the Berlin Wall, but "balance". In the late 1980s, the West still understood the importance of balance between governments, companies and the "social sector" – mutual societies, co-operatives and the like' (*FT*, 16 September 2003) (Mintzberg, 2001).

This chapter explores what a possible 'balance' between the various societal spheres in practice could look like and whether it is possible to identify successful societal arrangements that also have been economically successful. This requires, first, the identification of interactive principles of the institutional spheres *within* societies (section 2.2). Second, two additional dimensions will be explored that influence in particular the interaction *between* societies: culture (section 2.3) and openness (section 2.4). Economically successful (societal) models have adopted various combinations of these characteristics. Section 2.5 spots the most successful contemporary models and considers whether these models converge or diverge on relevant characteristics (section 2.6). Does this lead to one 'best-practice' or 'hegemonic' model or will institutional and model rivalry persist (section 2.7)?

2.2 BALANCING SPHERES, INTERACTIVE PRINCIPLES

The debate about the correct balance between the different societal spheres is ongoing. Many countries have relied solely on the state to realize rapid social and economic development, which has undermined market and civil society institutions. 'Failures of government' followed, indicated by bureaucratic rigidity, an unaccountable government and a concentration of political power. In Eastern Europe, the Soviet Union, but also in Argentina and South Africa, it limited the capacity of the two other societal spheres to denounce or compensate for the failures of government.

On the other hand, if the market is too dominant in society, 'market failure' can occur. This manifests itself in the concentration of wealth in a few, monopoly positions, passing costs on to others (for example, of environmental pollution, also referred to as negative externalities; Coase, 1988) and a shortage in the production of public goods. In cases such as these, the market is insufficiently regulated by the state, and civil society is incapable of articulating its interests effectively. This was the case in the earlier phases of capitalism in the US and England and in developing countries that embarked on a process of full liberalization in an attempt to attract foreign capital. Finally, when institutions of civil society dominate other institutions, the risk of 'civil society failures' (or societal failures) arises, which manifests itself in an obsession with a particular definition of the 'good' and a lack of tolerance towards other values and ideologies. Examples include the theocratic regimes of Iran and the Taliban in Afghanistan where the market and state are subordinate to religious principles, or specific elites in a country that create a clientist system with an oversupply of 'club goods' for the in-crowd of the family, the social class, or the special interest group that rules over all other spheres (and thus turn public goods into club goods). The debilitating 'logic' of these mechanisms was already signalled by Mancur Olson (1971) in his treaties on collective action.

The dominance of one specific societal sphere almost always leads to counter-reactions. Too much power in the hands of the state leads to rebellion by civil society. Too much power in the hands of the market brings new economic regulations and citizens that seek out alternatives to the market (from new age religions to the development of alternative monetary systems). Too much power in the hands of specific civil society groupings leads to counter-reactions of other groupings.

Three specific principles can be employed to give shape to the complex interaction between the three institutions of society (Linder and Vaillancourt Rosenau, 2000: 8): subsidiarity, substitution and complementarity.

Subsidiarity

The subsidiarity principle has its origins in the Catholic social doctrine and holds that society is hierarchically structured with the state at the higher, and the family at the lower end. As long as the family is capable of looking after itself, no other institutions are needed. The subsidiarity principle has also been adopted by the European Union as a leading principle of governance: the Union will regulate only those affairs that cannot be given shape by the individual member states. Civil society as the 'social capital' of the market economy is another dimension of the subsidiarity principle and has been particularly well developed in (Catholic) countries such as Italy.

But the system does not apply exclusively to these countries. Sociologist Robert Putnam (1995) concluded that a society's economy does not function well without sufficient social capital. The basic idea of social capital is that membership of community organizations, clubs or associations creates trust and a feeling of community by building shared values and norms. This idea does not fit easily with the economic orthodoxy of selfish individuals (*Homo economicus*). A well-organized civil society makes an important contribution to balancing the scales of society. But, spillovers of social capital formation are not necessarily always positive: the club goods that communities build also create barriers to entry for others or can even exclude them altogether. Economists have great difficulty linking the idea of 'social capital' to economic growth (OECD, 2001). In the case of a badly developed legal and regulatory system, social capital is of greater significance to economic growth than in the case of well-developed institutions (the European Union for instance) (Beugelsdijk and van Schaik, 2001). What can be considered 'sufficient' social capital in practice can differ from country to country.

Companies have traditionally acknowledged the importance of social capital by providing funding for civil society organizations. Two forms are traditionally employed: sponsoring and philanthropy. In Europe, according to European Commission estimates, 81 per cent of all sponsoring by business is dedicated to sports whereas the remainder is for culture and good causes. Annual European sponsoring of sports by business amounts to 5.7 billion euro. In turn, some sports clubs that started as 'amateur clubs' have themselves become thriving businesses. But many of them still obtain a considerable part of their income from sponsoring. Spanish and record-holding football club Real Madrid, for instance, receives a third of its sizeable budget – hundreds of millions of euros – from sponsors (*Vk*, 29 November 2003). Corporate philanthropy, on the other hand, is sometimes represented as a vital aspect of 'corporate citizenship' (Saiia *et al.*, 2003: 170). Of the 4.5 billion euro that circulated for instance in the Dutch philanthropic sector in 1999 (defined as voluntary contribution to non-profit causes), 37 per cent came from households and 51 per cent from companies (Schuyt, 2002: 496). In the US, however, corporate philanthropy only accounted for around 5.1 per cent of all philanthropic giving in 1999 (Saiia *et al.*, 2003: 171). Worldwide, it is estimated that philanthropy accounts for around 10 per cent of the income of the non-profit sector. More than half (51 per cent) is generated by membership contributions and more than a third (39 per cent) is funded by government (Johns Hopkins, 1997).

Substitution

One sphere can take over the function of another sphere – the market can take over a large part of voluntary work, the state can replace the market and vice versa. This can lead to interesting confrontations in practice: the greatest challenge of near-monopolist Microsoft in the area of software is not so much government that (still) imposes limited restrictions by means of anti-competition laws.[1] Neither is Microsoft threatened by other commercial competitors. Its greatest threat is Linux, the software system that was created by a group of highly qualified 'volunteers' from universities and companies who, 'in their free time' in the 1990s created a non-profit product or public good. Linus Torvald made the source code public to further the development of the system – something that Microsoft specifically did not do in order to operate as market player. Linux poses the biggest threat to Microsoft's hegemony since it introduced the Netscape browser in 1995 (*Business Week*, 3 March 2003: 48). The attractiveness of Linux has increased due to the search for lower computing bills (Linux is free) and the decision of Intel – another dominant player in the computer market – to make chips for Linux. But, most importantly, probably, because of the widespread resentment towards Microsoft's almost monopoly position in large parts of the computer systems market and its lack of transparency in revealing its source codes. Linux is based on the principle of open sourcing. Linux provides a 'democratic', 'transparent' and 'non-profit' alternative to the monopolistic, untransparent, excessively profit-oriented strategy of Microsoft.[2]

Complementarity and pragmatism

All sorts of combinations and alliances exist between the spheres whereby different spheres supplement each other. Such supplementation is necessary for a dynamic and robust society. In this regard, the rise of the Internet represents an excellent example. Tim Berners-Lee was an independent consultant associated with the European Organization for Nuclear Research (CERN) in Geneva (the public institution which, among other things, developed the large particle accelerator) when he developed the World Wide Web (WWW) and HTML around 1990 for his own use as database developer. Afterwards, he made the conscious decision to place his brainchild at the disposal of the global public free of charge, in order, among other things, to further develop the specifications (including such well-known acronyms as http, url, html and xml) in consultation with a group of 'volunteers' from all over the world.[3] Through these actions, the WWW became an internationally accepted standard at an unprecedented rate. Soon thereafter, it unleashed the opportunity for companies such as eBay and Amazon.com to develop commercial applications on the Internet. An interesting thought-experiment for the Business–Society Management drinks table is: what would have happened if Bill Gates, the founder of Microsoft, had developed the WWW? Or, put differently: what would have happened if Berners-Lee had patented his web software?[4]

2.3 THE ROLE OF CULTURE

Culture influences interaction within and between societies. Cultural differences become particularly apparent when people from different societies meet. There has been fierce debate among management scholars on the relative position of culture vis-à-vis institutions. The debate has been on whether structure and institutions create culture (the position of the 'structuralists') or whether culture creates structure and institutions (the position of the 'culturalists') (Schneider and Barsoux, 1997). The debate has not been closed, and probably never will be, because it is safe to assume that culture and structure are intertwined and interact. Taking this principle into account, culture can be identified as another benchmark for characterizing societies, firms and the way in which they operate along with being another dimension in the 'balancing act' of the various spheres.

The culture of a country is intertwined with the relative position of each 'sphere'. It is still common in cultural studies to use the insights of the classical studies conducted by Hofstede (1991) who tried to illustrate the impact of cultural differences on management.[5] He distinguished between four characteristics: (1) power distance (the extent to which a society accepts the unequal distribution of power in institutions and organizations); (2) uncertainty avoidance (the extent to which a society tries to create predictability and stability to lower general feelings of uncertainty); (3) individualism/collectivism (the extent to which people are inclined to take care of themselves and their immediate families); (4) masculinity/femininity (the extent to which people are biased towards 'masculine' values of assertiveness, competitiveness and materialism or towards 'feminine' values of nurturing and quality of life and relationships). In cultures with a significant power distance and extensive hierarchies, the state can take a more hierarchical position towards civil society. In cultures with a smaller power distance and flatter hierarchies, governments, business and civil society are often searching for more pragmatic societal arrangements.

On the basis of these characteristics, at least four rival cultures can be distinguished. In Anglo-Saxon economies, one can find low power distance and low uncertainty avoidance with individual flexibility, delegation and coordination through informal personal communication and output control. In Asian economies, uncertainty avoidance remains relatively low but it is embedded in relatively hierarchical systems, with centralized, paternalistic structures and high levels of social control. The continental European culture (in particular of the north-western countries) is somewhere in between the Anglo-Saxon and Asian models with a more feminine culture, low power distance, higher uncertainty avoidance and forms of individualism that also attach value to social communities. In Arab countries, a great power distance is generally combined with low individuality and a medium degree of uncertainty avoidance. Cultures overlap in some of their characteristics and specific cultures can simultaneously be associated with economically successful and economically less successful models. This renders it difficult to attach much explanatory value to culture, but as a factor in the interaction between business and society it is, nevertheless, very important to take into account.

2.4 A HIDDEN DIMENSION: INSTITUTIONAL OPENNESS

The three institutional spheres not only interact within the boundaries of the nation-state, such interaction can also take place across national boundaries. But the literature reveals remarkably limited interest for the degree of internationalization of the economy and the relative openness/closedness of national institutions. Countries are often presented as relatively closed and coherent systems. Most text books of economics, culture, institutions, 'business systems' and politics use the nation-state as level of analysis and comparison. Many cultures, economic and political systems, however, are not closed. The nature of interaction between national institutional spheres and their organizations critically depends on the openness or closedness of the arena in which the interactions between major actors appears (cf. van Tulder and Audet, 2004; Muller, 2004). The extent to which actors have economic interests with or within other institutional environments, in turn, affects the nature of domestic institutions. In civil society, international migration patterns, for instance, affect family structures and particularly the institutions of metropolitan areas. Inter-governmental and supranational organizations affect, and sometimes act as substitute for, national laws (see also Chapter 5). In the business environment, the degree of internationalization particularly affects the openness of the bargaining environment. Two primary macro-economic measures of economic openness can be identified: trade and Foreign Direct Investment (FDI).[6]

Openness makes domestic actors dependent upon the 'ups and downs' of international markets. The 'openness index' of the World Bank and the trade-balance assessments in most macro-economic models are based on export/import ratios. But exports as well as imports leave the national institutional system relatively untouched. Trading actors often remain firmly rooted within their (national) institutional environment. Large import flows can have an impact via 'embedded' technologies and practices from other institutions, but with exports the effects on the national institutions are more indirect and often smaller.[7]

The openness towards FDI is a stronger indication of the institutional openness of a country. FDI flows and stocks document the way in which multinational corporations invest in specific countries through the establishment of subsidiaries or the acquisition of assets. FDI signifies a much higher degree of commitment to local institutional environments. Firms engaging in direct investment create their own specific 'barriers to exit' from a local economy which they would not have if they were merely exporting to the country. Export flows can be redirected relatively easily, whereas investments imply considerable 'sunk costs', such as setting up factories, shops and the like in the host economy. A high share of inward FDI stock (as a percentage of GDP) gives an indication of the size of foreign actors' involvement in the domestic economy and its 'inward openness'. It measures the impact of host multinationals on the domestic economy. The subsidiaries of host firms participate in the domestic economy and thus can also directly contribute to the creation of domestic institutions and/or affect the nature of the interaction between the various national spheres. In the event that these firms are well rooted abroad, they are bound to introduce some of their institutional practices to the domestic arena. Outward FDI measures the degree to which domestic actors (home-based multinationals) invest abroad. Outward investment creates a 'leakage' effect on the domestic economy by exporting (productive) capital abroad. The higher the outward investment share, the greater the impact can be on the domestic economy and the greater the accompanying impact of foreign institutions on domestic institutions. Outward FDI only indirectly affects the openness of an economy,[8] whereas inward FDI does that more directly. Figure 2.1 shows how the world's major economies can be positioned along these two measures of institutional openness.

Developed economies provide the home base for more than 95 per cent of the world's largest multinationals (UNCTAD, 2003). Since the 1980s, around 85 per cent of total FDI flow has come and gone to developed economies. In this sense, most developed economies are strongly intertwined through FDI. But even within this group, the degree of openness varies. The degree of openness impacts the way in which the success or failure of the national model needs to be analysed.

- *Closed*: According to this yardstick, around a third of the world's countries can be considered relatively closed economic and institutional systems. They share negligible or small degrees of inward *and* outward FDI. Large countries such as India, Russia, the US and Japan belong to this category. Comparing the national institutions of these countries on a nation-to-nation basis as done in mainstream economics, would thus still make sense. Most of these countries are well known for their 'go-it-alone' strategy in international gremia (chapter 5). A number of developing countries that were either unattractive to foreign firms or imposed substantial barriers to entry also fall into this category. They include, in particular, Arab countries, which share negligible degrees of outward openness and small degrees of inward openness.
- *Outward open*: Countries that are outwardly open – and thus have more outward than inward FDI stock – are almost always developed countries. Two-thirds of the 193 countries, share very low degrees of outward openness. The number of countries that can ultimately be classified as outwardly open is very limited (3 per cent of all countries). These countries are host and home to major multinationals and suffer the greatest investment 'leakages' – productive capital that is not invested in the home market, but abroad. The success of the Norwegian, Finnish and French economies, is strongly related to (and dependent on) the European Union – host to most outward FDI from these countries. The success of the Taiwan economy is strongly related to China, where most of its outwards investments are headed towards.
- *Inward open*: All developing countries are inwardly open to varying degrees. A few countries combine very low degrees of outward openness with very high degrees of outward openness (more than 40 per cent). Studying these countries, in particular,

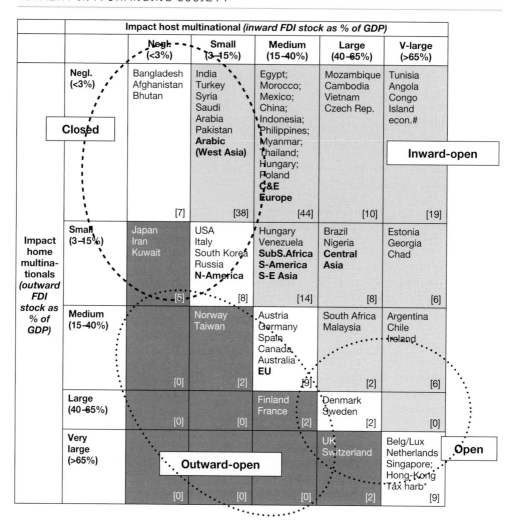

Impact host multinational *(inward FDI stock as % of GDP)*					
	Negl. (<3%)	**Small** (3–15%)	**Medium** (15–40%)	**Large** (40–65%)	**V-large** (>65%)
Negl. (<3%)	Bangladesh Afghanistan Bhutan	India Turkey Syria Saudi Arabia Pakistan **Arabic (West Asia)**	Egypt; Morocco; Mexico; China; Indonesia; Philippines; Myanmar; Thailand; Hungary; Poland **C&E Europe**	Mozambique Cambodia Vietnam Czech Rep.	Tunisia Angola Congo Island econ.#
	[7]	[38]	[44]	[10]	[19]
Small (3–15%)	Japan Iran Kuwait	USA Italy South Korea Russia **N-America**	Hungary Venezuela **SubS.Africa S-America S-E Asia**	Brazil Nigeria **Central Asia**	Estonia Georgia Chad
	[5]	[8]	[14]	[8]	[6]
Medium (15–40%)		Norway Taiwan	Austria Germany Spain Canada Australia **EU**	South Africa Malaysia	Argentina Chile Ireland
	[0]	[2]	[9]	[2]	[6]
Large (40–65%)			Finland France	Denmark Sweden	
	[0]	[0]	[2]	[2]	[0]
Very large (>65%)				UK Switzerland	Belg/Lux Netherlands Singapore; Hong-Kong Tax harb*
	[0]	[0]	[0]	[2]	[9]

Impact home multinationals *(outward FDI stock as % of GDP)*

Closed

Inward-open

Outward-open

Open

Figure 2.1 *Relative institutional openness: the impact of host and home multinationals on selected economies, 2002 (N = 193)*

Source: FDI data based on UNCTAD, 2003

Notes: * Cayman Islands, Bermuda, Virgin Islands, Panama; # e.g. St Kitts and Nevis, Saint Lucia; [ ] = total number of countries in this category.

without taking into account the impact of host players (multinational firms) on the domestic economy and institutions does not make much sense either.

- *Open*: The same also applies to some of the countries that combine relatively high inward openness with a high outward openness. Tax havens such as Bermuda and the Cayman Islands, and successful city-states including Hong Kong and Singapore, in particular, belong to this development category. The development path of these economies can only be understood within the broader context of their regional function (Hong Kong with reference to China, and Singapore with reference to the ASEAN region) or their position within the international regulatory system (taxes in particular). Developed countries that are open on both accounts are primarily the smaller countries of Europe. The only medium-sized economy (in terms of population) that in the 1990s developed a substantial degree of outward *and* inward openness is the UK. This combination has been relatively successful. Within the G7 group of largest economies (measured in political terms and in total GDP), the UK registered relatively high growth figures since the end of the 1990s. The country combined low inflation with a solid currency. Like Ireland, the UK has built its recent growth model on the basis of foreign capital. The 'price' the country has to pay for this development is that leading institutes and companies are run by foreigners – often from erstwhile colonies such as South Africa (leading in the British judicial system and with many firms), Australia and Canada (dominating the media), Americans (dominating the banking industry). Economic cornerstones such as Harrods, British Airways and British Telecom are being managed by non-British citizens (Sampson, 2004).

2.5 SELECTING SUCCESSFUL ECONOMIES

What have been the societal success formulas of the post-war era? Two measures are generally adopted to identify macro-economic success: *per capita* Gross Domestic Product (GDP) growth and the scores on the Human Development Index (HDI). GDP is a relatively straightforward measure of the size of the formal economy. The internationally acknowledged distinction between 'developed', 'developing' and 'least developed' countries are all based on per capita GDP measurements. The relative growth of GDP over a longer period of time for a developing economy reflects the speed at which it is 'catching up'. In international institutional comparisons, such an economy is clearly 'doing something right'. The HDI number, reported in the Human Development Report of the United Nations Development Programme (UNDP), is an indication of a country's level of development. The HDI ranks nations according to their citizens' quality of life rather than strictly by a nation's traditional economic figures.[9] On the basis of these selection criteria, three types of countries can be attributed the status of a post-war 'success'.

First, in the group of developed countries, during the 1975–2003 period, almost all small open economies of Europe consistently scored highest on the HDI and very high on GDP. Second, among the medium sized and large developed countries, the US stands out. It has by far the biggest GDP in the world, but its HDI – although in the High Human Development group – has not been among the best in the world. Other Anglo-Saxon countries such as Australia, Canada and the UK have experienced particularly strong GDP growth since the beginning of the 1990s. Germany and France have become the biggest continental European economies and the motor of the European integration process in various post-war periods. Like the US they score high on GDP per capita, but slightly lower on the HDI. Third, in the group of developing countries, only Eastern Asian countries apply for global 'star' status in the post-war period. According to World Bank estimates, nine Eastern Asian countries have been among the 12 fastest growing economies in the world since the mid-1970s. In this group of economies Japan, South Korea and China deserve separate mention for their relative economic and population size. Other successful East Asian countries ('tigers') are either minute city-states (such as Hong-Kong and Singapore) and/or occupy a very specific political position vis-à-vis mainland China (Hong Kong, having lost its relative independence in 2000; Taiwan still considered to be a 'dissident' province of China).

In other developing regions of the world, GDP growth, the HDI position, or both, make it difficult to classify countries as a 'success'. In Latin America, most countries have not been able to grow quickly and/or move towards a High HDI ranking. Only Chile and some smaller tax havens in the Caribbean scored reasonably, but not exceptionally, well. In the Arab/Middle Eastern region, some countries are included in the High HDI group (Bahrain, United Arab

Emirates, Kuwait, Qatar), but they are either very small states or scored much less impressively on GDP growth per capita. The larger countries (Iran, Saudi Arabia, Syria) generally are in the Medium HDI group and have relatively low GDPs per capita and/or relatively low growth. The 25 'least liveable' countries in the world in 2003, according to the HDI, are all located in Africa. The country in Africa that can be considered a relative economic success is Botswana, but its GDP growth over the period 1980–2000 has not (yet) been matched by a High HDI ranking (in 2003 it was among the bottom 46 countries in the HDI ranking).

2.6 RIVAL SUCCESS FORMULAS

The 'core' group of biggest and particularly successful post-war social and economic models – as distinguished in the previous section – displays very diverse combinations and ways of balancing the three institutional spheres.

The US: antagonistic relations

The US is by far the largest economy in the world. Together with the other Anglo-Saxon economies (Australia, Canada and the UK) it experienced the fastest growth in real GDP of the high-income countries since the 1990s – after decades of relative decline by these same countries. The market sector in the US is very big, the state is relatively small and there is almost no overlap between the three societal spheres. The Americans employ a '*trias politica*', a rather strict separation of powers, which leads to strongly antagonistic relations (the logic of substitution). In the constitution of the US, strict limits have been specified as to the intervention possibilities of the state. Most Anglo-Saxon countries have adopted this 'liberal' regime (Esping-Andersen, 1990; Salomon *et al.*, 2000). This institutional set-up contributed to the growth of the whole economy. Due to its success, many other countries – in particular in South America – copied large parts of the American constitution, but without achieving comparable economic growth. State-owned companies in the US barely exist. Trade unions, although very militant, are weak and barely centrally organized. The judicial system is based on jurisprudence, rendering the US a *litigation society*: a judge and/or a jury pass judgment or a verdict on everything and everyone. Moreover, in contrast with most countries, many functionaries (from judges to police commissioners) are appointed by means of elections.

Shareholder capitalism dominates, which leads to a short-term oriented society fixated on quarterly profits and marked by low savings quotas. The employment mobility of the population is relatively high as is the role of migration and immigrant labour in civil society and universities. The US is the leading example of the 'Anglo-Saxon' model. It remains a relatively closed economy even after the implementation of the North American Free Trade Agreement (NAFTA) in 1995 between the US, Mexico and Canada. As a regional integration agreement, NAFTA is much more 'superficial' than the European Union (it has, for instance, no regional competition or trade policy), and thus has a less pervasive effect on firm strategy and domestic institutions. In the 1990s, NAFTA has in fact further lowered the openness of the US to external trade and inward investment (Muller, 2004; Carillo *et al.*, 2004). The US is generally considered as a 'hegemonic' power that employs a go-it-alone strategy internationally and dominates the North American region.

Japan: loyalty and long term

Japan's economic success started earliest of all the East Asian economies and is without peers: its GDP per capita grew from US$276 in 1950 – comparable to developing countries – to more than US$23,000 in 1990 – comparable to leading industrial countries. Japan is the second largest economy in the world. At the same time, Japan moved towards a High HDI ranking (ninth in 2003). In Japan, the interface between state and market is very well developed: a limited number of clusters of large companies (*keiretsu*) and a relatively weak government often work in close cooperation and consultation. In the 1950s and 1960s, the state did attempt to be more controlling but could not realize it in practice. The Japanese state is sometimes portrayed as a 'developmental state'. In the case of Japan, this is not the sign of a particularly strong government, but of a tightly developed interface with business interests (cf. Ruigrok and van Tulder, 1995). The 'visions' of the famous Ministry of International Trade and Industry (MITI) played an important role in Japan's remarkable economic success, but these visions were always based on close pre-consultation with the biggest business stakeholders. Civil society is relatively small and not well organized, but very coherent. Foreign migration to and from Japan has been very modest. Trade unions are not centrally organized. These plant unions play an important role in the functioning of companies, but can easily be played off against one another. Strikes hardly occur as trade unions are simultaneously exceptionally loyal to the interests of the company they work for. Among other things, this has to do with the lack of public pensions and rudimentary unemployment benefits. The Japanese state can therefore not be classified as a 'welfare' state. People are extremely dependent on a job at one of the large employers. Consequently, savings quotas are high, which allows companies to finance investments at relatively low cost. As such, they are able to focus on the long term. The Japanese model was very successful in the 1970s and 1980s, but faced considerable difficulties in the 1990s. Japan has always adopted a go-it-alone strategy without engaging in regional integration, but the ASEAN region can in many respects be considered the 'annex region' of the Japanese developmental model (ibid.). It remains an extremely closed economy, which has profited greatly from exports to other countries and has only modestly engaged in outward FDI (cf. van Tulder, 2004c).

Germany: *Wirtschaftwunder* and *Mittelstand*

The biggest and strongest economy in Europe remains Germany, despite the signs of economic decline that has been afflicting the German economy since the mid-1990s. It is the third largest economy in the world and home to many innovative large multinationals. The German economic system recovered very quickly from the defeat in the Second World War. In many respects, the bombing of most of its factories and cities created an enormous boost for re-investment. The growth period it encountered in the period 1950–70, has become known as the German *Wirtschaftswunder* (economic miracle). Not only did it create a robust domestic economy, it also triggered growth in all its neighbouring countries. The German economy became the motor of European integration. The German model is also referred to as the *Rhineland* or *stakeholder* model (cf. Albert, 1993). The three institutional spheres are valued more or less equally and supplement each other in many respects. Trade unions have a legally fixed representation on the boards of companies and while state ownership in many sectors still exists, it is approached more pragmatically than in France. Consequently, wages are relatively high in Germany, but this triggered a very innovative economy. Germany is a Federal State in which most of the actual bargaining/negotiating and institutional interaction develops at state (*Bundesland*) level. The subsidiary principle applies in the institutional interaction between the various governments. Studies on the performance of the Rhineland *stakeholder* capitalism model (e.g. de Jong, 1988) show that the profitability of German companies is traditionally higher than that of companies which operate within the framework of Anglo-Saxon *shareholder* capitalism. Measured only in terms of so-called market capitalization (stock markets), American and English companies performed better in the 1990s. Capital markets in Germany are much less developed, but industrial banks, on the other hand, play a vital role in financing large companies. Banks and large industrial firms hold strong cross holdings.

The part of the German model, however, that has generally been considered the core of its success, is the smaller and medium sized, family-owned firms. This is the famous German *Mittelstand*. Many of these firms are engineering firms that, in close interaction with local universities (through a well-advanced system of vocational training), create the most dynamic and entrepreneurial part of the economy. The German *Mittelstand* is often more international than their better-known big German counterparts. German reunification in the 1990s had serious and relatively negative repercussions for the competitiveness of the German economy, with the unemployment rate rising at the same time. Nevertheless, and at the same time, German firms have vigorously expanded in Central and Eastern Europe, which has enabled them to become more cost-effective. The success of the German model is increasingly dependent on the course of the European Union and particularly on the role played by the new entrants from May 2004 onwards.

Small countries: corporatism as compensation for openness

Combined, the eight small continental European countries (Nordic countries, Benelux, Austria and Switzerland), would represent the fourth largest economy in the world with the size of the population of the UK or France. Up to the 1970s the 'Swedish model' represented a successful model for many countries – combining a welfare state with a competitive industry. During the second half of the 1990s, the Dutch '*poldermodel*' generated interest in its job-creating potential, high economic growth in combination with a welfare state. By the start of the twenty-first century, the 'Nokia model' of Finland allegedly has become the most innovative economy in Europe, combining high R&D expenditures with – again – a welfare state. Most small and successful countries in Europe share a number of characteristics:[10] their economies are 'more open' than average and they consequently have to cope with a process of interaction between institutions that is strongly affected by international actors. Export and imports represent more than 40 per cent of GDP, while FDI stock – both inward and outward – amounts to more than 40 per cent of GDP. Small, open economies share smaller populations, a lower GDP, a higher concentration of employment in production with a few large companies. Most leading domestic firms have larger interests abroad than in the domestic economy. Economic 'openness' would normally lead to domestic fragmentation with foreign interests prevailing over domestic interests. This has also become known as the 'small country squeeze'. Interestingly enough, however, the most successful smaller economies also share a higher propensity towards national consensus building. They have institutionally been faced with the challenge of internalizing external (political, economic and cultural) effects whereas larger economies have often been able to externalize some of their internal problems (cf. Katzenstein, 1985) thus creating all sorts of negative externalities for smaller (neighbouring) countries. The internalization of the effects of these negative externalities spurred compensatory governmental policies and a larger claim of the public sector on the national economy (cf. Cameron, 1978). Governments in the smaller countries thus developed relatively progressive policies for the environment, for labour market, welfare provisions and have been actively intervening in a large number of markets.

The more active government in the smaller countries, in turn, created ample motivations for larger firms to try to escape national regulation, or threaten to do so. Small economies have the most centralized and corporatist bargaining institutions of all developed countries. Relevant actors (firms, state, civil society) are permanently represented (cf. Esping-Andersen,

1990). In larger countries, such as the US and Japan, industrial bargaining is much more decentralized than in the smaller countries. In theory, a more closed national arena should facilitate bargaining and national institution building, because positive and negative externalities are confined to the same territory, while the players are more attached and loyal. But in practice, the smaller welfare states represent the most pragmatic and efficient bargaining settings. This has led to a very stable, democratic and hardworking country with a high level of industrial peace and where productivity is relatively high. It is typical for employers to be concerned when trade unions threaten to become weak and vice versa. What they fear is that there would be no credible discussion partner to do swift business with and that the (transaction) costs of negotiations would rise as a result.

France: *citoyens et écoles*

The country of the revolutionary citizenry still has a strong centralist state interlinked via a parliamentary democracy. A great number of government enterprises have become (partly) privatized in the 1990s, but they still have a semi-monopoly in France which otherwise does not damage their international competitiveness. Trade unions are strongly centralized and militant. Trade union representatives can be found on the Board of Directors of major corporations. Civil society is very well developed and many hybrid organizations (such as cooperatives and semi-public/private corporations) form an integral part of the fabric of the French economy. Family-owned firms are leading in many sectors. The system of the *Grandes Écoles* has led to exceptionally high mobility between state, civil society and market organizations: through the same educational background, civil servants have no problem moving on to companies and mobility in the opposite direction is also lively. Especially where interaction between the state and market is of importance – in the construction and development of complex so-called *turnkey* projects – French companies are international leaders: construction companies, water companies, telecommunications, fast trains, defence, electricity and aircraft construction. The system therefore creates its own (international) niche. On products for mass markets, French company achievements are significantly less impressive. The French institutional set-up remains semi-closed even despite its integration in the European Union.

China: size and *Guanxi*

With a population of around 1.2 billion in 2004, China was the fastest growing economy in the world in the period 1980–2000. Other transition economies – such as the former Soviet Union and a number of Central and Eastern European countries – scored much less impressively. China's pragmatic course of gradual reform has been considerably more successful than Russia's 'shock therapy'. In 1990, China's total GDP (in dollars) trailed behind Russia by 27 per cent; ten years later China had surpassed Russia by a margin of 189 per cent (World Development Indicators). More dramatic, perhaps, is that while China's life expectancy at birth increased slightly from 69 to above 70 years, the average Russian saw their life expectancy decrease from 69 to 65 (ibid.). In 2003, China became the world's fourth largest industrial producer after the US, Japan and Germany. In contrast to Russia, the Communist party in China kept matters under tight control. The excesses that marked Russia's transition (the legitimacy of the state caving in and the rise of 'oligarchs' in the economy controlling the recently privatized industries) could be kept at bay in China. The state, however, is far from democratic: critical representatives of civil society lead a very dangerous existence and companies cannot, strictly speaking, operate freely. NGOs in China are largely Government Organized NGOs (so called GONGOs, see Chapter 6).

37

In the 1980s and 1990s, foreign companies could enter China only via joint ventures with local companies. This was embarked upon with great enthusiasm, rendering China the annual recipient of more than 40 per cent of all FDI in developing countries since 1990 and the biggest absolute recipient of inward FDI in the world since 2003. There is (still) no evidence of a free market although small companies flourish like never before. State-owned companies still occupy more than three-quarters of all the relevant and strategic industries. For this reason, China also could not formulate any formal competition policy as was the case for Europe, Japan and the US (cf. Liang, 2004). As in most other Asian countries, China operates a relation-based informal system of interactions between the various spheres of society. This system is referred to as *Guanxi*, which literally means 'relationship'. Next to the formal bureaucratic institutions of governments, *Guanxi* provides an informal governance structure that is pragmatic and seems to function rather well, even for host firms (cf. Pearce and Robinson, 2000). Despite its entry to the World Trade Organisation (WTO) in 2002, China largely keeps following a go-it-alone strategy. The position of China in international negotiation arenas such as the United Nations Security Council and the WTO is strong, all the more so because political leaders have managed to maintain their national positions of power. After centuries of isolation, China again has to be reckoned with in all talks that determine the rules regulating the world economy.

South Korea: dirigism

South Korea is the only developing country that in three decades from the 1960s managed to work its way up to acquire the status of 'developed' country. In 1955, South Korea (like Taiwan) was as poor as Zaire and Sudan, and trailing behind developing economies such as Brazil and India. South Korea progressed from a Medium HDI score in 1975 to a High HDI score, no. 26 in the world in 2003 – the highest score for any previously developing country. This process was based in a strong and 'dirigistic' state that did not hesitate to intervene in the strategies of large conglomerates (*chaebol*) such as Hyundai, SK (Sungkyong), LG (Lucky Goldstar) and Daewoo. The large *chaebol* were still mostly family businesses.

The governments also imposed strict accession rules on foreign capital with the result that the country is still one of the least open countries in terms of FDI. South Korean civil society shares the same 'closedness' as Japan. On the other hand, and in contrast to Japan, it welcomed substantial trade volumes. The South Korean economy is much smaller than the Japanese economy and the number and sophistication of the leading conglomerates is also much smaller. Unlike their Japanese competitors, Korean *chaebol* could not develop fully fledged supply hierarchies within the Korean economy. Therefore, in order to become competitive, the South Korean economy could not rely only on exports, but had to import substantial volumes of components and products. The role of exports for the success of the model thus became much bigger than in the case of Japan and the necessity of relatively low wages equally important. This limited the importance of savings as a source of investment. At the same time, trade unions were prohibited (to keep wages low), democracy was largely absent and the interests of civil society were subordinate to those of the economy. Following the Asian currency crisis in 1997, South Korea has been one of the countries capable of quick recovery, for instance by means of an effective devaluation of the Won. It could engage in this policy, because of its go-it-alone strategy which implies that it did not engage in a regional integration initiative. But the Asia crisis did not leave the country unaffected: some conglomerates, such as Daewoo, had to retreat from their international expansion strategies that proved to be hazardously financed. Paradoxically enough, the economic crisis was accompanied by a process of democratization and the recognition of trade union rights.

2.7 CONCLUSION: MODEL AND INSTITUTIONAL RIVALRY IN THE TWENTY-FIRST CENTURY

A diverse range of (national) systems has been economically successful at one time or another. With interconnected economies through trade and investment, the success of one system also partly determines the failure of the other. Some countries have been successful precisely *because* they were different from the leading economy of the time. Measured over time, different actions and reactions can thus be registered. Periods during which the market model had the upper hand were alternated with periods during which civil society or the state took control. Social structures are far from static.

The examples also show that there is no a priori positive effect of openness, nor does a closed economic and institutional system, by definition, trigger inefficiencies and stagnation. The case in favour of openness, however, is one of the prevailing ideas in international economics. Rodrik (1999) has shown statistically that economic openness is neither a necessary nor a sufficient condition for economic growth (let alone a high ranking on the HDI). The examples above show that building up coherent institutions and exerting influence either by civil society, states or hybrid organizations on international firms can be considered a precondition for success. The nature of these institutions and interaction can differ considerably between countries and over time. As in national institution building, it is always a matter of 'balance'. No scientific consensus has yet been reached on the question of whether any one of these configurations and models is better than another. It is very likely that such consensus will never be reached. No single best practice exists; no single organizational concept guarantees the highest profits, the greatest continuity or the best job prospects.

The 1990s heralded the demise of plan economies and the consequential rise of transition economies. But instead of the creation of one model of capitalism, the variety and rivalry among countries and between economic systems intensified. Albert (1993) speaks of 'capitalism versus capitalism', whereas Whitley (1999) speaks of 'divergent capitalism'. While divergence does not necessarily lead to rivalry, rivalry can also exist between converging systems. In practice, both concepts are complementary. Diverging institutional settings interact with each other in international markets, within international organizations and in communication over the World Wide Web. Once confronted with each other, diverging institutions can also become rival institutions. The same applies to the carriers of these institutions in the international arena, individual persons and internationally operating corporations.

Chapter 1 specified the characteristics of all possible combinations of institutional arrangements around the world. This chapter identified the economically most successful models. If the main rivalry between institutional models is linked to the most successful models, it is possible to distinguish in particular between three rival models or regimes (cf. also Gilpin, 2002): (1) the 'liberal' or Anglo-Saxon model, (2) the 'corporatist/social democratic' or continental European model[11] and (3) the 'business-statist' or Asian model. Table 2.1 summarizes the main characteristics of these three models along organizational, cultural and interactive lines.

The liberal model is most prominently represented by the US, but prevails also in Anglo-Saxon countries such as Australia, Canada, New Zealand and – to a lesser extent – in the UK. It represents the dominance of the business sector in generally rule-based societies, with a clear separation of powers (complementarity) between each sphere and a 'lean' government. Although there are a variety of religious streams present in Anglo-Saxon countries, Americans are predominantly Protestant (60 per cent of the population in 2000; Huntington, 2004: 62). The Anglo-Protestant culture is distinct from the European Protestant culture.

Table 2.1 The main contenders: three rival institutional models

	Liberal	Business-statist	Corporatist/ Soc-democratic
Triangle relations	Liberal model	Business-statist model	Corporatist model
Prime regions	Anglo-Saxon countries	East Asia	Continental Europe
Interaction principle	Substitution	Complementarity and pragmatism	Subsidiarity
Position of three spheres	Division of labour separation of powers; dominance of business sector	Strong overlap business–government interface; small civil society involvement	Overlapping spheres Hybridization; equal importance to each sphere
Characterization	Competitive/ Antagonistic	Co-optation/ *Guanxi*	Cooperation/ Corporatism
Contracts	Rule-based	State rule-based and relationship-based	Mixture of principle- and rule-based
Orientation	Short-term	Long-term	Medium-term
Religious spiritual origins	Protestant; Anglican; Evangelic; Methodist; born-again Christians	Confucianism; Taoism; Shintoism; Buddhism	Catholic; Protestant (Calvinist); Greek-Orthodox; Judaic
State–church separation	Moderate	Moderate	Strong
Profit sector	Large	Medium–large	Medium
Non-profit sector	Large	Small	Medium–large
Schooling: private: public	1 : 3	Ranging from 1 : 2.5 to 1 : 4 (depending on level of development)	Ranging from 1 : 4 to 1 : 10
State-owned firms (% GDP)	Very low (c.3%)	Medium–high (c.20%)	Low–medium (c.10%)
PPP 'proneness'	High	Medium	Medium–high
Informal sector (average)	Low (13%)	Medium (25%)	Low–medium (19%)
Family controlled	Low–medium	Medium–high	Medium–high
Cooperatives	Low	Low	High
Power distance	Small	Large	Small–medium*
Individualism	High	Low	Medium*
Unc. Avoidance	Weak	Weak–medium	Weak–medium*
Closed/open	Closed	Semi-closed	Semi-open

* In the work of Hofstede (1991), this group would span the Nordic, Germanic and French welfare states, including the corporatist societal arrangements that have not been included in the work of Hofstede.

The business-statist model represents the dominant logic of most East Asian countries. It is based on a pragmatic mixture of state involvement and 'big business'. The largely informal and relationship-based (*Guanxi*) dynamics of these systems materializes at the state–market interface, whereas civil society is relatively marginal.

On most other organizational, cultural and institutional characteristics these three models show diverging characteristics as well – although it should be noted that the diversity within each model can be equally considerable (see the previous chapters).

The corporatist model, finally, represents a mixture of rule- and principle-based societies which prevail in northern continental Europe, but are also present in a number of central and southern European countries. It is the leading model used in the European unification process, thereby based upon the principles of subsidiarity and cooperation which often nurture overlapping/hybrid societal spheres of relatively equal importance. Continental European religious streams are often a mixture of Christian (Catholic, Protestant, Greek-orthodox) and Jewish influences.

Two contenders

These three models represent the main carriers of economic and political institution building around the world. They are economically the strongest and the basis for strong international expansion by firms originating in these systems. But they are not the only models available or possible. Taking into account the institutional logic presented in Chapter 1 and the characteristics of some of the other countries in the world, at least two contending models can be identified. They are less pervasive, because they have not really been very successful, but are nevertheless important to distinguish. Table 2.2 summarizes the main characteristics of these regimes.

First, the 'religious/autocratic' regimes that have developed in particular in Middle Eastern Arab countries (also classified as West Asia), in north-east Africa and to a more limited extent in some of the South Asian countries. The world's more than 1.5 billion Muslims are primarily located in these countries. Some of these countries have been very successful economically. The Islamic community consists of two main branches: a majority of more orthodox Sunnites and a minority of Shi'ites. Many of the 'petro-monarchies' that have accumulated the largest part of the oil riches, are reigned by Sunnite elites with a substantial Shi'ite majority. There are many varieties of the religious/autocratic model, but its basic interactive principle of the model is substitution, where the state and civil society – primarily on the basis of religious principles with no separation of state and Church – act as substitute for the market. Contracts are based on Islamic rules and Islamic laws and judges substitute (in particular in the case of Islam-inspired *Shari'ah*) an independent judiciary. Civil society under these regimes is relatively closed. Mobility between Arabic countries – even when people share the same language – is not particularly high due to strict imposition of national state rules. The big exception is the annual pilgrimage to Mecca, one of the five pillars of Islam that attracts millions of pilgrims to Saudi Arabia. The number of Muslims sent from each country is strictly regulated and no pilgrim remains in the country.

Second, a community-based model can be distinguished. This model can still be found in the original tribal structures of many of the Sub-Saharan African countries and in some of the basic communities organized by religious groups spread across the world. Nation building in many African countries has been fuelled by a legacy of colonialism, rather than being an autonomous development: certainly not along the often completely artificial borders defined at the end of the nineteenth century. African countries still know indigenous types of power distribution and societal – often participatory – structures of decision making (cf. Davidson, 1993). Pre-colonial participatory structures of power and decision making, including correction

41

Table 2.2 *Two contenders*

	Religious/autocratic	Community-based
Triangle relations	Religious/autocratic model	Community model
Prime regions	Middle East; North-east Africa; South Asia	Sub-Saharan Africa; local communities
Interaction principle	Substitution (religion substitutes for state) and complementarity	Complementarity and pragmatism
Position of three spheres	Strong overlap state–civil society	Overlap/hybridization market and civil society
Characterization	Hierarchy	Cooperation and Co-optation
Contracts	Islamic rule based	Principle and communal rule based
Orientation	Long-term	Medium-term
Religious spiritual origins	Islam (Shi'ite, Sunnite)	Animism, Amish, Mormon
State–church separation?	No	Not relevant
Profit sector	Small	Small
Non-profit sector	Medium	High
Schooling: private: public	Largely 'public'	Largely 'private'
State-owned firms (% GDP)	High (c.30%)	Low–medium (c.15%)
PPP 'proneness'	Medium–low	High (but unlikely)
Informal sector (average)	Medium (25–30%)	High (40–50%)
Family controlled	High	High
Cooperatives	Medium (Islamic cooperatives)	High?
Power distance	Large–very large	Small
Individualism	Low	Medium
Unc. Avoidance	Medium–strong	Medium
Closed/open	Closed	Semi-closed

mechanisms of checks and balances, of for instance the Ashante (living in what is nowadays Ghana) and the Igbo (Eastern Nigeria) have been difficult to eradicate. Examples of basic religious communities can be found everywhere around the world. Well-known communities are based in the US: the Mormons, dedicating years of their life to missionary work, or the Amish, who forgo modern technology, which provides their members with club goods that substitute for public and private goods. Iannoccone (quoted in *The Economist*, 17 January 2004: 64) found that the stricter a religious sect, the more public goods it provides. Many religious groups have also substituted the market economy with cooperative structures. The cost of providing the club good also weighs against the benefits otherwise provided by states (such as law and order, health care, schooling, old-age homes).

Both forms of basic communities have in common a very small or non-existent state, a strong overlap between civil society and market, whereby a large number of hybrid organizational forms exist that shape forms of 'barter trade' between the different spheres of society. Most of the economy is 'informal' according to formal national accounting principles. The local community model is also embraced as alternative model by many of the critics of globalization (cf. Korten, 1995). It is further developed in models of alternative local monetary systems and self-sufficient communities.

The challenges of 'being stuck in the middle'

The five different systems do not cover the whole world and, incidentally, also overlap geographically. Some countries and systems are somewhat 'stuck in the middle' between some of the five 'ideal' types:

- The United Kingdom has to cope with the Anglo-Saxon and the corporatist continental European models. If or when the UK effectively becomes part of the 'euro zone' – and thus accepts the euro as currency – there is a high likelihood that British institutions will start to converge even more with continental European institutions. The same applies to some of the Nordic countries that did not engage in deep European integration.
- A comparable trade-off between Anglo-Saxon and Continental European institutional arrangements has to be made by most Latin American countries. They share many of the European characteristics (due to a history of migration particularly from southern Europe), but are also geographically attached to North America and the US in particular. However, the days when Latin-America could be considered the 'backyard' of the US are over: certainly now that the Brazilian government – representing the biggest and the most European-oriented of all Latin-American economies – has become more assertive in multilateral and regional negotiations.
- Russia, the Caucasus states and the Central Asian republics run the risk of 'being stuck' between continental European corporatism and religious/autocratic institutional arrangements in particular. The Russian Federation (Commonwealth of Independent States (CIS)) could provide an institutional answer to these dilemmas, but for the moment it represents a relatively shallow form of regional integration.
- Many South and South East Asian countries try to integrate two institutional arrangements: religious Islamic and East Asian pragmatism. This creates considerable dilemmas, for instance, with respect to the role of schooling and the position of women in the economy. Both systems have very diverging views on the role of big business in society.
- Southern Africa is influenced by Anglo-Saxon, continental European, and traditional African community-based arrangements. This seems to pose the biggest challenge in terms of institution building, certainly taking into account the very low stability of most African countries.

Each of these regions have become 'stuck' between different and rival institutional systems, partly because of historical circumstances, partly because of the inroads of particular groups of multinationals and individuals in their institutional environment. On a more positive note, however, they could also offer fertile ground for developing alternative models which can perform the same hybrid function on a global scale as some organizational forms have done in the past within specific societies (see conclusion of Chapter 1). Time will tell.

43

Chapter 3

Rival trends: advancing business, towards globalization?

3.1 INTRODUCTION: ON MAPPING TRENDS

Advances, in particular of the business sector in society, have triggered one of the most debated, but equally ill-understood 'trends' since the beginning of the 1990s: globalization. Globalization of the business sector is generally equated with integrating national markets, increased competition and rapid technological advance by a multitude of small and medium sized enterprises that operate across borders (Figure 3.1). But by its opponents globalization is also equated with the dominance of 'big business', a lack of democracy, and the 'commercialization of society'. To what extent can these claimed changes be substantiated?

In mainstream management studies, processes of change are usually mapped by means of the so-called SEPT model. The letters in the model stand for S(ocial), E(conomic), P(olitical) and T(echnological).[1] This model was created by Ian Wilson, who worked as corporate planner at the American General Electric company. He compared managing a company with white water rafting. Sometimes the water is shallow and you have to make headway under your own steam, sometimes the water churns and the thing to do is to catch the right wave and steer the vessel in the right direction (Wartick and Wood, 1998: 20). But the SEPT model has a number of significant limitations. Although it deals with the three societal spheres that were identified in the previous chapters – where 'social' stands for civil society, 'political' for the state and 'economic' for the market – it treats them as separate units, as a result of which hybrid problems and solutions remain unaddressed. It is often at the interfaces of S–E–P that the real

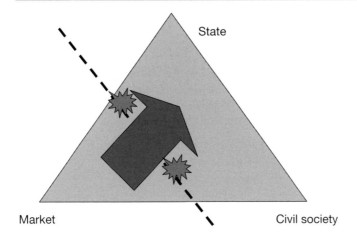

State

Market

Civil society

Figure 3.1 An advancing business sector

problems and challenges (and the real solutions) arise. As such, the SEPT model is a typically Anglo-Saxon model with clearly separated institutions. By including a separate 'T' factor in the model, it also creates the impression that technology develops autonomously, disconnected from the institutions and actors who operate within and between them. This chapter as well as the following two chapters (chapters 4 and 5) discuss technological development in relation to the developments that have taken place on the three sides of the societal triangle and in relation to the *actors* that are developing and using technologies.

Core actors in this respect are, on the one hand, big firms and big organizations that are the most important carriers of internationalization processes. But, since the mid-1990s, advancing markets, the 'commercialization of society' and the advent of 'big business' have been opposed by another core actor: the alternative/anti-globalization movement. Big groups of alternative/anti-globalists have been protesting against the negative consequences of 'globalization' at every major gathering of heads of state around the world since 1997 (e.g. in Seattle and Genoa). With explicit titles such as *Jihad vs McWorld* (Barber, 1995), *The Corporate Planet* (Karliner, 1997), *When Corporations Rule the World* (Korten, 1995), *Corporation Nation* (Derber, 1998), *No Logo* (Klein, 2000), *The Silent Takeover* (Hertz, 2002) and *Battling Big Business* (Lubbers, 2003), the intellectual segment of the alternative/anti-globalization movement clearly expresses their concern about the intensification of market thinking in all sections of society and the accompanying dominance of large (multinational) corporations. In this effort they sometimes also use simplifications and overstatements that obscure the analytical picture (see Box 3.1).

The critics of these critics, in turn, argue that it is good that the market mechanism is advancing worldwide. Plan economies have not delivered the desired results. In opposition to the anti-globalists, these groups hold that instead of suffering from globalization, developing countries, in particular, are suffering from a 'lack of globalization': internationalization of markets and subsequent trade would generate welfare for all. The protesters are reproached for opposing these developments without having an alternative to offer. Moreover, the term 'anti-globalists' has actually been coined by those who oppose the movement. Groups in the movement prefer the term 'alternative globalists' or 'social globalists' to convey the message that they are not against globalization *as such*.

But how much substance is there to these widely held ideas? In the 1990s, at least four related developments fuelled the idea of an advancing international market sector. They will

45

BOX 3.1 A SOMEWHAT OVERSTATED TREND: 'BIG BUSINESS' AS NATION-STATES

It is very popular to observe that many of the world's largest economies nowadays are corporations rather than nation-states. Serious textbooks (Spero and Hart, 2003) as well as anti-globalists use this comparison. An example is Noreena Hertz (2002) who, as introduction to further claims about the 'death of democracy' asserts the following:

> Of the world's 100 largest economies, 51 are now corporations, only 49 are nation states. The sales of General Motors and Ford are greater than the GDP of the whole of Sub-Saharan Africa, and Wal-Mart, the US supermarket retailer, now has a turnover higher than the revenues of most states of Eastern Europe.

These observations are far-reaching, but not entirely accurate. The Gross Domestic Product (GDP) of a country cannot be compared to the sales of a company; neither do states have 'revenues'. GDP measures the accumulated value added produced by domestic companies. Value added can differ considerably from revenues/sales. Retail organizations particularly blur the macro-picture. Their sales volumes – positioned at the apex of the supply chain – are extremely high, but their value added can be rather low. The difference between value added and revenues can amount to a factor '10'. Besides, the 'sales' of financial services companies – also indicated as 'assets' – are incomparable to the revenues of industrial companies. Value added in-house, is complemented by the level of outsourcing and dependent on the position of the company in the supply chain. National and sectoral differences also exist. Due to national accounting practices it is very difficult to measure and compare value added internationally. Some have used a 'general measure' (30 per cent of sales) of value added to fill in the blanks in international comparisons – in particular, left by American and Japanese firms that do not account for 'salaries and benefits' in a manner comparable to European firms (de Grauwe and Camerman, 2003; UNCTAD, 2002: 90; Bartlett *et al.*, 2003). Based on these measures, the world's largest transnational corporation (TNC) in 2000 would have been ExxonMobil with an estimated US$63 billion in value added (on US$206 billion). On the country ranking list, it would have taken 45th place and ranked equal to Chile or Pakistan. Apart from comparing the incomparable, these studies are also subject to a considerable margin of error, once again because, in the case of American and Japanese TNCs, value added is calculated at around 30 per cent of sales. This underestimates the value added of some of the firms.

Our own estimations (cf. van Tulder *et al.*, 2001) show that the largest firms in Europe have a higher level of value added (45–50 per cent) than the largest firms in the US (30 per cent) and Japan have. But the picture also changes per sector. In European telecommunications firms value added is very high (80–90 per cent). This is comparable to other service-oriented industries. Car manufacturers are somewhere in the middle (40–50 per cent), whereas the biggest wholesalers in Europe have shares of value added of 20–30 per cent. The absence of international accounting standardization renders it impossible to measure the power of large companies in terms of their total revenues/sales. The picture differs from economy to economy and in general needs to be adjusted downward with a factor two (in Europe) to three (in the US and Japan). Of the world's 100 largest economies, therefore, about 20 to 30 are companies – most ranked in the second half of the list. A remarkable finding nonetheless.

be the organizing principles of this chapter: the rise of multinationals as (alleged) carriers of 'globalization' (sections 3.2 and 3.3), a wave of mergers and acquisitions (section 3.4), increased financial insecurity (section 3.5) and the privatization of technology (section 3.6). What patterns can be observed, what are the societal levels at which business strategies materialize in particular (section 3.7)?

3.2 THE RISE OF MULTINATIONAL ENTERPRISE: UNDERSTANDING MOTIVES

Multinational enterprises have existed for a long time (Jones, 1996), but as of the beginning of the 1990s their number and influence have increased markedly. At the end of the 1960s, there were approximately 7,000 registered multinationals and by the beginning of the 1990s, the number had increased to 30,000. Ten years later, in 2002, the number of internationally operating enterprises amounted to more than 64,000 with more than 870,000 subsidiaries across the globe (UNCTAD, 2003: xvi). The overwhelming majority of these multinationals originate in OECD economies. The World Investment Report of UNCTAD – on the basis of research conducted in collaboration with the SCOPE research group of the Rotterdam School of Management/Erasmus University Rotterdam – annually lists the world's Top 100 largest 'transnational'[2] corporations. It presents the so-called 'Transnationality Index' (TNI) which measures the level of internationalization of firms by combining three indicators: the internationalization of sales, assets and employment. In 2001, the 100 largest multinationals in the world managed around US$3 trillion in foreign assets, generated US$2.2 trillion in foreign sales and employed 6.9 million employees abroad (UNCTAD, 2003: 5). On average, the level of internationalization (TNI) of the most international firms in the world was 55.7 per cent. Only on seven occasions did a multinational corporation from a 'developing' country appear at the bottom end of the list in the period 1990–2002.[3] Multinationals from smaller countries are the most international firms in the world, whereas petroleum, food, electronics, pharmaceuticals, chemicals, the media and automobile industry represent the most internationalized sectors.

Multinationals have been received with varying levels of enthusiasm, depending on the motives for internationalization attributed to them. A defining feature of multinationals is that they operate across home and host country borders with the result that they can less readily be controlled by social and political groupings. Specifically, many think that corporations move abroad to be able to play political and social groupings off against one other and profit from the 'rents' earned by its 'footloose' position. This idea is corroborated by intensified 'locational competition' in which host governments and communities compete with one another for the lowest wages, the highest subsidies and the best tax benefits so as to attract foreign investment (Schwartz and Gibb, 1999: 115; Mytelka, 2000). An important reason for this competition is that FDI has become the prime source of foreign finance for developing countries: after 1997 the flow of FDI to developing countries surpassed the flow of Official Development Assistance (ODA) and other forms of financial assistance – including IMF and World Bank loans – taken together (cf. Fortanier, 2004). This competition is feared to end in a *race to the bottom*, furthering the erosion of the preconditions for the development of balanced national economic and societal systems.

But often, opposite motives are equally relevant. The actual internationalization decision – and its relation with the business–society interface – involves a complex trade-off between various motives. Table 3.1 lists three clusters of internationalization motives that can be found in IB research: intrinsic, extrinsic and mixed motives.

Intrinsic motives refer to the efficiency gains to be won from 'being a multinational': 'internalizing' markets across borders in a global market economy characterized by considerable

Table 3.1 Strategic motivations of internationalization

	Internationalization motive	Entry repertoires
Intrinsic motives ⇒ transaction costs and efficiency approaches	❑ Market-seeking ❑ Efficiency-seeking ❑ Resources-seeking ❑ Asset-seeking	❑ Greenfield ❑ Brownfield (acquisition) ❑ Majority/minority shareholding ❑ Joint Ventures ❑ Export affiliate; distribution contract
Extrinsic motives ⇒ bargaining/ negotiation and game theoretical approaches	❑ Home: escape motives from home country ❑ Host: High/low barriers to entry	❑ Supply (sourcing) contracts ❑ Strategic alliance ❑ Technology sharing agreement ❑ Auctions ❑ First-entry-effects ❑ Wait-and-see
Mixed motives ⇒ competitiveness and positioning in sector	❑ Sector: bandwagon effects e.g. in country selection ❑ Monopoly/oligopoly effects	

'market failures'; exploring the resources where they are located and transferring them elsewhere; coordinating asset-specific advantages of particular locations that are normally unrelated (such as research institutions); gaining in efficiency through the integration of closed markets around the world, such as labour markets. In the classic work of Dunning (1993), these motives all belong to the so-called 'locational advantages'. A multinational distinguishes itself from non-multinational firms especially in terms of locational advantages. Studies of intrinsic motivations have been conducted especially in the scientific discipline of International Management (IM), building on 'transaction cost' economics and general management theory in particular. Well-known schools of thought that treat internationalization as a largely evolutionary process – involving stages and capability build-ups – are the Uppsala school (Johanson and Vahlne, 1977) and the 'learning school' (cf. Kogut and Zander, 1993). Both focus on the capability build-up in firms during internationalization.

Extrinsic motives include home and host country effects. The discipline of International Political Economy (IPE) focuses specifically on the political aspects of the internationalization process. In particular Vernon (1977, 1998) as the leader of the Harvard Multinational Enterprise project, has on various occasions documented the political storms that surrounded multinationals and that kept the sovereignty of nation-states 'at bay' (Vernon, 1971). On the one hand, companies can be motivated to move abroad to evade high taxes, strict environmental regulations or unfriendly labour relations in the *home country*. But this is not the whole story. 'Escape' motives can also be used to influence the domestic institutional setting. Threats to move abroad in pursuit of lower wages might also lead to more modest wage claims at home, which could, in the end, prevent the firm from moving abroad. The process then takes on game-theoretical properties. From tit-for-tat games it can be learned that a threat needs to be 'credible'. So, companies sometimes move part of their production abroad – even if this is not their ultimate ambition. Should unions modify their wage demands and governments lower their taxes, the threat might be more effective than actually moving abroad. The internationalization strategy of a firm is therefore closely tied up with its national and institutional origins. This mechanism is also referred to as the *Country-of-Origin Effect* (COE) (cf. Kolk and van Tulder, 2004a). The institutional environment of the home country provides the cognitive, normative and cultural 'frame of reference' or 'mindset' of senior managers who decide upon particular internationalization strategies (Prahalad and Doz, 1987). The few studies that systematically attempted to link national institutions to different internationalization strategies have generally found strong Country-of-Origin Effects. This finding also supports the idea of institutional divergence and rivalry as opposed to institutional convergence or institutional 'isomorphism' which is regarded as one of the clearest manifestations of globalization (cf. Kolk and Levy, 2001; DiMaggio and Powell, 1983).[4]

On the other hand, companies' strategic decisions are affected by *host-country* policies and considerations (cf. Gomes-Casseres, 1990). Host-country considerations provide the logical flip-side of escape motives: 'environmental' or 'industrial flight' from the home base is, for instance, only feasible if 'pollution havens' in the host base are available; escaping high taxes or inimical labour relations often implies a move towards tax-free zones and 'tax havens' with company-friendly labour relations. The host country is *inward* open to FDI. But host-country considerations can also involve regulatory barriers. Regulatory barriers include: 'voluntary' export restraints, tariffs, discriminatory tax arrangements or 'local content' regulation. As regards the FDI regime, most countries have engaged in considerable liberalization measures (cf. UNCTAD, 2003). But as regards the trade regime, with every successful round of multilateral trade liberalization that abolished direct trade barriers, a large variety of so-called non-trade barriers have been erected (Gilpin, 2002).

The existence of extrinsic motives as a trigger for internationalization is much more difficult to prove, not least because corporate strategists prefer to legitimize their decisions with reference to the more 'rational' sounding intrinsic motives. Management studies in the 1990s therefore concentrated on intrinsic motivations and the effects on host economies rather than on the more complex effects of extrinsic motivations in their interaction with host and home economies. The entry repertoires of firms (Table 3.1) especially, have been influenced by political motives. Many governments, for instance, did not allow majority ownership of foreign firms, which prompted many multinationals to engage in joint ventures, or minority ownerships ('brownfield'), often accompanied by technology-transfer agreements. In case of a dominant domestic actor, such as a state-owned company, only a 'greenfield' investment – establishing completely new facilities – proved to be a feasible entry strategy. In transition economies in central and eastern Europe, being the first to enter a market through a joint venture with a state-owned firm often implied 'buying' market share which effectively created entry barriers for latecomers (cf. Carillo *et al.*, 2004).

Mixed motives, finally, refer to the sectoral dynamics of internationalization. Therefore, they can also be dubbed *sector intrinsic motives* (cf. Slager, 2004). Internationalization processes differ from sector to sector. In the oil industry, for instance, great distances separate major exploration sites and markets. Asset internationalization can be greater than the internationalization of sales. The market structure of a particular sector and the intensity of competition strongly influence the internationalization trajectory. For instance, in financial services, firms have first consolidated national groups before embarking on internationalization (ibid.). The classic thesis of Hymer (1976) states that firms internationalize after they have gained sufficient market power in their domestic market. Vernon (1966) linked the international process to the state of the product-life-cycle, which is basically a sectoral process. Porter's (1990) cluster effects and competitiveness studies come to comparable conclusions: a firm's dynamism in its domestic market renders it more/less competitive and more/less able to operate in international markets. Sectoral dynamics concern what is being referred to as 'bandwagon' or 'herding' effects. This phenomenon is particularly relevant for oligopolistic sectors, where firms closely monitor and copy each other's behaviour. Bandwagon effects range from product portfolios to the choice for a particular country. The choice for China as the chief recipient of FDI in the 1990s reveals a major bandwagon effect. No big firm wanted to be left behind, although few managers could predict whether the investment would be profitable or not.

Appraising dominant motives

So, the strategic motives as well as the net effects of internationalization can vary. Most IB studies up to now have concluded that 'efficiency' considerations related to low wages generally have rarely been the deciding factors in the decision to internationalize. Gaining entry to a market or access to particular assets and resources have proven much more important intrinsic motives (UNCTAD, 2000c). The net effect of relocation on domestic employment can in fact be positive; particularly if the relocation increases the overall competitiveness of a firm, it could eventually create more jobs at home (cf. Van den Berghe, 2003). But this effect depends on the particular form of relocation, which in the 1990s was largely regional (ibid.). Relocation for low wages creates considerable trade-off problems. Lower wages are, for instance, often accompanied by higher transport costs, lower productivity, local currency fluctuations and lack of flexibility. Because of these trade-offs, global sourcing – although applicable to some firms and some sectors – has often been less important than 'regional' sourcing (cf. Mol, 2001; Mol and van Tulder, 2002). For comparable reasons 'local' sourcing prevails over global sourcing. New production organizations of facilities aimed at 'just-in-time' inventory and delivery and enhanced flexibility, for instance, require suppliers to be located near the production plant rather than at the other side of the world.

The increased 'tertiarization' or 'servitization' of society increases the importance of local economies at the same time. Services are more difficult to standardize and often have to be customized for local clients. Goods and services that cannot be traded beyond the local market are referred to as 'non-tradables'. Lawyers, hairdressers, shopkeepers, consultants are among the occupations that produce local services for local customers. Research by economic geographers shows that the share of non-tradable goods and services has increased substantially over the twentieth century. The findings of Krugman (1997) provide a classic example of this process: in Chicago in 1894 – the leading American production location of that time – more than half of all employment was dependent upon tradable goods and services (traded with the rest of the world); at the end of the twentieth century employment in the leading American location (Los Angeles) only has around one-quarter of employment in tradable goods and services. Even with the arrival of international 'call centres' spread around the world, service economies generally create localization. The consequence for multinational corporations is that they have to take into account the so-called 'integration-responsiveness' grid (Prahalad and Doz, 1987) that seeks to realize an optimal balance between international/global visions and local demands.

Companies that have relocated abroad have also found that tax incentives do not substitute for bad investment decisions. Most research on the motivations of multinationals shows that tax incentives are almost always relatively low on the priority list. Moving abroad is informed by a great number of complex and conflicting motives which also create divergent internationalization strategies. The growing pressure on multinationals towards greater corporate responsibility has (again) enhanced the importance of intrinsic motivations on internationalization strategies. Chapter 13 further explores the relevant dimensions and the related strategic dilemmas for firms.

3.3 THE RISE OF MULTINATIONALS: DECIPHERING RIVAL INTERNATIONAL TRAJECTORIES

In internationalization strategies, there exists a considerable gap between strategic intention and reality (cf. De Wit and Meyer, 2003). This holds true particularly for the concept 'globalization', which is best interpreted as a strategic objective rather than a realized strategy (Ruigrok and van Tulder, 1995). One of the first to use the term 'globalization' was Harvard marketing guru Theodore Levitt (1983). Accordingly, Levitt articulated the classical American ideal: 'The global corporation operates with resolute constancy – at relatively low cost – as if the entire world (or major regions of it) were a single entity; it sells the same things in the same way everywhere' (Levitt, 1983: 92). Standardized products based on relatively standard-ized production processes for integrated markets and corporate branding, has been the ideal of many American firms since the 1980s. Among them companies such as Ford (with global car ambitions), IBM, Coca-Cola, Nike, Wal-Mart or McDonald's. Globalization in this model promotes a global division of labour as well as the growth of international trade. The concept of 'global sourcing' (and 'offshoring') has been pioneered in the US as well (cf. Mol, 2001).

The alternative global strategy has been dubbed 'global localization' or 'glocalization'.[5] It does not aim at creating standardized products for standardized markets, but rather at being accepted as a 'local citizen' in each of the three major markets in the world (the Triad of North-America, Europe and Japan). Glocalization is often the response to barriers host countries create: activities will be localized abroad only if a firm is otherwise treated as an 'outsider' or if it is being hit by trade or investment barriers and thus losing market share. Glocalization often starts with 'screwdriver assembly', where the firm establishes a local production site in order to comply with 'local content' regulation and to circumvent trade barriers; only if the government puts further pressure on the firm, will it engage in further local outsourcing. This strategy is aimed at becoming 'local', but with the least possible international spread of activities. Glocalization was the response of Japanese manufacturers such as Toyota, Nissan, Honda, Sony or Canon to the threats of European integration (Fortress Europe) and American retaliation against the Japanese export success of the 1970s and early 1980s.

Since the 1970s, firms have also moved beyond these glocal/global strategies. Figure 3.2 depicts a general framework in which additional internationalization strategies can be placed. The framework is based on the original scheme by Porter (1986). The 'coordination' dimen-sion reveals the efforts that need to be made to manage subsidiaries; the greater the international division of labour among the various subsidiaries and the wider network of suppliers, the greater the need for coordination. The 'spread' dimension reveals the degree to which production is spread across a large number of countries. For most companies an *export-oriented* strategy is the logical starting point in the process of internationalization. Many smaller and medium-sized firms, as well as firms with an extended domestic network of suppliers often rely on this strategy. Traditional multinational corporations have pursued a *multi-domestic* strategy in

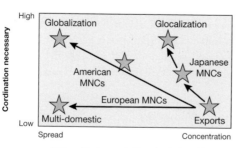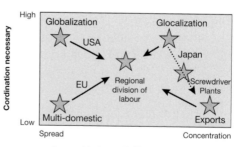

Figure 3.2 Dominant internationalization strategies: 1970–1980 and 1990–2000
Source: SCOPE databank; van Tulder, 1999

which foreign production was set up on a country-by-country basis. A multi-domestic firm is usually well equipped to serve relatively small local markets – but it suffers from an underdeveloped international division of labour. A *regional division of labour* strategy, finally, aims at concentrating most of the production and markets within one trade bloc. Regional divisions of labour often occur within regions that share common institutions and some degree of political integration.

In the 1970s and 1980s, European producers employed a variety of these strategies. Italy's most competitive producers – often organized in networks of smaller and medium-sized firms – better known as 'flexible specialization' networks (cf. Piore and Sable, 1984) – generally adopted export-oriented strategies combined with international franchises such as Benetton. The most international European firms originated in the smaller countries and almost all adopted a 'multi-domestic' strategy. The domestic market was not big enough to reap sufficient economies of scale and prompted many producers to internationalize relatively early in their growth strategy. Additionally they did not have the political leverage many companies from big countries have, so they had to adjust more to local governments and institutional conditions. Firms from medium-sized European countries that internationalized early faced a number of comparable barriers, certainly in the fragmented European region and generally also developed multi-domestic strategies (cf. Ruigrok and van Tulder, 1995).

From global ambitions to regional realities

This changed in the 1990s. The major Japanese producers had responded to the threat of a Fortress Europe (the '1992' trajectory) and to the opportunities an integrated market offered, but were now confronted with a sustained crisis at home. As a result, many of them gradually started to withdraw into the domestic market and/or divest part of their international activities. After 1992, Japanese FDI flows into Europe slackened dramatically, suddenly dropping from a peak of US$7 billion in 1992 to only US$2 billion in 1994. Europe and the US's share of the total outward flow of Japanese FDI decreased from 83 per cent in the peak period of 1989–91 to 58 per cent between 1994 and 1996 (UNCTAD, 1997: 48). According to JETRO (Japan External Trade Organisation) evaluations (1996), as many Japanese companies withdrew from as entered into the European Union during the first half of the 1990s. Concomitantly, the Asian region – in particular ASEAN countries – started playing host to a growing proportion of Japan's total overseas investment. In this way, many Japanese multinational firms – particularly in the electronics and automotive industries – created their own 'annex region' without even having a formal regional integration agreement (RIA). The average TNI of leading Japanese multinational companies decreased in the first half of the 1990s from 35.5 per cent to 31.9 per cent. Japanese banks such as the Mitsubishi Bank, Dai Ichi Kangyo and the Sumitomo Bank adopted a withdrawal strategy as well (cf. Slager, 2004). So, Japanese firms did what every military strategist would do in times of hardship: partly retreated to their own region in order to regroup behind relatively closed regulatory and institutional boundaries. In the second half of the 1990s Japanese multinationals slowly started to expand again, but now also in the ASEAN region.

European firms that had developed multi-domestic strategies as a response to national regulatory frameworks started to regroup their activities in the 1990s. Factories were closed around Europe in order to invest in one integrated production plant that could serve an integrated European market. A regional division of labour developed within the European Union. Anticipating the access of central and eastern European countries to the European Union, some of the sourcing and assembly activities were also relocated to these countries, thus establishing a dependent and low wage 'annex' region within continental Europe (cf. van Tulder, 2004b).

This further reinforced the regional division of labour and substituted for some of the sourcing activities in Asia and north Africa. Large American firms had been the strongest protagonists of the North American Free Trade Agreement and subsequently started to make more intense use of the low-wage potential in Mexico. This helped create another regional division of labour, which ultimately resulted in the North American home region gaining in importance – even for the most international American multinationals (cf. Muller, 2004; van den Berghe 2003). The net effect of NAFTA in the second half of the 1990s has been a de facto 'retreat' from the 'globalization' trajectory. For many firms the global trajectory has always been more of an 'intention' rather than a strategic reality. Consequently, the rhetoric of globalization also started to dwindle.[6]

Rival internationalization patterns

The patterns of realized internationalization strategies that can be identified among leading multinationals display considerable 'country-of-origin' effects. So, even if it seems a contradiction in terms it can still be valid to talk about 'American', 'Japanese', 'German' or 'Dutch' multinationals. The timing of internationalization has in many instances been linked to changes in the regulatory regimes of the home country (cf. Slager, 2004). For the overwhelming majority of multinational enterprises, home-country influences also largely prevail over host-country influences. This is, first, because the bulk of the sales and assets of only a very small group of the largest firms in the world is located outside the home country – outside the home region the number is even smaller (Rugman and Verbeke, 2004). The effects of the institutional and political integration of the European Union might soon justify referring to 'European' multinationals as a separate entity (Box 3.2).

Sectoral effects can also be observed. The intrinsic motivations of firms to internationalize display specific sectoral patterns, but the particular shape of the process is strongly affected by extrinsic factors – depending on the strategic nature of the sector. Industries such as oil,

---

BOX 3.2 THE AMBIGUOUS LEGAL IDENTITY OF MULTINATIONALS

Multinational enterprises, like all other non-governmental organizations, lack real international legal personality. This renders them only marginally subject to international law (cf. Malanczuk, 1997: 91). As regards liability questions and in case of international disputes – take, for instance, the Brent Spar oil platform which was sited in international waters (see Chapter 15) – multinational companies can only be held responsible within the confines of national jurisdictions. In some instances national judiciaries have facilitated extra-territorial claims on firms that are located within their territory, but in general it is very difficult for representatives of civil society to address the international activities of firms inside a courtroom; and vice versa (Chapter 12). Only in the case of some regional and bilateral agreements (the European Union, NAFTA, and bilateral tax and investment agreements) have private parties – including firms and individuals – legal personality and thus access to, for instance, dispute settlement panels. This is not the case for multilateral organizations, such as the WTO (ibid.: 101). A formal 'Societé Europeènne' (SE, a European 'Ltd' construction) has been the topic of continued debate in the European Commission, but by the beginning of the twenty-first century it still has not been formalized.

Table 3.2 Organizational form and internationalization strategy, 1990s

Form	Strategic trade-offs	Mechanism
For-profit – public companies	Dominant mode: Mergers and acquisitions. Top 10 examples*: Shell, ExxonMobil, General Electric, BP, IBM, Canon, Sony, BAT, Unilever, ABN Amro Bank, Citicorp, Barclays, Lloyds, Nestlé. Average TNI: >50% (with major variations)	– Strong 'home-country' and 'host-country' effects (depending on the stock exchanges where the company is listed) – Capital intensive – Rapid (de) internationalization – Sectoral dynamics: resource and market seeking – Early internationalization – 'Global' or bi-regional strategies prevail – Mixed and extrinsic motives prevail
Family controlled – public companies	Dominant mode: Aimed at greenfield investments and/or acquiring distribution networks. Top 10 examples: Wal-Mart, Peugeot, Ford (in the past), Toyota, Heineken, Carrefour, BMW, Fiat. Average TNI: 30%	– Interaction between family ownership and largest shareholders – Controlled and relatively slow internationalization – Depending on stock exchange: moderate home-country effect – Generations of multinationality: relative latecomer (in retail) – Domestic region orientation – Mixed motives prevail
Family controlled – private companies	Dominant mode: Greenfields and multi-domestic. Examples of biggest firms: Cargill, Aldi, C&A, SHV, Kroger. Average TNI: varies	– Family ownership makes it difficult to internationalize rapidly (no 'easy or risk taking capital'), slow strategy – Less capital intensive, more labour intensive; strong orientation on retail – There is no major local embeddedness needed; so no global localization – Globalization strategy possible, but strong home-country orientation – Early internationalization, depending on the line of trade or sector – Prevalence of intrinsic motivations
Not-for-profit Cooperatives	Dominant mode: Export oriented or multi-domestic; Alliances, limited greenfield. Examples of biggest players: Rabobank Group, Credit Agricole. Average TNI: 15%	– Cooperative structure makes it difficult to internationalize rapidly – Take-over of other cooperatives is also difficult; so alliances and international networks prevail; multi-domestic is important to establish strong local links – Relatively late internationalization; home region oriented – Strong home-country effects – Intrinsic motivations prevail

Not-for-profit Pension funds Islamic banks	Dominant mode: Export oriented (of capital); internationalization of shareholdings. Examples of biggest players: Calpers, ABP, company pension funds. Average TNI: < 10%	– Internationalization is directly linked to the domestic interests: pension funds invest global, operate local – Special position for company pension funds – Strong (domestic) regulation barriers to internationalize; no foreign stock quotations – Extrinsic and mixed motives
State-owned/controlled companies	Dominant mode: Export orientation and multi-domestic acquisition strategy (other state-owned companies). Examples: Deutsche Telekom, Electricité de France, Renault, France Telecom, NTT, US Postal, Landesbank. Average TNI: 30%	– The deep pockets of (home) governments provide a substitute for capital markets as financial source for internationalization – Internationalization is hampered by host-country opposition: (1) accusations of unfair competition; (2) fear of foreign domination From domestic orientation to regionalism – Generations of multinationality: relative latecomers (depending on timing of privatization abroad and at home) – Extrinsically motivated
Public–private partnerships	Dominant mode: Multi-domestic; project-based organizations. Examples: global construction and real estate companies, channel tunnel and airbus consortium. Average TNI: low	– International firms that participate in a partnership will always have to adapt to local (public) circumstances; otherwise: strong bound with home government (as financier) – Domestic company is often leader of the private consortium/conglomerate – Home region oriented – Extrinsically motivated
Not-for-profit hospitals, universities, infrastructure companies	Dominant mode: alliances, networks and semi-autonomous affiliates or franchises. Examples: Schiphol franchise (operates other airports as well). Average TNI: low, but growing rapidly	– Idem as cooperatives; strong embeddedness in local regulatory environment; only commercial parts can internationalize for instance through franchises – Host economies need to have comparable regulatory frameworks; so home region oriented – Extrinsically motivated

Source: Scope
* Top 10 examples: taken from the ten largest industrial firms and five largest banks in six major home bases of MNEs: Japan, US, UK, Germany, France and the Netherlands.

microprocessors, military equipment can hardly be considered independent of political motives. Exactly which mechanisms apply and under which conditions remains a question for further research in IB.

Finally, a firm's organizational form also greatly affects the entry-strategy followed, its timing and the extent to which it pursues this objective. Table 3.2 depicts the main organizational forms as discussed in Chapter 1. It lists a number of representative firms and seeks to identify a number of common features of internationalization. Research on internationalization strategies has strongly concentrated on the first two groups of (public) companies, often neglecting to examine the exact impact of the ownership dimension. Table 3.2 gives an overview of relevant, albeit tentative, mechanisms.

3.4 MERGERS, MARKET CONCENTRATION AND OVERLAPPING INDUSTRY BOUNDARIES

The 1990s were characterized by an enormous growth in the number of countries that opened up to foreign investment. It was argued that this would increase competition aside from many other positive consequences. It was expected that if foreign enterprises entered a market, the number of competitors would increase naturally – at least initially. But the 1990s was also a decade of an enormous wave of mergers and acquisitions (M&A). According to estimations by Thomson Securities, the number of mergers and acquisitions between 1980 and 1999 increased by 42 per cent each year. At the beginning of the 1990s, total Merger and/or Acquisitions were valued at around US$200 billion, in 2000 it was more than 17 times that amount (US$3.5 trillion) (*The Economist*, 27 January 2001). Most of these consolidations took place within national boundaries; but about 25 per cent crossed national boundaries, particularly within the OECD region.

In the early 1990s, many M&As were so-called 'conglomerate' M&As between companies in unrelated activities. During the course of the 1990s, two-thirds of all M&As became horizontal in nature, with firms in the same industry acquiring one another (UNCTAD, 2000c: 101). More than 95 per cent of these so-called 'mergers' were in fact 'acquisitions'. More than three-quarters of global FDI flows in the 1990s came in the form of M&As (UNCTAD, 2000c). The strategic 'epicentre' of the wave of cross-border M&As in the 1990s was around the Atlantic, primarily involving companies from the US, the UK, Germany, France and Canada.

The wave in M&As resulted in national and eventually even global oligopolies in a number of industries. A few examples: in the automobile industry the so-called C10 ratio (share of the ten largest manufacturers on the global market) increased from 69 per cent in 1995 to more than 80 per cent in 2000; in the pharmaceutical industry, the C10 ratio climbed from 33 per cent to 50 per cent in the same period. Totally different industries such as telecommunications (86 per cent), pesticides (85 per cent), computers (70 per cent), accountancy and financial services exhibited comparable levels of concentration by the end of the twentieth century (UNDP, 1999; van Tulder, 2002a; Liang, 2004). In most segments of the media industry, only three large firms dominate the flows of information: three press agencies (Reuters, AFP, AP), a few big broadcasting organizations (News Corporation, MCI, Vivendi), four big music producers (Bertelsmann, Sony, Time Warner and EMI) and a few big newspaper conglomerates.

At the same time, companies also tried to cross the boundaries of their sectors which could further increase general levels of concentration in the whole economy. Pharmaceuticals, food and chemicals are currently integrated in the so-called *life sciences*; telecommunications, computers and software are grouped together in information and communication technology; and banks, insurance companies and stockbrokers have become so-called 'financial service providers'. In a given sector, this can indeed lead to a temporary increase in competition, but the effect on the sectors combined suggests further concentration.

3.5 GROWING INSTABILITY AND INSECURITY

The wave of cross-border mergers and acquisitions in the 1990s was primarily financed by issuing shares. This made it possible for relatively small players such as Enron, Vodafone, WorldOnline, UPC, Vivendi or KPNQwest to grow and internationalize at a very fast pace. An additional effect, however, was that stock markets increasingly traded in 'inflated expectations' (the *bubble economy*). Entrepreneurs were under pressure to paint a rosier picture of their companies' short-term profits than was actually the case. Many CEOs also sought to safeguard their personal earnings. In 1996, more than half the salaries of top managers of the largest listed companies in the US were linked to the share price via stock options (Abowd and Kaplan, 1999). This appears to have set in motion a self-reinforcing mechanism of ever-higher share prices, inflated expectations and the manipulation of company results with the primary aim of driving up the share price. The collapse of share prices in 2001 and 2002 not only resulted in the demise of many a dotcom company, it also undermined the financial basis of many fast-growing conglomerates. In this way, the company share price of 11 of the 20 largest mergers in 2000 fell sharply within 12 months following their announcement, while 12 of the 20 companies also saw the value of their shares lagging behind that of competitors (*Newsweek*, 8 July 2002: 18). Shareholders – among them large institutional investors such as pension funds – accordingly suffered great losses on their investments.

Uncertainty regarding the stability of the American version of *shareholder* capitalism is growing. In the course of the 1990s, the number of times that audit committees of listed companies in the US asked their accountants to recalculate annual figures – for example, due to inaccurate reports on earnings – increased from around 50 per year in the first half of the 1990s to more than 240 *earnings restatements* in 2001 (*Business Week*, 15 July 2002). Large companies such as Enron and WorldCom have been proven to manipulate their figures so as to record higher profits and adjust the share price upwards. The financial perils of these companies appeared on the front pages of newspapers and journals. As a result of the scandals, the American government altered accounting rules for the US in July 2002. This adjustment is seen as the greatest correction of the rules of Wall Street since the Great Depression of the 1930s. In addition, the anti-fraud law was significantly tightened up (*FD*, 25 July 2002).

International uncertainty further strengthens 'speculative' capital which no longer bears any resemblance whatsoever to real economic transactions.[7] For example, by 2002, trade in foreign currency amounted to US$1,200 billion per day. In this way, the effectiveness of the foreign exchange policy of governments – and with that the strength of the currency – is to a great extent influenced by the decisions of what has been estimated as no more than 200 young foreign exchange dealers (Rodrik, 2000). With the rise of speculative capital, a succession of financial crises presented itself since the early 1990s. From the banking crises in Finland, Norway and Sweden (1987–92) and the *savings and loans* crisis in the US (1989), via the Japanese banking crises (1990 onwards), the Peso-'tequila'-crisis in Mexico (1994), the collapse of Barings (1995), the Asian currency crisis (1997), the Rouble crisis in Russia (1998), the Samba crisis in Brazil (1999) and back again to a Peso crisis, albeit this time in Argentina (2000–02). No economic system seems to have been spared. On the solutions, no one seems to be able to agree. Since the end of the 1990s, financial regulators have engaged in laborious talks on stricter international regulation – the so-called Basel-II talks – the outcome and, particularly, the effectiveness of which remain extremely uncertain.

3.6 PRIVATIZATION AND THE COMMERCIALIZATION OF TECHNOLOGY

Large market shares represent the present competitiveness and power base of firms. But innovation should guarantee or create firms' and countries' future competitiveness and power base. Innovation can be measured in patents, inventions, diffusion of innovation, but the most telling measure of relative innovative power can still be considered the budgets spent on research and development (R&D). In the past, governments were largely responsible for investing in R&D expenditures. This accelerated technological advancement in health, infrastructure, but also in military technology. Most governments have lost their lead in steering R&D trajectories through large-scale funding of government-owned laboratories and/or universities. According to the OECD databank on R&D expenditures, the share of OECD member governments in total expenditure on research and development dropped from 45 per cent to 31 per cent between 1981 and 1998. At the same time, the share of companies in the total of global R&D expenditures increased to almost two-thirds (63 per cent). At present, the American government is still by far the single largest investor in innovation, followed by Japan, France and Germany. But private investors such as General Motors and Ford already take fifth place. In 1998, Ford Motors spent US$7 million on R&D, more than the governments of the Netherlands, Denmark and Switzerland combined (cf. van Tulder et al., 2001 and DTI – innovation scoreboard).

The influence of the government (as representatives of common/public interests) on the direction of technological development is declining whereas that of companies (as representatives of private interests) is growing. Although innovative rookies regularly appear out of the blue and the garage can still be the site of radical inventions, the company or organization that spends the most on R&D is likely to succeed in creating a very favourable 'selection environment' in which innovation matures and gets diffused. Following Ford in the ranking of largest R&D spenders, at least 15 other industrial giants outspend any government. Figure 3.3 shows the relative impact of the largest ten corporate R&D spenders in the global R&D arena. The 50 biggest R&D spenders in the world in 1999 respectively spent an average of more than US$1.5 billion on R&D. Most of the biggest R&D spenders are 'public companies'. Family-owned firms generally compete less in high-tech markets. Jointly, these 50 companies spent a total of US$211 billion on R&D, which amounts to around half of all private investments in R&D (Gross Expenditures on R&D) in the OECD area as recorded by the OECD. All of them are among the largest firms in their respective home countries. The C10 concentration ratios in R&D for specific sectors in 2000 are excessively high: IT hardware (58 per cent), automobile (82 per cent), pharmaceuticals (62 per cent), electronics (77 per cent), chemicals (69 per cent). The global patenting system further reinforces the position of these key players. R&D intensity and internationalization levels are strongly related (ibid.).

The rise of corporations as directors of technological change is not necessarily harmful. The market sector can be a more efficient allocation mechanism than (bureaucratic) government funds. In the present phase of technological and economic development, technological advance, the diffusion and application of fundamental inventions is more important.[8] However, if the demand for specific technologies is not accompanied by great purchasing power, it becomes difficult to stimulate companies to focus their R&D efforts on, for instance, curing tropical diseases. The same applies to the problem of technology that is boarded up with patents. Despite the general recognition that patents are vital for safeguarding future innovation (see Chapter 6), the legitimacy of protection becomes questionable when companies are willing to take countries to court who copy their patents – as the pharmaceutical industry did in 2001/2002 in the case of African nations who wanted to launch cheaper antiretroviral drugs on their markets (see Chapter 17).

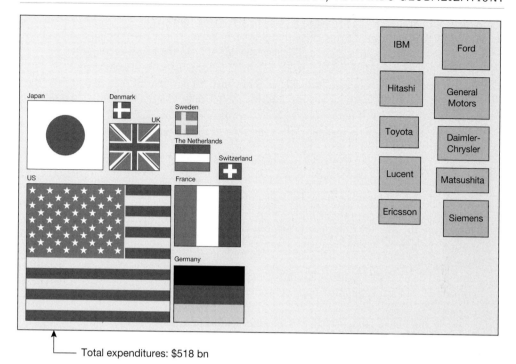

Total expenditures: $518 bn

Figure 3.3 The largest R&D players, 1999
Source: compiled from OECD, DTI and annual reports

The commercialization of technological development also carries the risk of creating unrealistic and constructed expectations: optimistic reports on technological breakthroughs that are (almost) exclusively aimed at raising money on capital markets. The growing influence and commercialization of technology is accompanied by higher expectations with respect to the ability of companies to bring about changes in the social and ecological sphere. Multinationals are increasingly acknowledged – especially in developing countries – as source of knowledge, capital and technology transfer (Dicken, 2003). As a result, companies are expected – rightly or wrongly – to take on ever-greater responsibilities. Seventy per cent of consumers in the Netherlands, for example, expect companies to make an effort to solve global environmental and social problems.

3.7 CONCLUSION: MULTINATIONALS, CARRIERS OF GLOBALIZATION?

Advancing business in society involves a greater oligopolization of sectors, a greater commercialization of technological development in the hand of a relatively small number of 'core players' as well as greater expectations as to the responsibilities of large companies. This chapter also argued that firms are not states and that advancing business does not necessarily equal globalization. By the beginning of the twenty-first century, after periods of expansion and retreat, of extrinsically and/or intrinsically motivated internationalization strategies, it is not easy to identify a dominant/particular trend in the internationalization repertoires of leading (core) firms. The following clusters of firms can be identified (cf. Muller, 2004; van Tulder *et al.*, 2001; Rugman and Verbeke, 2004; Oxelheim and Ghauri, 2004):

- A very limited number of firms can be classified as truly 'global'.
- A slightly larger group of firms expanded primarily beyond their own region and can be classified as 'host-region' oriented; this has very often been the result of a merger between firms from different regions or an active and rapid acquisition strategy.
- Non-international big companies that have more than 90 per cent of their activities in the *home market* are still a strategic reality, but this applies only in large economies and in specific sectors; some of these firms retreated to their home market after international expansion (for example in banking); the relevance of the national economy for big firms on average declines.
- A larger group has developed *bi-regional* strategies. In the case of the US and European firms, it has been primarily between North America and European firms and in the case of leading Japanese companies, it has been between Japan and the US.
- The biggest group of firms has adopted a regional strategy within their 'home region'; this is especially the case for European firms, but US firms within NAFTA and Japanese and South Korean firms within Asia have also attached most strategic importance to their home region.
- Almost all firms have adopted additional *local* strategies: they are becoming increasingly 'embedded' in local economies both as production sites and as markets.

In view of the above, it seems that while the leading multinationals are large enough to operate across the globe, their strategic core still lies in Europe, Japan and the US (the so-called 'Triad'), which renders them less *footloose* than many assume. The strategic core of the world economy is still situated around the Atlantic, although the ascent of multinationals from Asia – creating their own peripheral region – is noticeable. Should anyone therefore wish to summarize trends of internationalization around the world, it would be more adequate to talk of 'regionalization' and 'localization' than 'globalization'. This finding should not come as a surprise, it represents a certain business logic because of the increased instability and insecurity of the 'global' system, as this chapter also illustrated.

Chapter 4

Rival trends: an advancing and increasingly emancipated civil society?

4.1 INTRODUCTION: ASSESSING A LARGELY QUALITATIVE PHENOMENON

The worldwide protest against the war in Iraq in February 2003 led the *New York Times* to describe 'global civil society' as the 'second superpower' (quoted in Kaldor *et al.*, 2003: 3). Sweeping claims about globalization and empowerment are made not only with regard to the role of multinationals, but also with regard to international civil society. To what extent can the proclaimed advancement and 'emancipation of civil society' be substantiated (Figure 4.1)? One major problem is that national statistics do not capture the exact size of civil society, the 'free space between the state and the market, beyond family and the personal' (Anheier *et al.*, 2001: 17). Employment in the non-profit and 'informal' sectors is an approximation of the direct economic significance of civil society. It has increased in importance since the late 1980s (Hupe and Meijs, 2000), so it is safe to assume that the economic importance of civil society has increased. If taken separately the non-profit sector (excluding religious groups) would constitute the eighth largest economy in the world (Kaldor *et al.*, 2003).

Whether a growing civil society also implies a growing influence of citizens on society, however, depends to a large extent on the nature and organization of its most important representatives – NGOs. What and who do they represent and which interests are represented at which levels (section 4.2)? On balance, this assessment is influenced by four developments: (1) the relative growth of 'new' NGOs (section 4.3); (2) the relative demise of 'old' NGOs such

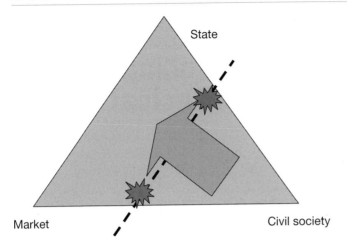

Figure 4.1 *An advancing civil society?*

as trade unions (section 4.4); (3) the creation of hybrid NGOs (section 4.5); and (4) the various ways technology is used and produced by civil society. As such, the emancipation of civil society could be accompanied by NGO representation of (1) individual; (2) group; or (3) collective preferences and interests (section 4.6)

4.2 CIVIL SOCIETY AND THE AMBIGUOUS NATURE OF INTEREST ARTICULATION

Since the so-called 'third wave' of democratization took off in 1974, the potential involvement of civilians in governing countries has increased around the world. According to the Stanford University Comparative Democratization Project:

> more than 60 countries in Southern Europe, Eastern Europe, Latin America, Asia, and Africa have made transitions from authoritarian regimes (of varying duration and repressiveness) to some form of democracy (however tentative and partial) . . . this wave of democratization (is) the greatest to date in the world system.[1]

Democratization of societies particularly involves the state–civil society interface along with the organization of collective preference articulation through the creation of political parties. However, an emancipated and empowered civil society is not a precondition for democratization. While the number of people living under democratic regimes has increased, the interest of people around the world in traditional democratic representation – through regular elections for political parties representing collective interests – has declined. In contrast with the past, individual preferences rather than collective needs are emphasized. Assertive citizens seek to exert direct influence on their environment rather than through the political process. Noreena Hertz (2002) identifies a hollowing out of democracies but at the same time advocates the rise of new instruments of individual representation through the market: 'do not vote, shop!'[2] The number of people that can use their buying preferences as a force for societal transformation or consolidation is bigger than ever. Around 1.7 billion people – including substantial sub-elites in many developing countries – have become part of a consumer society (ibid.).

Especially in the OECD region, companies and governments are faced with more articulate, assertive, demanding and critical *individual* citizens. The renewed assertiveness of citizens in developed countries seems simple to explain. Higher education and greater spending power in OECD countries have brought about the emancipation of citizens, employees and consumers who differ in their individual beliefs and are more strongly than ever before communicating their preferences in a range of areas. The real growth in income throughout the 1990s has created the possibility to move up to 'higher' levels in Maslow's pyramid: people's needs have grown from physical needs, safety and social security to recognition, appreciation and personal development. The emphasis has therefore started to shift to non-material individual values and needs, such as social cohesion, work/life balance, creating meaning, high quality of living environment and enhancing other qualitative aspects of society.

The effective emancipation of civil society critically depends on the position of their official representatives – the non-profit NGOs (see Chapter 1). In the 1990s, new social movements became organized around issues such as individual human rights, gender equality, environmental protection, third world development, peace and democratization (Kaldor *et al.*, 2003: 18), thus being 'more about equity than social equality, and more about self-determination of the individual and of society, than about power politics and the state' (ibid.).

While 'new' social movements grew in importance, 'old' social movements – particularly political parties and trade unions – came under increased pressure. It remains to be seen whether this will lead to the effective satisfaction of individual as well as collective needs. To some, the emancipation of International NGOs (INGOs) in this context represents a development towards 'global democracy'. But to others, it represents the formation of a new global counter-elite (Edwards and Gaventa, 2001) or 'epistemic community' (cf. Braithwaite and Drahos, 2000) with more or less the same needs and interests as multinational enterprises. These individual and group needs can diverge strongly from the 'common' interests of civil groups around the world.

4.3 LEVELS OF INTEREST ARTICULATION: THE RISE OF A 'GLOBAL CIVIL SOCIETY'?

In 2001, the first World Social Forum was organized in Porto Alegre (Brazil). It represents the first convocation of what is also dubbed as 'global civil society' (Korten *et al.*, 2002). Notwithstanding the optimistic rhetoric of a 'global' civil society, the overwhelming majority of the millions of NGOs still represent national and local groups and are organized at a national level (UIA, 2001). The nation-state and local authorities remain the prime actors for civil society groups to appeal to. In a study by the Johns Hopkins Comparative Non-profit Project of the share of International NGOs (INGOs) in the total number of NGOs of 28 countries (most OECD countries and a number of developing countries), it was found that by 2002, INGOs accounted for around 1–2 per cent of total non-profit sector employment, or 134,000 full-time equivalent (fte) jobs (Kaldor *et al.*, 2003: 11). Compared to both nation-states and multinationals, employment created by INGOs is therefore negligible. For example, in 2001, the average number of full-time employees at each of the 50 largest multinationals in the world in 2001 (see Erasmus/UNCTAD databank; UNCTAD, 2003) was 196,000 fte. Wal-Mart alone, the biggest employer in the world (and ranked 34th largest TNC) had around 1.4 million employees – ten times the number of all INGO employees combined.

The growth of INGOs since the mid-1990s is remarkable nevertheless. According to the *Yearbook of International Organizations* (UIA, 2001), the number of INGOs in 2000 was estimated at 30,000 compared to 6,000 around 1990 and less than 2,000 before 1980. With 204 members, FIFA, the international football association – also an INGO – unites more countries than the United Nations (*c.*180 members) does. Amnesty International has 1.8 million members spread across more than 140 countries. The World Wildlife Fund (WWF) has more than 5 million members and the Friends of the Earth Federation has more than 1 million members combined with 5,000 local groups (Kaldor *et al.*, 2003: 3).

Organizational characteristics of INGOs

Since 2001, the Centre for the Study of Global Governance at the London School of Economics publishes a *Global Civil Society Yearbook*. According to this yearbook, INGOs have three defining characteristics: (1) professionalism, (2) regionalism and (3) local embeddedness.

- *Professionalism*: INGOs are the most 'voluntaristic and donative' part of the non-profit sector. With approximately 58 per cent of revenue derived from volunteer input and individual donations, they are surpassed only by non-profit religious groups (73 per cent) (Kaldor *et al.*, 2003: 11; Johns Hopkins, 1997). The dependency on donations has triggered a greater urge to become professional and service oriented. Thanks to large financial contributions by members and donors, organizations such as Greenpeace, Amnesty International, Friends of the Earth and the WWF were able to appoint a large number of professionals. As a result, they are increasingly being regarded as expert discussion partners and some governments have even bestowed upon them the role of watchdog (a function they themselves are not always entirely pleased about). The managers of these INGOs also started to develop 'branding' strategies comparable to those of the biggest MNEs. Some of them did this in collaboration with MNEs such as Nike, Unilever or Starbucks. These concrete projects also require a high level of professionalism. Finally, co-financing and poverty relief INGOs, which redistribute development funds for governments, have been confronted by more demanding governments setting specific output targets, which increases the pressure for further professionalization (and decreases their independence). In the 1990s, professionalization was complemented with service provision and is the fastest growing area of INGO activity (Kaldor *et al.*, 2003: 8). As in the business sector, INGOs have started to merge and create alliances across borders. Especially in areas where international organization are an important source of funding, did this process result in an 'oligopoly' of NGOs. Ninety per cent of EU funding in the 1990s, for instance, went to only 20 per cent of the (largest) NGOs (Doh and Teegen, 2003: 96), whereas the 'Big Eight' NGOs in humanitarian, development and poverty relief receive the majority of all available funds. The 20 largest NGOs receive 75 per cent of all funds allocated by the UN (Rani Parker, 2003: 84).
- *Regionalism*: The presence of INGOs has a strong regional tendency. INGO density coincides with those countries and world regions that have been home to the headquarters of leading multinationals and the largest number of institutionalized NGOs. INGOs thus have a strong presence in Europe and, to a lesser extent, North America (cf. Braithwaite and Drahos, 2000). The growth of INGOs in central and eastern Europe (due to the fall of communism) has been strong, but started at a very low level. The lowest levels of interest articulation through INGOs can be found in the Middle East and north Africa, and also the presence and growth of INGOs in East Asia has remained relatively modest.
- *Local embeddedness*: Third, INGOs are strongly embedded in particular localities. The prevailing organizational form of INGOs is network-like and has a multi-domestic nature. Cities in the US and Europe serve as the 'NGO capitals of the world'. The general structure of 'global civil society' as a network of activities and activists is, in practice,

more or less bipolar with two centres in North America – more specifically at an axis, from Montreal to New York, Washington and Europe (Annheier and Katz, 2003: 247). The legal headquarters of INGOs are strongly linked to 'global cities' (cf. Sassen, 2001). As in the case of multinational firms, NGOs have their legal basis in national jurisdictions. 'Even where national law is subject to a supranational framework, as in the European Union [in particular], civil society law remains essentially reserved to national legal systems' (Anheier and Katz, 2003: 225). For Federal states, this implies that the legal basis is at state level, as is the case with most American NGOs. In the event that they want to organize nationally coordinated actions, the organizational form that is chosen is often a loose, ad hoc network of semi-independent organizations.

Rival organizational forms

INGOs and MNEs share a number of characteristics. Both can be considered to operate in a competitive market. Where MNEs search for customers and good products, INGOs search for members and meaningful projects. Both MNEs and INGOs show a tendency towards oligopolization. There are a number of 'core' INGOs that are on top of a hierarchy of NGOs, comparable to MNEs. INGOs also experience first-mover advantages in their competition with other INGOs to cover an issue and/or receive funding (Doh and Teegen, 2003). Particularly notorious is the rivalry that exists among aid INGOs in first reaching a disaster area. Consequently, the coordination and organization problems INGOs face across borders show remarkable similarities to those of MNEs. Figure 4.2 imposes on a number of leading International NGOs the same organizational framework in which multinational corporations were placed in Chapter 3 (Figure 3.2).

The organizational form adopted by INGOs is thereby strongly linked to the nature of their activities. Rani Parker (2003) distinguishes three categories of INGOs: (1) very political and

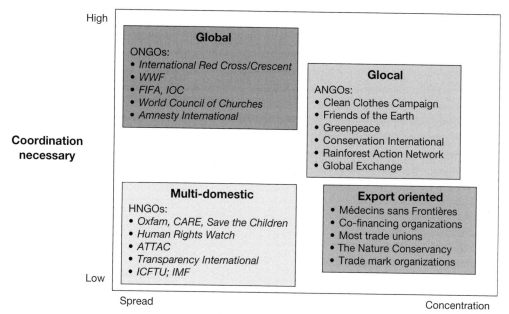

Figure 4.2 Organizational forms of INGOs

activist Advocacy NGOs (ANGOs), (2) a-political Operational NGOs (ONGOs) and (3) Hybrid NGOs (HNGOs) that operate in between these two extremes. NGOs that belong to the same category generally tend to adopt comparable internationalization trajectories and face comparable international coordination problems as MNEs that have chosen that internationalization strategy.

Advocacy NGOs share a strong political orientation and have strong local origins. As a result, they favour either an 'export' or a 'glocal' orientation in case they internationalize. It creates the least spread of activities. An export orientation and a glocal strategy are often part of the same strategic trajectory. In order to be effective ANGOs have to be strongly rooted in one or a limited number of countries. Examples of nationally oriented INGOs are big environmental organizations such as The Nature Conservancy (the world's richest environmental group, amassing US$3 billion in assets), trade unions and trademark organizations.

International co-financing organizations or support organizations such as Médecins sans Frontières (Doctors without Borders) or big environmental organizations such as Conservancy International can be characterized as 'export-oriented' organizations. Their presence in specific countries is only temporary and they operate mainly from the country/ies where they collect most of their funds.

In cases where these NGOs permanently spread some of their activities abroad, they tend to adopt a 'hollow' networked type of organization, which is loosely organized and can be activated whenever needed (cf. Rani Parker, 2003). This resembles the typical 'glocal' organization of MNEs. Glocal ANGOs are among the prime and most critical opponents of MNEs. Examples of Glocal NGOs are: Global Exchange (a US organization with partnerships around the world), Greenpeace and the Rainforest Action Network (in combination with the Whale and Dolphin Conservation Society).

Hybrid NGOs often adopt a multi-domestic organizational form by establishing alliances with sister organizations across borders in a loose (con)federal structure with modest international coordination. HNGOs operate often in between the strong political activist orientation of ANGOs and the a-political orientation of ONGOs. The multi-domestic orientation facilitates that the partner organizations are easier accepted as 'national' or 'local' organizations and, for instance, can get funds from 'home' governments.

Prominent examples of HNGOs are development aid organizations such as Oxfam International, CARE (both a consortium/confederation of 12 member countries) and Save the Children (a network of affiliates and 'sister organizations'). Other prominent multi-domestic organizations are international trade union confederations (International Confederation of Free Trade Unions (ICFTU), and International Metalworkers Federation (IMF)), Transparency International, Friends of the Earth and Consumers International. The international confederation form is necessary to represent their members in some of the multilateral organizations, such as the agencies of the UN, International Standards Organisation (ISO) and (informally) the WTO. But, multi-domestic HNGOs also experience comparable coordination problems to multi-domestic MNEs. For instance, in the 1990s several Oxfam groups in Mozambique worked on similar projects, without having any contact between them (*FT*, 26 January 2005). In response, the organization drastically restructured in 2004. It established a degree of coordination, by creating better communication networks, but also by making a few of the largest national organizations the coordination hub in Oxfam's response to emergencies.

Operational NGOs are NGOs that have explicitly pursued a global presence on global issues and have adopted a more centralized organizational form. ONGOs have made large-scale investments in an international organization, handle budgets of several hundred million dollars and have field offices in many countries operated as wholly owned subsidiaries (Rani Paker, 2003: 84). Consequently, they tend to be risk-averse and a-political. The so-called 'Big Eight

NGOs' in humanitarian, development and poverty relief NGOs are all international alliances dominated by ONGOs (ibid.). But like 'global' MNEs, they also experience a substantial tension between standardization and localization.

Examples include the WWF, FIFA, the International Olympic Committee (IOC), the International Red Cross/Red Crescent all located in Geneva (Switzerland), and Amnesty International (London). Many of these organizations still nurture a multi-domestic image, but on closer scrutiny, they are relatively centralized in their organization. Amnesty International, for example, coordinates its strategy from its London headquarters, where all research activities are also based. The International Red Cross is a single branding organization, but is managed as a federation of officially 'independent but affiliated' national organizations, similar to the organizational structure of a global corporation such as Royal Dutch Shell. This organizational form is known for generating problems of coordination. The international federation of the Red Cross, for example, engages in partnerships with firms at international level. This hampers the possibilities of forming national partnerships. The WWF is in a position comparable to the Red Cross: it is a federation of national organizations, but 80 per cent of all the national themes (to which the bulk of national budgets is dedicated) are managed by the international organization.

The formation of the European Union has also stimulated many national NGOs in Europe to create regional umbrella organizations. When centrally organized global NGOs seek to collaborate with decentrally organized multi-domestic NGOs, they are faced with organizational problems comparable to those of firms. Should Amnesty International, for instance, want to merge with the American-oriented Human Rights Watch organization, substantial coordination problems would arise. This is probably the reason why so few INGOs have actually merged. The prevailing network organization of the new social movement creates considerable and oft-cited international flexibility, but also makes it difficult to achieve sufficient coordination and sustained interest articulation.

4.4 THE PARTIAL DEMISE OF TRADITIONAL NGOS

While the rise of new social movements is celebrated, three 'old' international social movements gradually lost ground in one way or another: political parties, the Church and trade unions. This makes it particularly difficult – if not impossible – to assess the net effect of the proclaimed emancipation of civil society. In almost all countries formalized political parties have seriously lost ground (cf. Hertz, 2002 and Chapter 5). The position of institutionalized religion (Church) is more diverse, though. The overwhelming majority of the world's population is still religious. The annual overview of religions of the Encyclopaedia Britannica notes that the absolute number of atheists in the world even decreased in the 1994–2004 period by 40 per cent to around 148 million people. This represents 2.5 per cent of the world's population. The position of the Christian and Islamic faiths has remained stable or even grown, whereas in other regions a religious revival has been observed with serious political consequences. At the same time, however, religious movements have become more fragmented and, in particular in high-income countries, religion has become 'personalized'. The traditional geographical distribution of world religions (Christians in 'the west', Muslims in the Middle East and Asia, Hindus in India) is slowly eroding. The centralized organization of the Catholic Church is complemented by the much more decentralized organization of Islam and local religions. The societal position of institutionalized Churches, thus, has become weaker in many respects.

But, in particular, the gradual demise of the trade union movement as the most significant representative of the traditional ('old') social movement in the Business–Society Management interface deserves special attention. In most countries, labour movements are still the biggest and most active NGOs. The International Metalworkers' Federation (IMF), for instance, is the largest international trade union organization. It has over 180 member organizations in 95 countries with more than 21 million members in total. The membership of trade unions differs from the membership of NGOs such as Greenpeace or Amnesty International. There is a much clearer link with representation of group and collective interests in the economic realm. Due to their large constituencies and business-oriented agenda, trade unions have indisputably been the most important representative of civil society throughout the twentieth century and an integral part of the 'growth model' of many societies (Box 4.1).

With stepped-up internationalization processes, the historical compromise that was reached between nationally organized labour, employers and governments started to unravel. International comparative studies on industrial relations are relatively rare. In its World Labour Report 1997–98, the International Labour Organization (ILO) reports a sharp decline of trade union membership during 1985–95. In 1995, the world's workforce was estimated at 1.3 billion of which only 13 per cent were unionized. In only 14 of the 92 countries surveyed – mostly in Europe – did union membership exceed 50 per cent of the national workforce.

BOX 4.1 ORGANIZED LABOUR AS ENGINES OF GROWTH

The rise of 'organized labour' at the end of the nineteenth century signalled the departure of modern capitalism. The French regulation school (cf. Boyer and Saillard, 2002) considers the fact that trade unions successfully organized workers – which led to better labour conditions and higher wages – the strongest impetus for economic growth. Organized labour brought about the coupling of supply and demand growth. High(er) wages not only forced employers to organize work more efficiently and/or productively, but also made it possible to sell larger volumes of products. Henry Ford's 'five dollar working day' in the 1930s put workers in the position to buy the cars they manufactured, thus linking supply and demand. The new era also became known as the age of 'Fordism' in which high productivity and economies of scale (conveyor belts) were traded off against higher wages and more time off. So-called 'productivity coalitions' under Fordism created mass consumption and *virtuous growth cycles* for the whole economy. It created the preconditions for rapid growth on the basis of the emancipation of workers. Interestingly enough, a prime motivation for Henry Ford to introduce his 'five dollar working day' was to keep trade unions out of his factories. After a few years, Ford tried to roll back the productivity coalition within his own firm, but was overtaken by national events under the Roosevelt administration that led to the 'New Deal' of the 1930s. The New Deal laid the foundation for the rapid growth of the American economy by creating a national infrastructure and a certain welfare system that guaranteed some form of income for the unemployed. American industrial relations remained antagonistic and unions are very decentralized in local plant unions, and not formally represented in federal institutions – unlike in most European countries. Industrial relations have been embedded in a general anti-union climate, which has led to relatively low 'union density rates' (defined as the percentage of union membership among wage and salary earners). In many other parts of the world, particularly Europe, trade unions have however become a stronger part of the institutional fabric and successfully lobbied for workers' rights, better working conditions and higher wages at national level. In many respects, the rise of organized labour around the world created the preconditions for modern twentieth-century capitalism to flourish.

- *Collective bargaining*: In Europe, the coverage of collective bargaining is very high – at an EU average of around 80 per cent (EIRO, 2002). The coverage of collective bargaining represents the proportion of workers that have their pay and employment conditions to some extent set by collective agreements. These agreements largely take place at national and inter-sectoral levels. Even in countries with a relatively low trade union density, such as the Netherlands (26 per cent), France (9 per cent) or Austria (41 per cent), national legislation requires that sectoral collective agreements are extended to employers and employees who are not members of signatory organizations, creating in some cases almost 100 per cent coverage (ibid.). In developed countries such as Japan and the US where companies dominate, there is a sharp division between a (small) 'union sector' and a (large) non-union sector. The division is sharper in developing countries with the consequence that the degree of collective bargaining coverage in these countries is even lower.
- *Union membership*: In the 1985–95 period, membership levels declined in all but 20 countries. Interestingly, a number of Nordic European countries that had already recorded the highest union density even grew in union density. The sharpest drop in union membership was in central and eastern European countries. Trade unions were part of the 'old' institutional fabric and consequently shrunk with economic transition. Even Poland, where the role of the trade union movement in helping the country make the shift to capitalism cannot be disputed, was not unaffected. For many, the actions of trade union *Solidarnosc* (Solidarity) and its leader Lech Walesa at the beginning of the 1980s signalled the beginning of the end of communism. In 1982, more than 80 per cent of all Polish workers were organized in trade unions. By 2002, this figure had plunged to 14 per cent (ILO Highlights, 2003). In the Americas, trade union membership also declined, although less radically.
- The decline in trade union membership has been triggered by the technologization and 'tertiarization' of society. The weakest sector for unionization has always been the service sector which has also been the fastest growing sector. At the same time, public sector unions have been least affected in terms of membership. A relationship between the globalization of economies and sectors, and trade union membership decline has not been found (cf. Visser, 2002).

Reversal of a trend?

At the beginning of the twenty-first century, there are signs that the diminishing attractiveness of trade unions has come to a halt. But the trade union movement has changed very much since the 1970s. Three developments materialized at the same time: (1) consolidation and decentralization; (2) internationalization; and (3) so-called 'servitization' of trade unions.

- *Consolidation*: First, as in the case of companies, trade unions merged and consolidated in the 1990s. In many countries – including the US and Japan – trade unions consolidated specific, related sectoral activities. The impetus behind the merger between the Communication Workers of America and the International Union of Electronic Workers in late 2000, for example, was clearly the technological convergence of the two sectors and their workers. In Europe, the number of industry federations affiliated with the European Trade Union Confederation (ETUC) has been reduced by mergers in the food and agriculture, and service sectors (Carley, 2002). In many countries, a comparable trend can be identified among national employers' organizations – provided they exist.[3] At the same time, trade unions, particularly in Europe, tried to regain some of the lost bargaining ground by decentralizing their activities to the local level. Local activities nowadays complement national-level activities in many countries.

- *Internationalization*: Second, trade unions have also expanded their international activities. This was achieved primarily through collaborating with other NGOs in addressing the impacts of prominent multinationals such as Nike, The Gap, C&A and the like in developing countries (see Part III). A limited number of 'global works councils' were created in an effort to strengthen the bargaining power of workers. Most of these councils centre around European firms such as ABB, Alcatel, Ericsson and Renault and a pioneering group was initiated by Volkswagen. But the experience of global works councils has been very mixed: they are very difficult to organize, do not meet regularly, do not have access to the required information on strategic issues and sometimes weaken the bargaining position of existing trade unions rather than strengthening it (IMF, undated). The regional level has been a more promising level on which to recoup lost trade union influence. Since 1994, a European Directive exists that requires companies with more than 1,000 employees and facilities in two or more European countries to establish a European Works Council. Research conducted by the European Trade Union Institute (ETUI) in 2002, revealed that although 1,874 companies would be required to do so, only around 700 companies actually have European Works Councils (EWCs). The experience of existing EWCs is also mixed: they have to cope with different languages, representatives of the more developed countries dominate, getting hold of strategic information is difficult and involves deliberations with high-level managers, and they are in competition with national trade union organizations. But, as multinational corporations had to undergo a lengthy 'learning' period, this might very well also be the case for works councils. In the short run, however, it has not led to very effective international representation.
- *Servitization*: The third development among trade unions is that they too have noticed the growing individual needs of their members and are trying, in addition to protecting the collective interests of their members, to develop into service organizations. The service orientation which is aimed at individual members will lead to a more fragmented profile and could further hollow out the protection of members' collective interests.

The position of trade unions around the world is in a state of flux. On the whole, they tend to be on the defensive and reorganizing and re-orienting their activities. In almost all countries in the developed world, the days lost due to strikes and other forms of industrial action have been at a historic low. At the same time, in many countries working hours have increased instead of decreased. For instance, production workers in the manufacturing industry in the US and the UK worked more hours in 2000 than they did in 1980 (Carley, 2002). In Japan and the United States, the number of days leave is considerably lower than in EU countries.

4.5 THE RISE OF THE SUBSIDIZED NGO: FROM GONGO TO BINGO

The extent to which the growing number of NGOs is also indicative of a rising and active civil society is far from clear. The pool of NGOs is increasingly 'polluted' by many hybrid forms about which clarity lacks as to whom they actually represent. This problem concerns three types of NGOs in particular. First, there are NGOs that have been established by the government: so-called *Government Organized NGOs* or GONGOs. They fulfil a (semi-public) supervisory function and are part of the 'privatization' strategy of governments, although GONGOs cannot truly be considered private actors. GONGOs are almost entirely dependent on the government and are of great relevance to the functioning of companies and markets. NGOs that as private actors carry out specific projects on behalf of government, for example, work placement projects, export promotion or environmental decontamination – are referred to as *Government Interested NGOs* or GINGOs.[4]

Second, companies too, have established NGOs. Included are pharmaceutical companies, oil companies and chemical or airline companies who have set up their own consumer organizations (European Airlines Consumer Forum). All are examples of so-called *Business Organized NGOs*, or BONGOs.

Finally, there are NGOs that have started to participate on the market themselves such as the auto owners associations that operate service stations, and development NGOs (such as Oxfam) that manage clothing or 'fair trade' shops. They can creatively be referred to as *Business Interested NGOs* or BINGOs. The Dutch political scientist Van Schendelen draws the following conclusion: 'increasingly often, NGOs function as sly bypass in the lobbying struggle between companies and governments'. The rise of NGOs is not an entirely autonomous movement, influenced by developments in civil society alone. Chapter 7 will further go into the various roles NGOs have adopted vis-à-vis companies in particular.

4.6 TECHNOLOGIZATION: IN SUPPORT OF INDIVIDUALIZATION AND CONTROL

The rise of the Internet and the use of information technology triggered two parallel developments involving civil society: the creation of new communities and the further promotion of individualization. New societal groupings have become capable of mobilizing large numbers of people very quickly over the Internet and through mobile phone networks. This increases their impact and supervisory capabilities considerably. Information on companies can be collected more readily, which promotes the growth of international communities around a specific theme, for example by means of protest websites. Sometimes these communities organize against the very technological progress that makes their existence possible. An example is the international web communities that came into being around the issue of privacy protection. Additionally, consumers organize themselves in purchasing associations on the Internet through which quantum discounts can sometimes be obtained from companies. In this way, they sidestep the official distributors and for the time being boost the free market (system). As far as their production and distribution strategies are concerned, companies operate 'in an increasingly CNN world', which means that a company's alleged ethical wrongdoings can quickly reach the other side of the globe (Casado, 2000: 149; Carter and Deephouse, 1999). Nowadays, much less can be kept secret. Time and distance have acquired different meanings and companies are less capable of isolating civil society.

Technological progress also facilitates a double-sided 'individualization' process of civil society. Companies in the service industry are increasingly marketing customized products for the individual that are nevertheless based on standardization. This is the trend towards so-called 'mass customization'. At the same time, technology has enabled individuals to copy software, music and the like. Emancipated individuals can thereby act as 'pirates' which creates severe commercial challenges for leading firms. Companies claim to be losing more than US$14 billion in annual sales and are petitioning for stricter copy protection. Civil society, on the other hand, opposes this with the argument that copy protection and software codes have achieved a higher status than legal codes and thus impact the lives of citizens more pervasively than any other regulator (cf. van Wijk, 2002). Individual 'hackers' and inventors of Internet viruses have also become a threat to the stability of the network(ed) economy.

Whether individualization or group emancipation, free action on the Internet or control measures to contain possible 'abuse', will triumph in future, depends on the nature of the interaction between the respective spheres and will probably show considerable differences between countries and institutional systems.

4.7 CONCLUSION

The proclaimed 'emancipation of civil society' does not represent a clear and unequivocal trend. Whereas some NGOs grew in importance, others encountered major problems. The rise of subsidized NGOs has obscured the position of NGOs as interest articulators for civil society. A relatively small international civil society elite – or 'epistemic community' – has developed, primarily organized by INGOs and individuals from Western Europe and North America. The 'globalization' in civil society organizations is largely concentrated in two core regions. The 'new' social movement is only partly capable of substituting for the traditional social movement. The new social movement also has to operate largely outside of existing institutional frameworks, even in Europe where the degree of institutionalization of NGOs has been very high. So, new NGOs have greater difficulty in effectively representing the preferences of their constituencies.

New INGOs are only at the beginning of an internationalization process. They are largely multi-domestically organized and still strongly embedded in their local constituencies. The rivalry among INGOs has increased. Only a few real 'global' NGOs exist. They combine a high degree of professionalism in tackling single issues with an increasingly service-oriented approach. Organizations representative of civil society are therefore at the moment primarily oriented towards the articulation of individual and group preferences regarding isolated – single – issues. This signals a departure from the representation of collective preferences and interests that prevailed throughout the twentieth century. Technology, in particular, facilitates the articulation of individual interests and the individualization of societies. This development re-enforces the danger, signalled by Robert Putnam, that the stock of 'social capital' – with strong positive effects on the economic growth of societies – decreases. In his words: it is difficult to 'bowl alone' (Putnam, 2000).

On the other hand, the individualization of societies increases the vulnerability of the thus created 'network' economy and consequently could also lead to the introduction of new control measures for a (perceived) collective good. The use of technology, however, also allows multi-domestic and network organizations of civil society to operate more effectively than ever before. Table 4.1 summarizes the rival trends in civil society. What trend prevails depends on the nature of the institutional arrangements chosen in society, which in turn depend on the nature and outcome of the bargaining process between different interest groups. Chapters 6 and 7 and the remainder of this book will take a closer look at this.

Table 4.1 Rival trends in preference representation by civil society

Individual preferences	Group preferences	Collective preferences
– Has increased; 'do not vote, shop'! – Development of a 'consumer society', but only representing 27 per cent of humanity – Piracy and individual emancipation possibilities have increased – 'Bowling alone'	– Traditional NGOs versus 'new' NGOs – Growing service orientation, i.e. in favour of individual and member preferences – Single-issue orientation and professionalization necessary to generate support for NGO	– Democratic representation has lost most of its appeal, but 'democratic deficit' is rarely considered a problem – Global elite instead of global 'commons' – Labour movement as representative of collective interests (going beyond the members) on the retreat

Chapter 5

Rival trends: a receding state?

5.1 INTRODUCTION: A CERTAIN TREND, IS IT?

It has almost become part of economic and administrative orthodoxy to speak of a receding state: for seemingly good reasons. The 1990s were filled with talk of large-scale privatizations, de-regulation and liberalization, while developing countries, in particular, opened up to international firms which necessitated the denouncement of 'nationalist' policies and protectionism. This trend not only seems to be tangible, but also logical – contrary to some of the other trends discussed in earlier chapters.

The first reason for governments to start considering retreat, was financial difficulty. In the 1980s and 1990s, governments experienced serious budgetary difficulties. They viewed the (partial) sale of government corporations as an opportunity to overcome budget deficits. Developing countries that were confronted with exploding international debts had an additional urge to sell off their 'crown jewels' in a search for capital. In 1998, the wave of privatizations reached a total value of US$100 billion in the OECD region (*The Economist*, 29 June 2002; OECD, 2002). Second, many governments openly proclaimed a more humble role because they were confronted with many of the weaknesses of large state involvement (bureaucratization, rigidity). The welfare state reached its limits in many countries and led, according to many observants – not only neo-classical economists – to a decline in economic dynamism and competitiveness. Social groupings had had enough of a 'paternalistic' government that

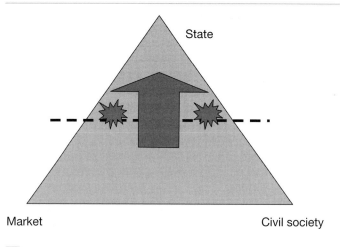

Figure 5.1 *A receding state?*

often seemed incapable of providing adequate public services. Third, New Public Management theorists advocated the professionalization of state bureaucracies by adopting management techniques from the market sector. One of these techniques involved 'outsourcing' of non-core activities. So governments started a search for their 'core activities' (the provision of public goods). Fourth, the moral authority of the government declined and the effectiveness of legislation in morally complex areas such as corporate social responsibility proved limited. In addition to privatization operations, most governments in the 1990s therefore also launched large deregulation and liberalization operations. Deregulation was thereby particularly aimed at facilitating the market mechanism and attracting internationally operating companies. In the 1991–1998 period, around 900 changes in foreign investment-related regulations were implemented globally. Ninety-four per cent of them were meant to create more favourable conditions for trade and investment (UNCTAD, 2001).

But does empirical evidence support the 'receding government' thesis? Trends partly contradict and complement one another and one can find best- and worst-practice cases with/without major state involvement. This chapter further considers the factors contributing to the changing domestic position of national governments (section 5.2). It seems that due to declining moral authority and a limited effectiveness, governments are clearly searching for a different role in society. But the changes that appeared throughout the 1990s have also reached a point of saturation (section 5.3). What seemed to be clear 'trends' have already been reversed in some countries. Besides, governments in general have never really retreated in any substantial manner (section 5.4). What does happen, however, is that states have started to reconfigure internationally. Section 5.5 documents the new configurations of states that have been developing in the 1990s and early twenty-first century. This chapter provides the final step in a nuanced assessment of (perceived) 'trends' in the world economy along the three corners of the societal triangle. In every chapter various levels of analysis are covered. Thus, summarizing these trends at the end of this chapter (section 5.6) should enable us to consider at what societal levels the biggest changes appear and assess the nature and intensity of the interaction between the three societal spheres.

5.2 FACTORS CONTRIBUTING TO RETREAT

Declining moral authority

The power of traditional authorities such as the government (but also the Church) to act as exclusive moral frame of reference – which everyone felt obliged to respect within reasonable bounds so as to regulate society – declined in the 1990s in the liberal and social democratic societies (Schwartz and Gibb, 1999; Roddick, 2000). Norms, values, principles, societal expectations and objectives develop in the interaction between different institutions. In this way, the regulatory power that western government traditionally exerted in their capacity as normative framework weakened in terms of effectiveness, impact and suitability (SER, 2000: 25). Governments that were confronted with increasing individualization, internationalization of companies, the disintegration of established socio-political groupings and a fragmentation of society, were particularly affected. The role of the state in most Asian, African and Middle Eastern countries changed less, because these factors did not play such a prominent role. These developments too, influenced the role and status of the government in the societal triangle. The number of people who align themselves to the Church and political parties steadily declined while membership figures of non-governmental organizations such as Amnesty International, Médecins sans Frontières and Greenpeace grew. Some of these NGOs took over part of the moral authority normally attributed to governments.

The limited effectiveness of sanctions and legislation

Despite a certain democratization of their moral authority in certain regions of the world, governments nevertheless reserve the power to impose binding minimum norms in the form of legislation. But in practice, the sanctioning role of (particularly western) government with respect to 'soft' issues such as corporate social responsibility, industry standards, environmental issues, employment and innovation, seems to be limited. Governments are usually not capable of imposing legislation across national boundaries (Bryne Purchase, in: Jeffcott and Yanz, 1999: 1). International governance becomes more difficult once laws apply to countries with different political priorities and backgrounds. When government interventions interfere with market mechanism the negative effects of the sanction due, for instance, to a lowered competitiveness of a sector might be bigger than the intended positive effect of the sanction. Rapidly changing technology areas are very difficult to regulate through laws: once a law is adopted, the technology has already reached a different level.

Legislation is a thoroughly blunt instrument: laws are very rigid, often lag behind technological and societal developments, and are ill-suited to articulate unambiguous guidelines for moral grey areas – which is exactly what the debate on many of the interface issues (see Chapters 1 and 2) in general and on corporate social responsibility (see Part II) is about. For example, it took two centuries to lay down laws prohibiting slavery (Schwartz and Gibb, 1999: 128) and a further century or more to get the laws accepted and implemented. Nowadays, forced labour and slavery still exist, but in more difficult to identify forms, such as 'trafficking'. A US Government report estimates that between 700,000 and 2 million women and children are trafficked across borders each year.[1]

Laws are not effective and have to be custom made if they are to have impact. In many areas that critically depend on the voluntary involvement of societal stakeholders, obligatory policies are difficult to design (Steiner and Steiner, 2000: 132) and the traditional instruments of government – laws and policing (see Table 1.1) – barely adequate. Therefore, many governments have been placing voluntary restrictions upon themselves in the use of legislation in areas

75

that are relevant to corporate social responsibility and other issues of Societal Interface Management. Governments around the world fear that compulsory disclosure of information and regulations would have a negative effect on the international competitiveness of national firms, and that companies would merely conform instead of setting the trend. Instead they started to appeal to the self-regulatory abilities of firms and civil society to make progress. Chapter 8 discusses the outcome and nature of these processes of self-regulation.

Moreover, the (proclaimed) retreat of governments in some societies was no more than an acknowledgement of the limited role national governments already played in many rule-making areas relevant for IB. Governments of developing countries in particular have experienced a limited autonomy for instance in setting industry standards. Most of the standardization appeared in committees and bodies that were either dominated by foreign governments or by the large firms from the leading industrial countries. The law-making abilities of governments in these countries have already been seriously eroded over the past decades, partly as a result of international regulation, partly as the result of the growing importance of technology and technological standards in the spread of de facto rules. Governments in the smaller and open developed economies face comparable problems (see Box 5.1).

In search of a different role for government

Governments, especially those of OECD member states are searching for a stimulating role for government, where proactive instead of conformist company policies are encouraged. The government of the companies are stimulated largely by means of policies on subsidies and

---

BOX 5.1 GLOBAL PRIVATIZATION OF PUBLIC LAW: A VIEW FROM AUSTRALIA

Outside Europe and the US and Japan:

> the extent to which states have become rule-takers rather than rule-makers is greater than most citizens think, largely because when governments announce new regulatory laws they are somewhat embarrassed to disclose that the national legislature voted for those laws without having any say in shaping them. . . . [F]or years some of Australia's air safety standards have been written by the Boeing Corporation in Seattle, or if not by that corporation, by the US Federal Aviation Administration in Washington. . . . Many of Australia's pharmaceuticals standards have been set by a joint collaboration of the Japanese, European and US industries and their regulators, called the International Conference on Harmonization. Its telecommunications standards have been set in Geneva by the International Telecommunication Union. The Chair (and often the Vice-chair) of most of the expert committees that effectively set those standards in Geneva are Americans. The Motorola Corporation has been particularly effective in setting telecommunications standards through its chairmanship of those committees. As a consequence, Motorola patents have been written into many of the ITU standards that we all must follow. This global privatization of public law seems benign to some, though not to the person who asked how many Microsoft engineers it took to change a light bulb. 'None', was the answer. Bill Gates simply declared darkness the industry standard.

(Excerpt from: Braithwaite and Drahos, 2000: 4)

quotas, along with fiscal privileges for socially responsible initiatives. An example of these are the tax breaks that were introduced in many countries in the 1990s with regard to investment in societal, sustainable and ecological projects and funds. Next to this, applications from companies, such as foreign trade contracts, are assessed on unambiguous and verifiable criteria so that unaccountable forms of business conduct are avoided in the use of instruments that promote export and investment (FD, 9 June 2001). Here attention is paid largely to fighting corruption, environmental and social conditions and themes that lend themselves to developing generally applicable criteria and which link up with international developments. The OECD and ILO guidelines are examples of this (see also Chapter 12).

For the implementation of the OECD guidelines, semi-autonomous National Contact Points were established – under the supervision of the government – where potential violations of the guidelines can be raised and possibly solved. In addition, complaints with respect to the conduct of (multinational) enterprises can be submitted. Information exchange, complaints procedures, and dialogue are increasingly becoming more important in the public approach to business issues in a number of, particularly, European, Anglo-Saxon and Asian countries than sanctions and (strict) legislation. But major differences exist even between the leading countries. The spending of tax income in many countries has been increasingly directed to semi-independent governing organizations (SGOs), and government organized/sponsored NGOs (GONGOs and GINGOs), which has consequently weakened the direct influence of central governments on spending (tax) income.

5.3 A SMOTHERED TREND: RE-REGULATION AND RE-PRIVATIZATION

The 1998 value of US$100 billion represented the peak of a wave of privatizations in the OECD region and around the world in sectors such as telecommunication, public utilities and financial intermediation. In particular in developing countries, privatization implied a complete take-over of state-owned enterprises by (mostly foreign) firms. In developed countries the process has been much more moderate. In many countries the government lowered its share in major companies, but did not leave them uncontrolled. In Norway, for example, the most significant privatization transaction accounted for US$1.5 billion in income for the government in 2001. This involved the sale of part of Statoil, reducing the government share to 80 per cent, which still is a more than controlling stake (OECD, 2002: 48). In other countries, such as Sweden and the Netherlands for instance, 'privatization' implied creating more or less 'independent' business units that could compete on the market, but that nevertheless remained under the indirect auspices of the government (see Chapter 1).[2]

But at almost the same time the wave of privatizations reached its peak by the end of the 1990s, governments started to have second thoughts about the vigour with which they had been selling off companies. In particular, the effective and sufficient provision of public goods had become questioned. In many instances 'underinvestment' had been signalled – implying that private firms did not invest enough to sustain the reliability, availability, safety and sustainability of the 'good' that had previously been delivered by the public sector (albeit at a lower rate of efficiency). An important motive for this is the renewed insight that infrastructure projects are perhaps more of a public than private good, and that society cannot afford huge disruptions in the infrastructure, for instance through market failures. At the same time, doubt is growing over the effectiveness of completed privatization and deregulation projects. Particularly as a result of large irregularities in the electricity and rail infrastructure, the governments of England, the US and the Netherlands have proceeded to partly reverse privatization.

Consequently, privatization has been reversed in some cases. For example, by mid-1998, due to the financial crisis in Hong Kong, the Hong Kong government started buying back shares of previously privatized firms in the stock market, as part of a policy of macroeconomic stabilization. By early September 2001, the Mexican government announced its intention to re-nationalize its heavily indebted sugar mills in order to save them from bankruptcy. In October 2001, the UK government announced the re-nationalization of Railtrack. For similar reasons, the New Zealand government in 2001 introduced a number of measures that indicated a de facto reversal of privatization programmes in airlines and banking. In October 2001, the Dutch government repurchased the high voltage electricity grid from the privatized power producers. By that year (2001), privatization proceeds in the OECD area had dropped to just US$20 billion (OECD, 2002).

The number of possible objects for privatization has sharply declined over the course of the years. This diminishes the likelihood of a further decline of government's share in society. But, it is very unlikely that all privatizations will be undone, particularly in developing countries. Developing countries – such as Argentina – face the additional dilemma that former state corporations could almost only be sold to foreign companies. As soon as a government wants to reverse already launched privatizations it will encounter enormous problems, among others, due to bilateral investment treaties with OECD countries that either prohibit or make re-nationalizations outrageously costly. Some actual re-nationalizations have met with international sanctions or laborious and costly dispute settlement procedures (see Box 5.2). Foreign parties were much less involved in most of the privatizations within the OECD region, thus creating less international conflict when governments chose to re-nationalize.

Particularly in developed countries, a shift can be observed in the nature and form of the private sector's involvement in areas that were previously the exclusive domain of governments. Given this changing role for the private sector, one can also observe changes in organizational

BOX 5.2 PRIVATIZATION AND RE-NATIONALIZATIONS: OUTLINE OF AN INCREASINGLY DISPUTED AREA

November 1999. The water company of Cochabamba, the second town of Bolivia, was privatized. The ownership was handed to an international consortium (the International Water Holding company) consisting among others of Bechtel of the US and the Italian Edison company. Directly after the change of ownership, the price of water supply was drastically increased. The inhabitants were also told that they could not use their own wells and surface water for free, because the consortium had obtained the monopoly over all drinking water in the whole province. Local inhabitants – supported by international campaign organizations like XminY – protested, and even barricaded the town. The row resulted in the re-nationalization of the water company by the Bolivian government. But the International Water Holding company did not recede. It demanded US$25 million in compensatory damages, more than three times the amount they had payed for acquiring the company. The claim is submitted – by a subsidiary of the ING group working on behalf of the Holding – to the International Centre for Settlement of Investment Disputes (ICSID) of the World Bank. At almost the same time, ING announced that they would support the proliferation of Max Havelaar (fair trade) coffee (see Chapter 8) in their own company to show their commitment to international corporate social responsibility.

(Source: *Osmose*, 29 April 2003: 5–6; XminY campaign)

forms and regulation. In particular, public–private partnerships (PPPs) are seen as potentially circumventing some of the hazards of full public ownership (with its dangers of bureaucratization, corruption and inefficiencies) or complete privatization (with its dangers of monopoly profits, underinvestment and self-enrichment by individual entrepreneurs). But PPPs are very difficult to manage, so even in this area it will not be clear whether they will really take off and provide the hoped-for alternative. So, the number of operational PPPs remains very small and their actual effectiveness highly disputed. This is partly to do with the paucity of academic research: as Linder and Vaillancourt Rosenau (2000: 2) have noticed, for instance, 'to date, organized assessments of partnering performance have been piecemeal and incomplete. Until scholarly research catches up, evidence will remain anecdotal and spotty'. At the same time Vaillancourt Rosenau (2000: 217) concluded that little is known about the effectiveness of PPPs basically because 'politics and discourse seem to drive the process'. Due to the complexity of their organizational forms and the economic environments within which PPPs operate, there are unresolved issues around regulation, accountability, and conflicts of interest. According to Pollitt (2003: 62), both the choice of the projects and the initial conditions that have to be met strongly influence the success or failure of PPPs (cf. also Mulder and van Tulder, 2004).

Finally, there is a 'natural' barrier to the retreat of governments. As soon as incidents occur (in areas such as food safety, privacy risks due to technology, growing international terrorism, poor labour conditions and the like) the debate surrounding mandatory public disclosure of social and environmental information and more stringent regulation of technology flares up again. The transaction costs that stick to the ever-flaring debates – and the possible reputational damage – are also high for companies. This is the reason why a number of entrepreneurs (along with NGOs such as the consumer organizations) who are less negative towards the principle of government regulation have come to the fore. The use of legislation to create a level playing field is slowly but surely being (re)discovered and the debate therefore won't die down soon. Growing internationalization creates growing risks that require new roles for governments. The threat of 'global' terrorism has already brought back the plea for a strong and vigilant state. International climate change has become acknowledged by binding agreements between states, where the role of governments increases rather than decreases. A joint study by the Centre for Research on the Epidemiology of Disasters (from Belgium) and A.T. Kearney, a management consultancy company, showed that growing 'globalization' (measured as the cumulative score of individual countries' openness) since the early 1990s, coincided with an increased frequency of both man-made and natural disasters (*The Economist*, 24 January 2004). In case of health threats, security problems and environmental disasters, public authorities have to act and consequently raise their influence and impact on society. Internationalization thus results in a trade-off between less regulation in business areas and more regulation in social areas. The net effect could be zero.

5.4 THE RE-APPRAISAL OF A 'TREND': SUSTAINED IMPORTANCE OF STATES

Taking the above trends and counter-trends into account, it should not come as a surprise that on balance the role of the state in societies has become far from obsolete, although different in nature. Perhaps the most frustrating statistic for many fanatical supporters of privatization in the 1990s is that – after all the rhetoric about a receding government – the involvement of the government in the economy actually increased slightly in the OECD region. This observation, however, remains a matter of the correct interpretation of national accounts. The relative position of governments in society can be measured in different ways. A relatively solid macroeconomic measure is the combined 'total outlays' of central, state and local governments (plus social security). It measures government expenditures as a proportion of GDP. Since 1989, the period most relevant for this study, the share of government expenditures in total GDP for the total OECD region as well as for the European Union increased slightly (Table 5.1).

But these statistics should be interpreted with great care and specified for groups of countries (see Box 5.3). In the 1989–93 period government expenditures in almost all countries rapidly increased. In the 1993–97 period expenditures decreased to pre-1989 levels, also as a result of sizable privatization efforts in many countries. Since 1998, the share of the state in most developed economies started to increase again. Depending on the (short) period of observation one can find support for the claim of an effectively retreating as well as of an expanding government. Over the whole period, it is safe to conclude that the proclaimed dramatic withdrawal of governments in most OECD economies has not appeared, its share has remained remarkably stable, while only the extreme – incidental – outliers got moderated in the course of the 1990s. A slight convergence of the relative position of governments in developed countries can be witnessed, but major differences still persist in particular between developed and developing/transition countries (with effectively retreating governments), and between Anglo-Saxon/Asian and continental European economies (see Chapter 1). Likewise the position of governments in these systems differs. The American government (with around 30 per cent of its GDP generated by taxes, one of the countries with the 'smallest' governments), for instance, can generate a tax income sum that is greater than the entire GDP of Germany, the third largest economy in the world (*The Economist*, 29 September 2001).

Table 5.1 Government expenditures, 1989–2003 period (as % of GDP)

	1989	2003	Highest % (year)
Large countries: stable or increase			
US	35.6	35.9	38.0 (1992)
Japan	30.5	38.3	38.7 (2002)
Medium sized countries: on average increase			
France	50.4	54.4	55.4 (1996)
Germany	44.0	49.4	50.3 (1996)
Italy	52.8	48.5	57.7 (1993)
Korea	18.9	29.1	29.1 (2003)
Spain	42.2	39.3	49.4 (1993)
Small countries: generally decrease			
Australia	37.2	36.2	40.3 (1992)
Austria	53.6	51.6	57.9 (1993)
Belgium	53.4	49.7	55.6 (1993)
Canada	45.8	40.1	53.3 (1992)
Denmark	57.3	56.6	61.7 (1993)
Finland	45.2	51.0	64.2 (1993)
Netherlands	54.5	48.6	56.0 (1993)
Norway	52.2	48.4	56.3 (1992)
Sweden	58.6	59.0	73.0 (1993)
Transition economies: generally decrease			
Czech Republic	38.0 (1992)	47.1	47.1 (2003)
Hungary	56.7 (1991)	48.4	60.3 (1992)
Poland	53.4 (1991)	46.8	54.9 (1992)
Euro Area	47.9	48.9	53.0 (1993)
European Union	47.4	48.4	52.7 (1993)
Total OECD	39.3	41.2	43.3 (1993)

Source: OECD

BOX 5.3 ARGUING WITH STATISTICS – OR HOW TO READ *THE ECONOMIST*

The Economist is the most influential magazine in the world. Its 'impact ratios' far outscore all other journals. At the same time the journal is a strange source of information. Its articles are very argumentative, but all are anonymously written. Articles in this weekly journal thus represent the 'institute' *The Economist* rather than the contribution of individual journalists (whom we don't know). What has been the agenda of this institute? *The Economist* was founded in the middle of the nineteenth century to defend the free working of markets in general and of free trade in particular. Its (non-overt) editorial formula is 'first simplify, then exaggerate'. In a bargaining society, certainly when written with the brilliance of its well-groomed staff, this formula has obvious appeal. But this background also makes it important for readers to make up their own minds on the arguments presented in the journal (cf. van Tulder, 1996).

A relatively simple example can explain this point. On 20 March 2004 *The Economist* published a short contribution in its 'economic and financial indicators' section on 'government spending'. It reads as follows:

> Public expenditure as proportion of GDP has fallen in most rich countries over the past decade, especially with the most generous welfare states. Between 1993 and 2003, government spending fell from 73% to 59% of GDP in Sweden and from 64% to 51% of GDP in Finland. Germany and Japan were the only two countries [in the chart published with the article] which have seen a rise in government spending as a fraction of output.

The source of the data is the highly respected OECD. So what is the problem?

The text does not make any incorrect statement, but is selective in its use of the statistics and suggestive in its analysis. A simple check with the original source – the very transparent OECD website – shows the following:

1   1993 has been a year of unprecedented and never repeated high government spending as proportion of GDP in almost all countries;
2   this phenomenon can partly be explained by incidental and accounting factors;
3   the decrease of this high figure appeared immediately after 1993 (in the 1993–96 period), while in the later period since 1997 the share in fact increased again (the article could as easily have been entitled: 'public expenditures have risen in the past five years');
4   if we take a strict definition of 'welfare states' – as those countries that have a share of government spending in GDP of more than 60 per cent – two actually faced an increase of government spending and only one a decrease; the article is particularly vague on what constitutes a 'welfare state';
5   different periods of study show different patterns, while a longer period of investigation – for instance since the Second World War – shows ever-increasing levels of governments spending, although with a clearly stagnating growth in the post-1986 period for the whole OECD region.

So, in juggling with statistics, one can make trends in government spending go either way. Over the whole period, however and excluding some of the timely 'outliers', which is an accepted statistical technique, it is safe to conclude that government share in the developed economies has neither grown nor decreased very much. The position of governments has, thus, hardly been affected by substantial privatization efforts, nor by the one-off revenues from, for instance, the sale of mobile telephone licences. Although the contents of *The Economist*'s contribution literally cannot be considered incorrect, its suggestion however shows considerable empirical flaws.

Paradoxically, government share in the GDP of developing countries – which was at a much lower level to start with – has indeed declined since the mid-1980s (World Bank, 1997). Development is generally helped along by public investment in infrastructure, education and health services, which makes it all the more striking that a decline has set in at this moment in time. To establish to what extent this is the result of mismanagement or international cost-saving operations imposed, for instance, by the IMF following the (factually inaccurate) example of a receding government of OECD countries, calls for closer examination.

5.5 THE RECONFIGURATION OF STATES: TRADING-OFF UNILATERALISM, BILATERALISM, REGIONALISM AND MULTILATERALISM[3]

Many governments have started reorganizing themselves at the international (and sometimes local) level. Some states internationalized in an attempt to simultaneously keep up with and enable international developments. The number of countries that have joined the WTO in the 1990s increased enormously which, in principle, consolidated the commitment of the majority of the world's populations to the idea of international free trade and free markets. The number of United Nations members also rose sharply in the 1990s: in four years 29 new member states joined, which had never happened in the preceding 20 years. So, the final decade of the twentieth century marked the start of major changes in the institutional and political framework of the world economy.

But, the direction of change still remains relatively obscure. The formalization of a multilateral free-trade system finally boiled down to the formation of the WTO in 1995 with unprecedented powers to press for further trade liberalization. But only slightly later, the efforts to create a Multilateral Agreement on Investment (MAI) failed miserably in 1998. For the first time in history, the role of non-governmental organizations in frustrating these talks has been acknowledged as substantial. Next, NGOs and developing countries frustrated the millennium round of further multilateral trade liberalization with a very bumpy start in Seattle in 1999 and an outright failure in Cancun in 2003. At the same time, the number of bilateral agreements between countries augmented at unprecedented pace. The cumulative number of Bilateral Investment Treaties, for instance, quadrupled from less than 500 in 1990 to around 2,000 in the year 2000 (UNCTAD, 2001: 7). Likewise, bilateral treaties on taxation increased threefold (ibid.).

In the first half of the 1990s, most countries still pursued multilateral strategies, thereby adhering to the call for 'globalization'. But other countries were much more hesitant and – despite the use of the rhetorics of globalization – even adopted relatively unilateral strategies (cf. Ruigrok and van Tulder, 1995). Sometimes, countries moved on both tracks. The US, for instance, is a fervent supporter of multilateralism and globalization, but at the same time does not back away from unilateralist strategies where national interests are involved (Nye, 2002). China's 2002 accession to the WTO seems a step towards integrating the country with the world's largest population in a multilateral trade regime. But some scholars contend that China's accession might equally well hollow-out the multilateral trade framework and lead to a further proliferation of non-tariff barriers – but now allowed within the bargaining framework of the WTO. The accession of Japan within the GATT (General Agreement on Tariffs and Trade) framework, for instance, did not prevent the US and EU governments from repeatedly complaining about 'structural impediments' and non-compliance to GATT's free-trade regime. Consequently 'voluntary' export restraints and other trade-related sanctions were imposed that had a major impact on Japanese industry. In particular the car and consumer electronics industries were hit by those measures (cf. Carillo et al., 2004).

The second half of the 1990s also marked the era of 'regionalism'. The number of regional trade agreements grew fivefold in the 1990–2001 period (Figure 5.2). We are facing a 'world of regions' (Scott, 1997). The effects of this trend have not been well understood. As the World Bank concludes 'the purpose of regional integration is often political, and the economic consequences, good or bad, are side effects of the political pay-off' (quoted in *FT*, 30 November 2001: V). At the start of the twenty-first century, there is hardly any country in the world that is *not* part of a formal regional integration initiative (Ethier, 1998; Atkinson, 1999; Muller, 2004). The number of countries that are *not* members of the WTO – the symbol of multilateralism – is larger. Nearly all of the WTO's 144 members by January 2002 had notified participation in one or more regional trade initiatives. This has been the result of the second wave of regionalism that materialized throughout the 1990s. Over the whole 1948–94 period the GATT secretariat received 124 notifications of formal regional integration initiatives relating to trade in goods. In the early 1990s the number of notifications grew quicker than in any period before. Since the formal creation of the WTO in 1995, the number of notifications boomed further with an additional 100 regional arrangements covering trade in goods and/or services. Some of the Regional Integration Agreements (RIAs) superseded previous arrangements, while some agreements were discontinued.

The definition of the WTO of regional integration initiatives does not cover all forms of regionalism, so the actual number of RIAs is larger. The WTO secretariat assesses that 43 per cent of all trade is exclusively conducted inside RTAs (which excludes for preferential trade agreements or partial customs unions). This is expected to rise to more than 50 per cent in 2005 when the number of RTAs in force and notified to the WTO may have grown to more than 180 from 124 in 2001 (*FT*, 30 November 2001). In addition, most extra-regional trade is also conducted to and from countries within a regional trade agreement, making the volume of international trade that is influenced by the existence of RIAs even higher. The importance of the second wave of regionalism for the dynamism of the world economy thus can hardly be underestimated.

The academic and policy debate on the institutional setting of the world economy in general and, specifically, trade/investment policy, developed along two axes of debate that are usually presented as dyadic pairs of opposing trends: unilateralism versus multilateralism and regionalism versus multilateralism. With the growing importance of regionalism, a logical third pair of opposing trends should be added, however: unilateralism versus regionalism. This section

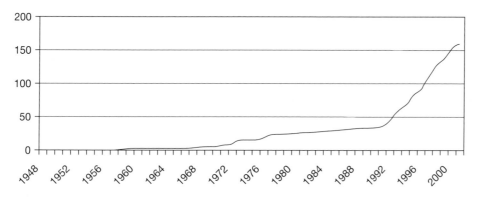

Figure 5.2 Regional Trade Agreements (notified to the GATT/WTO secretariat, 2002)
Source: WTO

83

will further confront the developments on regional integration and adherence to the multilateral trade system with these three debates in order to come to an international positioning of the various states.

Unilateralism versus multilateralism

The traditional debate in international political economy dealt with the question whether countries should/could adopt a unilateral go-it-alone strategy. The disruptive effects, in the 1920s and 1930s, of mercantilism and the breakdown of the closed planning economy as epitomized by communist economies has put protagonists of unilateralism at a disadvantage to the free-traders. Consequently, the number of countries that have become part of the WTO framework has rapidly decreased. Since the accession of China, three-quarters of the economies in the world – and most of its population – are organized within the WTO. Notable exceptions are Iran, North Korea and a number of minute states that have sometimes opted out of the multilateral institutional trade framework in order to function as a tax haven – which, in fact, is a sign of extreme integration in the global (financial) system. Around 25 countries have not yet considered membership of the WTO. Twenty-two countries – including most of the countries organized in the Commonwealth of Independent States – had observer status in the WTO at the beginning of 2002. Actual accession to WTO might still take some time and is dependent upon the outcome of specific bargaining in particular between the new ascendants and the European Union and the US – as proved to be the case with the accession of China to the WTO. This is particularly true for the accession of Russia.

Since most countries have, indeed, become members of the United Nations, one of the most clear indications whether or not a country is willing to adhere to multilateralism has been whether a country subscribed to the GATT regime. But the position of the GATT as an instance of supranational multilateral rule remained rather modest during the 1960s, 1970s and 1980s. The end of the Uruguay Round and the start of the WTO in 1995 signalled the effectuation of a much more powerful and independent supranational institution aimed at really implementing multilateral free trade. An independent dispute settlement procedure in which majority voting can be used, in particular, provides a drastic break with the old practice of dispute settlement in which every member country had de facto veto power. Since 1995, the boundaries to unilateralism and regionalism have been explored, in particular, through the dispute settlement procedures of the WTO. The jurisprudence of the WTO is likely to shape the content of the multilateral trade system. Due to a lacking multilateral investment regime, the WTO dispute settlement procedure might function as a lever in FDI as well.[4]

In the 47-year existence of the GATT, until 1995, 236 dispute cases were reported. This is an annual average of five cases. Between January 1995 and the end of 2001, more than 240 cases were filed by various countries, which represents an annual average of 34.[5] The stricter rules, better dispute settlement system and greater autonomy to enforce decisions (for instance by imposing retaliatory trade barriers against offending countries) of the WTO as opposed to GATT have contributed to the bigger use of WTO dispute settlement procedures. Under the new WTO rule, the number of developing countries that are involved, either as complaining or respondent country, increased. Under the GATT system around three-quarters of all complaints were solely between developed countries. Under the WTO system that number has decreased to 40 per cent, whereas the number of complaints involving developing countries as complaining parties amounted to 31 per cent. In particular a higher proportion of disputes (29 per cent) were complaints made by developed countries against developing countries – that previously had benefited from special and differential treatment under the GATT regime (Yin et al., 2001: 7). A final reason for the increasing number of trade disputes stems from the renewed attempt to tackle non-tariff barriers under the WTO system. Whereas the GATT regime substantially lowered traditional barriers such as tariffs and quotas, the new WTO regime opened up possibilities to address non-tariff barriers such as subsidies, anti-dumping measures, intellectual property rights, discriminatory tax and technical barriers, government procurement and measures related to investment. In the 1995–2000 period 80 per cent of the complaints brought to the WTO dealt with non-tariff barriers (cf. Yin *et al.*, 2001: 9).

So, even within the WTO framework, the unilateralism versus multilateralism debate is bound to continue. A number of important countries still follow a largely go-it-alone strategy – even despite their adherence to the multilateral framework of the WTO/GATT. Such a position could be dubbed 'unilateral multilateralism' and applies in particular to countries such as China, Japan, South Korea that are members of the WTO, but not yet very open to investment and trade, nor part of a major Regional Integration Initiative.

Regionalism versus multilateralism

Serving on the second wave of regionalism, the 'unilateralism versus multilateralism' debate was quickly superseded by a 'regionalism versus multilateralism' debate. The biggest fear – in particular within WTO circles – has been that regionalism could substitute for globalization and thus become a stumbling block towards further global trade integration. The WTO secretariat created a special commission to monitor the process of regionalism to consider whether trade diversion or trade creation would come out of booming regionalism. Leading scholars have tried to resolve this dispute by introducing the concept of 'open regionalism' (Bergsten, 1997). Closed regionalism would imply that regionalism substitutes for multilateralism/globalism and could, on balance, lower global free trade, whereas open regionalism complements global free trade.

The clearest effort of open regionalism is no doubt the APEC initiative that explicitly embraced the concept of 'open regionalism' at its inception in 1989. The official declaration emphasized that 'the *outcome* of trade and investment liberalization in the Asia-Pacific will not only be the actual reduction of barriers among APEC economies but also between APEC economies and non-APEC economies'(Bergsten, 1997: 3). But at the same time APEC – as a consequence of the adoption of this concept – is also one of the least advanced forms of regional integration. At the moment APEC should not really be counted as an RIA, although the intentions towards a free trade agreement by the year 2010 have been expressed.

A number of the largest APEC members, such as China, Japan and South Korea, have not entered into any other formal RIA. They can therefore be considered to still go-it-alone, while APEC cannot (yet) be counted as a formal RIA. APEC might, indeed, apply for open region status, exactly because it is no formal institutionalized region. Countries that belong to comparatively weak RIAs, such as India (in the South Asian Association for Regional Cooperation (SAARC)), can also be considered to belong to the go-it-alone group. They do not face the trade-off between regionalism and multilateralism/globalism, but have engaged in a sort of 'unilateral multilateralism' that is not necessarily beneficial to world trade.

On the other hand, within the WTO, the governments of these countries clearly form a counterweight against the countries that have partly transferred their autonomy to a supranational organization. The latter is particularly relevant for members of customs unions and beyond. Members of free-trade agreements (such as the US in NAFTA) are still somewhere in between a multilateral and unilateral strategy. Paradoxically, this could imply that the RIAs they strike are, in practice, relatively closed – being an extension of unilateral strategies.

Hardly any of the multilateral trade disputes within WTO have been intra-regional. Of the 242 WTO disputes in the 1995–2002 period, only nine covered disputes between members

85

of the same RIA. Four disputes within CEFTA and one within MERCOSUR perhaps illustrate the relative weakness of the region. The disputes also covered concrete agricultural products (wheat, sugar, poultry) and not general controversies over the institutional design of the regional trade regimes. In the case of NAFTA, Canada and Mexico, in 2001, used WTO dispute settlement procedures to explore the unilateral position taken by the US. These disputes did not concern concrete sector issues, but two general policy issues – which thus could also be relevant for the car industry – on subsidies and countervailing measures, and on dumping. In the former case Mexico and Canada (as first plaintiffs) were joined by a long list of countries. In the latter case, plaintiff Canada was joined by the European Communities. Both cases involved the erection of a formal panel – much to the disdain of the US. Only in 13 cases were individual EU countries addressed in a complaint. The European Commission always acted as plaintiff on behalf of all member countries. The advanced nature of the EU integration trajectory is also illustrated by the fact that no EU country filed a WTO complaint against another EU member state.

In the overwhelming majority of cases, therefore, signatories of RIAs abstained from WTO procedures to settle their trade disputes or only entered into relatively minor disputes (except for NAFTA). This illustrates the prevalence of regionalism over multilateralism or unilateralism. Almost all RIAs – even if they were rather weak – have functioned as a substitute for multilateral trade dispute settlement.

One final way to overcome the multilateralism versus regionalism dispute, would be in cases where regions come to bilateral (inter-regional) agreements with other regions. Except for the prospective European integration process in which CEFTA countries integrate with the EU, only agreements between MERCOSUR and SACU, and between MERCOSUR and the EU are under negotiation (and expected to materialize in 2005).

Unilateralism versus regionalism

The debate on unilateralism versus regionalism is part and parcel of the regional integration process in particular for individual member countries that entered a RIA. Each member country faces a continuous balancing act between regional and national interests. The more a region contains one strong economy which holds a hegemonic position, the more interests differ. The experience of the 1990s shows that a strong economy might initially speed up the process of integration, but also that it creates additional barriers to the depth of integration.

RIAs can range from extremely modest and shallow arrangements such as preferential trade agreements (PTAs) and partial customs unions (PCUs) to very intense and deep arrangements such as Economic Monetary Union (EMU) and Economic and Political Union (EPU). The rough assessments made by the WTO very often only make a distinction between Free Trade Agreements (FTAs, which are a more shallow form of so-called 'negative' integration) and customs unions (CUs, which are a deeper form of so-called 'positive' integration). As the vertical axis in Figure 5.3 indicates, FTAs and CUs occupy only the middle positions in a range of regional integration forms. A further step in between customs unions and monetary unions are Common Markets (CMs).

Figure 5.3 shows the position of the 11 most important and partly overlapping RIAs along the vertical axis.[6] Regions where no single strong economy (or hegemonic power) exists – in particular Europe and MERCOSUR (with two or more strong states) – have proceeded further on the track of deeper integration than regions with one dominant state such as NAFTA (US), SAARC (India), CIS (Russia). The dominant position of South Africa in SADC might be considered equally important, but for developing regions the dominance of a regional power-house could always be offset by external forces (see also Chapter 2).

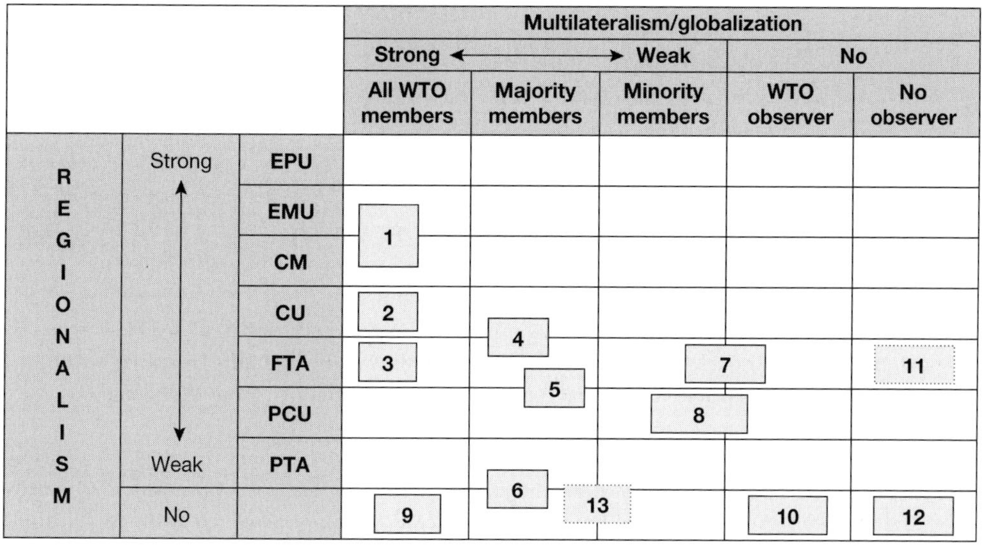

			Multilateralism/globalization				
			Strong ← → Weak			No	
			All WTO members	Majority members	Minority members	WTO observer	No observer
R E G I O N A L I S M	Strong ↑ ↓ Weak	EPU					
		EMU	1				
		CM					
		CU	2				
		FTA	3	4		7	11
		PCU		5	8		
		PTA					
	No		9	6	13	10	12

Legend

1 = EU; with Turkey a customs union exists since 1996
2 = MERCOSUR
3 = NAFTA, CEFTA, ANZCERTA
4 = SADC/SACU (13/14 WTO member)
5 = ASEAN/AFTA (7/10 WTO member)
6 = SAARC [INDIA] (5/7 WTO member)
7 = CIS [RUSSIA] (3/10 WTO member)
8 = AMU (3/5 WTO member)
9 = JAPAN, KOREA, CHINA (since 2002 WTO member)
10 = CHINA (1990s)
11 = SOMALIA, SYRIA, IRAQ (PART OF ARAB FREE TRADE AREA)
12 = NORTH KOREA, IRAN, TURKMENISTAN, ERITREA, 8 MICRO-STATES
13 = APEC (intended to create a free-trade area by 2010)

Figure 5.3 Position of regional integration initiatives

A number of go-it-alone strategies thus can materialize even within regions. The relative unilateralism of a country within a region additionally depends on the nature of bilateral agreements that have been settled within that particular region and beyond that region. Five examples can further illustrate the mechanism of relative unilateralism (go-it-alone) within a region:

■ Russia in CIS [7]: within CIS there exists a customs union with a few countries, but in addition a large number of bilateral trade agreements. Russia is the spider in this web of relations. The majority of CIS states have bilateral relations with Russia though often not with neighbouring countries (see, in particular, the Central Asian states Kazakhstan, Uzbekistan and Turkmenistan). Since the majority of the CIS states are not (yet) members of the WTO, the regional dominance of Russia remains strong.

■ India in SAARC [6]: SAARC is a very weak expression of regionalism in which India is clearly the leading force. Discussions on a regional Free Trade Agreement (SAFTA) are still in their initial stages and suffer from the India–Pakistan dispute over military hegemony. India has furthered its dominant position in the region by striking bilateral trade agreements with Bhutan and Sri Lanka. Because neither these two countries nor any other country in the region struck comparable deals with each other or with external countries, the position of India is further strengthened, despite its unilateralism.

- The US in NAFTA: next to NAFTA the US did not engage in any regional or bilateral trade treaties.[7] Contrary to the US, in particular, Mexico has struck various bilateral treaties with outside partners in Latin America, while more treaties (with the EC, EFTA, Japan) are under negotiation. The US has no other bilateral trade agreements under negotiation. The Free Trade Area of the Americas (FTAA) discussion has recently started. The hegemonic position envisaged by the US in this agreement is bound to lead to opposition by other leading countries – in particular Brazil.
- South Africa in SADC: South Africa has initiated a customs union within SADC with six neighbouring countries that are much smaller (South African Customs Union (SACU)), while additionally striking a bilateral free-trade deal with the EC. Both deals further reinforce its position as the region's hegemon.
- Brazil and Argentina in MERCOSUR: Part of the animosity between Brazil and Argentina has been over alleged efforts of Brazil in particular to make use of its economic size and establish a hegemonic position. But, the difference in relative size of the two countries is not so large that a dual hegemony is inconceivable which bars an inclination to go-it-alone. Nevertheless, the tension between regionalism and unilateralism within MERCOSUR is tangible. The accession of Chile to MERCOSUR might further balance the relative powers. Brazil and Argentina, further, came to separate deals with the Andean Community, but did not strike any separate bilateral agreements with individual countries.

ASEAN and the EU are clear regions without any of the countries going for a unilateral strategy, for instance, by separate bilateral agreements with countries or other regions. In these regions, no formal hegemon exists that dampens go-it-alone or opportunistic behaviour. This is not to say – of course – that individual countries do not seek to use their bargaining space to the full. See, for instance, the UK, Denmark and Sweden, who have not made the move towards a European Monetary Union. In the possible trade-off between deeper and more closed regionalism and multilateralism they clearly expect to reap more benefits from a shallow form of regional integration.

Figure 5.3 also positions countries and regions along a horizontal axis specifying the degree of multilateralism by the year 2002. It is possible to adopt a relatively unilateral strategy even when being a member of the WTO or belonging to an RIA. The weaker the region, the bigger the chances are for unilateralism within regionalism. Regionalism under these circumstances does not substitute for unilateralism or for multilateralism.

Redrawing the political map of the world?

Figure 5.4 summarizes the three basic strategic repertoires that governments have adopted in the final decade of the twentieth century, thereby choosing combinations of the three axes of debate exemplified above:

- *Regionalism*: with different trade-offs between globalism/multilateralism and open/closed regionalism. Very weak regionalism would be easiest to characterize as 'open regionalism', but it might also relate to more advanced versions of regionalism. This depends on the exact dynamism of the particular region. Within regionalism particular countries might choose a relatively unilateral strategy. There seems to be a difference

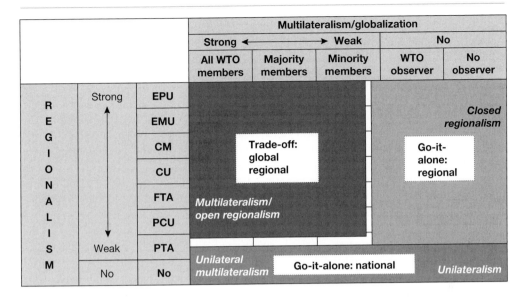

Figure 5.4 *State repertoires*

between regionalism containing only developed countries, regionalism between developed and developing countries and regionalism between only developing countries.

■ *Go-it-alone – national*: where the trade-off is between unilateralism/autarchy and unilateral/multilateralism.

■ *Go-it-alone – regional*: were the trade-off is basically between closed regionalism and unilateralism.

5.6 CONCLUSION: LEVELS OF RESTRUCTURING, LEVELS OF BUSINESS–SOCIETY MANAGEMENT

The world according to statistical sources, primarily consists of nation-states. This is more an expression of 'methodological nationalism' (cf. Kaldor *et al.*, 2003) than of sound statistical evidence. Most statistical bureaus are national bureaus and the nation-state therefore presents the prime level of analysis. But real societal, economic and technological developments have moved in directions that cannot be covered in national frameworks. Chapters 3, 4 and 5 identified a number of those directions. Interestingly enough, one of the consequences of methodological nationalism, is that everything that goes beyond the boundaries of individual states – and thus methodologically moves into relatively unknown and unobserved territories – immediately becomes part of methodological opportunism and evidence of certain claims. This is the case with the notion of 'globalization'. It is surprising to see how often the process of 'internationalization' has become synonymous with that of 'globalization', whereas in practice major developments took place either locally, regionally, or across two major regions. The previous chapters have illustrated that the 1990s, which have generally been proclaimed as the 'era of globalization' perhaps can better be indicated as the era of 'regionalism'. Although the formation of the WTO in 1995 represented an immense stepping stone for multilateralism in the area of trade (and intellectual property protection), most other multilateral initiatives since the second half of the 1990s failed. Likewise local (and multi-domestic) civil society prevailed, while advocacy-oriented NGOs actually helped in frustrating some of the most drastic multilateral initiatives.

89

It is undeniable that society is undergoing enormous change, but the direction it is going in is indeterminable. For very good reasons, government claims that it wants to recede but does not appear to do so in practice. The market is advancing but at the same time concentration is increasing, which could signify a shift away from free market processes. At the same time, confidence in financial market institutions is declining sharply. Deregulation is the slogan, but re-regulation is the practice. Civil society is becoming more assertive, articulate and demanding but remains strongly fragmented, which could stand in the way of further emancipation. The three spheres of interest are still exploring their boundaries. The importance of technology and internationalization (not globalization) is increasing enormously, as is the uncertainty about the appropriate social structure.

Figure 5.5 summarizes the relative intensity of change at the six geographical and institutional levels that have been distinguished in the previous chapters. Despite the claim of receding states, a large number of governments are still basically following a go-it-alone strategy – although often in pragmatic alliances with other partners around the world depending on the issue. The 'end of the nation-state' cannot be proclaimed. National levels still prevail in organizing the interests of NGOs and states, the regional and local level are particularly relevant for firms. Trade unions have tried to move to a more decentralized level, where NGOs have always operated, but at the cost of international interest articulation.

The bi-regional level across the Atlantic is particularly relevant for the outlook of the world, because firms as well as INGOs have been focusing on this axis. On the other hand, this is also the axis along which states and regions (the EU versus the US in particular) have been fighting many regulatory battles. Triadization represents, in particular, a political and business trend. Triadization is linked to the creation of 'dependent' or 'annex' regions along a dominant core country or region. In Europe and North America, states have initiated formal RIAs thereby providing the preconditions for firms to engage in a regional division of labour. In Asia, no pervasive political trajectory of regionalism exists, but Japanese firms have created an 'informal' region (ASEAN) that functions as their own 'annex' region. Whether this is a sustainable strategy with the coming of age of China, remains to be seen and partly depends on the internationalization strategies adopted by the Chinese (state-owned) multinationals.

On the global level the market dynamism comes from finance, media, pharmaceutical, telecommunications and oil companies in particular. Most of these markets contain global

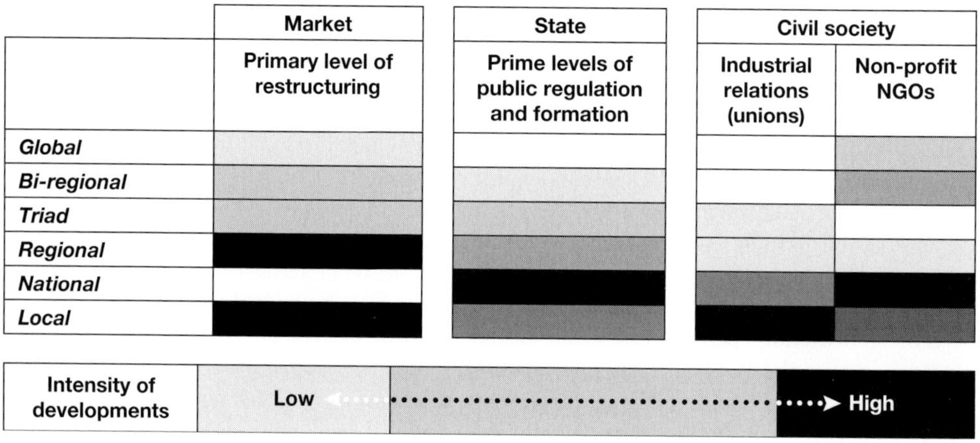

	Market	State	Civil society	
	Primary level of restructuring	Prime levels of public regulation and formation	Industrial relations (unions)	Non-profit NGOs
Global				
Bi-regional				
Triad				
Regional				
National				
Local				

Intensity of developments	Low ◁ ⋯⋯⋯⋯⋯⋯⋯⋯⋯⋯⋯⋯ ⋯▶ High

Figure 5.5 Levels of interaction and restructuring

players, but state regulation, especially in these sectors – not by accident – is predominantly national/regional. The WTO represents the only real global supranational initiative (next to a number of technical committees engaged in standardization and technical harmonization) that can give shape to global trade liberalization. A global civil society exists in a number of 'epistemic societies' and Internet communities that share common beliefs and cultures. The number of real global NGOs, however, remains relatively limited.

Chapter 6

Managing rivalry: the international bargaining society

6.1 INTRODUCTION: THE ADVENT OF A 'BARGAINING SOCIETY'

At the beginning of the twenty-first century, ideologies and societal visions have become increasingly intertwined. The dividing lines between institutions and between societies are more often drawn on pragmatic grounds than on the basis of ideological differences. The sociologist Kees Schuyt, refers to this as the 'multi-individual society' where everything is negotiable: 'Parents and children, trade unions and companies, liberals and social democrats have become skilled negotiators, but with fading convictions. Strategic behaviour is characteristic of negotiating politicians and calculating citizens' (*Vk*, 19 June 2002). The original concept of a 'bargaining society' developed in European smaller and open economies, where it became part of the constitutional framework in which institutionalized and collective bargaining, for instance, was used to set wages (Chapters 2 and 4). Studies from political sciences and sociology not only stressed the benefits of this particular type of collective bargaining (Hedström, 1986), but also pointed at the inefficiency (Johansen, 1979) and fragmentation (Wallerstein and Golden, 1997) that resulted from this particular type of institutionalized bargaining. A 'bargaining society' would fall victim to a self-defeating dynamic stemming from the 'inefficiency of bargaining' as a mode of policy making: 'bargaining has an inherent tendency to eliminate the potential gain which is the object of the bargaining' (Johansen, 1979: 520).

Exactly because of this criticism on its effectiveness, at present the concept of a 'bargaining society' applies more than ever to the processes of change appearing around the world. There is an increasing range of problems for which neither markets nor hierarchies are effective or acceptable (Metcalfe and Metcalfe, 2002). But now, because of the moving boundaries highlighted in Chapters three to five, bargaining is becoming less institutionalized at the national level, and more part and parcel of the new game of an international 'network economy' (Castells, 1996) or a 'deadline-based' society in which 'you need some threat of enforcement to get people to act'.[1] Nowadays, countries even identify themselves as a 'bargaining society'.[2] In practice this means that new institutions are the result of the formal and informal interactions between actors and are shaped at local, national, regional and/or global levels.

It is not by accident that the idea of a bargaining or negotiation society has matured, in particular, since the 1990s. The moving boundaries between the three societal spheres leave open considerable room for manoeuvre and tension and thus for bargaining. Figure 6.1 illustrates the institutional 'voids' that appear everywhere due to (partial) advancing market sectors, moving civil society and the attempts of governments to retreat. The figure illustrates the societal 'territories' within which the most important societal (interface) conflicts are presently being enacted.

The size of the spheres gives an indication of the intensity of the societal interface conflict. Civil society and the market in particular are currently moving most forcefully into each others' traditional territory – supported, among others, by technological developments. A retreating movement brings forth other interface conflicts. Four institutional centres of conflict have unfolded where fundamental choices have to be made about the structuring of society: between state and market (private/public), between market and civil society (profit/non-profit), between state and civil society (state/non-profit) and in the centre, on the boundary area of all spheres. Traditional institutional settlements do not suffice anymore. Powerful actors in all three spheres bargain, in particular, on how to fill the societal interfaces that are under dispute. In this context, business strategists have to decide what (future) strategies to develop. They are faced with many dilemmas.

Luckily, the characteristics and dilemmas of a bargaining society are receiving increasing attention in the social sciences. Thirty years of economic and business science – in a number of cases even awarded the Nobel Prize[3] – has yielded a long list of problems and challenges. These problems have in common that they draw attention to the fact that the economy cannot be seen as a transparent market, with many market players, in which exclusively rationally thinking and acting individuals operate with profit maximization as singular objective (Box 6.1).

The discussion about the institutional preconditions for steering the bargaining society in the 'right' direction – in fact, any direction – has not yet led to unequivocal insights. Not everyone has equally powerful means or equal amounts of time at their disposal in

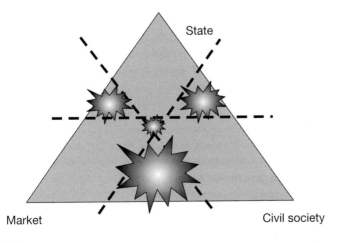

Figure 6.1 *Interface management conflicts, regulatory voids*

BOX 6.1 CHARACTERISTICS OF A BARGAINING SOCIETY: PROBLEMS IDENTIFIED IN MAINSTREAM ECONOMICS LITERATURE

- The problem of *information asymmetry*: as no two negotiators have the same information at their disposal, how to come to optimum results regardless? (Stiglitz)
- The *principal–agent* problem: who represents whom?
- *Transaction costs*: negotiations also involve costs that can be cut via procedures and institutions: who controls whom? (Williamson)
- *Positive and negative externalities*: to what extent are negotiators capable of considering the costs and benefits to other players who are not partaking in the negotiations? (Coase)
- *Opportunistic behaviour*: players take risks and are not willing to take into account common interests in decisions they take, e.g. the interests of future generations.
- The *moral hazard* problem: this is a major source of market failure. It implies that in a situation where two parties are coming into agreement, each party may take the opportunity to gain from acting contrary to the principles of the agreement. It involves so-called 'maximum behaviour' of people, when costs exceed benefits, the behaviour that the contract is supposed to prevent might, in fact, appear. Classic cases of moral hazard appear in insurance where fire insurance often encourages arson or automobile insurance encourages accidents. It leads to *adverse selection*.
- *Strategic behaviour* including *coalition building*: misrepresentation of one's preferences in order to vote against the least preferred option, not necessarily voting in favour of the most preferred options. (Arrow)
- *Rent seeking behaviour*: aims at getting a bigger slice of the cake rather than making the cake bigger. Rent seeking appears in zero-sum games such as lobbying, cartel agreements, or protectionism. (cf. Tullock)
- *Bounded rationality*: of the so-called *behavioural theory of the firm* that assumes that players do not act and reason in a vacuum. (Simon; Cyert and March)
- The *prisoner's dilemmas*: two negotiators attempt to act rationally, but due to lack of communication both end up with a sub-optimal outcome. (Nash)
- *Irrational behaviour*: emotions and psychological considerations in economic decisions that lead to exaggerated price fluctuations influencing, for example, the functioning of auctions. (Kahnemann, Smith)
- *Regulatory capture* where the 'gamekeeper turns poacher' and regulators are taken hostage by the (partial) interest groups they are supposed to regulate. (cf. Posner)
- *Credibility and time inconsistency problems*: problems in macro-economic policy making, which can be solved, for example, by designing institutions (such as Central Banks) that are sufficiently independent from political and market fluctuations. (cf. Kydland and Prescott)

negotiations. The arenas in which the future of society is negotiated are not arbitrary and the effectiveness of the outcomes is not neutral. Some individuals are better represented by organized interest groups than others. Some representatives are considered more legitimate than others, some actors are more independent and more powerful than others. The 'roles' chosen by these representatives are part of their bargaining strategy and influence the effectiveness of their strategies. These are all dimensions of a bargaining process that need to be taken into account when one tries to anticipate and assess the outcome of the process. Furthermore, an important part of the negotiations is moving into the international arena as Chapters 3–5 have illustrated. Firms operating in a bargaining society consequently experience problems in three areas: (1) legitimacy problems: who represents whom? (section 6.2); (2) outcome problems: whose interests are at stake? (section 6.3); (3) international problems: what is the nature of the international bargaining arena? (section 6.4).

6.2 LEGITIMACY: WHO REPRESENTS WHOM FOR WHAT?

The state: adequate parliamentary control?

With the fall of the Berlin wall in 1989 it seemed that the parliamentary democracy had proved itself as the 'best' way to elect and control governments. The electorate, however, is showing up in increasingly smaller numbers at elections, political parties hardly have members and the status of politicians is low – in England, it is even lower than that of car-park attendants (Hertz, 2002: 9). Whereas political parties around the world must make do with membership numbers of tens of thousands, INGOs such as WWF or Amnesty International have more than a million members. And these numbers are growing continually, sometimes at the cost of religious and politic membership (Chapter 4). Next to this, voter turnouts are slowly declining in almost all countries. At the American presidential and congress elections of 2000 only 47–49 per cent of registered voters cast their ballot. Even in the new democracies of Eastern Europe the number of voters rapidly took on Western European turnouts (two out of three people voted). For European Parliamentary elections and in most developing countries the figures are lower.[4] A government that claims to want to retreat, but does not do so in practice (Chapter 5) loses credibility and reliability, and voters, in turn, lose confidence in its representatives.

The market for corporate control

In the 1990s the issue of *corporate governance* arose: who represents those who are in charge of (large) corporations; are the shareholders really the principals and managers the 'agents' and do managers, in fact, act in the interests of their owners? How 'public' are 'public companies'? Much agreement prevails on at least one aspect of this question, though: small shareholders have very little influence on company policy which can put the legitimacy of company management in question in the same way as that of members of a government team. Research by the English banking consultant Manifest, on the extent to which shareholders of the largest companies of the UK (800, representing more than 70 per cent of the FTSE 250 index) actually exercise their right to vote, showed that in 2001 only 48 per cent of shareholders actually voted. It appears that in practice, only 4 per cent of these voters were opposed to management policy (*FT*, 5 July 2002).

'Corporate governance is concerned with the institutions that influence how business corporations allocate resources and returns' (O'Sullivan, 2001: 1). There is a 'market for corporate control' that is, in theory, leading to corrections of managers engaging too much in self-interested behaviour that could harm the profitability and stock value of the company. 'Under such circumstances, other management teams are likely to offer themselves to the shareholders as alternatives to the incumbent management. The *market for corporate control*, then is the competition among these management teams for the rights to manage corporate resources.' But the market for corporate control only serves as a 'discipline of last resort' (Fama, 1980). The discussion on good 'corporate governance' has been strongest in the Anglo-Saxon countries, where the importance of shareholder capitalism is largest. The two leading countries as regards the 'market for corporate control' discussion, thus, have been the US and the UK. These countries also have experienced the most profound changes in the composition of shareholders over the years (cf. Appeldoorn, 2004). In the 1950–2002 period in the US, the increase in percentage of pension funds (public and private combined: from 0.8 per cent in 1950 to 21.4 per cent of all shares in 2002), mutual funds (from 2.0 per cent to 18.3 per cent in 2002) and foreign shareholders (from 2 per cent to 11 per cent) has been noteworthy. American households remain the largest shareholder group in the American corporate governance system, but their share has rapidly decreased from 90 per cent in 1950 to 36.7 per cent in 2002. In comparison: in France (7 per cent), the Netherlands (19 per cent), Germany (14 per cent), Japan (19 per cent) private investors in 2002 made up a considerably smaller part of the firm's financial constituency (Appeldoorn, 2004; Peck and Ruigrok, 2000).

Institutional investors can be seen as more informed and more active shareholders than households. Thus, this growing group is asserting more pressure on corporate boards to perform and on governments to install good corporate governance legislation. In the UK the same three trends can be seen: the rise of institutional investors, the decline of private households (from 54 per cent to 14 per cent) and the increase of foreign investors (from 7 per cent to 32 per cent). By the end of the 1980s, the British market for corporate control had already become dominated by institutional investors and well-informed foreign banks. This also explains why pleas for serious changes in the corporate governance regime were made earlier in the UK than in other parts of the world.[5] In 1992, a number of bankruptcies in the UK triggered the installation of the Cadbury committee which published 'best corporate governance practices' (Monks and Minow, 2001).

In countries such as France, Germany and Japan, cross-holdings of shares by other industrial companies (including industrial banks) generally represents the most important group of investors. These companies are very knowledgeable, but exert influence over the companies through 'old boys' networks, which makes the inclination towards serious change in the corporate governance regime (and higher transparancy) smaller. In the discussion in some European countries the most frequently heard point of criticism is that the members of the Supervisory Board (recruited from this 'old boys' network) rarely make use of their power to discharge executives and follow company policies more critically. But, the constituents are changing in some of these countries. In particular, the share of foreign investors in Japan (18 per cent) and France (31 per cent) rapidly increased over the 1990s, which explains the growing awareness of corporate governance issues by the end of the 1990s.

After the publication of the Cadbury report over 60 reports on corporate governance were published in 30 different countries (Monks and Minow, 2001), mirroring the largely national approach chosen to the problem. The *OECD corporate governance principles* in 1998 were the first international effort to specify corporate governance 'best practices' and serve as a modest reference point for the OECD governments and their organizations (OECD, 1998). The definition adopted by the OECD of corporate governance is relational and thus gives room for a bargaining perspective in which the outcome of the process represents a trade-off between regulation and market forces. 'Corporate governance is affected by the relationships among participants in the governance system. . . . These relationships are subject, in part, to law and regulation and, in part, to voluntary adaptation and market forces.'[6]

Historical studies on corporate governance show that when economies prosper and stock markets rise, few people talk about corporate governance (Frentrop, 2002). The Internet hype or the dotcom bubble era proved no exception. Frentrop (2002) concludes therefore that so-called 'shareholder activism' has still been ineffective in its dealing with corporate governance due to the failing of the disciplinary mechanisms of take-overs and monitoring. But the growing number of stock exchange scandals and cases of (alleged) self-enrichment of well-known managers undermines the legitimacy of corporate management – be it executives or non-executive managers (see Part II).

Civil society: highest confidence, but moderate interest

NGOs appear to offer opportunities for private initiatives through participation in the public debate and the development of initiatives in areas which, in the past, used to be the exclusive terrain of governments. This is referred to as the *resource mobility* approach and also explains the rise of NGOs as an expression of an articulate and more assertive society (Tieleman *et al.*, 1996: 24). Research in a number of OECD countries shows that on themes such as the environment, human rights and health, society has relatively more confidence in NGOs than it has in government, companies and the media. (Wootliff and Deri, 2001: 158). With human rights issues the *confidence gap* between NGOs (59 per cent) and companies (4 per cent) is the biggest (Edelman, 2002). Only in the US were companies, until recently, more trusted than NGOs and governments on many of these themes. But an international poll conducted by Edelman, a US public relations firms, for the World Economic Forum (*FT*, 24 January 2005) revealed that trust ratings for NGOs in the US had climbed from 36 per cent in 2001 to 55 per cent in 2004, thereby relegating business to second place. This is largely attributed to the impact of major corporate scandals in the same period in the US.

In practice, it would however appear that civil society's traditional factors of failure are of undiminished importance (Chapter 1): sectarian behaviour (single-issue movements that make it difficult to take other interests into account), technocrats in power and eventual fragmentation and lack of continuity. A large part of the energy of NGOs is spent on securing the continuity of the organization through donor canvassing. Just like company shareholder meetings, NGO members usually don't turn up for meetings and it is also difficult to determine to what extent NGOs actually represent the opinions of their members. Sixty per cent of the Netherlands Committee of Directors (NCD), for instance, are members of Greenpeace. The rise of state and market sponsored NGOs (the BONGOs, GONGOs, GINGOs and BINGOs) waters down the number of 'true' *civil society* NGOs, weakens their legitimacy and therefore their effectiveness in talks with companies and governments. The determining factor for the legitimacy of NGOs, at the end of the day, remains membership figures. For governments, the most influential and institutionalized NGO – with the biggest membership – remains the trade union movement, despite lost members and trade union density in most countries since the 1980s (section 4.4). But trade unions have been seriously robbed of their strength and legitimacy as a result.

Recruitment of leaders and legitimacy

Leaders of each of the three societal spheres (business, state, civil society) predominantly come from the same sphere (Chapter 1, Figure 1.2). This adds to their legitimacy within their own constituencies and thus makes it easier for them to represent their group in bargaining arenas. But what happens to their legitimacy if they switch societal sphere in the course of their career? This question has been researched by the SCOPE team in the case of leaders of state. The research shows that in the year 2000, leaders of state in rich countries are twice as likely to have a business (market) background as government leaders in the poorest countries. The relationship between government and business in these countries is generally more uncomplicated and leaders of state gain credibility in the eyes of managers due to a shared background. Because of this background, the credibility of state leaders in the eyes of representatives of civil society, however, often declines accordingly. Recent examples include Prime Minister Berlusconi in Italy, Prime Minister Lubbers in the Netherlands, President Bush and Vice-President Cheney in the US. They represent this double split in legitimacy: a mistrust of the combination of their (former) business interests with their (current) position in the eyes of the general public. Even within business groups the 'firm-oriented' president/prime minister is always approached with suspicion for fear of representing 'partial interests'. Leaders of state in the poorest countries have a civil society background almost three times as often as leaders of state in the richest countries which may boost their legitimacy among citizens, but places their legitimacy in the market under pressure.

Far-sighted managers versus short-sighted politicians?

An important dilemma for a bargaining society is how to hold talks with current generations on matters that affect future generations (see section 6.3). Who is at present best equipped to reflect on sustainability issues? What exactly is the planning horizon of managers, politicians and NGOs? According to Rischard (2002) managers think further ahead than do politicians. Shell, for example, in the 1980s, started looking at future scenarios that examined how the world could look in ten years' time. The famous scenario planning of Shell, however, is only suited to specific trade sectors such as the oil industry and is applicable only to a limited number of companies. At the other end, there is the extreme short-term thinking of American managers who particularly focus on quarterly results, since these determine the share price and the value of their own share option packages. Often, company pension schemes are also linked to the share price. The traditional planning horizon of entrepreneurs in Europe and Asia seems to lie further in the future. Share prices are a little less important and societal institutions are less antagonistic than they are in the Anglo-Saxon system – in particular the US. This is more conducive to a long-term orientation. The planning horizon of managers can sometimes be exceptionally long, but (capital) markets are capable of very short-term punishment of inadequate policies. The planning horizon of entrepreneurs that are not dependent on the capital market (family businesses, state-owned firms and cooperatives) extends further, but they, too, are confronted with short-term fluctuations in their markets that can thwart long-term planning completely.

Politicians generally have a planning horizon that does not reach beyond the next election – the so-called *political cycle*. One of the most widely studied topics in political economy is therefore the relationship between political and economic cycles. The timing of elections matters for macro-economic cycles, although the exact relationship is multifaceted. Alesina and Roubini (1997) for instance found that the relationships between political and economic cycles are remarkably similar in most democracies, particularly those with a two-party system. Anglo-Saxon countries share a two-party orientation. But whereas in the US and the UK, elections are generally held every four years, in Japan prime ministers and cabinets are appointed for a period of only two years. Accordingly the planning horizon of Japanese politicians and the impact of political cycles on the economy can be even shorter. It weakens the bargaining position of governments considerably (and strengthens the position of the informal powers with civil servants), and heightens the opportunistic behaviour that surrounds elections in order to please voters. The term of office of politicians also presents a problem in the realization of public–private partnerships, given that the planning and realization of most of these projects often exceed four years.

But along the same line of reasoning, business leaders hardly have a longer-term horizon. According to a study of the outplacement agency Drake Beam Morin (DBM), it appears that in 2002 the average duration of appointment of CEOs of large listed companies was about three years – and that is declining. This means that, on balance, politicians bear responsibility longer than company leaders do.[7] In practice it is also the informal powers behind politicians (see section 1.1) who hold talks on behalf of government, certainly in the international arena. The planning horizon of these informal powers is longer than that of the politicians they serve, which might refute the assertion that entrepreneurs are better able to protect longer-term interests than are politicians. Politicians operate on the voters market and because elections are normally held only once in four years, the punishment mechanism of the voters market generally takes longer to take effect than that of the business market.[8]

Finally, the planning horizon of NGOs appears to be longer than that of entrepreneurs and politicians. Not only do many NGOs focus much more explicitly on longer-term issues – for example, the ecological environment – managers of the large NGOs often also occupy their positions for longer periods. As such, it would appear that these organizations have greater continuity. Exactly how this works requires more detailed research. NGOs operate on the 'market' of members and donors. If the confidence of members is betrayed, they can punish NGO policies by staying away or leaving – revoking donations or terminating membership. This correction mechanism generally takes longer to take effect than that of the business market, but it has swifter results than that of the voters market. When the high remuneration of the (interim) director of Plan International, a large NGO involved in foster children, in 2002 was published – in combination with a series of other bad publicity events – the organization lost 35 per cent of its members in less than three years. Consequently the (interim) director retired. In 2004, the director of a Cancer Foundation in the Netherlands was fired the week after his high remuneration became public. The board that fired him had earlier wholeheartedly approved his salary.

6.3 RELATIONSHIP DILEMMAS: ARE BARGAINING OUTCOMES OPTIMAL?

In a bargaining society companies and societies are simultaneously trying to achieve their objectives (Googins and Rochlin, 2000: 128) without settled rules and solid institutions to govern their activities. Is it possible to reach optimal outcomes and overcome the inefficiencies of their own sphere? For companies, market failures are the greatest problem; for governments the greatest challenge is a lack of efficiency and sufficient resources; while NGOs, which represent an articulate and demanding citizenry, usually struggle with a shortage of funds. Civil society organizations can receive assistance in the form of company sponsoring and government subsidies. At least three fundamental and interconnected problems present themselves in the relationship between companies, NGOs and governments: free-rider behaviour; the distribution of costs and benefits; short- and long-term perspectives. In practice, there is a high level of overlap between these problems.

Free-rider problems

Government provision of public services has always been justified with the free-rider argument: individual players assume that someone else will construct the required highway, road, army or dike. This will allow them to use it without having to pay for it. The end result is usually that the highway never gets built, unless the government cuts the knot and builds the road with public resources. If governments retreat or are confronted with budget constraints, how can an adequate social infrastructure be constructed at all? The idea of *public–private partnerships* has been experimented with since the 1990s (see Chapter 1), but has been faced with comparable free-rider problems. The private sector often wants a greater financial and political commitment than the government is willing to give (infrastructure projects are often politically thorny). In addition, in practice it appears that different public authorities are in competition with one another. Projects are often complicated, require time, and are non-recurrent and expensive which makes it difficult to estimate the efficiency with which resources are employed. In addition, governments remain mistrustful of the private sector, which would probably also be able to carry out the project without its assistance. Financial negotiations often seem to end in a zero-sum game, where the objectives, the achievement of synergy and coordination benefits are lost sight of: what the government gains the company loses and vice versa. Who carries the risk of the partnership and who might be burdened with a free-rider? The result of this dilemma is that both parties wait and see and the partnership never materializes. The (potential) free-rider problem thus results in a 'prisoner's dilemma'.

Free-rider problems appear in all areas of regulation and negotiation, where there is a bonus on 'wait-and-see' strategies and a penalty on 'being first'. An example is environmental regulation: firms that want to be first in environmentally sound strategies generally have to invest more in learning and the development of new equipment than 'lagging' firms that can profit from the experience gained by the frontrunners. Many countries that have allied themselves with a strong military power have received a 'free-ride' on the military umbrella of their ally. Post-war Japan and Germany, for instance, could invest in their civilian sectors thus gaining tremendous competitive pace, whereas the US had to sustain its military capacity which generally has a downward effect on the productivity of the economy and on advancements in civilian technologies. Lagging firms can get a 'free ride' on the good reputation of a branch through the efforts of leading firms. Firms and governments in particular plea for a 'level playing field' in which the same rules apply to everybody and no one can even be inclined to take a 'free-rider' role by staying behind. But who is setting the rules and to what extent can opportunistic individual behaviour be evaded in order to create the preferred public good? Rajan and Zingales (2003) formulate the free-rider dilemma as follows in their provocative book entitled *Saving Capitalism from the Capitalist*: 'While everybody benefits from competitive markets, no one . . . makes huge profits from keeping the system competitive and the playing field level. Even capitalists do not gain from defending it.'

Distribution of costs and benefits and optimum investments

Innovation is another area in which the interests of society and individual companies can diverge but still be complementary. The fundamental dilemma: the average return on R&D investments for companies is 20–23 per cent and for society more than 50 per cent (Stiglitz and Wallsten, 2000). Consequently, private-sector investments in R&D are below optimum levels. Companies are not able to get the full social returns on their investments – in part because capital markets do not function optimally in this area. This dilemma can also be described as the *trade-off* between static *in*efficiency (under-utilization of knowledge) and dynamic *inefficiency* (underproduction of knowledge). Shared R&D projects between universities, states and firms could be a solution. But significant problems present themselves the moment the question is raised as to who 'owns' the knowledge generated by shared R&D projects. Until recently, academic researchers hardly patented their knowledge, but with the decline of public funding of research this route is followed more often. As a consequence, companies are no longer willing to collaborate with universities. They conduct their R&D largely internally so as to patent it themselves, and technologies that are socially most useful receive sub-optimal investment.

Short–long term

One of the greatest problems of a bargaining society is that participants often appear to be short-term oriented, while responsible behaviour should also be adopted in the long term. The pursuit of sustainable development for instance (See Part II) implies that future generations should also be given adequate opportunities for welfare realization (SER, 2000: 13). The reason for this is that while these future generations are not participating in negotiations directly, they will certainly experience their consequences. Ecological issues illustrate, in particular, the trade-off problems between short- and long-term interests. A short-term societal interest (for example, a healthier environment through more stringent regulations and the imposition of process and production standards that can involve enormous investment costs) can lead to weakened corporate competitiveness and ultimately a lack of the sources of income to invest further in an environmentally friendly society. A short-term corporate interest (more profits), however, can lead to negative externalities (environmental pollution) that can only be solved by government measures (clean-ups). And those measures can be funded only by higher taxes for citizens or companies, at the cost of the future income of companies. In corporatist countries, the partnership solution currently takes the following form: conclude a covenant with the respective interested parties and come to voluntary agreements, for example, on CO_2 emissions. The criticism against such covenants is that the parties only reach agreement with one another if it involves a short-term win–win situation. Since it is sometimes more desirable to have short-term losers in order for society to win in the long-term, the optimum solution for society is never put in place if (potential) losers also partake in the bargaining process. Covenants appear to lead to compromises of 'the lowest common denominator', which are ultimately sub-optimal for the problem that needs to be addressed.

In a bargaining society, short-term interests tend to prevail over long-term interests because next generations are not represented in present bargaining. In economic terms: distributive efficiencies – aimed at immediate gains between powerful subjects – tend to dominate productive efficiencies that can only be created by interactions aimed at longer term gains. It also blunts the incentives to make the bargaining process as a whole more productive (Metcalfe and Metcalfe, 2002).

6.4 INTERNATIONAL: PLAYING FIELD OF THE STRONG AND SINGLE-ISSUE MOVEMENTS

Within national boundaries, there are laws that place limits on a bargaining society and institutions that can act as referee in conflicts. In the international arena it is much less the case. International law stipulates regulations for a much more rudimentary legal system in effect providing negotiators with only a few basic principles and courses of action. International law is the law of negotiators, where the 'law' of the strongest often applies. The process of international regulation is, in the words of the most insightful study by Braithwaite and Drahos (2000), a 'messy process'. Even more than in the national bargaining arena this process contains 'contesting actors', 'contests of principles' and 'webs of influence' in which the shape of regulation is 'accumulated in thousands of obscure technical committees of international organizations' (ibid.: 28), in which the use of economic coercion has become much more important and widely used since the Second World War. It has also been more cost-effective than rewarding actors who choose to comply with a regulatory regime (ibid.).

Coercion and sanctions are generally used by economically strong countries. They use sanctions against economically weak countries, not vice versa. In the 116 cases of international sanctions counted by Hufbauer *et al.* (1990) the average economic size (GDP) of the sanctioning countries was 187 times the economic size of the sanctioned country. In the twentieth century the US – sometimes in collaboration with the UK – used by far the highest number of unilateral sanctions (*Washington Post*, 12 July 1998). International regulation is governed by the rule of principle, rather than by the 'rule of law' (Braithwaite and Drahos, 2000: 30). The international community contains a transnational 'elite' of bureaucrats, scientists, regulators, business people and NGOs. They are also known as 'epistemic communities' that share a common culture and professional ethos that goes beyond national cultures. The OECD is the 'single most important builder of business regulatory epistemic communities' (ibid.: 29).

Consequently, in IB, 'negotiation rather than the perfect market equilibrium solution is the rule' (Agmon, 2003: 426). IB theory generally focuses on the interface between business and states:

> Globalization is the outcome of the interface between national states and MNEs. It is a negotiated solution rather than perfect market equilibrium. . . . [N]ational states are trying to generate as much welfare for their residents as they can, while MNEs try to maximize their value.

'This creates a bargaining situation' (Agmon, 2003: 416) in which both parties are often faced with oligopolistic markets and considerable information asymmetries between the parties that can expect to be in a negotiation situation more than once. Game theory shows that the credibility of both parties in this (repeated) bargaining situation is extremely important to reduce opportunity costs. International Business–Society Management approaches should thereby also focus on the interface with civil society in general and NGOs specifically.

Single-issue orientation

Entrepreneurs and governments reproach many of the around 30,000 INGOs for operating largely as single-issue movements, not controlled in a democratic fashion by their constituencies and often consciously ignoring and distorting the interconnectedness and complexity of international issues. This restricts their legitimacy vis-à-vis national governments and firms. But not only NGOs are 'guilty' of such blame; in the international arena, this trait is inherent in most important players of the market and state as well. The more than 60,000 multinationals operate as single-issue players who can only credibly defend their own business interests. In this, there is hardly any democratic control across borders. Nationally, trade unions and works councils are still able to exercise some control; internationally, unionized participation vanishes rapidly from the scene and is generally badly informed (Chapter 4). No internationally coordinated corporate governance regime exists, and neither, yet, does any internationally coordinated market regulation.

The most important international (inter-governmental) players that are of significance to the functioning of the international economy and that operate multilaterally, are the WTO, the IMF and the World Bank. The influence of strong states – primarily from the OECD region – in the post-war period resulted in shifts in the international bargaining arenas. With the shifting arena the principles that were involved in the issue also changed. For instance the principle that knowledge is the 'common heritage of mankind' (a type of 'hypernorm' in the 'moral free space' that characterizes the international bargaining society, see also Chapter 13) was 'defeated by shifting intellectual property issues from UNESCO and UNCTAD to the World Intellectual Property Organization (WIPO) and the GATT, where knowledge was treated as property subject to trade principles' (Braithwaite and Drahos, 2000: 29). But international relations constitute recurring bargaining games. So the developing countries that in particular had lost this battle over the 'location' of the intellectual property regime, frustrated progress in the consecutive 'millennium round' exactly because they had been outmanoeuvred in previous rounds.

The WTO, the successor of GATT acts explicitly as a single-issue player, with the exclusive aim to create free (not necessarily fair) trade. The organization is not democratically controlled in this ambition. Since its foundation in 1995, the arbitration procedure of the WTO made it the only multilateral organization in the world able to intervene in national legislation or policies. NGOs criticize especially this aspect of the WTO arbitration procedures. Governments that, for example, impose stricter environmental requirements on companies on behalf of their citizenry run the risk of being reprimanded by the WTO for engaging in activities that 'interfere with the free operations of international markets'.[9] The supranational authority of the WTO, however, can potentially also be used by NGOs and weak states addressing issues that can be related to protectionism in the developed countries, thereby overcoming the general dominance of the economically strong states in the WTO. In 2004, the Brazilian organization of cotton growers – in collaboration with the Brazilian government – successfully appealed to a panel of the WTO that ruled against the subsidies of the US government for its cotton growers. These subsidies were proven to influence the world market prices of cotton to the detriment of the Brazilian growers. But although historical, this example is probably bound to remain an exception, due to the labyrinth of exception rules that in particular apply to the agricultural sector, which is the most important for developing countries' exports. Only new rules could improve this position.[10]

In practice, the IMF also projects itself largely as a single-issue organization that is primarily concerned with capital interests. Moreover, the distribution of power within the IMF is proportional to the financial stake of the different nations in the organization. In practice, this means that the US in particular and, to a lesser extent, other large industrialized countries determine the general policy direction of the institute. Eight countries represent 48 per cent of the votes within the IMF (UNDP, 2002). As a single-issue organization, the IMF has its eye particularly on the capital interests of OECD countries.

The influence of member states in the World Bank is also proportional to their financial contribution – the same eight countries have 46 per cent of the votes – but due to its development objectives, the World Bank is less restricted in its orientation. Another influential multilateral organization, the United Nations Security Council, focuses exclusively on the question of safety and security. The five large nuclear powers (China, France, the UK, the US and Russia) have veto rights. As multilateral organizations have a broader mandate and member states have proportional voting rights on the basis of *one country one vote*, they become less single-issue oriented, but also less powerful.

The greatest evidence of the existence of a 'bargaining society' can therefore be found at the international level, characterized by strongly antagonistic relations and exceptionally few well-positioned supervising bodies or governments with the legal authority to put conflicts between the different spheres back on course. Cross-connections appear in dribs and drabs for instance when companies sponsor specific United Nations organizations from time to time. In addition, company representatives partake in important discussions of the ISO or in sector-specific consultations such as the International Telecommunications Union (ITU) – all single-issue organizations.

6.5 CONCLUSION: THE CHALLENGES OF THE BARGAINING SOCIETY

What are the consequences of looking at International Business–Society Management issues as part of an international 'bargaining society' (cf. also Ghauri and Usunier, 2003)? Size matters:

relatively resourceful actors have more influence than the poorer actors. Rules matter, but power and legitimacy often matter more. The nature of the process of interaction matters, which is influenced by the roles chosen and the relative dependencies of the players in repeated games. Chapter 7 will further elaborate these characteristics. The issues matter: some issues such as patents and the competitiveness of firms and sectors tend to matter more than other issues such as corporate responsibilities. In a bargaining society, issues tend to become simplified and confrontation rather than dialogue prevails in case of rival interests. It is also very difficult to come to any agreement on how to create sufficient international public goods. Rivalry in the form of races and contests as interaction means, prevail over co-alignment and co-habitation. The arena where actors meet each other, matters a lot. One of the preconditions for 'fair outcomes' of a bargaining game is the creation of a 'level playing field'. But this precondition is hardly ever met in either national or international bargaining arenas. Besides, it is possible to argue, on the basis of welfare theory, in favour of a non-level playing field (cf. Appelman *et al.*, 2003).

In an international bargaining society, there are no single decision-making centres, so the way international firms manage their various interfaces with international civil society and states requires the mastering of a complex game with a large number of stakeholders engaged in an increasing number of clashes that leave ample room for regulatory voids and conflicts. Apparent trends – such as a retreating government – appear significantly more complex in practice. By contrast, the three most important spheres of society (market, state and civil society) seem to be clashing increasingly. Each sphere is, after all, characterized by its own rationality, logic, ideologies, cultures and norms. And uncertainty is also growing. It appears that it is not that simple to make declarations about the best social arrangements without running the risk of being exposed or labelled as an ideologue. *Best practices* are difficult to identify if one has a competitive and flourishing economy in mind, but it is even more difficult if one also has a sustainable economy in mind. In a bargaining society, reputation among peers, perception and images play an increasingly important role. They provide additional legitimacy in bargaining processes in case power and size do not suffice.

Chapter 7

Managing rivalry: the challenge of Societal Interface Management

7.1 INTRODUCTION: ON INTERFACES AND POSITIONING

Managing in a bargaining society is complex and uncertain. From the perspective of market-oriented companies, two societal interfaces predominate: private/public and profit/non-profit (Figure 7.1). Along these lines, great redistribution and legitimacy battles, especially pertaining to companies, are presently being enacted. Along these two interfaces governments (section 7.2) and NGOs (section 7.3) have to decide upon their role and level of dependency in their relationship with companies. The bargaining society is enacted in the relative dependencies

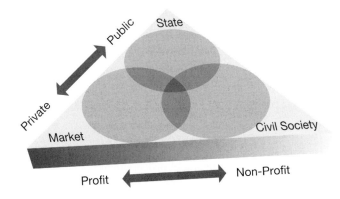

Figure 7.1 Societal Interface Management for firms

along these two interfaces and defines the boundaries and challenges for their interaction with society – their 'Societal Interface Management' (section 7.4).

7.2 GOVERNMENT AND GOVERNING ROLES

Studies on the bargaining relationship between governments and firms have often centred around the discussion whether states can be attributed (relative) autonomy in implementing and formulating public goals. The idea of state autonomy 'refers to the capacity of the state to act independently of social forces (particularly economic forces)' (Caporaso and Levine, 1992: 182). Marxist writers – and in their wake many writers that nowadays belong to the anti-globalist movement – tend to conceive of the state as an instrument or 'agent' of the ruling class and 'big business'. Poulantzas (1978) already moderated this view somewhat, granting the possibility of states having some 'relative' autonomy, especially when confronted with competing interests from groups of relatively equal influence. International comparative political-economic studies started to distinguish between 'strong' and 'weak' states or 'policy networks' (cf. Katzenstein, 1978; Krasner, 1978; Chapter 2). A strong state would have more autonomous power towards its own society and would often be able to resist pressures from particular interest groups. A weak state would contain a much less interventionist and less authoritarian government with fewer policy instruments and an inclination to leave economic restructuring to be determined by the operation of the market. Anglo-Saxon governments thus would be considered relatively 'weak' states, whereas continental European governments are much 'stronger'.

The strong/weak typology has a number of serious weaknesses, however. The direction of influence between state and market/firms can change over time and it can differ from sector to sector and even from firm to firm. There are historical examples of large French firms dominating state bureaucracies and of British and American state intervention (through the military budget for instance) that contradict the simple weak/strong state dichotomy. The weak/strong state dichotomy regards the national state as the 'core actor' and as a *unified* actor. In reality firms will often strike an agreement with one ministry to influence another, or team up with regional and local authorities to pressure national governments. Furthermore, the position of governments vis-à-vis firms changes with different ownership structures: subsidiaries of foreign multinationals have a different stake in national policy networks to domestic firms (cf. Ruigrok and van Tulder, 1995).

Four basic roles can be adopted by governments vis-à-vis business and civil society (Fox *et al.*, 2002). These roles involve increasing levels of dependencies – implying that the effectiveness of government roles becomes increasingly dependent on the actions and reactions of the bargaining partner: (1) mandating, (2) facilitating, (3) partnering, (4) endorsing (Table 7.1).

- *Mandating*: In their mandating role governments act primarily as regulators and standard-setters defining minimum behavioural norms. Governments have full autonomy over their inspectors and influence firms and civil society primarily through penalties (either legal or fiscal). Firms and civil society, on their part, can try to influence the (independent) government through lobby activities.
- *Facilitating*: In their facilitating role, governments search for more enabling instruments to create incentives for firms and civilians to move in the 'right' direction and build the appropriate capacities to do so. This could include the use of procurement policies focused on particular goals such as corporate social responsibility, national competitiveness or national security. The instrument of subsidies gives governments influence over the applicants of the subsidy. But the effectiveness of the subsidy in

Table 7.1 Government roles at the interface with business and civil society

	Endorsing	Partnering	Facilitating	Mandating
	Dependent State	Interdependent State		Independent State
Principle	Self-regulation	Semi-private regulation	Semi-public regulation	Public regulation
Instruments	Political support; publicity and praise; labelling; support of civil society initiatives; publishing 'best practices'; supporting voluntary labelling	Combining resources; stakeholder engagement; Dialogue; Public Private Partnerships; convenants	'Enabling legislation'; Strategic stakeholder dialogue; awareness raising; incentives, subsidies, tax rebates; voluntary labelling procurement policies; capacity building; supporting spread of labels; self-governing agencies	'command and control' legislation; regulators and inspectors; legal and fiscal penalties; FDI guidelines and trade policies; public labels and safety standards; anti-trust rules; generic policies in education, military, infrastructure
Corporate governance/codes	Own responsibility: voluntary codes and reporting; peer reviews/pressure	Multi-stakeholder code development; Shared monitoring	Implementing international principles; reporting stimuli/guidelines	Stock exchange regulations and codes; company law; mandatory reporting and disclosure rules
Common position of government	Local governments in 'company towns'; weak host governments towards strong multinationals; receiver of Business-community involvement (BCI); corporate philanthropy and sponsoring	State-owned corporations; joint membership of international technical committees; PPPs; regulators; joint training programmes; institutionalized consultation with business and civil society		National governments; regional governments; multilateral organizations; object of formal business lobby; generic policies

achieving the goals of the government depends on the professionalism of the beneficiary. The transaction costs involved in monitoring subsidy schemes can be huge. Subsidies towards firms in particular are risky, because the effectiveness of the subsidy depends on the market position of the firm. Subsidies for product development, for instance, make the government scheme dependent not only on the development skills of a company, but also on its marketing capabilities. The same applies for the instrument of tax rebates. The position of state-owned companies is particularly interesting in this regard. The idea behind state-owned companies is that governments have a bigger say in these companies. But that idea rapidly dissolves when state ownership becomes associated with the 'socialization of losses'. Loss-making state-owned companies often exert more influence over the government, than vice versa. The state is the hostage of company management, not least because it is almost impossible to sell the company back to the private sector again. Nationalizations in the past seldom gave government agencies a decisive say in company affairs. In fact, the nationalization of particular industries has led companies to colonize agencies of the state rather than vice versa (cf. Cawson *et al.*, 1990). Nevertheless, state ownership has also strengthened the bargaining position of governments to other firms in the industry, in particular to foreign companies wishing to enter the country (Ruigrok and van Tulder, 1995: 109). Governments have often created semi-public regulatory bodies to monitor developments in these areas.

- *Partnering*: Partnering implies that governments actively seek a combination of resources and stakeholder engagement. This can be done in the form of PPPs, but also in less formal organizational forms such as stakeholder dialogues and shared monitoring activities. The partnering role of governments often comes in the form of semi-private regulation and convenants. In cases where the regulator would be semi-public (see also below) the role of the government changes from being an equal partner into one with more powers to change the rules of the game. Partnering stresses the complementary assets and skills of the three spheres, which implies multi-stakeholder dialogues and capacity building. Partnering, and endorsing activities generally, hint at a relatively weak legitimacy and/or bargaining position of the public actor that engages in them. The United Nations, for instance, engaged in many partnering actions and multi-stakeholder dialogues due to lack of support by their member states for more stringent measures (such as mandatory codes).

- *Endorsing*: The endorsing role of governments is the least involved and makes them most dependent on firms and NGOs for achieving particular bargaining outcomes. Extreme dependencies can be found in so-called 'company towns', which are built around one particular company as the main employer which thus dominates economic, social and political life in that town. Almost all big (core) firms in the world have become dominant in at least one town somewhere in the world. Some towns, such as Toyota City, even adopted the name of 'their' company. A (bargaining) dilemma any firm dominating a company town will have to deal with is that *overt* influence of the local 'hearts' and 'minds' may easily provoke resistance from those local actors traditionally having the monopoly over these matters: local churches, teachers, the medical trades and local politicians. To overcome such resistance in the past firms such as Philips, General Motors, Volkswagen, Corning Glass and Nokia, often felt obliged to develop quite advanced social infrastructures (local museums, sports facilities, schools). In a more modern shape this has now become known as 'business-community involvement' (BCI) and corporate sponsoring. Whether the motivation for these activities has changed over the decades will be analysed in Part II. Where a (local) government finds itself confronted with a very dominant subsidiary of a multinational, headquartered somewhere else, its bargaining power is substantially less than in the case of a company town that also houses the headquarters of a company.[1]

Governance and control dilemmas

Governments and companies that lack legitimacy look for measures to control each other effectively. A solution is increasingly sought in the establishment of *intermediary organizations* and *agencies*, which oversee particular trade sectors or business conduct on behalf of the government or the public (civil society). In many of the OECD countries old and reputable institutes of this kind exist, such as Central Banks, Audit and Civil Rights courts, land registry agencies and the like. Throughout the 1990s, the privatization or partial privatization of various regulatory organizations proceeded relatively unsystematically and high-handedly, often leading to much uncertainty and concern. General employer organizations and representatives of specific branches demanded that a check be put on, as they put it, the 'unfair' competitition experienced from the commercial activities of semi-governmental organizations. This did not relate to state-owned companies. The hybrid nature of these organizations created confusion even then and the confusion has increased rather than decreased ever since.[2]

Semi-public market supervision

A significant number of national supervisory and executive bodies operate in between state and markets, to oversee different markets relatively independent of the government. In the Netherlands, the form of 'self-governing organizations' (SGOs) was invented to give these organizations a separate legal form. Comparable regulatory agencies exist around the world. They operate in between the 'rule of law' and 'the rule of principle' (Braithwaite and Drahos, 2000: 30). Many of them have the legal power to exert sanctions on wrongdoers, but are also aimed at stimulating the self-regulatory powers of the sector. These organizations include (among others) post and telecommunications authorities, securities commissions, pensions, insurance and competition policy (anti-trust) authorities, regulators for energy markets, food safety and the media. The status of these agencies can differ per country, but in all countries their operations are always the result and the object of considerable interest battles. The position and jurisdiction of major agencies also regularly change over time. The discussion over the position of many of these agencies, at the moment, runs parallel to the discussion on the question whether or not the state should withdraw (see Chapter 5). Some countries, for instance, (partially) privatized many of their former fully state-owned regulatory and supervision authorities to make them more efficient in the course of the 1980s and 1990s, only to seriously reassess that strategy following major exchange scandals, financial crises, energy supply disruptions and food safety problems since the end of the 1990s (see also Chapter 7).[3] The struggle is not only about power (who controls whom and who has jurisdictions), but also about the most effective manner of regulating markets, creating conditions for competitiveness and innovation and representing the interests of consumers. This involves complex trade-off processes.

Food and drug safety

One example is the institution of food and drug safeguards around the world. These have only developed after long battles between food and drug companies and (segments of) governments. Mostly companies and right wing political parties opted for a limited influence of government on business. Agencies around the world – most of them representing a hybrid form of semi-public regulation – have been struggling to find a balance between tougher and looser rules, and between the interests of consumers and the industry. Hilts (2003) has documented this extensively for the Food and Drug Administration (FDA) in the US. Tough rules are important for food and drug safety, whereas looser rules are important to stimulate innovation and secure food security in the future. Nestle (2002) further documented how the food processing industry in the US tried to obstruct any form of regulation, for instance, by a powerful lobby and the funding of congress people and presidential campaigns, mostly of Republicans, but also of Democrat candidates. The aim of these strategies is not necessarily to influence the independence of the supervisor, which in developed countries is often guaranteed by law and monitored by the media. One of the results, according to Nestle (2002), of the extensive lobbying of the food industry in the US has been that the FDA is under-staffed and under-financed which makes it difficult for it to fulfil its mandate. Furthermore, the FDA top is often recruited from the very food industry it is supposed to supervise. As a consequence, most food safety rules in the American food meat processing industry, for instance, still stem from 1906.

The regulatory problem increases when the (technological and sectoral) boundaries of a particular sector get blurred. Food, chemicals and pharmaceuticals are increasingly crossing each others' territories due to progress in biotechnology techniques – creating a new branch, that of 'life sciences'. Likewise, the various specialized agencies have also regularly struggled over each others' competencies. The US, at the moment has generally lower barriers to innovation in the area of biotechnology for food (genetically modified food) – whereas European governments, firms and consumers have a stronger emphasis on food safety. US producers – together with the Federal government – reproached Europeans for imposing non-tariff barriers on the imports of American food and food components (such as soy). Europeans, on the other hand, reproached Americans for being too indulgent on food safety – the FDA, for instance, does not require food producers to reveal on food labels whether they use genetically modified organisms (GMOs). In 2003, the US threatened to bring the case before the WTO – a specialized institution dealing with free trade and not food safety nor its security. Whether or not the case will be resolved, it reveals the bargaining dynamics of most regulatory disputes involving the international balance between tougher and looser rules.

Financial regulation

Another example is formed by the complex system of semi-public regulation of financial markets. Central Banks thereby function as well-established bargaining actors in most countries in the world. Their position, status and independence, however, differs from country to country. The US developed a mixed monetary regulatory system, a federation of 12 Federal Reserve Banks presided over by a Federal Reserve Board. It leads to rivalry between state and federal regulators. But the system of Central Banks are not the only (semi) public organizations regulating financial markets. For insurance and securities markets, often different institutions have been created, such as the Securities and Exchange Commission (SEC).

The mix of institutes regularly leads to power battles on overlapping jurisdictions between federal institutions (such as the SEC, the Treasury Department and the Federal Reserve Bank) and state institutions. For example, the New York attorney general (Elliot Spitzer) '[did] a fine job in illustrating the structural anarchy in America's supervision of its financial institutions' (*The Economist*, 24 January 2004: 67). *The Economist* continues more specifically:

> [the banking industry] is overseen by an assortment of regulators whose overlapping
> responsibilities are understood by almost no one. Local banks are overseen by the

Federal Deposit Insurance Corporation and state regulators. Some of the biggest banks, and all bank holding companies, are also supervised by states but in conjunction with the local branches of the Federal Reserve. Those that are not fall under the purview of the Comptroller of the Currency, a branch of the Treasury Department.

The anarchy is also the result of regulatory changes allowing for national banks and bank-insurance companies to develop in the US, where previously the sectors had been separated and local supervision prevailed.[4]

In other Federal states around the world, the Central Bank took over the function of local bank authorities, but was granted a higher degree of independence (as in Germany) from government and business alike. In all countries the overlapping semi-public regulatory regimes between banks, insurances, securities and general competition policy, lead to serious bargaining struggles. In Italy, for instance – following the Parmalat affair in 2003 – it was discussed whether the Bank of Italy (the Italian Central Bank) should hand over supervision of the banking industry to the anti-trust authority in Italy – deemed more independent. One of the points of discussion has been whether it would increase the likelihood that foreign banks could acquire Italian banks, which has always been barred by the Central Bank (*FT*, 26 January 2004). At the level of the EU, the Committee of European Securities Regulators (CESR) has been active in introducing capital adequacy rules and other harmonized standards and rules of conduct, which ultimately have the force of law in Europe. But some of the rules do not distinguish between banking, insurance, securities trading or fund management, which still leaves considerable room for different interpretations and limits the possibilities for services to be sold in different countries (*FT*, December 2004). A 2005 study by the Centre for the Study of Financial Innovation, noted that the overriding view of bankers around the 54 countries surveyed was that the financial watchdogs 'are out of control' (*FT*, 24 January 2005).

These two examples illustrate in particular two dimensions of the problems that are related to semi-public supervision organizations in a bargaining society: jurisdiction and constituency disputes.

Geographical jurisdiction border disputes

Jurisdiction disputes generally revolve around geography and industry. First, we will consider *geographical jurisdiction disputes*. In most countries centralized organizations negotiate with decentralized organizations over their jurisdiction. This problem is particularly tangible for federal states and regional authorities (in particular the EU). When in 2003 New York Attorney-General Spitzer addressed problems at the New York Stock Exchange, he operated within his own constituency, but also entered into a regulatory dispute with the SEC whose prime responsibility it is to deal with this issue. A second issue relates to the principle of 'extra-territoriality' of regulation. With the adoption of the Sarbanes-Oxley Bill in 2002, the US not only installed a stricter accounting regime on companies, but also expanded the extra-territoriality of its rules by requiring the CEOs of companies listed at its national stock exchanges to accept a certain degree of personal liability for which they could be held accountable in the US. This includes, therefore, also foreign CEOs who would normally only be judged in their country of residence and/or of the company's official headquarters. The measure immediately became disputed not only by companies, but also by regulators around the world, in particular in Europe. At the same time the SEC and the European regulatory committee (CESR) – which both draft rules and regulations rather than laws – are trying to establish more formal ties.[5]

Differences in regulations between Europe, the US and Japan have, for instance, also led to significantly different patent strategies, affecting the competitiveness of companies from these countries in turn. In July 2002, the European Patent office, for example, placed restrictions on a controversial patent concerning the growth of human and animal embryos – so-called stem cells – after protests from a number of countries, including the Netherlands (*Vk*, 25 July 2002). A similar discussion in the US is, for the time being, heading towards different results. Semi-public patent supervisory bodies are settling ethical discussions.

Another international dispute over jurisdiction appeared between the European and American competition policy authorities in the 2001–2003 period. European Competition Authorities seemed more critical than American anti-cartel regulators. A number of large acquisitions of American companies (e.g. General Electric's bid for Honeywell) in Europe were consequently thwarted, which led the Americans to reproach the Europeans for protectionism through its competition policy. Both Europe and the US accused each other of erecting impenetrable barriers. A lack of international coordination will necessarily result in further struggles over jurisdiction – especially when the players are political and economic heavyweights. But efforts to coordinate international regulation, also entail bargaining. The European Union in particular has been working on a number of harmonization initiatives, for example in the area of merger supervision and requirements for annual reports. This is a logical step given that the different supervisory systems of individual countries generated complications and delays, especially with respect to the regulation of international companies. In the aftermath of decentralized national negotiations, one part of the hard-won powers of national competition policy authorities to supervise national mergers and acquisitions was curtailed (once again) in October 2001 (*FD*, 29 October 2001).

In addition, there is a discussion under way on a European supervisory authority for banking, insurance and dealing in shares, which could yet again upset all the compromises that national supervisory bodies have struggled to reach. The problem with international (re)negotiations over semi-public supervision is, among other things, that players who 'lose' in one round of talks can use the next round to try to get their way. This is also why game theory distinguishes between singular and repeated games, as the two games have completely different logic. The bargaining society entails repeated games.

Industry jurisdiction disputes

Second, *industry jurisdiction disputes* appear in particular when technological developments and firm strategies create blurring of the boundaries between industries that were previously separated and the objects of separate supervision. In the course of the 1990s, thus, the following industries became the object of considerable supervisory disputes: (1) financial services (banking, securities, insurances, pensions); (2) life sciences (food, chemicals, pharmaceuticals, drugs); (3) communication (telecommunication, information technology, media); (4) infrastructure (automotive, rail, planes); (5) energy (electricity, nuclear, alternative energy sources). In addition, the regulation in these jurisdictions often conflicted with the general competition policy authorities. The UK and Greece for instance have started to integrate general competition supervision and the supervision on telecommunications and media. In most other countries, however, the supervising bodies are still separate and thus prone to mutual rivalry. European Regulation in this area is based on the subsidiarity principle, rather than on hierarchy and supervision. This sustains (modest) rivalry between the various countries and continued international diversity. In financial markets, the intensity of jurisdiction disputes seems particularly strong. The discussion on an optimal division of tasks among the financial supervisory bodies centres on the question whether to design a division by sector or by function. Since all financial services providers are increasingly performing comparable functions, this would make a division on sector increasingly impractical. In the Netherlands it was decided in 2002 to concentrate the activities of the Central Bank and the pension and insurance authorities on so-called 'prudential' (business economical) supervision, while the duties of the Securities authority focused on conduct-oriented supervision.

Constituency disputes

Constituency disputes revolve around the question of which prime stakeholders or interests are represented by the semi-public supervision organization: (1) producers or consumers; (2) present or future producers (innovation); (3) specific producers and the whole economy. In many countries constituency disputes have arisen, in particular, between a number of the semi-public authorities that were created in the 1990s to monitor the 'creation of markets' in previously publicly owned sectors (such as telecommunications, electricity, water, media and railways) and traditional authorities that had to monitor the proper 'working of markets'. The main constituency of the traditional group of supervisors are customers, whereas the main constituency of the new group of supervisors has been to also represent the interests of the firms that have overtaken the former state sector.

So, after their creation as semi-independent institutes in the 1990s, a fierce battle over jurisdiction flared up between the newly created and the traditional supervisory bodies. Objectives and fields of duty (sectors) partly overlap each other and the economy and technology are, of course, also developing. In this way, the discussion is raging on the question of whether supervisory bodies should only focus on business economical supervision, or whether they should also be supervising the conduct of companies, the task being to protect consumers. In financial markets the dispute revolves around the question of what regulators should do about credit rating agencies and hedge funds. In telecommunications and energy the dispute in many countries is how to match the interests of customers with sustaining the international competitiveness of the newly created private firms (often operating as private monopolies). The dispute revolves around the constituency of the general competition authorities and the branch-specific authorities.

For companies in the specific sectors, such transformation periods generate enormous uncertainty. Even if the tasks have been assigned, the uncertainty remains. What is awaited, after all, is the exact content of the duties of the supervisory bodies, which heralds yet another process of negotiations.

Semi-private supervision

Semi-public supervisory bodies complement organizations that have been appointed from within specific trades and which can be typified as semi-private. Examples include disciplinary tribunals, the Bar and associations of doctors, dentists, accountants, journalists or estate agents. The effectiveness of such internal disciplinary tribunals is, however, up for discussion, even within the professions themselves. The levels of secrecy are high (verdicts are seldom published), failing members are hardly ever expelled, the legal status of verdicts is dubious and the position of the client/patient is often unclear.[6] Legal provisions for 'whistleblowers' do not always protect them from serious repercussions (see Box 7.1).

Moreover, systems of self-regulation work much less in developing countries. Forced by the new demand for transparency and openness, and confronted with citizens who defend their interests increasingly explicitly, more and more professional associations in the OECD region have started to account publicly for results of disciplinary hearings. But their effectiveness in addressing the issues at stake remains unclear.

BOX 7.1 NOT TO BE ENVIED: THE POSITION OF 'WHISTLEBLOWERS'

Whistleblowing, is the act of raising concerns about misconduct within an organization. It is considered by many as a key element in raising the effectiveness of any governance system. But others consider it as an act of 'betrayal' and lack of 'loyalty' to the organization. Both aspects can indeed play a role and whistleblowing is certainly not necessarily without self-interest, although the position of a whistleblower is hardly ever to be envied. *Time Magazine*'s 2002 'persons of the year' award went to three whistleblowers – Cynthia Cooper (WorldCom), Coleen Rowley (the FBI) and Sherron Watkins (Enron) – who each had addressed serious misconduct in their respective organizations. According to *Time Magazine*, they 'reminded us of what American courage and American values are all about'. A 2003 *National Business Ethics* survey in the US, showed that the percentage of employees reporting misconduct increased from 48 per cent in 1994 to 65 per cent in 2003 (Tansey Martens and Kelleher, 2004). The act of whistleblowing is not limited to the US and not only a recent phenomenon – although certainly increasing in importance as another expression of the 'bargaining society'.

> In China, Dr Jiang Yanyong broke ranks [in 2003], finally persuading his government to publicly reveal and confront the spread of SARS. [In the 1990s] Harry Templeton looked media magnate Robert Maxwell in the eye and challenged his plundering of the pension fund.
>
> (www.pcaw.co.uk, consulted at 26 June 2004)

Reporting misconduct, however, is not easy, in particular when the internal communication procedures are not conducive to criticism and job protection is not in place. This is still the case with firms. Reporting misconduct by public servants is not only favoured by many governments but is even required by law and/or facilitated by organizational rules in two-thirds of the OECD countries. But, interestingly, only half of these countries offer general protection to the whistleblower (OECD, 1999). So, even with governmental organizations around the world, the act of whistleblowing contains great personal risk. Famous whistleblowers have experienced serious problems – even when protective laws were in place.

An example is provided by one of the most famous whistleblowers in the European Union. Internal auditor Paul van Buitenen, single-handedly brought the whole European Commission to a fall in 1999. In an internal memorandum he revealed fraud, nepotism and mismanagement in the Commission to senior Commission officials, but was ignored. In December 1998, he revealed information to the European Parliament, details of which were subsequently disclosed in the press. He was suspended on half pay, but the Commission had to appoint a Committee of Independent Experts to investigate the allegations. The March 1999 report of the Committee concluded, 'it is becoming difficult to find anyone who has even the slightest sense of responsibility'. Consequently, all 20 European Commissioners resigned. In 2004, van Buitenen, who had major problems in sustaining his work with the Commission, founded his own political party and was elected member of the European Parliament. In countries and in firms where adequate regulation is not in place, the act of whistleblowing is even more risky. Dehn and Calland (2004), the editors of a comparative study on whistleblowers explain, that only if 'the good intentions of any law are matched by a change in culture can a safe alternative to silence be created. Only then can the principle of accountability work in practice and protect the public interest'. Competition policy authorities in the US and Europe are increasingly using companies as whistleblowers to reveal acts of collusion in particular sectors. The first-comer whistleblowing firm gets absolved of sanctions, which makes the act less self-sacrificing than with individuals.

The problems encountered by six self-regulating groups that perform important functions at the interface between states and markets can further illustrate the breadth of the issue at stake: traders, accountants, journalists, scientists, credit raters and accreditors.

- *Supervising stock brokers*: This involves the semi-private supervision of insider trading on stock exchanges. Most stock exchanges in OECD countries – often privately owned – such as the NYSE, the Nasdaq, Euronext, and the Tokyo Stock Exchange have their own sophisticated surveillance mechanisms and staff to track insider trading and pursue investigations. These self-surveillance systems cannot prevent insider-trading scandals from appearing, but moreover have shown great difficulties in giving appropriate sanctions. These exchanges refer only the exceptional cases to the state and federal supervisors such as the SEC in the US[7] or the public prosecutor in other countries. Stock exchanges in developing countries do not have the financial muscle to invest in those systems, thus hampering the sophistication of self-regulation on insider trading or of timely and fair disclosure of information to analysts among others.[8]

- *Supervising accountants/auditors*: The supervision of accountants and auditors – functioning as supervisors of companies – in particular, has come into play since the mid-1990s. Do accountants/auditors represent the interests of management, of the investors, or of society as a whole? In the US the Financial Accounting Standards Board (FASB) is the standard setter in accounting rules. Its independence was challenged after the position of accountants came under attack. The SEC had also given substantial regulatory and self-serving powers to the accountants' professional association and lobbying group, the American Institute of Certified Public Accountants (AICPA), the national association of securities dealers and the stock exchanges. Comparable self-regulatory organizations (SROs) developed in almost all other developed countries. But, supervision over the activities by the profession itself – as is presently the case – appears to be inadequate. Moreover, the biggest accounting corporations started to merge in the course of the 1990s, which resulted in the 'Big Four' (KPMG, PwC, Deloitte & Touche, Ernst & Young) that do the great majority of corporate accounting. So the question asked by Sampson (2004) is a logical one: 'who audits the auditors?'. Furthermore, an old boys' network has developed between big companies and auditing firms. In 2003, the *Accountancy Magazine* found that 53 of the finance directors of the 100 biggest corporations were alumni of the Big Four (Sampson, 2004: 319).

  In addition, the accountant has increasingly become an advisor to the company, whereby the two functions (supervision and advice) can become entangled. Many countries require a strict separation of these functions, but the large consultancy firms have difficulties with it. The greatest blow for the profession occurred in 2001, when it came to light that the energy corporation Enron, worth about US$65 million in fees, was such an important client of Andersen Consulting that the Andersen accountants did not dare dissociate themselves from demonstrable fraud – which, incidentally, had been construed by their own consultants. This has at the same time regenerated the discussion on the hybrid status and 'degree of entrepreneurship' of accountants, which raises the question of whether a supervisor can or may be an entrepreneur at the same time. Governments throughout the world are considering stricter supervision and some are even contemplating bringing the function of accountants back under government control. Many governments are considering the introduction of compulsory auditor rotation.

- *Supervising journalists and media*:[9] Newspapers and television are regarded as having an important supervisory function in society – they are often called the fourth power or the fourth estate. But they are also run as businesses – which also face growing consolidation around the world[10] – whereas journalists are primarily regulated by boards of journalists themselves, sometimes complemented by supervision through an ombudsman. The effectiveness of boards of journalists and the ombudsman is low, as these institutions lack the power to enforce sanctions. In fact, any effective regulation other than self-regulation is internationally rejected by the sector. Journalists tend to emphasize the importance of a free press. In that frame of mind, powerful supervision can only lead to unwanted censorship. The organizations[11] that fight any shape of control on the press outnumber the organizations that supervise journalists.

In practice the only real counterforce to journalists are other journalists. The internationally accepted practice of checking stories of colleagues is taken even further in the US. Some media have adopted their own fact-checking branches[12] after having published false stories in the race to get hot news first. The debate on the independence of journalism is particularly ardent in the US. In Europe, this type of self-regulation is not common practice, although there is an ongoing discussion on whether the self-cleansing power of the media can deal with the aggressive competition that puts financial gains above the basic facts. For the US, Kovach and Rosenthiel (2001) conclude that many modern journalists do not know, or act upon, their societal responsibilities. Only in times of war will journalists be muzzled by government.[13] The independence of the media requires sufficient self-regulatory powers, otherwise its hybrid function between civil society and state/market actors disappears and it becomes yet another partisan actor. The relative independence of the editors and journalists vis-à-vis the owners of the medium, regularly requires debate and renewed bargaining. It basically depends on the contents and the function of the editorial charter adopted by the staff. This discussion becomes more acute the moment an entrepreneur fulfils an important political function, such as Prime Minister Berlusconi of Italy, who during most of his time in public office remained the owner of a number of very large newspapers and TV stations.

■ *Supervising scientists*: Associated to the self-regulatory powers of the media, is the issue of *peer review* as an increasingly important mechanism through which information and influence is regulated in the bargaining society. In particular in scientific communities around the world, peer review is commonly used as a way to select the 'good' from the 'bad' scientists. PhD titles are mostly awarded on the basis of a judgement of expert committees. But who can be considered 'experts'? The problem with such review procedures is easy to understand: the approval depends on the composition of the selection committee (which is the responsibility of the promotor who might not be completely objective), the committee members only approve what they like (which might be problematic because there are serious battles of insight in most sciences). With an increasing number of doctorates around the world, the pressure on the trade to approve PhDs has mounted. Many universities have initiated forms of quality control, but it has not yet happened that a PhD title was withdrawn *ex-post*, based on this self-regulatory mechanism. The basic correction mechanism remains the 'reputation' of the promotor, which could be negatively affected by a weak thesis.

Readers from prestigious scientific journals have to trust that the self-regulatory mechanism works well enough to guarantee that the research behind the articles published is reliable. Top journals use so-called 'double blind' referee procedures that are intended to make the selection procedure as objective as possible: the identity of neither the referees nor the writers of the article is revealed in the review procedure. This system has considerable drawbacks, however. (a) It takes a long time. Publishing an article in an esteemed (quarterly) journal can take up to three years. (b) Very specialized articles are difficult to judge by reviewers who do not belong to the particular discipline, but when they do, it is very difficult to keep the identity of the writer(s) of the article secret. (3) The reviewers often have contradicting opinions on the contribution, making it very difficult for the writer(s) to accommodate all reviewers without turning the article into an amorphous product that is intended to 'please everybody'.[14] (d) The rating of particular journals is also in the hands of peers – based on lists of cross-referencing for instance – which favours traditional journals and orthodox science managed by well-established scientific communities over more recent and heterodox science. (e) The publication of scientific journals has become 'big business'. A small number of international scientific publishers – in particular in natural sciences and medicine – demand booming prices for the top journals. Since 1993, the fees asked for scientific journals have increased by 200 per cent. This limits the distribution of these journals and therefore the public access to the knowledge generated.[15] (f) The system cannot adequately address various forms of 'cheating' as regards the authors. Co-authors regularly get a free ride on publications of their colleagues while supervisors use their position to become the first author. But, even more seriously, it can happen that articles have not been written by the revealed author(s) at all, but by a ghost-writer. The British newspaper the *Observer* in December 2003 suggested a link between drugs companies – which have immense interest in getting an endorsement for their medicine by a prestigious journal – and independent academics. Academics – falling victim to the 'deadline society' themselves – are helped by pharmaceutical companies to 'upgrade' their writing or even do the research. Whether these allegations can really be substantiated and whether this has resulted in many 'dubbed' publications representing the interests of industrial groups is open for debate, but the peer review system does not preclude this mechanism from appearing.

■ *Supervising the credit raters*: Rating agencies operate as increasingly powerful private 'watchdogs' or 'peer reviewers' of firms and even countries. Among the rating agencies, the New York-based Standard and Poor's Corporation and Moody's Investors Service stand out in size and impact. Their judgement on the solvency (creditworthiness) of firms and governments are favoured and feared. A Triple-A rating of these agencies – although not based on the same methodologies – is the most desired qualification for any CEO or state leader. Credit rating agencies earn income from the sales of their general (unsolicited) ratings to investors and from solicited ratings at the request of particular companies. The big credit rating organizations earn their income primarily from solicited ratings. In the case of solicited ratings, the company can provide secret information and/or informally question a disappointing rating. The independence of the credit rating organization can become jeopardized in this exchange of information. It has been found that solicited credit ratings usually result in higher ratings for the company involved, than in the case of unsolicited ratings (Smith and Walter, 2001).

Primarily governments get Triple-A ratings, because they do not run the risk of going bankrupt. These ratings affect the interest rates payed on loans and thus have tremendous influence in particular debt-ridden countries and companies. In addition, the rating has a symbolic function. When the rating goes up, it serves as an endorsement of the policy implemented by either a state government or a company board. In Europe, only three public companies had a Triple-A rating in early 2004 due to their impeccable credit position: Shell, Nestlé and Novartis (*Vk*, 3 February 2004).

The announcement of a downward grading – or even the announcement of a *formal review* – on the other hand, has brought many a country and firm into considerable trouble. The fiscal crisis of Argentina towards the end of the 1990s, for instance, was aggravated enormously by the downward ratings of Moody's. The country did not have the bargaining clout however to dispute the downgrading. When Russia was, for the first time, awarded a rating by Moody's (not by S&P, or Fitch) in October 2003, it was celebrated as a major event, which 'put Russia on the investment map' (*FT*, 9 October 2003). But when, in 2002 and 2003, the governments of Japan and Germany and some of their leading companies were slightly downgraded by S&P – for the first time in a long period and only from a very high credit rating – they not only became outraged, but also started to dispute the methods used by the rating agencies. Furthermore, their ministers, Central Banks and other regulators, started to put pressure on the rating agencies to change their judgement. Finally, these events triggered a renewed discussion on the regulation of the rating agencies. The rating agencies create a degree of transparency for investors (cf. Braithwaite and Drahos, 2000: 160) – that is for those willing to pay their fees – but are not very transparent themselves.

- *Supervising the supervisors*: The supervision of supervisors represents a separate category. Certification bodies and accreditation agencies (for instance of accountants) are two types of supervisors that have a clear function in the economy. Councils for accreditation grant certifying bodies – for example, of ISO quality standards – accreditation to fulfil their supervisory roles. The independence and discretionary powers (partly because of personnel shortages) of these organizations are, however, the subject of much criticism. All the problems associated with semi-public supervision relate to these organizations as well.

Effectiveness of intermediary organizations

Supervisory organizations are societal interface organizations of the highest order. They can be seen as monitoring bodies that oversee one of the cornerstones (state, market or civil society) of society on behalf of another cornerstone. The legal framework often makes life difficult for supervisors. In practice, however, these frameworks cannot always readily be applied which leaves much room for interpretation and thus for negotiation/bargaining. Five factors in particular determine the effectiveness of intermediaries: independence, objectives and resources, jurisdictions, coordination and legitimacy.

- *The degree of independence*, from politics, society and the market. Research into the functioning of Central Banks shows, for example, that Central Banks best promote their objectives of controlling inflation and maintaining stability of national currency rates when the president of the bank is neither appointed nor influenced by the Minister of Finance. The same has also been found for Competition Authorities and Audit Offices and probably will apply to most intermediary organizations: the more independent the more effective.[16] Most of the cases of abundant executive compensation, fraudulent accounting practices, lack of ethical standards in business, even insider trading, have also been associated with supervisory boards or non-executive directors that did not allow adequate independence of the executive directors. Most of the regulatory reform in corporate governance regimes is therefore aimed at restoring a greater degree of independence of the board of directors/supervisors. The degree to which this will be achieved depends on the bargaining dynamism of national systems (see Chapter 2 and Kydland and Prescott, 1977).
- *Clear objectives and access to sufficient (financial) resources* to realize objectives. It was only by the time the stock market fraud in the US had taken on massive proportions that the SEC was given the extra resources that it had been requesting for decades. The problem of many semi-independent organizations is that they lack sufficient resources or are used as a 'cash cow' for other purposes.[17]

- *Different jurisdictions* with respect to supervisors with complementary objectives and responsibilities. Unclear mandates have often led to unnecessary clashes over direction, but have also caused opportunistic behaviour in companies and citizens that is comparable to a territorial battle. Technological developments also made for shifting sectors and created a battle over jurisdiction between sector-specific supervisory bodies.
- *International coordination* of similar types of supervisory bodies. It is becoming increasingly important for intermediaries in an RIA to align their policies. Europe chose supervisory alignment in terms of the subsidiary principle; globally, however, supervisory alignment seems to be a matter of substitution, which decreases the effectiveness of supervision and increases the uncertainty for companies.
- *Recognition of legitimacy* of the supervisory body by those concerned. If a supervisor is not accepted by the business sector it is supposed to regulate, the effectiveness of supervision is limited. Players would probably not be very cooperative and would try to evade supervision; this is often occurring in the relationship between food companies, energy companies, telecommunication companies and their regulators around the world.

One of the clearest expressions of the existence of a bargaining society, is that the number of intermediary organizations increases. Unless the above preconditions are met, the confusion about their status and effectiveness will intensify as internationalization advances.

7.3 NGO ROLES ON THE INTERFACE WITH FIRMS

The function of NGOs is, first and foremost, to organize society and to create 'club goods' (see Chapter 1). Next to that, they operate at two interfaces: (a) between the state and civil society and (b) between the market and civil society. The first interface is the most traditional. Many NGOs appeal to government to obtain additional funding for projects they carry out on behalf of civil society. These are largely local projects for the benefit of the local population. As such, NGOs are taking over part of what is traditionally regarded as government responsibilities while still retaining part of their independence. Belonging to this category are those development aid organizations or co-financing organizations which, in many countries, receive government funding to carry out projects aimed directly at the local population in developing countries that cannot be realized through local governments. Moreover, the growing trend is for government to set specific targets that these NGOs are required to meet. They are increasingly judged on output, slightly reducing their independence again. Next to that, there are the so-called government NGOs. One of the reasons why receding central governments still succeed in obtaining the greatest part of the national income is that these funds are being redistributed to new semi-public supervisory bodies: (1) GONGOs – Government Organized NGOs – are NGOs that have been founded by the government and which fulfil a supervisory function on behalf of government; (2) GINGOs – Government Interested NGOs – carry out specific projects on behalf of government, such as promotion of exports or environmental decontamination. These NGOs are of great relevance to the functioning of companies and markets.

It is, however, the second interface in particular – market versus civil society – that is undergoing change. Since the early 1990s, with the advent of the bargaining society, NGOs have been calling companies to account for their social responsibilities in a variety of ways. Many NGOs believe that companies, more so than government, are/should be able to address certain issues. According to Elkington and Fennell (1998), NGOs can assume four roles in this regard: (1) sharks, (2) orcas, (3) sea lions and (4) dolphins. Sharks and orcas are inclined towards polarization and confrontation. They act more (sharks) or less (orcas) instinctively, strategically and in groups. By contrast, sea lions and dolphins are more inclined towards cooperation. Sea lions will accept sponsorship from companies (and tend not to criticize the hand that feeds them too much), while dolphins realize that companies can create important preconditions to achieve desired change but prefer to retain their independence in the process. Both confrontation and cooperation can be adequate strategies. Many NGOs start out as sharks: with direct action, debate and as much independence from companies as possible. According to a recent report by SustainAbility and the UN (2003), the categories of orcas and dolphins have gained in importance and appeal. Five strategies can be distinguished by means of which NGOs intervene in companies and markets so as to make their influence felt (see Box 7.2).

BOX 7.2 NGOS' INTERVENTION STRATEGIES

- *Anti-business campaigns*: effective in raising public awareness around an issue and generating pressure on companies. Tend to be effective only against well-known branded companies on black-and-white issues.
- *Market intelligence*: still largely focusing on individual companies, a growing trend involves building market intelligence on companies and facilitating pressure from employees, customers, suppliers, investors, boards etc. for improvements in performance on key issues.
- *Business engagement*: engaging businesses in partnerships aimed at collaboratively addressing key issues.
- *Intelligent markets*: potentially the most powerful way to intervene in markets is to try to do so at the level of the market – rather than with individual or groups of businesses. A small number of NGOs are attempting to do this by actively working to 'reframe' markets to reward positive behaviour and penalize negative behaviour.
- *Market disruptions*: come in the form of regulatory interventions or shifting liability regimes, to jump market frameworks to higher levels of sustainability.

(Source: SustainAbility and United Nations 2003)

The development of a shift towards NGO partnerships with companies (the 'business engagement' role) can be identified. Also notable is that next to, or perhaps because of, the emerging trend towards partnerships, national and international NGOs are increasingly confronted with demands of accountability and transparency. NGOs are being called upon to adopt codes of conduct. To meet these new demands, NGOs need to be managed in an increasingly professional manner.

Ten NGO roles

There is, however, a richer palette of NGO strategies than the inventory above suggests. A broad range of new roles is currently unfolding, especially in the area of multi and strategic stakeholder dialogues and project partnerships that move beyond a form of 'business engagement'. Roles such as broker, mediator and/or supervisor are appearing which, up until now, have hardly been discussed in academic literature. Moreover, it is often assumed that NGOs can fulfil only one role and/or that they migrate from one role to another. In practice, the situation seems much more nuanced. NGOs adopt different roles, both consecutively in a single process as well as simultaneously in different settings through which at one moment they seek to start a debate and the other they seek to start a dialogue.

The following ten NGO roles can be distinguished at the market–civil society interface:[18]

1 **BONGOs** (Business Oriented NGOs). Companies have helped to found a number of NGOs whose sole purpose is to represent their interests. That is not to say that these organizations also fulfil the function of one-sided representatives. In practice, many BONGOs provide a discussion platform for several societal groupings. The studies that are conducted – sometimes by independent researchers – can serve as input for all sorts of other forms of dialogue and debate. The principal problem of BONGOs, however, remains their credibility. BONGOs that represent the interests of a given sector are at risk of representing the 'lowest common denominator', just like official trade organizations and chambers of commerce. This was precisely the reason why some (large) companies elected to create new NGOs which could elevate the debate on a given issue to a higher plane. An example is the World Business Council for Sustainable Development (WBCSD) and some of its satellite organizations such as the Foundation for Business and Society (FBS) (which has come up with a global corporate governance benchmark). Another is the European Roundtable of Industrialists (ERT) which played an important role in the formation of the EU – an important public good for all Europeans – but which at the same time constantly calls suspicion on itself due to the fact that it only represents the interests of a limited number of industrial firms.

2 **PONGOs** (Partnership Oriented NGOs) often focus on one specific project which, in practice, is realized in collaboration with companies. The World Nature Foundation financed a number of its conservation projects with the assistance of companies. To a certain extent this amounts to a form of corporate sponsorship of NGO projects. 'Business–community involvement' projects are also characterized by different forms of partnership between local communities and participating companies (see Chapter 4). In the past, such initiatives were largely viewed as a form of philanthropy, but companies are increasingly adopting a strategic approach to these types of activities. At the very least then, one can speak of 'strategic philanthropy', but increasingly also of partnership. By starting a specific project with a company, however, an NGO does adopt a position of relative dependence in relation to the company, but that applies both ways. The partnership approach is more results oriented and focuses on concrete (partial) solutions. Consequently, partnerships are often more viable if relatively simple and practical single issues are at stake which may very well form a part of more complex, multi-dimensional issues.

BOX 7.3 PARTNERING PARADOXES: THE SPONSORING NEXUS

With US$100,000 General Motors sponsored the Chumbawumba band for its TV commercials. That band, however, in turn sponsors anarchistic groups acting against the domination of big companies in the world. One of these big companies is . . . General Motors.

Unilever acquired Ben & Jerry's, the ice cream maker and retailer. Ben & Jerry's is well known for its specific ice creams, but also for its more idealistic origins. The founders decided to dedicate five per cent of their revenues (before profits) to sponsoring charity funds. Some of the charities funded by Ben & Jerry's are anti-globalization activists that protest against the icons of globalization, a prominent representative of which is . . . Unilever.

3 **BINGOs** (Business Interested NGOs).[19] An increasing number of, not profit- but social accountability-oriented, NGOs seek to present themselves as alternative to companies on their own market. In this way, the Fair Trade Organization (integrated into the European Fair Trade Association) supplies products to many European countries while an organization such as Max Havelaar manages the quality labels and marketing. Automobilist associations are also active in this area. Dutch, German and English NGOs sometimes try to compete in their own markets by setting up their own filling stations and online travel agencies. Automobilist NGOs are united in an international organization for tourist and automobilist associations. The US has an automobilist federation that provides the same services in each state in which it is represented. Trade unions across the world are moving in the direction of 'service' organizations. They offer services to members such as insurance and training, which is direct competition for private insurance companies, pension funds and the like. These NGOs aim to raise company awareness of their responsibilities, but they also try – by modifying market conditions – to offer consumers a socially responsible or more favourable alternative. The dilemma these NGOs face, however, is that the effectiveness of their strategy depends on the market-related success of their products.

4 **SHANGOs** (Shareholding NGOs). These are NGOs that manage investment portfolios and aim to secure good shareholder value for their supporters, i.e. relatively small individual investors. As such, they can largely be described as single-issue NGOs. An important part of their strategy is the coordination and representation at shareholders' meetings of large groups of small shareholders. An increasing number of NGOs are springing up whose focus is especially on smaller shareholders interested in making sustainable investments. Since the mid-1990s, NGOs such as Greenpeace have also tried to exert influence on company policies through the acquisition of shares. Since the block of shares is never big enough to buy real influence via voting rights, these NGOs attend shareholders' meetings in the capacity of 'agitator'. As such, the role of the SHANGO is similar to that of the WONGO. This form of campaigning requires that NGOs buy shares, which puts them at risk of becoming dependent on stock market sentiments. For this reason, NGOs such as Greenpeace usually dispose of their 'right to vote' after the shareholders' meeting which means that they are not paid out dividends. The role of 'agitator', after all, does not sit well with gaining financially from the company whose operating procedures one has denounced.

5 **STRONGOs** (Strategic Stakeholder Oriented NGOs). As the interaction between NGOs and companies has more and more bearing upon strategic issues – the exact outcome of which cannot be predicted – mutual dependence in realizing shared objectives also increases. The participants acknowledge a shared responsibility for the end result and work towards it in alliance with companies. The *Marine Stewardship Council* seems to be one of the first initiatives towards genuine strategic stakeholder dialogue. The covenants, quality labels and other regulations that are agreed to in the Marine Stewardship Council have the objective of creating a common 'public good' (sustainable fisheries). The objectives will most likely have to be adjusted continuously and in close consultation with a large number of strategic stakeholders (STRONGOs).

6 **BRONGOs** (Broker Oriented NGOs). New NGOs are increasingly being founded that can meet companies' demand for a 'mediator' or 'broker' in the face of societal conflicts. The degree of independence of this NGO role is generally less than that of the supervisory NGOs (SUNGOs). Generally, it is not a permanent organization either. For each conflict, a new organizational form or 'arbitrator' can take shape. The parties to the conflict can delegate a

representative to the institution that is to be formed. Usually, the parties agree beforehand that they will accept the ruling of the mediator. Sometimes this role is started up by the government so as to create a more permanent forum – a 'third party'. The Environment Council is an example. All relevant sectors, NGOs, governments and civil society are represented in the 'council'. The Environment Council describes its role as that of 'honest broker', 'consensus builder' and an 'unbiased', 'unprejudiced third party'. Contributions of members in the form of donations, memberships and such are accepted on the condition that the donor accepts the independence of the Environment Council. As the role of broker/mediator becomes more permanent and members represent the primary stakeholders, one can increasingly speak of a strategic stakeholder dialogue.

7 **SUNGOs** (Supervisory NGOs). Companies, societal groupings and governments are increasingly seeking to identify organizations that can oversee compliance with codes of conduct, reporting requirements and/or quality labels that have been agreed on. As the role of civil society representatives (among others) in these initiatives becomes more prominent, the likelihood increases that supervision on compliance is placed in the hands of foundations or independent/autonomous governing bodies, which are financed by the participating organizations or government. Examples are the Global Reporting Initiative (GRI), various quality label organizations, but also the National Contact Points (NCP), which are a professional institute in all OECD countries that is intended to oversee compliance with the OECD Guidelines for Multinational Companies.

8 **DONGOs** (Discussion and Dialogue Oriented NGOs). NGOs that enter into discussion and dialogue with companies do not only focus on the moral superiority of their position, they also

---

BOX 7.4 BETWEEN DISCUSSION/SUPERVISION AND BROKER: TRANSPARENCY INTERNATIONAL

Transparency International (TI) originated in 1993 in response to frustration with working at the World Bank. The founder of TI, Peter Eigen, then a World Bank employee faced with corruption in Africa, was told that fighting corruption was not the Bank's mandate (*FT*, 13 October 2003). Now TI is active in more than 90 countries, with around 60 people employed in its German headquarters. Its Annual Corruption Perception Index has become the benchmark for many governments and – increasingly – also international organizations such as the World Bank. Conventions on bribe-paying and corruption by the OECD and the UN have been initiated by TI. In particular, it has had success in tackling corruption through addressing international big business and the public–private (procurement) interface. TI came up with a solution to help companies stop bribery without losing business to companies that still do it: pressure on governments to sign the OECD convention and subsequently inter-company agreements not to use bribery to win contracts. Anti-corruption codes of conduct have become relatively common among multinationals. TI's aproach has been based 'on building coalitions, not on confrontation' and has been successful among many multinational corporations (Eigen, 2003). The steering committee that helped build TI's 'business principles' consisted of NGOs, governments and big international companies such as General Electric Company, Norsk Hydro, PricewaterhouseCoopers, Rio Tinto plc and Shell International Ltd.

take an interest in the opinion and position of those companies. In their interaction with companies they try to understand the position of companies and vice versa. It is a question of mutual enlightenment without direct focus on resolving specific issues. The organizations remain relatively independent of each other. This applies to co-financing and voluntary organizations across the world. Médecins sans Frontières and Terre des Hommes, for instance, have their own responsibilities – essentially not (yet) focused on cooperating with companies – but reject conflict and confrontation with companies as means to draw attention to an issue.

9 **WONGOs** (Watchdog Oriented NGOs). NGOs that operate as 'agitator' or 'conscience' include organizations such as ATTAC, Greenpeace, McSpotlight, Friends of the Earth, Clean Clothes Campaign and Amnesty International. They intend to remain as independent as possible and actually seek confrontation and debate in order to draw attention to issues in as stark a manner as possible. They are strongly media oriented and make use of 'blaming and shaming' campaigns to highlight corporate responsibilities and inconsistencies.

10 **DANGOs** (Direct Action oriented NGOs). Hard-core action groups, such as the Animal Liberation Front, the former Rote Armee Fraction (RAF) or even al-Qaeda, employ anonymous cells to carry out (illegal) campaigns. They are oriented towards direct action without consultation, where animal liberation actions, sabotage and wreaking economic damage represent the primary components of their campaign repertoire.

The ten NGO roles discussed above signify an increasing degree of NGO independence from companies. Table 7.2 maps this. As NGOs operate more independently, their campaigns become less predictable for companies. Such campaigns are also almost always geared towards protest, debate and polarization. In such campaigns, NGOs chiefly adopt a single-issue approach and focus almost exclusively on exposing the problems. If NGOs are more solution and product oriented, and seek to operate as company representative (BONGO) or endeavour to carry out

Table 7.2 NGO roles at the interface with business

BONGO	PONGO	BINGO	SHANGO	STRONGO	BRONGO	SUNGO	DONGO	WONGO	DANGO
Role intensity (%):									
2	38	7	9	13	13	23	88	54	N/a

$\longleftrightarrow$

Dependent NGOs			Interdependent NGOs			Independent NGOs			
'Sea Lions'			'Dolphins'			'Orcas'		'Sharks'	
Product oriented; realization			Process oriented; integration			Protest oriented; polarization			
Operational NGOs (ONGOs)			Hybrid NGOs (HNGOs)			Advocacy NGOs (ANGOs)			
Single-issue approach; focus especially on (partial) solutions			Multi-dimensional approach; focus on problems and solutions			Single-issue approach; focus on problems			
Predictable			Interactive			Unpredictable			
Risks: complicity; excuse for finding more structural solutions; window dressing			Risks: weak compromises; co-optation; a too long-term vision; group thinking; lowest common denominator			Risks: simplification/exaggeration of issue; 'iconification'; reactionary; shirking of responsibilities			

a joint project with companies (PONGO), there is a great likelihood that they will focus on relatively simple (single) issues. Along with this, their dependence on and predictability for companies will also increase. It is only when NGOs seek a 'mutually' dependent relation with companies that it is possible to carry out a more multi-dimensional approach in practice, by means of which problems and solutions can be linked with each other.

Table 7.2 also depicts the results of research conducted on the 'intensity' of specific roles (van Tulder *et al.*, 2004). In a study of 60 large internationally oriented NGOs conducted in 2003, we enquired after the roles these NGOs were occupying at the time. One-fifth of the NGOs assume just a single role. More than 40 per cent assume more than two roles. Among the roles assumed, the centre of gravity clearly lies with the more protest-oriented roles (WONGOs and DONGOs). The partnership NGO (PONGO), however, is on the rise. The relative importance of DANGOs as a non-governmental organizational form is more difficult to establish due to the illicit nature of these groups' activities. These campaigns, however, have increased in significance – specifically in the form of terrorist attacks, but less so in the form of animal liberation actions.

Effective roles?

NGOs are increasingly struggling with the question of the degree to which their current roles are *effective* in achieving the objectives from which they derive their right to exist. Direct/hard core organizations (DANGOs), for example, run the risk of launching arbitrary campaigns lacking in strategy, where idealism degenerates into anarchy and violence and companies' reactions harden to such an extent that the NGO loses the sympathy of the broader public. This won't bring anyone closer to finding a solution to the issue at hand. The 'agitator' (WANGOs) strategy often leads to oversimplification and exaggeration of the issue. In this approach, only the large companies – the icons – can be confronted, sometimes with the opposite effect, for example, in the event that these companies are in fact leaders in their attempt to conduct business in a socially responsible manner. As such, they are 'punished' for their transparency and good intentions because the NGOs in question lack more subtle and/or sophisticated instruments to influence and interact with companies. Only relatively simple issues can be dealt with by NGOs through this 'David vs Goliath' approach. These NGOs can become 'trapped' in their single-issue role. Greenpeace in the US in 1991, for instance, tried to broaden its scope and campaigned against the first Gulf war. Two-thirds of the members left Greenpeace for mixing up the environment with the peace issue.

In the case of NGOs as 'discussion partner' (DONGOs) – the mild form of dialogue – the risk arises of simplification on the part of NGOs, and of a 'divide and rule' policy on the part of companies. At the other extreme of the scale (especially in regard to PONGOs and BONGOs), it is not entirely inconceivable for NGOs who collaborate with companies to serve as some sort of excuse for these companies not to make a sufficient effort to find strategic – and truly structural solutions for the problem at hand. The function that the cooperation between the parties acquires then becomes one of mere window dressing or ruse.

At the centre of the strategic spectrum of NGO roles, the mutual dependencies are greater which offers greater potential for a process-oriented multi-dimensional approach, but also carries with it the necessary risks. The NGO that operates as competitor on a market (BINGOs) makes the effectiveness of its activities dependent on the success of the market. Not only is there the risk of market failure, but particularly in an oligopolistic market the scope of such an NGO is strongly influenced by precisely those other market players who the NGO attempts to influence by entering the market. A comparable problem presents itself when an NGO acquires shares in a company in order to influence it (SHANGOs). While participation can be

125

bought, it often transpires that the shareholders' meeting is not necessarily the place where participation actually has an impact. An adverse by-product is that one becomes partly responsible for company policy – even if one votes against it – and that part of the NGO's capital becomes dependent on stock market sentiments. Moreover, in practice it appears that NGOs who exercise their influence on stock markets to prevent large investors – such as pension funds – from investing in certain 'dubious' companies, can achieve exactly the opposite effect. When critical shareholders carry out the threat to sell their shares, they can be replaced by less critical/exclusively profit-oriented shareholders. NGOs that position themselves as supervisor or 'mediator' (BONGOs) run the risk of losing the ability to advance their own ideas and interests as a result of exclusive preoccupation with mediating others' interests.

Accordingly, NGOs fulfil a broad range of roles that can be effective, but also involve significant risks. In practice, a balancing of different (complementary) roles among different NGOs appears to be most effective in creating minimum conditions for stakeholder dialogue. Thus organizations such as the WWF can more readily forge partnerships with companies given that the more radical alternative, Greenpeace, holds less appeal for companies. Due to a lack of financial means and professionalism many NGOs in the past have elected to assume a single role. This is currently undergoing change. NGOs are reconsidering the effectiveness of their actions and a move towards adopting of a multitude of roles can be discerned. This, however, generates internal management and coordination difficulties as well as external identity and legitimacy problems. Members and donors are not always able to identify with the different roles NGOs assume. Companies also sometimes have problems appreciating that an NGO can be a discussion partner and simultaneously approach the media to publicly criticize the company in connection with a different, or even the same, issue that's being discussed.

7.4 CONCLUSION: THE CHALLENGES OF SOCIETAL INTERFACE MANAGEMENT

Companies that want to take up position on the playing field of societal actors will have to take at least five interfaces into account:

- *Local/national/regional/bi-regional/global.* When companies internationalize, they become less connected to the national context within which they normally operate, while the importance of good relations with their local environment/s also increases due to outsourcing strategies and the increasing utilization of (local) social capital. How can this be dealt with? In addition it becomes increasingly important to assess whether regulatory regimes and institutions (1) converge or (2) diverge across borders. Diverging regimes require more coordination of activities if firms want to reap scale advantages. In the case of converging regimes it is relevant to assess whether this process represents (a) voluntary harmonization (such as in the case of the EU or the WTO) or (b) the predominance of one regulatory regime (such as the US government has been trying to do in various areas of company-relevant regulation). The latter is probably quicker to achieve, but is also less acceptable for the biggest contenders of the leading country. In speculating about the shape of international governance comparable scenario's are portrayed: (1) neo-liberalism in which states continue to be of importance and thus divergence will prevail; (2) neo-medievalism is based on the end of national sovereignty and the rise of non-state sectors as multinational firms, international organizations and NGOs; this leads to international chaos; (3) trans-governmentalism provides a renewal of the state, but now also through international convergence in policy networks (cf. Gilpin, 2002; Muldoon, 2003).

- *Public–private.* The absence of an adequate public infrastructure with regard to innovation, education, healthcare and transport also leads to sub-optimal outcomes and competitive disadvantages for companies. A company that operates in a country with a government that invests a lot in public infrastructures (both physical and knowledge) can, in the short term, gain significant competitive advantage. What, however, would be an optimal distribution of costs and benefits among companies, governments and civil society? Would public–private partnerships be functional? How many public goods do 'public' companies provide; how many 'private' goods do private (family-owned) firms provide? Would self-regulation without laws be effective?

- *Profit–non-profit.* Technological and economic developments hardly seem conceivable without a non-profit and informal sector, its social capital and the input and efforts of its volunteers. To what extent does an economy benefit from a (large) informal sector? How can firms more systematically interact with the non-profit sector?

- *Technology–society.* The hybridization of technologies (genomics, nano-technology, bio science), the overlap of formerly separated sectors (*life sciences, communication, financial services*) and the integration of production systems, lead to just as many societal interface challenges for the company. Technologically feasible innovations need not be socially desirable; take for example, genetic modification or cloning. Conversely, a socially desirable innovation technology need not yet be feasible. How can the two sides of the coin be connected?

- *Operational–visionary.* Societal developments require that entrepreneurs critically reflect on their technologies, the sector and the location in which they operate. This requires that discussions about corporate vision and leadership are re-introduced. Pharmaceutical companies, for example, came to the realization that they would rather be seen as 'care givers' than 'pill peddlers' exclusively pursuing the profit motive, and are thus returning to the vision of their original founders. To what extent can operational requirements for the short term be reconciled with strategic perspectives on the long-term future?

Technological and international conflicts are also taking place largely along these dividing lines. In Part II the idea and the discussion on various forms of CSR (generally translated as 'corporate social responsibility') from the perspective of companies will be elaborated in further detail. In doing so, these two interfaces will (and should) take centre stage. Companies are being confronted with a growing number of demanding and critical stakeholders, divergent social interests and expectations and therefore more social 'issues' than ever before. An increasing number of parties are affected by, and have an interest in, the conduct of companies. These are the stakeholders that take part in the reputation mechanism, as they determine the reputation of companies. Moreover, companies appear on the radar screen of social groupings with increased frequency. NGOs increasingly have their arrows focused on the market. The greatest territorial conflict can, therefore, probably be found on the profit/non-profit interface. It manifests itself specifically in conflicts between companies – as representatives of the market – and representatives of civil society.

International corporate responsibility

Principles of reputation and interface management

INTRODUCTION TO PART II

STARTER QUESTION . . .

In June 2004, the following question was put to an international expert audience at a conference in Amsterdam on international corporate responsibility: 'Will the concept corporate social responsibility – commonly referred to as "CSR" – ever be used in a concise, consistent and undisputed manner?' Eighty per cent of the audience replied that they didn't think so. The next question was: 'Is this a problem?' The largely academic audience replied (of course): 'It depends.' 'Yes', because the concept can also be abused by firms, governments and people that are not interested in it or want to use it for window-dressing purposes as a public relations (PR) tool. As long as CSR remains a catch-all phrase it can be taken hostage and it can also confuse the discussion if everybody is referring to something else. The concept becomes a management fad – a hype – and loses its value. 'No', because a concept such as this has to develop on the basis of new insights and experiences, and thus cannot escape a certain degree of ambiguity. And, besides, it also provides a steady source of work for scholars discussing the various concepts!

The very fact that different concepts and meanings of CSR have developed is an expression of the workings of an international bargaining society in which power and influence are also based in ideas, concepts and ideologies. Taking the theory and practice of CSR seriously, therefore, requires that its history and various dimensions be taken into account. This Part tries to do so by deciphering the components of 'CSR' and 'ICR' – the international dimension of CSR – which leads to the identification of at least four equally relevant (and sometimes rival) approaches to the concept: inactive, reactive, active and pro/interactive. Is it 'business as usual' or 'business as unusual'?

WHAT IS 'THE BUSINESS OF BUSINESS'?

According to Milton Friedman, the (grand) father of monetarism, it should be business as usual. A company has only one responsibility: 'to use its resources and engage in activities designed to increase its profits so long as it stays within the rules of the game, which is to say, engages in open and free competition, without deception and fraud' (Friedman, 1962). More succinctly formulated: 'the business of business is business' (ibid.). Or, as the heading of a *New York Times Magazine* article (13 September 1970) by the same author read 'The Social Responsibility of Business is to Increase its Profits'. Entrepreneurs are socially accountable only to shareholders and should maximize profits to the best of their ability. All other notions of primary corporate responsibilities would lead to non-rational actions, market distortions, the sub-optimal functioning of the market and ultimately a decline in social welfare. Friedman not only considers the current attention to the social responsibility of firms 'soft', but also wrong. In managing their companies, entrepreneurs should not venture beyond the boundaries of their core competencies. According to the economist and Nobel Laureate, one can even regard a company that concerns itself with 'other social responsibilities' as 'subversive' (*Vk*, 3 September 2002). One should simply allow the market and its players to go about their business, and thus contribute to welfare maximization and a 'better world'.

One problem with this fundamentalist neo-classical position is that in reality the number of companies that function purely according to market principles is very small (see Part I). There are many factors at work that cause market failures that render effective business practice without social regulations (institutions) inconceivable and that also carry the risk of under-investment in socially useful goods, services and infrastructure. The latter ultimately limits the opportunity for profit maximization for a large group of companies. Besides, hybrid organizations would lose a significant part of their *unique selling point* if they were to follow Friedman's principles. In practice, social and institutional capital is just as important as traditional production factors – people, natural resources and machines – which are the primary focus of neo-classical economists. Finally, it appears that 'soft' factors are becoming increasingly important also for purely market-oriented companies: consumer confidence, reputation, reliability and entrepreneurial spirit (innovation, ideals) play an important role in the success or failure of realizing profit targets.

The neo-classical school leaves little room for the importance of entrepreneurship, entrepreneurial ideals and the objectives with which a product can be launched on the market. Since the beginning of the 1990s, an entrepreneur who is perceived as doing something 'dubious' or who acts inappropriately in the eyes of customers or authorities can forget about profit maximization. It is therefore best to identify diverging societal, government (state) and company (market) expectations in order to adopt an appropriate approach.[1] Expectations with respect to company conduct, in the ecological and societal spheres, in any event, are growing. The role of the corporation in society is subject to change and, rightly or wrongly, the role assigned to companies is expanding. This is the field of activity of reputation management, issue management, business ethics and (international) corporate responsibility.

BUSINESS AS UNUSUAL

The ideas of Anita Roddick, founder of 'The Body Shop', an international enterprise which is grounded in ethical principles, seem to be referred to as often in the debate on the principles of management as those of Milton Friedman. In her book *Business as Unusual* she formulates these principles as follows: 'The business of business should not just be about money, it should be about responsibility. It should be about public good, not private greed' (Roddick, 2000). But Roddick's position has also become somewhat controversial.[2] One problem with her stance is that public goods are generally provided by governments. As Part I already showed, it does not suffice to substitute government failure with market failure. The provision of public goods is accompanied by considerable dilemmas that are very difficult – if not impossible – for firms to solve. Sometimes, private greed (profit maximization) can act as a powerful trigger for technological and entrepreneurial change. Moreover, the history of the Body Shop shows that business can never be driven purely by ethical principles alone. Principles offer a 'unique selling point' facilitating an entry strategy in an oligopolistic sector (personal care products). But serious problems exist in capturing the 'lower end' of the market, where many customers have started to regard a disjunction between price and quality that cannot be substituted for by ethical principles. In a survey on 'The Good Company', *The Economist* offers a 'sceptical look at corporate social responsibility' (*The Economist*, 22 January 2005). According to the survey, the present, rather superficial, attention to CSR detracts attention from genuine problems of business and business ethics. CSR needs to be complemented with 'wise' public interventions of various kinds. 'To improve capitalism, you first need to understand it. The thinking behind CSR does not meet that test' (ibid.).

So, the 'business as unusual' position also has its flaws. Whereas the Friedman position primarily advances theoretical, economical arguments, the Roddick position primarily employs practical managerial arguments. The result is a very intense, but perhaps not wholly insightful debate. In between, and even beyond, these extremes many other positions are possible and are relevant in studying the present and future dynamics of IB and capitalism. The success of international firms depends on the context (cultural, structural, historical and political) in which their general and CSR strategies are developed. There is not one, single, 'best-practice' formula for proper Societal Interface Management; there is a range of approaches available to defining the business of business.

ASSESSING THE CHARACTERISTICS OF INTERNATIONAL CORPORATE RESPONSIBILITY

Part II focuses on societal change from an IB perspective. This part builds upon the insights on the various dimensions of rivalry gained in Part I. The analysis in this part is largely descriptive, although using the insight gained from all relevant theoretical approaches. It examines what happens when firms are confronted with all the intricacies of the international bargaining society: conflicts of interests, badly functioning and competing international institutions, regulatory voids, rising expectations of citizens, retreating governments, information asymmetries, and non-level playing fields. Firms that move beyond regulatory and state borders face even greater challenges.

Part I discussed the challenges of 'Societal Interface Management' that entrepreneurs generally face. Part II examines the question of whether and how entrepreneurs can/should follow a socially accountable course in this dynamic and changing environment. Three aspects of this problem are considered.

The first concerns issues of corporate responsibility and how to engage with them *in principle*. Chapter 8 (The Logic) explores the 'logic' behind socially responsible behaviour of companies and whether there is a 'business case' for becoming a 'good corporation'. The second concerns the *practice* of CSR: what is at stake and what are the occasions and mechanisms that trigger a company to start thinking about CSR more proactively. Chapter 9 (The Occasion) identifies the timing of the triggering events and the operational challenges for issues managers. Chapter 10 (The Stakes) identifies the most important societal issues that have materialized. It discusses whether companies should consider themselves part of the problem, or part of the solution. Chapter 11 (The Mechanism) shows how reputation is a vital practical mechanism through which companies are allegedly corrected if they are not conducting their business in a socially responsible manner. These practicalities indicate to a large extent whether companies are indeed challenged to implement certain principles.

The third aspect concerns the *international dimension*: do Societal Interface Management challenges change in nature and size when firms move beyond regulatory and state borders? Chapter 12

(The Context) considers the relative success of particular ICR strategies as a confrontation between firm strategy and national and international CSR regimes. In interaction with national and international regulation, firms search for disciplining measures – in the development and implementation of codes of conduct, reporting practices, corporate governance and the introduction of labels. Chapter 13 (The Process) defines the principles of ICR by considering the various dimensions of 'distance' that accompany international operations. It takes a closer look at some of the practical dilemmas companies face in the international bargaining society. The study of IB–Society Management is a relatively novel field of expertise and research. In Part II, we therefore aim to discuss and integrate a number of conceptual frameworks, delineate relevant approaches and concisely present first empirical findings.

Chapter 8

The logic: the multifaceted notion of corporate responsibility

8.1 INTRODUCTION: ON FIRM BOUNDARIES AND HISTORICAL RESPONSIBILITIES

The notion of the social responsibility of corporations and of companies operating beyond their immediate (market) boundaries is as old as capitalism itself. What is currently referred to as 'corporate social responsibility' and customarily abbreviated as 'CSR' is an umbrella term that encompasses a hodgepodge of concepts and meanings that date back to the second phase of the industrial revolution in the mid-nineteenth century. The industrial revolution was accompanied by the advent of mass production for mass markets in the large steel and chemical factories, along with the widespread electrification of society. The third long wave (Kondratieff) of economic and technological development that emerged out of the industrial revolution demanded entirely different social structures and placed enormous pressure on existing networks such as the family, Church and community. Large-scale urban migration created societal and regulatory uncertainties within countries comparable with what we are experiencing today between countries – under the fifth Kondratieff (see Chapter 2). It called for new social structures at the interface of markets and civil society. The government generally kept to its role of guardian and was not yet ready for large-scale interventions.

Rising labour associations and trade unions at the time partly provided services such as pension funds and health support for widows. The loss of social cohesion was further set off by health and savings funds of manufacturers themselves. The founders of large industrial companies – many of them still key economic players today – became active in council housing and sometimes even built entire city quarters for their employees, including kindergartens, schools, libraries, sports facilities and shops. The Dutch industrialist Van Marken, for instance, admitted that enlightened self-interest lurked behind these initiatives: 'is the patron who neglects the rights of his workers truly acting in his own interests? To do so would be just as foolish as closing off the steam valve of his engine in order to save coals' (SER, 2000: 21). In Britain, the leading economy of the time, the Victorian social reformers adopted a similar type of paternalism to improve the living conditions of their employees. In the US, the anti-trust movement advanced arguments in favour of more corporate responsibility in protest against the 'robber barons' or big entrepreneurs, who attempted to monopolize the economy (McEwen, 2001). All over the world, 'enlightened' industrialists such as Siemens, Krupp, Philips, Edison (General Electric), Carnegie, VanderBilt, Rockefeller or the Lever brothers (Unilever) developed initiatives that ranged from corporate philanthropy to setting up whole villages. Their motives were more or less identical: fear of labour unrest and radicalism; keeping rising trade unions at bay; a sense of duty based in religious convictions; attracting labour forces from the countryside and using the initiatives for promotional purposes (ibid.: 21).

These initiatives were prompted not so much by legal obligations as well-intentioned self-interest and a desire to avert more stringent legislation (cf. Kolk, 2003). Research by various (parliamentary) commissions around the world into labour conditions in factories at the end of the nineteenth century often revealed the need for far-reaching social legislation which, among other things, resulted in industrial injuries laws. While these amendments were aimed at establishing a 'level playing field', 'socially responsible' entrepreneurs such as Van Marken were not altogether pleased with the new legislation. They objected not so much to industrial injuries insurance for labourers – after all, they already had one for their employees – but to the fact that the obligation was imposed upon them by government. The role of government with respect to corporate responsibility was therefore already a controversial topic more than a century ago. Protests by employers against too much government involvement at the end of the nineteenth and the beginning of the twentieth century also culminated in the establishment of the first employers' organizations and thus laid the foundation for the institutionalized bargaining society of much of the century to follow. Throughout the twentieth century, organizational policies slowly shifted from mere financial to industrial and market-oriented policies. Company policies also started to include wider groups of beneficiaries. The owner/manager was considered the sole beneficiary at the end of the nineteenth century. But since then beneficiaries slowly included employees since 1900, and the industry and the direct task environment of the organization, including customers, distributors, suppliers and creditors in the post-war period (Zenisek, 1979; Kolk, 2000).

Since 1960, the question of corporate responsibilities gradually acquired more 'societal' dimensions. The paternalism of the nineteenth century made way for an interpretation involving a more active stance of corporations and the involvement of large interest groups in society (stakeholders) (section 8.2). There are at least four approaches to corporate responsibility, each with its own logic and academic discipline. This chapter gives an overview of the different approaches companies can adopt in meeting their responsibilities towards society in general and to (groups of) stakeholders in specific: inactive, reactive, active and pro/interactive (section 8.3). This chapter considers whether CSR is merely a 'hype' which will whither away in a few years' time – particularly in the event of an economic downturn. This is a risk that looms large if CSR can only be operationalized as a 'moral' concept and managers are asked to do 'the right thing'. The argument is advanced in this chapter that if CSR can be integrated into mainstream management thinking and Societal Interface Management can occupy a new place in the organization of companies, the risk of CSR falling prey to fleeting trends and economic cycles is significantly reduced (section 8.4). The most comprehensive and proactive Societal Interface Management strategy embodies an approach that resonates strongly with the thinking of a number of business experts. This will require the adoption of a 'Triple-E' framework – instead of a 'Triple-P' framework – which is elaborated on at the end of the chapter (section 8.5). Together with the challenges specified in Part I (Chapter 7), they form the components to be considered in addressing the challenges of Societal Interface Management.

8.2 CONTEMPORARY APPROACHES TO CSR

The more active stance of business towards social and societal affairs since the 1960s ran parallel to the development of various academic disciplines and the creation of specialized/functional departments in companies. Management scholars started to talk of 'business *and* society management', 'business *in* society management' or 'business–society management'. As is common in academic and managerial thinking, the various approaches have overlapping origins, constituencies and conceptual frameworks. This has added to the general confusion about its precise meaning, but also added to status of the phenomenon as a 'hype'. In the 1970s, the term was said to be sufficiently 'catholic' to mean all sorts of things to all sorts of people (Sethi, 1975: note 9). At present, the term appears in a vast and still growing number of media publications[1] and academic journals, and is employed by thousands of organizations. The following international journals, for instance, appeared in the course of the 1990s: *Ethical Corporation*, the *Greenmoney Journal*, *Sustainability Journal*, *CSR Magazine*, *Journal of Corporate Citizenship*, and the *Accounting, Auditing and Accountability Journal*. Nevertheless, Harrison (2004: 1) predicts that 'the likelihood that any organization will gain a comprehensive understanding of the field is constantly decreasing'. The strategic management expert Michael Porter refers to the field of CSR as a 'religion with too many priests' (European Business Forum, Autumn 2003). But as was explained in Part I, rival definitions and elaborations of CSR reflect the complexities of (current) world trends. The meaning and content of CSR will therefore remain a contested concept (cf. Carroll, 1999). In order to move forward, however, a clear understanding of the various approaches is required. This section offers an – admittedly schematic – overview of the academic and societal roots of various complementary CSR approaches in order to delineate the various dimensions of corporate responsibility.

Business *and* Society Management

The establishment of critical consumer organizations in the 1950s and 1960s and the first protests against environmental degradation in the 1970s focused the spotlight on the responsibilities of companies vis-à-vis other societal actors. Howard Bowen's 1953 book *Social Responsibilities of the Businessman* started off the 'modern era' of CSR thinking (Carroll, 1999). In the 1970s, the concept of 'corporate responsibility' was introduced to operationalize the idea that companies should show their commitment to society more explicitly. In 1973 Davis formulated his 'iron law of responsibility' stating that 'in the long run those who do not use power in a manner that society considers responsible will tend to lose it' (Davis, 1973: 312–313). By the beginning of the 1980s, the attention shifted to 'corporate responsiveness'. In this framework management's response to the direct action of stakeholders is taken as the point of departure. Business and organizational models are characterized by an outside-in perspective which reflects the notion of 'Business *and* Society' (B&S). The contents and even the title of most contemporary books contained the business *and* society perspective. This expresses the perception that business and society (as external or environmental factors) are two spheres that are sharply separated. Responsiveness to external issues was seen as bridging the two worlds. In the 1980s, specialized corporate departments were created to pursue such bridging activities. External/Public Affairs departments were set up to deal with so-called 'issues management' and manage the various 'community relations' functions including media relations, customer relations, investor relations and governmental affairs. Societal responsiveness became a functional area of management – in modest form as 'public relations' (PR) and more ambitiously as 'Public Affairs' (PA).

Business and society as managing stakeholders

Stakeholder management in the B&S perspective adopts a rather minimalistic approach. It refers to the identification of the most important parties involved in a given issue (or those parties that can make an issue a real issue; see Chapter 10). Questions include: who are the most important players, what is the nature and duration of the relationship and what are their concerns? Companies are dependent on the social context in which they operate to realize their objectives. However, the commercialization of society (Chapter 3) renders this dependency mutual: stakeholders increasingly depend on companies to realize their ambitions (Wartick and Wood, 1999: 98).

According to the *behavioural theory of the firm*, each party that has a stake in the relationship strives to maximize their gain. A transaction is successful if both parties profit more than their individual investments are worth. Employees want a salary in return for their labour or intellectual input and consumers want a qualitatively good product in return for money. In the same way, stakeholders will grant a company its *licence to operate* if it creates added value in a sustainable manner.

A company accounts for the choices and inevitable trade-offs it makes in its communication with stakeholders. *Corporate communications* (*Public Affairs, customer relations, internal communications* and *investor relations*) often functions as an instrument in this (Grunig, 1992; van Riel, 2000). Communication with different stakeholders should align diverse interests and expectations. A distinction can generally be drawn between 'primary' and 'secondary' stakeholders (Clarkson, 1995), although such a distinction cannot be readily made and does not remain fixed over time.

Primary stakeholders

Primary stakeholders are those persons or groups of persons without whom the company cannot realize its objectives. Usually, this group includes employees, shareholders, investors, consumers and suppliers. Primary stakeholders represent the direct supporters of the company (Clarkson, 1995). In standard management terms, stakeholders are subdivided into consumer, capital and labour market stakeholders. In the International Business and Society literature (Wartick and Wood, 1998), the government is also regarded as primary actor, but the debate on this has not wholly taken shape yet. The problem with this discussion is that it is often assumed that a company stands with both feet in the market (type 1 in Figure 8.1). Most organizations, however, operate at societal interfaces.

The relevant group of primary stakeholders shifts depending on the position of the company in the societal triangle. Hybrid organizations, for instance, have to consider non-market parties as primary stakeholders much more. When companies operate at the interface of the market and state (type 2), the importance of specific government institutions and supervisors increases. Likewise, the importance of local communities and/or families increases when they operate at the interface of the market and civil society (type 3). Local communities or families are often regarded as secondary stakeholders; as groups or persons that do not directly influence the economic activities of a company, but that could indirectly influence or be influenced by it.

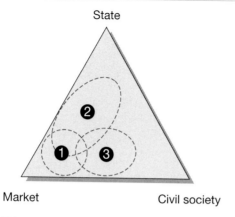

Figure 8.1 *Different groups of primary stakeholders*

Secondary stakeholders

Apart from local communities and families, secondary stakeholders generally also include the media, trade unions, competitors, analysts, the general public, environmental activists, supervisory bodies, non-profit organizations, the natural environment and future generations. It does however seem sensible to include only those stakeholders that can be negotiated with. The 'natural environment' and 'future generations' only really come into play in terms of stakeholder management when groupings are formed that represent the interests of the environment and future generations. Interests that are not represented do pose a problem. Stakeholder management is not a suitable means to address this, given the characteristics of the bargaining society (see Chapter 6).

The assessment of the position of competitors as secondary stakeholder forms another interesting topic of discussion. Issues surrounding corporate accountability can damage a whole industry. If foot and mouth disease in cattle breaks out on one farm, the overall consumption of beef declines. In that case, competitors might as well be identified as primary stakeholders. CSR issues have significant spill-over effects for the whole sector through the reputation mechanism. The classification of (primary/secondary) stakeholders is also dependent on the position of the company in the societal triangle and the type of issue involved. Companies that operate as supplier somewhere in the supply chain and in a purely market environment, seldom share any direct common ground with societal stakeholders. NGOs are therefore also only able to reach them via their most important customers or financial stakeholders. Unit branding companies such as Unilever that do not market products under their own name have such a buffer in place with respect to societal stakeholders. In practice, therefore, the degree to which primary or secondary stakeholders can exert influence depends on the positioning of the company in question, the nature of relationships and the issue at stake.

Mitchell *et al.* (1997) attempted to address this problem by means of a more specific categorization of stakeholders according to three attributes: power, legitimacy and urgency. The first two attributes fit directly into the framework of a bargaining society and the last pertains to the nature of the issue at hand. This model is intended as a tool to understand *and* predict stakeholder activity. *Power* is interpreted as the ability to get others to do what they otherwise would never do (Weber, 1947). *Legitimacy* refers to the mandate of the stakeholder – its right to exercise its powers (see Chapter 6) in relation to the claim on the firm. Finally, the *urgency* of a stakeholder claim influences the process of stakeholder interaction. It is also true that while

137

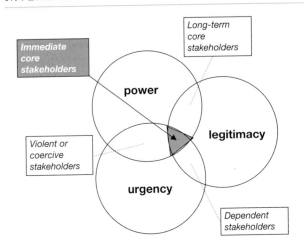

Figure 8.2 *Predicting stakeholder activity in a bargaining society*
Source: Mitchell *et al.* (1997)

primary stakeholders have power, they might not have legitimacy. Secondary stakeholders, on the other hand, score low on direct power but can be more influential than primary stakeholders if they score high on legitimacy and urgency. By combining these attributes, Mitchell *et al.* (1997) distinguish four types of stakeholders (Figure 8.2): (1) long-term core stakeholders who share the attributes of legitimacy and power but not urgency (e.g. shareholders); (2) stakeholders who share the attributes of power and urgency but not legitimacy and tend to become violent or coercive radical action groups; (3) dependent stakeholders whose claims are legitimate and urgent but who lack power (e.g. secondary stakeholders). Each of these three groups can move into the (4) immediate core stakeholder group (shaded) by acquiring the missing characteristic, thereby making it mandatory for managers to properly manage the stakeholder relationship with them. Stakeholders with two of the three attributes are likely 'to try to acquire the missing attribute, except in the case of long-term core stakeholders who feel their interests in the firm are met' (Wartick and Wood, 1999: 113).

Business *in* Society Management

In the 1980s, a more 'inside-out' perspective on the relationship between business and society developed. At the time the question arose whether firms can be considered and treated as moral actors. This signalled a shift from an instrumentalist towards a more goal-oriented approach to the study of corporate responsibilities. Edward Freeman (1984) was the first to point out that the relationship with stakeholders contains important strategic elements. He defined stakeholders as 'any group or individual who can affect or is affected by the achievement of the organization's objective' and argued that they have an important role to fulfil in defining the mission and aims of a company (ibid.: 64). An underlying thought of Freeman and others was that there is a direct correlation between the (financial) performance of a company and its relationship with its stakeholders. Managers became aware of the immense influence of their environment on the effectiveness of their company's operations. Stakeholders therefore had to be managed more actively (inside-out) in order to influence the company's performance in a positive manner.

The boundary between internal business processes and external actors became less distinct. In the 1980s, the concept of CSR was also imbued with fresh meaning by the United Nations appointed *World Commission on Environment and Development* – also referred to as the Brundtland

Commission. This Commission defined corporate sustainability as development that meets the needs of present generations without (negatively) affecting the opportunities of future generations to fulfil their needs (Brundtland, 1987). The Brundtland Commission also articulated a *specific* stakeholder group, namely, future generations of stakeholders (as primary stakeholders). Invoking the idea that the interests of others place limits on the unbridled pursuit of self-interest, it draws upon ethical principles that go back much further than the 1980s. These principles offer a moral solution to some of the dilemmas of the bargaining society (see Chapter 6), a view on economic conduct that can already be found in the *Second Treatise of Government* which was written by the philosopher and statesman John Locke in 1690. He argued that everyone has a right to claim land and the fruits of labour, provided enough of the same quality remains for others (also in future). This corresponds strongly with the Bruntlandt definition of sustainable development (1987).

The ethical foundations of CSR ultimately rest on two principles: the *charity* principle and the *stewardship* principle. The *charity* principle refers to the notion that privileged people are to protect the interests of the less privileged. The *stewardship* principle refers to the confidence interested parties place in managers to take into account the interests of those affected by business decisions (Frederick *et al.*, 1992: 35). Firms are not only to create wealth for themselves; they should also meet their social, ethical and ecological responsibilities and publicly account for it. The fulfilment of these responsibilities also requires undertaking initiatives that promote economic welfare, social well-being and a healthy environment beyond that which is legally required (Pride and Ferrel, 1997). The principle of *managerial discretion* (Caroll, 1979) complements these principles in that it views individual managers as moral actors who are capable of moral reasoning in reaching specific decisions.

The 'Business *in* Society' (BiS) school of thought further developed the academic foundations of these ideas. The International Chamber of Commerce, for instance, which acts as a strong force in favour of 'globalization' launched a 'business in society commission' to define the 'role of business in the context of globalization and changing societal expectations and [to] articulate messages on issues relating to business in society'.[2] A chief instrument of ICC's repertoire is to identify 'best practices' of responsible firms. 'Best practices' demonstrate a largely moral approach to CSR.

The apparent strong connection between financial and social performance stimulated managers to pay greater attention to 'corporate communication' and 'business ethics'. The latter aims to formulate ethical guidelines for responsible management and company conduct (Kaptein and Wempe, 2002). The communication with stakeholders became based upon ethical/moral concepts such as 'trust', 'reliability', 'social involvement', 'cooperation', 'accountability' and 'responsible entrepreneurship'. Management recognized the more visible role of business in society (cf. McWilliams, 2001: 117) and entered into various societal dialogues to discuss how to add social and ecological value for the company and society.

Stakeholder relations as explicit and implicit contracts

Stakeholder management in BiS approaches was further enhanced by insights from social contract theory. An examination of the nature of stakeholder relationships opened the way to more detailed stakeholder classifications. On the one hand, companies conclude explicit contracts with stakeholders: with employees via employment contracts, with government via legislation and with consumers via purchasing contracts. Comprehensive contracts in principle encompass all transactions that can have (external) consequences for another. But comprehensive contracts, no matter how explicit, are an illusion. Unforeseen circumstances can appear and very high transaction costs can be involved because the information required is either lacking or is too expensive. A smoothly running economy and society is therefore also dependent on implicit contracts that are based on norms, trust, previous transactions, agreements and expectations (Donaldson and Dunfee, 1999; Howard *et al.*, 1998).

A certain degree of information asymmetry, opportunism and strategic behaviour (Chapter 6) always exists between stakeholders. In a bargaining society, people do not always have all information at their disposal nor can they always process it all. They are *rationally* bounded. Incomplete and implicit contracts therefore have an important social function. Further elaboration and/or refinement are the result of negotiations between companies and stakeholders. Many entrepreneurs view a code of conduct as a deliberately incomplete contract, since not all dimensions of the different issues can (or should) be put in writing, while NGOs – due to a lack of confidence and explicit laws – would prefer explicit contracts. This process can be seen as a way in which groupings in a changing (bargaining) society can come to a new 'social contract' – the old ideal of the philosopher Rousseau.

The impossibility of pursuing the whole spectrum of economic, environmental and social interests and meeting all parties' expectations is what Kaptein and Wempe (2002) refer to as the 'issue of many hands'. Moreover, weighing up alternatives and choices almost always implies infringing upon some interests, which involves the 'issue of dirty hands'. To what extent may one dirty one's hands? An example of this issue is mass staff layoffs. The justification for infringing upon the private interests of employees lies in securing the continuity of the company and enabling it to make a contribution to economic growth, environmental protection and social progress in the future. In this way, more stakeholders' interests are served in the long term (Kaptein and Wempe, 2002). A company is continually required to weigh up public/private and profit/non-profit interests against one another. In practice, therefore, stakeholder management is a concrete form of Societal Interface Management.

In Anglo-Saxon countries the idea of corporate sustainability became first referred to as the quest for 'corporate social responsibility' or CSR. Wood (1991: 693) thereby developed the first – generally acknowledged – definition of corporate social performance (CSP) as 'the configuration of the principles of social responsibility, process of social responsiveness, and policies, programs, and observable outcomes as they relate to the firm's societal relationships'. The question as to whether it is possible to establish a positive correlation between CSP and corporate financial performance (CFP) (preferably in this order) is a topic of heated debate (see Box 8.1). The Anglo-Saxon approach to the link between CSP and CFP represents a more active approach to the business–society interface, but is nevertheless strongly utilitarian and shareholder-value oriented. It leaves considerable room for interpretation and is called into question the moment other (more stakeholder-value oriented) systems are taken into account. CSR has become the catch-all category that still includes a large variety of approaches: the PR approach that contains strong reactive elements; the International Business Ethics approach that is more active and tries to derive rules of engagement for firms from international ethical norms (Donaldson, 1989) and the International Business & Society Management approach that seeks for a more strategic perspective on IB. For the latter stream, 'corporate social responsibility is not the "do-gooding" version so many business voices object to; it is a broad, integrated, strategic view of business's vital roles and responsibilities in every society and in the global environment' (Wartick and Wood, 1999: 70). Since 1989, the International Association for Business and Society has been hosting many of these debates.

Business–Society Management

Since the end of the 1990s, an increasing number of authors started to talk about corporate *societal* responsibility so as to avoid a narrow interpretation of the term 'social responsibility',

BOX 8.1 IN SEARCH OF THE HOLY GRAIL: ESTABLISHING THE RELATIONSHIP BETWEEN CSP AND CFP

Proponents of socially responsible investment (SRI) are eager to point out that companies that actively pursued policies aimed at CSP since the 1990s have consistently scored higher market capitalizations than the average public company. The most popular and oldest index of CSP is the Domini 400 Social Index (DSI) (see Chapter 11 for other indices) published by the American social investment firm KLD (Kindler, Lydenberg & Domini). In the course of the 1990s, firms that were included in the DSI400 consistently scored higher on market capitalization than those included in the Standard & Poor's 500 (S&P500) index. Various other ethical investment funds make similar claims: it pays to invest in CSR because the returns are higher even on the capital market. The simple graphs accompanying the claims obscure the many complexities of the issue. First, market capitalization is not necessarily the same as profit-maximization and market capitalization is not the only measure of CFP. Second, not all relevant firms are listed on the stock exchange. Third, the selection of the sample is based on indicators of CSP that are open to debate, certainly when compared to different value systems. It is generally very difficult to identify meaningful and reliable quantitative CSP indicators, even when applying the classical definition of Wood (1991). Fourth, and related to the latter, the index reflects an American bias. Most of the lists are based on American firms. Finally, there is the problem of chronology. The so-called 'slack resources' theory proposes that a positive correlation between CSP and CFP can be identified because companies with higher financial performance can 'afford' – provide the slack resources – to invest in CSP.

In the more serious academic literature, most of these issues (except for American bias reflected in the indicators) have been addressed. The evidence supports a modest correlation between CSP and CFP, although enormous measurement problems still exist and a large number of studies have yielded inconclusive or even conflicting results. In a review of 95 studies on the relationship between CSP and CFP (Margolis and Walsh, 2001), 53 per cent identify a positive relationship. The weak statistical results and other difficulties encountered in operationalizing CSP have even prompted some scholars to call for a moratorium on CSP–CFP research (ibid.; Rowley and Berman, 2000). But, review studies often use a 'vote counting' technique, which has considerable analytical deficiencies (not every study needs to count the same in the voting, but how to weigh this?). These deficiencies have prompted others to call for more sophisticated reviews and more rigorous statistical techniques, in particular by conducting so-called 'meta-analyses'.

A meta-analysis of 52 empirical studies carried out over 30 years on the relationship between CSP and CFP was conducted by Orlitzky et al. (2003). They found that social responsibility and, to a lesser extent, environmental responsibility are likely to 'pay off' for managers engaging in it. They conclude that managers need not consider the choice for CSP and CFP as an 'either/or' trade-off. Managers who run ahead of the pack are not necessarily penalized. The public–private interface plays an important mediating role here: a company that scores high on CSP 'may especially benefit from receiving public endorsement from federal agencies' (ibid.). External reputation, as perceived both by public agencies and the general public seems to be an important intervening factor in the relationship between CSP and CFP. As regards the slack resources theory, the reviewed studies seem to hint at the following: the causation seems to be that CSP and CFP mutually affect each other through a virtuous cycle, in which 'financially successful companies spend more because they can afford it, but CSP also helps them become a bit more successful'. The authors, however, still have to acknowledge that considerable problems remain with the operationalization of CSP and CFP which is bound to moderate the positive correlations. They do suggest that the correlation is stronger for specific accounting-based indicators of CFP, which could indicate that the correlation applies particularly to Anglo-Saxon systems. New and internationally comparative research with better operationalizations of CSP is therefore required.

in particular 'when translated into Continental European cultures and languages, as applying to social welfare issues only' (Andriof and McIntosh, 2001: 15). With the introduction of the broader concept of corporate societal responsibility, the issue of CSR shifts from a largely instrumental and managerial approach to one aimed at managing strategic networks where longer-term relationships with stakeholders are prominent in the strategic planning of the company. In the words of Björn Stigson, president of the WBCSD:

> sustainable development is too big for companies to handle individually because it is critical to develop the right framework conditions, which can only be done by companies working together along the value chain. It also requires a broad interaction with stakeholders, to come to an understanding with society about how to address the challenge.
>
> (Stigson, 2002: 2)

Management literature has become peppered with concepts such as 'stakeholder engagement', 'trust building processes', 'dynamic interactions' and 'strategic corporate communication'. Baron (2002), for instance, asserts that successful executives integrate market and non-market strategies by effectively positioning their firm at the business–society interface.

It is increasingly acknowledged that both management and stakeholders can influence the profitability of companies. In the same way, active cooperation between companies and stakeholders is required so as to optimize the social contribution of companies. This mutual dependency can be found in new definitions of the concept 'stakeholders', as 'those whose relations to the enterprise cannot be completely contracted for, but upon whose co-operation and creativity it depends for its survival' (Slinger and Deakin, 1999). The interest of stakeholders in a company is gradually replaced by a strategic interest of the company in good stakeholder relationships. Thus the 'business–society' approach developed along with techniques such as (Strategic) Stakeholder Dialogue. It is only through the systematic and structural exchange of facts, opinions and values with stakeholders that companies can stay in touch with the new responsibilities imposed upon them. This development signals the quest for the 'balanced company'; a company which not only has a moral identity but also combines medium-term profitability and longer-term sustainability (Kaptein and Wempe, 2002).

A particularly influential and popular work in the exploration of Business–Society Management (B–SM) concepts is that of John Elkington (1999). In his book, *Cannibals with Forks*, he distinguishes between three dimensions of CSR, the so-called *Triple-P Bottom Line* (Shell, 2001) of *people, profit* and *planet*. The economic and financial basis (*Profit*) forms the precondition for guaranteeing the continuity of the company. In strategic management literature, this is also referred to as 'sustainable competitive advantage' that points towards the manner in which companies position themselves in relation to other companies in the same sector so that they can tap into profit sources for a prolonged period.

The social-ethical dimension (*People*) refers to the responsibility for issues of social justice, both internal (employees) as well as external (society) to the organization. Themes included in this dimension are sound labour relations, progressive social policies, opportunities for employee input and responsibility, work–life balance, a safe working and living environment, combating the use of child and forced labour in the supply chain, ethnic minority employment, respect for human rights and decent working conditions on national and international levels, and training and education.

The ecological and public dimension (*Planet*) focuses on the integration of environmental protection and operational management. In practice, the dimension of environmental management has been linked to 'corporate sustainability'. Sustainability refers to the responsible engagement with current and future generations' right to a clean and well-functioning environment. Themes that fall under this include: the precautionary principle (which refers to uncertainties regarding environmental impacts); 'zero-waste' and emissions; responsible use of natural resources; environmental protection; supply chain management (chain responsibilities as well as chain liabilities); eco-efficiency; sustainable development and eco-design; animal welfare and food security.

In Chapter 1, it was noted that each of these dimensions originally represented the primary interest of companies (*profit*), civil society (*people*) and government (*planet*). However, as indicated in Chapter 3, in a bargaining society these spheres – rightly or wrongly – are becoming increasingly intertwined with the result that primary interests and responsibilities have long since ceased to run parallel to the traditional institutional spheres of interest. In addition, significant 'governance voids' have appeared (Chapter 5) rendering it difficult to assign primary responsibilities to specific actors (see Chapter 10).

8.3 FOUR APPROACHES TO CSR

Four approaches to CSR have developed over the years. They are characterized by different procedural attributes: inactive, reactive, active and pro-/interactive (Table 8.1).

These approaches emerged at different stages of societal development and they are neither mutually exclusive nor do they represent 'best' practice models.[3] Each approach has its own orientation, logic and proponents. If these approaches can be shown to correspond with particular societal models, they could also become rival CSR strategies. This question will be elaborated on in Chapter 9.

The *inactive* approach reflects the classical notion of Friedman that the only responsibility companies (can) have is to generate profits. This is a fundamentally inward-looking (inside-in) business perspective, aimed at efficiency and competitiveness in the immediate market environment.[4] Entrepreneurs are particularly concerned with 'doing things right'; no fundamental or ethical questions are raised about what they are doing. The focus is largely on products and/or services provided: fast production, clever marketing, innovation in time and patenting or not. Good business from this perspective equals operational excellence. CSR thus amounts to 'corporate *self*-responsibility'. The slogan of sportswear manufacturer Nike, 'Just Do It!' is in line with this type of reasoning. The motivation for CSR is primarily *utilitarian* (Swanson, 1995), derived from so-called 'consequential ethics' where the focus is on the end result rather than the means by which it is achieved. In this goal-oriented approach, CSR is aimed at profit and sales maximization, return on investment and sales.

A slight variation on the inactive attitude is the *reactive* approach, which shares the focus on efficiency but with particular attention to not making any mistakes. This requires an outside-in orientation where entrepreneurs monitor their environment and manage their primary stakeholders so as to keep mounting issues in check without otherwise allowing it to give rise to fundamental changes in the business philosophy and primary production processes. Entrepreneurs are socially responsive and respond specifically to actions of external actors that could damage their reputation. Corporate philanthropy is the modern expression of the charity principle and a practical manifestation of social responsiveness (Post *et al.*, 2002: 89). During their protest campaigns against Nike for using suppliers in South East Asia whose factories allegedly resembled 'sweatshops', NGOs and activists rephrased the Nike slogan as: 'Just Don't Do It!' to get their message across (*The Economist*, 14 December 2002). In this approach the motivation for CSR is primarily grounded in 'negative duties' where firms are compelled to conform to stakeholder-defined norms of appropriate behaviour (Maignan and Ralston, 2002). The concept of 'conditional morality' (cf. Basu, 2001), in the sense that managers only 're-act' when competitors do the same, is also consistent with this approach.

Table 8.1 Four CSR approaches

Inactive	Reactive	Active	Pro-/interactive
'Corporate *self-* responsibility'	'Corporate social *responsiveness*'	'Corporate social *responsibility*'	'Corporate *societal* responsibility'
Inside-in	Outside-in	Inside-out	In/outside-in/out
'Doing things right'	'Don't do things wrong'	'Doing the right things'	'Doing the right things right'
'Doing well'	'Doing well and doing good'	'Doing good'	'Doing well by doing good'
'Just do it'	'Just don't do it'	'Do it just'	'Just do it just'
Efficiency		Equity/Ethics	Effectiveness
Utilitarian motive: profit maximization	Negative duty approach: quarterly profits and market capitalization	'Positive duty' or 'virtue based': values (long-term profitability)	Interactive duty approach: medium-term profitability and sustainability
Indifference	Compliance	Integrity	Discourse ethics
Business *and* Society Management		Business *in* Society Management	Business–Society Management
'Trust me'		'Prove it to me'	'Involve/engage me'; 'join me'

<--->

Multi-usage tools/concepts of CSR:

PR Brochures
  Press releases
    Sponsoring
      Transparency
        Accountability
          Corporate citizenship
            Corporate philanthropy
              Corporate volunteering
                Integrity
                  Business–Community
                  Involvement (BCI)

Economic Responsibility ←----------------------→ Social Responsibility
[Wealth oriented]   [Welfare oriented]
Narrow (internal) CSR   Broad (external) CSR

Both inactive and reactive approaches focus largely on output indicators such as (short-term) returns and productivity and are strongly means and wealth oriented. Relationships with societal and community stakeholders are relatively involuntary and room for managerial discretion is limited. Most entrepreneurs have a (neo-classical) perspective on CSR, and will probably conflict with societal organizations on a regular basis. Moreover, such efficiency thinking harbours the risk that an entrepreneur may indeed be doing something really well but that they are following the wrong course or pursuing the wrong objectives – inadequate technology or a bad product. Classical management examples are provided by manufacturers who develop the perfect gas bulb the moment electricity becomes widely used, or tobacco producers who gain loyal customers by increasing the addictive effect of tobacco. In the first case, it is a question of a normal business risk, but in the second, it is a question of ethics. Even then, it is problematic to classify a product or conduct as socially *irresponsible* (see Box 8.2).

An *active* approach to CSR represents the most ethical entrepreneurial orientation. Entrepreneurs who pursue this approach are explicitly inspired by ethical values and virtues (or 'positive duties') on the basis of which company objectives are formulated. These objectives are subsequently realized in a socially responsible manner regardless of actual or potential social pressures by stakeholders. Such entrepreneurs are strongly outward-oriented (inside-out) and they display a certain 'missionary urge' which makes them heroes to NGOs but an annoyance to 'true' entrepreneurs.[5]

Hybrid organizations are often characterized by such an ethical orientation in particular at the interface between the state and civil society. Entrepreneurs who adopt an active CSR approach share a strong orientation towards justice that is motivated by a healthy and clean environment, social equity, social progress and so forth. They are set on doing 'the right thing'.[6] While these entrepreneurs may have terrific relationships with NGOs, they do run the risk of neglecting business efficiency and jeopardizing the continuity of the company. In a society that is structured around the principles of business production methods, this can also be regarded as socially irresponsible.

All three perspectives on CSR have their managerial shortcomings: purely ethical business practice can result in managers doing the 'right things' wrong, while competitive market-oriented business practice can lead managers to doing the 'wrong things' right. Societal issues are almost always complex and involve a range of interests (Schumacher, 1973), with the result that a variety of 'right' answers are possible. A perspective is consequently required where the field of tension between ethics and efficiency is engaged with in a socially responsible manner. This requires a synthesis of the two approaches and the term *proactive* CSR can be employed to describe this orientation. One can speak of a proactive approach if an entrepreneur undertakes activities aimed at external stakeholders right at the beginning of an issue's life cycle (see Chapter 9).

BOX 8.2 SOCIALLY *IR*RESPONSIBLE?

It sometimes seems easier to determine what truly irresponsible conduct is than to establish what the characteristics of responsible behaviour are. But appearances are deceptive. Company fraud and price fixing can be readily classified as irresponsible behaviour given that it breaches compulsory legislation (competition law). But competition law is not the same around the world; cooperation between competitors can be very useful in developing innovative products and can be a prerequisite for 'responsible behaviour', for instance, in collaborating on establishing trade marks. Ethical investment funds and benchmarks always exclude the tobacco and the arms industry as clear examples of socially irresponsible sectors. But how socially unaccountable is the arms trade or the tobacco industry really? It is, in fact, difficult to pinpoint precisely why this may be the case. The arms trade is legally permitted and even socially responsible if it allows peacekeepers to defend themselves, for instance, in Eritrea or Afghanistan. The weapons industry stimulates trade, provides employment, triggers innovation, offers protection and is a means to peacekeeping. Likewise, the tobacco industry also escapes the label of being socially irresponsible. Tobacco, after all, provides pleasure, there is a need for it (whether created or not), it generates trade and employment and, via taxes, even welfare. It is therefore problematical to label whole sectors as socially irresponsible. This is why it is hard for companies to establish where the boundary between proper and improper conduct lies.

In a bargaining society, effective CSR is characterized not only by proactive business practices, but also by *interactive* business practices, where an 'inside-out' and an 'outside-in' orientation complement each other. In moral philosophy, this approach is also referred to as 'discourse ethics'. In discourse ethics, as developed by Habermas (1990), actors regularly meet in order to negotiate/talk over a number of norms to which everyone could agree. The motivation for managers to engage in CSR is based on what we might call 'interactive' duties and 'situational' and 'relativistic' ethics apply. The field of tension between ethics and efficiency is only resolved when entrepreneurs are willing to focus on the 'profitability of values' (SER, 2000) and think of efficiency as 'doing the right things right' (effectiveness).[7] This implies medium-term profitability and longer-term sustainability, not only for themselves but for the whole sector and sometimes even for the whole economy (adding a welfare orientation to a company's aims). Both active and proactive approaches to CSR share a considerable degree of voluntary action and managerial discretion.

8.4 CSR AS HYPE OR AS LASTING PHENOMENON: A GURU GUIDE TO SOCIETAL INTERFACE MANAGEMENT

Will the attention CSR is currently enjoying last? What is the 'business case' for CSR? Like all 'trends' (see Chapters 3–5), the interest in CSR will dwindle rapidly if it turns out to amount to little more than fashionable and ad hoc concepts. Concepts such as 'corporate citizenship', 'transparency', 'accountability', 'social entrepreneurship' or 'corporate responsiveness' are therefore bound to be exposed as fashion hypes if they remain narrowly defined, reactively inspired and ideologically used in PR campaigns. In terms of the four approaches to CSR, can CSR in practice move to the right of the spectrum? More specifically, the challenge CSR faces is whether it can realistically be operationalized in the organizational context and integrated in a more holistic view of CSR management and Societal Interface Management. As opposed to the various part-concepts, the likelihood that a holistic concept such as Societal Interface Management (or CSR as corporate *societal* responsibility) will become outmoded is much smaller. It is not built on fashionable concepts, it has existed since the advent of capitalism, it does not make claims to having the 'correct' answer and it is not moralistic.

Coincidentally, it can also be solidly grounded in the work of a large number of leading management experts. Internationally renowned authorities in all the major management disciplines, ranging from marketing to logistics, give substantial attention to issues related to the effective management of the societal interface. In the primary publications of most of these authors, this aspect more often than not lies at the core of their advice.[8] Almost all of them emphasize – in various ways – that profit maximization (the inactive approach to CSR) cannot be the ultimate goal of a firm. Business leaders themselves are increasingly supporting them in this idea. At the World Economic Forum in Davos in early 2004, less than one in five of the surveyed business leaders was of the opinion that profitability is the most important measure of corporate success (versus product quality – 27 per cent – and reputation and integrity of the brand – 24 per cent) (*The Economist*, 24 January 2004).

Most business gurus have attempted to develop a more active approach to management that combines efficiency and ethics/equity – either at the level of the organization, of the individual manager, or both. As this part of their advice is often the most sophisticated or qualitative, it is also the part that has been least understood and/or quoted. It might be worthwhile to reiterate their arguments – they already made the business case for various forms of proactive Societal Interface Management. Figure 8.3 depicts the various organizational layers and functional areas pertaining to Societal Interface Management (Chapter 6).

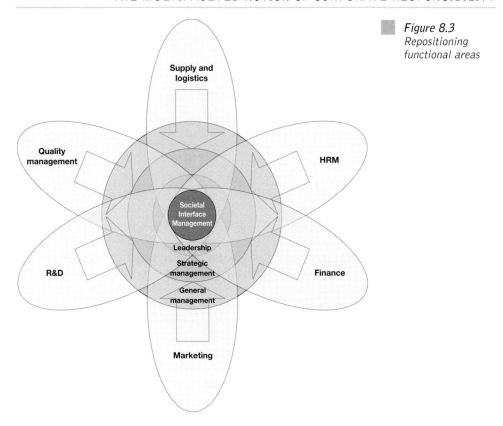

Figure 8.3
Repositioning functional areas

Organizational layer 1: leadership – on developing visions

Effective Societal Interface Management requires effective leadership. Leadership refers to the trade-off between more or less managerial control and the ability of individuals to influence a group to realize a given objective. Leadership distinguishes itself from 'normal management' on several essential points (Table 8.2). Most leaders are good managers, but good managers are not always good leaders.

The various leadership profiles that are discussed in the literature on leadership coincide with the approaches to CSR outlined above. Formal and informal leaders can be distinguished, both of which can have an important role to fulfil in the performance of groups and organizations (Capon, 2004: 95). So-called (a) 'transactional' and 'team' leaders are particularly good at specifying inactive and reactive CSR goals, clarifying roles and responsibilities and motivating their followers or subordinates to achieve group or organizational goals (ibid.). These leaders display a strong similarity to 'ordinary' managers, focusing largely on the internal operations of the firm. While (b) 'charismatic' leaders still focus primarily on internal operations of the organization, they also display an ability to present a vision of the future of the organization in combination with a strong personal commitment and a strong character. 'Visionary' and 'moral' leadership (c) is characterized by a more active stance on CSR. Both require an idea/vision of where the organization should be in the future. Moral leaders derive their legitimacy in particular from ethical principles on which their vision is based. Both types of leadership focus on communicating their vision to stakeholders inside as well as outside the firm. Visionary leadership, in particular, can be considered as a precondition for (d) 'transformational leadership'. This is the most outward-oriented type of leadership and directed at formulating and implementing a new

Table 8.2 *Leaders versus managers*

'Managers'	'Leaders'
Follow the established course.	Establish the course that managers follow.
Ensure that people do things.	Ensure that people *want to* do things.
Ensure that people do things.	Ensure that people do the *right* things.
Ensure that people do things better.	Ensure that people do *better* things.

Source: Whetten *et al.*, 2000: 498

organizational vision that is embedded in a broader vision of society and the active involvement of external stakeholders.

Warren Bennis and John Kotter are the leading leadership authors who emphasize aspects of leadership that are essential in meeting the challenges posed by Societal Interface Management. Bennis – who twice won the McKinsey Foundation Award for the best book on management – maintains that an open and democratic environment is essential for the effective functioning of an organization. Moreover, a leader is defined as someone who has the 'capacity to create a compelling vision, and to translate it into action and sustain it' (Bennis, 1989). Being a leader requires skills that can be learned and honed. Great leaders share three characteristics (*FT*, 14 August 2003): ambition, competence and integrity. Without integrity, ambition and competence can become dangerous attributes.

John Kotter (1990), a more contemporary expert on leadership, holds that there are significant differences between 'ordinary' management and leadership, although functionally they can be combined in the same individual (see also Chapter 3). The effectiveness of managers/leaders strongly depends on their relationships with others. The effectiveness of leaders, in particular, depends on their ability to conceive a vision of the future, communicate it through inspiring and motivating others, and create the preconditions to realize that vision. Like Bennis (1989), Kotter also states that leadership can – and even should – be taught (*FT*, 28 August 2003).

The relationship between leadership and CSP has also become a topic of research in the area of leadership studies. Corporate social responsibility requires Corporate Social Leadership (Hilton and Gibbons, 2002). This research, however, is still in its infancy. In the attempt to link top management (characteristics) with some form of CSP, three streams of analysis have developed: values, personal characteristics and compensation levels. Studies that focus on values reveal a strong link between social responsiveness and conservative values (Sturdivant *et al.*, 1985). Recent research (McGuire *et al.*, 2003) examined the relationship between levels of CEO compensation and CSP, but could not find any positive correlation. Other studies found evidence of a reversed correlation: high CEO salaries related to relatively poor social performance (Stanwick and Stanwick, 1998). Studies have been conducted that examine the professional background of leaders and its relation to CSP (Thomas and Simerly, 1994; Simerly, 2003). In cases where executives with experience in environmental management had been recruited, CSP improved. Most of these studies concentrated primarily on the Anglo-Saxon context (US firms, US CSP indices). This makes it difficult to arrive at general conclusions. The link between leadership characteristics, CSP and CFP still needs to be thoroughly researched before any general claims can be made.

Organizational layer 2: strategic management – on distinguishing yourself

Michael Porter is the world's undisputed expert in strategic management. Porter holds that firms that pursue an outright for-profit strategy will only achieve a 'sustainable competitive advantage' if they also score high on non-profit issues such as the environment. He is overtly critical of business leaders who only focus on their direct competitive (market) environment and short-term profits. In his view, they miss out on strategic opportunities to distinguish themselves from direct competitors. In a very influential article, Porter and van der Linde (1995) make a rather convincing case that companies that tackle environmental issues very proactively can also be very profitable. In this article, Porter and van der Linde attempt to beat neo-classical sceptics like Friedman about the ears with their own arguments. According to the two authors, long-term competitive advantage is only feasible if all sorts of 'sustainability' objectives (directly taken from the CSR literature) are pursued. Given that they endeavoured to convert neo-classical sceptics by linking inactive CSR visions with more (pro)active CSR visions, the debate that followed in the wake of this article was almost exclusively focused on *internal business* processes: the implementation of eco-efficient production systems, for example. Porter (2003) remains a strong adherent to a broad view on CSR. He recently accused company leaders of being defensive and unclear in their motives and challenged corporate leaders to link CSR to their business strategies. His position is succinctly captured in the following:

> My major criticism is that the field of corporate social responsibility (CSR) has become a religion filled with priests in which there is no need for evidence or theory. Too many academics and business managers are satisfied with the 'good feeling' as argument.
> (European Business Forum, Autumn, 2003)

Porter's criticism that CSR or corporate philanthropy programmes of companies do not suffice is actively supported by the second most important strategy author, C.K. Prahalad. In his recent work (Prahalad, 2004) he emphasizes that CSR needs to be integrated in the general strategies of the firm in order to command continued senior management attention and sustained resource allocation. Prahalad goes yet one step further than Porter into the direction of Societal Interface Management by explicitly addressing a societal problem such as poverty – which in his view cannot be solved without the involvement of particular for-profit strategies of big business. The idea of CSR in more traditional strategic management terms as enhancing a 'unique selling point' is further developed by authors such as Tapscott and Ticoll (2003) who conclude that the increased assertiveness of consumers and the societal demand for information (see Chapter 2) offer companies new opportunities to differentiate themselves. They provide numerous examples of the rewards of candour by firm leaders and thus redefine 'transparency' as a means to achieve a competitive advantage. Recently, strategic management and organizational thinkers have started to emphasize the importance of 'co-evolution' processes in which successful business strategies develop, in particular, when business strategy and institutional environment can be aligned (cf. Lewin and Volberda, 2003).

Organizational layer 3: general management – on how to get there

The most influential management experts can be found in the field of 'general management' or 'organization'. Peter Drucker, Charles Handy, Henry Mintzberg and Rosabeth Moss Kanter almost always appear among the first four in guru ranking lists (of either academic or consultants). Business scientists are primarily interested in the questions pertaining to the realization of certain objectives and the successful implementation and management of change. They have all stressed various aspects of Societal Interface Management.

The expert among experts, Peter Drucker, whose writings cover topics ranging from e-commerce to civilization, is the role model of the 'enlightened' manager (Drucker, 1999). Drucker has declared that the twenty-first century corporation consists of 'volunteers', which emphasizes the non-profit dimension of corporations and its interface with society. Drucker stresses the importance of organizations that are able to operate apart from governments, on a non-profit basis, not operated as (for-profit, market-oriented) companies. Drucker (1994) states explicitly that organizations should meet their societal responsibilities. If they do not, nobody else will. This has to be done in a responsible manner, within the boundaries of their competencies and without jeopardizing their ability to perform.

The second most widely read management expert in the world is Charles Handy (*FT*, 25 August 2003). He examines the nature of work and the role of organizational management in society. Handy argues for a more holistic and ethical view of business. He puts it as follows:

> We need to be more accepting of paradox and change, and more humanistic in our approach. The new corporate score card should include factors such as the knowledge and welfare of employees and contributions to society and the environment. Personal welfare is more important than profit.
>
> (ibid.; Handy, 1989)

Managers are not technicians, they are moral beings, and without a sense of ethics, and indeed faith, they become no more than unthinking servants of their organization and in time both they and the organization will lose their creative impulse and wither away (Handy, 1994).

Henry Mintzberg ranks third among International Management experts. He convincingly argues that the ideal corporate model (or best-practice) does not exist. According to Mintzberg: 'Corporations are social institutions. If they don't serve society, they have no business existing. The argument that they serve society by making money and creating jobs is coming apart' (Mintzberg, 2001). He continues: 'Enron is the illegal corruption. The real problem is the legal corruption. It's the executive corruption' (*FT*, 16 September 2003).

Number four on the list of experts is former Harvard Business Review editor Rosabeth Moss Kanter. Most of her studies have focused on the business–society interface. She became famous for her work on organizational change (*The Change Masters*, 1989), specifically in large companies (*When Giants Learn to Dance*, 1983) and leadership. She is particularly well known for her conclusion that women do not manage differently than men, but she supports the idea that social capital along with the social embeddedness of organizations is the most important form of 'capital' to take into account when trying to effectively change companies.

Finally, Arie de Geus can be mentioned as an expert who has added a relevant dimension to the area of 'general management'. His focus is specifically on the historical dimension of firm strategy. De Geus (1997) introduced the concept of the 'living company', also dubbed the most original and innovative business model to emerge in the latter half of the twentieth century (*FT*, 21 August 2003). He examined why some firms do, and many others do not, survive societal turbulence. His holistic view – strongly inspired by Peter Senge, another leading general management expert – anticipates the notion of Societal Interface Management as discussed in this book. According to de Geus, companies should harmonize their values in consultation with important stakeholders. Companies cannot exist in isolation: in order to be a 'living company' they have to be(come) 'learning companies'. According to de Geus (and Senge) this involves knowledge management, communication, corporate culture and ethics.

Functional areas – on the realization of goals

CSR is not only a topic of interest for scholars in the area of general and strategic management. The importance of integrating CSR ideas and orientations into more functional areas of management is also gaining ground. Six functional areas can be distinguished: (1) marketing; (2) quality control; (3) financial management; (4) supply management; (5) research and development; and (6) human resource management (HRM).

- *Marketing*: In simple terms, marketing concerns the questions of how products or services are made attractive to (potential) consumers. But Philip Kottler, the leading expert in marketing, defines marketing in much broader terms, linking it to CSR: 'Marketing serves as the link between society's needs and its patterns of industrial response' (Kottler, 2000). Central to Kottler's view is the belief that marketing does not simply concern commercial transactions but that it also involves social values. Marketing is a social activity. The most sophisticated approach to marketing, in Kottler's view, is one where the organization sees it as its task to determine the needs, wants and interests of target markets and to achieve the desired results more effectively and efficiently than competitors, in a way that preserves and enhances the consumer's or society's well-being. One of the results of such an approach is that ethical behaviour is linked with the profit motive and the satisfaction of consumer wants (*FT*, 8 August 2003). CSR strategies are increasingly judged from the perspective of the consumer. The nineteenth century has been dubbed the 'age of the producer' (with the development of new production techniques); the twentieth century as the 'age of the employee' (with strong trade unions and high wages); and the twenty-first century is expected to become the 'age of the consumer'. The increasing buying-power of individual consumers (Hertz, 2002; cf. Chapter 5) has increased the impact that individual consumer decisions have on company strategy and on the direction of society. Whether this leads to a 'better world' depends on the preferences of consumers.
- *Quality control*: At first glance, quality control appears to be a purely operational discipline. Joseph Juran, one of the most influential thinkers on quality management points out that 'if the goals are poorly chosen, the planning will be done to reach the wrong goals. We shall be "doing things right" but not "the right things"' (Juran, 1988: 139; cited in Zwetsloot, 1999: 22). This idea also reflects the second dimension of excellence in the quality thinking of Conti (Conti, 1993). Therefore, quality thinking is essentially concerned with 'doing the right things right'. More specifically: 'getting it right the first time' is emphasized (Zwetsloot, 1999). By doing things properly from the outset fewer problems will arise in future. Quality control thus becomes a proactive strategy. The quality management model propagated by the European Foundation for Quality Management (EFQM) includes a leadership and a societal dimension, which is explicitly aimed at corporate responsibility and excellence defined as: 'exceeding the minimum regulatory framework in which the organisation operates and to strive to understand and respond to the expectations of their stakeholders in society'.[9]
- *Financial management*: A topic of growing interest in financial management is the regulation of markets and the issue of SRI. The theory of financial intermediation is concerned with the efficient and effective allocation of capital in an economy. The 'raison d'être' of financial intermediaries such as banks, insurance companies and the like is partly to address market imperfections which create the need for 'interface' organizations that operate in between markets and societies. SRI is a booming area for investment funds (including institutional investors) that want to capitalize on the trend of (alleged) high CFP associated with CSP.

CSR issues have also appeared in the more traditional area of financial management and accounting which, to a certain extent, can be ascribed to the 'unethical behaviour' and accounting scandals that have occurred since the mid-1990s (see Chapter 10). This has increased the need for 'ethics' in accounting, although it has largely taken on the form of reactive CSR. More proactive concepts have also been developed. In 1996, Robert Kaplan and David Norton, leading experts in financial management, introduced the concept of the 'balanced scorecard'. Customer satisfaction, internal process improvement and organizational learning are aims that need to be integrated during planning and budgeting (*FT*, 22 August 2003). In this respect, their thinking coincides with quality management (Juran), HRM and organization learning (Handy, Mintzberg).

- *Supply chain management*: From a CSR perspective, supply chain management is one of the least advanced areas in business studies. A study conducted in 2003 by the Chartered Institute of Purchasing & Supply in the UK, revealed that 83 per cent of the purchasing directors are under pressure from company boards to prioritize price over matters of ethics and social impact (*Ethical Corporation Magazine*, 10 October 2003). CSR issues in supply chain management are, however, gaining in importance. Companies have traditionally been confronted with the problem of 'chain liability' which refers to the degree to which they can be held accountable for deficiencies in a final product due to supply irregularities. Critical NGOs are increasingly calling on firms (particularly business-to-consumer organizations) to account for their *chain responsibilities* which refers to the degree to which firms can be held responsible for the conditions under which products and services with their suppliers are produced. The more complex the supply structure, the more complex the link between liability and responsibility becomes, and the more supply strategies become an integral part of a CSR strategy.

- *R&D*: In the past, R&D strategies were viewed as an internal process. Nowadays, the process of invention, production and marketing is becoming more interactive and outward oriented. Suppliers – through black box engineering principles – as well as customers are increasingly involved in the innovation process in order to produce products for which there is a market. 'Technology-push' considerations have become strongly linked with 'demand-pull' effects. Increasingly, regulatory provisions are included in the design and search process. This has, among other things, led to the specialization 'design for recycling' which aims to include environmental considerations already at the beginning of the research process.

  The dictum that applies to quality control is also gaining ground in R&D: try to develop something 'good' from the start. At the same time, companies are increasingly dependent on patent regimes to reap the benefits of their innovation strategy. Interactive innovation, therefore, becomes part and parcel of the Societal Interface Management function. This is referred to as 'intellectual asset management' which includes the effective management of patents and intellectual property rights (cf. Van Wijk, 2002). In the event that intellectual property rights are under dispute – as in the case of, for instance HIV/Aids drugs or software piracy (see Chapter 10) – the R&D function is already linked to societal marketing strategies. The bigger the investment in innovation, and the longer the pay-back time, the more the R&D strategy of a firm has to become part of 'visionary' leadership strategies. As such it automatically acquires overtones of Societal Interface Management.

- *HRM*: Some HRM experts (in particular Drucker, Handy, Senge and Kanter) have also been involved in developing theories on leadership, general management and organizational change. HRM is becoming 'strategic human resource management'. In literature, the distinction is generally made between the Michigan approach to strategic human resource management – which entails a utilitarian and instrumentalist approach to HRM – and the Harvard approach – which entails a developmental humanist model (Legge, 1995). The Harvard approach comes closest to the recognition of the strategic importance of systematic Societal Interface Management for HRM. In keeping the motivation of employees alive and linking up with society, companies are developing 'volunteers' programmes, investing in 'integrity' training. Internal HRM programmes are becoming part of the company's external identity. Companies more active in CSR have a direct cost advantage, because it has been found that employees want to work for them for less. Companies with a bad reputation on CSR issues have more difficulty in hiring personnel and have to pay them more (Frank, 2003). Thus, the PA function and the external HRM function are increasingly starting to overlap.

8.5 CONCLUSION: FROM TRIPLE-P (CSR) TO TRIPLE-E (INTERFACE)

> *Good intentions are no excuse for bad results, and the arrogance of the ignorant good-doers turns them into do-gooders and undermines that necessary function of doing real good, without which society cannot exist for very long.*
>
> Kenneth Boulding (1981: 124)

Via the detour of a discussion of the various dimensions and approaches to the catch-all concept of 'CSR', we have arrived at a fundamental problem encountered in at least three scientific disciplines. In economics, philosophy and political science this is referred to as the conflict (or *trade-off*) between efficiency and equity. This chapter demonstrated that the solution to this trade-off should be sought in explicitly posing the question of effectiveness. The *Triple-P* of CSR (*people/profit/planet*) can therefore justifiably be replaced by the *Triple-E* of Societal Interface Management: efficiency, equity (*ethics*) and effectiveness (Figure 8.4).

The principal practical challenges of Societal Interface Management can be found at the interface between ethics/equity and efficiency. In addition, the two most significant institutional interface challenges for companies are situated at the public/private and profit/non-profit interface (see Chapter 7). Three 'strategic' interfaces can thus be distinguished that constitute the biggest challenges for companies. Table 8.3 summarizes these interfaces and some of their key indicators.

The challenges related to efficiency include the standard operational repertoire that middle managers employ to distinguish themselves from competitors in the same consumer and capital markets. Efficiency is means oriented. The challenges related to ethics and equity are goal oriented and pose an ever-growing agenda of issues and benchmarks company leadership has to take into account. Both lists are indicative. The ultimate managerial challenge is to take effective decisions at these three interfaces. This will require the effective application of the available instruments, which, in turn, will require effective interaction with stakeholders in society. Societal Interface Management is a combination of two forms of 'Triangular Management' (Figure 8.5).

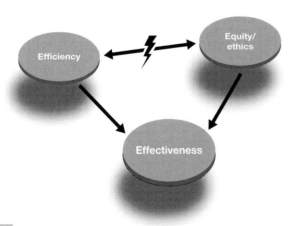

Figure 8.4 Triple-E

153

Other organizations in society also face a comparable triangular challenge. The trade-off between equity/ethics and efficiency, is increasingly acknowledged by governments and new NGOs. Since the 1990s, new public management scholars focused first on applying business and market (efficiency) principles to government operations. This trend was an understandable reaction to the inefficiencies related to the primarily equity-oriented focus of governments in the past. It formed the basis for large-scale privatization operations. The latest public management approaches, however, are again searching for a synthesis (effectiveness) in which they are rethinking some of the 'old' equity principles of governments (cf. Pollit, 2003). While the more traditional NGOs focused primarily on the 'ethics' dimension, they too have become progressively interested in the 'efficiency' with which they communicate their message and organize their constituencies. The question of the 'professionalization' of these organizations – with the obvious criticism of 'bureaucratization' – became particularly relevant in the 1990s. The same challenge arises for governments. Newer types of NGOs have been more professional from the start, and have often addressed the trade-off between ethics and efficiency in a more direct manner. Transparency International, for instance, 'has a global agenda of simultaneously ending corruption (the abuse of power) and improving economic efficiency through good governance reforms' (Braithwaite and Drahos, 2000: 36). NGOs face additional management problems at the interface between non-profit and public and non-profit and profit.

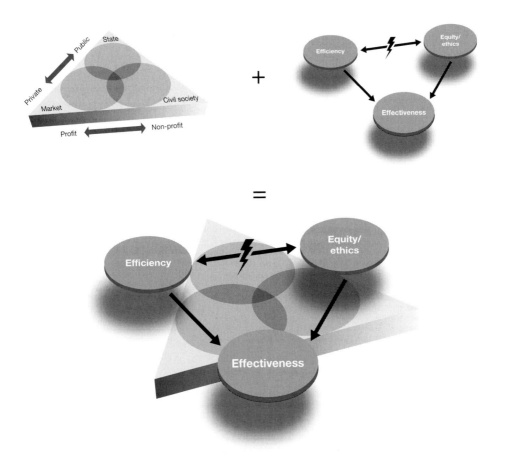

Figure 8.5 Societal Interface Management = Triangular Management

Table 8.3 Strategic challenges of Societal Interface Management

Public ⚡ private	Profit ⚡ non-profit	Efficiency	⚡ Ethics/equity
Relationship with government (local/regional/international).	Hybrid position or not.	Profit maximization.	Fairness.
Relationship with supervisors.	Relationship with family.	High productivity.	Justice.
Relationship with branch organizations.	Relationship with different types of NGOs.	Low wages.	Democracy.
Quality labels/trade marks or not.	Relationship with suppliers and consumers.	Production speed.	Decent wages.
Intellectual property protection.	Use of informal sector.	Flexibility.	Emancipation.
Public–private partnerships.	Relationship with members (in case of cooperatives).	Supply chain control, efficient outsourcing (just-in-time).	Diversity.
Adopting international codes.	Relationship with neighbours.	Research.	Innovation.
In-house or external education.	Business–community involvement?	Chain liability.	Responsibility.
Legislation or self-regulation.	Relationship with shareholders (small–large).	Horizontal differentiation.	Equality: equal opportunities.
Paying for negative externalities.	Relationship to culture and values.	Core business.	Truth.
War/conflict profits.	Strategic HRM.	Standardization/rationalization.	Dignity.
Relationship with public media.	Relationship with volunteers.	Single brand.	Freedom.
Regulation evasion.		Image branding.	Citizenship rights.
Provision of (global) public goods		Quality control.	Integrity.
		Economies of scale.	Accountability.
		Patent protection	Transparency.
		Competition.	Sustainability.
		Free trade.	Security/safety.
			Health.
			Quality of life.
			Economies of scope.
			Cooperation.
			Level playing field.
			Fair trade.

Chapter 9

The occasion: issues and issues management

CHAPTER CONTENTS

9.1 INTRODUCTION: ON THE OCCURRENCE OF ISSUES

When are corporations called upon to contribute towards the realization of equity and the effective provision of public goods in society? What occasions such a demand? When does 'global warming', 'child labour' or 'obesity', for instance, become an 'issue' for individual companies? In the post-war period corporate responsibilities first became an 'issue' because of a number of major triggering events – either through major incidents involving big companies or through NGO awareness-raising campaigns. Reputation-threatening societal discontent landed on the corporate agenda and the response was to 'manage' the issue. In the past, issues management amounted to a reactive form of crisis management – required in the face of critical incidents. Issues management largely involved problems encountered on consumer markets leading, for instance, to recalls of particular products. The challenge for the Public Affairs department was to come up with a strategy that would minimize (long-term) reputational damage.

Since the 1970s, the number of critical incidents for which firms are held partly responsible, has increased. As societal expectations with respect to the social and ecological policies of companies increased, companies were also expected to develop ecological and social initiatives. This chapter explains what gives occasion to issues (how they come about), inventories the main triggering events since the 1960s, how they develop (the issue life cycle) and how, in principle, they can be managed by firms.

9.2 FRAMING ISSUES

Jones and Chase (1979), the founding fathers of issue thinking, defined an issue as follows: 'an issue is an unregulated question or matter that is about to be straightened out'. Moore (1979: 45) added a risk element to this definition: 'a trend or condition, internal or external that, if continued, would have a significant impact on how a company is operated over the period of its business plan'. Ansoff (1980: 133) also defined issues as risky developments or topics that could have a great impact on the ability of the company to realize its objectives. Schoonman (1995: 16) spoke of 'a fiercely mounting matter, consisting of disputes that are subject to discussion and awaiting settlement'.

Issues are therefore:

- unresolved subjects of societal discontent that exist due to regulatory gaps;
- which involve great expectational gaps;
- leading to controversies;
- which (could) have an impact on the company and its reputation.

Unsettled, regulatory gaps

Issues are first and foremost societal matters that lack unambiguous legislation (Jones and Chase, 1979). Such matters are yet to be institutionalized, regulated or settled. As long as moral consensus has not been reached on a given social issue, legal regulations are not likely to be forthcoming (van Luijk and Schilder, 1997). This means that a controversial subject will remain an issue as long as there are no clear, compelling rules that govern it or consensus is still to be reached. Examples of lacking compulsory legislation in the 1990s include the sinking of Shell's Brent Spar storage tank in the Atlantic Ocean in the summer of 1995, and the question of whether or not to do business in Burma. There was no international legislation that prohibited the sinking of the Brent Spar (Chapter 15) and there was also no ban on doing business in Burma (Chapter 16), so there was considerable room for negotiation.

Serious negotiations can only take place when unambiguous legislation is lacking. In a bargaining society, legislation is lacking either by design (for instance, in countries governed by Common Law), due to the circumstances (for instance, in the international arena where no central legal authority exists) or because of changes in society for which no laws have yet been designed (for instance, due to technological change). Many issues arise as a result of major societal change. Part I showed the underlying dynamics of these changes. Issues are therefore generated by the bargaining society; but at the same time they also fuel further negotiations. Consequently, three types of interrelated issues can be distinguished that all relate to the dynamics of the bargaining society:

1   *Institutional issues*: old bargaining compromises have left a number of institutional voids. As a result, no rules of the game have been specified. It *leaves* considerable room for interpretation due to a relatively poorly developed legal framework. The international legal environment, in particular, creates sizeable regulatory gaps where incidents regularly appear that cannot be captured in international regulations. It is difficult, for instance, to define who is responsible for cleaning up oil spills in international waters. The issue represents a *search for clarity* on the assignment of responsibilities, not necessarily on the design of new laws.
2   *Stretch issues*: the changing bargaining environment as a result of the shifting boundaries between state, market and civil society has put existing institutional arrangements in

many countries under pressure. It *creates* considerable room for interpretation, but often within relatively well-defined legal frameworks. In this type of regulatory void, actors try to stretch the rules of the game by testing 'how far' they can go with specific activities. The accountancy 'scandals' of the early twenty-first century belong to this category. They have often proved difficult to classify as 'illegal' because legal provisions as well as auditing rules were ambiguous – certainly across countries. The issue represents a *search for the correct interpretation of existing rules*.

3   *Agenda-setting issues*: issues that exist for which no legal provision could have been made, for instance because they relate to technological change. Privacy became a 'new' issue once the application of Information Technology created completely new opportunities for infringing on privacy. The technological possibility of stem cell research generated moral and legal issues nobody ever had cause to think of before. NGOs, in particular, put these issues on the agenda through protest actions and critical reports. The issue represents *a search for new institutions* that should trigger further change, but also define the relative responsibilities of actors.

Expectational gaps

Issues exist particularly as a result of *expectational gaps* (Wartick and Wood, 1999: 175). Expectational gaps are created when stakeholders hold different views on what acceptable corporate conduct is and/or should be with regard to societal issues. It concerns the disjunction between the factual and actual interpretation (what is) and the desired interpretation (what should be). In this way, an issue creates a gap between being and belonging, between perceptions of corporate conduct or performance, and expectations of what it should be. These normative expectations are the subject of business ethics. They can sometimes be in tension with one another. Wartick and Mahon (1994) identify three gaps: factual gaps, conformance gaps and ideals gaps.

- *Factual gaps*: A gap, doubt or disagreement about the facts that lie at the basis of an issue. The discussion surrounding the deployment of biotechnology through genetic modification in the food chain primarily concerns the factual disagreement and doubt about the use and accuracy of assessments of the dangers of genetic modification. The factual gap becomes more serious for an MNE when the different countries it operates in interpret the basic facts differently. Part I showed that two developments in particular contribute to factual gaps: (1) the 'nationalism' of statistical bureaus that leaves many relevant empirical indicators unresearched; (2) the tendency towards 'trend-thinking' that leads to 'improper deduction', only taking into account those facts that support the favoured trend and leaving out most of the facts that would refute it.

- *Conformance gaps*: Parties may agree on the facts, but not on the consequences for conduct. A company may confirm the dangers of a product, but keep it on the market (as tobacco and alcoholic beverages companies have done), or a company may draw up a code of conduct, but not act accordingly. The conformance gap leads to disputes about the question of 'who bears responsibility' for addressing the issue.

- *Ideals gaps*: An inconsistency between norms, values and ideals. Appraisals with respect to permitting or prohibiting child labour, doing business in countries with totalitarian regimes or paying bribes can partly be traced back to differences in norms and values. Ideals gaps are particularly relevant for MNEs that operate across borders. They have to find a way to cope with these ideals gaps.

Controversy as a result of societal discontent

Controversies (Wartick and Mahon, 1994) arise due to societal discontent or doubt about corporate conduct and are often fuelled by irreconcilable stakeholder and company interests. Discontent can also grow as a result of society's changing demands, values and expectations (Schoonman, 1995). In this way, differences in opinion, lack of clarity, doubt or uneasiness exist with respect to, for instance, what constitutes food safety, 'civilized' working conditions, a living versus minimum wage, child labour (due to controversy, for instance, over the age at which a 'child' stops being a child), or the implications of biotechnology. In the face of controversies, at least two moral standpoints are possible which gives rise to a discussion between proponents and opponents. The expectations that give rise to gaps with respect to corporate policy and conduct can be deep seated and give rise to huge conflicts.

The growing attention to CSR in society functions as a self-reinforcing mechanism (van Riemsdijk, 1994). Due to technological advancements (Part I), it has become increasingly necessary to rely more or less blindly on the expertise of innumerable anonymous experts and technicians. At the same time, considerable risks seem to be involved in the new technologies, which in turn undermine the confidence the public places in experts. This gives rise to a fundamental feeling of insecurity and discontent – a state of being almost inherent to Western culture and further strengthened by stepped-up institutional changes (Part I). Society, therefore, desires reliable and verifiable information. The new keyword of the twenty-first century – far from applying only to discussions on CSR – is, therefore, 'transparency' even when the exact meaning of the concept is context bound and far from clear.

Impact on company and reputation

A societal issue only becomes a business-specific issue if it can have a significant impact on the company and its reputation (Ansoff, 1975; Moore, 1979). Not all issues affect every company. An oil company, for instance, will not have much to do with the discussion on genetic modification, while an Internet company will hardly have to deal with environmental degradation. Impact is of importance because it distinguishes issues from non-issues (Johnson, 1983). Next to issues and non-issues, silly issues and witch-hunts can also be found. The media sometimes creates such issues for want of news. They can, however, have a serious impact on a company and its reputation. A 'silly issue' is characterized by its short life span and lack of support. In the issues management literature – where a relatively reactive approach to issues is the norm – it is generally held that it is often only in hindsight that one can determine whether an issue was a witch-hunt or represents fundamental discontent in society. This book adopts a different analytical approach. By departing from processes of fundamental institutional change in society, it should be possible to identify the most relevant issues – even when the exact effect on specific companies is always contingent upon circumstances. This is the objective of Chapter 10.

9.3 ISSUES MANAGEMENT, CRISIS MANAGEMENT?

Since the original introduction of the notion of issues management by Jones and Chase (1979), the concept has largely been used to refer to the communication strategy of companies confronted with an (external) crisis. That is: issues management as crisis management. Now that attention from a management perspective has increased strongly, broader and more future-oriented views on the components of issues management are developing (see Table 9.1).

Table 9.1 Components of issues management

Public Affairs Council (1978)	'consists of (a) *monitoring* issue arena, (b) *identifying* important issues, (c) *evaluating* their impact, (d) *prioritizing* issues, (e) creating *response*, and (f) *implementing* issue action programming.'
Brown (1979)	'(a) issues *monitoring*, (b) corporate *performance*, and (b) issues *communication*.'
Chase (1982)	'the capacity to (a) *understand*, (b) *mobilize*, (c) *coordinate*, and (d) *direct* all strategic and policy planning functions, and all public affairs skills, towards achievement of one objective: meaningful participation in creation of public policy that affects personal and institutional destiny.'
Johnson (1983)	'the process by which the corporation can (a) *identify*, (b) *evaluate*, and (c) *respond* to those social and political issues which may impact significantly upon it.'
Heath and Nelson (1986)	'an array of activities and attitudes which are designed to (a) *adjust* the company to the public and (b) help the public *understand* the complexity and requirements of the company.'
Weiss (1998)	'(a) *detect* and *address* issues that may cause a firm and its stakeholders problems or harm, and (b) *contain* or *solve* issues that could become potentially damaging crises.'
Van Ginneken (1999)	'all efforts that are aimed at the (a) *identification*, (b) systematic *monitoring* and (c) *analysis* of mounting issues in the media and public opinion, that in any way may influence the future functioning of the company.'

Three streams of thinking can be distinguished in issues management. First, an *outside-in* (*reactive*) approach that employs a public relations and communication perspective on issues where the interaction between external parties and the company is central (cf. Johnson, 1983). In the 1990s, this stream was supplemented with an *inside-out* (*active*) perspective that focuses on the internal factors that play a role in the engagement with and interpretation of issues (cf. Heath and Nelson, 1986). An integrated approach (*pro/inter-active*) by the name of 'strategic issues management' is slowly gaining ground (Heugens, 2001). Strategic issues management aims at integrating the outside-in and inside-out perspectives and requires a more forward-looking attitude of managers. A successful strategic issues manager should be capable of preventing an issue from arising in the first place.

Central to all issues management is the dynamic process of identification, evaluation and response to issues that can significantly affect the company (Johnson, 1983 in: Wartick and Wood, 1999: 172). The view is held that while issues as such cannot be managed, it should be possible to identify the discontent and controversies in society and prepare a response to them. How do stakeholders think about issues such as child labour, conducting business in countries with dictatorial regimes and genetic manipulation/modification? The potential impact of confrontation on the reputation or continuity of the corporation has to be established. The identification of issues takes place through scanning the environment. The second step, evaluation, takes place through the classification of issues according to impact on reputation and likelihood of the issue developing into a business-specific issue. A matrix can be used to classify and prioritize reputation-threatening issues (see Figure 9.1). Threatening issues can thus be identified and perhaps dealt with proactively. Shell is one of the companies that systemati-

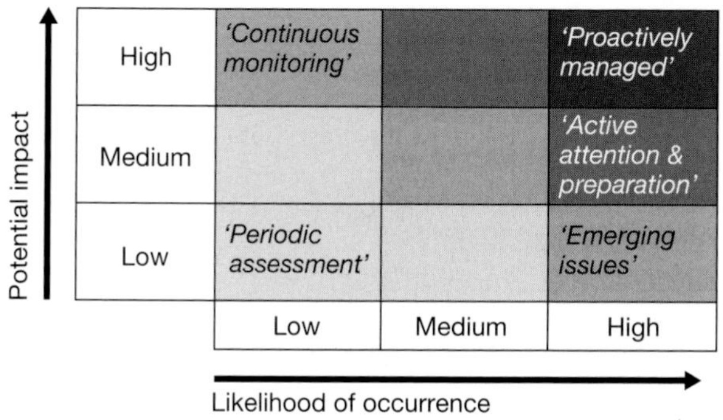

Figure 9.1 Issues priority matrix (company perspective)
Source: based on Steiner and Steiner, 2000: 174

cally makes use of this method. Of course, policy choices have to be made since not all issues can be addressed simultaneously. Moreover, not every relevant issue is immediately placed on the management agenda. Choices have to be made, alternatives have to be considered and, if necessary, scenarios have to be developed (Van der Heijden, 1996).

A vital role and aim of issues management is the timely acknowledgement of an emerging expectational gap and closing or narrowing it before the issue can have a negative impact on the company and its reputation (Wartick and Wood, 1999: 191). This can be achieved by adapting corporate policy and practice to the normative expectations of society and its stakeholders, for example, by means of a code of conduct. At the same time, an attempt can be made to influence the expectations of stakeholders and society through initiatives aimed at gaining support for the policy pursued. An example is so-called *issue advertising* which has the objective of creating understanding for the dilemmas a company is struggling with. In this way, issues management becomes stakeholder management.

Effectiveness of issues management

The effectiveness of any approach to issues depends on the type of gap that exists. A factual gap can be bridged by providing more or less objective facts. A conformance gap can only be closed if one of the parties adjusts its position, for instance, by fine-tuning its code of conduct. The ideals gap is the most difficult and can only be resolved through debate, discussion and dialogue. Ideals gaps widen if clarity is lacking about the primary responsibilities of actors. Primary responsibilities are linked to the rules that govern their day-to-day realization. Ideals gaps, therefore develop particularly along the societal interfaces positioned between the state, market and civil society. An ideals gap often forms the basis of CSR-related issues. The employment of an issues strategy generally appears to have a positive effect on the performance of a company, irrespective of the approach chosen (Heugens, 2001). Moreover, the employment of a well thought through issues strategy yields economic, strategic and reputation benefits. In this manner, issues management acts as a form of protection against the loss of elbowroom that accompanies the institution of government regulations. The strength of issues management is represented by the structural and proactive capacity to predict and prevent societal discontent before reactive communication offers the only recourse (Chase, in: Heath and Nelson, 1986).

Issues management essentially fails if an entrepreneur is only able to respond to a crisis such as an oil spill, employees leaving or a crashing share price. An incident is a crisis for a company the moment it has significant consequences for people, financial resources, or its property or reputation (Mitroff and Anagnos, 2001; O'Higgens, 2002). The company has then clearly made an inaccurate assessment of its susceptibility to a crisis. If important stakeholder opinions of the company subsequently threaten to take a turn for the worse, a reputation crisis looms (Zyglidopoulos and Phillips, 1999: 335). A bargaining society is marked by uncertainty. With changing and overlapping institutional boundaries, the likelihood of crises increases which further limits the effectiveness of reactive crisis management.

9.4 ISSUE LIFE CYCLE: FROM DISCONTENT TO SETTLEMENT

Companies, sectors, technologies and even entire economic systems can exhibit cycles of rise and decline. In the case of products, it is called the product life cycle and in the case of economic systems, this ebb and flow is referred to as prolonged cycles or Kondratieffs (Chapter 5).

The issue of CSR itself has been going through a life cycle. Some even regard it as a 'hype cycle' (cf. Harrison, 2004). In all cases, the cycle is S-shaped and the discussion is not about the basic shape, but the duration of the cycle and the possibility of the cycle starting anew. Issues also often run along a fixed pattern towards regulation or settlement. The so-called *issue life cycle* (Ackerman and Bauer, 1976; Mahon and Waddock, 1992) essentially consists of four stages: birth, growth, development and maturity. In each stage different stakeholders involved in an issue usually adopt a different attitude (see Figure 9.2).

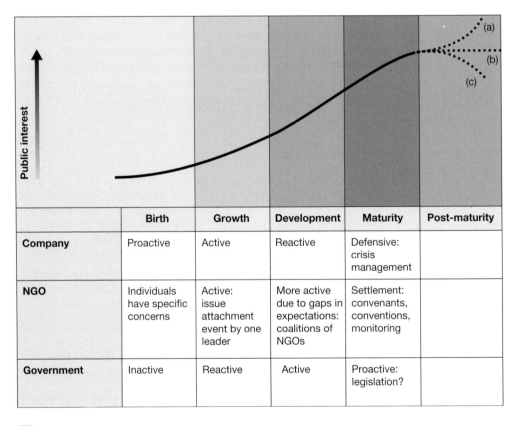

	Birth	Growth	Development	Maturity	Post-maturity
Company	Proactive	Active	Reactive	Defensive: crisis management	
NGO	Individuals have specific concerns	Active: issue attachment event by one leader	More active due to gaps in expectations: coalitions of NGOs	Settlement: convenants, conventions, monitoring	
Government	Inactive	Reactive	Active	Proactive: legislation?	

Figure 9.2 Issue life cycle

Birth: shifting expectations

The birth of an issue or societal discontent comes about under the influence of changing expectations somewhere in society, for instance the louder sounding call for corporate social accountability. Societal discontent arises with regard to a specific issue such as genetic modification, slavery, immigration or child labour. A single societal grouping becomes more actively concerned with the specific topic (Ewing, 1980; Schwartz and Gibb, 1999) and issues flow forth from the complex and intangible concerns of certain segments of society. Issues in this phase always concern a matter on which – in public opinion – the government is slack (inactive), which has created a regulatory void. Even issues that have been forgotten can unexpectedly surface again. True CSR issues are very tenacious (see Figure 9.2). The moment an issue is 'born' is very difficult to judge. Companies that anticipate an issue in this phase can be classified as strategic and proactive.

The birth of major issues since the 1960s, often involved the action of multinational enterprises (Table 9.2).

Andriof and Marsden (1999) identify three phases in this period: awakening (1960s–early 1980s), engaging (early 1980s–mid-1990s), and networking (mid-1990s–present). Over time,

Table 9.2 Major triggering incidents since 1960

Phase I: 1960–83 Awakening/governments	Phase II: 1984–92 Engaging/markets	Phase III: 1993–present Networking/governance
– United Fruit Company's involvement in central American 'banana republics', several occasions. – Nestlé baby food scandal (dying African children), 1970. – ITT role in overthrow of Allende government (Chile), 1973. – Role of oil majors in oil shocks of the 1970s. – Seveso chemical disaster (Italy), 1974. – Amoco Cadiz oil spill (French coast), 1978. – Ford Pinto fuel tank fire, US (and punitive damages), 1978.	– Bhopal chemical disaster (Union-Carbide, India), 1984. – Chernobyl nuclear disaster (Ukraine), 1986. – Chico Mendes killed (Brazilian environmentalist, rubber industry), 1988. – Exxon Valdez oil spill (Alaska), 1989. – Speculative raid on British pound (speculator – now philanthropist –Soros), 1992.	– Shell Brent Spar, North Sea, 1995. – Ken Saro-Wiwa Execution (Shell, Nigeria), 1995. – Barings Bank bankruptcy, 1995. – Nike child labour and sweatshops (South East Asia), 1996. – Long-term capital management crisis, Asia crisis, 1997. – Health claims against 'Big Tobacco' become successful. – 'Mad cow' and various other livestock (food safety) diseases, from 1996, UK/Europe. – Dotcom collapse, from 2001 (US, Europe). – Enron and consecutive accountancy scandals (US, Europe, Asia), from 2001. – Merck, Vioxx medication recall, 2004.

Source: Andriof and Marsden (1999), SustainAbility (2004) and own additions

the intensity of the societal response in particular, increased. In the earlier phases, ecological issues predominated while in later phases, these issues were increasingly complemented with issues concerning human, political and labour rights – all related to the generic issue of 'sustainability'. The last phase is characterized by Andriof and McIntosh (2001) as the 'networking' phase. It refers to the growing need for corporations and societal networks to work together to create institutions and standards to regulate corporate conduct.

A study of SustainAbility (2004) adopts a slightly broader analytical perspective by focusing on more general waves of pressure shaping the Corporate Responsibility and the Sustainable Development agenda of OECD countries. Three periods are identified: (1) 1960–1977: governments were in the spotlight and the issues focused on wars (Vietnam war) and the environment and limited natural resources; (2) 1977–1998: markets and business were in the spotlight while the issues focused on the integration of the environmental and socio-economic aspects of sustainable development; (3) 1998 onwards: the nature of globalization and governance (both of international organizations and corporations) is in the spotlight.

Despite slightly differing periodizations, both studies recognize that the last wave of issues is characterized by a 'network economy' in which no single actor dominates and in which the biggest challenges are posed by governance issues – i.e. how to cope with the institutional voids associated with the international bargaining society. The recent wave of triggering events brings together three different types of issues: (1) stretch issues (internal governance), (2) institutional issues (joint or external governance), and (3) agenda-setting issues (new governance).

Growth: intensification of public interest

The growth phase occurs specifically when those first in command fail to address an issue adequately (see Figure 9.2). The discontent grows even further when the issue can be clearly defined, is given a popular name and the media latches onto unsuspecting protagonists. Examples include: 'banana republic', 'Frankenstein food' (introduced by Prince Charles), 'global warming' or the 'greenhouse effect' (supported by Nobel Prize Laureates) and 'genetic manipulation' (instead of the original term 'genetic modification'). The transition to this second phase is often initiated by a *triggering event*, usually organized by a visible stakeholder. The triggering event does not necessarily have to represent the biggest incident that has taken place in connection with the issue (Box 9.1). Examples of such *events* include: media attention, calls for a boycott, documentaries, lawsuits, publications, conferences and eruptions (Schoonman, 1995). The growth phase is characterized by media attention and the emergence of the issue in the public debate (Wartick and Wood, 1999: 177). The issue is 'attached', so to speak, to a party who is then made the 'owner' (*issue owner*) of the social issue. Governments usually respond reactively and even defensively, by denying the issue. Companies that attend to the issue in this phase can be classified as 'active'.

Development: striking while the iron is hot

The controversy enters the development phase when important stakeholders, individually or collectively, demand changes to corporate policies (Eyestone, 1978; Rowley, 1997; Frooman, 1999). In the first instance, stakeholders can call the company directly to account for a gap in expectations or controversial corporate conduct. An example is a consumer boycott or pressure groups demanding a full explanation. Naturally, it is preferable for a company that a controversy or expectational gap does result in public campaigns so that damage to reputation is avoided. Next to this, stakeholders can choose to propel the issue into the broader public debate and they can attempt to get the government to enforce legislation. Between 1996 and 2001,

BOX 9.1 TRIGGERING AND IMPACT

The Exxon Valdez spill of 37,000 tonnes of oil in 1989 severely affected an ecologically sensitive area of Alaska. It acted as a strong triggering event for the ecological movement. Strangely enough, it only ranks 35 on the ITOPF (International Tanker Owners Pollution Federation, 2003) list of major oil spills since 1967. At the top of the list is the 1979 Atlantic Empress spill of 287,000 tonnes of oil off Tobago in the West Indies. This and many other, much larger, oil spills have gone largely unnoticed. The Exxon Valdez, however, has acted as trigger for various reasons: (1) the identifiable American mother company (Exxon), while most other oil spills involved tankers with names that could not be directly linked to any well-known brand; (2) the direct impact on the coast of the US, while many of the largest oil spills occurred on open sea or affected developing countries; (3) the perceived arrogance of the company's chairman in handling the crisis – he left it to subordinates to manage the crisis and initially denied any major responsibility for the damage caused; (4) the unprecedented damage claims following the event which can partly be attributed to the American litigious bargaining system (see Chapter 2).

Nike, for instance, was the subject of more than 1,000 newspaper articles (Connor, 2004) linking the company's name to allegations of child labour and sweatshop conditions. If the issue is propelled into the broader public domain, the company and its reputation are at risk of becoming the plaything of unpredictable and whimsical public opinion (Schoonman, 1995). Companies that respond to an issue in this phase can be classified as 'reactive'. In this phase, the media often jolts the public awake with sensational images. For a media scandal to break, a number of conditions need to be in place (Lull and Hinerman, 1997). First, prevailing social norms must appear to have been violated. Second, specific persons or entities that can also be empirically verified/factually identified must be at stake. Third, the parties involved must have acted consciously and in accordance with their own needs and interests. Fourth, the actions must have diverse consequences for those concerned, and it must be possible to pin the blame on the company. Fifth, the information must be widely disseminated via the media, fashioned into a coherent story and evoke widespread interest and discussion. It is a self-reinforcing process (ibid.: 75). Gradually, the issue becomes *hot*, requiring that the iron be struck in the following phase.

Mature: settlement

In the mature or settlement phase, the issue has to be addressed and the expectational gap has to be bridged. Companies that are confronted with the issue for the first time at this stage will always view the situation as a crisis and be inclined to respond purely defensively (making the best of a bad situation). In this phase, public interest grows exponentially until measures are taken (settlement). According to Bos (1995: 18), societal organizations play an important role in the settlement phase of an issue as they usually represent the issue and are therefore crucial to the company to legitimize the proposed solution (Chapter 3). Settlement does not necessarily imply legislation. Technological developments and societal changes are complex and often happen too fast to be adequately captured in legislation and regulations that involve long, drawn-out processes. Parties must therefore often content themselves with interim solutions or disciplinary measures. In joint consultations, covenants and conventions can be concluded that address issues such as environmental degradation and working conditions. Covenants and conventions are more flexible instruments than legislation. In this way, the rigidity of legislation is avoided which allows us to speak of a socially *more acceptable* business practice. Covenants and conventions only have judicial bearing upon the parties that were involved in drawing it up and that endorsed it – unless a declaration of 'generally binding' is made, which is less frequently the case.

Post-maturity: dying, dragging or disappearing

A CSR issue can indeed seem settled through the conclusion of a covenant, but that is not to say that it has been resolved. Cultural differences can lead to interesting differences in viewpoints on the status of a settlement. Western cultures, for instance, regard a covenant or a law as a sort of social contract that can no longer be negotiated. By contrast, Eastern cultures (and companies) regard a law, contract or covenant not as the end, but the beginning of negotiations (cf. Ruigrok and van Tulder, 1995). The bargaining society also displays fundamental dilemmas of effectiveness – for example, in looking after collective goods – where the over-negotiation of issues is unavoidable. There are thus three possible scenarios for an issue that has reached the mature phase. In the first place, an issue can reappear at a later stage if the solution is not stable or if new expectational gaps open up ((a) in Figure 9.2). The cycle will then have to be repeated once more, for instance, in the case of an inadequate code of conduct or settlement. In the event that the legal environment encourages repeated claims, an issue can drag on for a very long time (Box 9.2).

In the second place, equilibrium can be reached ((b) in Figure 9.2). In this case, the solution or the initiative undertaken by the company balances the expectations of the relevant parties. Modified policies or initiatives are also regarded as acceptable. Parties have come to an acceptable resolution of the controversy. In this way, the issue, by definition, ceases to be an issue.

In addition to the fact that an issue can be resolved, an issue can, in the third place, also disappear completely ((c) in Figure 9.2). This can take place in four ways.

- Due to a loss of *momentum*. Societal and cultural change makes expectational gaps disappear or renders the issue irrelevant. A good example of this is the issue surrounding doing business in apartheid South Africa. Whereas Shell was first asked to leave South Africa, the company was asked to stay after democratization so as to make a contribution to the country's development (van Riemsdijk, 1994). This resolved the issue for Shell in Europe, but in the US legal environment, the claim culture made it possible for the issue to resurface (see Box 9.2). Loss of momentum truly occurs when a company ceases to exist. This was the case with the bankruptcy of Enron. But if a company is taken over by another company (Baring by ING, Union Carbide by Dupont) or changes name (Enron into CrossCountry Energy or Philip Morris into the Altria Group) momentum can gather once again.
- Through *issue fatigue*. Stakeholders are no longer impressed by the topic. Issue fatigue occurs when there have been so many similar affairs that the relevance or urgency of the issue is undermined (Schoonman, 1995: 98). World hunger is such an issue where the response to the most shocking images on television is channel zapping rather than societal mobilization.
- On the basis of *legislation or government regulations*. After legislation the matter is, by definition, no longer an issue. Indeed, it can be that there are groupings for which the issue continues to exist despite legislation, but they then have to adjust their strategy in

BOX 9.2 DRAGGING ISSUES

- **Bhopal.** On 3 December 1984, a deadly chemical cloud escaped from the Union Carbide factory in the Indian city of Bhopal causing 3,000 casualties directly and 12,000 (according to the government) to 30,000 (according to activists) more casualties in the following 20 years. In 1989 the company reached a settlement in Indian courts in which the company paid €360 million to the Indian government. In 1999 Dow Chemical acquired Union Carbide. Dow still faces protests of the International Campaign for Justice in Bhopal (of which Greenpeace is a member) to accept liability for health and clean-up issues 20 years after the incident even though Dow did not own Union Carbide at the time of the disaster. A major problem is that the local government has not been able (or willing) to effectively distribute the settlement money among the people directly affected. Amnesty International claims that of the original amount, €270 million is still to be distributed to the victims. The factory premises are still heavily polluted, which has, as recently as January 2005, led activists to demand extra compensation and measures from Dow.
- **Exxon Valdez.** In the 15 years after the 1989 Exxon Valdez oil spill, Exxon was forced to pay US$3.5 billion in clean-ups, rehabilitation and compensation (van de Wateringen, 2005). But the case is not over yet for the company in 2005: punitive damage claims amounting to a sum estimated between US$1 billion to US$5 billion against Exxon (now also teamed up with Mobil) were still pending, dragging the company and its critics from court room to court room.
- **Apartheid.** In 2004, 14 years after the demise of the apartheid regime in South Africa, three dozen multinational corporations (among them IBM and General Motors) that invested in South Africa during the apartheid regime, found themselves in an American district court again. Under the Alien Tort Claims Act, they were accused by plaintiffs representing black South Africans repressed under the apartheid regime of complicity in murder, torture and other human rights violations. In December, the judge ruled against the plaintiffs – much to the relief of the US government, the South African government, and the National Foreign Trade Council – a coalition of US multinational companies. Moreover, the judge in his ruling warned against a proliferation of future cases that might harm international commerce. The ruling also armed business groups urging Congress to modify the Alien Tort Claims Act (see Chapter 13) (*FT*, 2 December 2004).

order to focus attention on the issue once again, often at a higher level. This, for example, is the case for women's liberation movements and movements against racial discrimination: in many countries there are clear laws for this – often after constant and tough campaigns led by civil society groupings – but ingrained patterns are difficult to eradicate.

- Through *self-regulation* or *self-disciplining*. Company initiatives can take the sting out of an issue. A controversy can cease with the development of credible codes of conduct or divestment in countries with dubious regimes. It is, however, far from clear what a credible international code is, as will be illustrated in further detail in Chapter 12 and the cases discussed in Part III. Divestment can resolve the issue for the company in question, but it does not necessarily mean that the issue has ceased to exist. The effectiveness problems of semi-private or semi-public supervision have already been outlined in Chapter 7 (section 7.2).

The path to the regulation or settlement of issues remains controversial, though. NGOs often want issues regulated by government so as to give companies fewer opportunities to evade their responsibilities (Heath and Nelson, 1986: 196). NGOs try to propel issues such as GMO and child labour into the cycle as quickly as possible, if necessary, by deliberately bringing the company's reputation into discredit. But in doing so, they risk damaging their own reputations or imposing an inadequate solution on the issue at hand. NGOs can 'create' new issues and put them on the agenda of companies and society so as to raise consciousness and attract attention. The media is an effective instrument in getting issues on the public agenda and influencing behaviour and opinions (McCombs and Shaw, 1972). A field of tension is thus created, given that companies are generally not in favour of legislation as a means to resolve issues since it limits their operating freedom. This was the case at the end of the nineteenth century and still is.

9.5 CONCLUSION: TOWARDS A REAPPRAISAL OF PUBLIC AFFAIRS

This chapter showed that modern issues management has to deal with the characteristics of the international bargaining society as identified in Chapter 6. Growing institutional voids and regulatory gaps (Part I) have created the opportunity for bigger conformance and ideals gaps. Bigger, recurring, more complex and increasingly international issues have thus materialized. The difficulty is that no a priori primary responsibility can be assigned to any of the societal actors for resolving an issue. The occurrence of issues is bound to context and time: what is considered a problem in one societal system is not a problem in another societal setting or at another moment in time. An issues manager of a multinational corporation that takes the characteristics of an international bargaining society into account identifies particularly those issues that develop along the societal interfaces and for which the chief bearers of responsibility are undetermined and therefore open to the biggest controversy.

Following the four approaches to CSR as explained in Chapter 8, modern issues management in the first place presents a challenge for the function fulfilled by the department of Public Affairs (PA) in the firm. Table 9.3 lists the characteristics of the different approaches that can be adopted by the PA department. With each approach a reconsideration of the position in the company and, consequently, the name of the department is at stake.

Depending on the role of Public Affairs in a particular company, the various tools of CSR (brochures, sponsoring, corporate volunteering, BCI, see Table 8.1) acquire different meanings. A corporate volunteering initiative in a largely reactive firm can easily become part of a PR campaign. In some companies, Public Affairs still fulfils a primarily PR function, with core responsibilities being the publication of glossy information brochures and maintaining the company website. At best, the entrepreneurial vision of the company director will also be communicated to the outside world. As management becomes more aware of the importance of safeguarding the company's reputation, the reactive PA function acquires the added dimension of 'issues management' and relations management with relevant primary stakeholders (particularly with investors, governments and communities). In the event of product recalls or other issues, the PA department seeks to restore the public's trust in the company as fast as possible. In cases where firms are faced with a critical incident, the function of the PA department is to 'buffer' the company against claims of stakeholders. The interaction with stakeholders takes the shape of a 'debate', in which the company largely intends to reiterate its own stance on the issue, not to modify it.

The more active a company becomes, the more Public Affairs takes on a 'corporate communication' role so as to communicate (inside-out) the values and vision of the company to society. The 'trust me' stance of reactive firms, mitigates towards the perspective of assertive

Table 9.3 Functional orientation of PA: from reactive to proactive

Inactive	Reactive	Active	Proactive
'Corporate *Self-Responsibility*'	'Corporate Social *Responsiveness*'	'Corporate Social *Responsibility*'	'Corporate *Societal* Responsibility'
Public relations Entrepreneurship Principal–agent	Public Affairs Community/investor/ government relations Issues management Corporate reputation Corporate philanthropy	Corporate communication Business ethics Responsible entrepreneurship Corporate identity	Strategic corporate communication Strategic issues management Strategic philanthropy Strategic management Leadership
Buffering		Bridging	
Stakeholder information: no organized interaction other than via markets	Stakeholder debate	Societal dialogue and (informal) stakeholder contract	Interactive: (strategic) stakeholder dialogue

stakeholders into a 'prove it to me' stance. Business ethical principles are introduced and corporate philanthropy is engaged with in a more systematic manner (as opposed to the ad hoc philanthropy related to the inactive CSR stance, or the *opportunistic* philanthropy associated with the reactive CSR stance). The idea of 'corporate citizenship' embodies the active operational-ization and integration of CSR principles and stakeholder theory (see Chapter 10). Considerable controversy remains over the question of whether a corporation can (or should) be seen as autonomous agent (Waddock, 2002) – not least because it challenges the conceptual distinc-tion between civil society and the market (Chapter 1). Companies are also increasingly employing CSR principles to help shape their corporate identity.

In the fourth approach, PA moves beyond its specialist role to acquire a more integrated role in the form of strategic corporate communication and strategic issues management (as opposed to issues management as a responsive form of crisis management). Its function is to 'bridge' the gap between company and society through engaging (strategic) stakeholders in dialogue (rather than debate) in the formulation and implementation of company strategy. This also requires that PA is treated as part and parcel of the general (strategic) management and leadership responsibilities of the company's CEO. Whereas CSR in the active approach is linked with 'moral' leadership, CSR in the interactive approach is linked with 'strategic' leadership.[1] The adoption of any given approach depends as much on a manager's own choices as it does on the institutional characteristics of the bargaining society/societies in which they operate.

Whatever PA orientation is chosen by companies, the analysis in this chapter has shown that it is sensible for firms not to wait until an issue matures, but to come to a priori issue rank-ings and a more fundamental identification of primary and secondary responsibilities. This requires that the nature of the most important issues is considered in more detail, while the possible consequences for societies and firms are assessed. So, issues management becomes content bound as well, instead of an instrument of general management. It becomes important to identify in greater detail what is at stake and move from issues management as reactive crisis management to a form of strategic issues management that aims at new governance models. Are firms part of the problem and to what extent should they (or do they want to) be part of the solution? These questions will be addressed in the next chapter.

Chapter 10

The stakes: firms – part of the problem or part of the solution?

CHAPTER CONTENTS

10.1 INTRODUCTION: IDENTIFYING ISSUES, ASSIGNING RESPONSIBILITIES[1]

American sociologist C. Wright Mills warned not to 'allow public issues as they are officially formulated, or troubles as they are privately felt, to determine the problems that you take up for study' (Wright Mills, 1959: 226). A first prerequisite for effectively addressing societal issues is to analyse them as objectively as possible. But, in practice, issues are habitually approached and regarded as important on the basis of the (perceived) self-interest of firms. The strategies of issues managers thus tend to be relatively reactive, short-term and occasion oriented. This orientation is often reinforced by the relatively weak internal bargaining position of the Public Affairs/Corporate Communications department. A second prerequisite for effective Societal Interface Management is that societal issues *themselves* are tackled (see Chapter 8), not least because the most important issues have become governance issues (Chapter 9). The formulation and implementation of new societal goals takes place in 'bargaining arenas' (cf. Chapter 6). Previously, government played the role of facilitator in many of these arenas. Growing regulatory and institutional gaps, however, have made governance itself a subject of negotiation. The issues not only define the stakes, but also the bargaining arena: firms, governments and other stakeholders regularly convene in changing network constellations to discuss the 'hottest issues', often also in surprising locations. Can or should firms thus be considered part of the (societal) problem or part of the solution? Should food firms be expected to take responsibility for solving world hunger? Should car manufacturers contribute to slowing down global warming? Should toy manufacturers help to address child labour? In short: who is to be(come) the 'issue owner'?

The objective of this chapter is to identify what is at stake and who should be considered chiefly responsible for tackling major societal issues: companies, governments or citizens? There are hundreds of societal issues that demand the attention of managers. On what basis should issues be selected, assessed and prioritized? So-called 'global issues' might provide a starting point for identifying the most relevant issues. Simmons and de Jonge (2001) define global issues as concerns that cannot be addressed successfully in the present international institutional framework. Such issues are global challenges in areas 'where changing settings are altering familiar assumptions about who sets policy, how, and with what results' (ibid.: 3). Prioritizing global issues, however, proves to be a difficult task (see Box 10.1).

Disputes about the institutional design of society – whether and what rules should be adopted – lie at the heart of all major issues (Chapter 9). In the assignation of primary and secondary responsibilities, three categories of issues emerge that will be discussed in this chapter.

1   *Stretch issues (Firms as cause of the problem).* When specific actors cause a particular problem, it seems reasonable that they take primary responsibility for solving it or addressing its consequences. Since issues necessarily arise in regulatory voids, it could also imply that other actors first stipulate the regulatory and moral boundaries within which the responsible actors are to take the appropriate action (section 10.2).
2   *Institutional issues (Firms as partially responsible).* When actors from various backgrounds are considered part of a problem it follows that they should also become part of the solution. While no individual actor bears primary responsibility, some may have a greater part in the problem or may be in a more powerful position than others. These actors can thus be considered more responsible for initiating solutions (section 10.3).
3   *Agenda-setting issues (Firms as only part of the solution).* Sometimes, specific actors are targeted to come up with solutions for extremely complex problems, anticipated problems or problems related to the primary responsibilities of other actors. These targeted actors may not be in a position to address the source of the problem directly, but can nevertheless broaden the range of possible solutions (section 10.4).

10.2 STRETCH ISSUES AND PRIMARY RESPONSIBILITIES

A popular Latin aphorism reads '*sibi quisque peccat*' – each person is responsible for their own sins. In most cultures there are similar sayings denoting the same simple truth: those who are the cause of a problem bear primary responsibility for solving it. In other words: clean up your own mess! Strictly speaking, an actor's primary responsibilities are related to those areas where society has granted them a licence to operate (Wood, 1991). Managers of firms are responsible for the impact of their policies, practices and operations on society. The latter is also referred to as the principle of 'public responsibility' and 'accountability'. Primary responsibilities thus also depend on the position of actors in the societal triangle. What the principles of public responsibility and accountability imply in practice strongly depends on circumstances. For instance, the degree to which firms should provide product information depends on government regulation, which differs from country to country and from product to product (see Chapter 12). But when firms are the source of particular problems – for instance, when managers stretch the rules that govern their accountability by means of very creative bookkeeping practices – they are necessarily part of the solution as well. Figure 10.1 positions major societal issues that coincide with the primary responsibility of each sphere in the greater context of the societal triangle.

BOX 10.1 PRIORITIZING GLOBAL ISSUES?

As soon as complex issues arise, efforts are undertaken to come to a priority ranking. The ranking process itself is an integral part of international bargaining processes. Most rankings prioritize issues that are pertinent in developing countries. Three recent priority-setting initiatives that employ different methodologies and occupy different positions in the Triple-E framework received widespread public attention.

- **Equity orientation: Millennium Development Goals.** In 2001 the members of the United Nations gathered in New York for the Millennium Summit to formulate the Millennium Development Goals. They identified eight issues: (1) poverty and hunger, (2) primary education, (3) gender equality, (4) child mortality, (5) maternal health, (6) HIV/Aids and diseases such as malaria and tuberculosis, (7) environmental sustainability, including deforestation, water and sanitation, (8) global partnership for development. These issues feature prominently in the policies, the rhetoric and around the bargaining table of governments, NGOs and international organizations. Firms that invest in developing countries are increasingly requested to comply with the Millennium Development Goals. The targets are very ambitious – for instance, halving global poverty and hunger and making primary school education accessible by 2015. The means to achieve these goals, however, were hardly specified. In 2005, an evaluation commission (http://unmp.forumone.com) concluded that on the basis of current efforts, only one goal could feasibly be realized.

- **Efficiency orientation: The Copenhagen Consensus.** In 2004, the controversial Danish economist Lomborg invited a select group of economists (including three Nobel laureates) to draw up a priority list of global issues that could be *efficiently* addressed in the short term. The group criticized the Millennium Development Goals for a lack of clear choices. The Copenhagen Consensus group concluded that contagious diseases such as HIV/Aids and malaria, malnutrition, water and sanitation should be at the top of the issues list. Migration and climate change ranked low on the list. The selection principle employed by the group was quite arbitrary, though. It *excluded* a number of issues due to (1) lack of data (corruption), (2) their complexity (several issues) or (3) because the panel could not come up with good proposals to effectively address the issue (education and security).

- **Process orientation: Twenty global problems.** The World Bank's vice president for Europe, J.F. Rischard, is the author of the book *High Noon* (2002). Even though the World Bank has not officially endorsed the ideas contained in this book, it has become quite influential. Rischard specifies 20 'Global Issues Networks' as the arena in which 20 global issues can best be discussed. Rischard distinguishes three categories of global issues: (1) issues that concern all inhabitants of earth (*the Global Commons; Sharing our Planet*), (2) issues that require international commitment (*Sharing our Humanity*) and (3) issues that require international regulation (*Sharing our Rule Book*).

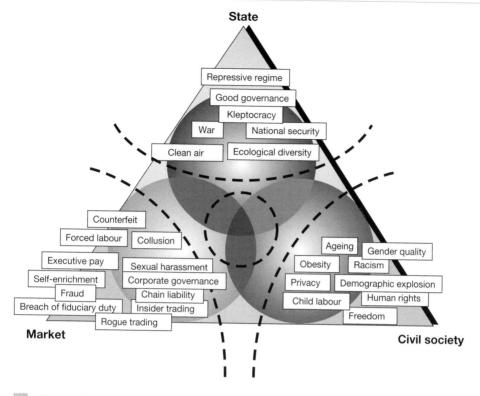

Figure 10.1 *Primary responsibility issues*

States: government as source of the problem

The primary responsibility of government is to represent the common interests of its citizens. This responsibility boils down to the effective provision of public goods such as national security (including defence and policing), a solid legal framework, preventing public bads (environmental degradation and pollution) and sufficient public access to basic resources (such as water, energy and clean air). There are no means available to price 'externalities' sufficiently (see Chapters 1 and 2), so the provision of public goods and services remains a primary responsibility of public officials. Governments that do not adhere to 'good governance' practices in providing public goods and services lose their legitimacy either at home or abroad. 'Good governance', however, is not a neutral concept and it is a topic of heated debate around the world. Conversely, 'bad governance' is slightly easier to describe, certainly when rulers forcefully extend their primary responsibilities to other countries (war), or when they abuse their position for personal gain (kleptocracy) or abuse their power for political gain (authoritarian or repressive regimes).

Civil society: citizens as source of the problem

Citizens find legitimacy in dealing with their 'personal' and 'social' realms, which include their choices for particular consumption patterns, their choice to engage (or not) in specific organizations such as churches, sport clubs and associations that give their life a social and cultural

173

meaning. Individuals' primary responsibility pertains to the way they deal with global issues that can be related back to themselves such as ageing, gender inequality, number of children (leading to population explosions), eating habits (leading to obesity or other health problems), individual freedom and privacy. Individual citizens can be held responsible by others for their conduct so long as they have access to information about the consequences of their choices. For example, if adults knowingly purchase products that are the direct result of forced labour or that have serious environmental impacts, they are responsible for their actions even if they do not have any alternatives. But reliable information on the *indirect* consequences of particular consumption patterns is not that readily available.

Most communities uphold some notion of basic human rights. Some cultures emphasize individual human rights, while in other cultures group or collective rights prevail. With rights also come duties. If basic social rights – such as the right to privacy – are violated by the stretching behaviour of individuals, it can be argued that the primary responsibility lies with the community (the family, the village, the club) to deal with this. The way such a violation is dealt with is largely context and culture bound. Incidents of racism, gender inequality, or violation of privacy, for instance, can be addressed by government action, but the traditional instrument of governments – laws – can never substitute for structural activities of the people themselves in these areas.

Markets: managers and firms as source of the problem

The primary responsibilities of firms and managers are related to the efficient and effective operating of markets in order to produce and distribute goods and services that society needs. Most societies have given firms considerable independence, trust and legitimacy in operating market institutions on behalf of society. Managers who attempt to stretch their primary responsibilities jeopardize this legitimacy. When companies fail to meet their primary responsibilities, they can, in principle, be held *accountable* for their actions. Three types of stretch issues for firms can be distinguished: (a) personal and company internal: involving abuse of fiduciary powers; (b) competitive: frustrating effective markets through collusion and corruption; (c) strategic: problematic choice of industry.

Stretching personal duties

The public responsibility of corporate managers is represented by the principle of 'fiduciary duty', the obligation to act in the best interest of the owners of the company. In Anglo-Saxon countries the fiduciary responsibilities of managers focuses largely on the interests of the shareholders, while in non-Anglo-Saxon countries other stakeholders such as employees are usually taken into account as well. The discussion on the fiduciary duty of managers became more acute in the second half of the 1990s following a large number of corporate 'scandals' involving top executives of big corporations. As a result the legitimacy of business has decreased considerably. Table 10.1 lists prominent cases in the OECD region for the period 1998–2004. Few countries were spared some form of corporate 'scandal' involving allegations of insider trading, executive compensation, the bending of accountancy rules, self-enrichment through excessive bonuses, or fraud and corruption.

Are these 'scandals' incidents or do they reveal structural patterns? A number of the scandals resulted in the sentencing or resignation (or worse) of the people involved. Thus it could be argued that the outcome of these scandals testifies to the effective functioning of the firms' auto-correction powers, or to the effectiveness of the judiciary system in enforcing existing rules. But the scandals also revealed faultlines in institutional arrangements and an inaptitude

Table 10.1 Corporate 'scandals' involving top executives* of leading companies, 1998–2004

Insider trading	Fraud/corruption	Bending of accountancy rules	Excessive executive payments
Brink# (World Online), Boonstra## (Philips), Stewart@, Waksal@ (Imclone), Messier# (Homestore, AOL Time Warner), Rankin*+ (RBC Dominion Securities), Tsutsumi (conglomerate)@	Parmalat (Tanzi@, Tonna@, Bassi+), WorldCom (Ebbers@#, Sullivan@)~, SK Group (Chey Tae-won@, Son Kil-Seung), Hyundai (Chun Mong-Hun+), Enron (Lay#@), First Allied (Rusnak)&, National Australia Bank** (Cicutto#**), Sumitomo bank (Hamanaka)**, China Construction Bank/ Central Bankε, Arthur Andersen~, JP Morgan++, Citigroup++, Merrill Lynch++, Boeing (Condit#), Coca-Cola, Yukos (Chodorkovski, Lebedev@), Elf (Le Floch-Prigent@)	Enron (Skilling@, Fastow@)~+, Tyco (Kozlowski#@, Swartz#@), Ahold (Van der Hoeven#, Meurs#), Vivendi – Universal (Messier#@), Adecco (Weber#), Resona (Japan), SembCorp (Singapore), Lernout&Hauspie (Belgium), Global Crossing~, KPNQ west (Neth.)~, Healthsouth, Xerox, Reliant Energy, PWC, AOL Time Warners, Shell (Watts)#, Computer Associates (Kumar, Richards)@, Fannie Mae (Raines#, Howard#)	Ahold (Van der Hoeven#, Moberg), KPN (Scheepbouwer), New York Stock Exchange (Grasso)#, Skandia, ABB (Sweden), Adecco (Switzerland), Mannesmann (Germany)##, Hollinger (Canada) (Black)#, GlaxoSmithKline (Garnier), Carrefour (Bernard)#

Source: press clippings; * CEOs, CFOs or other directors; @ jail sentences, imprisoned; ~ bankruptcy or taken over; +suicide/deceased; ε executed; ## case acquitted; # resigned; ++ financial settlement of charges (without admitting guilt); ** 'Rogue trading'; *+ suspended

in dealing with new business trends and strategies, which invite managers to explore the boundaries of their fiduciary duties.

In most of the cases it is difficult to distinguish between company and personal strategies. Executive salaries increasingly took the form of stock options in the company – legitimized by the notion that it enhances loyalty of relatively mobile CEOs (see Chapter 3). Influencing or manipulating the market capitalization of their companies thus became all the more important for top managers. Several studies have suggested that the primary motivation for the wave of mergers in the 1990s was not the (supposed) performance-enhancing effects of the new combination, but the promise of higher earnings for top managers.

The succession of affairs coincided with the timely appearance of regulatory voids. The 'rogue trading' scandals (Barings, Sumitomo Bank, National Australia) of the mid-1990s largely involved financial professionals who created fictitious options positions in order to hide current losses and hedge real positions. But the scandals also reflected an attempt by corporate managers to find a way of dealing with the relatively new futures and derivatives market. This new market was difficult to regulate and even to define. All managers were, therefore, to a certain extent, stretching the rules that govern their fiduciary duties to participate in a new market. The scandals highlighted the difficulties of interpreting (extensive and ambiguous) rules that also made it difficult to prove wrongdoing in court. The firms involved all claimed that the managers acted without the consent of top management, but given the widespread incidence of these practices, it remains a point of debate.

Since regulation can only solve part of the problem, and lags behind the strategic realities of firms, the discussion has shifted to the principles of governance for publicly owned corporations. The discussion focuses on the separation of ownership and control, and an increase in transparency, control and accountability. But the discussion also touches on a more fundamental matter: the limited personal liability of owners (shareholders). What has been an important condition for growth in the early phases of capitalism (risk-taking on the basis of limited liability) has turned into a formula for irresponsible management behaviour and low levels of shareholder commitment. An increasing number of observers (Micklethwait and Wooldridge, 2003; Mitchel, 2001; Kamp, 2003) are calling for the abolition of the limited liability of shareholders. They argue that abolishing the system of limited liability altogether would make business more accountable and responsible. This proposal would revolutionize the system of modern capitalism, though, and is not really seriously considered in any country. The Sarbanes-Oxley Act, which was enacted in the wake of the Enron and other financial debacles in the US, imposes greater personal liability on top managers of companies, but not on shareholders. No other country has yet followed the American example.

Stretching competition

Institutions are required for the optimal functioning of markets. And market institutions are principally vested in the operational practice of companies. So a chief responsibility of managers is to ensure that existing markets function as optimally as possible. It is generally considered inappropriate for firms to deceive consumers. But, markets take many forms and contain considerable information assymetries and 'failures' (cf. Chapter 1). The regulation of competition in markets around the world takes many forms as well (see Chapter 12). Divergent conceptions of markets and appropriate competitive strategies lie at the heart of the international rivalry between different models of capitalism (see Part I). As a result it is difficult to draw a clear distinction between abusive and non-abusive behaviour of firms. This also holds for two main issues that stretch the rules that govern the competitive strategies of firms beyond their primary responsibilities: collusion and counterfeit.

Collusion is defined as a secret activity undertaken by two or more actors for the purpose of fraud (the deliberate misrepresentation or concealment of information to secure illegal or unfair gain). Collusion takes place when rival companies in the same industry cooperate in a manner that is mutually beneficial – for instance, through price fixing or forming cartels to divide the market. But the boundary between explicit and implicit collusion is not always clear. Collusion is difficult to prove in oligopolistic industries where companies could raise prices as a matter of industry dynamics rather than fraudulent conspiracies. In many countries (see Chapter 2) there are networks of collaborating firms that in other countries would be considered collusive. From the perspective of a liberal governance regime, the 'collaborative' behaviour of big firms operating in Japanese *Keiretsu*, Korean *Chaebol*, Chinese *Guangxi* networks or in Italian networks of smaller and medium-sized firms, for instance, is generally considered to be improper.

Counterfeit business is less difficult to identify, but equally difficult to tackle. Counterfeit refers to the production and distribution of fake or imitation products that often carry the name of a popular brand, but do not have the product qualities associated with it. Trade in counterfeit goods includes items from French designer labels being copied by Italian producers (Italy being Europe's largest producer and consumer of counterfeit products), the illegal production of cigarettes in Paraguay (Latin America's biggest counterfeit base), American pharmaceutical products and Swiss Rolex watches and Japanese game controllers produced by Chinese producers (China being the world's largest producer representing two-thirds of counterfeit goods) (*Business Week*, 7 February 2005).

176

Stretching strategy

Some industries clearly experience greater legitimacy problems than other industries. Companies whose products are a direct source of health problems or that violate fundamental rights of states and citizens can be regarded as the primary cause of the problem and therefore chiefly responsible for solving it. Business dealings that involve trade in human organs, hard drugs and illegal weapons or slavery and human trafficking are universally considered to be illegitimate. Those in charge of these transactions knowingly engage in activities that pose serious risks to the health and well-being of the users of their products and/or other people involved – which is why it is illegal in most (not all) countries. But what about products such as tobacco, alcohol or soft drugs (see Chapter 8)? Government regulations on these products are relatively ambiguous. Consumers are considered capable of judging for themselves the consequences of the trade-off between short-term pleasure and longer-term health problems (see above). However, if cigarette producers deliberately add addictive substances to their product without informing their customers, or if they target children who are less capable of making a well-considered trade-off, they are responsible for the negative consequences of their actions. Whether consumers will, indeed, be appropriately compensated in the event that a company crosses this line depends on the national institutional set-up (see Chapter 12). With due reference to the dangers of the product on packets and a responsible marketing strategy, producers essentially pass the primary responsibility back to consumers. After all, the sovereignty of the consumer includes the choice *not* to consume a product.

10.3 INSTITUTIONAL ISSUES AND INTERFACE RESPONSIBILITIES: FIRMS AS PARTIALLY RESPONSIBLE

The most pervasive global issues develop along the societal interfaces where the absence of adequate institutions is particularly tangible. No actor bears complete and sole responsibility for creating the problem, which makes the search for a solution an intricate process as well. Interface issues embody all the dilemmas of the bargaining society: (1) the potential undersupply of solutions to the problem due to underinvestment; (2) the sub-optimal distribution of cost and benefits; (3) short-term solutions are favoured over long-term solutions; (4) actors operating in one institutional setting try to shift the burden on to others (so as to free-ride on the efforts of others); (5) issues are strongly intertwined – addressing one problem could aggravate another; (6) the definition of the problem itself becomes subject to negotiation; (7) solutions are sought in increasing the operation of 'markets'– even when this is not feasible or sensible. Figure 10.2 positions most important institutional issues along the three societal interfaces.

An interactive and discursive approach to ethics (see Chapter 8) where the parties involved negotiate the institutional framework in which they are to operate is particularly suited to interface issues. Distributional questions lie at the core of all interface issues: although solutions are available the uneven distribution of burdens renders the designation of responsibilities controversial. The problem of hunger, for instance, cannot be attributed to worldwide food scarcity, but to the unequal distribution of food and nutrition around the world. Most of the issues involve challenges for developing as well as developed nations. It is true that developing countries often confront these problems in their most extreme form, but hunger, illiteracy, contagious diseases, human trafficking and over-fishing have long ceased to be problems restricted to developing countries.

Since it is seldom clear which actor should take primary responsibility for addressing an issue, the focal point of disputes between NGOs, governments and firms is often on the

177

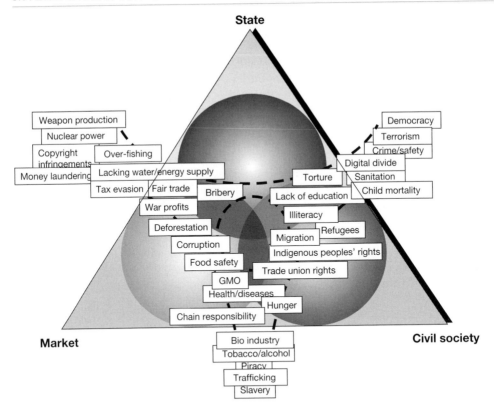

Figure 10.2 Interface issues

question of who has (or might have) the 'moral authority' in a particular issue. van Riel and others (in Schultz *et al.*, 2000) depict this as the quest for a 'sustainable corporate story' – you can only protect your interests if you have a good story. In terms of the Triple-E model introduced in Chapter 8, a sustainable corporate story operationalizes the pursuit of Effectiveness by making a reasonable trade-off between Equity and Efficiency. In practice, this ambition often requires new concepts that enable a richer understanding and more adequate indicators/ measures of 'progress'. A sustainable corporate story is challenged at three junctions: (1) at the public–private interface (core issue: ecology); (2) at the profit–non-profit interface (core issue: health); and (3) at the market–society interface (core issues: economic growth, unemployment and poverty).

Sustainability challenge #1: ecology – a trade-off between public and private interests

Macro-economic and generic rights are at stake at the public–private interface and are linked to the availability of, and access to, resources and public goods. One of the biggest controversies between firms and governments concerns the allocation of responsibilities for ecological issues. The world faces an unequal distribution of pollution, energy and clean water, a rapid depletion of forests and fish stocks and the (seemingly) universal problem of global warming. Several ecological issues have a geographical dimension with benefits and burdens, causes and consequences unequally distributed over countries and regions.

Take the issue of global warming for instance. Who is to blame for the issue in the first place? Industrialized countries with their 'unsustainable' economic growth models that are based on the consumption of huge quantities of non-renewable and highly polluting energy resources can be considered chiefly responsible. Due to their high levels of consumption, the distribution of pollution in the world is decidedly uneven. Industrialized countries produce more than 80 per cent of the world's pollution while around 15 per cent of the world's population live there. The American economy produces around 25 per cent of all greenhouse gases. These figures are relatively undisputed. Additionally, in an effort to assign responsibility for specific issues, environmental groups often single out specific groups of firms and consumers. The discussion becomes 'personal' and part of a bargaining process that (whether intentional or not) often obscures rather than facilitates the discussion. In 2003, for instance, Friends of the Earth International published a report, 'Exxon's climate footprint', which states that since 1882 when it was founded as Standard Oil Trust, the company's operations and the burning of its products have contributed between 4.7 and 5.3 per cent of all human-made carbon dioxide emissions. In February 2004, partly in response to FoE, ExxonMobil released a report stating that the fuel consumption of consumers by far accounts for the greatest part of emissions (87 per cent) while petroleum industry operations account for the rest (13 per cent). Chapter 18 discusses this case in more detail.

Other observers place the primary responsibility for global warming on the 'military industrial complex' in general and the US military in particular. The US military is the single largest consumer of fossil fuels and thus the single largest 'customer' responsible for emissions. Yet other studies assign primary responsibility to power companies. According to research of the WWF (Graus *et al.*, 2004), the power sector is the single biggest emitter of greenhouse gases, responsible for 37 per cent of CO_2 emissions from the burning of fossil fuels. The difficulty with these statements is that they can all be correct simultaneously. Consumers such as the military, power plants or individuals driving cars all use fuels that are produced and distributed by oil firms, of which ExxonMobil is one of the biggest. Assigning responsibility to single actors in a long and international supply chain is never simple.

An ecologically sustainable corporate story?

A 'sustainable corporate story' (Schultz *et al.*, 2000) involves both strategic and operational choices. A credible and realistic sustainable corporate story takes into account industry dynamics and delineates the role that individual firms can or should adopt. The dynamics of the industry for a large part determines the role other actors such as government and civil society can realistically adopt. Ecological problems related to renewable natural resources such as timber, for example, exhibit a different dynamic to ecological problems related to non-renewable resources such as oil and coal. It is clear that the strategic alternative to fossil fuels and the solution to ecological problems in general and global warming specifically, lies in the diffusion of safe, renewable energy sources such as solar and wind energy. But these alternatives are not yet economically viable. Global warming poses a strategic problem for consumers of fossil fuels and their consumption patterns. The pollution related to greenhouse gas emissions first affects the quality of consumers' lives. But the price of existing resources and the availability of alternatives strongly influence the choices consumers make. Even if a large number of consumers are prepared to limit their consumption of fossil fuels, this will not necessarily result in the appropriate behaviour by the energy providers. Prices are influenced by oligopolistic competition within the industry, cartel agreements among producing countries (such as OPEC) and levies imposed on fuel products by governments. If governments do not assume their responsibility to prevent or limit negative externalities or are not prepared to abandon economic growth in favour of longer term ecological sustainability, individual consumers will have great difficulty exerting enough buying power to influence the strategies of firms.

Government attempts to articulate a sustainable story on global warming have been rather ambiguous. The US (federal) administration is most sceptical of the risks and dangers of global warming and least willing to support multilateral approaches such as the 1997 Kyoto Treaty. Liberal regimes in general are more inclined to adopt a voluntary approach to the issue, at the same time expecting much from technological solutions that give rise to a particular dilemma. In order to invest in technological solutions, firms have to grow and reap profits. So short-term measures that increase cost and lower profits (certainly when aimed at very vague issues such as global warming) would jeopardize economic growth and thus limit the ability of firms to come up with future solutions. Individual US states as well as parts of the business community, in particular the insurance industry, which face claims by people suffering from pollution, are taking the threat more seriously (*FT*, 4 February 2005). Major developing countries such as China or India have not indicated a willingness to support the multilateral regulation either. As developing countries they are not yet required to ratify the Kyoto Treaty, which partly accounts for their reluctance to take measures that might have a negative impact on economic growth. Moreover, these countries' per capita contribution to global warming amounts to less than one-tenth of the average European or American citizen. Transition economies such as Russia ratified the Kyoto Treaty under major political pressure from Western European governments. Looking to the future, the International Energy Agency expects a 60 per cent rise in energy use in Asian countries by 2030. With the bulk of emissions to be generated by non-Kyoto countries in the future, Europe for example will only be responsible for 8 per cent of global CO_2 emissions.

The Kyoto Protocol is considered insufficient (too limited, too late) and bound to be ineffective especially since emission rights and standards can be traded between countries. Critics claim that the production of energy-intensive goods will be relocated to countries that have a less effective energy regime – so-called 'pollution havens'. The degree to which the internationalization of multinationals has really been triggered by the lower environmental costs in pollution havens however has been disputed (cf. Kolk and van Tulder, 2004a). Multinationals tend to have stricter environmental rules than their host countries. The relocation of production can thus be considered positive for the local ecology (and economy), although it lowers the pressure on polluting industries to reduce their emissions significantly. The Kyoto Protocol, nevertheless, can have perverse and even unintended effects. Instead of effecting a direct reduction of CO_2 emissions in their home countries, it further encourages industries to relocate activities to developing countries – and earn additional emission rights to boot. It helps industrialized countries to reach their target under the Kyoto Protocol, but without contributing to overall CO_2 reduction.

Sustainable industry initiatives?

In the short term, it seems unlikely that governments and consumers – given the instruments and bargaining arenas available to them – will come up with a suitable sustainable story on global warming. What about the producers of goods and services that generate the majority of CO_2 emissions? Their strategic challenge is to offer economically feasible alternatives with lower emissions to consumers. In an overview of the climate-change strategies of a large sample of *Fortune* Global 500 companies, Kolk and Pinkse (2005) identify a number of emerging strategies. More than two-thirds of all firms are classified as so-called 'cautious planners' and 'emergent planners'. Cautious planners are extremely vague on the issue and reactive.

Emergent planners have yet to implement a comprehensive climate strategy. The firms that are attempting to develop a more proactive stance, through a combination of the active pursuit of reduction targets and active emissions trading, represented the smallest group (4 per cent) of all *Fortune* 500 companies analysed.

If we were to identify and assign primary responsibility to the industries whose products are most implicated in climate change, three seem particularly relevant: the car industry, the oil industry and power companies. First, many car firms have supported initiatives to putting global climate change on the bargaining agenda. Many car firms have been active in developing hybrid and/or hydrogen cars that are less polluting and more fuel efficient. Bottlenecks still exist in the full-scale commercialization of these cars and the further technological development of critical parts such as fuel cells. Part of the problem is a lack of appropriate national regulation – the costs of negative externalities (pollution) are still not included in the price of petrol. Consumer preferences and purchasing behaviour also seem to be for fuel-guzzling cars. At the same time that car manufacturers were engaged in a modest attempt to market hybrid cars, four-wheel drive vehicles became the biggest car sales success of the twenty-first century. These vehicles are less fuel efficient and more polluting than previous generations. Should car manufacturers cease manufacturing four-wheel drive cars?

Second, major multinationals in the oil industry have also voiced a commitment to the Kyoto Protocol as far as their operations are concerned (Kolk and Levy, 2001). While none of the oil majors have plans to move out of oil in the foreseeable future, most actively engage in efforts to search for more sustainable alternatives to fossil fuels. British Petroleum has repositioned itself as a 'green company' (together with a major rebranding strategy). It is now the world's largest producer of solar energy systems. Shell invested US$500 million in the creation of a renewables business. Texaco invested substantial resources in hydrogen-powered fuel cells. But ExxonMobil has maintained its main strategic orientation and is focusing on improving petroleum manufacturing efficiency, as well as the development of advanced vehicles and fuels together with automobile manufacturers. The strategy is legitimized by the perceived value of the company by investors, as expressed on the capital market. In 2004, ExxonMobil was the company with the highest market capitalization (US$383 billion) in the world (see also Chapter 18). Compared to the alleged gravity of the issue of global warming, the greening efforts of the oil majors still seem somewhat modest.

Finally, the WWF conducted a study of 72 of the world's leading power companies to establish whether these companies, which produce around two-thirds of all electricity in OECD countries and Russia, have made any attempt to change to more renewable energy sources. American and Japanese companies came out worst, European companies fared slightly better. None can be said to have made significant changes. Of the European companies, only one-fifth has a greater than 2 per cent share of renewable energy in their fuel mix. According to the WWF, the power sector's contribution to climate change 'threatens the very development that electricity promotes' (www.wwf.org, consulted February 2005). It can thus be concluded that strategically, industry, governments and consumers are 'stuck in the middle' in their approach to major ecological issues such as global warming and deforestation.

Operational challenges: developing concepts and trademarks

On an operational level, a sustainable corporate story requires that a company's environmental strategy is aligned with its environmental management systems (Kolk, 2000; van de Wateringen, 2005). A number of conceptual and practical challenges also need to be overcome. Global warming and negative externalities associated with the unsustainable use of renewable and non-renewable resources are difficult to quantify. Various interesting concepts and practical instruments (such as trademarks) have, however, been developed to gauge the overall environmental impact of products. The concept 'ecological footprint' is one such effort. Mapping the ecological footprint of particular products from cradle to grave enables consumers to form an opinion on its sustainability. Research by UNESCO, for instance, focused on the amount of water that is required to produce goods and services that are consumed on a large scale in developed countries. To produce one cup of coffee 140 litres of water is required. The production of one hamburger requires 2,400 litres of water, whereas a cotton shirt requires more than 4,000 litres of water (www.waterfootprint.org). The implementation of this conceptual instrument shows that the unequal distribution of clean water over the world, including sanitary and health problems associated with a lack of access to clean water, is strongly influenced by the nature and organization of the international value chain across borders.

Other ecological initiatives that facilitate responsible conduct of critical *consumers* have developed in two areas in particular: air travel and forest products. First, consider air travel. *Treesfortravel* is a non-profit foundation that sells certificates to travellers so that new forests can be planted to compensate for greenhouse gas emissions as a result of air travel. The measure is based on research of the Dutch National Institute for Health and Environment which has established the exact number of new trees that are required to compensate for the volume of greenhouse gases that are released in the course of travelling from A to B. This initiative – and a rapidly growing number of related initiatives – addresses the problem of deforestation in conjunction with global warming in a very practical manner.

Second, ecological product labelling and certification is primarily aimed at the (critical) consumers of particular products. But labelling is fraught with a large number of practical and regulatory problems (see Chapter 12). Ecological issues have generated a wealth of labelling and certification schemes. Very broad and difficult to quantify problems such as global warming, however, are difficult to capture in a label. More concrete problems such as deforestation are easier to communicate. The Forest Stewardship council (FSC) trademark – a tick and tree symbol – has, therefore, become one of the most successful and most international initiatives. The FSC provides standard setting, trademark assurance and accreditation services for companies and organizations interested in responsible forestry. The trademark should enable customers to recognize responsible forestry products in the store. Major retailers in Europe, North America, South America and Japan have adopted FSC certification. FSC claims that since its inception in 1993, '48 million hectares in more than 60 countries have been certified according to FSC standards while several thousand products are produced using FSC certified wood and carrying the FSC trademark' (www.fsc.org). To put this effort into perspective: in 2000, more than 12 million hectares of forests were cleared and the amount is still growing. So the FSC trademark addresses a relatively small – but not insubstantial – part of the deforestation problem. Other NGOs still have doubts whether FSC presents the right approach.[2]

Sustainability challenge #2: health – trade-off between profit and non-profit

Along the market–civil society interface, individual and social rights are at stake. These rights include negative rights such as the right not to be forced into labour and not to be discriminated against, as well as substantive rights to health, safety and security. Interface controversies very often revolve around the question of whether the unequal distribution of individual and social rights is caused and/or can be solved by a greater involvement of markets and for-profit actors. One such controversy is health, which is strongly related to unequal levels of vulnerability to disease and unequal access to medication in particular. Health as an issue has two dimensions: prevention of health problems and treatment of health problems.

Health problems and disease are strongly related to other issues such as hunger/malnutrition, living conditions (sanitation), education and relative poverty.[3] Yet even widespread structural prevention measures cannot stop the occurrence of health problems and these need medical treatment. Medical treatment issues have four dimensions: (a) treatment of 'avoidable' diseases, (b) expensive treatments for diseases, (c) treatment with unintended side-effects, and (d) future treatments for diseases.

Avoidable diseases are diseases for which relatively cheap (generic) medicines are available and for which only basic access to the national health system (hospitals, general practitioners) is required. According to the WHO, approximately 30 per cent of the world's population have no access to any form of health care. The WHO calculated in 1999 that 48 per cent of the people who die before the age of 45 are victims of infectious diseases.

Expensive diseases are diseases and health problems for which treatments are available, but at high cost. The cost of these treatments is sometimes due to the experimental stage of the research or sometimes due to the pricing strategies of, for instance, the pharmaceutical companies that developed the medicine. High prices of medicine are a necessary – but strongly disputed – part of the international patenting regime which was essentially adopted to stimulate private companies to invest in the development of new medicines. The controversy surrounding HIV/Aids medication provides an excellent example of the consequences of pricing and patenting rules.

Unintended side-effects refer to medication that creates other health problems. This problem bears upon the trade-off between appropriate safety and security regulations vis-à-vis the desire of companies (but also of patients) to quickly bring treatments onto the market.

Future treatments apply to diseases for which no cure (yet) exists and which thus rely on the development of new cures. The growing commercialization of research (see Chapter 3), including partnerships between pharmaceutical companies and universities, has resulted in sometimes peculiar research priorities. Considerably more research funds are, for instance, allocated to cosmetic and plastic surgery than to developing affordable basic treatments for diseases typically found in developing countries such as meningitis, malaria or tuberculosis. According to assessments of the Global Forum for Health Research (2002) less than 10 per cent of global spending on health research is devoted to diseases or conditions that account for 90 per cent of the global disease burden. It is – wrongfully – assumed that current technical tools are sufficient for effective disease control. There is a global 'drugs gap' (Reich, 2000), in which the private sector invests almost exclusively in drugs for the developed world. Can (pharmaceutical) firms be held accountable for *not* investing in the development of certain medicines?

Sustainable corporate stories: health through prevention

Health through prevention can be considered a primary responsibility of civil society in interaction with national governments. Citizens and governments make the choice for a basic health model – including a view on hygiene. Strategic decisions on investment in basic health care or sanitation infrastructure are difficult to implement without government support. Even if certain parts of a town privatize their health system, they remain vulnerable to negative externalities and spillover effects of contagious diseases originating in other parts of the town. It is difficult to keep disease geographically contained. Investment in sufficient basic health care requires a 'positive duty' approach (Chapter 8) aimed at creating the preconditions for further development, long-term profitability and economic development.

Prevention is also in the direct interest of industries that are either confronted with the negative health effects due to a lack of prevention or preventative health products. There are three main industries that face the challenge of articulating a sustainable corporate story on health: food, insurance and sanitation.

HEALTHY FOOD

The main industry that needs to consider the link between healthy eating habits and more nutritious dishes/products is the food processing industry in general and the 'fast/junk food' industry in particular. Major food processing firms such as Unilever have traditionally adopted a technological and product-oriented approach to the issue. At the moment, some investment projects aim at the development of so-called 'designer foods' that are aimed at preventing health problems from appearing. Genomics is applied to create healthy dishes that are primarily aimed at up-market consumers. Fast-food chains and mass food producers such as General Mills, Kraft, Nestlé or Coca-Cola, on the other hand, are particularly well positioned to lower fat and salt in their products. Their approach to promote sustainable eating habits is not considered very convincing by many critical NGOs. McDonald's only expanded its menu to include healthier options and smaller portions, after the release of Morgan Spurlock's documentary film 'Supersize Me' in 2004. Most companies seem to include more healthful food items in their product range or promote balanced meals primarily as an effort to avoid new obesity litigation (*FT*, 24 February 2005). General Mills launched a web-based campaign called 'Mix-Up Dinner; Get Your Greens!'; Kraft Foods voluntarily pledged to stop advertising certain junk foods to the under-11 market (*FT*, 24 February 2005). Whether these initiatives will lead to a full-scale upgrading of their product range, however, is doubtful. The trade-off between healthful and cheap food poses serious dilemmas. The production of cheap food is also strongly related to ecological problems.

The 'slow food' movement, which has a much more comprehensive approach in that it can almost be said to endorse a particular lifestyle that appeals largely to high-end consumers, is rapidly gaining ground throughout the world. Founded in Italy, the slow food movement is grounded in equity principles such as greater enjoyment in eating and drinking (higher quality of life through food), and consumption of seasonal foods, which is aimed at increasing the consumption of local produce and reducing the negative environmental impact of importing exotic and out-of-season foods from far-away countries. The biggest challenge of the slow food movement – in order to really develop a 'sustainable corporate story' – is to get a foothold in the lower end of the market and thus provide an economically viable alternative for the fast food movement.

HEALTHY RISKS

Health insurance companies have always based their risk acceptance profiles on an assessment of the relative health of their prospective customers – within the boundaries of national legislation. Recently, some health insurance companies – in collaboration with food companies – have started to show an interest in supporting good eating habits to lower the incidence of specific diseases. This approach is still in its infancy, though.

HEALTHY GROWTH

The easiest approach to disease prevention, however, remains economic growth coupled with an equitable distribution of income and/or access to a public health and education system. Governments that accept their primary governance responsibilities provide adequate sanitation infrastructure and show active support for initiatives by citizens to maintain/improve basic health standards. For sanitation and water utility companies, disease prevention presents more of an operational challenge: how to reach as many 'customers' as possible (not only the ones with sufficient purchasing power). These companies can consider cross-subsidizing poorer customers by lowering the prices for them. This will contribute to the well-being of these customers, increase their disposable income and, ultimately, expand the potential market for the companies as well. For most of these utility companies, however, this strategy proves difficult to implement because they have concentrated their short-term activities on the 'marketable' part of the population. This leaves a large part of the operational challenge of providing a basic health infrastructure to philanthropists, development organizations and foundations. The Bill and Melinda Gates Foundation, for instance, has committed more than US$3 billion in the period 1998–2000 to improve access to basic health care in developing countries (*Business Week*, 5 May 2003).

Sustainable corporate stories: health care and treatment

Health as a problem of access to treatment allows more scope for a negative duty approach in which short-term profitability and market capitalization can act as triggers for corporate responsibility. This applies, in particular, to the pharmaceutical and the medical appliances industries. Multinational firms that operate in developing countries where public health problems are most acute are confronted with a number of additional operational challenges. If they pay their workers below subsistence level wages, companies indirectly contribute to local health problems and will probably face higher transaction costs related to employee dropouts, low levels of productivity or high levels of extended sick leave. Even companies that scarcely contribute to poverty reduction as a result of low wages, often invest in some form of basic health care for their employees. The biggest problem for most companies in developing countries is the rapidly increasing spread of HIV/Aids. According to ILO estimates, around 70 per cent of the HIV/Aids infected people are aged 15–49, representing the most productive segment of the labour force. International corporations set up a large number of organizations (BINGOs, see Chapter 7) to combat the spread of HIV/Aids, such as the Global Business Coalition on HIV/Aids (GBC) and the Funders Concerned about HIV/Aids (FCAA). The members of these organizations have invested in partnerships with international organizations such as UNAID which have been specially designed for creating these kinds of partnerships. A study of the HIV/Aids programmes of a group of leading companies,[4] reveals that while education on prevention forms part of all the programmes, the focus tends to be practical (provision of condoms) and workshops are available to employees only, rather than the wider community. The focus of attention in the majority of programmes is the provision of antiretroviral treatment to infected employees (cf. van Rijsbergen, 2004: 72ff.).

The pharmaceutical industry, in particular, is challenged by the trade-off that needs to be made between profit and non-profit (see also Chapter 17). Their product development and marketing strategies are at stake. Patenting fully developed drugs ensures that pharmaceutical companies earn a very high return on investment. The pharmaceutical industry has been among the most profitable industries in the world for several years. In 2002, the total profit of the ten drug companies listed on the *Fortune* Global 500 represented more than half of the total profit of the *Fortune* 500 companies (van Rijsbergen, 2004). If the pharmaceutical industry is to develop a real sustainable corporate story, five strategic and operational challenges have to be overcome.

1 **Healthy aims.** It is argued that listed pharmaceutical majors have lost sight of their original purpose, that is, to improve people's health. Since they have become marketing, patenting and money-making machines with profit maximization as the overriding goal, these firms have lost their legitimacy and licence to operate. One way of extricating themselves from this predicament is to change from a focus on research and drug development towards health

promotion and disease prevention. Joining forces with food and chemical companies, pharmaceutical companies can become real 'life science' companies. If pharmaceutical companies were to communicate their strategic commitment to health more convincingly, they may have less difficulty attracting new employees and could face fewer class action lawsuits where they are required to convince courts and regulators of their good intentions.

2 **Healthy prices and patent protection.** Pharmaceutical majors have to find a way of matching an effective international patenting regime with a 'fair' pricing system. High prices of medicine are a necessary – but strongly disputed – part of the international patenting regime adopted *in principle* to stimulate private companies to invest in the development of new medicines. This part of the health issue strikes at the heart of the global patenting system that was negotiated under the new WTO provisions and is better known as the agreement on Trade-Related Aspects of Intellectual Property Rights (TRIPS). The TRIPS agreement imposes obligations on the participating countries to grant the owner of a patent exclusive rights to prevent third parties from making or selling the patented product for a period of not less than 20 years.

Most pharmaceutical companies pursue a 'one world – one price' strategy (Flanagan and Whiteman, 2005). In the past, this strategy enabled them to recover the enormous investments in the development of new medicines fairly quickly. But as far as life-saving medicines for the poor are concerned, the strategy backfired and jeopardized its very foundations. Although the TRIPS Agreement is intended to safeguard the longer-term interests of pharmaceutical firms, in practice these interests can only be protected if pharmaceutical firms do not abuse their position in the marketplace by reaping monopoly profits. In the case of HIV/Aids drugs for instance, it was soon clear that firms from developing countries such as India and Brazil could produce generic HIV/Aids drugs at considerably lower prices – estimates of the World Bank run as low as 2 per cent of the price for these drugs in developed countries. Soon it was also clear that the TRIPS Agreement also contains certain provisions that allow national governments to resort to 'compulsory licensing' – use of a patent without authorization from the patent holder. Compulsory licensing is allowed under TRIPS if authorization from the patent holder on 'reasonable commercial terms' has not proven possible, or in situations of a 'national emergency', 'urgency' or 'in cases of public non-commercial use' which allow parties to negotiate and settle on a 'reasonable period of time' during which voluntary licensing is waived.

The threat of a number of developing countries (e.g. Thailand, South Africa and Brazil, supported by a coalition of NGOs) to resort to compulsory licensing of local producers of generic versions of patented HIV/Aids drugs were met with fierce opposition from the US government and pharmaceutical majors. Despite their public commitment to address the problems of developing countries, many pharmaceutical majors responded decidedly reactively to the operational solutions presented by the developing countries – even though the latter were acting in accordance with the TRIPS Agreement. In response, the Brazilian government ran a successful advertising campaign in OECD countries, which highlighted the fundamental choice between 'patient and patent rights', but emphasized that it was not against pharmaceutical companies in general. Flanagan and Whiteman (2005) conclude that 'through the threat of a compulsory license, Brazil was able both to negotiate lower prices and develop its own domestic capacity to produce HIV medications'. Access to affordable HIV/Aids medication became a primary issue in international trade negotiations under the auspices of the WTO. In the 2001 *Doha Declaration on the TRIPS Agreement and Public Health*, the strategy of negotiated price reductions through the threat of compulsory licensing was more or less legitimized. It helped governments of some developing countries to negotiate significant price reductions. The operational challenge for the pharmaceutical industry in future is to find a way of applying a differentiated pricing strategy across different regions, to further develop a CSR strategy that uses the provisions of the TRIPS Agreement in a non-defensive manner and find a way of reaching the poor in developed and developing countries without undermining its capacity to invest in the development of new medicines in the future.

3 **Healthy safety regulation.** The third challenge for the pharmaceutical industry is to match commercial interests with safety regulations in a manner that is not reactive or defensive. Food and drug administrations around the world have not always proven capable of exercising effective control over food and drug safety. Medicines (and other health products) can be brought onto the market too quickly and can have severe repercussions for consumers, undermining the legitimacy of the entire industry. The problem is exacerbated by the fact that a whole industry is facing the expiry of patent protection for top-selling drugs, the entrance of cheaper (generic) drug producers and a lack of real new (blockbuster) alternatives. So the temptation to take some risks in bringing new products to market is considerable, as is the risk of causing damage to reputations. How to solve this dilemma? Collaborating with regulatory agencies on developing new joint and high-quality safety regulations presents an option. This regulatory dilemma also applies to using controversial new techniques in developing new treatments, such as stem cell research and genomics. What would be the appropriate framework and research focus for pharmaceutical companies: a lenient regulatory environment where scientific progress can proceed uninhibited or one that is geared towards major consumer markets even if it means slower scientific progress?

4 **Healthy neglect?** The fourth strategic challenge is to encourage the development of vaccines and cures for neglected diseases such as malaria and sleeping sickness that do not represent a 'market' now or in the near future. Intensive collaboration with the WHO, national health institutes and development foundations, presents a course of action that is being pursued by some pharmaceutical companies (cf. www.who.org). Another initiative worth mentioning is the Drugs for Neglected Diseases Initiative (DNDI), which was set up in July 2003 by a French academic to 'tackle the imbalance between the priorities of first world drug development and the health needs of developing countries' (*FT*, 25 February 2005). The organizational model of DNDI is that of a virtual network using partners around the world (a PONGO, see Chapter 7). It is funded by big NGOs such as MSF and some public research laboratories. A first achievement of the group has been to perfect a new therapy to treat malaria, which has also attracted the interest of Novartis. Sizeable intellectual property problems remain, along with other types of 'most-neglected diseases' such as sleeping sickness and Chagas disease that plague developing countries but which are virtually ignored in terms of drug development (Berman *et al.*, 2001).

5 **Healthy employees.** The last challenge is primarily operational and concerns the question of how companies are to go about providing health care to employees. Should this imply prevention as well as treatment, and should it be provided only for the employees or for the whole community? Should it be aimed only at life-threatening diseases or also at prevention and other health-promoting habits?

Sustainability challenge #3: unemployment/poverty – the nature of growth regimes

All bargaining dilemmas are a fortiori related to the basic economic 'fabric' of societies – their so-called 'growth' or 'accumulation regime'. Economic growth issues require a fundamental

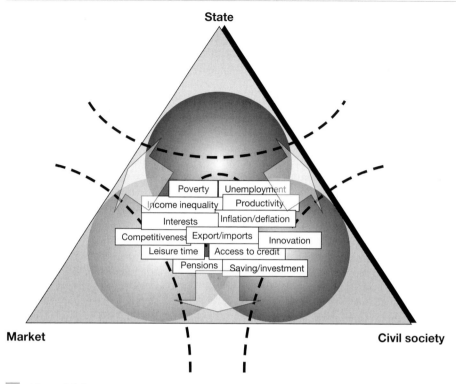

State

Poverty | Unemployment
Income inequality | Productivity
Interests | Inflation/deflation
Competitiveness | Export/imports | Innovation
Leisure time | Access to credit
Pensions | Saving/investment

Market

Civil society

Figure 10.3 *Growth regime issues*

trade-off between equity and efficiency, which affects all societal spheres and has significant spillover effects for all other interface issues. Growth issues can be positioned at the core of the societal triangle (Figure 10.3) and, therefore, involve shared responsibilities for governments, firms and citizens. Chapter 2 already identified a number of different societal arrangements marked by rival growth regimes. Addressing interface problems in times of economic prosperity (a virtuous growth regime) is always easier than in times of economic downturn (a vicious growth regime). Arguably the two most pressing sustainability issues at the core of the societal triangle are (un)employment and poverty. Poverty and unemployment often represent two sides of the same societal coin.

Unemployment

Paraphrasing C.Wright Mills (1959: 9), the following observation can be made: when one person is unemployed, it is a personal tragedy, but it may be attributable to his/her own personal efforts (*private problem, private solution*); when a large proportion of the population is unemployed, it is a structural matter closely connected to the nature of the growth regime, which cannot be overcome by personal effort alone (*private problem, public issue*). Beyond the 'natural' unemployment rate – a certain level of unemployment that can be beneficial for economic growth – unemployment represents a waste of human talent and public resources, threatens societal stability and inhibits economic growth. Unemployment and poverty often go hand-in-hand. In 2000, nearly a third of the world's labour force of about 3 billion was 'either unemployed/underemployed in terms of seeking more work or earn less than is needed to keep their families out of poverty' (ILO, 2004). At the end of 2002, the global unemployment figure officially stood at approximately 180 million people, which was 40 million more than before the peak of the Asian financial crisis in 1998 (ibid.).

In the period 2000–2004, unemployment grew in most developing countries, partly caused by slower economic growth in industrialized nations. Export-oriented, labour-intensive sectors such as the garment industry (employing largely women) were particularly hard hit. Asia suffered most severely from the bursting ICT bubble, which cut exports to industrialized countries. In the Middle East reductions in the size of the public sector pushed up unemployment to sometimes double-digit levels. Gulf countries, in particular, responded by replacing migrant workers (from Asia) with their own nationals (ILO, 2003). In industrialized countries, official unemployment figures have been rising steadily since 2000, to 7.4 per cent in the European Union and 5.6 per cent in the US in 2004. In 1998, Japan had an unemployment rate of more than 4 per cent for the first time since the Second World War. In Germany, the unemployment figure rose to 12.6 per cent in 2004, a post-war high. Even where employment grew in industrialized countries, it was at the cost of falling productivity.

Poverty

Whereas the overall number of people living in extreme poverty – on less than US$1 a day – decreased by 10 per cent in the 1990s, the number of people living on less than US$2 a day increased to 2.5 billion. Poverty is unequally distributed over the world. Although the greatest part of the world's poor live in the least developed countries, the number of poor people living in industrialized countries is not insubstantial. According to the UN Human Development Report 1998, the percentage of poor people in the US was 19 per cent, in the UK 13.5 per cent, whereas in France it was 7.5 per cent of the population. Poverty lies at the heart of almost all interface issues. The reduction of poverty is generally acknowledged to be the most important condition for worldwide economic growth. The FAO calculated that the negative effect of absolute poverty on economic growth can be calculated at between 0.23 and 4.7 per cent less annual growth in general. A number of variables explain this relationship. Poverty goes hand-in-hand with a lack of human assets and a high degree of economic vulnerability. Poverty leads to chronic malnutrition due to a lack of resources to purchase (nutritious/safe) food and water (FAO, 2002). Poverty is associated with forced labour and one of the major causes of child labour as children are put to work to complement the insufficient income of their parents. The incidence of child labour is strongly related to poverty: in the 43 countries where the average annual income is below 500 dollars, 30 to 60 per cent of children often do hard labour (UNICEF, 2004). This number decreases sharply with higher income. Poverty causes an unequal distribution of disease in developed as well as developing countries. Poverty and a lack of education (illiteracy in particular) are mutually reinforcing and create the social and economical conditions for social and political discontent and unrest. Poverty leads to social and political discontent. Poverty triggers migration and creates a breeding ground for terrorism. Poverty stands in the way of adequate investment due to the low creditworthiness of the poor (De Soto, 2000). Poverty triggers unsustainable agricultural practices and a less than efficient use of other scarce resources. Poverty and corruption go hand-in-hand.

Working poor and the poverty/unemployment trap

Working poor people work a substantial number of hours per week (at least 27 hours in the US) but earn an income below the poverty line.[5] At the end of 2002, the number of working poor – defined as workers living on US$1 or less a day – was estimated at 550 million globally. According to UNCTAD (2002):

the incidence of poverty is so high because most of the LDCs are caught in an international poverty trap. Pervasive poverty in LDCs has effects at the national level that cause poverty to persist and even to increase, and international trade and finance relationships are reinforcing the cycle of economic stagnation and poverty.

The working poor represent a substantial group of the workers also in developed countries. In 2001, the US department of Labour registered about 6.4 million 'working poor' people, representing around 5 per cent of the work force.[6] When someone disqualifies themselves from social security benefits or raises their tax liability by entering into an employment contract, they can fall victim to the 'poverty/unemployment trap' – losing more benefits than can be gained by entering a job. If a large enough number of people fall victim to this poverty trap, the economy as a whole might slide into a vicious cycle of growth – with low prices, but also low productivity, low wages and thus low economic growth. This could happen, for example, if a large core company in an economy place their employees in these kinds of dilemmas. Some observers have started to refer to this mechanism as the Wal-Mart effect (see Box 10.2). This effect builds partly on the idea that the sociologist Ritzer (1993) called a 'McDonaldisation of society'. The latter referred primarily to the standardization/rationalization of society – with increased efficiency as the sole benchmark starting with food production and sales, and spreading to all areas of society, such as education. The Wal-Mart effect adds to this sociological perspective the danger of a vicious growth regime through lower wages and, ultimately, insufficient purchasing power.

Sustainability challenges

A key sustainability challenge for society is to keep unemployment levels to an acceptable minimum (not necessarily zero) and limit the number of working or employable poor people that are caught in a poverty or unemployment trap. The sustainability challenges for companies are different, though. Do companies have a responsibility to create jobs for the unemployed, avoid lay-offs or pay decent wages? In principle, companies cannot be expected to create jobs for the unemployed, but they can be encouraged to contribute to enhancing the capacity of the unemployed to re-enter the labour market, for instance through sponsoring retraining programmes. This argument is especially relevant to companies that operate in the lower end of the market where a substantial number of existing or potential customers could be unemployed. For this category of firms, good unemployment programmes are more important than for companies competing at the higher end of the market.

It is almost impossible for companies to take an individual responsibility for solving structural unemployment. But companies face divergent consequences of structural unemployment. Companies serving the lower end of the market are more directly affected by structural unemployment. The unemployed are their potential customers. In case these very companies actively try to evade paying sufficient taxes to fund public employment programmes, they can indirectly contribute to vicious growth cycles and to their own lack of turnover growth. In practice, however, most companies tend not to be overly concerned about high unemployment rates as it moderates wage demands, increases the loyalty of their own workers and creates flexibility in the labour market. A relatively high unemployment rate creates a docile labour reserve. Even companies with a bad reputation can get sufficient people to work for them if the labour reserve is large enough. The sustainability challenge for companies might be to establish the minimum employment conditions that would allow the pool of reserve labour to meet their basic needs and the nature of a good trade-off between lower wages coupled with higher transaction costs involved in keeping social unrest at bay and getting caught up in a downward economic spiral which ultimately has a negative effect on all parties involved.

BOX 10.2 VICIOUS GROWTH REGIMES – A WAL-MART EFFECT?

On 6 October 2003, *Business Week* ran an article entitled 'Is Wal-Mart too powerful?'. With US$245 million revenues in 2002, the US retailer is the world's largest company and by far the largest retailer (three times the size of the no. 2 retailer, France's Carrefour). With 1.6 million workers it is also the largest private employer in the world and has considerable power over the distribution of a large variety of articles, such as household staples. The company uses its core position in networks of distribution and sales also to diversify into banking, for instance, by offering customers credit card arrangements (*Business Week*, 6 February 2005). *Business Week* cannot be reproached for upholding any ideological anti-business attitude. Nevertheless, the magazine has become critical of the Wal-Mart formula, arguing that it threatens to pull the rug out from under the American growth regime. On the one hand Wal-Mart follows a simple strategy that is to great benefit of consumers. The relentless pursuit of efficiency has resulted in bargain prices for shoppers (on average, 14 per cent cheaper than direct competitors) and hugely cost-efficient supply chains. Economists refer to a broad 'Wal-Mart effect' that suppresses inflation. On the other hand, *Business Week* continues, this formula is fraught with complications and perverse consequences. Wal-Mart is a family-controlled and strongly anti-union company and has managed to keep retail wages extremely low. *Business Week* claims that Wal-Mart sales clerks live below the federal poverty line. Rather than suppressing inflation, Wal-Mart might trigger deflation or a negative growth spiral – a phenomenon feared, perhaps, even more than inflation. According to *Business Week*, 'Wal-Mart might well be both America's most admired and most hated company'. *Business Week* also cites a number of academic studies that debunk the notion that a new big-box store boosts employment and sales and property-tax receipts. The dominance of Wal-Mart has other negative effects: Wal-Mart stores replace local stores, shoppers have to travel farther (higher pollution) and wages go down not only at supermarkets, but also at suppliers. Critics also argue that Wal-Mart's intensifying global pursuit of low-cost goods is partly to blame for the accelerating loss of US manufacturing jobs to China and other low-wage nations. The US$12 billion worth of Chinese goods Wal-Mart bought in 2002 represented 10 per cent of all US imports from China. In the mid-1980s, Sam Walton, founder of Wal-Mart, launched a 'Made in America' campaign which, 'for obvious reasons', is now de-emphasized. The consequences of the Wal-Mart strategy have important spillover or 'herding' effects. Its core networking position and dominant position in retailing compel other retailers to operate within the same rules of the game. Thus, the Wal-Mart effect could also bring about the gradual erosion of the American growth model if enough people lose the purchasing power required to keep the economy afloat. A growing group of 'working poor' is being created that has no way of escaping their position in the system. The Wal-Mart effect has, thus, also triggered a rather heterogeneous 'stop Wal-Mart' social movement.

Responsible discharge?

The unemployment challenge becomes more direct once companies start laying people off. The announcement of lay-offs always heralds major societal battles between trade unions and companies. It is often relatively straightforward to create a credible sustainability story when a company is compelled to fire people to remain competitive in the domestic market. If it has to relocate plants to off-shore production sites as part of the pursuit of an internationalization strategy, legitimizing lay-offs becomes significantly more complex. Such a company will have to present a persuasive *counter-factual* argument: how would not relocating the plant affect competitiveness? If it can be proved that staying put would jeopardize even more jobs – perhaps even the continuity of the company as a whole – it may gain some legitimacy. If a manager uses this argument without grounds, however, they will rapidly lose their legitimacy and bargaining position.

Publicly listed companies face a rather perverse logic in implementing a responsible hiring–firing strategy: the announcement of (massive) lay-offs often has a more positive impact on companies' market capitalization than the announcement of higher profits or bringing an innovation to market. Laying employees off has become part of the standard set of crisis management techniques of listed companies – even when CEOs know that the long-term survival of a company depends on employees' tacit knowledge. One of the sustainability challenges of publicly listed companies is thus to break through this mechanism. The unemployment/poverty trap looms large for many unemployed people. Companies that aim to develop a truly sustainable corporate story should acknowledge this issue and develop realistic solutions to the problem. One option could be to acknowledge more explicitly the 'value' of workers and their accumulated knowledge for the competitive position of a company. Thus, instead of stressing the 'liability' of employing a large number of people, they should be regarded as a substantial 'asset' – even if this type of asset is more difficult to measure than tangible assets such as cash flow, buildings, machines or patents.

Smaller and medium-sized as well as family-owned firms have always shown the greatest capacity to absorb unemployed (lower-skilled) workers, have often been the last to lay massive numbers of workers off, and are less confronted with complex legitimization exercises due to internationalization decisions. Companies that lay workers off in a society with a good social safety net are in a different position than companies operating in societies where unemployment can equate with poverty. The safety net sustains (part of) the purchasing power of the unemployed and thus supports a virtuous economic growth cycle. The lack of a safety net makes the lay-off decision more dramatic and the personal consequences more severe. Should this affect the company? The strategic challenge of companies is to design or support a social security system that sustains the purchasing power of the economically inactive population, while maintaining a sufficiently flexible labour market and adequate incentives for people to retrain so as to qualify for other jobs and contribute to higher productivity after a period of involuntary leisure time.

10.4 AGENDA-SETTING ISSUES AND INDIRECT RESPONSIBILITIES: FIRMS AS PART OF THE SOLUTION?

All issues that involve a trade-off between macro/public and group/club rights can be situated at the interface between state and civil society (Figure 10.2). These trade-offs affect the accessibility of public goods such as security, education, general health care, democracy and information. Group rights include the collective and emancipatory rights of specific population groups such as indigenous peoples, (illegal) workers, women, refugees, children or the elderly. These rights become issues when regulatory, expectational and ideals gaps develop, particularly in the not-for-profit part of society – often in the interaction between central and local governments/communities.

Whereas the primary responsibility of governments is to provide sufficient public goods, the actual distribution of many of these public goods is decided in interaction with citizens. If one group dominates, the public good in effect becomes a 'club good' and the government is ensnared by the logic of specific interest groups. This is also referred to as 'regulatory capture'

(Chapter 6) and is often considered detrimental to economic growth and social progress. Goods and services that can be efficiently provided by markets require a certain degree of 'exclusiveness' and discrimination between groups of citizens (customers). Issues that develop at the interface between state and civil society always revolve around the question of how exclusiveness and unequal distribution – caused by regulatory capture and the domination of market principles – can be avoided. Unequal access to information and education can create technological and knowledge divides, unequal access to democratic decision making can produce democratic deficits, and unequal access to safety and security can cause migration and force people to become refugees.

Firms only have an indirect responsibility for issues located at the state–civil society interface. They are often only marginally part of the problem, and as main supporters of markets (and thus primarily interested in exclusivity of goods and services), they are neither a sufficient nor a necessary condition for the solution of these issues. The impact of such issues on the operation of companies can be substantial. Chapter 1 discussed the importance of 'social capital' for instance for the effective operation of companies. The quality of the 'public sphere' – also referred to as the 'public space' (www.public-space.com) – is a factor that directly affects the competitive position of companies. Consider the issue of criminality, for instance. Countries with a high income inequality have higher crime rates. High crime rates and unsafe environments increase the transaction costs for companies (in particular retailers). Investing in armed security or installing security systems does not address the source of the problem and, even if successful, merely diverts the problem to other parts of town.

How can firms contribute to solving these kinds of public problems? Often, business leaders – either directly or through their associations – set the agenda for public policy formulation on issues of common interests. Firms are also assisting local communities through various social programmes or philanthropic deeds aimed at improving general quality of life in communities. These activities are often grouped under the rubric of 'corporate citizenship'.

Corporate citizenship as an act of agenda setting

The concept of 'corporate citizenship' is, perhaps, even more ill-conceived than the catch-all notion of CSR. It mixes two societal spheres whose logic often conflicts: markets and civil society. The concept of corporate or business citizenship draws on the notion of individual citizenship. Citizenship refers to the rights and duties of individuals in the communities in which they operate. Proponents of corporate citizenship apply these principles also to firms. Companies should be responsible members of the local community in which they operate (cf. Andriof and McIntosh, 2001). Some scientists are strong proponents. Zadek (2003) distinguishes a 'third generation corporate citizenship'. Others question whether it is theoretically and ethically possible to consider corporations as 'citizens' (Van Oosterhout, 2005). Does the idea of 'corporate citizenship' make any sense? Contemporary views of corporate citizenship contain significant limits and redundancies (Matten and Crane, 2005). From a political sciences perspective, Matten and Crane (2005) argue in favour of an extended notion of corporate citizenship defined as the administration of a bundle of individual citizenship rights – social, civil and political – in particular, the participation of corporations in processes of governance. Whatever the outcome of the academic discussion will be, corporate citizenship is a concept increasingly used by corporations themselves. For the moment, therefore, corporate citizenship is perhaps best understood as a metaphor for the ambitions of companies to be accepted as responsible actors in society that show some interest in the fairness of the outcome of the various trade-offs for citizens. Following the framework applied in the previous chapters, four approaches to corporate citizenship can be distinguished.

Inactive corporate citizenship is the most limited approach to corporate citizenship. Before an audience of fellow chief executives in Boston (MA) in March 2005, Nestlé's (Austrian) CEO, Brabeck Letmathe, expressed one version of this stance in provocative terms. In his view a company's obligation to the community is simply to create jobs and make products; 'companies should not feel obligated to "give back" to the community, because they haven't taken anything away' (*Boston Herald*, 9 March 2005). In the inactive approach, corporate citizenship is therefore only applicable to companies that are able to frame their contribution to the efficient functioning of markets and the provision of goods and services to customers as acts of 'citizenship'. Philanthropy is separated from the company in the sense that it is not companies that engage in philanthropy, but CEOs in their personal capacity as individual citizens.

Reactive corporate citizenship is applicable to companies that respond to public policy/social issues when it is in the interest of the company to do so. Lack of safety and security and education, for example, can have a negative impact on business interests. Corporate philanthropy (sponsoring and volunteering) is then employed as a PR instrument. Reactive corporate citizens tend to opt for solutions to inadequacies in the public sphere that are relatively easily linked to their own interests: setting up of company universities, donating products such as computers or software to local schools (by the producers of these products); supporting local security activities without addressing the wider causes of the issue; engaging in branch associations with a limited mandate. Another manifestation of reactive corporate citizenship is to withhold support for a particular regime or practice. Companies can refrain from investing in countries that openly abuse labour and human rights. This is part of a complex international trade-off that will be further analysed in Chapters 12 and 13. In pursuing this negative duty approach, companies can contribute to creating the conditions under which the issue may cease to exist or be resolved. The interface issue of torture is a case in point. While organized torture is mostly in the hands of governments (not necessarily always dictatorships) and civil society groups (such as the mafia), someone has to manufacture the instruments of torture. Research of Human Rights Watch (2002 report) shows that the number of companies worldwide that are known to produce or supply electro-shock equipment rose from 30 in the 1980s to more than 130 by 2000.

Active corporate citizenship implies an attempt by firms to make a more positive contribution to addressing some non-profit interface issues, albeit largely within the company's operational context. For instance, firms can address gender inequality by actively pursuing 'equal opportunity' policies through HR programmes; they can set up illiteracy programmes for employees and their families;[7] they can engage in corporate volunteering schemes or support local communities through the sponsoring of certain activities provided they are accessible to various groups (gender, age, religion); firms can sponsor organizations that are dependent on private sponsors to protect the interests of socially marginalized people such as refugees (e.g. UNHCR). The risk of active corporate citizenship is that it may generate unwanted side-effects. By providing schooling, health care and the like to employees, for instance, companies compensate for lacking public provisions by governments. This can diminish the resolve of governments and citizens to conceive more lasting solutions to the root cause of the problems at hand.

Proactive corporate citizenship focuses on the structural causes of major social issues and tries to address them through the development of realistic plans without reference to any specific or short-term interest of the company involved. Since the mid-1990s, a large number of research initiatives around the world have been founded to further develop the idea and concepts of corporate citizenship. Companies sponsor these initiatives in various ways. Operational (company-oriented) approaches to corporate citizenship have been developed primarily by research groups with a large number of members,[8] while more fundamental approaches seem to have been developed by research institutes sponsored by individual companies.[9] Another proactive approach to corporate citizenship is to organize multi-stakeholder dialogues and to collaborate with civil society in building local capacity. Civil society is particularly poorly organized in developing countries. Instead of seeking to replace government or civil society action through their own initiatives, companies can try to assist these groups in meeting their primary responsibilities.

Proactive corporate citizenship amounts to acts of what can be dubbed 'proactive philanthropy' – even when this goes far beyond what is commonly understood under the term of philanthropy. Proactive philanthropy makes an explicit selection of issues: support for girls' schooling instead of general support, support for general democratization programmes, investment in local infrastructure and sanitation. Proactive corporate citizenship often fits better with individual leaders who act in their personal capacity in an informal bargaining setting than with leaders who represent their firms in an official capacity in a formal bargaining setting. Individual CEOs have less difficulty dealing with the fundamental dichotomy between citizens and companies. As citizens they can exercise their influence in business associations that have a mandate from their corporate members to propose solutions and lobby for equitable access to and sufficient provision of public goods. The greater the number of members of international firms, the more they act as representatives of firms and the greater the difficulty for these associations to move beyond the issues that influence the direct responsibility of companies (Box 10.3). Proactive corporate citizenship requires CEOs to display a strong personal commitment to the public interest or common good.

BOX 10.3 THREE ASSOCIATIVE APPROACHES TO 'CORPORATE CITIZENSHIP'

- **Reactive:** The International Chamber of Commerce (ICC) is the largest institutionalized business organization in the world, representing thousands of member firms. This large (and diverse) constituency affects the topics it puts on the international bargaining agenda. This is reflected in the fact that its programme hardly makes any reference to public interest issues. Its primary concern lies with addressing issues that have a direct impact on firms and the market: corruption, biosociety, trade regulation, intellectual property, taxation, trade and investment policies, and governance. The ICC represents a *business in society* approach to public policy issues.

- **Active:** The World Business Council on Sustainable Development (WBCSD) is a medium-sized coalition of around 170 international companies – not individuals – 'united by a shared commitment to sustainable development via the three pillars of economic growth, ecological balance and social progress.' (www.wbcsd.ch). The main themes of the WBCSD are closely connected to the direct interests of business and the advantages and opportunities of sustainability are emphasized. The issues it focuses on include sustainable livelihoods, risk management, HSE systems, responsible forestry, eco-efficiency, sustainable mobility, energy and climate, water. The WBCSD represents a *business and society* approach to public policy issues.

- **Proactive:** The European Roundtable of Industrialists (ERT) has been the most successful of all associations in setting the agenda for non-profit action in the public sphere. The ERT has actively lobbied the EU on general interest issues that determine the general environment in which they operate. The issues focused on include education, enlargement, environment, pension reform, governance, development, infrastructure (next to firm-specific issues). European industrialists have taken it upon themselves to define what they consider to be an appropriate public setting in which to do business. The efforts of the ERT literally resulted in broadening the geographic and administrative space in Europe: by successfully lobbying for Europe's enlargement (broadening) with more than ten new member states, and the 'deepening' of many regulatory provisions implemented by the EC. The members of the ERT are required to participate in their personal capacity, not as representatives of their companies, the group was kept relatively small (around 45 members) and decision making takes place on the basis of consensus. Being all Europeans, they can all be identified as European 'citizens', which enhances their credibility from the perspective of policy makers. As acting CEOs of big national champions, members also have the persuasive power to get the ERT points on the appropriate tables, at the right moment. The ERT represents a *business–society* approach to public policy issues (see Chapter 8).

Prevailing practices of corporate citizenship

In 2003, the Center for Corporate Citizenship conducted a survey of 515 American business leaders from a broad mix of companies of various sizes and industries, which revealed that the inactive and reactive versions of corporate citizenship largely prevail (CCCB, 2004). Corporate citizenship is driven chiefly by internal corporate values (75 per cent) and customer feedback (53 per cent). A majority of the surveyed firms offer cash and volunteer time to local communities regardless of size. But a much smaller group (20 per cent) explicitly aims at providing solutions to core interface issues such as improving conditions in poor communities. A company secures its licence to operate through being seen as a good member of society. Consequently, most companies believe that good corporate citizenship is just 'good business': 82 per cent claimed that good corporate citizenship helps the bottom line, while 74 per cent said that the public has a right to expect companies to act as good citizens. Only a minority stated that they developed corporate citizenship programmes because the community expects it (30 per cent) or due to legislation or political pressure (24 per cent) (ibid.).

Corporate citizenship as corporate efforts to contribute to the resolution of societal issues is still in its infancy. Public statements on corporate citizenship, as a selection of recent statements reveals (Box 10.4), are still rather vague and often remarkably similar in wording. Corporate citizenship is randomly linked to 'being part of this world' and 'being a member of the community'. American companies in particular have embraced the notion of corporate citizenship for reasons that will be explored further in Chapter 12. Their statements about corporate citizenship are indicative of the traditional pursuit of a 'licence to operate' and often reiterate the primary responsibilities of companies as meeting societal needs through operating market institutions and generating healthy profit margins (section 10.2). Most corporations adopt a relatively reactive version of corporate citizenship. ExxonMobil and Pfizer provide an excellent example of this orientation, especially if one considers the recent furore over their stance on issues such as global warming and drug patenting rights. These companies seek legitimization primarily as in/reactive corporate citizens, with due reference to the preferences of existing customers and the dominant logic of present markets. The interface issues discussed in this chapter are neither mentioned nor confronted, and the community tends to be regarded either as an external issue or object of (corporate) philanthropy.

BOX 10.4 EXPRESSIONS OF CORPORATE CITIZENSHIP

Home Depot: 'The Home Depot invests company resources to secure safe and affordable homes in the hundreds of communities where it does business and where its employees and customers live. That includes providing supplies and volunteers for rebuilding areas hit by natural disasters and encouraging Home Depot employees to work with local organizations and youth to design and build neighborhood playgrounds. Home Depot also funds affordable homes for low-income individuals and families in cooperation with national builders such as Habitat for Humanity and Rebuilding Together, as well as community-based developers around the country. The company also collaborates with YouthBuild in more than two dozen cities to put young adults with troubled pasts in classrooms where they acquire basic skills before receiving training on inner-city construction sites. Some of these young people have joined the ranks of the company's full-time employees' (Corporate Citizenship Report, 2003).

General Motors: 'Our citizenship today takes many forms, not the least of which is our commitment to maintain a financially healthy company that can continue to provide for the well-being of hundreds of thousands of active and retired employees. There's our commitment toward a sustainable future, through our research to develop affordable, pollution-free, fuel-cell vehicles that could one day take the automobile out of the environmental debate. And there are our employees' countless efforts to be good citizens through donations of time and money that improve daily life in the hundreds of communities we call our home the world over. . . . [I]t's worth noting here that GM has never lost sight of the value we place on being a responsible corporate citizen, around the globe' (Annual Report, 2003).

ExxonMobil: 'The demands placed by society on energy companies today are ever changing. What is undeniable is that the demand for energy is growing, not shrinking. As a responsible energy company, we believe that good citizenship means helping meet that growth in demand in an economically, environmentally and socially responsible manner' (Lee Ramond, chairman's letter, 2004, www.exxonmobil.com).

Pfizer: 'What is Corporate Citizenship? Citizenship defines our role in local and global communities and how we strive to conduct business responsibly in a changing world. Being a good corporate citizen includes listening to, understanding, and responding to our stakeholders about their needs regarding Pfizer's policies and operations. Stakeholders are people or groups who affect, or are affected by, Pfizer's business activities. Our relationship with them is at the heart of our citizenship because they define what it means for Pfizer to create value. They are the ones who will determine when Pfizer fulfills its mission to become the world's most valued company to stakeholders' (www.pfizer.com, 2005).

Proctor and Gamble: 'P&G's vision is to link business opportunity with corporate responsibility to create a concept we call "corporate social opportunity." We believe that we can build our businesses while contributing our part to help address some of the toughest global health and social issues' (P&G Sustainability Report, 2004).

Novartis: 'At Novartis, corporate citizenship – or corporate social responsibility – is a top priority. As a corporation, Novartis wants to act the same way as responsible and conscientious individuals would act in their community. We do everything we can to operate in a manner that is sustainable – economically, socially, and environmentally – in the best interest of long-term success for our enterprise. The cornerstones of our commitment to corporate citizenship are: (1) active engagement in society in areas where we are competent; (2) helping where help is most needed; (3) establishing and implementing transparent, ethical corporate standards and policies' (www.novartis.com, visited August 2004).

Siemens: 'As a global company, we believe that business success along with sound principles of environmental stewardship and corporate citizenship are all essential parts of an inter-locking whole. . . . Our ideas, technologies and activities help create a better world. We are committed to universal values, good corporate citizenship and a healthy environment. Integrity guides our conduct toward our employees, business partners and shareholders. Our employees are the key to our success. We work together as a global network of knowledge and learning. Our corporate culture is defined by diversity, by open dialogue and mutual respect, and by clear goals and decisive leadership. . . . We believe in being a good neighbour and socially responsible corporate citizen wherever we do business' (website, corporate citizenship, 2004, www.siemens.com).

Toyota Motors: 'Toyota Industries is respectful of the people, culture, and tradition of each country and region. It also works to promote economic growth and prosperity in those countries. Through its corporate activities, Toyota Industries works to contribute to regional living conditions and social prosperity and, as well, strives to offer products and services that are clean, safe, and of high quality'. (Basic philosophy of Corporate Citizenship Toyota Industries, 2004).

Mitsubishi Corporation: 'Humanity has to address its impact on the environment of the earth – the only home we have. At MC, we constantly ask ourselves what we can do to protect the natural world and human communities residing on this precious planet and what we can do to build a sustainable future' (Corporate Citizenship, sustainability vision, 2004).

Most companies stress some form of environmental stewardship, but remain relatively vague on implementation principles. Life sciences and food companies such as Proctor and Gamble, or car manufacturers such as General Motors and Mitsubishi exhibit a greater propensity towards explicitly addressing interface issues such as global warming and individual health. Firms whose local communities represent not only the 'surrounding population' but also its main market are particularly adept at exploiting an active form of corporate citizenship. Large retailers such as Home Depot explicitly address some of the more structural local problems including housing and youth criminality.

The mechanism: reputation and correction

11.1 INTRODUCTION: 'REPUTATION, REPUTATION, REPUTATION – THE IMMORTAL PART OF MEN'[1]

In a rapidly changing international society a long list of unresolved, controversial and hotly debated issues has been brought back to the negotiating table (Chapter 10). But international societal change also introduced one mechanism that was deemed particularly appropriate to address the social responsibility of companies: reputation. Governments around the world were asked by NGOs to start regulating the behaviour of companies more strictly, to introduce new laws and standards and to impose strict sanctions on the culprits. Instead of following this advice, most governments put their faith in the so-called 'reputation mechanism'. It was believed that companies that 'do something wrong' would immediately be corrected by the reputation mechanism. Reputation build-up can take ages, but it can disappear in an instant. Critical NGOs and customers would 'punish' the company for irresponsible and unaccountable behaviour. Governments additionally argued that a legalistic approach would probably only result in unwanted 'escape' behaviour by the companies. Besides, they had just decided to lower their profile in society, so stepping up regulation seemed an ideological anachronism. Thus, instead of warding off the bargaining society, governments increasingly tried to use its mechanisms to solve some of the issues.

The non-interventionist stance of governments has traditionally enjoyed the support of companies. Now they could also agree with the importance of the reputation mechanism. A strong reputation was increasingly acknowledged as an enduring source of competitive advantage. A strong reputation helps to mobilize support of customers, employees, investors, the media and – last but not least – financial analysts (Fombrun and van Riel, 2004). A strong reputation has financial value as a corporate asset, and can stave off disaster in the face of a crisis (ibid.). Is it correct to assume that the reputation mechanism will help to address societal issues effectively and encourage managers to develop genuine Societal Interface Management policies and practices? This chapter explores the functioning of the reputation mechanism in CSR issues.

The reputation of a company represents the 'big stick' when it comes to observing explicit and implicit contracts with society and interested parties. Reputation has many dimensions and there are many definitions of the phenomenon. Economists, for instance, often refer to game theory: 'in game theory the reputation of a player is the perception others have of the player's values . . . which determines his or her choice of strategy' (Weigelt and Camerer, 1988: 443). Business strategists, particularly, regard reputation as a valuable asset in markets as it creates barriers for newcomers and competitive advantage for existing competitors (Caves and Porter, 1977). For marketeers, it is about 'images' in the minds especially of customers with respect to products – hence the term 'corporate image'. Image refers to an impression that exists among people which is created by a network of associations that are retained in the minds of stakeholders (Maathuis, 1999). Reputation is the sum of different images in the minds of stakeholders that forms the overall perception that is held of a corporation. Then there are the organizational experts who regard reputation primarily from the perspective of culture and identity (Dutton et al., 1994), and the sociologists who define reputation as 'aggregate assessments of a firm's performance relative to expectations and norms in an institutional field' (Shapiro, 1987). Accountants, finally, view the reputation of a company chiefly as an 'intangible' asset that can nonetheless be debited to the balance sheet, such as goodwill, for example.

This chapter illustrates that all these dimensions are significant for an accurate understanding of the function of reputation and the reputation mechanism in regard to corporate social responsibility in general and Societal Interface Management in particular. The most important ingredients of reputation can be portrayed by means of a temple, complete with pillars and a foundation (section 11.2). Reputation has a number of general (section 11.3) and specific CSR-related functions (section 11.4) for companies. The reputation mechanism can have a corrective effect on companies that do not score well in the area of CSR (section 11.5). The corrective mechanisms of reputation management combined with the self-disciplining behaviour of companies provide the behavioural frame in which CSR strategies materialize (section 11.6).

11.2 A TEMPLE OF REPUTATION

Reputation exists in minds of consumers, clients, shareholders, journalists, environmental activists and citizens (van Riel, 1995). Reputation, therefore, concerns the perceptual representation of a company as seen through the eyes of different stakeholders. Perceptions inform individuals' attempts to interpret and give meaning to their experience (Robbins, 2000: 23). This renders reputation, and also the reputation mechanism, a dynamic phenomenon that takes shape in the relation and interaction with stakeholders. A unanimous account of a company's reputation is impossible. After all, each stakeholder makes a judgement on the basis of their individual perceptions, personal experience, interests and expectations. 'Business is a battle of perceptions' (Ries, 1997). Just like people have different views on one and the same company, the company essentially has a reputation to uphold for *each* stakeholder group (cf. Brown and Dacin, 1997; Barich and Kotler, 1991; Garbett, 1988; Gregory, 1991; Dowling, 2001). In practice, it amounts to identifying relevant stakeholders (Chapter 8).

Pillars of reputation

Fombrun and Gardberg (2000: 13) assert that the reputation of a company rests on six pillars of perception that together form the Reputation Quotient® (RQ).[2] Perceptions are closely aligned to belief systems – in this case, ideologies (Chapter 1) – which renders it quite appropriate to depict the pillars of reputation as a temple (see Figure 11.1).

The pillars of the temple are:

1 *Emotional*: a company's emotional appeal is represented by general sentiments, respect, admiration and (perceived) reliability.
2 *Products/services*: perceived attractiveness and quality of products and services. Core values: quality, innovation, value for money, support.
3 *Financial*: perception of the financial results of a company, also its competitiveness, profitability, investment risks and growth prospects.
4 *Vision and leadership*: perception of the vision and the leadership qualities of management.
5 *Work environment*: perception of work atmosphere, culture and work environment.
6 *Social and environmental responsibility*: perception of corporate social responsibility and observance of relevant norms and values in the social and environmental domain and the issues at stake in these areas. Policy on sponsoring, voluntarism and donations is also included.

The 'reputation temple' comprises three generic pillars (emotion, vision and CSR) and three pillars that are grafted on specific components of operational management (work, finance and products). The respective pillars are linked to three specific (primary) stakeholders: those in the labour market, the capital market and the consumer market. Direct reputational effects will arise especially in relation to these stakeholder groups.

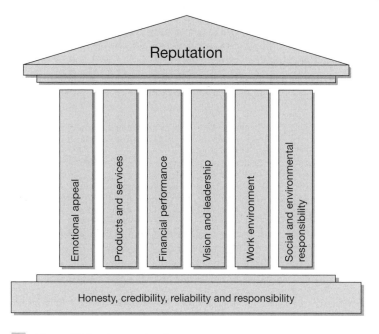

Figure 11.1 The temple of reputation

In the reputation temple, socially responsible conduct has a pillar of its own (social/environmental responsibility). Stakeholders partly judge companies on the basis of such conduct. In the area of CSR, there is thus something to 'win' or 'lose' with regard to reputation. Moreover, the pillars are connected to one another. Sustainable initiatives in the food industry not only influence the CSR pillar, they also affect product quality, which forms part of the products/services pillar (McWilliams and Siegel, 2000: 605). Sustainable initiatives are also influenced by the vision/leadership pillar and have an effect on the emotional pillar. Investment in the respective pillars strengthens reputation as a whole. Initiatives that contribute to environmental awareness and social justice strengthen a company's general appeal and reliability (Keller and Aaker, 1998). It is therefore not coincidence that Ben and Jerry's and the Body Shop have both relatively robust CSR, emotional and vision/leadership pillars. Sustainable initiatives, however, only add value to reputation if they are made public. For this reason, a company can only benefit from reputation enhancement if it discloses information about the work atmosphere, its vision, financial policy and products. In this way, companies are challenged to be transparent and disclose information on initiatives. Information is the key word and the media is indispensable when it comes to establishing the reputation of a company. The perception of consumers, investors and potential employees is only influenced if initiatives are made public. At the same time, the disclosure of CSR policy ensures that stakeholders can exercise their role as evaluators (Chapter 8).

Not every pillar is important to all stakeholders. Companies, after all, deal with several stakeholder groups, each of which employs its own set of criteria in evaluating a company (Freeman, 1984). Specific pillars in specific sectors and in specific markets function as important drivers of reputation (van Riel, 2001). Investors, for instance, are particularly interested in the financial performance of a company, graduates will pay greater attention to the quality of the work environment and an environmental group will attach the greatest value to a company's efforts to protect the natural environment. The reputation of a company creates expectations among stakeholders (Fombrun, 1996).

The foundation of reputation

The foundations of the pillars are, in the first instance, formed by three core ethical values: 'responsibility', 'honesty' and 'reliability'. 'Credibility' as a criterion for effective reporting, for instance, can also be distinguished as a value that underpins reputation. In total therefore, four core values form the foundation of a reputation. The moment consumers or investors decide that an entrepreneur is conducting business in an irresponsible, dishonest and untrustworthy manner, and that their confidence has been betrayed, the foundation of the pillars is undermined. The temple then starts showing cracks which could compromise the continuity of the company. Whether the perception of stakeholders is based on verifiable facts or not is essentially irrelevant in such a situation. In this way, a company gets caught up in a treacherous game.

Alsop (2001) adds 'respect', 'attractiveness' and 'admiration' to the four core values. These values form the foundation of the perceptual representation of a company's reputation. The more reliable, credible, honest and responsible a company is in the eyes of its stakeholders, the stronger and more sustainable its reputation (Fombrun, 1996). Past performance and philanthropic initiatives, such as donations and free medicine for employees, also influence reputation (Williams and Barrett, 2000: 342). Perception can be adjusted in two ways: through the company and its conduct, or through the perception and expectations of onlookers. Information about and disclosed by the company is continuously evaluated against the pillars of reliability, honesty, credibility and responsibility. In this way, the pillars and the foundation form the main ingredients for success.

Stakeholders evaluate a company's reputation by integrating a large number of signals. They draw their information from a range of sources, a number of which are difficult to manage.

The most important sources are printed media, television and radio, the Internet, friends and colleagues (cf. Saxton, 1998: 393). In addition, stakeholders employ all past and present opinions, rumours and statements in connection with a company to form expectations of future conduct. Stakeholder perceptions are further shaped and influenced by experience, images and symbols (van Riel, 1995: 75). The reputation of a company is thus the result of an interaction between a company's policy and assertions and stakeholders' evaluation of it. Clear communication is also of great importance if a company is to be evaluated positively – or in any event not negatively. Stakeholders, after all, filter the signals they receive and test them against their own perceptions, experience and assumptions.

In this way, each individual has a different image of the company as each attends to different aspects, receives different information and has different experiences. In this regard, one's experience of a company is more important than one's knowledge of it. Stakeholders evaluate the social principles, 'soul' and 'character' of a company on the basis of information about socially responsible activities a company has undertaken (Brown and Dacin, 1997; Keller and Aaker, 1998). On this basis, an evaluation of company reliability, honesty, responsibility and credibility is reached.

11.3 GENERAL FUNCTIONS OF REPUTATION: TIES THAT BIND

The relationship between reputation and operating performance is not easy to measure. It is regularly found that corporate reputation is strongly correlated with performance, but the correlation is generally more applicable to prior financial performance than subsequent financial performance, which might imply that good reputation is the result rather than a cause of good performance (Fombrun and van Riel, 2004: 28). Others stress that reputation works through a sort of 'value cycle' in which 'general reputations are heavily influenced by a company's size, advertising, operating performance, market value and media visibility – thereby confirming the idea that a company's operating performance, market value, and strategic behavior are heavily intertwined' (ibid.; Fombrun and Shanley, 1990). Corporate reputation therefore fulfils diverse and valuable functions: it is the binding and magnetic factor in relation to stakeholders, the basis for continuity, a buffer in the event of calamities (reservoir of goodwill), provider of information to customers and consumers, a corporate governance instrument, a strategic resource and the crucial factor in the relation between a company and its brands. Much is at stake.

Binding and magnetic factor

Reputation, just like trust, must be earned. It is the binding factor in the relationship between company and stakeholders. It coincides with loyalty and trust, which repeated interaction especially with primary stakeholders promotes (Saxton, 1998: 398). Due to social fragmentation (see Part I) the loyalty of individuals to an organization such as a company has become subject to 'permanent reflexivity' (Giddens, 1995). Loyalty has become less self-evident while the opportunity to switch to another employer, brand or share has increased. The licence to operate that companies are provisionally granted by stakeholders, is under pressure from competing loyalties. A company's real or symbolic engagement with issues can have an important impact on the choices stakeholders make in the face of competing loyalties.

Basis for continuity

Game theoretical insights show that companies that are not oriented towards the sustainable maintenance of relations and transactions also do not have the advantage of a good reputation. And because business consists largely of a succession of actions ('games'), reputation plays a significant role in short-term actions if the continuity of the company is at stake. Former one-off 'cheats' will be mistrusted more readily than those perceived as 'fair' players. From the moment a transaction is intended to be more than a one-off, opportunistic behaviour is punished (Etzioni, 1988). The reputation mechanism thus has a corrective function and provides the basis for repeated transactions and future relations (Beatty and Ritter, 1986).

Reservoir of goodwill

In times of economic crisis and in the face of controversies surrounding CSR themes, a good reputation functions as a buffer or cushion – a *reservoir of goodwill* (van Riel, 1999; Fombrun and Rindova, 2000; Jones *et al.*, 2000). Companies with a strong reputation are often given the benefit of the doubt (McGuire *et al.*, 1988; Patterson, 1993). By contrast, companies with a bad reputation have a harder time in such situations.

Bridging information asymmetries

Reputation could bridge the inevitable information asymmetry that exists between a company and its stakeholders, and which is part and parcel of the bargaining society (Stiglitz, 1989; Chapter 6). In their assessment of a company, stakeholders use not only the direct messages they receive from the company, but also the signals of financial analysts, investment colleagues and the media (Fombrun, 1996). In forming alliances, a company's reputation appears to function as an additional source of information (Anderson and Sorensen, 1999). For stakeholders, reputation fulfils a function that is related to expectations, knowledge and consistency, which helps them to process information (Lilli, 1983). Consumers and business-to-business (b2b) customers increasingly see company reputation as an indication of the quality of products and services (Barney, 1986; Keller, 1993).

Corporate governance instrument

The split between owners and managers leads to inadequate supervision and limited legitimacy (see Part I). Shareholder meetings seldom overcome this problem. Given the importance of perceptions, reputation can partly fulfil the function of letting shareholders – especially small shareholders – know that the company is managed in a manner that serves their interests. A negative reputation among small shareholders can cause enormous damage to the interests of a company (Carter and Dukerich, 1998; Weigelt and Camerer, 1988).

Intangible resource for strategic advantage

Reputation is an intangible resource that can create and sustain a competitive advantage and enhance the performance of companies (Deephouse, 2000; Hall, 1992). On the list of the most valuable intangible assets for CEOs, reputation is invariably number one (McMillan and Joshi, 1997; Fombrun and van Riel, 2004). It is a valuable asset that meets the requirements of Barney (1991): it cannot be imitated faultlessly (because it arises from a complex interaction with individual stakeholders), it cannot be replaced (and needs time to be established – there is neither an open nor standardized market for reputations; Caves, 1980; Peteraf, 1993) and is rare. Moreover, reputation as a resource is irreplaceable, as other resources that serve the same strategic purpose do not exist. Barney (1991) pointed out that reputation implies a psychological contract between a company and its stakeholders. Warranties, quality marks and contracts can only partly substitute a good reputation. Two companies with the same warranty terms can have significantly different reputations. A resource is scarce when other companies do not have access to the same resources or can imitate them only with difficulty (Barney, 1991: 107), as in the case of reputations.

Corporate reputation and corporate branding

The reputation of a mother company (*corporate reputation*) influences the brand image of the company. A company that uses the same brand name for its products and its company, referred to as *corporate branding*, can create and jeopardize new opportunities. Corporate reputation makes a company recognizable and gives meaning to the company as a whole, while brands add an emotional, distinctive meaning to products. If the company name and the most visible brand is the same, as in the case of Heineken and Shell, then damage to the *corporate reputation* has repercussions for the brand and sometimes also its turnover. *Corporate associations* can therefore have an impact on the evaluation of individual brands (Brown and Dacin, 1997). The principle of *corporate branding* can also have positive effects (Maathuis, 1999). A good reputation is therefore functional and valuable although there are differences between companies that pursue a corporate as opposed to a unit-branding strategy.

Reputation is a necessary, but not a sufficient, precondition for an effectively functioning company. Reputation is the outcome of the manner in which a company engages with issues and stakeholders combined with its marketing and branding strategies. Reputation is exceptionally difficult to measure (see Box 11.1). Over and above that, it is difficult to establish whether a respectable reputation does indeed contribute to higher sales (Brown and Dacin, 1997). It is, however, clear that a bad reputation has adverse effects on internal and external management, the relationship with financiers and, ultimately, the continuity of the company. Consequently, many entrepreneurs regard reputation management as an incidental activity, as a manifestation of crisis management (see section 9.3). Accordingly, reputation management is deployed defensively – when something goes wrong. More than half (55 per cent) of companies pay no structural attention to reputation management.

BOX 11.1 MEASURING (CSR) REPUTATION: A THORNY MATTER

Corporate reputation is traditionally measured by the value of the brand (in case of corporate branding). The **100 Top Brands**, the most commonly referred to listing is by Interbrand and annually published in *Business Week*. In 2004, Coca-Cola topped the list (representing a brand value of US$67 billion), followed by Microsoft (US$61 bn), and IBM (US$54 bn). Except for Nokia and Toyota (places 8 and 9, respectively, valued at US$30 bn and US$21 bn) all in the top 10 were American firms (*Business Week*, 2 August 2004). Of the 100 most valuable brands, 64 are owned by US companies. This has been a relatively stable finding since the 1950s. But there are some indications that US brands abroad suffer from the negative image of the current American administration (*FT*, 30 December 2004).

In 1990, *Fortune Magazine* started to list America's (and from 1997 onwards the world's) **Most Admired Companies**. In the *Fortune* ranking, reputation is measured on the basis of the individual opinions of thousands of top managers, directors and financial analysts. They rate companies on management qualities, product quality, innovation, long-term investments, financial performance, capacity for attracting and retaining talented employees, responsible community and environmental policies, and the use of financial resources. Over the years, these criteria changed, with different categories and headings; in 2004 for instance 'social responsibility' replaced 'community policies' as a category. *Fortune*'s measurement method turns the column 'quality of management' into the most important pillar of reputation. In 1994, the *Financial Times* started to compile a **World's Most Respected Companies** list, following a more or less similar method, which gauges the opinions of 1,000 senior officials and opinion formers across 25 countries. The two lists show considerable overlap. In 2004/2005 for instance 70 per cent of the top 10 firms overlap (although at slightly different places). General Electric of the US is at the top of both lists. In both lists, Toyota is the only non-American firm that reached the top 10. The *Fortune* and *Financial Times* lists also largely overlap with the 'best brands' list of *Business Week*. The lists expose the high level of visibility of these companies. It also makes them potentially more vulnerable to reputational damage, as well as targets for NGOs that employ the 'reputation' mechanism to focus attention on CSR issues.

But can these listings be considered good yardsticks for CSR? It has statistically been shown that the ranking on the *Fortune* reputation list correlates positively with financial performance (McMillan and Joshi, 1997; Roberts and Dowling, 1997; Srivastava *et al.*, 1997). But this correlation can also run in the opposite direction. The cigarette producer, Philip Morris, for instance, has ranked among the top five of the *Fortune* list for years, while the cigarette brand Marlboro, valued at US$22 billion, ranks 10th on the brand list. The financial pillar in the reputation temple has a significant *HALO*-effect on the other pillars: financial performance unintentionally overshadows all other measures in the individual perception of the 'peers' that are surveyed to compile the list. A good *ranking*, therefore, says little about the sustainability performance of the company and absolutely nothing about smaller companies (Deephouse, 2000). In 2001, Enron ranked 25th on the *Fortune* list, an achievement that was attributed to the fact that: 'no company illustrates the transformative power of innovation more dramatically than Enron'. A year later, after Enron collapsed, the company had disappeared from the list altogether, accompanied by an apologetic note from the *Fortune* editors stating: 'never mind; we meant "fiction" not "innovation"'. The different approaches to ranking – specifically of corporate responsibility – lead to strongly diverging results. The *Financial Times* top 10 sub-list of 'best for corporate responsibility' has a 30 per cent overlap with its general top 10 list, with Microsoft, Toyota and BP scoring the highest. *Fortune*'s Most Admired Companies list has no overlap with the general list with United Parcel Service, Alcoa, and Anheuser Busch (all American companies) scoring top positions in 2005. Many SRI funds – see below – boycott Anheuser Busch because of its alcoholic beverages production. The *Fortune* and *Financial Times* methods essentially amount to 'best in class' rankings, but this underestimates the effect of 'bad reputation' on a company's position. The weaknesses of the peers survey method is illustrated by other, more time-consuming research among consumers. Research in Europe (in 2000) and the US (in 2001) on the most visible companies paradoxically found that many companies simultaneously score high as well as low on reputation. In 2001, General Motors, Ford and AT&T for instance belonged to the top 10 companies in the US with the best as well as with the worst reputation (Fombrun and van Riel, 2004: 45ff.). It also shows that European consumers tend to harbour more negative feelings towards American producers, while American consumers tend not to draw comparisons, due to their focus on American companies.

11.4 REPUTATION AND CSR

There is an overlap in the meaning of reputation and the various dimensions of corporate responsibility: in both cases it concerns the development of initiatives which are positively valued by interested parties. Three of the six pillars of reputation have bearing on the relationship with concrete stakeholders in (1) consumer markets, (2) capital markets and (3) labour markets. But what does a reputation for 'socially responsible' business practice yield in these three market segments?

CSR reputation and consumer markets

It seems that companies with a good reputation, for instance with regard to product quality (the second column of the reputation temple), can ask higher prices for standard products (Shapiro, 1983; Bromley, 1993; Fombrun and Shanley, 1990). Moreover, reputation erects a barrier against competition and mobility (Caves and Porter, 1977) as customers tend to be more loyal to a company with a good reputation. A good CSR reputation acts as a distinguishing feature that yields a competitive advantage (Kreps and Wilson, 1982; Milgrom and Roberts, 1982). It seems that next to quality and price, consumers are increasingly taking social and environmental performance – and the related reputation – into account in their purchasing decisions. Positive associations with CSR can have a positive effect on the reputation of specific products, the company reputation in general and consumer behaviour (Creyer and Ross, 1997; Ellen *et al.*, 2000; Davids, 1990; Sen and Bhattacharya, 2001). In this regard, Brown and Dacin (1997: 79) speak of the relation between *corporate association* and *consumer product responses*. The strongest relation can be found in consumer perceptions of the expertise of a company to deliver products and services. Negative CSR associations have a demonstrably detrimental effect on product evaluations, while positive CSR associations have a fairly positive influence on product evaluations (ibid.: 80). Therefore, adequate communication of information about perspectives on corporate sustainability is important as it affects product evaluations (ibid.: 81).

According to research by the largest consumer organization in Europe (based in the Netherlands) more than half of consumers take societal considerations into account in their purchases. By means of environmentally friendly products, quality marks, donations, sponsoring, philanthropy and voluntary work, companies are increasingly attending to strategies that strengthen the CSR pillar of reputation.

CSR reputation and capital markets

Companies with a good reputation cannot only count on a greater likelihood of receiving loans from financial institutions, they also pay lower interest rates (Roberts and Dowling, 1997). Returns on investment and *price–earnings* ratios generally seem higher for companies with a good reputation in the area of corporate social responsibility than for those with a bad one (Little and Little, 2000). A good reputation renders companies more attractive to investors, both in the short and long term. Listed companies, in particular, can reap the benefits of a good social reputation when it comes to capital providers. They are, however, more at risk than unlisted companies – such as family businesses – of being punished for a bad reputation in the capital market. An increasing number of players in capital markets allow their investments to be influenced by the CSR reputation of companies. Around the world a variety of organizations have been founded that specialize in representing the interests of institutional and private investors who wish to contribute to sustainable development. With this, the market for socially responsible investment (SRI) was born.

SRI was initially based on the principle of avoiding companies that engaged in certain activities. As a result, SRI was about 'negative screens' on the basis of 'exclusionary criteria' and involved primarily firms active in the alcohol, tobacco, gambling, nuclear energy and weapons industries. Due to its direct and negative relationship to health problems, tobacco has become the most common negative screen, used by more than three-quarters of all SRI funds around the world (SIF, 2003). A comparable argument can be used for the gambling industry. Negative screening of industries to which primary responsibility for particular issues is less easily attributable is more problematic. So the number of SRI funds that exclude alcohol or nuclear energy is generally lower than in the case of tobacco. Tolerance of some industries (see section 10.2 on strategic stretching) is greater in some countries than in other countries. The military industry, for instance, is more acceptable as an object of investment in the US than in Canada. Whereas more than 66 per cent of Canadian SRI funds and around 80 per cent of European SRI funds (www.sricompass.org) use negative military screens, around 50 per cent of American funds do the same (SIF, 2003: 30).

Since the mid-1990s, a new generation of investment funds and indices developed which, in addition to disqualification criteria and negative screens, also employed positive and 'inclusionary' sustainability selection criteria such as a progressive social and human rights policy, proactive environmental policies, corporate citizenship and community participation. In 2003, the mutual funds in the US that used 'positive screens' on human rights and environment had already grown to 31 per cent and 48 per cent respectively (ibid.). In Europe, comparable positive screens developed for environmental issues (around 50 per cent). Positive and negative screens can be mixed up of course and lead to various assessments: whereas 52 per cent of European SRI funds use 'human rights violations' as a negative screen, only 18 per cent use 'preventive measures to avoid human rights violations' as a positive screen (www.sricompass.org).

Capital markets comprise a number of actors, each of which engages with company reputation in the area of CSR in its own way: investment funds, analysts and investment rating agencies, pension funds and financial services firms.

Investment funds

The number and size of investment funds that concentrate specifically on socially responsible business practice have grown exponentially. In the US, the leader in SRI, assets involved in social investing in the period 1993–2003 grew 40 per cent faster than any other professionally managed investment assets (SIF, 2003: 4). By 2003, there were around 700 SRI funds in the OECD region. In the same period investment portfolios in SRI grew by 240 per cent amounting to a total of US$2.14 trillion, the bulk of which (93 per cent) is managed on behalf of individuals and institutions, with the rest managed by mutual funds (ibid.). The downturn in shareholder investment in the first years of the twenty-first century was considerably smaller in SRI. In the US SRI embraces three strategies: screening, shareholder advocacy and community investing. In the period 1997–2003, screening increased in relative importance from 45 per cent to around 99 per cent. The relative importance of shareholder advocacy in the same period decreased sharply from 62 per cent to less than 2 per cent. Qualitatively, however, shareholder advocacy increased as measured by the number of resolutions submitted on CSR relevant issues in shareholder meetings. In the period as a whole, community investing – as a strategy by investment funds – remained negligible (ibid.).

Initially the funds that represented the interest, for instance, of religious groups such as churches applied CSR principles. Later on, specialized ethical investment funds and SRI investment screening agencies such as KLD were founded. They have become an important, but not yet leading force in the SRI market. Some ethical funds have recently started to pool their resources in order to get more leverage on specific items. In 2003, six investors in the UK created the Social Investment Forum (SIF). It aims at 'institutionalizing' a number of other initiatives on climate change and pharmaceutical issues in particular (*FT*, 24 August 2003). Ethical investment funds have also been the driving force behind the claim that SRI correlates with higher performance (see 'Business *in* Society Management' in Chapter 8). This claim is surrounded by causal controversy and statistical difficulties. Using an international database containing 103 German, UK and US ethical mutual funds, Otten *et al.* (2002) examined the performance of ethical mutual funds. They found little evidence of significant differences in risk-adjusted returns between ethical and conventional funds in the period 1990–2001. The introduction of some time variation, however, leads to a significant under-performance of domestic US funds and a significant out-performance of UK ethical funds, relative to their conventional peers.

Gradually, generic asset management companies have also started to apply SRI principles, for instance, by setting up ethical committees that set criteria and use CSR accreditation bodies. SRI compass (www.sricompass.org), a European SRI consultancy, notes that 70 per cent of all the SRI funds in Europe have an ethical committee. But generic asset managers remain faced with a large number of dilemmas, not least because investing in 'vice' instead of 'virtue' can still yield solid and above average returns for investors – no matter what SRI fund managers claim. Not including these companies creates a fiduciary duty problem for asset managers. They can be reproached for not appropriately representing the interests of their clients. So, separate 'vice funds' have been created (Box 11.2).

In practice, top fund managers have difficulty operationalizing ethical criteria. An excellent example of this was found in the UK. In 2003, research on the combined holdings of 30 top fund managers in charge of 41 UK equity funds, revealed that they had three leading tobacco companies (BAT, Imperial Tobacco Group, Gallaher Group) as their favourite investment target among the FTSE 350 companies (*FT*, 7 July 2003). These three companies are barred from inclusion in the FTSE4Good and the Dow Jones Sustainability Index, and are among the worst rated on the blacklists of many SRI funds. So tobacco companies are still considered a good investment and the widespread acceptance of ethical investment still a long way off.

BOX 11.2 INVESTING IN VICE

That all tastes are catered for also holds true in the world of investment funds. Whereas the more ethical investment funds have branded the alcohol, tobacco, gambling and weapons industry as 'unethical' or 'socially *un*accountable', the American Vice Fund selects these industries purposefully. The fund was founded in 2002 as an 'innovative' mutual fund product for individual investors and institutions. It claims that 'under normal market conditions' the fund will invest at least 80 per cent of its net assets in equity securities of companies that derive a significant proportion of their revenues from products often considered socially irresponsible' (2004 prospectus, p. 2). In 2005 the fund traded in defence (25 per cent), gambling (24 per cent), alcohol (23 per cent) and tobacco (14 per cent). Top shareholdings are: Altria Group, Fortune Brands, International Game Technology and Anheuser Busch. The founders are convinced that these sectors will always do well, irrespective of economical downturn, terrorist attacks or threatening wars. Apart from that, fund manager Mutuals.com claims that the Vice Fund yields better returns than the general index. The website (www.vicefund.com) quotes Lipper Analytical Services, a leading provider of global (mutual) fund data and owned by Reuters, who ranked it second out of a total of 711 funds in February 2005.

Indices, analysts and rating agencies

Investment advisors no longer rely solely on financial-economic indicators such as profitability and higher turnover. By the end of the 1990s, more than one-third of financial analysts and advisors had started to include a measure of the environmental and social performance of companies in their assessments (Business in the Environment, 2001). Worldwide, hundreds of specialized rating agencies have sprung up alongside – or as part of – SRI funds. The best-known international 'best in class' indices are the Domini 400 Social Index (DSI400), the FTSE4Good and the Dow Jones Sustainability Group Index (DJSGI) (Box 11.3).

All funds employ combinations of negative (human rights and trade union rights violations, use of child labour and activities in sectors such as the tobacco, weapons and gambling industry) and positive criteria (a proactive environmental policy, or active in the areas of organic farming or wind energy). All indices are reviewed on an annual basis. Almost all indices exclude companies that are active in the tobacco, gambling, alcohol, weapons or bio-industry, that use nuclear energy or carry out animal testing – the so-called *sin-stocks*. But there are major differences between the indices as well. The exact combination of positive and negative screening measures varies considerably in the various indices. The weighting of specific criteria in the indices also varies considerably (or is not even revealed). The content and meaning of one and the same criterion vary among the different indices. Even when funds adopt a seemingly simple criterion such as the exclusion of tobacco firms, definitions can vary from 'named tobacco companies', 'companies involved in the production of tobacco', 'companies with major interests in tobacco', and 'over five per cent of turnover yielded by tobacco-related business' (Louche, 2003).

BOX 11.3 LEADING SUSTAINABILITY INDICES

DSI400 The Domini 400 Social Index (DSI400) was established in 1990 by Kinder, Lydenberg, Domini & Co., Inc. (KLD) and is the oldest sustainability index. Investments are made in the 400 companies that are frontrunners in the area of CSR. The performance of the DSI400 scores more than 1 per cent higher than the Standard & Poor 500 Index (Statman, 2000). The preference is for companies who endorse the labour guidelines of the ILO. (www.domini.com/DFEF.html)

FTSE4Good In July 2001 four new indices were launched in Europe: the FTSE4Good. The most important criteria employed are stakeholder relationships, sustainable development in the environmental dimension and human rights policy. The criteria that are included in these indices draw, among others, on the conventions of the Coalition for Environmentally Responsible Economies (CERES), UN Global Compact and the OECD (Chapter 13). The indices are divided into four regions: US, UK, Europe and Global. With the indices, the FTSE seeks to create a new global standard for investment in socially responsible companies. The proceeds of the index were donated to UNICEF in its first year. (www.ftse4good.com)

DJSGI A large number of the indices of the Dow Jones Indexes, STOXX Ltd. and the SAM Group are aimed at the sustainability levels of company reputations. The indices focus on the US as well as Europe. One of the indices of the Dow Jones Sustainability Group Index (DJSGI) is the Dow Jones STOXX Sustainability Index. This index follows the economic, social, ethical and ecological performance of the largest international companies per sector. In 2002, the DJSGI listed 232 companies from 27 countries. (www.sustainability-indexes.com)

The admission criteria to the respective indices have therefore been subjected to criticism, especially the funds, institutions and indices that employ the *best in class* method. They are criticized for being inconsistent and lacking standardization. Companies can be included in one index, but excluded from another. For example: in November 2001 Fortis Bank was included in the FTSE4Good index but not in the Dow Jones Sustainability Index, while exactly the opposite applied to ING Bank (Louche, 2003). The leading indices are also criticized for including companies such as Shell and BP who are active in unsustainable and severely environmentally degrading sectors and whose products are sourced largely in countries with dubious regimes. The inclusion of pharmaceutical manufacturers such as GlaxoSmithKline or Pfizer, for example, is also controversial due to their refusal to supply developing countries with cheaper HIV/Aids medicine. The admission requirements of specialized 'idealistic' sustainability funds such as Triodos are much stricter.

Finally, transparency and openness of a company are mostly a precondition for inclusion in a sustainability index. The FTSE4Good indicated that approximately 50 per cent of companies are excluded from the index due to a lack of information on their CSR policies and practices.[3] Interestingly enough, the funds themselves are far from transparent about the criteria and methodologies they use. Lack of transparency on criteria and methods can serve as a means of power exertion by well-positioned intermediary actors in a bargaining society (Chapter 6). In response, a number of smaller and medium-sized SRI retail funds, under the auspices of Eurosif – the European Sustainable and Responsible Investment Forum – released Transparency guidelines in 2004 (www.eurosif.org) to create more clarity, help enhance the quality of the indices and thus contribute to their reliability. The chaos in sustainability indices, however, is bound to persist not least because an international bargaining society creates a continuous craving for rival indices. So, next to SRI rating agencies, business organizations such as the World Economic Forum ('Global 100 Most Sustainable Corporations in the World') or the ICC ('ICC Company Showcase list') have their own listings.

Pension funds

Investors who concentrate on long-term returns have become most interested in CSR. Institutional investors such as pension funds in particular have started to take corporate social and environmental performance into consideration in their investment portfolio. This orientation is, in the first place, inspired by legal provisions specifying the aims of pension funds. The Dutch Pension and Savings Funds Act (PSW) for instance prescribes that pension fund investments should be 'solid' and represent the longer-term interests of their participants. Since the end of the 1990s, the largest pension funds in the world such as ABP, PGGM of the Netherlands or TIAA-CREF and Calpers of the US – each representing US$150 billion or more in total assets – started to express their intent to dedicate substantial parts of their investment portfolio to CSR goals. These pension funds were not only the largest in the world, but also represent civil servants, teachers and semi-public officials who are generally more interested in social responsibility and public goods. A survey by Eurosif in October 2000 revealed that 59 per cent of the UK's largest pension funds (with over £230 billion in assets) had incorporated social responsibility criteria into their strategies.

The extent to which pension funds actively employ strategies to pursue CSR also depends on the legal framework and national idiosyncrasies. Calpers – the California Public Employees Retirement System – the largest pension fund in the US has become quite aggressive in its pursuit of social responsibility via shareholder advocacy. Calpers uses a black list – the so-called 'Focus List' – of companies that perform below the market average and/or have legal or ethical problems. The fund, for instance, played a leading role in ousting Richard Grasso, the NYSE chair. It uses its financial muscle not to pressurize companies, but also governments, such as the government of the Philippines (*Vkt*, 19 December 2003).

In Europe, national regulatory frameworks aimed at creating greater transparency in SRI portfolios of pension funds also contributed to the interest in SRI. The UK is a leading example of how this mechanism works. The UK Pension Act of 2000 requires the top management of the funds to make explicit in their Statement of Investment Principles (1) to what extent they adhere to social, environmental or ethical considerations in the selection of an investment portfolio and (2) how they apply their shareholder rights to implement these principles. Even though the Act does not *oblige* the funds to apply SRI, the disclosure provision has stimulated many funds to step up the use of SRI criteria. It is claimed that this strategy raised the proportion of pension funds incorporating SRI into their strategies from 25 per cent to 59 per cent (Eurosif). Comparable legislation is under way in the Netherlands, Belgium, Switzerland, Sweden, Germany and France (SIF, 2003). Currently US pension law does not require pension funds to assess the significant impact social and environmental factors have on financial performance and risk.

However, implementation of intentions can be a laborious process. More than three-quarters of pension funds in the UK are still not really taking SRI seriously. Research conducted by Ashbridge Centre for Business and Society in 2003 (*FT*, 26 January 2004) revealed that pension funds lack procedures for taking social, ethical and environmental factors into account. Most pension funds have opted for a gradual transition strategy. First, most funds adopt a code of conduct and criteria for SRI (on a variety of indices – both internal and external). Second, firms are assessed on the basis of these criteria, but existing investments in companies that pay inadequate attention to sustainability are not immediately removed from the portfolio, nor are companies openly criticized for not complying with the standards. Institutional investors around the world – including Calpers – rarely use their official powers to exert influence on shareholder meetings. Their vote on the management of public companies generally coincides with that of management. Of the almost 800 shareholder governance proposals submitted at annual shareholder meetings in 2003 – ranging from bans on protection against takeovers and the repricing of stock options, to calls for moderate executive pay – only 30 were submitted by mutual and pension funds (*FT*, 7 October 2003). Institutional investors tend to work behind the scenes. In 2002, Calpers targeted 13 companies with proposed resolutions only to withdraw all of them after talks with management (ibid.). In the Netherlands, PGGM, a large shareholder in many companies, employs open dialogue to urge policy change. If the dialogue has a satisfactory effect, an investment is reconsidered. In practice this approach has, indeed, sometimes led to the pension fund's withdrawal.

Financial service providers

Financial service firms active in securities have also initiated specialized SRI funds and – albeit it more modestly than pension funds – have started to apply SRI principles in their mainstream securities activities. In addition, SRI principles are gradually being used in retail and industrial banking activities. Also in the case of unlisted companies, a reputation for sustainable business practice is playing an increasingly significant role. As time progresses, more banks are including environmental risks in assessing loan applications. US banks have realized that under certain circumstances they can be held directly accountable for socially irresponsible conduct of their business relations (SER, 2000: 39). A direct appeal is also being made to financial service providers to review their policies. In the Netherlands, ING and ABN Amro, among others, have been called to account for indirectly financing suspect regimes and for investing in environmentally degrading industries, such as logging and coal mining (*Vk*, 6 October 2001).

Insurance companies have agreed to modify their portfolios in view of global climate change issues. With the endorsement of the *United Nations Environment Programme* (UNEP) *Insurance Initiative*, more than 250 financial service providers have chosen for investments that contribute to slowing down global climate change (Houlder, 2000). Of the world's largest firms, banks and insurance companies are most reluctant to reveal their involvement in CSR, for instance, through sustainability reports (Kolk, 2003). This is not really surprising. The CSR challenge represents the same fiduciary dilemmas for banks as it does for specialized securities firms: their customers as well as shareholders are especially interested in high-performing portfolios, which does not necessarily coincide with responsible investments.

CSR reputation and labour markets

The reputation of a company is an increasingly important distinguishing factor in the struggle to attract talented employees, especially in a country, a sector or a region that experiences labour shortages. A good reputation can boost labour forces, certainly as far as graduate recruitment is concerned. But it is not only the pillars 'products and services' and 'working environment' that determine the reputation of companies in the labour market. Research by Ethicon, the Centre for International Ethics Management at Erasmus University Rotterdam, shows that two out of three final-year business students attach value to the social and environmental performance of potential employers. If there is little difference in salary and secondary labour conditions, potential employees seek out other distinguishing features; a company's CSR policy in particular. This also fulfils a corrective function: one-third of those surveyed would not even consider working for an employer who has not adopted a CSR policy. In this way, the switch from one employer to another is made on ethical grounds. Not only are existing employees more motivated to work for a socially responsible company that radiates social consciousness, but efforts to recruit new personnel also benefit from it. Companies around the world are awarded quality marks such as 'Investor in People' (Netherlands) or 'the best boss to work for' for their efforts. A socially accountable human resources policy implies that the company values lifelong learning, health and safety, work/life balance, equal pay and equal opportunities for women and minorities. It is increasingly acknowledged that these features of a human resources policy lead to enhanced productivity, lower staff turnover, greater flexibility, more innovation, more reliable products and, ultimately, higher profits (EU, 2001). Leading gurus in HRM have already acknowledged the importance of a good reputation. That is the Triple-E in practice (see section 8.4).

11.5 REPUTATION AND CORRECTION

Three important CSR self-disciplining methods exist: codes of conduct (input oriented), quality marks (process oriented) and reporting (output oriented). The reputation mechanism can trigger these forms of self-disciplining by correcting firms that are 'doing something wrong'. Correction refers to the appraisal of company reputation, reprimanding a company or improving a company's reputation. Corrective acts can have a positive or negative effect on the reputation of a company. The function of the reputation mechanism is one of punishment and reward. Building a reputation not only costs plenty of time and money, it is also extremely vulnerable and very easily damaged. Reputational damage can theoretically be interpreted as the 'collapse' of one of the six perceptual pillars of reputation. 'Nothing deflates faster than a punctured reputation!' (Dewar, in: Lieberman, 1983). Loss of trust and credibility can shake the foundation of the 'reputation temple', put the *license to operate* at risk and jeopardize the continuity of the organization. If this happens, the buffer or reservoir of goodwill (section 11.2) that reputation represents in the face of controversies also disappears.

Restoring a severely damaged reputation is a painful process irrespective of the amount of time and money spent on it. The foundation of trust that underpins reputation takes time to be established but is easily damaged. A reputation is destroyed faster than it is created; it takes one day to earn a bad reputation and years to get rid of it. Publicity surrounding a conflict has a negative effect on stakeholder perceptions and jeopardizes the underlying relationship of trust. It appears that ExxonMobil is still scoring low on the *environmental responsibility* component of its reputation as a result of the Exxon Valdez oil spill off the Alaskan coast in 1989 (Alsop, 2001). The reputation of Ben & Jerry's was dealt a blow as a result of its sale to Unilever, despite the latter's assurance that its policy would remain unchanged (ibid.). Prevention is therefore always better than cure. Some reputations, such as that of Philip Morris, will probably never recover from controversies. The advertising campaign the company launched as a vehicle for its social responsibility principles was regarded as highly unconvincing. A particularly large amount of energy, time and money is required to restore credibility.

The course of a reputation crisis

A reputation crisis often unfolds according to a pattern similar to that of an issue life cycle (Chapter 9). First of all, a *triggering event* occurs by means of which stakeholders acquire information about an issue. Thereupon, stakeholders interpret the information and, if necessary, prepare a response. Finally, company management will also have to assess the situation and react.

Triggering event: starting point for damage

An accident or explosion, or the release of issue-related information in the form of a report, article or research about the moral conduct of a company can act as a *triggering event*. A company has little influence on determining the moment and the manner in which information is disclosed if the initiative is taken by an NGO. As a rule, as far as company reputation is concerned, 'no news is good news' (Fombrun, 1996).

Stakeholder interpretation and reaction

The reaction to a triggering event and accompanying issue-related information depends on stakeholders' interpretation of it. The interpretation is, in the first place, based on a previously established opinion of a company's reputation. A good reputation in the area of CSR could result in the company being given the benefit of the doubt (Zyglidopoulos and Phillips, 1999). How do stakeholders react to new issue-related information that is subsequently released by means of NGO campaigns? Three scenarios are conceivable in stakeholders' appraisal (correction) of company reputation (van der Zwart, 2002): appreciation, rejection and indifference.

- *Appreciation*: Stakeholder relations are enhanced as a result of the manner in which the company has engaged with the issue. The number of consumers and investors in the company increases which boosts turnover and the share price. The company reputation undergoes a positive correction, or is strengthened. The company is seen as heroic, concerned and considerate (or victim!) and becomes more attractive to consumers, employees and investors (Pearson and Clair, 1998: 69).
- *Rejection*: Stakeholder relations deteriorate and explicit or implicit contracts are severed. The company reputation is damaged. The new information that stakeholders obtain, conflicts with their normative expectations. Consumers, investors and employees never

'expected' that 'their' furniture supplier, shoe brand or petrol station would handle the issue concerned in such a manner. It requires correction in terms of trust and credibility. The company's reputation is negatively corrected which creates a crisis. The *license to operate* is under threat of being revoked.

- *Indifference*: Stakeholder relations remain unaltered or the reputational damage is difficult to discern. This is because the company deals with issue exactly as expected. It could also be that the expectational gap is not that great which is why the company is 'forgiven' this time. After all, companies with a good reputation have a sort of buffer that can absorb social or financial blunders. As discussed in Chapters 9 and 10, not all expectational gaps evoke such a mild response. The *reservoir of goodwill* can show signs of depletion, causing growing concern. Nevertheless, when NGOs finally present the issue to stakeholders, it leaves them cold. They are not interested in the issue or place higher value on matters such as product quality or price. In such a case, the CSR pillar of reputation is deemed of minor importance.

Management interpretation and reaction: bridges or buffers?

In the face of accusations from NGOs, company management first has to assess the situation. How does one, confronted with a critical NGO on a CSR issue, respond to stakeholder demands? The reaction from management depends on the assessment that is made of the power, urgency and legitimacy of stakeholders and their demands (Mitchell *et al.*, 1997). If a grouping is regarded as powerful, the issue urgent and the demand legitimate, managers will be quicker to take action (Zyglidopoulos and Phillips, 1999: 337). A powerful stakeholder with a legitimate demand can easily get the support of other stakeholders. In the event of a truly ethical dilemma, managers will largely want to meet legitimate stakeholder demands (Freeman, 1984). In the event of such a confrontation two managerial approaches are possible: *bridging* or *buffering* (van den Bosch and van Riel, 1998). Managers can try to shield the company from stakeholders' demands (*buffering*) or try to build bridges between the company and the stakeholders concerned (*bridging*). In the case of *bridging* one can imagine managers providing shareholders or societal groupings with information about matters such as environmental policy or labour conditions. The aim of bridging is to align the interests and expectations of the company with those of its stakeholders so as to guarantee the continuity of the company, avoid reputational damage and retain the *license to operate* (Scott, 1987: 185). In this regard, the behaviour and activities of the company will be adapted to the expectations of stakeholders (Meznar and Nigh, 1995: 976). The company can then proceed to embark on disciplining.

Management can also choose to buffer or shield the company from the demands of external stakeholders (Meznar and Nigh, 1995). In this strategy, management keeps quiet or refuses to account for, justify or adjust its policy. This style of communication is also referred to as *corporate silence* (van den Bosch and van Riel, 1998; Grunig, 1992).

Bridging is associated with dialogue. Dialogue can be important for a company that is confronted with normative issues (Schwartz and Gibb, 1999: 128). Different gradations of *bridging* and *buffering* exist along with their various styles of communication. The choice for one of the two strategies depends on the strategic importance of the issue, the power of the NGO, the size of the company and the attitude of the dominant coalition in top management.

11.6 INDICATORS OF REPUTATIONAL DAMAGE

Reputational damage can be sustained in the relationship with governments, the media or other societal groupings. With respect to the primary processes of the company, reputational damage is sustained especially in the relationship with the three stakeholders groups and markets already discussed: the consumer market, the capital market and the labour market.

Consumer market: 'rather purchase that other brand'

Consumers can make or break reputations. The reputation mechanism requires a certain degree of competition to function. A customer should, after all, be able to move on to a competitor if a supplier throws away its reputation. Certainly in the area of CSR, consumers have acquired increased power. Consumers have become more critical, vote with their feet more often and could break a brand in this way. Shopping has almost become a political act: *don't vote, shop!* (Hertz, 2002). The consumer is led largely by trust. As long as the media provides no immediate reason to withdraw that trust, there is little to be concerned about. Moreover, consumers' reactions depend on personal perceptions (Sen and Bhattacharya, 2001: 227). Reputational damage in the consumer market manifests clearly in a decline in turnover and/or market share. Such a decline can be the result of interest groups' participation in a consumer boycott of a company's products or services. It is the most powerful indication of reputational damage. But the damage can also be temporary. Graig Smith of the London Business School studied the impact of an NGO campaign against a big European food firm and found that sales initially dropped but recovered within a few months. (*The Economist*, 9 August 2003: 49).

Capital market: 'money talks'

Reputational losses associated with crises amount to an average of 8–15 per cent of the market value of affected companies (Fombrun and van Riel, 2004: 38). The reputational effect is not only direct for the company involved in the crisis, but also has a spillover effect on the whole sector. A company that has squandered the goodwill of capital providers will have to spend more to raise capital, whether it is by issuing more shares or by paying higher interest rates. Reputational damage in the capital market manifests in different ways. In the first place, companies that have sustained reputational damage will find it more difficult to access new capital (Karpoff, 2002: 79). In the second place, such companies lose their appeal which leads analysts to adjust their advice on which shares to buy. In the third place, a company can be removed from one of the sustainability indices. This was the fate of the German publisher *Springer Verlag*, which – known among other things for its environmentally friendly printing process – was dropped from a major SRI index. The company met all CSR requirements, but it was nevertheless decided to strike the company off the list due to the sexist and discriminating content of a number of its magazines.[4]

Finally, long-term investors – pension funds and banks – and short-term investors – small investors – may decide to withdraw their investments. In financial markets, so-called 'relevant information' is quickly assimilated into the prices on the stock exchange. News of higher than expected profits, a technological breakthrough, an acquisition or promising figures of a competitor generally results in a rise in the share price. By contrast, reports on profits lower than expected (even in the case of very high absolute profits), a deteriorating market and unsuccessful acquisition negotiations generally have a negative effect on the share price. Indications of socially irresponsible or unethical conduct are often also interpreted as relevant facts in financial markets (Karpoff and Lott, 1993: 757). Publicity surrounding fraud, for example, generates a negative return of approximately 1.6 per cent on the day before (sic!) it is made public in the media. The share price generally drops by 5.1 per cent in the month after fraudulent practices have been made public. Fraudulent behaviour is likely to incur fines and compensations to third parties, or a lower market turnover. Investors thus partly respond to expected outcomes in the near future. At the same time, there is also the so-called *reputational penalty*: the loss on returns when unethical behaviour is publicized is significantly higher than the sum of fines and damage claims. Trust forms part of the price. Reputational effects play an important role in the disciplining of companies in cases of fraud (Karpoff and Lott, 1993: 797; Karpoff, 2002). Whether the inverse is also true – that CSR coincides with a rise in share prices – has hardly been researched.

Labour market: 'do you want to work there?'

To deliver quality products and services, companies are strongly dependent on current and potential employees. Companies benefit from a motivated team. A team is demotivated if the company's reputation falls into discredit. The greatest influence on employee perception is the company itself. Employees, in turn, have a great influence on the perception of consumers and other groups in their environment (Saxton, 1998: 395). Indicators of reputational damage are fewer job applications, losing one's position on the list of 'most wanted employer', more hefty conflicts with the works council and/or the labour union and (involuntary) dismissals. Name changes of companies that have experienced bad publicity, are often also primarily inspired by labour market considerations. The existing employees are less burdened by the negative old image. Improving a bad image through a name change because of a previous accounting scandal was tried by Enron (now Cross Country Energy and Prisma Energy International), AOL/Time Warner (became Time Warner again, but especially the NYSE ticker symbol made the difference), PriceWaterhouseCoopersConsulting (became Monday), Conseco Capital Management (changed into 40/86 advisors). Other major reasons for a name change have been to get rid of a bad sectoral image (Philip Morris became the Altria Group) or after privatization to get rid of the bad image of state-owned companies (French Général des Eaux for instance became Vivendi). The problem with the new name, however, is that it can lead to confusion in consumer markets. If the underlying business practices do not change, the name change brings only temporary relief. What's in a name?

11.7 CONCLUSION: THE TRADE-OFF BETWEEN CORRECTION AND DISCIPLINARY MEASURES

Reputation management too, is based on the Triple-E principles that were discussed in Chapter 8. For a company to be able to interact effectively with stakeholders, efficiency in the three reputational markets (labour, finance, consumers) must be brought into line with the four core values that form the foundation of the temple of reputation (Figure 11.1). In this way, reputation management amounts to the management of the several private–public and profit–non-profit interfaces of society (Figure 8.2) rendering it an integral part of Societal Interface Management. Companies partly discipline themselves on issues related to CSR through introducing codes of conduct and trademarks, annual reporting, engaging in stakeholder dialogues, and corporate citizenship. These CSR tools were discussed in Chapter 8. The more companies discipline themselves, the more they exhibit an active approach to CSR. This chapter highlighted another aspect of the dynamics: companies are also disciplined in their interaction with stakeholders. In this regard, one can speak of correction due to (imminent) reputational damage. The discussion concluded with an overview of the most important indicators of correction.

In practice, (self-)discipline and correction are intertwined. Correction does not occur in the absence of demonstrable damage to reputation in one of the three core stakeholder relations. Apart from that, the response of stakeholders may also be one of indifference. In addition, it is also possible that the company has such a strong reputation – and consequently a *reservoir of goodwill* – that significant reactions simply fail to occur. The corrective effect of the reputation mechanism will be great if demonstrable damage is sustained in all three markets. If, during a conflict, the share price as well as the consumer market reacts strongly and job applications fall significantly at the same time, then one can speak of demonstrable reputational damage.

It is more difficult to classify corrections in grey areas. Reputational damage in labour markets is particularly difficult to demonstrate and its connection with a reputation conflict can least clearly be shown. It is conceivable that companies may attract sufficient new recruits despite damage to their reputation – particularly if the labour market is large. Reputational damage in capital markets is taken more seriously as a correction mechanism, but hybrid companies that are not listed on the stock exchange and/or do not borrow money can position themselves relatively independently of this market. It therefore seems logical that demonstrable reputational damage in consumer markets represents the most important corrective effect for companies. In Figure 11.2 the successive columns depict what this classification of different combinations of reputational damage yields.

The reputation mechanism utilized by so many governments is only effective if correction actually initiates some form of disciplining – the grey area in Figure 11.2. There are roughly three forms of disciplining conceivable with respect to CSR issues: none, negligible and demonstrable.

- *None*: No initiatives are undertaken to meet the demands and expectations of NGOs. The issue at stake remains unresolved. Disciplining does not take place. An entrepreneur who is capable of avoiding any form of reputational damage in the face of an obvious issue seems to be in a position where the reputation mechanism has no hold on the enterprise. If reputational damage sustained in consumer markets remains limited, damage in capital markets and the labour market is also easier to contain. Conversely, companies that sustain enormous reputational damage in consumer markets, but who are not willing to discipline themselves run a real risk of going bankrupt. The greater the reputational damage, the smaller the chance that a reactive (*buffering*) CSR strategy of such a company will lead to settlement of the issue. The reputation crisis continues and threatens the continuity of the company.
- *Negligible*: It is unclear whether the initiatives undertaken denote disciplining. A company could for instance withdraw from a country or activity but may have been planning to do

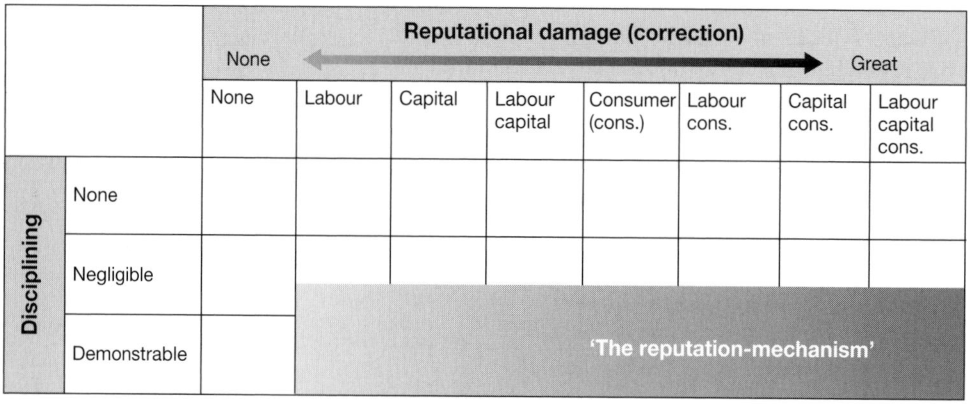

		Reputational damage (correction)							
		None ← → Great							
		None	Labour	Capital	Labour capital	Consumer (cons.)	Labour cons.	Capital cons.	Labour capital cons.
Disciplining	None								
	Negligible								
	Demonstrable			'The reputation-mechanism'						

Figure 11.2 Positioning the reputation mechanism

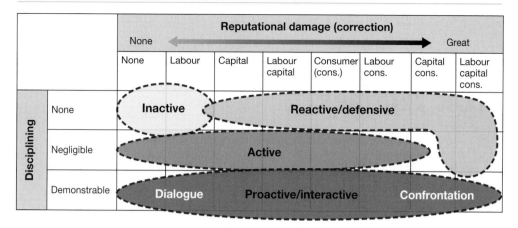

		Reputational damage (correction) None ⟵⟶ Great							
		None	Labour	Capital	Labour capital	Consumer (cons.)	Labour cons.	Capital cons.	Labour capital cons.
Disciplining	None	*Inactive*		*Reactive/defensive*					
	Negligible			*Active*					
	Demonstrable		*Dialogue*	*Proactive/interactive*				*Confrontation*	

Figure 11.3 Strategy repertoires in disciplining and correction

so all along. Quality labels are introduced but more as a means to compete with others than as an attempt to provide consumers with clear information. A company may report on social, environmental and ethical aspects of its operations, but refrain from integrating it into a sustainability report and have no inclination to strive for international coordination or integration of standards. A code of conduct could be drawn up, but contain no reference to international standards and implementation is barely monitored. Undecided controversies can also be situated under this heading.

■ *Demonstrable*: The company has undertaken initiatives, such as the development of a code of conduct or adopting an international standard that meet stakeholder expectations and demands to review company policy on a CSR issue. This settles the issue. This can occur in the absence or presence of demonstrable reputational damage. The reputation mechanism has a corrective effect if demonstrable reputational damage is sustained in the process of settling a conflict. If strong disciplining occurs in the absence of demonstrable reputational damage there is evidence of a proactive strategy, which is usually accompanied by close consultation with relevant stakeholders whereby serious reputational damage is avoided. In such a case, the company and stakeholders will most probably have entered a dialogue already in the early stages of the issue's appearance.

Figure 11.3 places the different types of CSR strategies discussed in Chapter 8 (inactive, reactive, active, inter/proactive) in the disciplining/correction framework of this chapter. With that, the analytical framework within which we can discuss Societal Interface Management challenges in general is complete. The analytical challenge that is left is to determine whether the international dimension adds complementary characteristics and/or another dynamics to Societal Interface Management. This dimension is explored in the next two chapters.

The context: rival CSR and ICR regimes

12.1 INTRODUCTION: FROM CSR TO ICR

In International Business (IB), context determines relative success. What is considered appropriate Societal Interface Management in one country is often deemed inappropriate in another country. Different countries represent different institutional contexts for CSR strategies – their so-called 'CSR regime'. CSR regimes reflect the national societal 'selection environment' in which corporate strategies develop and are judged as successful or not. Corporate philanthropy, for instance, can be lauded as an excellent expression of the voluntary social engagement of companies in one country while it can be considered obligatory on religious grounds in another, and in yet another country it can be regarded with great suspicion or dismissed as 'window dressing'. The very definition of what constitutes an adequate measure of firm performance (profits, market capitalization, return on investment, profits before or after taxes) differs across national accounting systems and cultures. The success of internationalization strategies critically depends on understanding these differences. Appropriate international issues management takes the relevant societal context into account (Chapters 9 and 10) and appropriate international stakeholder management takes heed of society as a whole (Getz, 2004).

The international dimension of CSR is referred to as international corporate responsibility (ICR) (cf. Hooker and Madsen, 2004). It is as multifaceted as CSR – so the ICR acronym can have various meanings. ICR adds three complicating dimensions to national CSR:

a   *increased bargaining dynamics due to larger regulatory voids*: the international arena lacks a common legal and institutional framework encompassing, instead, around 200 national

governments as well as an innumerable number of other potential stakeholders in varying constellations and spread over a large number of bargaining arenas;

b   *increased importance of rivalry*: instead of a relatively predictable institutional environment, companies are confronted with diverging and often rival legal, cultural, institutional, value and societal systems; and

c   *increased complexity of issues*: issues manifest differently and can be judged differently in different societal contexts.

The growing importance of these dimensions introduced an era of *multilateral diplomacy* where companies, governments, NGOs and, sometimes, IB associations, bargain over the formulation and implementation of principles, codes, rules and regulations pertaining to ICR. As yet, hardly any multilateral authority imposes rules and/or sanctions on MNEs in the event of non-compliance with CSR standards across borders. None of the original treaties that ushered in the most important post-war international organizations, for instance, mentioned MNEs – let alone their conduct – as parties to contend with.[1] In the course of the post-war period, the importance of MNEs for the effective operation of these international organizations was increasingly acknowledged by a large number of subsidiary arrangements. The result is a *mixture of* models, regimes and principles in the international arena.

The most important international arenas in which the ICR regime is negotiated centre on issues of trade (WTO/GATT, regional trade agreements), Foreign Direct Investment (OECD, World Bank, UNCTAD), development (World Bank, IMF, UN), corporate governance and tax regimes (OECD), international standards (ISO, ILO), and international security (UN, NATO). In addition, a host of other international issues exist on which countries try to settle either regional agreements (EU, NAFTA) or bilateral agreements such as efforts to harmonize accounting standards and coordinate competition policy regimes of the US and the EU. Alongside these efforts, national regulation and practices continue to exist with the result that corporate ICR strategies are shaped and directed in a multiple-tiered environment.

This chapter first analyses the different national CSR regimes of the three regions that represent more than 85 per cent of all inward and outward FDI stock (as a percentage of GDP): North America, Europe and East Asia (section 12.2). This is followed by a discussion of the different dimensions of the current international CSR (or ICR) regime. It starts with an overview of the guiding principles agreed upon in international institutions and the question which of these principles enhance divergence or convergence among CSR regimes (section 12.3). It is followed by an overview of two earlier phases of development of the ICR regime during the 1970s and 1980s (section 12.4) and concludes with an examination of the characteristics of the current ICR regime (section 12.5). The leading question that runs through this chapter is: 'To what extent does the interaction between national CSR regimes lead to an international ICR regime that enhances inactive, reactive, active or proactive ICR strategies?' (section 12.6).

12.2 NATIONAL CSR REGIMES

A CSR regime comprises more than the roles adopted by governments. It consists of all the actions, interactions and rules that influence the nature of societal interfaces. It determines to what extent CSR strategies are voluntary or mandatory and whether they can be considered successful or not. A CSR regime is the result of past bargaining processes and sets the framework for future bargaining processes. A CSR regime has three main elements:

- *Legal requirements*: Legal tradition of the country; reporting requirements for financial, social, environmental or sustainability reporting; extraterritoriality provisions (the degree to which companies can be held liable in national courts for their CSR practices abroad); other CSR-relevant regulation, such as competition policy, intellectual property policy, security and safety regulations, transparency rules.

■ *Government policy practices*: general strategies or roles of government (adversarial, cooperative, 'mandating', 'endorsing', 'facilitating'; see Table 7.1); public procurement (CSR criteria incorporated into government procurement policies and subsidy schemes); public advocacy (promotion of CSR awareness among the general public by local and central government); tolerance of corruption or 'clientism'; adoption of ICR regulation in national policy frameworks (defining a CSR regime as more 'open' or 'closed').

■ *Nature of interaction between business and civil society*: Community involvement of companies (as embedded in tradition, legal provisions for philanthropy or sponsoring, or religion); adoption and implementation of minimum standards for labour, supply chain responsibility and human rights either in codes or other business principles; corporate governance and accountability regimes (relevance of particular stakeholders; stimulation of social investment; voluntary transparency and accountability); receptiveness to labelling and trademarks.

Classifying and comparing national CSR regimes is problematic for a number of reasons. First, most CSR measures have only recently been introduced, rendering it difficult to assess their full meaning and potential impact. Second, the recent ICR trend has resulted in much copying behaviour, also referred to as the 'bandwagon' or 'herding' effect. Governments adopt measures in words, but not necessarily in deeds. Third, CSR regimes consist of unwritten as well as written rules, rendering a comparative overview extremely problematic. International classifications often rely on written rules or personal perceptions measured in surveys. Sophisticated comparative studies on CSR regimes do not exist as yet. National case studies, overviews of interesting practices and anecdotal evidence seem to prevail (cf. Fox *et al.*, 2002). Studying CSR regimes is therefore weighed down by huge empirical difficulties that can only partly be addressed in this chapter.

This section first presents a number of general observations on the characteristics of comparative national CSR regimes throughout the world. Three distinguishing characteristics are discussed: (1) the attitude to governance, accountability and transparency; (2) the perceived role of competition; and (3) the expected involvement of business in the community. Second, the three leading and best-established CSR regimes – that are home or host to all but a few multinationals in the world – will be further classified in terms of their general (from inactive to proactive) approach to CSR. In accordance with the institutional models identified in Chapter 2, leading CSR regimes are: the liberal, the (neo)corporatist and the business-statist models.[2]

Governance, accountability and transparency

CSR regimes differ particularly in their attitude towards corporate governance. In liberal countries publicly listed companies share an 'outsider' orientation and generate a significant part of the GDP (Chapter 2). Outsider systems are more short-term oriented, and are basically geared towards the interests of shareholders (Monks and Minow, 2001). Most other regimes share a variant of 'insider' orientation for their publicly listed firms. The insider system is based on 'network finance' consisting of particular groups of stakeholders whose influence derives particularly from their investments. In the continental European (neo)corporatist regime, workers, industrial banks and sometimes governments are strong insiders. In the Asian system other firms in the same conglomerate, industrial banks, family owners through minority shareholding and sometimes governments (in China) represent strong insiders. In the religious-autocratic regimes of the Middle East, the governing elites are influential insiders in large companies. In community systems, the corporation *is* the community and public listings do not exist.

The World Bank Institute provides profiles of the different governance systems of its member countries.[3] National governance systems are not necessarily identical to corporate governance systems. Two dimensions of national governance systems are directly relevant for concrete CSR regimes: (1) voice and accountability and (2) the control of corruption. A direct link can be discerned between the national level of economic development and the sophistication of the governance regime. Corporatist continental European countries have a consistently high score on both voice/accountability (highest) and on control of corruption (high). Liberal countries score high (but not the highest) on voice and accountability and highest on control of corruption. Business-statist regimes in East Asia display a wider variety of development levels. They exhibit a more dispersed and lower (medium) score on both accounts. Voice and accountability scores in particular are relative to national levels of development. Religious-autocratic regimes portray a much more coherent picture relatively independent of level of development. Middle Eastern countries have the world's weakest voice and accountability regimes, combined with a medium score on control of corruption.

Voice and accountability are directly related to transparency. Liberal countries score high on fighting corruption by means of sanctions and stricter accounting rules as stipulated for instance by the Sarbanes-Oxley Act. But this also creates certain risks. The ever-present threat of litigation in liberal countries has a negative impact on efforts to be more transparent on CSR-relevant company characteristics (unless strictly required by law). The less antagonistic and more cooperative institutional system of continental Europe makes it easier for companies to disclose their intentions on CSR. They are also considerably less likely to be held account-able in court. Research by SNS Asset Management (*P+ Magazine*, Autumn 2003) shows that large European companies are generally more transparent as regards the publication of information relevant to CSR than American firms. The biggest US–Europe differences in transparency appear in the services industries such as banking, diversified financials and software. Hardly any differences in transparency were found in the pharmaceuticals industry. Pharmaceutical companies around the world often employ similar marketing strategies (see Chapter 10) and are therefore also confronted with a more uniform pressure to enhance transparency. The research did not include companies from other countries but, on average, companies from other parts of the world are considerably less transparent than either their American or European counterparts.

The role of competition

Competition policy (or the lack of it) is an important element of a national CSR regime. Competition policy rules define the concrete limits on power accumulation in the market sphere. In some liberal regimes such as the US, the national CSR regime was first and foremost prompted by anti-trust considerations (see Chapter 8). The anti-trust legislation in liberal countries is primarily aimed at consumer interests and the efficient operation of markets. It regulates the abuse of market dominance, is not opposed to market dominance as such and is relatively ambiguous on concrete sanctions. Only very high market shares (more than 66 per cent of the market) are considered a possible sign of market dominance (cf. Liang, 2004). Should firms make use of their market dominance to invest in technological progress and/or to lower prices for consumers, dominance is not necessarily viewed in negative terms. Abuse has to be proven in court, which is not easy. In Anglo-Saxon countries such as Australia, New Zealand and the UK, the notification system for potential market-disturbing mergers is voluntary (UNCTAD, 2000a).

In continental Europe, the competition policy regime represents an intricate trade-off between efficiency and equity goals. It is aimed at the interests of both producers and consumers. The threshold for addressing market dominance is much lower than in the US (40–50 per cent). Both the US and the EU use a pre-merger notification system. This implies that more mergers (potential market abuse through collusion) are reported to the EC. The political room to manoeuvre to sanction firms – but also to come to settlements – is greater in the case of the EC.

In most East Asian countries, competition policy is either very pragmatic or non-existent (China). The system is primarily aimed at the interests of the producers. This efficiency orientation has the effect of allowing sometimes very high market shares (up to 75 per cent market share is not considered market dominance) and essentially adopts a non-interventionist stance (World Bank, 2002a). Notification of mergers is mandatory only *after* the deal has been closed. In most Middle Eastern countries the anti-trust regime is even more weakly developed, but if a regime does exist, it comprises rather strong equity (fairness) rules in terms of which a rather low market share already amounts to 'market dominance' (as low as 20 per cent). As a consequence, 'Islamic competition policy' – if such a classification can ever be made – strengthens the position of small and medium-sized corporations.

Business–community involvement

Corporate volunteering and corporate philanthropy as part of relatively sophisticated business–community involvement programmes (Meijs and van der Voort, 2004) are typical of the liberal CSR regimes of Anglo-Saxon countries. BCI is primarily a response to inadequate government involvement in building up social capital. The American system of corporate volunteering in particular is more task and output oriented. It is also characterized as the workplace model (ibid.), which is strongly aimed at efficiency. Anglo-Saxon countries are the breeding ground for 'business in the community' initiatives. In the formulation of the national CSR regime, business in the community schemes are characterized by a relatively moderate involvement of NGOs. For example, the UK 'Business in the Community' initiative established in 1982, is the oldest and perhaps the most influential in stimulating business involvement in (local) communities. No NGOs participate in it.

In continental Europe, corporate volunteering is much less advanced, and more process oriented; participation and membership is more important than output (Meijs and Bridges Karr, 2004). BCI – if it exists – is strongly equity oriented. In corporatist states there is hardly any tradition of overt corporate philanthropy. The welfare state creates a system of indirect philanthropy (via taxes). The ideological retreat of the welfare state in some European countries has stimulated a shift towards direct philanthropy such as BCI. BCI initiatives in corporatist states are often undertaken in collaboration (partnership) with NGOs due to their prominence in local communities. European companies that are leaders in this area seem to be those companies that have invested heavily in Anglo-Saxon countries. Their BCI initiatives thus signify an attempt to harmonize their ICR strategies. Whether efficiency, equity or effectiveness considerations prevail in such a case is a topic for further research.

In Asia, the phenomenon of corporate volunteering and philanthropy hardly exists. One could postulate that BCI in community regimes is inverted: citizens volunteer to work for companies as part of their community service. In the Middle East, the Islamic practice of *Zakat* lies somewhere in between the community-based and corporatist BCI regimes. *Zakat* is the third of the five pillars of Islam (Esposito, 2004). The act of *Zakat* (almsgiving) purifies one's wealth and applies to both companies and individuals. It is obligatory for all Muslims each year to give 2.5 per cent of wealth and assets to the poor. *Zakat* therefore represents an institutionalized version of CSR – and an alternative to taxes. The *Zakat* regime for companies is rather detailed and well specified. The Islamic CSR regime stimulates managers and civilians to adopt a relatively active ethical stance towards business, with only limited reference to economic efficiency.

The neo-liberal approach to CSR: CSR America

The liberal or neo-liberal approach to CSR is well advanced and stimulates a relatively narrow approach to the efficiency–ethics trade-off (Triple-E). It has been pioneered in particular in the US, which remains its most prominent representative. The US CSR regime originated more in anti-trust regulation aimed at curbing firms' abuse of power in consumer markets, than in social regulation (as in Europe) opposed to the abuse of power by firms in labour markets. The CSR regime is strongly rooted in the protection of property rights, including intellectual property and the rights of shareholders and creditors. The relatively antagonistic bargaining environment in liberal countries stimulated a legalistic CSR regime based on common law. The regime is shaped by jurisprudence rather than strong (centralist) regulation. CSR tends to be compliance oriented rather than voluntaristic. Generally, governments have adopted a mandating and facilitating role in order to maintain their independence from societal groups. These particular government roles also entail a strong emphasis on sanctions (for instance in combating corruption and abuse of governance regimes) and rules, rather than subsidies and partnerships. According to research of the National Policy Association (Aaronson and Reeves, 2002), public advocacy and promotion of CSR in the US is modest. At a decentralist level, however, a variety of government roles exist alongside one another. The principle that guides many practical CSR regulation discussions is that of 'substantial equivalence'. The safety of food (or medical devices, or drugs) in the US does not raise regulatory concern as long as the new product does not differ materially from its predecessor (Doh and Guay, 2004). Labelling is therefore deemed unnecessary if it interferes with the free trade of the product.

American companies are leaders in the formulation of codes of conduct. This is often regarded as an indication of their active stance on CSR. Some companies have tomes for manuals that specify *dos* and *don'ts* in the finest detail for employees. The motivation for many American companies, however, has been largely reactive. First, codes are an expression of the general business culture in the Anglo-Saxon world where antagonistic labour relations have led to the formulation of explicit and rule-based contracts (see Chapter 2). Second, the reasons behind the enormous proliferation of ethics officers and ethics hotlines are remarkably banal. In 1991, the federal government issued the *Federal Sentencing Guidelines* (FSG). These guidelines imposed significant fines on companies whose employees engaged in 'criminal' activities. Companies could however count on significantly reduced sentences if they could demonstrate that a system is in place to prevent, or at least detect, illegal activities. This led to a tidal wave of ethics officers, codes of conduct and ethical training programmes in companies and even the institution of chairs in Business Ethics and Business–Society Management at American universities. But a compliance regime hardly encourages real reflection on ethics in the business environment. Empirical research shows that the Federal Sentencing Guidelines have not led to a significant reduction in violations (McKendall *et al.*, 2002).

The specific CSR and ICR approach of large American companies is regularly put to the test in court. The US is the only major country that enables host country citizens to call US multinationals to account for conduct in host countries that is in breach of US legislation.[4] A 2004 Supreme Court ruling now also enables foreigners to use the 1789 Alien Tort Claims Act. The Act allows citizens to sue American transnational corporations if they are implicated in human rights violations and other breaches of international law. Cases brought to court in the US include Burma/Myanmar (Unocal), Apartheid regime support (IBM, General Motors, Exxon Mobil, J.P. Morgan Chase, and Citigroup), and Argentina's military rule (DaimlerChrysler). The use of the Alien Tort Act is strongly opposed by the Federal government and the business community, but not necessarily by local state governments.[5] Other liberal countries have also organized opposition to its implementation: the UK, Australia and Switzerland filed a complaint with the US Supreme Court supporting the Bush administration's bid to stop the use of the Alien Tort Claims Act. They argued that domestic courts should not interfere in matters that fall under foreign jurisdictions.

The potential threat of local (indigenous people) filing tort claims against American multinationals affects the way these companies operate abroad. It further entrenches the 'universalist' approach that is firmly rooted in the domestic CSR regime of the US. The US legislative regime represents the dominant selection environment for US CSR. An example of such a universalist approach, based on domestic considerations, is the embracement of 'universal' human rights. The US government and US multinationals, in particular, have become passionate advocates of the development of (universal) human rights around the world. It is worth noting that the UN Declaration of Universal Human Rights includes a number of individual human rights that representatives of non-OECD countries question strongly. These countries, however, were not invited to partake in the original formulation of the Declaration in 1948.

The rule-based orientation of CSR in the US is demonstrated by its tough stance on corruption. Whistleblowers enjoy relatively strong support under the US CSR regime. Together with Transparency International and the ICC, the US government has become the most active actor in combating corruption around the world. The US already outlawed the acceptance of bribes in IB in 1977 through the Foreign Corrupt Practices Act. However, according to Transparency International, the US has, in practice, been relatively lenient in its sanctioning of firms and has itself become susceptible to payment of bribes (as measured by Transparency International's Corruption Perception index). A common law (jurisprudence) and rule-based approach with a small central government generates considerable enforcement problems. In the past, other countries (e.g. France) actually allowed firms to treat bribe payments as tax-deductible expenses. This led to protests from US firms that they faced a competitive disadvantage vis-à-vis CSR regimes that tolerated widespread corruption and bribery.

The legalistic and instrumentalist-oriented CSR regime of liberal countries creates a largely reactive and instrumentalist CSR orientation. The liberal CSR regime will only adopt higher labour or environmental standards if it will boost short-term profitability – for instance if consumers are willing to pay more for goods produced at higher standards.[6] In the liberal CSR regime, corporate responsibility is still primarily mediated through shareholders and the stock exchange. The increased attention to corporate social responsiveness and responsibility has given rise to measures that either directly or indirectly support SRI.[7] The basic philosophy underpinning SRI has strong reactive and negative overtones ('don't do things wrong'). The American Quakers were the first group to implement SRI principles through a process of 'negative screening' in order to avoid investment in the armaments sector (Park, 2004). It is therefore not entirely surprising that Anglo-Saxon countries are known to score highest on SRI as a percentage of total market capital (IFC, 2003). In 2002, in the US, 12 per cent of total market capital, representing US$2,300 billion, was dedicated to SRI.[8] 'Corporate governance' is an important screening measure of SRI funds in Anglo-Saxon countries, whereas continental European SRI funds rarely apply this principle when they attempt to identify 'best in class' performance.[9]

The neo-corporatist approach to CSR: CSR Europe

The European approach to the efficiency and equity trade-off (Triple-E) is much broader. Governments and well-organized NGOs have become deeply involved in the actual implementation of national and regional CSR regimes. In consequence, governments adopt facilitating and partnering roles in an effort to work together with firms on developing CSR practices that combine both efficiency and equity. Public advocacy of CSR (e.g. corporate citizenship, sponsorship and legislation) in most European countries is relatively strong (Aaronson and Reeves, 2002). An inactive approach to CSR is not really an option for any of the parties. The stock market is generally not considered to be the main arena for influencing CSR strategies, which explains why SRI in Europe remains fairly low (with the exception of the UK): in 2003 it amounted to US$260 billion (SIF, 2003), representing around 1 per cent of total market capital (IFC, 2003). European SRI funds exhibit a more holistic approach to screening than the liberal regimes. Not only do environmental and labour screens feature prominently, SRI also tends towards a positive duty approach while screening amounts to more than merely employing single exclusionary measures (SIF, 2003: 33).

As a rule, stakeholders from all three spheres of society are included in the formation of national and regional CSR regimes. This characteristic of the formation process has an important impact on the implementation of standards and codes that have been agreed upon in that it renders them 'more or less' obligatory. This process is underpinned by the continental European practice of civil law which is characterized by stricter rules, but is often only marginally monitored by the authorities. The latter is typical of corporatist and social democratic regimes: standards are formulated to conclude past negotiations, but also to facilitate future bargaining between societal stakeholders. Sanctions are weakly formulated in the European CSR regime, the objective being to encourage companies to adopt an active stance, but also to discourage 'evasive' behaviour as has been observed among so many American companies (as a result of a predominantly reactive and rule-based approach to CSR).

Austria provides a typical example of the way in which a corporatist regime engages with CSR. It is characterized by a largely voluntary, but nevertheless extensive, process of tripartite code and standards building. The development of a code of conduct for the Austrian economy, for instance, was carried out by the (tripartite) Federation of the Austrian industry and the Austrian business council on sustainable development. The Austrian CSR guideline employed ISO 14004 (Guideline for environmental management systems) as a basic framework, but has added a number of specific issues relevant to internal and external stakeholders in Austria. The code's implementation is aligned with the implementation of the environmental management system. The Austrian Standards Institute adopted this code of conduct as more or less obligatory.

As a result of the institutionalized bargaining process, the CSR regime in European countries generally contains more and stricter stipulations on labelling, environmental reporting and codes of conduct than it does in liberal countries. This is reflected, for instance, in explicit reporting laws on environmental strategies in Denmark and the Netherlands (requirement for a separate environmental report), Norway, Sweden, France and Spain (integration in financial annual report). Consistent with the leading principle of subsidiarity in Europe, however, companies are also actively encouraged to do more than what is legally required. A good example of this approach is the 'Multi-stakeholder forum on CSR' which was organized by the European Commission and included some 40 representatives from businesses, trade unions, consumer groups and NGOs. The Commission defines CSR as the 'voluntary integration of social and environmental concerns into a firm's business operations. To realize this objective, firms' investment in human capital, environmental protection and sustainability, and stakeholder relations will have to exceed that which is *"required by law"*' (italics added, Commission of the European Communities, 2001).

The regulatory principle that guides the European CSR regime is the 'precautionary principle'. A new product (from genetically modified foods to refrigerators) must be proven safe before it is launched on the market. The development of labelling strategies as a means to ensure cautiousness is encouraged. Free trade is therefore not the most important factor guiding international trade. The European CSR regime is more open and displays stronger support for multilateral regulations and international standards (through OECD guidelines and ILO conventions) especially on social/labour rights and environmental protection. In small open European countries, a great number of pioneering CSR/ICR initiatives have been launched that seek to create partnerships through dialogues between the three societal spheres (business, government and civil society) and develop national standards based on international standards (cf. Fox *et al.*, 2002):

- In 2002, Belgium was the first country in the world to enact a legal provision for a social label. Companies can put this label on their products if they protect basic worker rights as recognized by the ILO, among others. This requirement applies also to the subsidiaries of foreign multinationals in Belgium.
- By the start of the twenty-first century, the Danish government was the first in the world to support the formal assessment of CSR performance: a 'Social Index' assessing the degree to which companies live up to their social responsibilities and a 'Human Rights Impact Assessment' to identify the aspects of their business that may directly or indirectly violate human rights. In 1994, it was also one of the first governments to launch a national CSR campaign to stimulate small and medium-sized companies to support local community projects in Denmark.
- In 2002, the Netherlands was the first to link export credit insurance, development aid and other financial support of companies to a written declaration expressing familiarity with the OECD Guidelines for Multinational Enterprises and a commitment to adhere to the guidelines. However, neither sanctions nor monitoring are anticipated.
- Norway established a tripartite consultative body on business and human rights under the auspices of the Norwegian Ministry of Foreign Affairs. Norway is considering the installation of an Ombudsman for Norwegian Companies abroad. The Ombudsman can ask development agencies and embassies to withdraw support for companies that violate guidelines on human rights and the environment (Abrahams, 2004).
- In 2002, Sweden established a partnership for global corporate responsibility between the Ministry of Foreign Affairs and Swedish businesses.

The corporate-statist approach: CSR Asia

According to the Heritage Foundation's Index of economic Freedom (www.heritage.com), the leading economies of East Asia rate among the most liberal (Hong Kong, Singapore) and the least liberal economies (India) in the world. They do, however, share a very pragmatic approach to business and a strongly efficiency-oriented CSR regime that tends to avoid opposing firms' abuse of power unless it undermines the competitive position of the national economy. Consequently, Asian CSR regimes are not very well advanced and often do not even trigger a reactive stance from business vis-à-vis imminent regulation. Public advocacy of CSR and corporate citizenship in countries such as Japan is negligible (Aaronson and Reeves, 2002). The Asian CSR regime does not display any major trade-off between efficiency and equity. It is primarily aimed at the efficiency and international competitiveness of the industry itself. A number of the East Asian countries are still in a relatively early stage of economic development. Consequently, the East Asian CSR regime is not only shaped by culture and institutions, but also by levels of development. CSR regimes in Asia hardly set any relevant minimum standards of their own, unless they can be related directly to efficiency goals and control. The weak and inactive CSR regime in Asia also implies that funds dedicated to SRI are negligible and primarily employ environmental screens (SIF, 2003: 33). In the event that CSR guidelines are adopted in the Asian regime, it is often accompanied by intimate consultations with large firms and motivated by the need to secure the given industry's international competitiveness. Once adopted, however, implementation is actively pursued. The adoption of codes of conduct is not stimulated, neither is labelling. CSR regulation has developed primarily in the area of environmental protection, i.e. the area that directly affects the internationalization strategies aimed at markets of developed countries.[10] On labour and human rights and working conditions, the Asian CSR regime generally exhibits an inactive CSR and ICR orientation.

Regime interaction

The liberal, neo-corporatist and business-statist CSR regimes organize the bulk of FDI, of trade and of the world's GDP. Their orientation and characteristics show considerable divergence (Table 12.1) and can be classified as 'rival' because they tend to emphasize and stimulate different business approaches to the issue of CSR: a largely inactive approach in East Asia, a reactive approach in liberal countries, and a more (inter)active approach in neo-corporatist countries. All systems, however, also show some overlap, which could lead to converging interests and practices. The interaction between these CSR regimes strongly influences the nature of the ICR activities of MNEs across borders. The representation of these CSR regimes in international organizations strongly influences the nature and formation of ICR regimes.

Table 12.1 Three leading CSR regimes

Inactive	Reactive	Active	Pro/Interactive
Corporate *self-*responsibility	Corporate social *responsiveness*	Corporate social *responsibility*	Corporate *societal* responsibility
	Efficiency	Equity/ethics	Effectiveness

Liberal approach: 'CSR America'

Moderately open: 'mandating'/'facilitating'; shareholder/consumer oriented; common law; litigation-oriented codes and reports; moderate transparency; strong sanctions; substantial equivalence principle; strong corporate volunteering and philanthropy tradition (BCI); public advocacy: weak; SRI: strong

(Neo) Corporatist approach: 'CSR Europe'

Open: 'facilitating'/'partnering'; employee/ consumer/producer oriented; civil law; voluntary and regulation-oriented codes and reporting; high transparency; weak sanctions; precautionary principle; weak corporate volunteering and philanthropy tradition; public advocacy: moderate–high; SRI: weak

Business-statist approach: 'CSR ASIA'

Moderately closed: partnering/endorsing; producer oriented; customary/communist law; informal codes; pragmatic principle; low transparency; no corporate volunteering and philanthropy tradition; public advocacy: very low; SRI: negligible

12.3 INTERNATIONAL INTERACTION: PRINCIPLES AND PRACTICES

International regime interaction not only represents the articulation of country interests, it is also guided by a number of principles that have been the result of various rounds of previous international negotiations, by various constellations of parties in a large number of bargaining arenas. Regime interaction can be characterized by two dimensions: the degree of rivalry (process dimension) and the degree of convergence or divergence (outcome dimension). The result is (1) a race, (2) a contest, (3) co-alignment or (4) co-habitation (See introduction to Part I). Table 12.2 classifies leading principles and practices that have been introduced since the Second World War under one of these four headings.

Convergence-enhancing interaction

In the post-war period, two of the most pervasive principles guiding interstate interactions have been embodied in the GATT and WTO treaties on international trade liberalization. They are the principles of 'national treatment' and 'nondiscrimination'. Applying the first principle on trade requires that foreign goods and services that enter the national market are treated the same as domestic goods and services. The second principle has been embodied in the *most-favoured nation* (MFN) rule, which is a prohibition against discrimination and requires all (WTO) members to treat each other as well as they treat their most favoured trading partner. The 'most favoured' idea contains an element of rivalry and stimulates a downward pressure on official trade barriers.

Comparable international principles apply to the *harmonization of standards*. In this case the members of a harmonization initiative work on a common set of shared standards. This has proven particularly relevant in technology areas where market growth and international exchange are vitally dependent upon the interoperability of technical standards across borders. The International Standards Organisation (ISO) was established in 1946 to help achieve exactly this. It is the prime arena in which actors get together to bargain over technical standards. ISO can use a top-down approach and come up with completely new standards, which then create a *de jure* international standard. It can also apply a 'bottom-up' approach and endorse an existing standard as the de facto international standard. The first option establishes a minimum playing field for further rivalry between actors, the second option in principle settles the rivalry between competing standards by limiting the playing field. The imposition or harmonization of standards has been criticized because it can inhibit further innovation, by limiting the changes

Table 12.2 International dynamics

		Process: rivalry	
		Strong	Limited
Outcome	Convergence	Race Harmonization, benchmarks, MFN, continuous improvement, best available practice, arbitration, reciprocal adjustment	Co-alignment National treatment, multi-stakeholder dialogue, conventions, guidelines, codes, charters
	Divergence	Contest Reciprocity, separate standards, adverse selection, de facto standards, contests in principles	Co-habitation Mutual recognition, non-reciprocal coordination, coalition, partnership

that can be made to rival standards and products. On the other hand, harmonization and *de jure* standards enable 'network effects' which facilitate economies of scale.

In other CSR-relevant areas, international convergence has been enhanced by establishing *guidelines*, *conventions*, *codes of conduct* or by defining *benchmarks*. They are typical instruments that are embraced by international organizations when institutional rivalry is considerable and efforts for harmonization have not been, and never will really be, successful. Guidelines and benchmarks are often used to suggest a direction for conduct in conditions of uncertainties (Braithwaite and Drahos, 2000: 21). It also makes it possible to identify 'best practices' or 'best in class' and stimulate companies or countries to follow this lead. Guidelines and benchmarks specify the minimum requirements beyond which a 'race to the bottom' should not proceed. Conventions and codes, in particular, aim at supporting a process of self-regulation through the specification of a number of 'principles' and 'rules'. Benchmarks, conventions, guidelines and codes are therefore also typical instruments introduced in a bargaining society in which, due to sizable institutional voids, firms are stimulated towards self-regulation. The effect of the benchmark critically depends on the building blocks of this 'best practice'. In cases where the benchmark is strongly inspired by one national model, its effect in regulating rivalry between the actors of diverging models will probably be limited. Benchmarks have primarily been developed by international industry associations – international conventions by inter-state organizations such as the ILO, UN or the EC; guidelines have been the prime target of specialized international organizations such as the OECD.

Dynamic convergence can be enhanced by applying process principles that guide the benchmarking process in a particular direction. The principle of 'continuous improvement', for instance, has this function. It is practised by the ISO and other international standard-setting bodies. Process principles try to cover for the dilemmas attached to 'rule compliance', which requires that rules have to be changed every time a new situation develops and which in practice always implies that standard-setting bodies follow way behind the business practice (and are, therefore, in practice, either irrelevant or a stumbling block for further progress). A comparable pragmatic idealism is contained in applying the principle of 'Best Available Technology' (BAT) or 'best available practice'. These terms were originally introduced in life cycle analyses and environmental management and policy models. Instead of defining a static 'best practice' example or rule/guideline that needs to be redefined – and thus renegotiated – every time technology changes, crises appear or new insights are gained, a process ambition is specified that aims at a 'race to the top'.

A *multi-stakeholder dialogue* is a more recent instrument of international interaction between actors in the CSR arena that is aimed at enhancing international convergence. The organization(s) that initiate the dialogue acknowledge that the traditional bargaining arenas are not sufficient to discuss issues in a non-rival manner. Multi-stakeholder dialogues represent an effort in co-alignment. The participants share the ambition to establish new common goals through a process of dialogue rather than through debate or confrontation. In particular, international inter-governmental organizations have initiated international multi-stakeholder dialogues on CSR-relevant issues (Box 12.1). A more concrete form of convergence-enhancing co-alignment is formed by *partnerships*. In particular, UN organizations, the ILO and the World Bank started to establish partnerships with major companies in an effort to increase their effectiveness, but also to overcome budgetary shortcomings.[11] Critics of this approach argue that the UN organizations are aligning more towards the (efficiency) interests of companies than vice versa. The UN might gain credibility with business, but might lose its effectiveness in achieving its main (equity-oriented) goals.

Convergence, finally, can also be enhanced through the way in which international *disputes* are settled. In cases where no effective dispute settlement procedures are available, convergence

BOX 12.1 MULTI-STAKEHOLDER PROCESSES

Agenda 21, one of the outcomes of the United Nations Conference on the Environment and Development (UNCED) hosted in Rio de Janeiro 1992, was the first UN document to explicitly acknowledge the role of stakeholders (Hemmati *et al.*, 2002). Stakeholder participation and involvement is described as crucial for sustainable development. Agenda 21 even specified the so-called 'nine major groups' that need to be involved in the international dialogue on development: women, children and youth, indigenous people, NGOs, local authorities, workers and trade unions, business and industry, scientific and technological communities and farmers. Although these groups cover the whole societal spectrum, the identification of separate groups revealed who the UNCED regards as primary stakeholders in development, both in terms of contributing to the process and in terms of those most affected.

The Rio Conference was followed by several gatherings where stakeholders were invited to participate in discussions on governance issues in particular. The UN Commission on Sustainable Development (CSD) has contributed to the design and development of multi-stakeholder engagement. The CSD approach has become exemplary for all multi-stakeholder dialogues initiated by the UN on sustainability. The UN also stimulated other international organizations to apply multi-stakeholder engagement principles, either independently or in collaboration with the UN. Two types of global issues are discussed in multi-stakeholder forums: (1) those that address the question of how to reconcile economic growth with ecological and social sustainability, and (2) those concerned with the question of how to develop and implement core technologies in an ethically just manner while taking into account societal risks. Multi-stakeholder processes can be conducted over a limited period of time, but they can also be ongoing. Major examples include:

- The *World Commission on Dams* (1998–2000)
- The *Global Reporting Initiative* (since 1997)
- The WBCSD/IIED *Mining, Minerals and Sustainable Development process* (1997–2001)
- The UN *Global Compact initiative* (since 1999)
- The *Global Alliance for Workers and Communities* (since 1999) partnership between the World Bank, companies and NGOs
- The OECD *Biotechnology discussion* (1999–2000)
- The OECD *Guidelines for Multinational Enterprises* (1999–2000)
- The *Extractive Industries Review* (since 2000) commissioned by the World Bank
- The *European Multistakeholder Forum on CSR* (since 2002) initiated by the European Commission.

will only be weakly enhanced or divergence only weakly countered. Effective dispute settlement is strongly influenced by the possible imposition of sanctions by the dispute body. Due to the lack of supra-governmental organizations, the strongest mechanism that enforces international convergence in case of international disputes, is *arbitration*. The parties that agree to submit their case with an arbitrator also agree to consider this ruling 'binding'. International arbitration has been part of a number of international treaties and can be carried out between private parties, between states, or between states and private parties. International arbitration between private persons is dealt with by a variety of organizations, such as the International Chamber of Commerce Court of Arbitration. When states are concerned, the Permanent Court of Arbitration (also known as the Hague tribunal, established in 1899), the International Center for the Settlement of Investment Disputes (ICSID, since 1966 under the administrative support of the World Bank) and the WTO Dispute Settlement Body (since 1995) are among the most relevant arbitration institutes.

Arbitration procedures have proven a force in shaping the CSR nature of the 'free trade' regime, following the foundation of the WTO in 1995. In the period 1995–2004, 324 cases were brought to the WTO Dispute Settlement Body by member countries. Many of these disputes concern issues that are relevant for ICR. For instance, many disputes deal with the imposition of taxes on alcoholic beverages, trade-inhibiting safety regulations, or whether or not specific industries can be subsidized. WTO disputes therefore almost always represent the trade-off between efficiency (as represented by free trade and the WTO treaty) and equity (as represented by the efforts of individual countries). A notorious CSR case brought before the WTO Dispute Settlement Body was on the question of whether developed countries in particular had the right to impose import barriers in order to protect endangered species (such as dolphins or sea turtles) versus the rights of, especially, developing countries to exploit natural resources to commercial ends. In 1998, the WTO body came up with a pragmatic multilateral solution. It stipulated that developed countries assist developing countries in acquiring the technologies to protect endangered species so as to remain commercially competitive (Gerber, 2005: 165). Increasingly the WTO dispute settlement procedures are used by developing countries to protest against neo-mercantilist practices of developed countries, in particular for agricultural products. The WTO framework thus can help in creating a 'level playing field', but it cannot help in creating a 'fair playing field' as is requested by critical NGOs. 'Fair trade' is anathema to the WTO.

Divergence-enhancing interaction

The strongest trigger for enhanced international divergence, remain the efforts of governments to sustain national sovereignty. The stronger the government and the more closed the economy, the bigger the chance is that the representatives will raise barriers to international principles that do not comply with their own regime. One of the strongest principles in international relations remains the principle of *reciprocity*. It states that favours, benefits and penalties granted by one state to the citizens or corporations of another state, should be returned in kind. Specific tariffs, copyright provisions, visa requirements have thus become the area of 'exclusive deals' between two countries. Reciprocity ties one transaction to another. In domestic market transactions, reciprocity is usually considered illegal. In international transactions it is widely practiced, for instance in the area of counter-trade. Reciprocity, is particularly imposed by strong and/or big states and – like most bilateral deals – frustrates multilateral deals and international convergence on the basis of multilateral or universal principles (see Chapter 5). Smaller states generally do not refer to reciprocity, out of fear of retaliation.

Reciprocity can also appear without coercion. First, in the form of *reciprocal adjustment* which is used as a form of cooperation between two actors that share a common interest. Reciprocal adjustment appears in areas of intellectual property rights or in such practical areas as agreeing to drive on the right side of the road. This process produces a rule outcome or a convergence or harmonization of a set of rules (Braithwaite and Drahos, 2000: 22). *Non-reciprocal cooperation* occurs when parties do not have a common interest in any common set of rules but, by trading-off various interests, come to a temporary coalition on a specific topic. Non-reciprocal cooperation appeared for instance between some of the developed countries, in establishing a common intellectual property rights regime (ibid.: 23).

Every convergence-enhancing multilateral initiative can at the same time also create divergence. First, in cases where the treaties or conventions specifying the principles do not include

233

all possible actors or in the same manner. For instance, the WTO does not organize all countries in the world, ISO members are not all full members, and specialized organizations such as the OECD, by definition, organize only a limited number of (developed) countries. Internal convergence leads to external divergence, and international rules become a club good rather than a public good. Second, the principles initiated by many international organizations need not be adopted by all members, leaving substantial divergence in the enactment of principles. In 2000, for instance, ILO's eight core labour standards had only been ratified by 97 of the 177 member countries. The US had ratified only two of the eight conventions (www.ilo.org). ILO is a tripartite organization and particularly weak in enforcing its standards on its member countries.

Third, the principles often leave sufficient room for interpretation – often by design in order to reach consensus. 'Open standards' or 'framework' agreements are often so broadly defined that they leave considerable room for rivalry and divergence. In cases where there are no sufficient dispute settlement procedures available, seeming convergence in theory, could imply substantial divergence in practice. ISO standards leave considerable 'managerial discretion' to the firms implementing the standards. ISO supporters emphasize its flexibility, whereas opponents criticize its vagueness (Kolk, 2000: 114). The WTO treaties focus primarily on formal trade barriers. Consecutive rounds of trade liberalization have effectively lowered formal tariff barriers. But informal – or non-tariff – barriers at the same time have increased in importance. They are not addressed by the WTO. Informal trade issues are perhaps more important to CSR regimes, than are formal trade barriers. The MFN principle never prevented any of the WTO members engaging in regional and bilateral trade agreements, even when these clearly discriminate in favour of the participants to the agreement. Regional and bilateral trade agreements are therefore becoming more important to CSR regimes than multilateral global agreements. According to trade economist Baghwati (2004) an immense 'spaghetti bowl' of bilateral, regional and other kinds of arrangements exists that signals international divergence.

Fourth, the principles formulated by an international organization rarely cover all dimensions that are important to the issue. Not all trade in goods and services fall under the WTO agreements, which has been the reason for follow-up rounds on further liberalization. The 'national treatment' principle creates a level playing field only in those areas that are covered by the WTO treaty. The OECD proved incapable of harmonizing international tax standards, for instance. It is as important to consider which areas are *not* covered by rules as to study the characteristics of rules that are established.

Other divergence-enhancing interaction is triggered by the principle of *mutual recognition of standards* as practiced, for instance, by the ISO. It is comparable to the national treatment principle in the WTO. The mutual recognition principle departs from the notion that countries can keep their own standards (for instance, in product safety, labour, environment, education, tax regulation), but accepts the standards of other countries as equally valid and sufficient (Gerber, 2005: 151). The mutual recognition of standards is often the topic of bilateral negotiations between countries. The strongest form of rivalry and mutual exclusion, exists when countries keep their own standards *and* refuse to recognize other standards. *Separate standards* are the rule rather than the exception in many CSR-relevant areas. In accounting standards, reporting requirements, corporate governance or the regulation of trademarks, many countries still have separate standards, requirements or accreditation principles. Imposing separate standards upon foreign companies active in the own economy thus can become part of an international rivalry in regulation resulting in reciprocal actions of other countries and increased divergence.

Finally, *contests in principles* enhances divergence in sometimes unintended directions. Less inclusive principles with weaker sanctions, compete with more inclusive principles with stronger and stricter sanctions. The lack of international coordination or harmonization can lead to a plethora of codes, principles, benchmarks and guidelines that decreases their effectiveness in disciplining companies. Companies that are confronted with the wide variety of contesting international codes might be inclined to opt for the 'easiest' code. This is the problem of *adverse selection* that stimulates companies that have the highest risk of suffering from reputational damages, to adopt international codes or standards that involve the lowest degree of commitment. Where these codes are initiated by the UN, this process has also become dubbed 'bluewashing'. The bigger the rivalry between principles in a given issue area, the bigger the chance of adverse selection and free-riders becomes.

12.4 ICR REGIME DEVELOPMENT – THE 1970S AND 1980S

Over the years, the behaviour and the role of MNEs, in particular, called for the establishment of new international standards and organizations. Table 12.3 lists the key standards and organizations that were launched in the aftermath of high-profile incidents (triggering events) that occurred during the three different phases identified in Chapter 9. They include the Nestlé baby food scandal (Phase I, 1970), the Bhopal Chemical disaster (Phase II, 1984) and Shell's Brent Spar affair (Phase III, 1995). The present ICR regime came into being in waves. Many forms of regulation and self-regulation have come about as a result of what can be described as the *bandwagon effect*: companies, organizations and societal groupings copy one another's behaviour. Nobody wants, or can afford, to lag behind. This section discusses the first two phases of the development of the ICR regime and the section that follows (12.5) discusses the institutional arrangements that characterize the present ICR regime.

Phase I: initial codification

The institutions and standards of the first (awakening) phase of ICR regime formation focused primarily on environmental issues, the rapid rise of MNEs and growing concern of governments over their unchecked power. In a number of cases – ITT in Chile, companies in banana republics – it transpired that multinationals were abusing their position of power. The role of oil multinationals in the oil crises of the 1970s was also regarded with great suspicion. The general attitude around the world was therefore very critical of MNEs. INGOs such as Greenpeace were founded (1971). This was reinforced by the fear of dominance by American multinationals who stepped up their internationalization efforts, giving rise to negative sentiments in Europe in particular. Multinationals were considered to be undermining Keynesian (demand-oriented) national policies. Following a number of clear cases of power abuse, the operations of multinationals in developing countries also came to be regarded with suspicion. At that time, theoretical discussions centred on 'growth limits' (Club of Rome) and the establishment of a New International Economic Order (NIEO).

In the 1970s, the UN (Centre on Transnational Corporations), the OECD and the ILO almost simultaneously undertook to set down guidelines for MNE conduct. Threatened by the creation of stringent codes by these organizations, the ICC was the first to introduce some sort of 'code' (*ICC Guidelines for Multinational Investment*, 1972). The lack of international consensus on the purpose of the code, its wording and, particularly, the potential for sanctioning non-compliance, moderated the original intention to make the codes mandatory. Instead, voluntary codes were agreed on with limited effect. The UN, OECD and ILO still represent the leading international arenas in which codes, charters and guidelines for the general conduct of multinationals are explicitly negotiated and updated (see Box 12.2). There is increasing cross-reference in these initiatives to each other's guidelines, which indicates a

Table 12.3 Three waves of standards and institutions regulating MNEs

	Phase I: 1960s–1983 Awakening/governments	Phase II: 1984–1992 Engaging/markets	Phase III: 1993–present Networking/Governance
MNE view	Negative	Positive	Ambiguous
Triple-E	Equity >> Efficiency	Efficiency > Equity	Efficiency ↔ Equity
New standards, principles, initiatives	■ FAO/WHO Codex Alimentarius, 1963 ■ UNESCO: cultural and national heritage, 1972 ■ NIO resolution accepted, 1974 ■ ILO, OECD, UNCTC, ICC codes of conduct for MNEs, 1975–78 ■ Sullivan Principles, 1977 ■ Eco-label Der Blauer Engel, 1978 ■ Convention on discrimination against women, 1979 ■ Brandt Report, 1980 ■ UN: Control of restrictive business practices, 1980 ■ UNICEF/WHO code of marketing breast-milk substitutes, 1981	■ World Bank and IMF: Introduction of Structural Adjustment Programmes and continuation of Washington Consensus, 1980s ■ UN Guidelines on consumer protection, 1985 ■ Responsible Care, 1985 ■ FAO code of conduct on pesticides, 1985 ■ 'Sustainable development' (Brundtland Report), 1987 ■ Torture and inhumane treatment convention, 1987 ■ ISO 9000 series, 1987 ■ Fair Trade Label (Max Havelaar), 1988 ■ Child Rights Convention, 1989 ■ CERES Principles, 1989 ■ UN Summit for Children, 1990 ■ ECO-O.K. Certificate, 1991 ■ Agenda 21: e.g. Environment and Development and Forest Principles (Rio Earth Summit), 1992 ■ ICC Business Charter on Sustainable development, 1992	■ FSC certificate, 1993 ■ FAO Code for Responsible Fisheries, 1995 ■ Rugmark, 1995 ■ ICTI code of Business Practice, 1996 ■ ISO 14000 series, 1997 ■ FIFA Code of Labour Practice, 1996 ■ OECD, bribery convention, 1997 ■ SA 8000 series, 1997 ■ GRI, 1997 ■ Kyoto Protocol, 1997 ■ CCC code of labour Practices, 1998 ■ Triple-P concept, 1998 ■ 'Greenwash' concept in Oxford Dictionary, 1999 ■ AA1000, 1999 ■ UNESCO Charter for sustainable tourism, 1999 ■ OECD, corporate governance principles, 1999 ■ UN Millennium Development Goals, 2000 ■ Amended OECD MNE guidelines, 2000 ■ EITI, 2002 ■ Kimberly Process Certification, 2002 ■ Equator Principles, 2002 ■ Corporate governance rules and benchmarks, from 2002 ■ UN Human Rights Commission: human right norms for MNEs, 2003 ■ WHO Framework Convention on Tobacco Control, 2003

New institutions and organizations		
■ Amnesty International, 1961	■ Third World network, 1985	■ NAFTA, side agreements, 1995
■ CEP, 1969	■ Caux Round Table, 1986	■ WTO, 1995
■ WEF, 1971	■ SustainAbility (Elkington), 1987	■ EBNSC, 1995; CSR Europe, 1996
■ Club of Rome, 1972	■ Basel Accord, 1988	■ American Apparel Industry partnership, 1996 (1998: FLA)
■ Greenpeace, 1972	■ CERES, 1988	■ Marine Stewardship council, 1997
■ UN Environment Programme, 1973	■ PWBLF, 1990	■ ETI, 1997
■ World Resources Institute, 1983	■ (W)BCSD, 1991	■ Business partners for development, 1997
■ ERT, 1983	■ European Union, 1992	■ CEPAA, 1998
		■ Global Compact, UN, 2000
		■ WSF, 2001

Sources: Andriof and Marsden (1999), Abrahams (2004) and own additions; NIO = New International Economic Order; CEP = Council on Economic Priorities; WEF = World Economic Forum; PWBLF = Prince of Wales Business Leaders Forum; WBCSD = World Business Council on Sustainable Development; EBNSC = European Business Network for Social Cohesion; EITI = Extractive Industries; CERES = Coalition for Environmentally Responsible Economies; WSF = World Social Forum; EMU = European Monetary Union; ICTI = International Council of Toy Industries; FIFA = Fédération Internationale de Football Association; CCC = Clean Clothes Campaign; FLA = Fair Labour Association; ETI = Ethical Trading Initiative; ERT = European Roundtable of Industrialists

process of international convergence in the development and implementation of minimum principles. The ILO, for instance, is one of the most prominent supporters of the implementation of the Global Compact principles. Updates of the guidelines of the three international organizations have increasingly become formulated in consultation with NGOs and business representatives. However, the approach to implementation of the various codes differs substantially. The ILO, UN and ICC guidelines are entirely voluntary whereas the OECD Guidelines are more or less legally binding (for the 38 signatory governments).

BOX 12.2 THE DEVELOPMENT OF FOUR INTERNATIONAL APPROACHES TO 'PROPER' MNE CONDUCT

ICC: Benchmarks and Charters

The International Chamber of Commerce (ICC) has concerned itself with corporate conduct and multinational investment since 1972. The ICC does not use the term Multinational Enterprise. In 1991, the ICC developed the 'Business Charter for Sustainable Development' which is aimed at providing environmental benchmarks or 'good practices' for corporations. The most recent of these guidelines also refers to UN, OECD and ILO guidelines. The ICC is committed to the 'precautionary principle' approach, but does not enforce its guidelines.

OECD: Guidelines

In 1976, the first version of the *Guidelines for Multinational Enterprises* was signed by all OECD member states. In June 2000, the sixth version was formulated. The OECD guidelines consist of voluntary CSR norms and principles that encourage stakeholder engagement and are intended to achieve sustainable development. The signatory countries are responsible for about 90 per cent of all FDI. The most recent guidelines were established in consultation with the IB community, trade unions, governments and public interest organizations. The 2000 review emphasizes adherence to national legislation in the host country. Important issues such as child labour, forced labour, human rights, the environment, corruption, payment of taxes and consumer protection are included in the guidelines. In the 30 OECD member countries National Contact Points (NCPs) were established to oversee the implementation of the guidelines. In the May 2001–June 2004 period, 42 cases were brought before NCPs, the bulk of which concerned employment and industrial relations issues initiated by trade unions or related NGOs (cf. OECD, 2004). The operations of home multinationals in a developing country were at stake in 60 per cent of the cases. The complaints were filed particularly against MNEs from France, the UK and Germany.

ILO: Principles

In 1977, the ILO Governing Body – an organization based on consensus between government, employers and trade unions – adopted a *Tripartite Declaration of Principles Concerning Multinational Enterprises and Social Policy*. The principles refer to compliance with labour rights – such as the right to free association – and decent working conditions, which include combating child labour, forced labour and discrimination. The declaration has been updated a number of times. It is the leading set of global guidelines on social and labour policies for multinationals. It offers a procedure for addressing disputes. The Tripartite Declaration was amended in November 2000 to incorporate commitments to the four principles enshrined under the ILO's *Declaration on Fundamental Principles and Rights at Work*, respecting commitments involving child labour and the minimum working age. The ILO principles are supported by NGOs, employers and employee organizations, but problems of ratification generally apply to governments. ILO conventions are increasingly included in other codes, for instance the ICFTU Basic Code of Labour Practice, and thus act as a springboard for the development of other codes.

United Nations: from Code to Compact

In the 1970s, the UN (Centre on Transnational Corporations) initiated the most radical attempt to codify MNE behaviour. The code never got beyond the status of a draft. Eventually, in 1992, these endeavours were officially halted and the bureau that had initiated the codes disbanded – paradoxically just at the moment international environmental organizations (UNCED) launched new initiatives in the area of 'sustainability'. In the second half of the 1990s, negotiations on international guidelines started anew which resulted in an appraisal or adjustment of the ILO and OECD guidelines. In December 1999, the UN secretary general, Kofi Annan, initiated *The Global Compact for the New Century*. The initiative challenged leading figures in the business community to develop the social and ecological pillars of the global economy in a sustainable manner. It is not a code, but a set of voluntary principles rooted in key UN declarations and conventions. It encompasses ten foundational principles with respect to human rights, labour rights (*people*) and environmental rights (*planet*) and is, among other things, based on the *Universal Declaration of Human Rights*, the ILO *Fundamental Principles on Rights at Work* and the *Rio Principles on Environment and Development*. Shortly after it was officially launched, 50 companies (e.g. Shell and Unilever), dozens of international trade organizations and countless NGOs had joined the *Global Compact*. In the period 2000–05, nearly 2,000 companies became signatories of the Global Compact. It is considered an important trigger for firms to grow into new issues that are not covered by existing industry or company codes.

Phase II: first expressions of business leadership

In the 1980s, which represents the second phase of the ICR regime build-up, the general attitude towards multinationals became more positive. It was clear that socialism as an alternative societal model to capitalism had failed. At the same time, the dominance of US multinationals had diminished and competition between developed countries increased. MNEs became vital for the competitive position of countries. Since MNEs had also managed to put a check on flagrant abuses of power, negative sentiments dwindled even further. International organizations and standards focused on the 'feasible' society: sustainable development and sustainable management were introduced as concepts in which economic growth was considered vital for further ecological progress. Conceptual discussions centred on 'sustainable business', 'responsible care', and 'green capitalism'. Eco labels became better established and the first 'fair trade' certificates were issued that enabled goods to be sold through conventional distribution channels. The 1988 introduction of the *Max Havelaar* label in the Netherlands is considered to mark the beginning of the second generation of fair trade initiatives.

This period is also marked by a declining interest in an international governmental code of conduct for MNEs. Instead, the emphasis shifted to self-regulation. Networks of business leaders began drafting general guidelines for potential members to follow. Examples are the 1986 Caux Round Table Principles for business and the 1989 CERES Principles. A number of leading business councils and leadership forums also originate from this period, all of them addressing generic problems of CSR. Prime examples are the Prince of Wales Business

Leadership Forum (1990) and the Business Council for Sustainable Development (1991) which later merged with the World Industry Council for the Environment to become the World Business Council for Sustainable Development (WBCSD). Most of these organizations invited firms to adopt their principles, which thus acted as a benchmark in a process of rival convergence. In the period 1989–2004, the CERES Principles for instance were endorsed by around 75 companies of which nine included *Fortune* 500 companies. The Caux Roundtable Principles are claimed to be the most widely adopted code of business ethics in the world. At the same time, the first specialized private CSR consultancy firms were established. One of the most influential private consultancies, SustainAbility, stems from this period. It was founded in 1987 by John Elkington (and Julia Hailes) in the UK. They concluded that business and markets have to be involved in the pursuit of a sustainable future, which is why they have been working closely with business leaders. Books such as *The Green Capitalists* (1987) and *The Green Consumer Guide* (1988) laid the foundation for the very influential 'triple bottom line' and the 'Triple-P' (People, Planet, Profit) concepts that were introduced in the 1990s.

12.5 ICR SINCE THE 1990S – SEARCHING FOR NEW GOVERNANCE PRINCIPLES

In the third phase of ICR regime formation – beginning in the early 1990s – the attitude towards MNEs became ambivalent once again. MNEs were seen as the drivers of 'globalization' and the ICT revolution, a positive force in the opening up of many countries. The number of triggering events (oil spills, industrial accidents) that came to light without outside intervention was relatively low. The regional integration processes in North America and Europe supported by business coalitions of leading MNEs, combined with the structural crisis in Japan, reinforced the prevalence of economic over social considerations. Only by the end of the 1990s and the beginning of the twenty-first century did accounting scandals, the end of the dotcom boom and excessive executive remuneration packages rock the trust that was placed in industry.

At the same time, however, incidents were increasingly shaped and exposed by critical NGOs who sought direct confrontation in order to get their message across. These events gradually gave rise to the 'anti-globalization' movement which addresses the problems associated with an extreme reliance on markets and protests against the dominant position of MNEs. A large number of new initiatives, new concepts and new organizations duly appeared, while existing international organizations tried to revive some of their old principles. The present ICR regime is shaped by these efforts in four bargaining arenas: codes of conduct; trademarks and labelling; corporate governance regulation; and non-financial reporting. The key question is whether these initiatives have led to regulatory convergence and thus a homogeneous ICR regime as is often the intention of such initiatives, or do national CRS regimes continue to diverge?

Codes of conduct

A code of conduct is a system of agreements and basic principles through which a company communicates the kind of conduct its members – and possibly business partners – are expected to exhibit in specific situations (van Luijk and Schilder, 1997). This implies that the code should indicate what is acceptable and what is not, and how issues such as child labour, human rights, working conditions and trade unions are engaged with. A code of conduct can, therefore, serve as a compass in the maze of current international norms, and fill in some gaps in legislation (cf. Kolk and van Tulder, 2002).

In the early 1990s, a few leading international civil society NGOs put forward concrete proposals for codes of conduct. Church organizations such as the Catholic Institute for International Relations (CIIR) presented concrete codes conferring a modern guise on the age-old ecclesiastical practice of codification. Amnesty International UK developed a set of 'Principles for Business' (1991). Some of the trade unions (International Confederation of Free Trade Unions (ICFTU) and the International Building and Wood Workers) drew up codes or model frameworks. The Clean Clothes Campaign (CCC) developed a Fair Trade Code aimed at fair and equitable trade and a Code of Labour Practices (1998). The number of international codes that were drawn up by other INGOs, however, remained relatively modest. Drafting a generic code of conduct is not easy and requires considerable financial and human resources. As a result, NGOs started to turn their attention to specific issues and introduced specific instruments, in particular, trademarks.

In response to the often rather strict codes proposed by INGOs, a large number of companies started to formulate their own ethical values and guidelines for conduct in a 'code of ethics', 'corporate code', 'Leitmotiv' or 'declaration of basic policy principles', 'corporate values statement' and 'business principles'. All these documents can essentially be situated under the term 'code of conduct'. In industries where few players operate and oligopolistic competition prevails, there has been a particularly strong tendency to follow others' conduct closely. That applies also for codes of conduct. Possession of such a code may simply mean that one conforms to specific modes of conduct within a given industry. Nike and Reebok use more or less the exact same wording in their codes of conduct. By the end of the 1990s, 85 per cent of the 2,000 largest US companies had a code of conduct (KPMG, 2002).

Corporate self-regulation initiatives were paralleled by a number of – largely voluntary – industry codes or charters introduced by international industry associations. These codes initially focused on environmental issues and later, increasingly on labour conditions or more generally on 'sustainable development'. These industries include: Hotels (1992), Tourism (1992), Mining and Metals (1993), Tea (1995), Toys (1995), Apparel (1997), Sporting Goods (1997), Fertilizers (1990, 2002), Iron and Steel (1992, 2002), Cyanide (2000), Mining and Metals (2000), Diamonds (2000), Coffee (2004). Most international industry associations started with general policy statements in the early 1990s, which were later reformulated into voluntary guidelines. Sector or trade organization codes correspond with the more established practice of developing profession-specific codes such as those for accountants, journalists, doctors, advertising companies and lawyers (Deephouse, 2000).

The 1990s were further characterized by an increasing number of coalitions (or networks) consisting of corporations, governments and NGOs that formulated standards, declarations or guidelines. Leading coalitions became the Forest Stewardship Council (FSC, 1993), the Marine Stewardship Council (1997), the Ethical Trading Initiative (1998), the Fair Labour Association (1998), the Global Alliance for vaccines and immunization (1999), the Kimberley Process (2000, on conflict diamonds) and the UNDP Sustainable Tourism Development Project (2001). A telling development at the time was that some international organizations – in varying coalitions – started to use their position to advocate rule compliance of firms that wanted to do business with them. In 1996, FIFA (an international sports NGO whose member countries exceeds that of the UN in number) designed a 'code of labour practice' in alliance with three international trade union organizations to improve working conditions of sporting goods suppliers (van Tulder and Kolk, 2001). The World Bank also tried to act upon the demands of its (anti-globalization) critics by establishing greater transparency, particularly in troubled industries such as mining (The Extractive Industries Review, in 2001) and forming a coalition with prime private banks to increase the accountability of project finance (The Equator Principles, Box 12.3).

241

BOX 12.3 THE EQUATOR PRINCIPLES

In 2002, the International Finance Corporation (IFC) – the private lending arm of the World Bank Group – convened a meeting of ten big international commercial banks to address environmental and social risks in the financing of large projects. This meeting resulted in the Equator Principles, a set of guidelines for managing environmental and social issues in project finance lending. The guidelines were introduced as 'voluntary' to banks active in IFC projects. But the concern that the IFC might stop 'doing business' with non-compliant banks, provided sufficient incentive for a rapid diffusion of the principles. At the same time, the IFC developed a framework for improving corporate governance. In April 2004, 21 banks had adopted the Equator Principles, covering over 80 per cent of all development projects financed by banks. The participating banks apply these principles globally to project financing in all industry sectors, including mining, oil and gas, and forestry, and to all projects with a capital cost of US$50 million or more. Project finance is an important method of financing in which loans for new investments are structured around the project's own operating cash flows and assets. The Equator Principles include, for instance, appropriate consultation with affected local stakeholders. Projects must also demonstrate compliance with IFC's safeguard policies, which cover management of crosscutting impacts such as natural habitats, indigenous peoples, and involuntary resettlement (cf. www.equator-principles.com). INGOs such as Friends of the Earth remain critical of the principles due to their voluntary nature. They are concerned over the lack of transparency and of regular complaint procedures.

Likelihood of compliance, sanctions and effectiveness

The codes of conduct proposed by INGOs are generally much stricter, specific and inclusive of measurable criteria than company codes. INGOs also place high value on external monitoring and verification, as well as clear sanctions in the event of failure to comply with the codes (cf. Kolk and van Tulder, 2002, 2005). By contrast, research on the content of codes of conduct (Kolk and van Tulder, 2002, 2005) shows that companies favour *internal* monitoring of compliance with the code. Hence, NGOs questioned the *likelihood of compliance* with codes – the probability that companies will conform to their codes of conduct and behave responsibly (Kolk *et al.*, 1999).

The codes issued by international industry associations in particular are weak where likelihood of compliance is concerned. This can be attributed to a lack of specification. In the case of the Chemical Industry's Responsible Care programme (King and Lenox, 2000; Prakash, 2002), for example, it has been found that the codes of individual companies within the sector are often more advanced and detailed.

The codes drawn up by international governmental organizations are often much stricter than individual company codes. Still, the likelihood of compliance with these codes was generally not very high either, partly due to conflicting interests of participating countries. Stricter formulations were often hampered by competing policies of national governments representing rival CSR regimes.

Furthermore, some of the international organizations' codes were never intended to be implemented or to coordinate other codes. They were developed largely to serve as 'model codes' and to stimulate other coalitions and code development. A model code can serve as a point of reference in the continuous pursuit of greater clarity, detail, strictness and compliance.

It can, however, also lead to *adverse selection* where poor performing companies elect to adopt this type of code (cf. Lenox and Nash, 2003). An example is the UN Global Compact which was designed as an umbrella code that represents a set of voluntary principles rooted in key UN declarations and conventions. The objective of the UN Global Compact was to function as a very general benchmark, with an associated rather low level of compliance likelihood. Progress on implementation is difficult to measure and compliance hard to enforce. This increases the risk of 'bluewashing' – companies entering into a coalition with the UN (blue) largely for PR reasons (cf. Van Lindenberg, 2003). The main problem with this is that the UN could be seen as offering credibility to corporate efforts while asking very little in return.[12]

In sum, the content of most international codes is still relatively weak. They are hardly objectively monitored for compliance, contain often only a few verifiable criteria and they tend to lack a thoroughly worked out objective. For a large part this can be attributed to the nature of CSR issues that are often too complex to capture in codes. The strict adherence to minimum ages as set down in a code on child labour, for instance, could aggravate the issue, not least because it seems that governments are less interested in combating child labour than companies are. In certain contexts it may be wiser to formulate codes of conduct in broader – more vague – terms or even not at all, so as to accommodate the complexities involved in combating child labour (cf. Kolk and van Tulder, 2002; Chapter 13).

Quality marks, labelling and accreditation

Company efforts with regard to societal interface issues referred to in a code of conduct can be made recognizable for consumers by means of a quality mark, label or certificate. Such a quality mark or label enables a company or a group of companies to communicate its commitment to society and provide stakeholders with information on the quality and contents of products. There is great diversity and enormous overlap among quality marks and labels. There are sector quality marks, labour condition quality marks (Oké bananas, Fair Wear, Rugmark, Fair Trade), production conditions quality marks (FSC certificate, Rainforest Alliance), recycling or organic quality marks (Eco-O.K.), human resources policy quality marks (Investor in People) and product quality marks. CSR-related quality marks are often classified as 'idealistic quality marks'. A small country such as the Netherlands alone boasts about 100 'idealistic' quality marks and an additional 100 green logos. Europe has about 30 international eco labels. In the face of such diversity in quality marks, the potential is great that the consumer may not be able to see the wood for the trees. Moreover, due to the large number of quality marks, the instrument is threatening to lose its force, as indicated by studies of the OECD (1997), which showed that generally, eco-labelling has been, at best, moderately successful with individual consumers. Research conducted in the Netherlands in 1999 showed that the majority of respondents did not know what the label actually meant. Accreditation councils around the world inspect whether a label does what it promises, but not whether its promise also reflects the perception of consumers.[13]

It remains exceptionally difficult to address a complicated CSR problem by means of a quality mark or label. Some eco-labels, for instance, are awarded to a product if it is 'one of the least environmentally degrading of its kind', which may refer to anything from the production process or product properties to recycling. Other eco-logos that hint at the recyclability of a product fail to be clear on whether the product/the packaging is made of (supplied) recycled material or if the product/packaging itself can be reused. It is impossible for the consumer to establish which of these qualifications apply to the product.

Also, while almost every consumer knows what the Fair Trade or *Max Havelaar* labels stand for, some confusion surrounding these labels also exists. Consumers tend to be under the impression that Fair Trade is the manufacturer and not just the quality mark. In practice, a manufacturer could therefore 'spoil' the market for other manufacturers who use the same label. If the label is awarded also to other products, the potential for confusion between product characteristics and quality mark further increases.

In most countries, the issuing of marks or labels is subject to (some) regulation but in practice that does not do away with problems of overlap, diversity, confusing or inadequate information and a lack of international coordination. Effective control and international coordination, however, is exceptionally difficult. Control and coordination of CSR themes are essential, but quality marks hardly supply any information about this. National accreditation and certification institutes appear not to have been able to curb the number of quality marks. And internationally too, there is hardly any evidence of coordination.[14] In Europe, governments and environmental organizations have been trying to integrate different national labels since the 1990s. Thus far, it has not been successful and has also led to the present situation where quality marks could mean something completely different from one country to the next – which decreases their effectiveness enormously. The so-called quality mark the 'Green Dot' (*Grüne Punkt*) is a clear example. Germany, Spain, Sweden, Norway and also Canada are Green Dot countries. The logo guarantees that the manufacturer has paid for the processing of the packaging and that the consumer can also return the packaging to the shopkeeper. However, products with this logo can be found in other countries where it also enjoys a high level of consumer recognition. In these countries the logo is to a large part meaningless – unless consumers are prepared to travel to the adhering countries to return it there.[15]

Confusion can also be deliberately created. In 1993, the issue of deforestation was first addressed by the FSC who introduced a global quality label. Following the early lead of this scheme, however, several regional forest certification schemes were set up. To a certain degree it can be interpreted as an authentic response to the alleged shortcomings of the label, but it can also be seen as an attempt to water down the original objectives of the FSC scheme. A large NGO, the World Rainforest Movement (WRM), in the field characterizes the many competing certification schemes as the 'greenwashing' of logging activities. The rival certificates have increased the confusion surrounding sustainable logging and have probably withheld the FSC from formulating more stringent rules (in order not to lose its appeal as a leading label).

Certificates could replace the role of labels. The most successful approach to certification has been implemented by the ISO in the area of environmental management (ISO 14001) or quality management (ISO 9000).

Particularly with regard to environmental management systems (ISO 14001), ISO became a very prominent standard-setting institute. In the period 1996–2000, more than 20,000 firms applied for ISO 14001 accreditation. But the impact of this international regime is rather diverse. Japanese companies, in particular, have adopted ISO standards (Kolk, 2000). But the application of ISO standards does not guarantee good performance in the area of CSR. It is possible to be accredited with ISO 14001 without improving much in environmental management (cf. Van de Wateringen, 2005). The implementation of ISO standards allows considerable managerial discretion, and its effectiveness therefore depends on how companies choose to use them (Ammenberg, 2003). The various ISO standards thus do not necessarily lead to increased convergence between countries, sectors and firms, nor do they lead to an average increase in CSR performance.

Following ISO's approach, a number of independent certification institutes have already propagated specific CSR certificates. The most detailed certification initiatives at present are SA8000 and AA1000 (Box 12.4).

BOX 12.4 INDEPENDENT CERTIFICATION

SA8000

The Social Accountability Institute (SAI), formerly the Council on Economic Priorities Accreditation Agency (CEPAA), has introduced the SA8000 in 1997 as guideline for monitoring working conditions. The issues that are addressed derive from the ILO guidelines, such as child labour, forced labour, discrimination, health and safety, freedom of association and the right to collective bargaining. The SA8000 is related to the social performance of a company. Companies that uphold these norms can acquire a certificate that shows that they meet fundamental labour norms. According to Amnesty International, the SA8000 is the best standard in the area of social issues. At the beginning of the twenty-first century, 118 production facilities around the world, employing 70,000 people were certified to SA8000.

AA1000

The AA1000 guideline was launched at the end of 1999 by the Institute of Social and Ethical AccountAbility (ISEA) and focuses on the process of social, ethical and environmental accounting and verification. Central to this guideline is the quality of the dialogue with, and participation of, interested parties. It offers organizations a systematic framework for conscious and transparent engagement with issues surrounding CSR. In spring 2002, the AA2000 Accountability Management was launched. It linked with the already existing quality model EFQM and the *Balanced Scorecard*. The EFQM model includes a section on outcomes that focuses on an evaluation by society. Here, the relationship with the social environment is measured by means of the principle of reciprocity: the influence on and evaluation by society.

Corporate governance

National discussions on new corporate governance principles resulted in a number of initiatives. A certain degree of regime convergence can be detected especially in the period 1999–2003 when all codes and laws adopted aimed at greater transparency for shareholders. However, none of these provisions give shareholders more rights, only more information (Appeldoorn, 2004: 46). National CSR regimes also started to converge on the role of the board of directors. In most codes (except for the US) it is proposed to separate the functions of the CEO and the chairman.

On other corporate governance issues, however, important differences still remain, largely along the lines of traditional differences between governance regimes. For instance, while both the Japanese 'revised corporate governance principles' (2001) and the US Sarbanes-Oxley Act (2002) mention insider trading as an explicit problem of corporate governance, the US enacted a law, while Japan and other countries (including France, the UK, Netherlands and Germany) formulated (voluntary) self-regulating principles or codes. Similarly, the codes and laws of liberal countries (US and UK) explicitly aim at abolishing the use of anti-takeover devices such as poison pills and controlling minority shareholdings by companies (Appeldoorn, 2004). The French, German, Dutch and Japanese codes do not make this explicit, while their system builds much more on these principles. While all codes, except the American and French, provide guidelines for the chairman of the board, each is different in practice.

In international regime interaction, laws have a greater impact than voluntary codes. The legalistic US approach to corporate governance has therefore become more pervasive and has prompted many publicly listed (non-US) companies to respond to these new rules: adopting them, lobbying for changes in the law, or withdrawal. After the passing of the Sarbanes-Oxley Act in the US large companies from Europe and Japan seriously contemplated withdrawal from the US stock exchanges.[16] Adaptation to US governance laws leads to an informal spread of the US corporate governance regime via multinational corporations that are listed in the US. Companies, as well as governments, have objected to this form of imposition but to no avail.

The question is to what extent this process of national rivalry is mediated by international initiatives. The guidelines for corporate governance, points of reference and benchmarks formulated by international industrial associations and organizations (e.g. EU, OECD) contain no formal sanctions, relying instead on the function of the reputation mechanism. The OECD is the most important multilateral arena in which bargaining takes place over general principles of corporate governance. In its 1999 'Principles of Corporate Governance', the OECD secretariat acknowledged that a standard model of good corporate governance is not desirable. A 'one-size-fits-all' approach to corporate governance would not be able to accommodate the pluralist interests of most member countries. It is not possible to identify best practice that can be universalized. Nevertheless, the OECD formulated a number of general principles that emphasize the importance of access to information for shareholders. Notable also is that the principles include explicit provisions regarding the treatment of stakeholders other than shareholders (cf. Appeldoorn, 2004). This provision clearly indicates a compromise between rival national governance regimes. Nevertheless, implementation of the Guidelines is bound to be particularly weak in liberal regimes that do not emphasize the rights of stakeholders other than shareholders.

Another relevant initiative was undertaken by the non-profit-oriented Foundation for Business and Society (FBS), a spin-off of the WBCSD. In 2002, it embarked on the development of the 'Global Corporate Governance Benchmark' (GCGB). This initiative was undertaken in close consultation with the ICC. The benchmark was intended to focus primarily on the key characteristics of corporate governance – the 'DNA of good governance'. The difficulty of the exercise is illustrated by the fact that the final benchmark contains primarily 'outsider' system characteristics, whose relevance is limited to firms listed in liberal countries. Applying these principles to public companies around the world reveals that firms that are listed in the US rank better than other firms (cf. van Raamsdonk, 2004). The GCGB is not a neutral benchmark, though, if widely adopted, it could contribute to international convergence.

Reporting

As part of the bargaining dynamics among societal actors, reporting relates to the discursive power of firms – the power to 'frame debates'. Multinationals – confronted with a variety of regimes – can employ reporting as a means to influence or respond to society (cf. Kolk and van Tulder, 2004b). Internally, reporting fulfils an important communication and management function. The spate of environmental, social and ethical reports of the 1990s can be viewed as a manifestation of Societal Interface Management. Analysing the quality and consequences of reporting on these non-financial issues is extremely complex. On the one hand, as reporting becomes more professional and expensive (full-colour and glossy), companies run the risk of their efforts being dismissed as an exercise in PR (*window dressing*). On the other hand, reticent companies sometimes do more in the area of sustainability than they openly communicate (Mauser, 2001). What types of reports can be found and what is the likelihood that the different types of reports will be integrated and standardized?

The diversity of reports is great and growing. Departing from the Triple-P categorization (planet, people and profit), Figure 12.1 offers an overview of various types of reports that have existed since the early 1990s; they overlap and supplement one another.

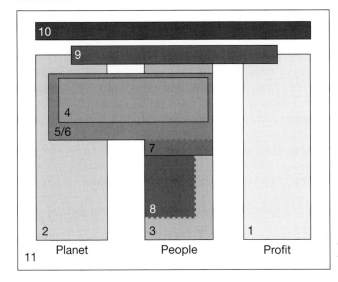

1. Financial report
2. Environmental report
3. Social report
4. Environmental and social report
5. HSE report
6. Responsible care report
7. WHSE report
8. Social-ethical report
9. Societal report
10. Vision on sustainability
11. Sustainability report

Figure 12.1 Reporting around the world

The three main areas of reporting are: (1) financial, (2) environmental and (3) social (numbers relate to those on Figure 12.1). Internationally, *financial reports* are most stringently regulated. In almost all countries, companies are required by law to account for financial matters on an annual basis. Still, significant differences exist across countries – and even within countries – as to the kind of information that should be disclosed. In Europe, a movement towards standardization can be discerned which coincides with the adoption of the International Accounting Standard (IAS) in 2005. However, since the US, in particular, will continue to lay down other rules, the probability of worldwide standardization of reporting is slight.

Hugely divergent norms and practices also apply to *environmental reports*. In many smaller European states, some form of environmental reporting is legally required. Other European countries tend towards voluntary reporting through the promotion and adoption of the Eco-Management and Audit Scheme (EMAS). American and Japanese companies are subject to other reporting laws and practices. The likelihood that environmental reporting standards will be standardized globally seems small.

In practice, the *social report* focuses particularly on human resource matters such as the remuneration policy and the training, safety and welfare of employees. Broader social themes – such as human rights and child labour, in particular – are less often addressed. Again, a broad spectrum of social reports exists, driven in part by divergent regulatory requirements. For example, there are no laws or guidelines for social reports in the Netherlands, whereas in the US, there are.

To add to the diversity, a large number of hybrid forms of reporting developed in the course of the 1990s. These include: (4) 'Environmental and Social Reports'; (5) HSE (Health, Safety and Environment) reports; (6) 'Responsible Care' reports; (7) WHSE (Welfare, Health, Safety and Environment) reports; (8) 'Social-ethical reports'; (9) 'Societal report'; (10) 'Vision on sustainability' statements; and, finally, (11) 'Sustainability reports' which are the most comprehensive attempt at incorporating the different elements of the *Triple bottom line*.[17]

Still, even sustainability reports often contain few hard facts and evidence is often anecdotal. Most reports do not explain how the information is collected and only rarely do the reports

BOX 12.5 GLOBAL REPORTING INITIATIVE (GRI)

The Global Reporting Initiative (GRI) guidelines were established in 1997 by CERES and UNEP. In addition to CERES and UNEP dozens of organizations assisted in setting up the initiative. Different indicators, now amounting to about 50, and quality requirements must make it possible to compare social, ecological and economic performance (GRI, 2002). Moreover, the guidelines also provide an outline of the structure of a sustainability report. The business community and public interest organizations are increasingly regarding the GRI guidelines as the norm for social and environmental reports. Both the government of the Netherlands and the European Parliament endorse the GRI. In August 2002, the third version of the GRI guidelines was published. The GRI institute works closely with the most important organizations concerned with the development of codes of conduct: the Global Compact, the ILO and the OECD (section 5.1). On 6 April 2002, Amsterdam was chosen as the new location for the UN institute (*FD*, 9 April 2002). Interesting to note is that a contributory factor in this decision was not only the fact that a number of Dutch multinationals with head offices in Amsterdam and with the reputation of being leaders in the area of sustainability reporting participated in the lobbying process, but that the head offices of both Greenpeace and Amnesty International are in Amsterdam. All three societal institutions were therefore represented in the lobbying process. The GRI guidelines distinguish between environmental reports, fragmented reports, three-dimensional reports and completely integrated reports (GRI, 2002). Just like the application of the GRI guidelines, external verification of the report is not compulsory. The objective of the GRI is to enhance the credibility of sustainability reporting by means of six qualitative characteristics: relevance, reliability, comprehensibility, comparability, timeliness and verifiability.

contain concrete verifiable objectives (SustainAbility, 2000). Even in the case of *best practice* companies, a significant gap exists between stakeholder demands and the actual content of reports (Elkington *et al.*, 2001). To counter this criticism, however, and to promote harmonization of non-financial reports and standards, many *best practice* companies are starting to adopt the Global Reporting Initiative (GRI) guidelines in the compilation of their sustainability reports. The GRI is currently the most integrated and ambitious international standard that has been developed by an independent international organization (Box 12.5).

12.6 CONCLUSION: THE SHAPE OF THE ICR REGIME

Corporate reporting as yet is characterized by a significant degree of chaos, inadequate external verification, a lack of coordination and, to a certain extent, a lack of resolve of the different parties to cooperate. This places severe limitations on the effectiveness of initiatives in the area of ICR. One cannot speak of an international *level playing field* in ICR. Legislation is often absent, institutions are fragmented and even function in a manner that further promotes rivalry. The rules of the game have not yet crystallized and are being negotiated in a large number of arenas, which renders it awkward, complicated and uncertain for all parties to arrive at an 'accurate' interpretation of ICR. This chapter outlined a number of trend-setting international concepts, initiatives and institutes – largely initiated by NGOs, international industry organizations or international governmental organizations – that could combat overlap and stimulate best practices. Some of these initiatives have been embraced by a large number of companies and governments. Moreover, codes of conduct, quality marks, certificates and reporting are not only the manifestation and result of past negotiations between companies and stakeholders; they are also a source for continued negotiations in the future. A number of divergent approaches can be found in the leading arenas in which the ICR regime is being negotiated (Table 12.4). The orientation of dominant member countries or the overall historical mandate of the respective institutions render them more or less active in establishing rules, benchmarks and the like.

An *inactive ICR* approach is primarily adopted by efficiency-oriented international institutions such as the WTO and the IMF. The dominant view of these organizations is that the shape of globalization and ICR should be primarily defined by markets. Open markets are the best guarantee for efficiency, growth and, ultimately, equity. These institutions therefore embody the risk that the discrepancy between formal rules and informal practices will become more pronounced. If official international rules do not sit well with national interests as defined by governments or conceptions of social justice as defined by NGOs, the likelihood is strong that the rules will be contested. The one-size-fits-all (efficiency) approach of these institutions leads to considerable divergence in practice. One way of tackling the tension between efficiency (open markets, free trade) and national equity (sovereignty, fair trade) was to include a social clause in the WTO treaty that links trade and labour standards. However, the discussion on including such a clause soon petered out (Abrahams, 2004) and a dispute settlement procedure was adopted instead – a pragmatic trade-off whose main objective is international efficiency.

A *reactive ICR* approach is exemplified by the ISO and the OECD. Their main objective is to create a minimum level of harmonization between otherwise rival principles and standards. The ICR regime propagated by these organizations represents what is internationally feasible – given the present distribution of power among members. The risk of reactive ICR institutions is that a dominant member imposes its ICR regime on other participants. Or formulated

Table 12.4 ICR orientation of international organizations

Inactive	Reactive	Active	Proactive
International efficiency		Global equity	International effectiveness
Contest	Race	Co-alignment	Co-habitation
Rival divergence	Rival convergence	Non-rival convergence	Non-rival divergence

WTO
IMF
ICC, FBS + Branches
ISO
OECD
World Bank
United Nations
ILO
European Union
Indep. Accreditation

| Risks: imposition of efficiency rules on ICR agenda; discrepancy between formal rules and informal practices | Risks: imposition of one dominant model; danger of lowest common denominator and ceiling for progress | Risks: weak compliance likelihood; 'blue/green/whitewash'; adverse selection | Risks: weak implementation; Partnership 'capture'; temporary alliance |

differently: a harmonization approach is only feasible if the rules that are adopted coincide with the interests of dominant countries or companies. Many harmonization initiatives (for instance on tax harmonization or on specific international standards) that did not take these 'realistic' considerations into account, have consequently been ruled out. If a dominant model or standard is not adopted, reactive ICR regimes risk adopting only 'lowest common denominator' standards or benchmarks. This could frustrate 'frontrunner' firms or countries that pursue higher ICR standards.

An *active ICR* approach has been pioneered by multilateral development institutions such as the World Bank, the UN and the ILO. These institutions can be considered the most active drivers of ICR (Vives, 2004). Their more idealistic approach of non-rival convergence has prompted them to search for guidelines and ambitions instead of designing strict codes or reporting guidelines. This might lead to a 'race to the top', but could also have the opposite effect. Through a process of adverse selection, companies that subscribe to the vague principles propagated by international organizations could use their commitment to these principles largely for PR and 'blue/green/whitewash' purposes. In this way, the international organization may gain legitimacy, but the 'issues' the guidelines or principles address are not effectively dealt with.

The first contours of a *proactive ICR* approach are only gradually emerging. Independent accreditation agencies in particular have come up with interesting initiatives. However, initiatives that aim at a high level of compliance run the risk of weak adoption rates (partly due to other standards with more scope for lower levels of compliance). The principle of 'continuous improvement' in a dialogue with important stakeholders, as for instance adhered to by the GRI initiative, might solve some of these dilemmas. The partnership strategy that has been developed especially by multilateral development institutions as well as some multi-stakeholder dialogues could lay the foundation for further progress in this area. Partnerships are formed around particular issues and do not encompass whole industries. In this sense they do not lead to convergence, but sustain a degree of non-rival 'healthy' divergence between participating and non-participating actors. The risk of the partnership strategy is that coalitions are only temporary and/or that international organizations are 'captured' by their partners. The latter resembles the risk of 'regulatory capture' that has been experienced by so many national governments. Braithwaite and Drahos (2000) illustrate this by citing the experience of Codex Alimentaris Commission of the FAO which was captured by large food corporations and lowered food standards worldwide – for instance in the area of genetically modified foods.

Finally, the overall outcome of the interaction between the various ICR and CSR regimes remains extremely hard to assess and predict. Judging by the prevalence of ICR regime articulation at the inactive and reactive side of the ICR spectrum (Table 12.4) it appears that rivalry is likely to remain a leading principle in the international interplay between the parties. Some non-rival principles are slowly emerging, but they are not yet operational to the extent that the rivalry-enhancing principles are. This is especially due to the lack of international institutions and organizations that forcefully represent these principles. It is also not clear whether such a shift in emphasis would lead to convergence or divergence or whether it would bring about a 'race to the bottom' or a 'race to the top'. In one of the most comprehensive and sophisticated studies on this topic, Braithwaite and Drahos (2000: 516) concluded that international harmonization and deregulation in the 1990s worked in tandem to produce downward pressure on regulatory standards. But they tended to characterize this as 'shifts' or 'ratchets' rather than a 'race'. They also concluded that 'for the last quarter of the twentieth century, the ratchets driving the regulation of environment, safety and financial security have predominantly been upwards ratchets; with other domains of economic regulation the principle of deregulation has driven predominantly downwards ratchets' (ibid.: 522).

Clear downward shifts can, for instance, be observed in tax regimes and labour standards. A race to the bottom is less likely to occur in food safety and quality regulation. Should the price of downward shifts be too high, all parties (firms included) have an interest in increased regulation (see Chapter 10). This has been the case, for instance, in international financial regulation where the financial crises of the 1990s threatened to undermine the stability of the whole system. International rule convergence could have an adverse impact on weaker parties if the interests of the strongest party take precedence over that of others. Whether convergence, divergence or rivalry will ultimately prevail strongly depends on the strategies of the only actor that truly operates across borders: MNEs. The final chapter of Part II will therefore examine in more detail the strategic ICR repertoire (and dilemmas) of multinationals.

Chapter 13

The process: ICR as managing distance

CHAPTER CONTENTS

13.1 INTRODUCTION: ON THE IMPORTANCE OF DISTANCE

In 1997, at the peak of the globalization wave, Frances Cairncross, editor of *The Economist*, compellingly proclaimed the 'death of distance'. She argued that the communication revolution would bring down communication costs to such an extent that distance would no longer be a relevant barrier for social and economic interaction (Cairncross, 1997, 2000). A distinctive competitive advantage of an MNE – compared to a domestic company – is precisely its ability to manage distance. Across distant borders, product and factor markets are very imperfect. The key competitive edge of a multinational is generally considered to be the company-internal exploitation of these international market imperfections. If distance became obsolete, it would lose its competitive advantage and render a separate approach to ICR superfluous.

This chapter explores whether distance is still a relevant factor for firms and what this implies for the IB case for corporate responsibility. The study of ICR focuses on the responsibilities of firms, governments and civil society across borders. ICR theory and practice surpasses CSR as an 'evolving area of inquiry still at an early stage of development' (Windsor, 2004: 47). ICR is an even more multifaceted notion than CSR and requires external (regime) characteristics. At the international level, free-rider problems intensify, institutional voids expand and the sufficient supply of (global) public goods becomes fraught with difficulties. International stakeholder relations become more complex not only because more and diverse stakeholders are involved, but also because contracts, societal systems and norms and morality tend to differ more across than within borders.

Activity across borders, often offsets and sometimes magnifies firm rivalry. State and cultural rivalry complicate matters further. Rivalry across borders generates considerable challenges (increased insecurity), but also a host of opportunities (playing governments off against one another) for MNEs. Across borders the potential increases for firms to 'do good' along with the potential to 'do wrong'. Why would MNEs abstain from their ability 'to do wrong' if it enhances their performance? Or, alternatively, why should MNEs try to act responsibly if their competitors benefit from being irresponsible? ICR strategies have to address problems of principle, but also problems of practice (five ICR issue boxes throughout this chapter will illustrate the trade-off between principle and practice in more detail).

ICR strategies are influenced (1) by generic internationalization strategies adopted by firms (from an export orientation to globalization), which in turn are influenced by (2) home and host country CSR regimes, and (3) international CSR regimes. The nature of these relationships is largely determined by (4) the relative distance between home and host countries (Figure 13.1).

The 'business case' for ICR critically depends on the effective management of the various dimensions of distance that exist between home and host countries. Insights on the principal dimensions of distance (and ICR) largely developed along comparable (historical) lines as distinguished in Chapter 8. Relevant theory building and empirical testing occurred over three consecutive phases and in three distinct fields of inquiry: International Business and Political Economy; Ethics; and Stakeholder Management.

ICR as managing geographical distance

International Business (IB) and International Political Economy (IPE) in the 1970s and 1980s examined business–society interaction primarily at the interface with host governments, institutions and cultures. Since many cultures and institutions are relatively static, most dynamic (bargaining) interaction took place between companies and governments. International management focused on conducting risk assessments and smart cross-cultural management practices. Political or Country Risk Analyses (PRA) entailed primarily host country characteristics, with the objective of achieving economic success 'despite' risky political environments.[1] Risk

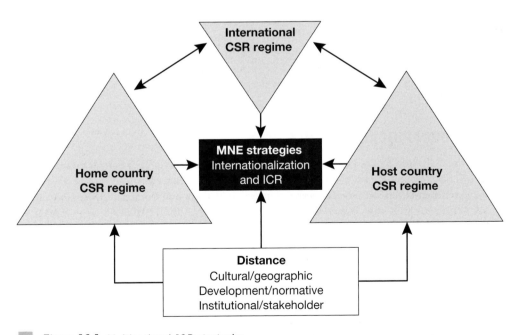

Figure 13.1 Multinational ICR strategies

analyses focus on the 'liabilities of foreignness'. They are reactive at best and presuppose a relatively adversarial position of the multinational firm vis-à-vis host stakeholders such as local
governments, citizens, firms and suppliers (Wells, 1998a; Moran, 1998). 'PRA encourages
firms to overlook ethical concerns and issues of social responsibility in favour of single-minded
self-interest' (Getz, 2004: 22). The dimension of distance in this context (i.e. as risk-enhancing
factor) was first conceived of as 'geographical distance' (section 13.2).

ICR as managing normative and cultural distance

An International Business Ethics (IBE) perspective on ICR developed in the late 1980s.
Divergent systems of norms and values reflect diverging societal configurations – which can all
be economically successful (see Chapter 2). For multinational companies, the tension between
different systems of norms is the rule rather than the exception (Donaldson, 1996: 47). Business
ethicists in the late 1980s were the first to address specific CSR dilemmas associated with IB
operations. International Business Ethics and Business and Society scholars focused particularly
on the potential 'to do harm'. In addition, international HRM scholars in the 1990s, started
to focus on the potential of ethical capabilities in improving the competitive advantage of MNEs
(Bowie and Vaaler, 1999, Buller and McEvoy, 1999). Others (Watson and Weaver, 2003)
noted that the level of internationalization is strongly related to the level of concern company
executives display towards ethical issues. Executives of international companies are more
aware of ethical dilemmas (ibid.: 85). The relevant dimension of distance can be described as
'normative' or 'development' distance (section 13.3).

ICR as managing stakeholder and institutional distance

First efforts to integrate some aspects of IB, IPE and IBE have been undertaken in the second
half of the 1990s in the study of International Stakeholder Management (ISM). This approach
opened up a whole new field of research around the creation of opportunities 'to do good'
(Getz, 2004) in a pragmatic manner by coordinating personnel and stakeholders across cultures,
values and borders. Business opportunities can be created by aligning individual internationalization strategies with the interests of home and host stakeholders. This approach requires quite
a sophisticated assessment of the *impact* of investments on home and host stakeholders. The
relevant dimension of distance in this context can be described as 'stakeholder' or 'institutional' distance (section 13.4).

13.2 GEOGRAPHICAL DISTANCE

In empirical IB studies, geographical distance normally functions as 'control variable', for
instance in accounting for trade and investment flows (Disdier and Head, 2004) and the consequences of international activity for firm profitability (e.g. Lu and Beamish, 2004; Contractor
et al., 2003; Ruigrok and Wagner, 2003; Fortanier *et al.*, 2005). While a large stream of
research focused on the impact of geographical distance on internationalization strategies and
firm performance, the nature of the connection between geographical distance and ICR strategies and performance has been more difficult to establish. Nevertheless, geographical expansion
often has considerable social and environmental consequences. The prime effect is relatively
straightforward and negative: the movement of goods and people across great distances
contributes to global environmental problems, created by pollution and, in particular, the
depletion of non-renewable resources. Industries such as tourism, transportation and logistics,
whose business depends on geographical distance are particularly relevant in this respect.

Another dimension of the relationship between geographical distance and ICR is that geographically dispersed operations can result in increased stakeholder pressure on MNEs to step up their ICR efforts. But the very question of 'distance' can also be an incentive for firms to internationalize precisely because it enables them to exploit the divergence in stakeholders' capacity to exert pressure in different countries. The discussion on these effects has become better known as the 'industrial flight' or the 'pollution/tax haven' discussion. 'Rent-seeking' firms would evade home government regulation and relocate to company-friendly regulatory environments (the 'havens'). This discussion has three dimensions: (a) the importance of the escape motive in the decision to relocate production; (b) the degree to which host countries in practice encourage a 'race to the bottom' in order to attract FDI; and (c) the degree to which geographical dispersion prompts MNEs to develop 'state of the art' ICR strategies.

- *Escape*: First, many empirical studies seem to suggest that escape or flight motives do not play that important a role in the decision of MNEs to internationalize. The most important reason for this being that the costs of compliance connected to environmental and labour regulations are not that high compared to total costs of production (Meyer, 2004). Moreover, the potential cost savings from relocating to low-standard countries need to be balanced with high transportation costs, including the higher risk of supply disruptions. This argument, however, does not necessarily apply to polluting sectors such as petrochemicals or low asset-specific, labour-intensive sectors such as software engineering, textiles production, furniture and toy production. The higher labour or environmental costs as a percentage of total production costs the greater the likelihood that escape motives may play a role in firms' decision to internationalize.

  Even if strict home country social and environmental legislation is not a key incentive for internationalization, escape motives often inform arguments employed in the bargaining process with domestic stakeholders: even a cursory reading of the newspapers is sufficient to know that the pressure to internationalize as a result of 'burdensome regulation' is an oft-recurring theme in many countries.

- *Race*: Second, the evidence of a 'race to the bottom' in host country standards due to the investment strategies of MNEs is mixed. A race to the bottom in environmental standards has been difficult to establish, although conclusive evidence to the contrary has not been found either (cf. Kolk and van Tulder, 2004b). Necessary conditions for a race to the bottom according to Spar and Yoffie (1999) are (1) considerable mobility of firms and goods across borders due to free trade, and (2) considerable institutional distance – in their words: 'regulation and factor costs are heterogeneous' to such an extent that 'the heterogeneity leaves gaps that can be turned into the firm's competitive advantage'. Meyer (2004: 270) adds that (3) products should be relatively homogeneous so that price is a key competitive parameter, and that (4) the sunk costs related to the relocation should be relatively low.

- *Halo*: Third, and in contrast with the emphasis on escape motives and races to the bottom, recent studies tend to stress the so-called 'halo effect'. This view holds that the most internationally dispersed firms could play a 'cutting edge' role in developing and implementing sophisticated ICR strategies. Such strategies would help MNEs to realize economies of scale, to reduce potential liabilities due to regulatory change (Dowell *et al.*, 2000) and to buffer potential damage to their reputation for instance if they are reproached for 'managing with double standards' across borders. Furthermore, as Kostova and Zaheer (1999) explained, MNEs are expected to do more than domestic firms in building reputation and goodwill.

255

Additionally, Sharfman *et al.* (2004) suggest that global competitive and institutional pressure lead MNEs to develop high level, environmental management systems that make them more competitive. The combined pressures of global integration and local responsiveness (Bartlett and Ghoshal, 1989; Prahalad and Doz, 1997) would lead MNEs to opt for the highest rather than the lowest common denominator. But, real empirical substantiation of these expectations is still absent. It is also difficult to establish whether the 'highest common denominator' suffices to effectively address the ICR issue (for instance of global warming or child labour).

13.3 CULTURAL DISTANCE

Research on cultural distance complements the research on geographical distance by focusing in particular on *entry modes* in host countries (Kogut and Singh, 1988; Brouthers and Brouthers, 2000; Padmanabhan and Cho, 1999; Slangen, 2005), in addition to the relation between cultural distance and trade and FDI flows (Slangen, 2005). The impact of cultural distance on ICR performance has two dimensions. First, not taking into account cultural distance can negatively affect (ICR) performance. Second, actively managing cultural distance has important effects on ICR strategy and corporate performance. Managing cultural diversity entails greater coordination costs. Consequently it has been assumed that cultural diversity would have a negative impact on performance. Nevertheless cultural diversity has also been shown to be of strategic advantage to a company: greater creativity and innovation; targeting of a greater variety of customers; greater adaptability to environmental changes; more diverse teams of employees are more likely to disagree with each other and thus find fault with the status quo.

Nowadays, when scholars and managers talk of ICR, they primarily build on the work of business ethicists, who since the end of the 1980s started to pay attention to the dilemmas faced by multinationals operating in different economies and value systems.

How are overseas managers to act in the face of practices that seem immoral to them? What should they do if the ethical norms of the host country differ from, or even conflict with, that of the home country, or if legislation is simply absent? Can a company justify investment in a country where human and political rights are systematically violated? Should a company resign itself to discriminatory practices of suppliers in the host country? Is a company obliged to influence the politics of a country in order to maintain or raise minimum wages?

These issues are often characterized by what Donaldson and Dunfee (1999) identified as the *moral free space*. In this space, unequivocal rules of conduct and legal prescriptions are absent and ethically accountable conduct is not necessarily synonymous with socially accountable conduct. In the moral free space, each person, each stakeholder and each company is entitled to formulate their own individual point of view. The acceptability of the perspectives will however be determined by societal stakeholders and public opinion. Donaldson (1996) and Donaldson and Dunfee (1999) developed an integrated social contract approach (ISCT) to IB that draws on the social contract theory of the philosopher John Rawls. They distinguish two principles that can serve as a compass in the maze of normative approaches that exist in the moral free space: relativism – or moral pluralism, and hypernorms – or universalism.

Relativism is succinctly captured by the adage 'When in Rome, do as the Romans do'. In this perspective, the ethics of one culture is no better or worse than that of the next. Consequently each country has the right to formulate its own environmental, labour, health and safety laws (Donaldson, 1996: 40). This approach allows competitors who have a more flexible approach to norms and values to take advantage of the conditions prevailing in the host country.

From the perspective of moral pluralism companies should respect local traditions and cultural differences. 'Promotional gifts' in one cultural and institutional setting can be a 'bribe' in another setting. This approach is often justified by the explanation 'if we don't do it, someone else will'. The relativist approach is therefore often criticized for being 'ethically blind'. It ignores the normative expectations of progressive societal groupings in the host country and stakeholders in the home country.

But respecting local traditions and cultural differences does not automatically amount to cultural relativism. Donaldson (1989) examined the dilemmas created by differences between home and host country norms and values. He argued that while international firms should respect fundamental human rights,[2] they are not responsible for honouring human rights in precisely the same manner as nation-states or individuals (ibid.: 145). The focus of Donaldson's research was the problem of conflicting home and host country norms and the viewpoint that it is often not acceptable to abide by the principle that 'if our practice does not break one of their laws, it's OK' (ibid.: 146). Donaldson adapted the quest for universal principles for IB practice to accommodate relative levels of economic development. This led him to conclude that international companies do not always have to apply the highest standards possible for instance when dealing with repressive regimes (Box 13.1).

BOX 13.1 COMPLEX ICR ISSUE #1: DEALING WITH REPRESSIVE AND CORRUPT REGIMES

In 2003, a special report to the United Nations Commission on Human Rights by Freedom House (2003) rated the 'most repressive regimes' in the world. Repression was measured as the lack of political rights and civil liberties. Of 192 countries, nine countries were judged 'the worst of the worst': Burma, Cuba, Iraq, Libya, North Korea, Saudi Arabia, Sudan, Syria and Turkmenistan. Seven additional countries appeared near the bottom of the list, because 'they offer some very limited scope for private discussion, while severely suppressing opposition political activity, impeding independent organizing, and censoring or punishing criticism of the state' (ibid.: vii): China, Equatorial Guinea, Eritrea, Laos, Somalia, Uzbekistan and Vietnam. Of the 192 countries of the world nearly half can be considered free in the sense that they respect a broad array of basic human rights and political freedom. A quarter are not free and suffer from systematic and pervasive human rights violations. This has not prevented firms from investing in these countries. China, Vietnam and Saudi Arabia, for instance, have been prime targets of FDI. Should companies do business in countries with a repressive regime?

Problems of principle: What are repressive regimes exactly? What constitutes civil liberties? Should governments be democratically elected? Authoritarian rule is often combined with kleptocracy. Kleptocracy has a very negative effect on the development of a country and its stability. Should companies have an opinion on kleptocracy if their own governments support the corrupt regime?[3] If home governments of MNEs do impose an official boycott, why should companies move ahead quicker in boycotting countries than their own government? Local opposition leaders sometimes ask companies to withdraw, but how is one to determine whether they are legitimate? In countries with reprehensible regimes it is always difficult to act in a socially accountable and engaged manner. Nevertheless, entrepreneurs also argue that 'through our presence we can set an example' (constructive engagement). According to one ethical norm, a multinational should not meddle with a country's politics, but when it concerns human rights violations it seems to be acceptable and even expected (hypernorms). Corporations that stayed in South Africa under the apartheid regime argued that they were acting in accordance with civil and political rights and were trying to support democratic change (Donaldson, 1989).

NGOs on the other hand held that companies that choose to operate in such countries are necessarily implicated in sustaining the repressive regime. Finally, withdrawing from a country creates other ethical problems. Will the company that replaces it do better? What will become of employees after the factory has been closed down?

Problems of practice: Empirical research shows that remaining in a country ruled by a repressive regime imposes a penalty, not only on the company's reputation among consumers, but in particular on its reputation on the stock exchange with institutional investors. In the event of a more or less formal political boycott – as in the case of South Africa – the costs 'imposed by the boycott eventually exceeded the costs of withdrawal' (Kumar *et al.*, 2002: 159). In the absence of a formal political boycott – as in Burma/Myanmar – the trade-off is more difficult to make. In the case of China, for instance, there is a boycott of defence equipment, but no general boycott.

The practical problems are particularly big in resources industries. They often have to operate in countries with oppressive regimes that are rarely subject to international boycotts. Many of these firms present this as a fact of life – as an environmental factor that cannot be changed and for which a thorough political risk analysis is the best tool. But in these industries it is notoriously difficult to separate business from politics. Daniel Yergin (1991), an internationally respected expert on the oil industry, once characterized the dealings of the oil industry as 90 per cent politics and 10 per cent business. In most countries, only a few multinational firms dominate the exploration, refinement and/or distribution of these resources due to the demand for 'exclusivity' in contract negotiations. Should the big influence of a company in a country, not be matched by equally big responsibilities? The presence of big resources companies in relatively poor countries has coincided with distributional fights among local groups, kleptocracy, poor governance and the breach of basic human rights. Human rights issues and incidents are strongly associated with the international operations of oil firms (see, e.g., Haller *et al.*, 2000; Tomei, 1998). Although natural resources firms might not be held directly responsible for these conditions, they can definitely be considered part of the problem. For instance: should firms engage in bribery or commissions? The stance on bribery depends on the degree to which the home government is prepared to tolerate the praxis of bribery. Western countries, in particular, implemented sanctions on bribing firms. But, in France, until recently the payment of 'commissions' in other countries was tax deductible (*Vk*, 17 January 2004).

Universalism advocates a universally applicable set of standards and rights and risks being branded as ethically imperialist. The conviction that one must always uphold the norms of the home country even if, as is the case for many MNEs, they differ from those of the host country is on a par with ethical imperialism (Donaldson, 1996: 39; Wartick and Wood, 1999: 151). The ethical imperialist believes that people, including managers, should always and everywhere act as they would at home (Donaldson, 1996: 40). This viewpoint is founded in absolutism, the conviction that there is only one set of values that can only be expressed through one set of concepts. It requires that everyone acts the same, irrespective of the context.

The perspective holds that international firms should respect the fundamental principles that function as minimum requirements for socially, ecologically and ethically responsible corporate conduct ('hypernorms'). These principles are the object of an overlapping consensus – in the words of Rawls. They should be acceptable to all cultures and all organizations (Getz, 2004: 21). They are universally recognized minimum norms and include the right to life, quality of life and economic progress, freedom of speech, dignity, respect for human rights and good citizenship. Hypernorms resonate with the principle of reciprocity that lies at the core of the teachings of the Chinese philosopher Confucius: 'do not do unto others what you do not want done unto yourself' (Donaldson, 1996: 42).

It is evident that a universalist approach clashes with respect for cultural differences and the notion that ethics is acquired in specific cultural and ideological contexts. The question is whether firms should follow such a 'universalist' or a more 'relativist' approach. Is it socially responsible for companies to impose their (Western) norms, standards, values and ideologies on other countries? Is it responsible to demand that companies leave countries in the face of ideological controversy and turn thousands of employees out on the street in the process? Low wages and child labour appear immoral in rich, highly developed countries, but can one condemn developing countries for accepting lower wages if it attracts foreign investment, creates employment and ultimately improves the living standards of its citizens?

Some international HRM scholars have stressed that adopting universal moral standards also improves the competitive position of multinationals (Bowie and Vaaler, 1999). Others, however, have modified this claim by stressing strategic contingency factors. Rational universalism appears particularly relevant for MNEs that have chosen global strategies, whereas the relativist strategy is more appropriate for multi-domestic MNEs (Buller and McEvoy, 1999). Box 13.2 gives a concrete example of this multifaceted problem of universalism versus relativism.

An integrative approach: development distance

The principles of moral pluralism and hypernorms combined, constitute Donaldson and Dunfee's (1999) integrative approach to solving some of the ethical dilemmas of IB: a minimum set of universal human rights combined with a moral free space that allows local 'contracting' provided global norms are not violated. The 'integrative' approach requires strongly coordinated strategies and norms and is particularly appropriate for MNEs that are somewhere in between the global and multi-domestic strategies. As Chapter 3 explained, the observed trend of MNE internationalization strategies in the 1990s, has been more towards regionalism than towards globalization. In practice this implies first that MNEs have to take into account the extent to which they want to build on a company-internal division of labour across regional borders. The more firms rely on an international division of labour, the greater their need for an integrative approach.

Second, MNEs have to take the level of development of the host economy relative to the home economy into account. The relative economic development of home and host countries has the biggest impact on what can be considered normatively appropriate strategies for MNEs. MNEs investing in the least developed countries face challenges that cannot be solved by either adapting to local customs, or imposing their own norms on the economy. Reed (2002) speaks of 'development ethics' in searching for an integrative approach to international stakeholder management vis-à-vis developing countries.[4] Issues that are related to levels of development include, in particular, child labour and working conditions, not necessarily corruption, collusion or bribery. It has already been recognized that effectively addressing these development issues, requires a separate – more integrative – approach which, for instance, uses broader and positive-duty oriented codes of conduct (cf. Kolk and van Tulder, 2002, see Box 13.2).

Thus, in practice, managing normative distance by modern MNEs increasingly boils down to managing 'development distance': the bigger the development distance between the home and the host country of a firm is, the bigger the 'moral free space' becomes, the bigger the ethical dilemmas are and the bigger the need for an integrative approach to ICR. Development

259

BOX 13.2 COMPLEX ICR ISSUE #2: CHILD LABOUR

An estimated 246 million children under the age of 15 are currently working on the streets, in workshops and on plantations earning money for themselves and their families. Almost three-quarters work in hazardous situations (UNICEF, 2004). Child labour is very unequally distributed over the world with 99 per cent of child labour located in developing countries. The ICR issue of child labour contains problems of principle and practical problems.

Problems of principle pertain to definitions, cultures and economic models. The argument against child labour appeals to a universal ethical value (hypernorm) that carries significant moral weight: every child has a right to go to school. Universal values take precedence over context, disregarding, for instance, the possibility that child labour might stem from economic necessity. Before the introduction of child protection laws in the mid-nineteenth century, child labour was morally acceptable in Europe. Today there are people living in developing economies that are economically worse off than people who lived in nineteenth-century Europe. In Western countries, the general norm has taken root that children should go to school and do not belong in the workplace. The strict separation between adulthood and childhood in the Western world is often not shared by other cultures. Simple moral judgements on the issue are therefore problematic. Even in Western countries children work in various occupations (in the family business, delivering newspapers) which is generally considered a good learning experience for children (Pierik and Houwerzijl, 2004). In consequence, clear international legislation on the issue of child labour does not exist. The ILO conventions on banning child labour were not ratified by all members.

Practical problems relate to addressing child labour *effectively*. Only a small fraction of working children work in export-related industries (cf. Kolk and van Tulder, 2002), which makes it difficult for Western companies to address the problem directly. Nevertheless many companies have included child labour provisions in their codes of conduct. However, the remedy can be worse than the disease. The application of strict codes, in some cases, has led to children being laid off only to end up in prostitution or on the streets (Schwartz and Gibb, 1999: 144). In practice, protectionist motives play a role in the opposition to child labour as well. Sectors that are under threat from cheaper imports raise the issue of (alleged) child labour in order to bar products of these countries from their home markets. In the international negotiations there is little room for nuanced viewpoints, such as the one that holds that child labour in combination with schooling might be a more effective approach to the issue than absolute condemnation. Broad and positive duty-oriented codes of conduct – that include the provision of educational opportunities to children who continue to work are more effective than strict and negative duty-oriented codes (cf. Kolk and van Tulder, 2002, 2004a). A broad code on child labour was adopted by Swedish clothing retailer Hennes & Mauritz (H&M). A strict code was adopted by Nike that defined a minimum age of 18 for the production of footwear, which exceeds the generally accepted minimum age of 16.

distance can be operationalized as the difference in GDP (factor endowments). It has been found in IB research, that firms tend to engage in horizontal affiliates (market-seeking and multi-domestic strategies) in case of big differences in relative factor endowments (a small developmental distance), and in vertical affiliates (implying an internal international division of labour) in case of relatively big differences in relative factor endowments (Carr *et al.*, 1998).

The preference for vertical affiliates is easy to understand: MNEs' affiliates in the least developed countries have less chance to ally with local companies, face bigger uncertainties and thus require more control from headquarters. So, in case of ethical dilemmas connected to a large development distance, the likelihood increases that firms can consider this as a 'company internal' challenge. This enables a particular kind of corporate leadership. It has been suggested that in cases of big development distance the most effective approach towards typical ethical dilemmas such as child labour seems to imply that managers show 'transformational leadership' in which they are not afraid to adopt strategies and codes of conduct that deviate from the 'common denominator' in the sector (cf. Kolk and van Tulder, 2004b).

13.4 STAKEHOLDER AND INSTITUTIONAL DISTANCE

Aside from geographical and normative distance, another important dimension of distance – not entirely unrelated to the previous ones – is stakeholder or institutional distance. International stakeholder management adds considerable complexity to local stakeholder management by adding more actors with diverging – and often conflicting – interests across geographical, cultural and normative borders. Shell, for instance, estimates that in local projects it engages approximately 10–25 stakeholders who often share a common interest. In the case of strategic international issues, Shell claims that there are over 100 different stakeholder groups with highly diverse interests (cf. van Tulder *et al.*, 2004). In International Stakeholder Management, managers have to consider a number of additional dimensions vis-à-vis 'national' stakeholder management: a distinction has to be drawn between home and host stakeholders; secondary stakeholders can take on the status of primary stakeholders and vice versa; the concept 'corporate citizen' often acquires a different meaning in an international setting; and the impact of international stakeholder groups has to be assessed more systematically. Kostova and Zaheer (1999) were the first to introduce the term 'institutional distance'. On the basis of theoretical reasoning they expect that the greater the institutional distance is between the home country of an MNE and a particular host country, the greater the challenges an MNE subsidiary will face in establishing and maintaining its legitimacy in that host country. This section first discusses the home country dimension of stakeholder and institutional distance, and then the host country dimension. Subsequently, the consequences of the distance between home and host institutions for both general corporate strategy and ICR strategy are discussed.

Assessing the process: home country effects

In 1999, Wartick and Wood made a first attempt to map international stakeholder relationships. They set out by charting intercultural differences in stakeholder environments through the introduction of a hypothetical example in which they distinguished between home and host countries. In their hypothetical example, the list of home country stakeholders is longer than that of the host country stakeholders. This seems logical in general. *Ownership*, for instance, is often concentrated in the home country of the firm. In the home country, the company also has its original customers who can still exert considerable influence even if the importance of the domestic market has diminished. In consequence 'country of origin' effects continue to influence a large range of strategic and organizational characteristics of MNEs (Harzing and Sorge, 2003). As regards ICR strategies, strong country of origin effects have been identified for: codes of conduct (Kolk and van Tulder, 2004a), environmental reporting strategies (Kolk and van Tulder, 2004b), reputation effects, the self-representation of international companies on CSR issues (Maignan and Ralston, 2002), environmental management practices in general and the approach towards specific issues such as global warming (Kolk and Levy, 2001).

The nature of the CSR regime in the home base – under specific circumstances – thus exerts a strong influence on the ICR orientation of MNEs. In consequence, it has been found that Asian firms, in general, tend to adopt relatively inactive ICR strategies, American firms tend to favour reactive ICR strategies and European firms are inclined towards more (pro)active ICR strategies.

Assessing the process: host country effects

Host country stakeholders are most likely to be affected by IB transactions at *the time of entry* (Getz, 2004: 25). Local governments, local communities and local competitors are particularly affected just before and after a foreign firm's arrival – during the bargaining surrounding the locational decision. The media at this stage is often also more active and important to the success of a new entrant. The influence of host country stakeholders on the ICR strategies of MNEs is bound to increase should the host countries represent bigger markets and should they at the same time represent 'institutionally distant' countries with strongly diverging CSR regime characteristics.

This process has been particularly relevant for Japanese and South Korean MNEs – as the first and archetypal Asian MNEs – when they internationalized to North America and Europe in order to profit from these large host markets. In terms of their national CSR regimes, Asian MNEs would be largely efficiency oriented, inclined to inactive ICR strategies, which also implies relatively low obedience to international codes and standards. But their growth strategies required entering particular markets and, thus, a certain degree of adjustment to host country regulation. International minimum standards provide an alternative to adapting to host country regulations, but only where they are clearly established. So, Japanese multinationals have been hesitant in embracing international factory automation standards which were not well established and related to their production process (cf. Dankbaar and van Tulder, 1999), but they became most active in embracing ISO 14001 standards, which are well established and strongly related to their marketing strategy. The latter, in turn, encouraged their reporting on environmental management. Both the Ministry of the Environment and the Ministry of International Trade and Industry (MITI) were strongly involved in this process, which mirrors the link made between environmental and export interests. MITI had already actively stimulated certification at an earlier stage, based on the expectation that ISO 14001 would become a condition for entering the European market. Such a development occurred earlier also in the case of the ISO 9000 quality system to which Japanese firms initially objected because it did not conform to their internal approach to quality management (Kolk and van Tulder, 2004a). So the adoption of some international standards by Japanese companies can be largely considered as a reactive strategy to ensure market access abroad. Only under such circumstances will host country influences exceed home country influences on the general strategy.[5]

Addressing the outcome: distance and economic consequences

MNEs that are not confronted with significantly different CSR (and other) requirements in the host countries in which they operate can be expected to perpetuate their home CSR (and other) strategies abroad. To what extent is this accurate? An often quoted study by Globerman and Shapiro (2003) found that liberal countries whose legal systems are rooted in English Common Law – with less market regulation, less codification and more case law, providing better protection of shareholders, creditors and property rights – are more likely to receive FDI. This finding hints at the fundamental importance of specific regimes, as opposed to the importance of their distance. On closer observation, however, the findings of Globerman and Shapiro contain a significant empirical bias. The empirical proof only came from the foreign investments made by US firms. Furthermore, the research accredited the liberal regime with the highest degree of governance infrastructure 'quality'. Empirical bias is a common problem with empirical studies in IB. What Globerman and Shapiro found, therefore, was not an absolute measure of the sophistication of any institutional model, but a context-bound impression of the importance of institutional and regime distance: US companies tend to invest more in countries with a *comparable* legal orientation and governance regime. So, the shorter the regulatory and institutional distance between countries is, the greater the likelihood of mutual FDI flows.

Support for the effect of institutional distance on flows of FDI has also been found in the relationship between former colonies and the UK, also known as the 'commonwealth effect' (Jones and Lundan, 2001). Jones *et al.* (1997) argue that an average advantage of 10–15 per cent accrues from being attached to the former colonial network. This pattern reveals the considerable 'sunk cost' effects related to FDI flows, but also the effect of low transaction costs that accompany investment in a country that shares the same legal and governance regime.

Studies that focused on corruption revealed comparable patterns. Habib and Zurawicki (2002), for instance, found that corruption creates a serious obstacle to FDI; but they also found a negative effect due to the *difference* in corruption levels between the home and host countries. This implies that firms experience considerable operational pitfalls when confronted with a different – not necessarily higher or lower – corruption level than in their home base.

Addressing the outcome: a trade-off between home and host stakeholders

In internationalization strategies, a complex trade-off always takes place between the interests of home and host stakeholders. The home–host trade-off is particularly intricate for stakeholders that are the least mobile, i.e. who, compared to MNEs, are very restricted in their ability to move to other locations. This involves especially three groups of stakeholders: employees, governments, and local competitors/suppliers. The trade-off has two dimensions: (1) what would happen if the company did not internationalize (the so-called *counterfactual* dimension), (2) to what extent can the outcome be considered 'fair' – 'fair wages', a 'fair tax' base and 'fair competition'?

Employees: what constitutes 'fair wages'

Home country trade unions are particularly interested in the net effect of internationalization on employment in the *home* economy. A relocation decision always feeds traditional stakeholders' fear of 'slipping down the hierarchy'. In the event that the relocation of a factory to a low-wage country requires the closing down of the site in the home country, trade unions in the home and host country clearly have conflicting interests. But examples of such 'narrow relocation' strategies are relatively rare. Mostly, MNEs develop broad relocation strategies in which part of the activities are outsourced or relocated, while other activities at home are reorganized and can even be upgraded. In order to correctly assess the net effect of relocation, the counterfactual argument should be taken into account: what would happen if the company did not relocate (part of) its activities? If the company would lose its competitive edge, the net result could be that even more jobs would be lost in the home base. However, counterfactual arguments are very difficult to substantiate. The same is true for effects of relocation strategies on wages in the home country (Box 13.3).

The history on realized relocation strategies since the early 1990s shows that the effects of relocation on employment are intimately connected to specific internationalization strategies of firms. A study of the impact on home/host employment of the internationalization strategies

BOX 13.3 COMPLEX ICR ISSUE #3: A RACE FOR LOW WAGES?

Problem of principle: People need sufficient income to lead a decent life. This is a basic human right. National economies thrive on higher income (see Chapter 10). But nations that are faced with a lack of development often only have low wages as a competitive advantage in the international market place; why shouldn't they use that advantage? Low wages cut the costs of production of goods and services and lead to immediate welfare gains for consumers. MNEs can make use of the sizable differences in the cost of wages across borders and secure a competitive advantage. But firms can also actively pursue excessively low wages by playing one location off against another through their relocation policies, which reduces part of their workforce to the 'working poor'; people who produce goods that they themselves cannot afford to buy (see Chapter 10). How far may international firms go in stimulating 'locational competition' through offshoring?

The pursuit of low(er) wages is a recurring theme in the media and is presented as one of the strongest incentives for firms to move production abroad. Trade unions are particularly critical of firms that 'relocate' to low-wage countries that are often devoid of unionization. Relocation debates are highly politicized. Where a company's decision to relocate is coupled to shutting down facilities, it is perceived as the 'exportation' of jobs abroad. In the 1990s, the fear of *direct* job displacement due to the complete relocation of factories was complemented with the fear of *indirect* job displacement due to the integration of low wage locations into a global division of labour. Global offshoring or outsourcing, particularly to low-wage countries such as India and China, has become a 'hot' issue in many a presidential campaign. The Economist Intelligence Unit (February 9, 2005) found that India, China and the Czech Republic are the primary candidates for relocation with MNEs. In interviews with company managers on the issue of internationalization, the prospect of relocation is often cited to influence local bargaining relations, for instance by stressing regulation and red tape in the home market (*FT*, 2 February 2005).

Problem of practice: The stakeholder debate is more often led by sentiments and short-term considerations than by actual insights. Serious IB studies up to now have concluded that 'efficiency' considerations linked to low wages have generally rarely been the deciding factor in the decision to internationalize. Lower wages are often accompanied by higher transport costs, lower productivity, local currency fluctuations and a lack of flexibility. So the transaction costs involved in the pursuit of low-wage production locations can be considerable. Only in sectors where the work is relatively standardized and labour costs are relatively high do low wages provide a dominant motive for relocation. This is the case particularly with respect to offshoring and outsourcing activities to India, where wages are low, but education levels are relatively high and transaction costs (for instance due to the high number of English-speaking people) are relatively low. Gaining entry to a market or access to particular assets and resources have generally proven much more important intrinsic motives for internationalization (UNCTAD, 2000c). The net effect of relocation on domestic employment can, in fact, be positive. Particularly if the relocation increases overall competitiveness of a firm, it could eventually create more jobs at home (cf. van den Berghe, 2003). This effect depends on the particular form of relocation and sourcing, which in the 1990s was largely regional (ibid.; Mol, 2001; Chapter 3).

of the world's largest corporations in the 1990s, reveals that the bulk of employment in most large companies still remained in the home market (van den Berghe, 2003; van Tulder *et al.*, 2001). Home employees and their trade unions continued to be strong primary stakeholders for most large companies. The impact of internationalization on the composition of labour across borders strongly depends on the nature and motivation for the internationalization strategy (van den Berghe, 2003). In the 1990s, multi-domestic firms, for instance, revealed a favourable effect for host workers – although not necessarily at the expense of domestic workers. The relocation strategies of the largest 'global' MNEs were accompanied by a decline in total employment with these firms. This decline was primarily at the cost of employment in the home country, while host country employment remained stable. The generation of multinationals that only started to internationalize in the 1990s – the 'new generation' of MNEs – exposed positive effects on their employment volume in both home and host economies. MNEs aiming at a regional division of labour faced rather mixed effects.

Finally, a proper assessment of the net effects of internationalization on employment also includes the indirect effects on suppliers and local communities. Foreign firms in host communities not only generate direct and indirect positive impacts, they can also destroy local employment by 'crowding out' local firms. In general, foreign firms are considered to contribute positively to employment, but there is still considerable debate as to the 'quality' of this employment (cf. Fortanier, 2004). A number of international companies have started to assess the 'indirect' impact on employment in their sustainability reports.

Governments: what constitutes fair taxes?

Occasionally, governments explicitly discriminate against foreign companies in favour of domestic companies. For instance, in 2005 the government of Argentina (successfully) stimulated consumers to boycott Shell after the company had raised the price of petrol. In many countries, more subtle 'buy national' campaigns are still implemented in which consuming products from home companies is favoured over 'foreign' products.

However, with the increasing foreign content of domestic products, and increasingly ambiguous ownership structures of leading companies, the distinction between 'foreign' and 'domestic' has become increasingly fluid. In addition, national and local host governments have good reasons to attract (or retain) large foreign MNEs. International companies affect the macro-economic policies of individual countries particularly through their (potentially) positive impact on trade and investment flows, competition, technology transfer and tax income. In consequence, governments prefer to use incentives rather than sanctions, and non-discrimination principles rather than discriminatory practices in their policies towards MNEs (UNCTAD, 2000b).

In some instances, this can lead to policy competition among governments. Policy competition is the outcome of governments' sustained efforts to develop and maintain an attractive investment climate. Two instruments are generally available to governments: financial incentives (such as subsidies) and fiscal incentives (such as tax holidays, export processing zones and tax havens). The 1990s saw an increase in the intensity of 'locational tournaments' and policy competition; a development that involved governments of developing as well as developed countries (Mytelka, 2000). On the one hand developed country governments increased their financial incentives. In 1995, for instance, local governments in the US alone offered a package of US$32 billion in financial incentives for MNEs (Clearinghouse, 1996). On the other hand, developing countries lowered fiscal burdens: from an average corporate tax between 30 and 35 per cent in 1990 – equal to the average OECD level – to a tax rate below 20 per cent (Oxfam, 2000) by the end of the 1990s. The financial incentives of some developing countries went to such extremes that they effectively turned the whole country into a tax haven. In 2000,

BOX 13.4 COMPLEX ICR ISSUE #4: FAIR TAXES, TAX EVASION AND TRANSFER PRICING

Problem of principle: governments need tax income to sustain the provision of adequate public goods and services. The tax basis of many governments is eroding. This is particularly relevant for developing countries that face the biggest gaps in the provision of public goods. But who decides what 'adequate' means? It can be agreed in principle that the distribution of the tax burden should be 'fair'. Many governments have implemented 'progressive' tax regimes that put a heavier tax burden on the 'strongest shoulders'. But who decides what a 'fair distribution' of the tax burden is? The national sport in most countries is to try to pay as little taxes as possible. When it is within the confines of national regulation, this is an accepted strategy. But tax evasion on an international scale represents different dilemmas. By directly incorporating in tax havens such as Bermuda or the Cayman Islands, companies fuel suspicions of 'unfair' tax evasion. Three of the most criticized firms in the US – Tyco, Global Crossing and Accenture/Andersen Consulting – were incorporated in Bermuda before they filed for bankruptcy (*FT*, 9 March 2004).

Problem of practice: one of the clearest competitive advantages of multinational corporations is that they can increase profits by making smart use of rival tax regimes around the world. Tax authorities of developed and developing countries compete among each other in two ways: (1) lowering taxes ('tax dumping') to capture FDI, (2) issuing new regulation on the appropriation of global profits in an attempt to capture a greater share of MNEs' (tax) revenues. But to what end? The phenomenon of 'transfer pricing' is particularly relevant to MNEs. Multinationals trade many goods 'in-house' between their subsidiaries. An increasing share of global trade – assessments run from 30 per cent to 60 per cent – consists of intra-firm trade. The value of these transactions is not based on market prices, but on internal (transfer) prices agreed upon by the parent and subsidiaries of the same company. Transfer prices affect different types of goods and trade flows: imports (for example, of intermediate goods), sales (exports or to other subsidiaries, for example) and royalties (licensing fees or other forms of technology transfer). Transfer prices in company-internal transactions are a necessity for multinational firms – many having become multinational because of failures in the effective and efficient operation of international markets. Transfer pricing is therefore not synonymous with manipulation or abuse. But in the 1990s, the idea of 'transfer price manipulation' became firmly rooted in critical social movements as well as governments. Pharmaceutical companies provide an interesting example. In the period 1994–2003, the foreign profits as a percentage of overall income of the six largest US pharmaceutical companies increased from 38 per cent to 65 per cent. At the same time, taxes paid on those profits fell from 31 per cent to 17.5 per cent – half the US corporate tax rate (*FT*, 17 October 2004). Relatively broad consensus exists that MNEs engage in transfer pricing manipulation with some regularity (Eden and Yu, 2001; Eden and Rodriguez, 2004). MNEs have the opportunity to exploit international contradictions and loopholes in complex tax laws, and corporate structural and organizational laws. If they don't make clever use of these loopholes, their competitors will, and they will be at a competitive disadvantage. The pervasiveness of the reasons for transfer price manipulation renders it an international problem with costs to the tax collectors estimated as high as US$200 billion worldwide. In 2004, the US Congress estimated annual losses in tax revenues due to transfer price manipulation at around US$40 billion for the American economy alone (Muller *et al.*, 2004). Consequently, the Internal Revenue Service (IRS) in the US has been stepping up litigation on disputed income and 'inflated and undervalued transfer prices' (*FT*, 3 February 2005).

the OECD identified 35 countries as tax havens. These governments, however, occupy a relatively weak bargaining position with respect to MNEs and not least because of the fierce competition among host countries for FDI. Oxfam assessed that the combined loss of tax income of developing countries due to tax competition amounted to more than US$35 billion.

This would not be a problem if the net effect of inward FDI – for instance, on economic growth or sustainable job creation – were positive. But the effectiveness of these measures in actually attracting MNEs or stimulating relevant investments is hotly disputed.

For instance, despite US$2.5 billion in fiscal incentives in the Philippines in 2000, foreign investment in the country actually declined, partly as the result of even more generous incentives in neighbouring countries (Easson, 2001). UNCTAD (2000b) notes that the advantages and disadvantages of FDI incentives are difficult to assess, not least because it is impossible to measure what would have happened in the absence of those measures.

In the car industry, *financial* (rather than fiscal) incentives have become a very important factor in policy competition. In 1980, the average government subsidy per newly created job in the car industry amounted to US$4,000, while by the end of the 1990s subsidies of from US$150,000–200,000 per job created around the world were the rule rather than the exception (Arbix and Zilbovicius, 1999). Often, however, the location decision is already made and government subsidies are an interesting 'bonus' for the company (Oman, 2000). The public dilemma thus becomes that, because the company would have invested anyway, the government could have spent the subsidy on other – perhaps more CSR-relevant – causes.

INSTITUTIONAL DISTANCE AND EFFECTIVENESS

Morisset and Prinia (2001) argue that fiscal and financial incentives have a substantial effect on the decision where to invest only under certain conditions: more or less equal infrastructure, transport costs and political and economic stability across countries. Institutional and development proximity could, therefore, spur governments to engage in policy competition. While the advantages of (tax) policy competition for countries can be disputed, the disadvantages for certain countries are straightforward. The tax burden shifts from mobile production factors such as capital to less mobile production factors – in particular labour (Gropp and Kostial, 2000). The emphasis on fiscal incentives for incoming (big) companies leads to a greater reliance on smaller and medium companies, a more regressive tax system and an overall reduction in the provision of public goods. Consequently, multilateral development agencies such as the IMF and the World Bank have tried to introduce FDI guidelines and add conditions to their loans in order to prevent developing countries from engaging in fiscal incentives. But the practice proves more steadfast than the principle (Easson, 2001).

Local competitors and suppliers: what constitutes fair competition?

An accurate assessment of the impact of FDI and MNEs on host country economic growth and development is particularly difficult to make when it comes to the issue of market structure and the nature of competition. In competition policy thinking the 'contestability' of a market has been considered more important than the exact degree of concentration in the market. But this also requires a definition of the 'relevant market'. Would that be the national market, the local market or the regional market? There is no international coordination in national competition policy regimes, while at the same time the degree of concentration in many sectors has increased – although exact data are difficult to assemble (cf. Liang, 2004 and Chapter 3). In particular, the impact of FDI on host market structures, has generated considerable controversy, not only among directly affected host stakeholders, but also in academia. On the one hand, worldwide growth in FDI since the 1980s is regarded by many as a blessing since it

BOX 13.5 COMPLEX ICR ISSUE #5: ERADICATING POVERTY AS SELF-INTEREST?

Problem of principle: Around 2.5 billion people live in absolute poverty – defined as living below an income of US$2 a day. Poverty is at the core of many societal problems and is a fundamental problem of failing human rights. Whether the size of the problem is increasing, decreasing or stabilizing depends on the definition of poverty that is employed (see Chapter 10). Since the mid-1990s poverty reduction has become top priority on the agenda of all international organizations. Some national governments are requiring companies that do business in developing countries to either integrate poverty in their ICR approach – or lose export credits and other subsidies. The 'business case' for MNEs to 'do something' about poverty eradication becomes more and more compelling. Poor people are increasingly being regarded as 'primary stakeholders'.

Problem of practice: Multinational corporations are increasingly confronted with stagnation in their home markets in the industrialized world. So they are searching for extra growth opportunities. Some developing countries such as India and China are rapidly growing and present excellent business opportunities. It is not surprising that 'poor people' are being recognized as a potential market. This has most provocatively been proclaimed by strategy thinkers C.K. Prahalad and Stuart Hart. In this regard they speak of 'The Fortune at the Bottom of the Pyramid' (Prahalad and Hart, 2002; Prahalad, 2004), referring to the four billion people that live on a per capita income below US$1,500 (PPP). Combined, these people represent a 'multi-trillion dollar market' that outsizes industrialized countries – certainly for basic commodities such as food and clothing. In a later book, Prahalad (2004) outlines how culturally appropriate and ecologically effective goods and services can be developed to reach this bottom of the pyramid. A 'fundamental re-conception of the business value proposition' and an 'intimate understanding of local needs' are required.

So far, so good. But it is also suggested that these strategies can eradicate poverty ('through profits' as the subtitle of the book reads). As Prahalad and Hart presented it in their opening statement of the initial *Harvard Business Review* article: 'Low-income markets present a prodigious opportunity for the world's wealthiest companies to seek their fortunes and bring prosperity to the aspiring poor.' The claim for this form of 'inclusive capitalism' seems somewhat of an (ideological) overstatement. The approach introduced by Prahalad strongly resembles the original concept of 'local responsiveness' by Prahalad and Doz (1987) (see section 12.2). It primarily applies to MNEs that are not yet represented in these locations. The 'market' at the bottom of the pyramid is, in practice, of course, already served by local firms and the informal economy. Where MNEs – with their extremely efficient production methods and deep financial pockets, let alone transfer price methods – focus on this market segment, there is no doubt that they can out-compete local firms. They therefore also 'crowd-out' local firms and local employment, which in the end might generate more poverty than it alleviates.

A sustainable corporate story that includes the ambition to eradicate poverty has to take medium- and longer-term structural effects into account – positive as well as negative spillovers such as crowding-out effects. Not many business strategists have attempted to do this, even if they realize that eradicating poverty is a typical 'shared problem' that requires action of all stakeholders (see Chapter 10). Prahalad and Hart, for instance, state: 'Corporations are only one of the actors; MNCs must work together with NGOs, local and state governments, and communities' (ibid.). How this should be applied in order to prevent negative spillover effects on the local economy has not been specified by the authors. Research on the approach of firms to poverty in codes of conduct shows a comparable lack of sophistication. Of the frontrunner CSR companies in the world – as included in the ICC 'Company Showcase' list – not many are very outspoken on poverty alleviation. Only one-sixth of the companies explicitly showed an ambition to 'reflect local conditions' in their code (Westdijk, 2004).

promotes economic growth, particularly in developing countries. FDI is viewed as an important means to stimulate competition and to promote economic growth and social development (Fortanier, 2004). But FDI also tends to 'crowd out' local employment and less competitive firms. In a social sense crowding out always entails considerable hardship. In a strict economic sense, crowding out does not have to be problematic, so long as local firms are replaced by more efficient competing firms. However, if crowding out leads to increased market concentration, the risk of market power abuse, monopoly rents and deterioration of resource allocation also increases (ibid.).

Crowding-out effects of local firms due to inward investments by MNEs were found in a number of studies, while other studies (OECD, 2001) tend to emphasize the net positive effects of FDI on the economy of host countries. At best it can be concluded that the empirical evidence is far from conclusive (cf. Caves, 1996; Rodrik, 1999; Meyer, 2004). Simplistic statements either in favour or against MNEs, in any event, are invalid (Box 13.5).

13.5 CONCLUSION: THE CHALLENGES OF ICR

Distance in IB is alive and kicking. The proclaimed 'death of distance' (Cairncross, 1997) proves grossly exaggerated. Geographical distance still plays an important and often decisive role in the international strategies of companies. Distance is a multifaceted phenomenon. This chapter added cultural, ethical, development, institutional and stakeholder distance to the analytical picture. Most multinationals have to manage all dimensions of distance simultaneously. It is difficult to make a straightforward and attractive business case for any specific ICR approach. The international arena contains all varieties of ICR strategies and their performance depends on the competitive position and internationalization strategy adopted by firms. The scattered and often anecdotal evidence presented in this chapter, nevertheless, suggests that MNEs can gain substantial competitive advantage in managing these dimensions in a sophisticated manner.

Four basic types of ICR can be distinguished: inactive, reactive, active and proactive. Table 13.1 summarizes the characteristics of each approach. Each approach tends to favour a particular definition of relevant stakeholders, emphasizes a particular dimension of distance, propagates a particular view on globalization and is likely to utilize a distinctive set of ICR management tools.

An *inactive ICR* approach is likely to be followed by managers that primarily focus on responsible action within the firm. The decision to invest abroad (either through offshoring or outsourcing) is largely based on the costs associated with transportation and wages. The ethical orientation is dominated by company-internal (corporate culture) or domestic considerations. An inactive approach to ICR favours a liberal global trade and investment regime that takes care of a 'level playing field' – which, through efficiency-enhancing international trade, is expected to lead to greater prosperity for the world. Interestingly, it is suggested elsewhere that a true 'globalization' regime is bound to render the MNE superfluous and obsolete (Ghemawat, 2003). An inactive strategy is therefore probably favoured by those firms that have not yet become dominant multinationals or hope to internationalize primarily through exports. The issue orientation is relatively narrow, which makes this type of ICR an example of relative indifference towards international corporate responsibilities.

Reactive ICR focuses on not making any mistakes in the international arena, hence its much stronger emphasis on political risk management and cultural distance. The concept of 'context-focused philanthropy' seems particularly well suited to multinationals with reactive ICR ambitions. The greater the cultural distance, the greater the risks firms face and thus the greater the potential negative impacts on their performance. When the concept of 'global corporate citizen' is introduced by this type of firm, it seems reactive at best; or it might imply unspoken

269

Table 13.1 Four typical ICR approaches

	Inactive	Reactive	Active	Pro-/interactive
	Indifferent Corporate Responsibility	International Corporate *Responsiveness*	International Corporate *Responsibility*	International *Community* Responsibility
Prime distance dimension	Geographical distance	Cultural distance	Normative distance	Institutional/ stakeholder distance
Prime home–host dimension	Corporate culture and home country oriented	Home country as precondition; host country as risk	Home and host country norms conflict	Integrated home and host country approach
Prime responsibility for shape of globalization	Leave it to the market (minimum state involvement to create efficiently operating markets)	Each actor's own responsibility; if actors do not take up their responsibility, nobody is to blame for taking advantage	Search for ethical minimum standards of globalization and 'best of class' examples as benchmark and inspiration	Globalization as a discourse process towards defining joint responsibilities; active search for partnerships
Issue Strategy	Narrow (defensive)	←	→	Broad (offensive)
ICR tools:		←	→	

PR brochures
Strict (internal) codes of conduct
Global citizenship reports
Context-focused philanthropy
International ICR label
Sustainability reporting
Broad (external) codes of conduct
Multi-level stakeholder
Dialogues, partnerships

'ethical imperialism' at worst. Reactive ICR stresses especially international corporate *responsiveness*. The issue orientation is primarily oriented towards checking the responsibilities of other actors (governments, civil society).

An *active ICR* approach is required especially when the norms of home and host country conflict. In that case a more integrative approach is helpful. The ethical approach to IB focuses on moral distance and tries to adopt a number of hypernorms that create a minimum level of morality in its international operations. Political risk analyses are less important than ethical and social risk analyses. ICR becomes focused on international corporate *responsibilities.*

A *proactive ICR* strategy is particularly appropriate should external factors exist that could decisively affect the international performance of the firm, for instance because of changing transfer pricing regimes and increased bargaining power of local stakeholders. The challenge for ICR managers thus is to interactively link home and host countries' norms and values through various interactions with home and host stakeholders. Thus, proactive ICR also strives towards an active synthesis of all motivations for internationalization (intrinsic, extrinsic and mixed motives). Only on the basis of multi-level stakeholder dialogues with a large number of (host/home) stakeholders spread over local communities can an appropriate strategy be developed. In this way, ICR becomes international *community* responsibility. A proactive ICR approach is particularly appropriate to address international interface issues, which requires a broad issue approach and the use of broad ICR tools (such as broad instead of strict codes of conduct).

The brief characterization of these four ICR types – admittedly sketchy and to some extent even relatively mechanistic – shows that the 'business case' for ICR is more complex than the general business case for CSR. The performance of firms operating across borders can benefit from responsible as well as irresponsible behaviour. In the international arena, it is easier to 'get away' with irresponsible behaviour than in any national arena. The opportunities for tax evasion, and transfer price, wage and cost manipulation and the like are abundant and arguably greater than within the legal environment of a single country. But at the same time, working across borders entails an increasing number of business risks that fall beyond the scope of political risk analyses. Increasingly powerful and unpredictable stakeholders require ethical and social risk analyses as well, which, in turn, necessitate a more active attitude towards society.

This chapter quoted several authors who expressed their discontent with the limited relevance and sophistication of the traditional approaches to IB and international management. In IB, the societal interface always demands close attention. In the international arena, multinational companies tend to have more discretionary power over their own operations and strategies. This requires them to reflect about their ICR approach in more detail and adopt a more active approach than the one followed domestically: for instance by setting down rules on HRM across borders or by managing cultural and political differences between the home and host countries they operate in. An interactive and bargaining oriented perspective on ICR recognizes that various constellations of home and host stakeholders should be taken into account.

The international bargaining society in action

Cases, conflicts and consequences

INTRODUCTION TO PART III

MACHIAVELLI'S SOCIAL RESPONSIBILITY ...

Asked before an audience consisting of graduate business students and middle managers what reading he had profited from most in his career, the European Chief Executive Officer (CEO) of one of the biggest multinationals in the world replied without hesitation: Niccolo Machiavelli's *The Prince*. For those who are not familiar with the work of this fifteenth–sixteenth-century Italian political writer, the central message of *The Prince* is that expediency takes precedence over morality. Machiavelli describes in some detail the use of cunning and deceit by a ruler to maintain his authority and implement his policies. The CEO acknowledged that his personal and his company's success could largely be attributed to the smart, appropriate, timely and balanced exertion of power. It is not surprising that leading IB scholars in the 1990s classified his firm as representative of best practice, exemplary of the 'transnational solution' (Bartlett and Ghoshal, 1989) – an international firm based upon network structures which is considered optimally suited to effectively coordinate activities across borders in a globalizing world. What is perhaps more surprising, but all the more telling, is that at the same time, leading IB ethics scholars hailed this firm also as one of the 'best in class' performers in CSR, adoption of codes of conduct and trademarks, and articulating a 'sustainable corporate story'. The CEO, thus, managed a company that had successfully linked globalization and corporate responsibility. The interesting question, of course, is whether he did that in spite of, or precisely because of, his Machiavellian views.

Within the conceptual framework developed in the first two parts of this book, this seemingly contradictory combination of identities is not extraordinary – on the contrary: successful (international) business strategies are shaped in the interaction between business and society. In Part I, this notion is referred to as 'Societal Interface Management'. The context in which Societal Interface Management strategies have materialized since the early 1990s, has been referred to as the 'bargaining society'. Societal Interface Management strategies are developed in consultation and through negotiation with stakeholders. The more firms develop international strategies, the bigger the institutional voids they encounter and the greater the significance of the 'laws' of the bargaining society in guiding the actions of individual players. The insights of scholars such as Machiavelli are particularly relevant in a bargaining society in which the use of power is not regulated by strict laws. Part II further considered the business case for corporate responsibility in such an international context. It was found that power plays an important role in the articulation and execution of ICR. Expediency (pragmatism) and morality (idealism) are two equally important attributes of IB. The exertion of power is a reciprocal (two-way) process that is employed by business to influence society and vice versa and manifests in complex patterns of self-regulation and correction. One of the prime mechanisms through which this process is executed is the 'reputation mechanism'. Although the reputation mechanism seems quite modern, Machiavelli understood its power – himself the subject of the often contradictory impact of reputation. *The Prince* was, in fact, nothing more than an ingenious pamphlet, which was aimed at gaining influence with the ruling de Medici family in Florence. The same text also gave him the particularly bad reputation for which he still is remembered today – for ostensibly being an intellectual supporter of corruption and totalitarianism.

But let us return to the modern-day CEO of the introduction. It might already be clear that the impact of Machiavelli's thinking on the development of corporate responsibility is not entirely far-fetched. The multinational in question had hardly been affected by the reputation mechanism. It was pragmatism that fuelled its adoption of a 'unit branding' strategy and a cultural relativist strategy – adapting to local cultures, tastes and values. Despite the fact that its products can be found in hundreds of millions of households around the world, not many would relate its products to the company. Even though it was relatively unaffected by the reputation mechanism in its consumer markets, the company nevertheless pioneered a number of 'sustainability' initiatives for a number of its most critical products. Enlightened self-interest prompted the company to consult and negotiate with important stakeholders across the globe to come up with adequate solutions to important sustainability problems that had arisen. One of the proposed solutions was a 'sustainable fisheries' initiative launched in 1996, which entailed a commitment to source all the company's fish products from sustainable stocks. The company is one of the world's largest fish buyers. The initiative would not have been possible or successful had the company not exerted its power 'smartly' and had the company not taken responsibility for major (interface) issues encountered in its supply chain. The firm – with its emphasis on bulk consumer products – also became one of the first multinationals in the world to target the 'bottom of the pyramid'. Rather than treating poverty as a problem, the company started to view it as a strategic 'challenge'. Its name? Unilever – the Anglo-Dutch food and personal care products multinational.

Unilever is an interesting example of a pragmatic-idealist approach to ICR. A company's approach to corporate responsibility does not develop in a vacuum, it involves a complex trade-off between interests and aims that are context and issue dependent. The bargaining approach of Unilever illustrates the importance of what in moral philosophy has been referred to as 'integrative ethics' or the 'discourse approach' to ethics (Chapter 8). The approach of the company can also be classified as (pro)active and interactive, an approach which has been identified as particularly fitting to European CSR regimes (Chapter 12). Whether this employment of power, accompanied by the use of the reputation mechanism, is smart, appropriate, timely and balanced still depends on the implementation process, the issue at hand and whether the case is considered from the perspective of the firm or other stakeholders. Other questions that arise are as follows: does the company indeed contribute to solving sustainability issues? Are firms on whom the potential impact of the reputation mechanism is greater (for instance due to a corporate branding strategy) more forced to contribute to the resolution of societal issues? Are American MNEs more at risk of suffering reputational damage than European or Asian MNEs? Would a more 'global' firm have to adopt a different strategy?

'ISSUES CAN'T BE MANAGED, CONFRONTATION CAN'[1]

The effectiveness of a particular approach to ICR depends on the nature and the outcome of the interaction with societal stakeholders – i.e. the nature of the bargaining process. Part II showed that concrete CSR initiatives are often developed when confrontation with stakeholders is imminent (Chapters 9 and 11). The reputation mechanism is activated in particular by conflicting expectations and interests, and large institutional gaps. Part III considers a number of cases in detail in which NGOs and firms clashed over a specific international issue.

In Parts I and II, three dimensions of corporate Societal Interface Management were discussed: (1) the private/public and profit/non-profit societal interfaces; (2) the question of effectiveness with respect to (international) CSR at the interface of efficiency and ethics (Triple-E); (3) the effectiveness of the reputation mechanism for CSR at the interface of correction and discipline. Part III tests these three dimensions against 18 cases of CSR conflict that have been thrashed out since the early 1990s. Conflicts between NGOs and companies serve the purpose of defining the responsibilities of companies given the institutional voids left by retreating governments and the advent of the international bargaining society. Reputation is considered the most important means of disciplining companies.

Since the beginning of the 1990s, particularly large (multinational) enterprises have been confronted with disciplining demands from NGOs. In the confrontation spearheaded by NGOs to give concrete content to corporate responsibilities four main issue clusters have emerged: (1) health (food safety, GM, medicine); (2) labour/human rights and conditions (such as forced labour, child labour); (3) environment (waste dumping, global warming); (4) dictatorship and wars (Burma/Myanmar, Nigeria, blood diamonds). Some cases show how issues can evolve over time (for instance, the treatment of dictatorship in Burma), other cases show the evolving strategies of NGOs over time (e.g. Greenpeace and the Clean Clothes Campaign). As for the multinationals that were the target of NGO campaigns, the cases were selected to be as representative as possible. Shell is represented twice, because of the enormous impact of the two cases in 1995 and 1996 (Brent Spar and Nigeria) it was involved in. Figure III.1 depicts the different actors and the dates of the 18 confrontations that were selected for further analysis in this book.

Five cases were selected for inclusion in the printed version of this book, which encompass a variety of large icon multinationals from different countries and industries and deal with some of the most significant 'triggering' events since the early 1990s (Chapter 9). The five cases are also more or less spread over the period 1990–2004 and reveal distinct bargaining dynamics. The cases are chronologically presented: Nike – labour issues (Chapter 14); Royal Dutch Shell – environmental degradation (Chapter 15); Triumph – dictatorial regimes (Chapter 16); GlaxoSmithKline – health (Chapter 17); ExxonMobil – global warming (Chapter 18). Thirteen other major cases are published on the website (www.ib-sm.org) and are included in the integrated case analysis in Chapter 19. The website offers the opportunity to add recent information, to add cases and to include graphic material such as photos, tables and graphs. Major issue conflicts have largely involved multinationals from Europe and the US. Hardly any major conflicts have erupted between INGOs and Asian MNEs – testifying to the fact that reputation conflicts often involve 'home companies' and illustrating the relatively inactive bargaining setting of East Asia (Chapter 12). Issue conflicts are very often unique and therefore difficult to compare.

Each case study (in this book as well as on the website) discusses the following aspects of the conflict:

- the characteristics of the societal interface challenges: public/private; profit/non-profit; efficiency/ethics;
- the characteristics of the company (or the subsidiary in question) and the most important stakeholders in the conflict at hand;

275

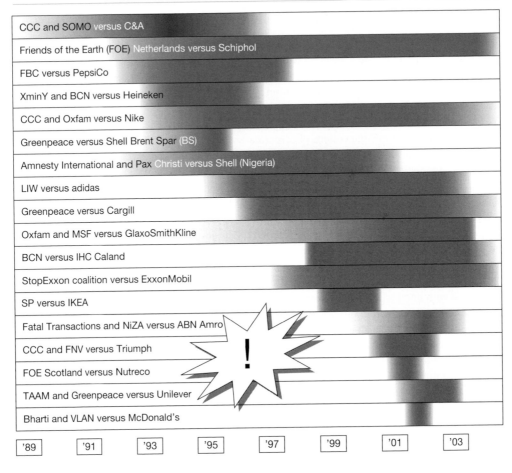

CCC and SOMO versus C&A

Friends of the Earth (FOE) Netherlands versus Schiphol

FBC versus PepsiCo

XminY and BCN versus Heineken

CCC and Oxfam versus Nike

Greenpeace versus Shell Brent Spar (BS)

Amnesty International and Pax Christi versus Shell (Nigeria)

LIW versus adidas

Greenpeace versus Cargill

Oxfam and MSF versus GlaxoSmithKline

BCN versus IHC Caland

StopExxon coalition versus ExxonMobil

SP versus IKEA

Fatal Transactions and NiZA versus ABN Amro

CCC and FNV versus Triumph

FOE Scotland versus Nutreco

TAAM and Greenpeace versus Unilever

Bharti and VLAN versus McDonald's

'89 '91 '93 '95 '97 '99 '01 '03

Figure III.1 Cases of societal interface confrontation

- a description of the conflict;
- indications of correction signals related to reputation damage – in the (1) consumer market, (2) capital market and (3) labour market;
- indications of disciplining that was initiated by the company through quality labelling, reporting, drawing up codes of conduct or otherwise;
- an assessment of the outcome of the conflict and the contribution the conflict has made to resolving the issue.

FROM 'PROVE IT TO ME' TO 'INVOLVE ME' OR 'ENGAGE ME'...

The objective of the case analyses in this book and on the website is to establish whether proactive or reactive, inactive or active entrepreneurial strategies on the identified interfaces have led to a different type of confrontation. Have companies that adopted a proactive strategy come closer to solving concrete social responsibility issues? Has there been an identifiable role for the reputation mechanism in the case of companies that initially pursued inactive or reactive strategies? Chapter 19 gives an overview of the 18 corporate responsibility conflicts' outcomes in terms of discipline and correction. Negative correction, which functions effectively in conflicts, appears to be somewhat different from positive discipline. Chapter 19 therefore evaluates the effectiveness of the reputation mechanism. The reputation mechanism seems to be a blunt instrument that can also have undesirable side effects for companies. In addition, a large group of companies – depending on where they are situated in the value chain, their marketing strategy, their dependence on external financiers and the presence of primary civil society stakeholders – is beyond or barely within the grasp of the reputation mechanism.

As yet, the confrontation between the focus on efficiency of international companies and the focus on ethics of NGOs has barely led to truly effective solutions to societal issues. It would appear that steps in the right direction are being made and that a reorientation with respect to the societal positioning of companies is also under way. The assertion in Part II, that interactive and proactive stakeholder management seems the most adequate approach to CSR is confirmed in practice. The returns on confrontation – as a form of interaction – are perhaps too low for truly socially responsible business practice. Even settled conflicts cast a shadow on future negotiations. The transaction costs involved in an international bargaining society may be high, but the transaction costs of a society steeped in conflict and confrontation are enormous. Instead of getting involved in conflicts or debates with stakeholders, the value of engagement in dialogue – especially by European companies – even at the beginning of an issue's life cycle, is increasingly acknowledged. In the final chapter of this book, the central question is how this dialogue can be given strategic content. Chapter 20 specifies the preconditions of a *strategic stakeholder dialogue* so that the challenges of Societal Interface Management (see Part I), corporate *societal* responsibility (CSR) and international *community* responsibility (ICR) (see Part II) can be addressed in a constructive manner.

Chapter 14

Do it just

Oxfam and CCC
versus
Nike

Since the early 1990s, a large number of sporting goods manufacturers have been under fire for their alleged unaccountable engagement with employees in countries of production. Nike was at the forefront of the issue. The company was called to account due to the appalling working conditions in factories in South East Asia (e.g. Indonesia and Vietnam). Oxfam, CCC, CorpWatch and NikeWatch, in particular, confronted Nike about the discrepancy between the huge salaries of icons such as Michael Jordan and Tiger Woods and the extremely low wages of workers and the alleged miserable working conditions prevailing in the factories of suppliers. The critics have suggested that Nike should publish all of its contract factories, and allow independent inspection to verify conditions there. Any auditing carried out by Nike should be made public according to the NGOs.

Table 14.1 Nike Inc. – Societal Interface Management challenges

Public ⚡ private	Profit ⚡ non-profit	Efficiency	⚡ Ethics/equity
Playing governments off against each other can be very effective	Large sponsoring contracts especially with wealthy athletes versus low wages for factory workers	Seeking lowest wages? Image marketing Hollow company: subcontracting leads to enormous cost savings	Good working conditions Supply-chain responsibility
Governments are keen to attract foreign investment	Business community involvement		Combating child labour
Official minimum wage is adhered to so what is the problem?	Basketball courts in disadvantaged American neighbourhoods	High salaries for management High market capitalization	Human rights Fair wages Trade union rights 'Do it just'
Is it up to Nike to change local legislation?	Nike as a 'way of life' Consumer organizations versus human rights NGOs	Marketing essential for sustaining demand	
Nike was one of the first companies with code of conduct	Establishing own NGO? Relationship with NGOs, universities and trade unions	Code as means to monitor supply chain	
Constant adjustments to codes and to monitoring of compliance			
Member of the Global Compact			

NIKE INC.

Nike Incorporated is an American company that sells sports apparel and shoes. Nike was founded in 1964 by athlete Philip Knight and named after the Greek goddess of victory, Nike. The company's headquarters are in Oregon. Acting as counterpart to brands such as Puma and Adidas, Knight started out by importing shoes from Japan where labour costs were low. Nike does not manufacture and sell merchandise itself, but contracts manufacturing to third parties and issues licences to outlets. Nike obtains its goods from approximately 900 suppliers in 55 countries in Asia, Central America and Eastern Europe. The company focuses largely on marketing and product development. In 1988, Nike started 'sub'-contracting the manufacturing of its products to factories. Nike employs approximately 23,000 people worldwide, from its World Headquarters in Oregon and European Headquarters in the Netherlands, to nearly every region around the globe. Including manufacturers, shippers, retailers and service providers, nearly one million people help bring Nike to athletes everywhere.[1] Nike has 11 offices of its own in the Asia Pacific region and are located in: Australia, China, Hong Kong, Japan, Korea, New Zealand, South East Asia (Singapore, Malaysia, Philippines, Thailand), and Taiwan. In addition to these offices, Nike also has manufacturing offices in Vietnam and Indonesia. An overview of the subsidiaries and (contract) factories of Nike is presented in Figure 14.1. At the end of the financial year ending on 31 May 2003, Nike realized a worldwide turnover of US$10.7 billion, an 8 per cent increase from the fiscal year 2002. This was the best year of the company's 31-year history.

OXFAM AND CCC *ET AL.*

Oxfam Community Aid Abroad focuses on influencing Nike and other transnational companies to respect basic employee rights. Just like Novib in the Netherlands, this Australian organization forms part of Oxfam International. Oxfam Australia is behind the watchdog NGO NikeWatch.

One of the coalition members was the Dutch branch of the international Clean Clothes Campaign (CCC). Research into working conditions in the garment and sportswear industry had already been conducted for ten years, first in the Netherlands (illegal garment workshops) and later also in other countries and regions. The Clean Clothes Campaign came into being as a result of the exposure of misconduct in the workshops of (Western) companies, largely in developing countries and free trade zones. The aim of the CCC is to improve working conditions in the garment and sportswear industry. Other organizations dedicated to enhancing living and working conditions which were active in this conflict are: Press for Change and NikeWatch.

CONFLICT

Since the early 1990s, Nike has been the target of different societal organizations in connection with the unacceptable working conditions at the factories of suppliers in Asia and Central America. In the eyes of human rights NGOs, Nike was more or less the black sheep of the 1990s (Werner and Weiss, 2002; Klein, 2000). In 1997, it once again led to an explosive confrontation between the Transnational Resource & Action Centre (TRAC)[2] and Nike over working conditions at sweatshops in Vietnam. Nike's glowing image threatened to become tarnished. At first, the Board brushed aside the allegations. However, when the conflict reached the front page of *The New York Times*, the share price decreased, contracts with universities were revoked and sales figures fell, Nike decided in May 1998 to demand serious improvements of working conditions at suppliers' factories by means of stricter controls and prohibiting the use of child labour.[3] This led Nike to revise its code of conduct in 1998, which included raising the minimum age of employees to 18 years – going beyond the international ILO Guidelines

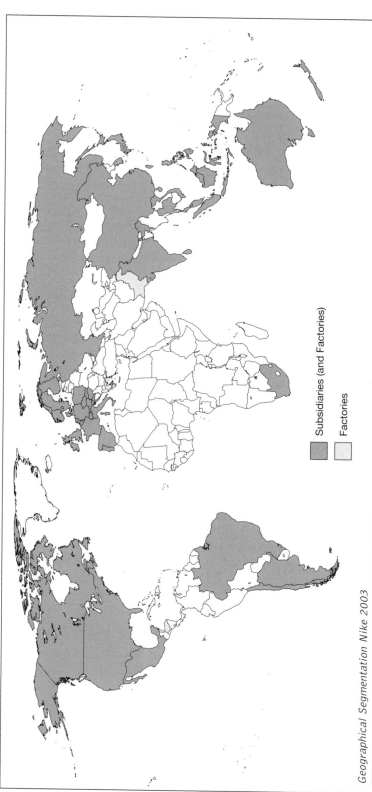

Geographical Segmentation Nike 2003

	Net revenue		Pre-tax income		Net property, plant and equipment	
United States	4793.7	39%	1015.1	44%	193	21%
Europe, Middle East, and Africa	3834.4	31%	750.7	33%	232	25%
Asia Pacific	1613.4	13%	354.9	15%	379.7	42%
Americas	624.8	5%	101.9	4%	12.7	1%
Other	1386.8	11%	75.3	3%	94.3	10%
	12253.1		2297.9		911.7	

■ Subsidiaries (and Factories)

□ Factories

Source: Nike 2004 Form10-K p57/58

Note: Year ended May 31, 2004.

Figure 14.1 *TNI Nike Inc. (Nike, 2004)*

(van Tulder and Kolk, 2001). According to societal organizations, however, these measures were insufficient and were regarded with suspicion. After 1998, negative reports of miserable working conditions in factories in Indonesia continued to dominate the agendas of NGOs. Approximately a third of all Nike shoes are manufactured in Indonesia.[4] Nike employed about 104,000 people in that country in the year 2001.[5]

STEUN DE CAMPAGNE

Nike

Fair Play?

Samenwerkende organisaties: Alternatieve Konsumenten Bond (AKB), International Restructuring Education Network Europe (IRENE), Komitee Indonesië, Schone Kleren Overleg (SKO), Stichting Onderzoek Multinationale Ondernemingen (SOMO). Ill.: P. v. Dongen

Figure 14.2 'Support the Nike Fair Play Campaign'. Dutch fair play campaign initiated by various European NGOs. Courtesy of Clean Clothes Campaign

RACE TO THE BOTTOM?

Reports circulated of unsafe working conditions, lack of freedom to unionize, sexual intimidation, forced labour, child labour and unacceptably low wages. A working week of at least 60 hours was regarded as normal. The CCC, Oxfam and CorpWatch in particular, condemned the practices they came across in the contract factories of Nike's suppliers. An hour's surfing on the Internet produces dozens of civil society organizations that are actively following the working conditions of suppliers to Western multinationals. Although Nike hires expensive celebrities to promote its cult of success and 'rebellion', the company frequently stumbles over its famous slogan: 'Just do it'. Alert activists skillfully employed the slogan to confront the firm on working conditions in production units: 'Do it Just' and 'Just do Just'. People were asking themselves how it could possibly be that employees who manufacture shoes that sell for US$140–180 dollars per pair did not earn more than 1.5 dollars a day, while marketing genius Nike paid its management and icons such as Michael Jordan and Tiger Woods millions of dollars. Nike was reprimanded for making false promises. According to NGOs, the textile industry in the sports sector is *the* example of the race to the bottom regarding wages and working conditions. This, they argue, was set in motion by economic internationalization (see Chapter 2) and the field of tension between efficient and ethical business. In Indonesia, the following was reported: more than 30 per cent of the workers had personally experienced, and more than 55 per cent had observed, verbal abuse. An average of 8 per cent of workers reported receiving unwelcome sexual comments, and more than 3 per cent reported being physically abused. In addition, sexual trade practices in recruitment and promotion were reported by at least two workers in each of two different factories, although a subsequent investigation was unable to confirm this.[6]

GLOBAL ALLIANCE RESEARCH

In response to the allegations, Nike collaborated in setting up a research project to investigate misconduct at the factories of Indonesian suppliers. The research was conducted by the Global Alliance for Workers and Communities, an American organization collaborating with companies such as Nike, clothing company Gap, NGOs, universities and the World Bank.[7] The objective of the organization is to improve the lives of – what are often female – employees in Asian factories. Critics regarded the founding of the Global Alliance by the International Youth Foundation (IYF) as a way for Nike and Gap to 'buy' a socially responsible image. 'Got problems with NGOs? Start your own!'[8] Nike joined the Global Alliance in 1999, and membership cost the company US$7.8 million.[9] In the study on working conditions in Indonesian factories, 4,000 employees were interviewed. According to the report, female factory workers were subject to large-scale verbal and sexual harassment by supervisors. They also had little access to medical care, had difficulty taking sick leave and were forced to work overtime. It was thus evident that suppliers were, indeed, frequently disobeying the strict guidelines Nike had set down.

On 22 February 2001, in response to the 50-page report, Nike for the first time openly acknowledged the abominable working conditions in Indonesian factories.[10] Oxfam, NikeWatch and the CCC were pleased with Nike's recognition of abuses in Indonesian factories. But according to the NGOs, it was not sufficient to agree to the unacceptability of the situation, it also needed to improve significantly. Nike subsequently declared that it would address the situation and that supervisors would be appointed to monitor matters of sick leave and wages. According to the CCC, Nike is not always well informed about the conditions in Asia. In order to make Nike's supply chain more transparent, Nike decided in 2005 to publish all their suppliers for end products on the Internet. More initiatives made by Nike can be found under the 'Demonstrable indicators of disciplining' section of this chapter.

DEMONSTRABLE INDICATORS OF REPUTATIONAL DAMAGE

Consumer market

Reactions on the consumer market did not fail to occur when the confrontation was as its height. US universities, such as the University of Oregon, refused sponsorship as a result of the negative reports in the media. They saw through the expensive advertising campaigns and refused to be associated with Nike.

The annual figures, to be sure, increased steadily over the past few years. In 2001, an increase in sales of 4 per cent to 9.9 billion euros can be discerned, but closer observation shows that it was largely European sales that were responsible for this.[11] In 2000, shoe sales in the US declined by four per cent.[12] And in 2001, sales on the domestic market also had a rough ride. In the US, sales declined by 1 per cent, while shoe sales in Europe increased by 9 per cent. In the first quarter of 2001 – the Global Alliance report was published on 21 February 2001 – US sales in Nike shoes fell by 50 per cent compared to the same quarter the year before. The next quarter, ending on 31 May 2001, shoe sales increased by 1 per cent, whereas in Europe, a 13 per cent increase could be discerned. The third quarter, ending on 31 August 2001, once again shows a lagging demand for Nike shoes on the domestic market with a decline in turnover of 7 per cent. Sales in Europe increased by 1 per cent.[13] In the quarter ending on 30 November 2001, US shoes sales declined by 2 per cent in comparison to an increase of 24 per cent in Europe.[14] Sales figures in the US were therefore structurally under downward pressure while sales in Europe and Asia were growing steadily. In view of the negative reports surrounding misconduct in the factories of suppliers, it is plausible that the reputation of Nike suffered, particularly in the domestic consumer market.

Capital market

The Nike share price fluctuated strongly in the week that the Global Alliance report on working conditions in Indonesia was publicly disclosed. Figure 14.3 depicts the price movements of the Nike share during this period.

On the day of publication of the Global Alliance Report, 21 February 2001, the share price decreased by 1.5 per cent, which represents a market value decline of more than US$150 million. The Dow Jones Index also decreased, but not at the same pace. The share price subsequently rose 2 per cent on the day Nike publicly admitted to the abuses and promised to do everything in its power to address it. A few days earlier the price dropped several per cent. On 26 February 2001, the management of Nike announced a profit warning. The firm warned investors that the earnings would be most disappointing, partly due to problems with stock management and weak domestic demand. As a result, on 27 February, the share suffered a decline of 19 per cent. Software firm I2, which supplied Nike's stock management systems, received even greater punishment with a share price decline of 22 per cent. The market appears to have reacted more vehemently to the news of a profit warning than it did to unacceptable working conditions. From April 2001, the share price started to recover.

A second interesting date is 10 October 2001. On this day, Nike published its first Corporate Social Responsibility Report which included a discussion of the improvements that have been made in the working conditions of Indonesian factories. On that day, the share price increased by more than 3 per cent.

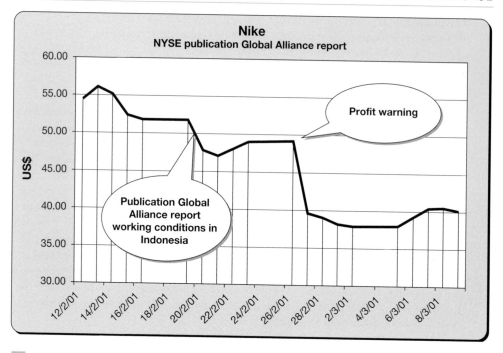

Figure 14.3 Nike share development, February 2001

Labour market

There is still a large number of people in developing countries who want to work for Nike suppliers. Specifically due to higher wages and improved working conditions – thanks to the struggle of the 1990s – Nike's popularity is not expected to abate. Nevertheless, Nike is not included in the annual list of the *Fortune* 100 Best Companies to work for. Nike itself has indicated that it has experienced no trouble on the labour market in connection with the allegations of unacceptable working conditions at suppliers' factories.

On the basis of our findings, it can be concluded that demonstrable indicators of reputational damage can be discerned on consumer and capital markets.

DEMONSTRABLE INDICATORS OF DISCIPLINING

The overall approach of the management of Nike in this matter can be described as one of bridging. In the 1990s a more defensive attitude (buffering) was adopted despite initiatives to draw up codes of conduct and partaking in international conventions. The company eventually took the initiative to solve the matter itself. In the process, much use was made of consultations with societal organizations. It seems that society judges the end supplier and holds it accountable. Under Philip Knight's leadership, Nike had great difficulty dealing with the criticism from external parties. The blame was continually laid with others, to the immense frustration of stakeholders. In the past years, Nike has embarked on several (disciplining) initiatives to manage issues surrounding working conditions in contract factories. Nike has revised and refined its code of conduct on a number of occasions. Additionally, the management of Nike requires that manufacturers in South East Asia comply with its code.

285

- Nike insisted on the research the Global Alliance conducted.
- Nike allow independent and systematic audits by the Fair Labor Association (FLA) of suppliers' factories, the results can be consulted online.
- In 2001, Nike published its first Social Responsibility Report, using the GRI guidelines as guiding principle. Nike supports the GRI as an organizational stakeholder in developing common reporting and assurance frameworks and systems to measure a company's corporate responsibility progress. Nike believes all stakeholders should have the benefit of common performance criteria through company reports in order to evaluate a company's record and progress on corporate responsibility activities.[15] The second CSR report had been postponed to 2005 (over the 2004 year) due to the Kasky case (see section on 'The aftermath'). Nike did, however, in the meantime, publish a 2002–03 Community Investment Report.[16]
- Nike has established a special staff department consisting of 70 employees who carry out audits.[17]
- Released the names and locations of hundreds of contract companies manufacturing Nike-branded finished products on their website. Nike believe disclosure of supply chains is a step toward greater efficiencies in monitoring and remediation and shared knowledge in capacity building that will elevate overall conditions in the industry. No one company can solve these issues that are endemic to the apparel industry. Nike believes the future demands more collaboration among stakeholders.
- External audits of practices in factories worldwide are conducted by organizations that have been approved by the FLA. The FLA announced on 12 May 2005 it has accredited Nike's workplace programme – signifying satisfactory completion of the company's three-year initial implementation period. This accreditation signifies Nike fulfilled the requirements set forth by the FLA and is in substantial compliance with the FLA's rigorous workplace code of conduct in contract factories making Nike-branded products.[18]
- The large number of adjustments to the code of conduct has led Nike to set the minimum age for children working in factories even higher than the ILO guidelines stipulate. According to the report, NikeWatch employees have noticed improvements in the factory of Nike suppliers in Indonesia.[19]

OUTCOME

Whose interests were met?

NGOs (among them, the CCC and Oxfam) witnessed Nike repeatedly launching new and better initiatives and improvements. The pressure exerted on Nike therefore ensured that a start was made in meeting the interests of factory workers (and the NGOs involved). In the case of Indonesia, Nike promised to take steps immediately. Endorsement of the GRI guidelines and the AA1000 standard in its CSR report is also a step towards sustainability. As yet, it appears that the CCC and Oxfam have held out longest.

Issue resolved?

Despite the fact that problems such as overtime and harassment of female workers are now being addressed, controversial matters, such as a living wage and freedom of association remain on the agenda of the CCC and Oxfam (e.g. NikeWatch). The issue surrounding working conditions, compliance with codes and the enormous difference in salaries of 'marketing' stars and factory employees will continue to haunt Nike. Many are still suspicious of Nike and several social reports are not enough to restore trust. The marketing and production formula that has made Nike so successful would have to change radically if Nike truly wants to take the wind out of its critics' sails. Nike remains very active in communicating about the issues the company is confronted with. In March 2002, Oxfam started a new campaign against Nike and Adidas with the slogan 'We Are Not Machines'. This campaign is once again aimed at the working conditions of women in Asian factories.[20] The Mexican factory, Kukdong, is also followed closely. In response to the pressure, an independent trade union has been established and planned dismissals related to reorganizations have been struck off the agenda (Werner and Weiss, 2002: 263).

The aftermath

NGOs such as the CCC, NikeWatch and Oxfam conceded that Nike has taken many steps in the right direction, certainly compared to competitors who are reported to have come off worse. NikeWatch and CCC have started a new campaign in 2004 called 'Play Fair at the Olympics' demanding that sports brands and the IOC play fair and ensure sportswear workers' rights. The particular focus this time was not on Nike, but mainly brands that haven't received campaign attention in the past, including Fila, Asics and Puma. A market leader, however, will be targeted first so as to bring about change in the industry. Nowadays, Nike is investing a lot of energy in improving monitoring and enforcing compliance with its code. The company is sensitive to the media and thus a useful target in drawing attention to certain issues. Ultimately, the end supplier is held accountable. Societal organizations are watching Nike closely. Despite all the CSR initiatives, its shoe factories are the object of the harshest criticism from human rights organizations and the anti-globalization or alternative globalization movement. Nike is presently participating in multiple international initiatives to promote and shape socially responsible policies. The company is involved in the Global Alliance for Workers in Communities, Business for Social Responsibility and the FLA (Nike, 2001, 2004), endorses the UN Global Compact and the CERES principles and employed the GRI guidelines in compiling its Responsibility Reports. The report discusses compliance with the code and working conditions in factories. Nike is listed on the Dow Jones Sustainability Group Index (DJSGI).

In 1997 clouds started to emerge above Nike's corporate ground. In 1997 Mark Kasky, a labour activist from San Francisco, sued Nike for making false statements for the first time. In 2002 he accused Nike of false advertising in the company's public claims about working conditions in its foreign factories and in 2003 of inappropriately promoting its CSR record. These lawsuits had a 'chilling effect' on corporate social responsibility reporting.[21] The likely consequences of a Kasky victory would be to set back the corporate accountability movement immeasurably by making any kind of active/proactive corporate disclosure or initiatives a vastly higher-risk activity than it currently is, according to critics. Nike may be the only one that has so far pulled back from its reporting activity.[22] Nike tried to have the case stopped based upon the US's First Amendment right to free and open debate. However, the US Supreme Court concluded that it would allow the controversial lawsuit against Nike to go to trial. The lawsuit was recently settled out of court. In September Nike agreed to pay US$1.5 million to the FLA to improve working conditions worldwide through monitoring and factory worker programmes.

In 2005 the company decided to publish a CSR report (over the year 2004) again. The 108-page report, Nike's first public corporate responsibility report since it made the decision to stop reporting in October 2002 when it petitioned the US Supreme Court to hear the Kasky *versus* Nike First Amendment case, was released in conjunction with the annual CERES conference in Boston, MA. CEO Philip Knight stated in his opening letter in the report that they are using the last report to 'play a little catch-up and draw a more complete picture'.[23] Nike feels it must balance the need to communicate and be transparent with the risk of litigation. The company is currently redefining its process for data collection and is developing the necessary tools to help guide both their internal and external reporting, including data validation and assurance systems.[24]

Chapter 15

The ocean as rubbish dump?

Greenpeace
versus
Shell

In 1995, Shell became embroiled in the most analysed and oft-cited CSR controversy of the 1990s: the Brent Spar affair. After years of research, the British government finally gave Shell UK permission to sink the old and defunct oil platform off the Scottish coast. Like David against Goliath, Greenpeace entered the battle to prevent Shell from using the ocean as a rubbish dump.

Table 15.1 Shell Plc – Societal Interface Management challenges

Public ⚡ private	Profit ⚡ non-profit	Efficiency	⚡ Ethics/Equity
Relationship with governments of countries situated around the North Sea (England and the Netherlands) was well-managed (or so it was thought) No violation of international treaties	Consumer relationship toughened Greenpeace and critical consumers particularly in Germany Attacks on petrol stations	Cost-effective disposal of defunct platform Sets the example for remaining installations Efficient management of joint venture	Can the oil industry ever be environmentally friendly? What is less damaging to the environment: sinking or onshore dismantling? Licence for remaining defunct platforms?

ROYAL DUTCH SHELL PLC

Shell, in full, the Royal Dutch Shell plc came into being in 1907 through a merger concluded between NV Koninklijke Nederlandsche Petroleum Maatschappij and The Shell Transport and Trading Company (Shell Transport). The two parties merged their interests on a 60:40 basis while retaining their separate identities. The parent companies do not carry out operational activities. The Royal Dutch Shell plc is the collective name for the holding companies, while service companies and operating companies are largely referred to as 'Shell' (although Shell always points out in a footnote in its commercials that national Shell companies are largely autonomous). In 2005 the two parent firms decided to unify completely and base their headquarters in The Hague, the Netherlands. The firm operates in more than 155 countries worldwide and its core activities are: Exploration and

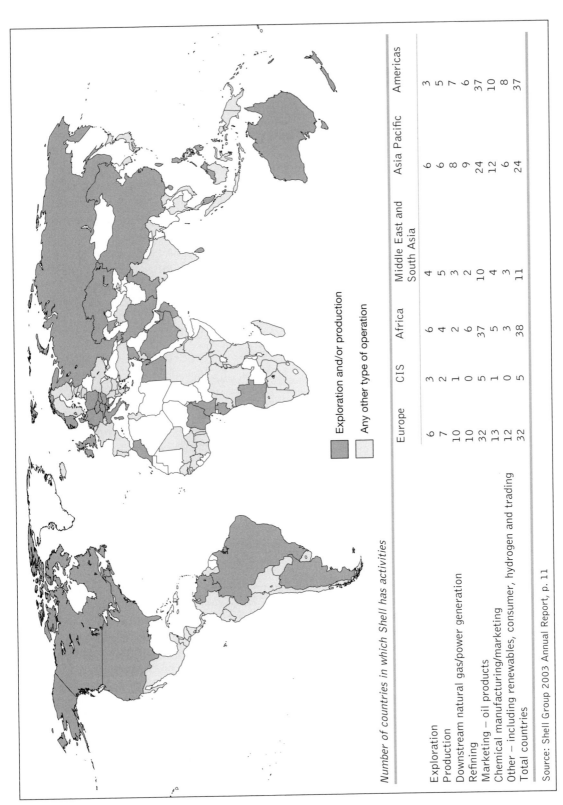

Number of countries in which Shell has activities

	Europe	CIS	Africa	Middle East and South Asia	Asia Pacific	Americas
Exploration	6	3	6	4	6	3
Production	7	2	4	5	6	5
Downstream natural gas/power generation	10	1	2	3	8	7
Refining	10	0	6	2	9	6
Marketing – oil products	32	5	37	10	24	37
Chemical manufacturing/marketing	13	1	5	4	12	10
Other – including renewables, consumer, hydrogen and trading	12	0	3	3	6	8
Total countries	32	5	38	11	24	37

Exploration and/or production

Any other type of operation

Source: Shell Group 2003 Annual Report, p. 11

Figure 15.1 Shell's operations worldwide

Production, Oil Products, Chemicals, Gas and Power and Renewables (see Figure 15.1). In 2003, the net earnings of Shell worldwide amounted to more than 11 billion euro. Shell controls the entire chain of production – from well to pump. It is both a business-to-business and business-to-consumer enterprise. Shell is listed on a number of stock exchanges, but in the Netherlands it is listed on the AEX Index under the name Royal Dutch Shell plc. According to the magazine *Fortune*, Shell is one of the largest companies in the world and according to *Forbes* magazine, in the year this conflict played out it was also the most powerful. Shell's most significant competitors are ExxonMobil, BP Amoco, Chevron, TotalFinaElf and Texaco. Through joint activities in some parts of the production chain, competitors are sometimes also partners – also referred to as 'co-competitors'.

GREENPEACE

Greenpeace Netherlands is dedicated to the protection of the natural environment. The conservation of 'unpolluted' international bodies of water, such as oceans, is high on the agenda. Greenpeace is an independent international organization which exposes global environmental issues and forces solutions which are essential for a green and peaceful future. Greenpeace strives to safeguard the conditions for a sustainable relationship between humans and nature. Greenpeace Netherlands is one of the largest environmental organizations in the Netherlands with 611,000 donors in 2004.[1] Greenpeace Netherlands has 85 full-time salaried employees and its headquarters are in Amsterdam. One of the active supporters of Greenpeace in this affair was the Dutch Foundation 'Natuur en Milieu'.

CONFLICT

In June 1976, Shell UK installed a new oil storage tank in the Brent oil field in the Atlantic Ocean: the Brent Spar. The Brent Spar was jointly owned by the American Exxon and the Anglo/Dutch Shell, but was operated by the latter in a joint venture named Shell Expro. In September 1991, the more than 150-metre-high storage buoy from which tankers loaded oil, concluded its service because it became obsolete. Between 1991 and 1993, the Board of Shell, with the assistance of the British government and countless external advisors, conducted extensive research into the best option for disposing of the Brent Spar.

In February 1994, Shell submitted a proposal, the Abandoment Plan, which was based on research conducted by Aberdeen University, to sink the Brent Spar in the Atlantic Ocean off the Scottish coast. The cost of dismantling oil platforms at the time was estimated at about 11 million euros for small, and double the amount for larger types. In addition to being costly, the dismantling process would also be an extremely dangerous exercise. At least as far as the environment and public health and safety were concerned, sinking the Brent Spar was a scientifically accountable undertaking. In December 1994, the British Ministry of Trade and Industry approved the sinking of the Brent Spar. In February 1995, the British government officially announced its approval. This news was also communicated to the 13 parties to the Oslo Convention. No objections were submitted during the 60-day term set aside for this purpose.

THE OCCUPATION OF THE BRENT SPAR

On 30 April 1995, a month before an important North Sea conference in Denmark, 30 activists from the environmental organization Greenpeace, proceeded to occupy the Brent Spar. In the process, they made clear to the outside world that it was a 'toxic time bomb' containing 5,500 tonnes of oil and that 'no justifiable grounds' existed for sinking the Brent Spar.[2] In addition, Greenpeace posited that the sinking of the Brent Spar would open the way to 'dumping' the 400 other obsolete oil platforms, which, just like the Brent Spar, were disused and bobbing around the ocean.[3, 4] This potential domino effect was part of the core of the issue. The symbolic battle had begun: David against Goliath under the watchful eye of a benevolent media.

Greenpeace started a large-scale campaign with the motto 'The ocean is not a rubbish dump'. Formulated in somewhat demagogical and unnuanced terms: the most powerful and profitable multinational dumps its waste in the the ocean! According to Greenpeace, the Brent Spar also contained about 100 tonnes of sludge, including chemicals such as cadmium, lead, zinc, PCB-containing liquids and also more than 30 tonnes of scale consisting of radioactive waste.

LICENCE AND REMOVAL

On 5 May 1995, a permit was issued to Shell to sink the oil platform on a carefully selected site in the Atlantic Ocean (the North Feni Ridge) as Best Practical Environmental Option (Elkington, 1999). Within a short space of time, the stakeholder model Shell UK was oriented towards expanded significantly as other European operating companies and even European governments, became involved in the issue. On 9 May 1995, the German Minister of the Environment publicly opposed the sinking of the Brent Spar in the light of Greenpeace's protests. In Germany, in particular, support for Greenpeace had been growing at a tremendous pace for years. Moreover, German politics were being swept along by the 'green' transformation of political relations in government at the expense of the liberals. In the weeks that followed, independent British scientists confirmed that sinking was the best course of action, both for humans and the environment (health and safety). In response to this announcement, on 23 May 1995, the Scottish police removed the Greenpeace activists from the Brent Spar and transported them to a Scottish island. Greenpeace publicly called for a pan-European boycott of Shell and held protest demonstrations at Shell headquarters in The Hague, among other places.[5] The second phase, during which the media followed the issue closely, broke out, with moral panic gaining the upper hand.

TOWARDS SINKING

Shell and the British government seemed to be more isolated in the matter than expected at first. On 9 June 1995, at the fourth North Sea conference in Denmark, a number of European delegates appealed for the onshore dismantling of defunct oil platforms. Great Britain and Norway appealed for decision-making on a case-by-case basis (Jordan, 2001). On 10 and 11 June 1995, Shell, under voluble protest from Greenpeace, set out on the journey to the sinking spot in the Atlantic Ocean.[6] An army of journalists, photographers and camera people was transported by Greenpeace to the Brent Spar in its campaign boat, the *Moby Dick*. In full view of the cameras and the rest of the world, the most mediagenic scenes were subsequently played out to the advantage of the environmental movement. That same evening, images of activists in rubber boats caught up in a battle against a towering enemy were broadcast on the news across the globe.

Greenpeace chained four activists to the Brent Spar which would have amounted to murder had the platform been sunk. At the G7 summit in Halifax, Canada, the German Chancellor Kohl made it clear to then British Prime Minister Major that he did not approve of the present state of affairs.[7] The Dutch Minister of Economic Affairs, Wijers, also stated that he 'would not mind' if his chauffeur avoided Shell filling stations in future. Public opinion on the European continent slowly (but surely) turned against Shell.[8] Between 14 and 20 June 1995, approximately 200 Shell petrol stations in Germany were besieged and vandalized with anti-Shell slogans such as 'Shell go to Hell'. Fifty stations sustained serious damage and two were set on fire with weapons and fire bombs. German petrol station owners reported a 20–30 per cent decline in turnover in one week.[9] In some places, more than a 50 per cent decline in turnover was established.[10] The largest daily newspaper in Germany, *Bild*, forcefully called upon the public never to fill up at Shell again. An opinion poll in the Netherlands showed that 82 per cent of the Dutch population supported Greenpeace in this affair. The city council of Leiden called on policy advisors to stop refuelling at Shell petrol stations,[11] especially since there were enough competitors around to supply fuel. Shell petrol stations became the target of public discontent also in Denmark (Backer, 2001: 245). Emotions gained the upper hand, shutting out the technical facts and arguments Shell advanced in its defence. Everything Shell claimed was regarded with suspicion. Involuntarily, the company became the owner of the issue. Greenpeace and other societal groupings got a hold on the previously elusive giant and turned it into an icon of unacceptable corporate conduct with respect to the environment.

ON ITS KNEES

By the end of June 1995, the debate on the facts and scientific evidence had intensified. At Shell petrol stations and in daily newspapers, Shell made it clear that the sinking of the Brent Spar was the best option both from a costs and environmental perspective.[12] On 19 June 1995, the Board of Shell stood firm in its decision to sink the Brent Spar.[13] One day later, it made a turnabout when it appeared that the majority of European governments were reconsidering the matter and the security situation in Germany and Denmark was threatening to get out of hand. Grudgingly, the Board changed tack and yielded to public pressure, to the intense displeasure of British Prime Minister Major. In his view, it confirmed the waning power of government with respect to societal organizations. Newspaper headings in the *Daily Telegraph*, the *Independent*, *The Times* and the *Daily Mirror* published detailed reports of the victory of David over Goliath in the service of planet Earth. This day is seen by environmental NGOs as one of the greatest victories in the history of the environmental movement. Soon the grumbling started. *Trouw* (a Dutch newspaper) wrote of a 'dark day for democracy' where Greenpeace, without a mandate and with vague and superficial arguments, managed to force the Brent Spar onto dry soil while Shell had been acting completely in accordance with the law. A choice had been made for a decommissioning process that was more dangerous, more expensive and more environmentally degrading than sinking.[14] On 7 July 1995, the Norwegian government offered to stall the Brent Spar in one of its fjords before its dismantling. With the assistance of an independent Norwegian organization, Det Norske Veritas (DNV), Shell UK launched an investigation into the contents of the Brent Spar and the allegations of Greenpeace. The British government requested Shell to come up with a better and more responsible proposal for the Brent Spar given the lack of international guidelines.

LIES

On 5 September 1995, Greenpeace admitted that the information that was used to sway public opinion had been somewhat exaggerated. The tank contained much less oil than claimed and the activists who fell into the water had not been run over by Shell boats.[15] Greenpeace offered Shell an apology.[16] On 18 October 1995, the research by DNV was complete and it emerged that Shell had been more accurate than Greenpeace.[17] Greenpeace was accused of manipulating the facts. This led to fierce reactions from different newspapers and journalists who felt 'betrayed'. The reputation of Greenpeace as a reliable and trustworthy organization was damaged (Schwartz and Gibb, 1999: 30). Despite the dent in its reputation, Greenpeace membership increased by 4 per cent (22,000) to 600,000 in 1995. That year, the environmental movement had three million members.[18] In the wake of this incident, the director of

Shell Netherlands called for a code of conduct for NGOs.[19] With this appeal, it was hoped that organizations such as Greenpeace and Amnesty International would realize that their existence depends on their supporters.

In 1998, countries situated in the eastern region of the Atlantic Ocean signed an extension of the OSPAR convention. The convention now includes a stipulation that prohibits the dumping of oil and gas installations and the discharge of toxic and radioactive substances into the ocean. The first version of the OSPAR convention was signed in Oslo on 15 February 1972. In June 1995, the EC expressed support for the recycling and reuse of offshore installations. However, the most important international documents on disused offshore oil and gas installations are diverse and difficult to interpret. Among them are the 1958 Geneva Convention on the Continental Shelf; the 1982 United Nations Convention on maritime law; the 1972 London Dumping Convention; the 1989 International Maritime Organization guidelines and rules for the disposal of offshore installations and constructions on the continental shelf; the 1989 Basel Convention in connection with controlling cross-border traffic and the disposal of hazardous substances; the 1972 Oslo and 1992 Paris Conventions; the 1992 Helsinki Convention concerning the protection of the North Sea marine environment; the 1976 Barcelona Convention for the protection of the Mediterranean against pollution. These conventions concern minimum standards only.[20]

DEMONSTRABLE INDICATORS OF REPUTATIONAL DAMAGE

Consumer market

It is difficult to determine the effect of the campaigns on the turnover of Shell in the Netherlands. It is plausible, however, that the conflict did not have a positive effect on its turnover. The decline in turnover is easier to establish in Germany. German Shell petrol station owners reported a decline in turnover of 20 to 50 per cent in June 1995. This amounted to a loss of a few hundred million euros.

Capital market

Assessing the effects of protest actions on Shell's position on capital markets, the price movements of the Royal Dutch share listed on Amsterdam Stock Exchange (AEX Index) were analysed. Two periods were selected for this purpose: 28 April–31 May 1995 and 1 June–30 June 1995.

28 April–31 May 1995. On 30 April 1995, Greenpeace activists occupied the Brent Spar. The share price showed a slight increase of 1.38 per cent on the Monday. In the days leading up to receiving permission to sink the Brent Spar, the share price registered a slightly upward trend. Figure 15.2 shows the price trend of the share during this period.

Until 19 May 1995, the share price registered a daily increase on the Damrak (as on the German stock exchange in Frankfurt). In the US, the price of the Shell share decreased by a few per cent during the first weeks of May. On 19 May 1995, it became clear that the 30 activists were not going to leave the Brent Spar without a struggle. A court case had to provide the definitive answer. On that day, the share decreased by 3.5 per cent. On 23 May, the activists were taken to court to hear the judge's verdict. This was followed by a call for an international boycott of Shell petrol stations. Despite the price fluctuations, at the end of May 1995, the share price was still more than three per cent higher than before the Greenpeace activists occupied the Brent Spar. That month, the AEX Index exhibited a steady upward trend.

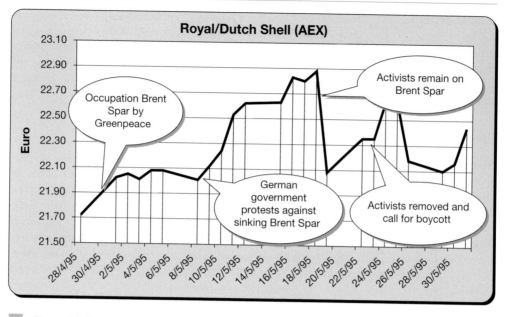

Figure 15.2 Shell's stock price fluctuation during occupation

1 June–30 June 1995. In June, the debate surrounding the Brent Spar intensified. The number of media reports increased drastically. Especially between 14 and 19 June, loud protests sounded across Europe (see Figure 15.3). In the first three weeks of June, the Royal Dutch share lost 3 per cent of its value, which amounted to a market value decline of 2.3 billion euros or a loss of about 11,550 euros per shareholder. This loss contrasted with the slightly upward

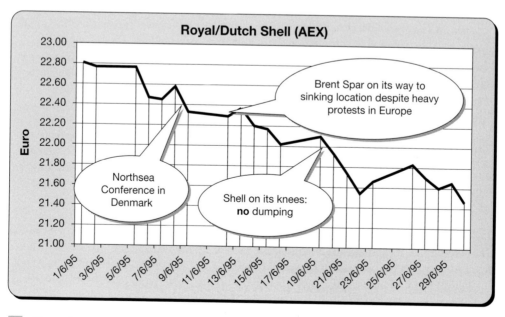

Figure 15.3 Shell's stock price during intensifying debate in Europe

trend of the AEX. In the three days following Shell's change of tack and decision not to sink the Brent Spar, the share price decreased by more than 2.5 per cent while the AEX showed an increase of one per cent. Over that month as a whole, the share price decreased due to negative reports. By contrast, the AEX Index remained stable. In the course of August, the price settled and a slight recovery could be discerned. This recovery would gain thorough momentum at the time of Shell/Nigeria affair which erupted in November 1995.

Labour market

According to Shell, the Brent Spar and Nigeria issues as such did not much influence the company's attractiveness as an employer. In combination with the economic decline of the oil industry (low crude prices) from the mid- to late 1990s, the issue resulted in a lower intake of new recruits. In addition, the Corporate Image Barometer published by *De Telegraaf* and the annual corporate image research conducted by Intermediair (Intermediair, 2002: 30), show that at the time of the Brent Spar and Nigeria affairs, Shell was regarded as a significantly less attractive employer. The company quickly recovered. The surveys show that after the debacles of 1995, Shell's image on the labour market improved markedly. In 2002, Shell ranked second among the nation's favourite employers, compared to 1999, when the oil company occupied fourth place.

Research conducted by Shell shows that the number of people who had an unfavourable or favourable view of Shell, respectively, increased and decreased in connection with this issue.[21] This is a clear indication of reputational damage.

DEMONSTRABLE INDICATORS OF DISCIPLINING

Shell undertook several (disciplining) initiatives to manage the issue.

- Instead of sinking it, the company decided to dismantle the Brent Spar onshore.
- Shortly after the Brent Spar affair (and the controversy surrounding Nigeria, see Chapter 13), the Board of Shell revised the Statement of General Business Principles (SGBP) with the assistance of, and in consultation with, numerous stakeholders. The principles of conduct Shell endorses apply to all Shell companies and suppliers. The principles express the core values of 'integrity', 'honesty' and 'respect for people' and must be upheld to support and protect the reputation of the company (Shell, 1997). The SGBP were originally formulated in 1976. Their establishment was prompted by the societal discussion at the time about the role and position of multinationals in society. In 1997, two new concepts were added, namely 'sustainable development' and 'human rights'. The Shell principles apply to all business conduct within Shell: objectives, responsibilities, economic principles, integrity, political activities of operating units and employees, health, safety and environment, society, competition and communication. The principles describe the conduct Shell expects of employees worldwide and are available in 30 languages.
- Since the revised version of the SGBP, hundreds of contracts with supplies have been cancelled for being inconsistent with the code of conduct.
- The Board decided to publish an annual report that covers compliance with the code and the company's social and environmental performance. In addition, periodical audits are carried out. Shell's first and widely lauded sustainability report was published in 1998: 'Profits and principles: does there have to be a choice?' In this report, an account is given of the activities Shell has embarked on to meet its economic, social and environmental

responsibilities. The report also describes the dilemmas and issues Shell is confronted with. The 2000 sustainability report was awarded the first prize in the European Environmental Reporting Awards (ERA). Shell took the initiative to structure core activities along the Triple-P Bottom Line. The importance of accounting for its conduct was brought home by the Brent Spar and Nigeria affairs. These issues served as wake-up calls and made Shell realize that change was imperative.

Shell employs its website to maintain the dialogue with its societal interface and supporters and opponents can hold discussions with each other via the Tell Shell option.

- Shell has instituted a Social Responsibility Committee; through this commission, top management supervises the implementation of Shell's sustainability principles.

Apart from revising its code of conduct and reporting annually by means of the Shell Report, Shell has also made internal structural changes. The company switched from a decentralized matrix structure to a more centralized structure, especially in the areas of external affairs and public relations (van den Bosch and van Riel, 1998). Decisions were taken too much in isolation – without taking into account the effects on the Group as a whole. According to Shell, more coordination was required.[22]

OUTCOME

Whose interests were met?

In this case, Greenpeace succeeded in realizing its objectives. The Brent Spar was dismantled in a Norwegian fjord. Moreover, an EU convention was adopted that prohibits the sinking of offshore installations. The Brent Spar issue shows that pressure on companies from society can bring about significant policy change.

Issue resolved, case closed?

The issue is solved: the Brent Spar was not sunk and an EU convention should ensure that the remaining 400 platforms won't end up at the bottom of the ocean.

The aftermath

Over a period of seven years and influenced by the issues surrounding the Brent Spar and Nigeria, Shell has become a pioneer in the area of CSR. The company has secured a listing on a number of sustainability indices such as the FTSE4Good, DJSGI World and Stoxx Index or best of sector.[23] Shell has developed its own instrument, the Sustainable Development Management Framework (SDMF) in order to integrate sustainable development in decision making. This framework is structured around three core themes (performance with a long-term view, dynamic and caring innovator and acting on strong business principles) and is characterized by a 'plan, do, check feedback' learning cycle. Through this framework, employees are engaged in integrating social aspects into decision making. Shell has learned to listen to the voices in society. The company does not shy away from holding a dialogue with parties such as Friends of the Earth and Greenpeace. It offers the company new ideas and nourishment in the form of knowledge and viewpoints. The dialogue was entered into at as early a stage as possible and is now eliciting criticism that Shell seems intent on smothering also its enemies.

Chapter 16

Provocative bras from Burma

Clean Clothes Campaign, FNV Global and BCN versus Triumph International

Lingerie manufacturer Triumph International came under fire for its presence in Burma some time after PepsiCo, Heineken and IHC Caland.[1] Burma has a military regime, and people disappear, are being tortured and deployed in forced labour camps. Triumph's factory was situated on property that is owned by the military government. Renting this site was therefore regarded as directly financing the military regime. The political opposition in Burma, under leadership of Nobel Prize winner Aung San Suu Kyi and the independent trade unions urge the international community to refrain from doing business in Burma so as to force the rulers to the negotiation table. In 2001, the NGO Clean Clothes Campaign, in collaboration with, among others, The Burma Campaign UK, Burma Center Netherlands (BCN), The International Confederation of Free Trade Unions (ICFTU), labour unions FNV Global and CNV, requested Triumph to withdraw from Burma.

Table 16.1 Triumph International – Societal Interface Management challenges

Public ⚡private	Profit ⚡non-profit	Efficiency	⚡Ethics/equity
Totalitarian regimes are a government matter, thus government should take the lead; why should companies do so? Should the absence of a functioning State in a developing country automatically imply a wider moral responsibility upon MNEs and their home states? Junta as owner of terrain; does it pose a problem? Conform to international regulations/or not?	Relationship with representatives of workers (trade unions), consumers (CCC) and sector organization Guarded, but social status of family business might ultimately require different approach	Efficient buying from and supplying to consumer markets, the largest among which is Asia Relationship with largest customer in the Netherlands	Business and Human rights Supply-chain responsibility Responsibility to retrenched employees in Burma

TRIUMPH INTERNATIONAL

Lingerie manufacturer Triumph International (Triumph) was founded in Germany in 1886. It is a traditional family business and not listed on the stock exchange. Triumph's market is divided into units, each with its own director. Headquarters are in Zurzach, Switzerland. The company had factories in Portugal, Austria and Morocco which moved to Vietnam, Indonesia and other South East Asian countries, including Burma. This move took place not only due to costs, but also to be closer to Triumph's largest consumer market, Asia, and Japan in particular (see Chapter 3 for internationalization strategies). Triumph is a world leader in the underwear and lingerie market, employs 38,699 people and had a worldwide turnover in 2003 of 1.6 billion euro (2003). In addition to the brand Triumph, the company also markets the brands Hom, Bee Dees, Valisère and Sloggi.

NGO COALITION: CCC, FNV AND BCN

In collaboration with other societal organizations, CCC (both in the Netherlands as well as in Switzerland) was one of the first to call upon the apparel and footwear industry to adopt a code of conduct based on ILO conventions and to commit themselves to reasonable wages and the independent monitoring and verification of working conditions. The campaign took place in association with e.g. FNV Global (Mondiaal), Novib (Oxfam Netherlands), Burma Center Netherlands and the India Committee of the Netherlands (LIW).

The labour union FNV Global (Mondiaal) is the International department of the Dutch Federation of Trade unions. It is actively involved in the development of a robust independent international labour movement. FNV Global is also active in the ILO.

Burma Centrum Netherlands is an independent foundation that aims to inform the Dutch society on developments in Burma and to initiate and coordinate activities that benefit democratization and sustainable development. BCN also aims to contribute to a constructive dialogue between the various groups in Burma. The Burma Campaign UK was also actively involved in this campaign.

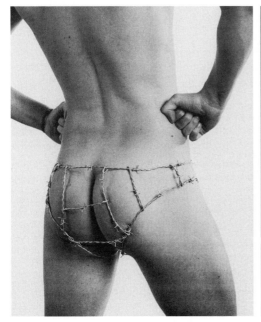 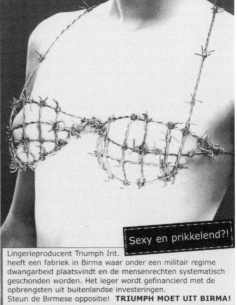

Figure 16.1 Provocative images from Burma. European poster campaign by various NGOs. Picture by Harry Meijer

THE CONFLICT

Triumph had a lingerie factory in Myanmar, formerly Burma. For years, companies had been called upon to abandon investments in Burma due to its dictatorial regime and the violations of human rights. The democratically elected government had been overthrown by a military regime. The Triumph factory was located on property owned by the government with the result that Triumph was held responsible for financing the military regime. The conflict started in December 2000 with a letter to Triumph from the CCC.[2] According to the CCC, the Board of Triumph failed to respond. In January 2001, protest campaigns in the Netherlands, Belgium, the UK, Norway and Switzerland followed, which were organized by different groupings under the leadership of the CCC and Burma Campaign UK. In Asia, no protest actions were organized. Triumph attributed this to a completely different attitude to this 'Burma issue' in Asia, which was informed by a different culture. Triumph also stated that investment decisions were made in Hong Kong where the Burma issue was not deemed important at all.

Closing the factory implied the compulsory dismissal of their 845 employees.[3] According to Triumph, withdrawal was an option, but not the best solution to the situation in Burma. The firm was more inclined to fulfil the role of catalyst – making a contribution from the inside (constructive engagement). According to the CCC and FNV Global, Triumph should not have invested in Burma in the first place. Especially not after the Heineken and PepsiCo affairs (www.ib-sm.org). Doing business in Burma necessarily implied support for a reprehensible regime, but the company chose to ignore the signals. The organizations demanded that Triumph shut down the factory, draw up a social plan for redundant employees and develop a credible international code of conduct.

PUBLIC DEBATE IN EUROPE

In the first months of 2001, the CCC and Triumph exchanged viewpoints. Triumph refused to change its position. As a result, the pressure was stepped up. Through card and poster campaigns, free protest postcards, protest actions on streets and in stores,[4] press releases, the attendance of youth fairs, the deployment of a genuine 'Lingerie protest train' and a call to boycott Triumph, the groups put Triumph in the public moral spotlight in various European countries. Triumph subsequently announced that it would immerse itself in the ILO guidelines for conduct. In summer 2001, a delegation from the CCC, the ILO and Triumph visited Burma to assess the situation.

On 22 October 2001, follow-up protest actions at the Night of Lingerie, a night for the promotion of the lingerie branch in the Netherlands, reached an even wider public. That evening, the Board of Triumph was presented with an artwork: a large steel needle threaded with a thick length of barbed wire mounted on a large white cushion. Protest cards were also distributed. The press was well represented that evening and the story was also relayed by regional newspapers.

In response to the negative publicity surrounding Triumph, Bodyfashion Netherlands – the trade organization for the lingerie sector – decided to exclude Triumph from all promotions during the Lingerie Week. This implied that Triumph would no longer have access to any of the sector's collective activities in connection with Lingerie Week. The trade organization's members were informed in writing of the steps taken against Triumph.

The parties held their breath at the end of 2001. In Norway, the sports federation suspended its contract with Triumph to supply the Norwegian Olympic Team's underwear.[5] The victory for this step was claimed by Burma Campaign UK.[6] At the end of January 2002, Triumph buckled under public pressure and decided to withdraw from Burma.[7] The company strongly regretted that it could only offer its 845 employees financial compensation and not more. In a press release, Triumph acknowledged that it was 'due to the public debate in Europe' that it was ceasing production of bras and other underwear in Burma.[8] Triumph is a family business with a strong traditional culture, which would not yield to just 'any fashion whim'. The decision to close down the factory was prompted by a public debate, also picked up by national and international governmental institutions in Europe on the political situation in Burma – a debate that became increasingly emotional and which led to planning uncertainties that Triumph could no longer accept.

DEMONSTRABLE INDICATORS OF REPUTATIONAL DAMAGE

Consumer market

Triumph claimed that it had not discerned a decline in sales. An above average increase in sales could even be detected on the European market in 2002. The annual figures of 2001 nevertheless show that sales that year declined by almost 5 per cent.[9] Large retail customer VendexKBB (the Netherlands) confirmed that sales in Triumph underwear in its shops showed no decline at the time of the conflict. However, there have been frequent consultations between the two Boards. On several occasions, VendexKBB urged Triumph to find a way to settle the issue. VendexKBB insisted that the Board of Triumph would reconsider its presence in Burma and respond appropriately to the international outrage in Europe. Triumph has a 35 per cent market share in VendexKBB retail shops (Bijenkorf, V&D, Hunkemöller). A decrease in sales cannot be substantiated, but neither one of the Boards of the two firms could deny the number of protest cards they received. Thousands of cards were sent to the headquarters of Triumph and VendexKBB. Furthermore, at the youth fair, Megafestation, 2,900 photos were submitted to Novib's (Oxfam Netherlands) protest plate. There are clear indications of a negative change in the perception of customers, such as the above-mentioned response of the Norwegian Olympic Committee and the trade organization Bodyfashion Netherlands. Access to consumer markets was impeded by this. The worldwide sales figures have increased steadily in 2002 and 2003 up to a turnover of 1.6 billion euro in 2003 (a 4.7 per cent increase on 2002).[10]

Capital market

Triumph is a family business and not listed on a stock exchange. According to Triumph, it did not experience any problems on capital markets as a result of the Burma conflict.

Labour market

The Board of Triumph could not establish whether employee motivation declined at the time of the conflict. The number of job applications did not fluctuate either. In the Netherlands, the involvement of the FNV, which employees regarded as 'their' trade union, did however cause confusion and raised concern.

DEMONSTRABLE INDICATORS OF DISCIPLINING

Triumph undertook several (disciplining) initiatives to manage and solve the issue:

- Divestment in Burma.
- In 1996, Triumph set up a European works council and, in 1998, it refined its code of conduct (Leitmotiv). The NGO campaigns resulted in an interest to adopt the ILO code

and make reference to the UN Declaration of Human Rights. Triumph International has implemented a revised code in December 2001 based on these institutions.[11] As a member of the European Apparel and Textile Organization (EURATEX) Triumph subscribes to the Code of Conduct negotiated with the European Trade Union Federation of Textiles, Clothing and Leather (ETUF: TCL), which includes the ILO forced labour convention. The Code also affirms the right for workers to form and join a trade union and to negotiate freely – a right denied to workers in Burma.[12]

- ■ Societal organizations, including the CCC were invited to attend Triumph's general meeting in 2002 to share viewpoints. The dialogue and consultations between the parties will continue in the future and are going on today as well.

OUTCOME

Whose interests were acceded to?

At the end of January 2002, Triumph annouced its withdrawal from Burma. The interests of the CCC, BCN and the FNV were thus acceded to most. In the meantime, the code of conduct (Leitmotiv) of Triumph has been refined several times. However, the whereabouts of, and the consequences for, the 845 former Triumph employees is still unknown. Can this be considered an effective solution to the issue?

Issue resolved and closed?

The issue of Triumph International at their factory in Burma was resolved a couple of years ago, but the Burma issue in general was not. As long as the junta in Burma remains deaf to international critique and doesn't improve the political and human rights situation the issue will persist. Aung San Suu Kyi was released from house arrest in May 2002.[13] After her release, there was widespread hope that it would be a step towards democracy in Burma and lead to serious political reform. However, during a tour of Northern Burma, Aung San Suu Kyi and her supporters were attacked by a government-sponsored mob. The attack took place on 30 May 2003.[14] As many as 70 people were killed in the attack and over 100 people arrested, including Aung San Suu Kyi. She remains in detention and all National League for Democracy (NLD) offices have been closed. The US Congress has since put stricter sanctions in place in 2003 in regards to Burma, prohibiting Burmese imports for the next couple of years and has extended the visa ban on high-ranking military officials if the situation is not improving.[15] Also, the EU has stiffened economic sanctions on the military regime since the crackdown of Aung San Suu Kyi on 30 May 2003 resulting in the third house arrest for the Nobel Prize laureate.[16]

The junta has made an effort a year later (November 2004) by releasing dozens of political prisoners. It is said that this was done under pressure of being thrown out of the ASEAN coalition. Any proposal of a road map to political change in Burma will fail to bring about democracy in this country unless it is formulated and executed in an atmosphere in which fundamental political freedoms are respected, all relevant stakeholders are included and committed to negotiate, a time frame for change is provided, space is provided for necessary mediation, and the restrictive and undemocratic objectives and principles imposed by the military through the National Convention (ensuring continued military control even in a 'civilian' state) are set aside.[17]

The INGOs are now to proceed with a call on European tour operators and related parties such as the Asian Way of Life, Lonely Planet, Far Holidays International, Outsight Travel, Summum Travels, Djoser and Shoestring to suspend trips to Burma. Various tour operators have complied with the request.[18] The Dutch National Contact Point (NCP), which monitors the OECD guidelines, has however concluded that the investment context which is necessary in order to fall under the guidelines, is missing in regards to the travel industry and has merely given out general consideration and discouragements when organizing travels to Burma.

The aftermath

The management of Triumph International is aware of the responsibilities that arise from its IB activities and the employment of a labour force worldwide. Triumph acknowledges that these responsibilities extend to all employees who produce their products regardless of whether they are employees of the firm or not. Both the management and the European Works Council of Triumph emphasize the paramount importance of the protection of human rights laid down in the 'General Declaration of Human Rights'. The parties are governed by the relevant agreement from the ILO and Global Compact of the UN for the regulation and furtherance of working and economic relations. Triumph International, the European Works Council and the Europäische Gewerkschaftsverband der Textil-, Be- kleidungs- und Lederarbeitergewerkschaften (EGV/TBL) are setting up a committee for the supervision of the regulations of their Code of Conduct. Triumph is sending two representatives to this Monitoring Committee, likewise the European Works Council two representatives and EGV/TBL two representatives. The committee dictates the tasks and authority of the Monitoring Committee according to the principle of unanimity.[19]

Triumph International has first-hand experience of the far-reaching effects of the reputation mechanism. The company has acknowledged that the presence and pressure of societal organizations accelerated change and greater transparency. Triumph was not prepared for the conflict and did not see it coming. In future, Triumph will hold more consultations with societal organizations, particularly in the Netherlands, Switzerland and Belgium. Greater care will be taken when opening new factories in the future. This case illustrates that it is in the interest of family businesses to be more open and be sensitive to their environment, certainly with respect to societal issues. In managing the issue, Triumph was assisted by the management of Heineken which confronted the same issue a few years earlier.

Chapter 17

'Do more, feel better, live longer, but only if you can afford it?'

MSF and Oxfam
versus
GlaxoSmithKline

For several years market leader in the pharmaceutical industry, GlaxoSmithKline, and other large multinational pharmaceutical companies, have been condemned for excessive pricing through patent strategies, which limits access to so called antiretroviral medicines (ARVs) (used to treat HIV and Aids) in areas where the disease is most prevalent: developing countries. Over the last ten years, the media, NGOs and even international governmental institutions have focused heavily on events relating to the industry's ARV patent strategies. Oxfam joined with Médecins sans Frontières (MSF), VSO, Treatment Action Campaign, and other partners to cut the cost of the vital portfolio of HIV/Aids medicines. The NGO's campaigns call for and bargain for reform of global patent rules, and challenge drugs giant GlaxoSmithKline (GSK) to take the lead within the pharmaceutical industry to promote poor people's access to medicines by e.g. lowering their prices.

Table 17.1 GlaxoSmithKline – Societal Interface Management challenges

Public ⚡private	Profit ⚡non-profit	Efficiency ⚡	⚡ Ethics/equity
The production and distribution of ARVs involves doing business with governments in developing countries	Clients are civilians, governments and NGOs	Africa is largest, but also poorest market for medicines	Is the right to (accessible) healthcare a universal human right?
Cooperate with government, even though they might be corrupt?	Role of shareholders and institutional investors	The firm is market leader	Should the absence of a functioning State in a developing country automatically imply a wider moral responsibility upon MNEs and their home states?
Relationship with the UN, WHO, World Bank, WTO and Ministries of Development		Different prices for different geographical markets?	HIV/Aids has a great impact on the economies of developing countries
Dealing with intellectual property rights (IRP, patents, copyrights and trademarks) and international agreements		Patents protect R&D investments efficiently	Transparency needed in regards to pricing of ARVs
Patents and the role of the WTO?			Free trade versus the availability of medicines as a human right

GLAXOSMITHKLINE

GlaxoSmithKline (GSK) is a leading research-based pharmaceutical company with a powerful combination of skills and resources that provides a platform for delivering strong growth in today's rapidly changing healthcare environment. The company was formed in December 2000 through a merger of the British Glaxo Wellcome and the American firm SmithKline Beecham. The merger created the largest pharmaceutical worldwide. Headquartered in Brentford (UK) and with operations based in the US, the company is one of the industry leaders, with an estimated 7 per cent of the world's pharmaceutical market (2004). Based on 2004 results, GSK had sales of US$37.2 billion (US$31 billion accounts for the pharmaceutical division) and profit before tax of US$11.1 billion. Total pharmaceutical turnover was US$29 billion in 2003.[1] The company also has a Consumer Healthcare portfolio comprising over-the-counter (OTC) medicines, oral care products and nutritional healthcare drinks, all of which are among the market leaders. GSK has over 100,000 employees worldwide. Of these, over 40,000 are in sales and marketing in 40 countries, the largest sales force in the pharmaceutical industry. Around 35,000 employees work at 85 manufacturing sites in 37 countries and over 16,000 are in R&D. GSK's R&D is based at 24 sites in seven countries. The company has a leading position in genomics/genetics and new drug discovery technologies. The GSK R&D budget is about US$4 billion. The US accounts for 52 per cent of the companies market (by sales). GSK scored 68 per cent on the 'Transnationality Index' (TNI) over 2003 (see Figure 17.1). This index is the average of the ratios of foreign to total assets, sales and employment, and captures the foreign dimension of the firm's overall activities. Europe is GlaxoSmithKline's second largest market, accounting for 28 per cent of sales. All other geographic areas (Latin America, Asia Pacific, Canada, Japan and Middle East/Africa) are minority markets, each contributing less than 7 per cent to total sales.

The company produces ARV medicines such as Retrovir (since 1987), Epivir (since 1995), Combivir (since 1997), Ziagen and Agenerase (since 1998), Trizvir (since 1999). Combivir is GlaxoSmithKline's best-selling ARV drug, and the company held a 45 per cent global market share in HIV/Aids drugs in 2003. Glaxo's (FTSE UK listing) main competitors in the ARV market are Boehringer Ingelheim (privately owned), Abbott Laboratories, Bristol-Myers Squibb, Pfizer, Merck (all S&P500 US listings), and Roche (listing on SMI Switzerland). In the R&D of AVR medicines these key players in the industry are collectively responsible for producing the top ten HIV Antiviral Products in terms of global sales[2] (Liddell et al., 2004: 3).

OXFAM INTERNATIONAL

Oxfam International was founded in reaction to the growing poverty and accompanying inequality and injustice in the world. The organization's aim is to heighten social awareness that economic and social justice is crucial for sustainable development. In pursuit of this objective, it has launched several campaigns such as 'Cut the Cost' in February 2001 against the pharmaceutical industry and 'Make Trade Fair' to focus attention on (un)fair international trade practices. Oxfam International is a confederation of 12 organizations that are active in more than 100 countries on four continents.

MÉDECINS SANS FRONTIÈRES

Médecins Sans Frontières (MSF) is an international humanitarian aid organization that provides emergency medical assistance to populations in danger in more than 80 countries.

AIDS HEALTHCARE FOUNDATION

The mission of the Aids Healthcare Foundation is to provide cutting-edge health care and advocacy to people with HIV and Aids regardless of their financial situation. The organization provides care

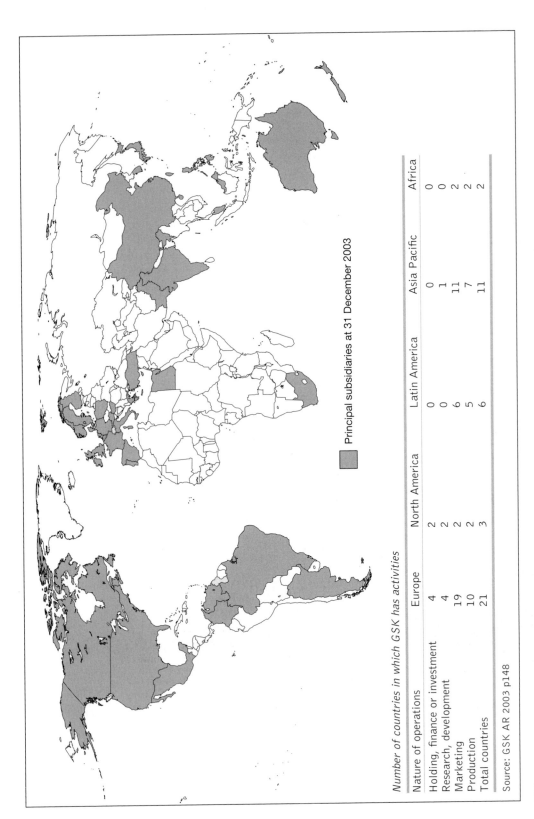

Number of countries in which GSK has activities

Nature of operations	Europe	North America	Latin America	Asia Pacific	Africa
Holding, finance or investment	4	2	0	0	0
Research, development	4	2	0	1	0
Marketing	19	2	6	11	2
Production	10	2	5	7	2
Total countries	21	3	6	11	2

Principal subsidiaries at 31 December 2003

Source: GSK AR 2003 p148

Figure 17.1 Transnationality GlaxoSmithKline

in specialist healthcare centres, focuses on education and research, and is dedicated to protecting the rights of people with HIV and Aids in the US and across the world. In the US, it has 14 healthcare centres, in Africa it has two, and in Central America it has one. The organization employs about 500 people.

THE CONFLICT

Development and distribution of Aids and HIV

The process of economic interconnectedness on a global scale – often referred to as globalization – is accompanied by growing inequality between and within countries. The gap between rich and poor has grown over the past years. This gap is clearly visible if one considers the accessibility of medicines, and ARVs in particular. In 1981, the first case of Aids was diagnosed. This was the start of what has been described as 'a new type of global emergency' (UNAIDS/WHO, 2004: 7). In just over 20 years, more than 20 million have died from Aids. The number of people living with HIV/Aids has been steadily increasing since 1990 from an estimated 10 million people to an estimated 38 million as of the end of 2003. The disease is most prevalent in sub-Saharan Africa, where two-thirds of those with HIV live, despite the fact that just over 10 per cent of the world's population are located here. At present, no cure has been developed for Aids. ARVs that have been developed since the mid-1990s have the ability

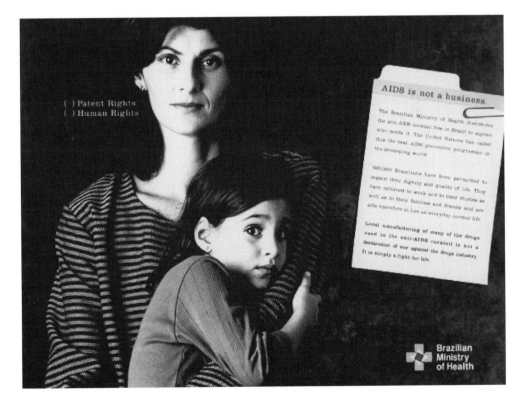

Figure 17.2 'Patent Rights or Human Rights?' This ad has been published by the Brazilian government in The New York Times. The advertisement argues that 'Aids is not a business' and the local manufacturing of HIV medications is not a 'declaration of war against the drug industry'. The ad is taken from and has the print permission of Flanagan and Whiteman (2005)

to prolong life significantly and reduce the physical effects of the infection. Worldwide, five to six million people are in need of access to antiretroviral therapies (ART). However, in low and middle-income countries, only 7 per cent are estimated to have access (UNAIDS/WHO, 2004). In those countries where there has been wide availability, a dramatic reduction in HIV-related illnesses and death has been observed (e.g. Brazil, see also Chapter 10).

Various causes are attributed to the lack of access. Insufficient health infrastructures, lack of health education and the high cost of ARV medicines are some of the most commonly cited reasons (Topouzis and van Wijk, 2003: 1). Rich people often have a range of treatments to choose from while large groups of poor people do not even have access to essential medicines. The spending of research budgets is also strikingly asymmetric. More than 90 per cent of funds for health research from pharmaceutical MNEs is spent on Western diseases. Less than 10 per cent is used for research on epidemic tropical diseases. In addition, many countries do not have sufficient, affordable healthcare. There is a shortage of medicines and vaccines and the available medicines are often frightfully expensive. The HIV/Aids crisis, in particular, reveals what the consequences of too costly medicines can be. Globally, more than 38 million people are infected with HIV, of which 95 per cent live in developing countries. More than 21.8 million people die of Aids-related diseases each year.

TRIPS

Especially in South Africa, poverty and a resultant lack of education and information has led to an Aids epidemic on an unprecedented scale: one in ten South Africans is infected with HIV. At an average income of US$3,000 per year, HIV/Aids cocktails costing US$10,000 per year are unattainable to most. This gave former president Nelson Mandela cause to pass legislation in 1997 that made it possible for South Africa to by-pass trade agreements and patent laws to purchase cheap Aids medicines. One of these trade laws concerns the so-called Trade-Related Aspects of Intellectual Property Rights (TRIPS) agreement (see also Chapter 10). In 1994, the WTO Uruguay Round resulted in, among other things, the signing of the TRIPS agreement. The 147 member countries of the WTO, must comply with the provisions of the WTO agreements that deal with intellectual property and thus the TRIPS agreement (Flanagan and Whiteman, 2005). This agreement 'aimed at extending worldwide the type of intellectual property protection that had up until that point been granted to firms established in the most developed countries' (Coriat et al., 2003). The signing of TRIPS has been the birth of the issue. TRIPS was developed in order to align the protection regimes of all countries across the world. TRIPS also allows for disputes regarding breaches of the TRIPS agreement to be settled at the WTO Dispute Settlement Body (DSB). However, the agreement lacks clear rules and regulation on how countries could make use of the 'included safeguards when patents increasingly present barriers to medicine access' ('t Hoen, 2003; Liddell et al., 2004). Pharmaceutical companies in developed countries seized the opportunities caused by the advantages and deficiencies of TRIPS, creating the foundation for an unregulated social topic awaiting settlement. The establishment of TRIPS on the one hand and the development and distribution of Aids is actually a coincidence. However, these issues have become intertwined (Liddell et al., 2004; Coriat et al., 2003). In 1996, with the arrival of tritherapy treatments, patenting of all ARV drugs in the developed countries came into being.

PATENTS, PHARMACEUTICALS AND ANTIRETROVIRALS

Intellectual property legislation allows a limited monopoly for companies owning a patent. 'Profitability of many of the largest pharmaceutical companies depends on a handful of products'

(Ambrosini *et al.*, 1998). Increasing competition and a number of challenges such as growing R&D expenditure, have made ownership over patents and trademarks a powerful source of competitive advantage, for example in price setting and production distribution (Topouzis and van Wijk, 2003). Pharmaceutical companies argue that the high cost of R&D, which was estimated at US$802 million per new drug in 2000 makes it difficult to provide affordable medicines to developing countries.[3] These costs are recuperated through patents that prevent other pharmaceutical companies from producing and providing cheaper generic forms of the branded drug. The world market for branded ARV medicines consists of approximately 20 ARVs. The top ten branded ARVs combined account for a market share of 86 per cent. The patents of 17 branded ARVs (including the top ten) are held by seven firms, all of whose headquarters are located in developed countries (Topouzis and Van Wijk, 2003; Coriat *et al.*, 2003). The ARV market is therefore oligopolistic, within which the UK firm GlaxoSmithKline (GSK) plays a significant role. GSK is much in favour of international agreement due to the fact that GSK spends around US$500 million or more to bring one new drug to market. GSK argues that it would have no incentive to undertake the risky and costly process of R&D without strict patent protection rights (Lawrence *et al.*, 2005: 467).

However, under TRIPS there is a rule that permits exceptions to protect public health. The agreement states that in case of a national emergency or other circumstances of extreme urgency compulsory licences can be granted by the governments of countries by e.g. GSK, allowing them to by-pass the patent law. The Doha declaration gives the freedom of WTO members to grant these licences, and determine the grounds upon which they are granted. Since August 2003, the WTO council on intellectual property rights has allowed developing countries to manufacture cheaper generic drugs under 'compulsory licensing', or import cheaper generics made under compulsory licensing if they are unable to manufacture the medicines themselves. Governments could in this way compel a patent holder, such as GSK, to license another firm to a generic, low-cost version of the drug. Governments of nations could also engage in parallel importing in such emergencies. This is referred to as cross-border trade that was not sanctioned by the patent holder, e.g. importing cheaper generics from another country such as India.

SOUTH AFRICA TRADE DISPUTE

In 1997 the South African government, under Nelson Mandela's presidency, passed the Medicines and Related Substance Act. The act authorized parallel importing and compulsory licensing in order to tackle the HIV/Aids epidemic in South Africa. GSK, among other large pharmaceutical firms, viewed both provisions in the Act as an assault on its intellectual property rights. The period of 1998 to 2001 is characterized by growth and development of the issue. This period shows how an ideals gap results in controversy. While multinational pharmaceutical companies such as GSK argue that they are not the cause of HIV/Aids and act upon their limited monopoly, NGOs become increasingly active in forming alliances and drawing attention to (the publics view of) the responsibilities of these companies (WHO, MSF, UNAIDS). Multinational pharmaceutical companies ultimately react to the rise of generic manufacturers (South Africa trade dispute). At the same time, governments of some developed countries (US and EU) react to the development of a pharmaceutical industry in Brazil, India and Thailand via lawsuits, while other governments of developed countries (for instance France) become active in donation and negotiated special prices programmes. Pharmaceutical companies have repeatedly been blamed and criticized for the expanding crisis, which was demonstrated for example in the 1998–2001 South African trade. In 1998 GSK and 38 pharmaceutical manufacturers including the South African Pharmaceutical Manufacturers Association filed a lawsuit against the government of South Africa 'alleging that the Medicines and Related Substances Control Amendment Act No. 90 of 1997 violated TRIPS and the South African constitution' (Pharmaceutical Shareowners Group, 2004). The US and the EC support 'their' manufacturers and pressure South Africa to repeal this amendment. GSK pursued the lawsuit against the South African government because the government wanted to buy generic (brand-free and lower-priced copies) versions of drugs GSK had under patent (Lawrence *et al.*, 2005: 464). The largest Indian generic drug manufacturer Cipla (Chemical, Industrial and Pharmaceutical Laboratories) had offered to sell sharply discounted copies of Glaxo's ARV medicines to NGOs. The large pharmaceuticals had to follow suit. In the meantime, the South African government decided not to implement Mandela's law as yet. South Africa, after all, had aspirations to become a significant global trading partner. But times do change. In December 2000 Glaxo was accused in the media of blocking access to generic Aids drugs in Ghana for instance (*Wall Street Journal*, 1 December 2000). A shift in international opinion became apparent early in 2001 when the case was brought before the Pretoria High Court. This became known as the 'PMA versus RSA': Pharmaceutical Manufacturers Association against the Republic of South Africa. Early in 2001 the pressure on GSK increased due to societal demands for cheaper drugs. Cipla offered to sell medicines at a heavily discounted price and focused media attention on pricing policies for patented medicines (Lawrence *et al.*, 2005). On 8 February 2001, *Wall Street Journal* carried the headline: 'Drug Industry Jolted by Cipla Aids-drug offer'. India, being a developing country in the eye of the WTO, has an extension on putting TRIPS agreements and obligation into effect. This means Indian producers such as Cipla are able and allowed to produce copies of drugs that are patented and developed elsewhere. Cipla offered its drug Duovir (a copy of GSK's Combivir) to Médecins Sans Frontières and also the African government at a very low price and even cost price for a year's supply (between US$350 and US$600 a year). Due to the worldwide attention and media coverage the lawsuit in South Africa received, Oxfam launched a campaign 'Cut the Cost' in February 2001. In this campaign, the international aid organization accused the Western pharmaceutical industry of waging an 'undeclared drug war' on poor countries (www.oxfam.org, 2003). They alleged that the 'pharmaceutical monopolists' placed millions of human lives at risk while the production costs of their patented Aids inhibitors amounted to less than a quarter of the retail price. The Oxfam campaign specifically targeted the pharmaceutical giant and world market leader GSK (GSK patented Combivir in 1996). In its annual report, the company claimed to be actively striving to make affordable medicines accessible to the least advantaged. GSK and other pharmaceuticals were accused of indirectly contributing to the Aids crisis and the death of victims.[4] Oxfam demanded that the industry drop their lawsuits against countries that produce cheaper generic medicines.

DROP THE CASE

In May 2001 the pharmaceutical companies decided to drop the case against the South African government due to lack of support from home governments and international public pressure, and started lowering their drug prices. Oxfam was involved in this success. It achieved great success at several shareholders' meetings, where activists dressed in white laboratory coats protested and distributed boxes of medicine which included a leaflet calling on GSK to show leadership in the industry and take significant steps to develop more affordable medicines for the poorest of the poor. In addition, Oxfam warned the pharmaceutical industry in a new report entitled 'Dare to Lead' that it would lose public support if it persisted in its patent strategies and again called on GSK to take the lead in the transformation process.[5] Oxfam called on the company to act according to the principles it explicitly states in its annual report, which include making medicine more accessible to the poor.

Later in 2001, 32,000 people in 163 countries signed a petition calling on the WTO to change its patent rules when it met in Doha. The final deal – the Doha declaration – reaffirmed that public health is more important than patents. This was an important step forward in making medicines affordable for developing countries.

MEANWHILE IN THE US . . .

Critical voices from stakeholders in the US could also be heard in 2002. At the beginning of the year, the largest Aids organization in America, the Aids Healthcare Foundation, placed GSK under strong legal pressure. First the company was accused of having acquired the patent on AZT illegitimately. According to the Aids Healthcare Foundation, this first HIV/Aids drug had already been discovered by the federal health organization in 1960. At the time, it was used to treat cancer patients, but it was also found to be a means to fight Aids symptoms. When this came to light, GSK appropriated the patent and brought it on the market at a price 32 times its production costs. The case, referred to as the 'Smoking Gun', is still pending (www.aidshealth.org, 2003).

On 15 April 2002, the CEO of GSK, Jean-Paul Garnier, received a letter from the California Public Employees Retirement System (CalPERS is the largest and one of the most influential pension funds in the US). In the letter they demanded a change in the 'corporate behaviour' of GSK. The letter focused on three management aspects: company policy on prices in developing countries, humanitarian efforts of the company with regard to HIV and Aids, and that company conduct regarding both these factors could result in a tarnished reputation and a decline in its share price. According to CalPERS, the last aspect, especially, would have severe financial repercussions. CalPERS therefore requested GSK to make a concerted effort to find a balance between the supply of medicines in developing countries at the lowest possible price and the long-term survival of the company. According to the pension fund, economic costs and reputational damage had to be bridged. The pension fund, for Californian government officials and teachers in California, also suggested that it was planning to sell its shares (worth US$760 million) in GlaxoSmithKline. The Aids Healthcare Foundation was actively involved in drafting the letter and providing CalPERS with factual information about GSK.[6] GSK not only decided to lower the prices once again (also in 2000, 2001 and 2003) but also secured some 120 arrangements to supply preferentially priced HIV/Aids medicines to 50 of the world's poorest countries. In September 2002 and also April 2003, GSK further reduced the preferential prices of their HIV/Aids medicines by up to 33 per cent (GSK AR, 2002: 2; *FT*, 28 April 2003).

TIMELINE

A short timeline of events constructed from the *Financial Times* is provided to sum up several events in relation to the HIV/Aids medicines and patent negotiations concerning GSK:

Cost-cutting events

12–02–2001	Oxfam urges charitable stance on drugs patents
12–02–2001	GSK facing crusade over drugs for poor; investors support Oxfam campaign
16–02–2001	GSK to review drug-pricing policy
22–02–2001	GSK cuts price of HIV medicine
11–06–2001	GSK to extend the distribution of cheaper ARVs
20–06–2002	GSK announces two-year price freeze on HIV/Aids medicines

| 06–09–2002 | GSK cuts its drug prices for poor countries |
| 28–04–2003 | GSK again reduces its not-for-profit price of HIV/Aids medicines for the developing world |

South African court case events

05–03–2001	Drugs companies in challenge to South Africa over patent rights
06–03–2001	South Africa judge throws patents trial into doubt
07–03–2001	South Africa trial put on hold till April
19–03–2001	WHO supports South African law on drug patents
16–04–2001	Mandela attacks drug companies over patents
17–04–2001	Patents case holds key for drug groups
18–04–2001	Drugs companies set to drop Aids patent suit
19–04–2001	Drugs groups still seeking patents law deal
22–05–2001	Compromise on cheap Aids drugs

Doha events

17–10–2001	Campaigners attack drug companies on Aids patents
25–10–2001	Stage set for clash at WTO meeting over drug patents
15–11–2001	Declaration on patent rules cheers developing nations

According to GSK however, counterfeit pharmaceutical products are a growing problem and can put patients' health at risk through the use of low-quality or harmful ingredients. Effective enforcement of intellectual property laws can help prevent the distribution of counterfeit products. GSK is now working in close cooperation with governments and others in the pharmaceutical sector to tackle this problem.

DEMONSTRABLE INDICATORS OF REPUTATIONAL DAMAGE

Correlations between key events pertaining to patent strategies, and trends in the capital, consumer and labour markets could provide a valuable insight into the influence that patent strategies relating to ARV medicines have on the reputation of GSK.

Consumer market

The total sales of GSK were not particularly affected by the controversy surrounding the company's HIV/Aids medicines in the past years. In 2001, in particular, the company's turnover increased markedly. This was the period during which the conflict with Oxfam International seemed serious. However, GSK has many different kinds of product so we have to look at the antiviral sales. Given the strong position of the company in the world market and the dependence of the 'ill' on the company's medicines, a decline was not really expected.

The sales of GSK's products in the HIV therapeutic area show interesting developments. The total sales of the ARVs (including the popular Combivir) increased steadily since 2000 by around 12–14 per cent annually. This increase could be found in both the US and Europe and Rest of the World (as GSK formulates it). However, the sales of antivirals in 2003 declined in both the US and Europe by 4 and 7 per cent respectively. Also, the beginning of 2004 showed problems in the antiviral sales in the aforementioned regions accept in the GSK defined business region Rest of the World (including developing countries). In 2004 the total sales of antiviral drugs increased by 'only' 4 per cent in relation to previous years (also for Combivir alone). Profits in 2001 were significantly lower which could be the result of the ever-increasing price-cuts the company actively started to implement in 2001. The percentage of profits allocated to R&D in 2001 is also lower than it was in preceding years (GSK AR, 2001, 2002, 2003 and 2004).

Whether the fluctuations of the sales figures can be related to the HIV/Aids patenting issues and lawsuits remains unclear, but probable.

Capital market

In order to find a link between all the events in the past years regarding the HIV/Aids ARVs pricing and patenting disputes we decided to look at a couple of events and the reactions of shareholders reflected by GSK's share price in relation to the FTSE index.

In February 2001, investors publicly supported an ARV price cut. The effect of GSK's announcement on 16 February 2001 to review drug-pricing policy might show a little impatience on behalf of the investors (–0.79 per cent). However, on the day that the price cut finally was announced (22 February), stock prices climbed 2.34 per cent in a calm market (+0.34 per cent).

The announcement of extending the low pricing policy of GSK on 11 June 2001 shows only a small drop in stock price (–0.61per cent) in a negative market (–1.36 per cent). A year later, 20 June 2002, a two-year price freeze on HIV/Aids medicines was announced, showing also a small drop in stock price (–0.14 per cent) in a negative market (–1.50 per cent). On 6 September 2002, another price cut, showed a 1.34 per cent rise in a positive market (+2.13 per cent). Finally, 28 April 2003 shows a small rise (+0.32 per cent) in a positive market (+1.63 per cent). It is clear that these investors do not negatively correct low-pricing behaviour.

5–7 March 2001: South African Trade dispute

The South African Trade dispute is a fine example of how the pharmaceutical companies handle infringement and face the pressure of NGOs (Liddell *et al.*, 2004). The announcements on 5, 6 and 7 March 2001 show heavy drops in stock price averaging per day for Glaxo's American competitors (also involved as part of the total of 40 pharmaceutical firms filing the lawsuit): –1.74 per cent for Abbott, –1.90 per cent for Bristol-Myers Squibb, –2.44 per cent for Merck and –1.26 per cent for Pfizer in a positive market (+0.74 per cent a day). This result is the same for GSK, –1.15 per cent in a positive market (+0.72 per cent FTSE). Roche does not seem to be affected, averaging +0.44 per cent a day in a positive market (+0.32 per cent). Company stock prices are negatively corrected within two days of reports on abandoning the lawsuit and seeking a deal. Averages per day: Abbott –1.47 per cent, Bristol-Myers Squibb –2.74 per cent, Merck –1.61 per cent, Pfizer –3.12 per cent, GSK –3.54 per cent in positive markets S&P +2.57 per cent and FTSE +0.96 per cent. Roche is the only company with a positive average during these two days of +0.91 per cent in a positive market (+0.27 per cent).

Advocating legal protection: WTO negotiations 2002

With regard to the Doha Declaration, investors do not seem to applaud or negatively correct the outcome of the companies' advocacy. The events relating to the import licences debate shows a mixed picture. Cheap drugs boost trade talks on 16 November 2002 leave Abbott (–0.91 per cent), Pfizer (–0.39 per cent), Roche (–0.47 per cent) and GSK (–1.89 per cent) going down in relatively calm markets.

A strong decline was expected around May 2002; at the time when CalPERS (the largest pension fund of the US) got involved in the conflict. Given that GSK took direct action immediately and lowered prices even further, a clash has been avoided. Also the Pharmaceutical Shareowners Group (PSG) has expressed deep concern with regards to the ongoing public criticism and consequent negative impacts that this will have on the industry.[7] Although drug pricing and misconduct in clinical trials and marketing areas within the industry have been the focus of such criticism, the response of the pharmaceutical sector to the HIV/Aids crisis over recent years is one of PSG's key concerns, fearing that it will have a long-term effect on shareholder value.[8] PSG has expressed concern regarding CSR issues and reputation, with respect to their effect on staff morale and recruitment prospects, if companies fail to be proactive in addressing these issues. Knowledge workers, on which the industry is based, are particularly 'sensitive to criticisms from friends and family about working for "unethical" or "uncaring" companies' (Pharmaceutical Shareowners Group, 2004). The pharmaceutical industry views its approach to drug development as a sales problem, which is evident in the '10/90 gap'[9] of R&D expenditure. The source of the industry's labour force means that there is little direct impact of the HIV/Aids epidemic on their workers. This relationship is in contrast to labour-intensive work such as that of the textiles industry, where there is a strong chain of responsibility regarding ethics and labour conditions, as their employees are at the heart of the issue. With a growth in significant talent pools from up and coming educational systems such as China and India (where Aids is more prevalent), these issues may have greater prominence in the near future (Pharmaceutical Shareowners Group, 2004: 9).

Labour market

The relationship between reputation and effect on labour has been difficult to measure; trends within company rankings are affected by a multitude of factors and hence attributing the affect of reputation on labour (or any other single factor) as a cause of shifts within these ranking is not a reliable approach. Although we appreciate this caveat, by examining rankings both within industry and across all markets, we can gain a limited insight into the possible effects of reputation. Rankings within the industry give an indication of how pharmaceutical companies are performing in comparison to their competitors. The analysis is based on the 'Top 50 Pharma' reports, dated between 2001 and 2003. It is clear that the pharmaceutical industry is highly competitive, with Pfizer, GSK and Merck maintaining the top three positions over the last four years, while Roche has maintained its 12th ranking. Notable, however, is that GSK was not included in the list of '100 best companies to work for' which the UK *Sunday Times* publishes every year. 'Associate' HIV/Aids medicine manufacturers Boehringer Ingelheim and Aventis Pharma are, however, listed in 66th and 72nd place respectively.[10]

In view of the above information, it can be said that it was especially on the capital market that the company was confronted with demonstrable indicators of reputational damage.

DEMONSTRABLE INDICATORS OF DISCIPLINING

Leading pharmaceutical companies (including the pharmaceuticals mentioned before, such as Merck, Phizer and GSK) tend to engage in bridging strategies, as this reduces the opportunity for further attack, by explicitly explaining their actions and engaging in stakeholder dialogue to correct 'irresponsible' behaviour. GSK CEO Garnier realized after his appointment that the criticism on their account could be turned around. He made the developing countries one of his focal points by stating in his January 2001 speech:

The pharmaceutical industry today sells 80 per cent of its products to 20 per cent of the world's population. I don't want to be the CEO of the company that only caters to the rich . . . I want those medicines in the hands of many more people who need them.[11]

We have found several indicators of disciplining related to the HIV/Aids medicines and patent debate:

- GSK was one of the first companies to offer its HIV/Aids medicines to developing countries at preferential prices.
- GSK donated £116 million worth of drugs to developing countries in 2003 (Liddel *et al.*, 2004).
- Its so-called 'Positive Action' Programme, now in existence for over a decade (since 1992), is an international programme of partnership with communities affected by HIV/Aids, aiming to provide more effective education, prevention, enhanced care, support and treatment. The company supports partnerships with networks of people living with HIV/Aids, community groups, international agencies, NGOs and governments to intensify community responses to HIV/Aids. In its first ten years, 'Positive Action' has worked with partners in 49 countries. Positive Action was instrumental in the establishment of the Global Business Council in 1997, under the Chairmanship of Sir Richard Sykes, also the Chairman of Glaxo Wellcome at that time. The objective of this action programme, which is an example of public/private collaboration, was to bring about dialogue between GSK and people infected with HIV.[12] On its own, the programme could not stop the criticism against the company, which became increasingly vehement during the 1990s. When Oxfam subsequently started its campaign 'Cut the Cost' in 2001 GSK decided that it had to do more and launched a second programme 'Facing the Challenge'.
- The 'Facing the Challenge' programme focuses on three aspects: (1) specially reduced prices for least developed countries and sub-Saharan Africa; (2) investing in research on and the development of medicines for diseases that are particularly prevalent in the developing world; (3) adopting a leading role in community activities that promote effective healthcare.
- GSK uses various separate CSR-like reports available. This includes reporting on sustainability in environmental health and safety, global community partnerships, improving healthcare in the developing world, and commitment to society and the environment. A Corporate Social Responsibility Committee was established in 2001, which focuses on the social strategy of the company and reports about it in the Corporate Social Responsibility Report. The breadth of information available is indicative of GSK's long-term commitment to addressing these issues. Aids and HIV initiatives are given much attention, with 'access to medicines' being one of the company's ten Corporate Responsibility Principles, which were adopted in 2003.
- Various drug price reductions (even though under pressure by Indian exporters, pension funds and public opinion) for various sub-Saharan African countries.
- Allowing various local producers production licences for making patent-protected ARV products. In October 2001, a significant step was taken in breaking through the patent strategies of the pharmaceutical industry. GSK issued a licence to the South African company Aspen Pharmacare to manufacture the Aids inhibitors Retrovir, Epivir and Combivir. Aspen Pharmacare was given permission to produce and sell the drugs to the

South African government and non-profit organizations at a lower price. GSK has granted another three voluntary licences to Thembalamni (South Africa), Feza Pharmaceutical and Cosmos Ltd (Kenya). While Oxfam, in particular, welcomed this step, the aid organization emphasized that it was only meaningful if it signified the start of a further review of patent laws.

■ Joining in the UN's 'Accelerated Access Initiative', through which drugs are being provided at discounted prices in poor African countries. The Accelerating Access Initiative (AAI) constitutes a partnership between UNAIDS, the WHO, UNICEF, the UN Population Fund, The World Bank, and seven pharmaceutical companies including GSK and its competitors Abbott Laboratories, Boehringer Ingelheim, Bristol-Myers Squibb, Merck & Co. Inc. and Roche.

GSK has been applauded for the initiatives by being ranked in various CSR indices: GSK is currently ranked in the FTSE4 Good Global 100 index and the global DJSGI. GSK was still ranked in the top seven of the pharmaceutical sector in the DJSGI in 2004.

OUTCOME

Whose interests were acceded to?

Time and again, GSK reacted to campaigns by launching more focused initiatives (even though filing a lawsuit can be considered very much a buffering strategy). The pressure from both organizations has therefore ensured that a start was made in meeting the needs of HIV and Aids victims in developing countries. Oxfam International has indicated that there is still a long way to go before all Aids patients in the world receive equally advanced medical treatment. Most striking is that the moment that CalPERS became involved in the conflict and reputational damage became a potential reality, the price of Aids medicines was lowered within a matter of days. This underlines the strong influence of shareholders on a company whose customers are as good as dependent on it. In conclusion we can say that the interest of the stakeholders has been acceded to most looking at the GSK initiatives and price cuts

Issue resolved, case closed?

The commotion surrounding the price of HIV/Aids medicines persists. Disputes such as that of the South African Trade dispute, have arisen as a result of lack of systematic regulations concerning the issue of patent infringement in countries experiencing matters of national emergency. This has been viewed as a CSR issue – through patent policy, pharmaceutical companies are restricting access of ARV drugs to those most in need. In 1996, the 'cocktail' of Aids inhibitors cost US$10,000 per patient per year, five years later (2001) it cost US$1,100. Since 2001, more price cuts have been implemented. The last is dated May 2003; on 2 May 2003 GSK lowered the price of Combivir,[13] the most important component of the so-called combination therapy, from US$1.70 to around US$0.90 per day. With this, GSK still is not the cheapest producer in the world: the Indian Ranbaxy has a course of treatment, which has been approved by the WHO, that costs US$0.73 per day. For this reason, critics are questioning the sincerity of the initiatives of GSK and, consequently, are uncertain as to whether it amounts to more than window dressing. Accordingly, a call was made for public verification to clarify whether the company's efforts amount to more than buffing up its tarnished reputation. These have been made because it is often not clear what the duration of the initiatives is and precisely who the beneficiaries of the medicines are.

A resolution to the issue is therefore still forthcoming. While the conflict drags on, the acuteness of the clash has diminished somewhat thanks to the initiatives GSK has launched.

The first report GSK has published with reference to the latest initiative indicates that the company does not see itself able to resolve the above outlined problem surrounding prices on its own. In the report, GSK seems to favour partnerships with various organizations and governments to address the problem.

Following the issue

HIV cannot be cured yet. There are currently only preventative approaches to mitigate the spread of the virus, and its effects. In this sense, the role of pharmaceutical companies must be made clear. Antiretroviral therapies provided by the pharmaceutical companies have the ability to prolong life significantly and reduce the physical effects of the infection. However, it is important to recognize that medicine is not a solution, it is only a mitigation to the major problem (Liddell *et al.*, 2004).

Over past years, high prices of ARVs were seen as one of the main access barriers to ART in developing countries. High drug prices were a result of patents, limited volume, limited price competition, high import duties, tariffs and local taxes, high mark-ups for wholesaling, distribution and dispensing, and individual country pricing strategies (WHO, UNICEF, UNAIDS, MFS, 2002). Now, due to competition from generic manufacturers and public pressure, prices of ARVs have been reduced and donations by pharmaceutical companies increased (WHO, UNICEF, UNAIDS, MFS, 2002). Pharmaceutical companies use at the same time, differential pricing strategies, applying their 'own criteria for countries, sectors and institutions that may benefit from reduced price (or donations)' (WHO, UNICEF, UNAIDS, MFS, 2003). Although access to ART has increased during the past years, there are still enormous numbers of people in developing countries in need of access to ART. The business community as a whole (not counting the pharmaceuticals) has not yet embraced HIV/Aids as a core business issue, an increasing number of companies are now implementing comprehensive HIV workplace programmes. In some countries with sub-optimal political commitment or poor public sector health facilities, businesses implemented workplace programmes unilaterally, providing the necessary infrastructure and expertise. The goal must be to mobilize the business community to support, rather than substitute government leadership.[14]

The question that remains is whether a large-scale attack on the pharmaceutical industry is indeed sensible. History has taught us that companies that have come under fire in the public domain can fulfil the role of leader in the field of socially responsible business practice. Recent examples include the former 'pariahs' Shell and Nike. In the conflicts surrounding both companies, critics departed from their oppositional stance to engage the companies. The pharmaceutical industry, too, could fulfil such a pioneering role, but its opponents would then be required to enter into dialogue on behalf of the victims of HIV/Aids in developing countries. According to GSK, patents and other intellectual property rights play a vital role in encouraging the innovation needed to develop new treatments for many of the most serious and life-threatening diseases. If a new product could immediately be copied and sold by others, GSK would not be able to continue to fund new research. This would, according to GSK, discourage innovation and limit research into newer and better medicines and vaccines.

There are concerns that patents and the TRIPS Agreement limit access to vital medicines, such as those used to treat HIV/Aids, for people in the developing world. GSK believes that neither patents nor TRIPS are a key barrier to access to medicines in the developing world and focus on them takes attention away from the real barriers.

Chapter 18

A changing climate for a sleeping tiger?

StopExxon coalition versus ExxonMobil

In May 2001, INGOs such as Greenpeace, Friends of the Earth and People & Planet called upon US oil giant ExxonMobil to account for its negation of international environmental regulations to slow down global climate change. The perception of ExxonMobil as the number one global warming villain prompted INGOs to launch the Stop ExxonMobil Campaign. They believe that climate change will continue unabated as long as ExxonMobil controls the US policy on energy and climate change. Activists and concerned citizens in the US, Australia, UK and the rest of the world demand that ExxonMobil end its sabotage of international efforts to combat global climate change, support mandatory reductions in greenhouse gas emissions and invest in renewable energy technologies.

Table 18.1 ExxonMobil – Societal Interface Management challenges

Public ⚡ private	Profit ⚡ non-profit	Efficiency	⚡ Ethics/equity
Pollution related to extraction and use of fossil fuels as a public or private responsibility? Should companies be allowed to give donations to I politica parties? Investing in sustainable and renewable energy sources as private or public responsibility? Respect for international environmental treaties? Lack of level playing field	Who are the most important stake-holders of the company? Public as consumers, neighbours, or future generations? How can a company respond to climate change without damaging its short-term economic well-being? Renewable energy is potentially less profitable To what extent can civil society representatives be brought to court for their actions?	Competitive advantage over competitors from developing countries such as China and India. Cost of investment in developing alternative energy sources is high and it is unclear whether they can be marketed profitably It seems more efficient to further present technologies, than to invest in new technological trajectories	Care and respect for the natural environment Should oil companies take responsibility for the longer-term environmental impact of their products? Should companies mitigate the strong demand for cheap energy? Should developing countries be exempt from responsibility for global warming?

EXXONMOBIL

ExxonMobil came into being in 1998 as a result of a merger between the oil companies Mobil and Exxon. The objective of the merger was to form an effective global competitor in a volatile world economy and in an industry that was becoming increasingly competitive. ExxonMobil is the largest player in the energy business. The company operates in more than 200 countries and territories, it has approximately 88,000 employees and its net profit in 2003 was around US$21 billion with a total turnover of US$237 billion (ExxonMobil, 2003). These figures represent the largest profits ever announced in the corporate world. The company, with its headquarters in Texas US, tops the 2004 *Fortune* 500 list of companies with the highest profits. The Transnationality Index (TNI) of ExxonMobil was 62 per cent, based on 2002 figures (see Figure 18.1). ExxonMobil brands include Exxon, Mobil, Esso, On-the-Run and Speedpass. ExxonMobil comprises four businesses: Technology, Downstream, Upstream and Chemicals. Ninety per cent of ExxonMobil's petrochemical assets are in businesses that are ranked at number 1 or number 2 in the market.[1] ExxonMobil's goal is to continue to be the world's premier energy company.

STOPESSO/EXXONMOBIL COALITION: GREENPEACE, FRIENDS OF THE EARTH AND PEOPLE & PLANET

International environmental NGOs Greenpeace, Friends of the Earth and People & Planet are largely responsible for organizing the StopEsso campaign.[2] Greenpeace and Friends of the Earth are both well-known INGOs dedicated to protecting the natural environment. Greenpeace is an independent, international campaigning organization that uses non-violent, creative confrontation to expose global environmental problems and to enforce measures for a green and peaceful future. Greenpeace is dedicated to safeguarding the ability of the Earth to sustain life in all its diversity. Friends of the Earth International (FoEI) is one of the world's largest grassroots environmental networks, uniting 68 diverse national member groups and some 5,000 local activist groups throughout the world. FoEI promotes solutions that will help to create environmentally sustainable and socially just societies. People & Planet is the largest student network in the UK that campaigns to alleviate world poverty, defend human rights and protect the environment.

CONFLICT AROUND CLIMATE CHANGE/GLOBAL WARMING

Climate change issues are among the most urgent global challenges in International Business–Society Management. This international environmental issue has attracted much attention from politicians, civil society, the media and business because of its actual and potential impact. It involves issues around human-induced emissions, greenhouse gases and global warming. Our atmosphere contains naturally occurring gases such as water vapour, carbon dioxide, zone methane and nitrous oxide, which capture light reflected off the earth. Together with clouds, these gases help keep the Earth's surface warmer than would otherwise be the case. This is the so-called greenhouse effect. Human activity, such as the burning of fossil fuels and agriculture, produces carbon dioxide and other greenhouse gases. These man-made emissions lead to increases in greenhouse gases and an enhanced greenhouse effect. Fossil fuels are the greatest source of man-made greenhouse gases. The impact of this enhanced greenhouse effect on weather patterns is referred to as climate change.

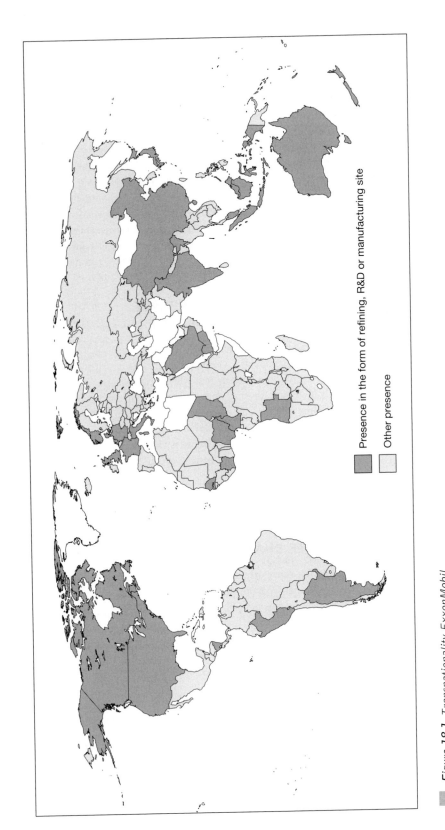

Figure 18.1 Transnationality ExxonMobil

Source: Based on SCOPE data the TNI = 62 per cent

Presence in the form of refining, R&D or manufacturing site

Other presence

HEATED INTERNATIONAL POLITICAL NEGOTIATIONS: THE KYOTO PROTOCOL

After months of agitated debate and political wrangling, thousands of international policymakers and corporate advocates travelled to the Japanese city of Kyoto to attend the UN Convention on Climate Change (UNFCC) (Rotman, 1997: 25). There, in Kyoto, on 11 December 1997, industrialized countries around the world agreed to significantly reduce the emission of environmentally destructive gases such as carbon dioxide (CO_2). This convention can be viewed as another attempt to come to an international agreement on stabilizing emissions after the failing negotiations of the 1992 Rio de Janeiro 'Earth Summit'. The Kyoto agreement is regarded as a concrete first step towards stabilizing the world's changing climate. The commitments that form the substance of this international agreement were incorporated in the so-called Kyoto Protocol. The protocol sets targets for reducing harmful emissions to below 1990 levels. The EU accepted a reduction target of 8 per cent, the US 7 per cent and Japan 6 per cent to be reached by 2012. The Kyoto Protocol, however, would only come into force once 55 countries, representing 55 per cent of the total emissions discharged in 1990, had ratified it. In other words, these countries would have to enact legislation to meet the terms of the Kyoto Protocol.

Former US President Clinton agreed on the protocol and even came up with a framework for flexible mechanisms such as emissions trading, the Clean Development Mechanism (CDM) and Joint Implementation (JI).[3] This would allow companies to achieve a reduction in emissions in cooperation with other companies or governments, either by trading emission credits or through partnership in an offset project once the protocol had been ratified. In March 2001, however, just weeks after his inauguration, President G.W. Bush announced that the US would not ratify the Kyoto Protocol. He declared it 'dead'. In July 2001, in Bonn the international community demonstrated that the protocol was still alive despite the withdrawal of the US by reaching a political agreement on the rules for its implementation. The details of the rules were finalized at the Seventh Conference of the Parties (CoP7) to the Kyoto Protocol in Marrakech, Morocco in October 2001. With the protocol ready for ratification, most countries set the deadline for September 2002, the date of the World Conference on Sustainable Development which was to be held in South Africa. Developing countries such as China, India and Brazil are exempt from any formal obligations.

Since the US withdrew from the treaty, the fate of the Kyoto Protocol rested with Russia (responsible for 17 per cent of total emissions). The US would have been pleased if Russia had rejected the Kyoto Protocol, but the EU put pressure on Russia by promising that Russia could enter future negotiations with the EU on becoming a member of the WTO. The EU had ratified the treaty and was in danger of becoming one of the sole supporters of the protocol, together with Japan. In April 2004, the advisor to Russian president Putin, Andrei Illarionov, likened the expected effect of the Kyoto Protocol on the world economy to an 'international Auschwitz'. Hopes of Russia ratifying the treaty were all but crushed. If Russia refrained from ratifying the protocol it would have been an immense disappointment for all who endorsed it. The Russian vote was crucial for the treaty to come into effect. A minimum of 55 country signatures was needed from the states responsible for 55 per cent of greenhouse gas emissions in 1990. On 22 October 2004 the Russian Douma finally gave in and ratified the Kyoto Protocol despite doubts about its impact on the country's economy. With this, the treaty officially came into effect for 128 countries on 16 February 2005 – albeit with a seven-year delay and without the participation of the US. Russian Foreign Minister Fedotov admitted that Russia did not want to be blamed for the failure of the protocol if it didn't sign. Putin and Russia have even been referred to as the 'saviours' of the Kyoto Protocol. Representatives of Greenpeace, FoEI and the UNEP were extremely pleased that this milestone had been reached even though it is only a first step towards possible effective control over the global warming matter. Some argue that it will be fairly easy for Russia to reach the Kyoto targets given that this country's greenhouse gas emissions have decreased dramatically (approximately 30 per cent) since the benchmark year 1990. It may therefore even be profitable given that surplus emission rights can be traded on the market.

US AND EXXONMOBIL AS 'EVIL' ICONS OF CLIMATE CHANGE

The debate over climate change and the role of (international) business fundamentally centres on two issues. One relates to the scientific evidence that climate change can be attributed to human activity, particularly the burning of fossil fuels. The other concerns the question whether developed countries should also be legally bound to a reduction in the use of fossil fuels and greenhouse gas emissions. A fifth of the world's population live in the developed world but they are responsible for three-fifths of the world's greenhouse gas emissions. The US alone produces 25 per cent of emissions worldwide, and a third of the developed world's greenhouse gases despite being inhabited by only 5 per cent of the world's population.[4, 5] It is said that the poorest people of the poorest countries in the world are likely to suffer most from climate change due to their dependence on farming for their livelihood and because their governments lack the resources to protect them from droughts, hurricanes and floods. The US is the largest polluter in the world and the pressure on the US government and its corporations is increasing.

ExxonMobil is one of the world's largest oil companies. It has profited much from the extraction of fossil fuels and has been a strong opponent to measures to slow down climate change. It is one of the last to persist in challenging the scientific consensus on climate change. European competitors BP and Shell have already taken steps to address the challenges posed by climate change. ExxonMobil's refusal to accept the link between its business and global warming comes right from the top of the company. In 2002, Lee Raymond, Chairman and CEO of ExxonMobil said: 'We in ExxonMobil do not believe that the science required to establish this linkage between fossil fuels and warming has been demonstrated – and many scientists agree.'[6] In the week before US President George Bush was inaugurated, ExxonMobil placed an advertisement in a leading US newspaper stating, 'the unrealistic and economically damaging Kyoto process needs to be rethought'. The month before President Bush announced his rejection of Kyoto, ExxonMobil again placed adverts in major US newspapers. Entitled 'Moving past Kyoto . . .', the first advert claimed that at the top of the list of 'fundamental flaws' of the Kyoto Protocol 'is the growing recognition that most governments cannot meet the politically chosen targets without resorting to economy-wrecking measures'. ExxonMobil went on to say that 'Kyoto was too much too soon'[7] and that 'the Kyoto Protocol approach would be a serious mistake'.[8] This standpoint, which many argue is also explicitly aimed at influencing government policy, was met with outrage and prompted the numerous (and almost endless) anti-ExxonMobil campaigns.

Environmental NGOs do not merely put pressure on national governments, they also target individual companies. According to various INGOs such as Greenpeace and FoEI, ExxonMobil can be held partly responsible and accountable for lobbying against the Kyoto Protocol. According to the NGOs, there is no other company that has done as much as ExxonMobil to sabotage the Kyoto negotiations, misinform US policymakers and confuse the US public. They regard ExxonMobil as one of the main architects of President Bush's energy policy and responsible for the decision to reject the treaty. In fact, the President's plan includes everything

Figure 18.2 Stop ESSO campaign. Downloadable stickers from Greenpeace, Friends of the Earth and People & Planet

ExxonMobil's CEO Lee Raymond had been calling for, largely through the lobby group Global Climate Coalition. The GCC was (it has been dissolved as 'the industry voice on climate change has served its purpose by contributing to a new national approach to global warming') a powerful organization of trade associations established in 1989 to coordinate business participation in the international policy debate on the issue of climate change and global warming. According to activists, GCC attempted to 'frustrate' international negotiations on climate change. The coalition also opposed Senate ratification of the Kyoto Protocol on the grounds that it would lead to such stringent targets for lowering greenhouse gas emissions that economic growth in the US would be severely hampered and energy prices for consumers would skyrocket. The GCC opposed the treaty also because it does not require the largest developing countries to reduce their emissions. GCC members collectively represented more than 6 million businesses, companies and corporations in virtually every US business sector, agriculture and forestry, including electric utilities, railroads, transportation, manufacturing, small businesses, mining, oil and coal.[9] Previous GCC members, such as Ford, General Motors, Texaco, Shell and BP left the Coalition as the scientific consensus on climate change became stronger (e.g. Kolk and Levy, 2001: 502). Exxon and the then separate Mobil both remained members until the group was disbanded. ExxonMobil also took part in a US$6 million American Petroleum Institute (API) public relations campaign that challenged the scientific consensus on climate change. The API's campaign plan said: 'victory will be achieved when those promoting the Kyoto treaty on the basis of extant science appear to be out of touch with reality'.[10]

323

WHY 'STOP EXXONMOBIL CAMPAIGNS'?

One of the largest StopEsso/ExxonMobil campaigns was launched on 8 May 2001 after the US Government rejected the ratification of the Kyoto Protocol.[11] Activists and concerned citizens across the EU, US and world demanded, among other things, that ExxonMobil:

- Stop denying the scientific link between climate change and the emission of greenhouse gases. *The Economist* has also commented on ExxonMobil's position (December 2004): 'ExxonMobil, the biggest (oil company), is also the world's most powerful climate change sceptic. If the world's biggest purveyor of fossil fuels ever accepts openly that global warming is real, that may turn out to be more important to the planet than any Kyoto deal.'
- Support the ratification and implementation of the Kyoto Protocol as other energy firms do, and call upon the US government to do the same.
- Invest in renewable energy. According to ExxonMobil, the development of cleaner, alternative energy sources is still far in the future. In 1997, CEO Lee Raymond, offered the following explanation: 'With no readily available economic alternatives on the horizon, fossil fuels will continue to supply most of the world's energy needs for the foreseeable future.'[12]
- Assess its potential liability for current and future damage caused by climate change and set up a fund to meet claims that may in future be made against it.[13]
- Use its extreme wealth to put measures in place to limit its (direct and indirect) contribution to global warming.
- End its sabotage of international efforts to address global warming and support the reduction in greenhouse gas emissions. Esso/ExxonMobil was one of the main financial contributors to George Bush's election campaign. As soon as George Bush was elected as president, he announced that the US would pull out of international agreements to slow down global warming – the exact stance Esso/ExxonMobil had been promoting (see also next section).[14] The Greenpeace report, 'Decade of Dirty Tricks' cites 25 tricks Exxon used in the last ten years to sabotage the Kyoto Protocol.

USING POCKETBOOKS TO INFLUENCE PUBLIC POLICY?

The Washington-based finance reform group, the Center for Public Integrity, claims that the US oil industry has contributed US$67 million to federal political candidates and has spent another US$381 million on lobbying since 1998.[15] The report indicates that 73 per cent of the industry's political campaign contributions have gone to Republican Party candidates, mostly House of Representatives members from oil-rich states such as Texas (home of President Bush and ExxonMobil headquarters). The largest single recipient of oil industry donations is President George Bush, who has allegedly received more than US$1.7 million in contributions from the oil industry since 1998. Although the report does not accuse the industry of any wrongdoing, it does point out that oil companies have taken advantage of the current political climate to advance their interests at the expense of environmental concerns. The report states that ExxonMobil tops spending on lobbying in the industry at US$55 million. According to the report, ChevronTexaco, Marathon Oil, BP Amoco and Royal Dutch/Shell each spent more than US$25 million on lobbying. In its 'Standards of business conduct' the corporation states that it refrains from making any contributions to political parties, except as permitted by law (Standards of business conduct, 2004).[16] On this issue, ExxonMobil spokespeople reason that, 'it's not surprising that as the largest company in the US, we're asked by officials to comment on substantive issues, it is part of the American political system that interest groups and companies can participate in public discussions'.[17]

EXXONMOBIL'S POSITION ON THE KYOTO PROTOCOL AND THE SCIENCE OF CLIMATE CHANGE

At the annual shareholders' meeting of 31 May 2001, CEO Lee Raymond explained his position on Kyoto as follows:

> We see the Kyoto Protocol as unworkable, unfair, ineffective and potentially damaging to other vital economic and national interests. The debate over Kyoto has distracted policymakers for too long. I am encouraged to see more constructive discussions focusing on more realistic approaches. That said, the overall issue remains to be addressed. We think the best path forward is through attention to longer-range technological approaches and economically justified voluntary actions, as well as a strong program of climate science.[18]

Activists argue that the opposition to the Kyoto Protocol amounts to a lack of concern about climate change. According to the energy corporation's management, this is simply not the case. ExxonMobil does not believe Kyoto is the right approach. It fears that it would impose an enormous economic burden on the developed world while achieving precious little in terms of slowing down climate change. The reason for this is that there is an increasing demand for cheap energy, most of which will be consumed by developing nations in order to grow their economies (e.g. India and China, the fastest growing and consuming economies today). These countries, however, have no comparable obligations to reduce their emissions. In the eyes of ExxonMobil, the protocol is an unworkable and inappropriate public policy response to a complex issue. If implemented, the protocol will not achieve its goal of significantly reducing greenhouse gas emissions. It will however have negative repercussions for the economies of both the developed and developing world.[19] ExxonMobil seems cynical about the cynics (Alsop, 2004: 255). In the EU and the US, this stance brought about fierce protests and blockades of petrol stations, but also shareholder resolutions during shareholder meetings. One of the numerous actions undertaken by Greenpeace and Friends of the Earth in 2004 was the projection of 40-foot images of storms and floods onto the building where the company held its annual shareholders' meeting. One of the captions read 'Global warming fuelled by ExxonMobil'.

In early October 2004, ExxonMobil admitted that its greenhouse gas emissions had increased by 2 per cent in the past year to 135.6 million tonnes. The corporation said it did not have targets for reducing CO_2 emissions, but that it was working hard on 'energy efficiency' gains (the *Guardian*, 7 October, 2004). According to the *Guardian* newspaper, this means that the company generates more than twice the amount of CO_2 emissions an entire country the size of Norway produces, and nearly 50 per cent more than rival BP despite only slightly higher oil and gas production levels. The admission comes as the energy giant faces a consumer boycott in Europe over its hard-line stance on climate change and follows a report released by Friends of the Earth this year. The report claims that in the past 120 years – since the company was founded in 1882 as part of Standard Oil – ExxonMobil's operations and products have generated about 5 per cent of the global increase in CO_2 emissions.

DEMONSTRABLE INDICATORS OF REPUTATIONAL DAMAGE

General

Due to the frequent mentioning of ExxonMobil in rankings and lists, we include a paragraph on 'general' indicators of reputational damage in this chapter. ExxonMobil's stance on climate change has ensured its reputation as one of the icons of environmentally irresponsible companies. The many articles in newspapers, books, academic journals and on the worldwide web, which criticize the company, testify to this widespread perception. A poll conducted by the *Wall Street Journal* in 2001 showed that nearly half of the people familiar with ExxonMobil give it a poor rating for environmental responsibility (*Wall Street Journal*, 2 July 2001.) The company's CEO, Lee Raymond, has already been called 'the face of Global Warming' and has been awarded a Greenwashing Award by NGOs at the 2002 Johannesburg Summit.[20] Besides this, various reputation studies show the negative impact of the company's stance on the Kyoto Protocol and the Exxon Valdez oil spill of 1989 (it has been excluded from the list of America's Most Admired Companies since 1989).[21] In 2001, the year the US rejected the ratification of the Kyoto treaty, ExxonMobil came second among US companies with the worst reputation (Fombrun and van Riel, 2004). In the GMAC ranking (*Fortune* list) ExxonMobil fell from 6th to 110th position due to the Exxon Valdez spill. Since then, it has climbed back to 10th position in 2001 (cf. van de Wateringen, 2005). In 2003 and 2004 the company won the 32nd place on the *Fortune* GMAC list. Nevertheless, it still holds second place on the list of America's Most Admired Companies in 2003 and 2004, leaving Royal Dutch Shell behind. The *Financial Times* reputation ranking shows that in the period 2001–02 ExxonMobil lost its leading position vis-à-vis European oil giants such as Shell and BP. The company's stance on global warming has affected its reputation in Europe more than it has in the US. In a PriceWaterhouseCoopers poll of the World's Most Admired Companies in 2004, ExxonMobil plummeted from 16th (2003) to 42nd position (2004).[22] The November 2004 issue of British *Ethical Corporation Magazine* states that 'the company [ExxonMobil] seems to go out of its way to earn its reputation as Public enemy No. 1'.[23] Researchers have found out that key stakeholders in Europe tend to engage in more collaborative negotiations, resulting in a more consensual system (e.g. Kruck *et al.*, 1999; Kolk and Levy, 2004).

Consumer market

On the European consumer market, ExxonMobil had to deal with fierce consumer boycotts in countries such as the UK and Luxembourg where its petrol stations were blocked and protest campaigns by environmental groups such as Greenpeace and Friends of the Earth were staged. Even petrol stations throughout Australia and Canada were blockaded at times.

The continued pressure from NGOs did have an impact on the consumer market. In a report of 17 September 2002, Deutsche Bank pointed out that the worldwide interest in climate change is mounting.[24] According to the report, ExxonMobil's negation of this important trend could have a detrimental effect on the company in future. The profits of other large oil companies such as Shell, BP, ChevronTexaco grew steadily in the period between 2001 and 2004 whereas ExxonMobil's turnover and profits fluctuated a lot in the same period. An important business unit to examine in this regard is the company's 'downstream' operations or retail. Both US and non-US earnings fell by two-thirds in 2002. The total net income and turnover of all operations showed a steady decline between 2000 and 2002 (both showed an annual decline of approximately 10–15 per cent). The year 2003, however, was spectacular with both turnover (total and downstream) and profit rising considerably (ExxonMobil, 2003). Never before have a profit of US$21.5 billion (a 90 per cent increase compared to 2002) and turnover of US$246.7 billion been recorded by a privately owned corporation. Whether the decline in the period 2000–02 has anything to do with the Kyoto issue remains unclear. The company itself cited oil prices and international pressure on profit margins as important contributing factors. Of course, it can be held that the negative assertions in the media caused some reputational damage on the consumer market, especially the numerous boycotts at petrol stations. Clear and strong indicators to substantiate this claim, however, are absent.

Capital market

In examining reputational damage on the capital market, we focus on various types of indicators such as the response of institutional investors and analysts, and the ExxonMobil share price on the US stock exchange. Some investors, mainly in the US, regard ExxonMobil as an excellent company to invest in due to its focus on shareholder interests. However, more and more of Exxon's shareholders are interested in the issue of climate change and are urging the management to take measures. Here are some indicators of investors who question ExxonMobil's stance on the issue of climate change:

- In May 2003, a major US shareholder, Institutional Shareholder Services (ISS), encouraged shareholders to vote in favour of two proposals on climate change at the AGM of ExxonMobil. This move made ISS one of the first mainstream groups to apply pressure on a company board with respect to an issue of this kind. One proposal called upon the company to report risks to its operations, finances and reputation arising from climate change, and to explain how it mitigates those risks. The other proposal requested an explanation from the company regarding its approach to renewable energy. ExxonMobil rejected the motions, arguing that they are unnecessary in the face of an already clearly articulated policy. ISS disagreed, saying that the proposals are intended to provide shareholders with key information that would enable them to assess future financial risks.[25]
- In July 2003, the UK-based Social Investment Forum criticized ExxonMobil – together with other American companies such as TXU and General Electric – for being among the least proactive companies concerning the issue of climate change (*FT*, 24 August 2003). This point of criticism is backed by research conducted by CERES where the three aforementioned companies finished at the bottom of the Climate Change Governance Checklist. European competitors such as BP and Royal/Dutch Shell were lauded by CERES (Cogan, 2003: 19).
- According to CalPERS (pension fund, holding US$166 billion in funds in 2004), the Kyoto Protocol is one of the most influential drivers of environmental regulations. It has already had a considerable impact on international environmental regulations. In Europe and Japan, strict emission standards combined with strong incentive programmes have contributed to the growth in technology opportunities.[26]
- In 2003, the UK-based consultancy firm Claros (whose clients include fund managers and pension funds, corporations, policymakers and NGOs) identified ExxonMobil as the only oil giant that is refusing to acknowledge climate change risks, which signifies a major internal governance failure. The risks of investing in ExxonMobil are discussed in the Claros report 'Sleeping Tiger, Hidden Liabilities'.[27] Claros conducts research on behalf of investors on the potential impact of social and environmental issues in different sectors. ExxonMobil has been rated as the most environmentally irresponsible of the largest four oil companies in the world. The report was influential in attaining over 20 per cent of investors' support for shareholder resolutions on renewable energy and climate change. The report mentioned in the previous section (by Deutsche Bank in 2002) can also be considered damaging, the Exxon stock price lost almost 4 per cent on the NYSE. According to the report, ExxonMobil's negation of this important trend could have a detrimental effect on the company in future. Figure 18.3 shows the stock-price movement.
- As soon as ExxonMobil's stance concerning climate change became known, a group of shareholders combined their efforts to launch the so-called 'Campaign ExxonMobil'.

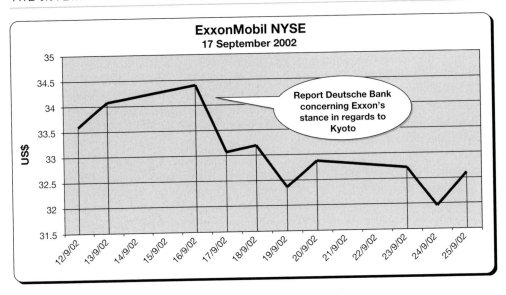

Figure 18.3 *ExxonMobil's stock-price fluctuation*

This is a shareholder campaign aimed at convincing ExxonMobil to adopt a responsible position on climate change. Campaign ExxonMobil was founded by religious and environmental groups who collaborate with institutional investors, corporate governance activists and financial analysts to highlight the financial risks of ExxonMobil's current position. According to the ExxonMobil shareholders they are looking for leadership, but all they are getting is confrontation. There is only one company in the US that has more shareholder resolutions on its agenda than ExxonMobil.[28]

- Proxy measures were filed with ExxonMobil at the annual shareholders' meeting in May 2004. The shareholder filers, collectively representing over US$250 billion in shares, include the New York State pension funds, a foundation, socially responsible investment firms, and a number of major religious pension funds associated with the Interfaith Center on Corporate Responsibility (ICCR), a coalition of 275 religious institutional investors that helped coordinate the filings. The resolution filings were partly coordinated by CERES, a coalition of investors and environmental groups, that has been active in promoting investor awareness of climate change risks. However ExxonMobil successfully challenged the resolution at the Securities and Exchange Commission (SEC) after putting out a report, which it claimed, and investors disputed, documents the company's plans on the matter.[29]
- Investment firm LENS Investment and Ram Trust Services has demanded Lee Raymond's resignation. According to LENS/RAM CEO, Robert Monk, the negative publicity around the oil firm's stance on climate change initiatives had resulted in lower share prices compared to ExxonMobil's competitors.[30]

Labour market

In order to establish whether ExxonMobil has been affected on the labour market we consider a few events that have occurred over the past few years.

- As part of the StopEsso campaign, People & Planet has targeted the company's campus presentations to inform potential recruits about ExxonMobil's stance on climate change. For the last two years (2002–03), People & Planet student groups have attended most of ExxonMobil's recruitment presentations in the UK to hand out leaflets and 'Esso sucks' lollypops and to ask them to reconsider working for such an unethical company. At Oxford Brookes, for example, Esso representatives were interrupted 20 minutes into their speech by the arrival of a 'tiger' who explained that he was retiring as Exxon's mascot due to the company's earth-trashing behaviour. According to a source inside a leading university's careers service department, ExxonMobil decided not to tour university campuses at all in 2003. ExxonMobil's major competitors, Shell and BP, continued to tour UK universities as usual.[31] ExxonMobil employees have, according to People & Planet, contacted the campaign to voice their concerns about the company's stance.

- The Paper, Allied-industrial, Chemical and Energy Workers international union (PACE) wrote a letter to Exxon CEO Lee Raymond on 12 April 2003, urging him to use his company's resources to stop global warming instead of pursuing frivolous lawsuits against Greenpeace for holding protests at the Texas headquarters. PACE union represents over 8,000 ExxonMobil employees.[32]

- ExxonMobil has been excluded from the '*Fortune* 100 best employers' since 1997.[33] The continuous pressure from NGOs could, perhaps, have had an impact on the labour market.

Whether these above-mentioned protests have resulted in demonstrable indicators of reputational damage on the labour market is unclear, but very plausible.

DEMONSTRABLE INDICATORS OF DISCIPLINING

In contrast to its more proactive and cooperative competitors BP, Royal Dutch Shell and Texaco, ExxonMobil still opposes the Kyoto treaty. BP and Shell support a significant reduction in CO_2 emissions (including internal trading schemes) and investment in renewable energy, and Texaco appears to be moving in the same direction (see Figure 18.4). Although it still rejects generally accepted views on many issues, a shift can nevertheless be discerned in the energy giant's strategy.[34] According to a model developed by Gladwin and Walter (1980), the company can be seen as assertively resistant while moving towards a more cooperative compliance strategy (Levy and Kolk, 2002: 289). The differences between the various companies can be explained in terms of home-country, firm-specific, industry-specific and issue-specific factors (Kolk and Levy, 2004: 178).

- ExxonMobil claims that it has put a number of measures in place to promote conservation and energy efficiency, and to advance the use of alternative energy sources. For example, it continues to build cogeneration facilities at its refineries that can save up to 30 per cent of energy normally used. Exxon also continues its research and development of environmentally friendly technology such as fuel-cell powered vehicles, clean coal technology for power generation and technology for the separation and storage of CO_2 emissions. It also supports scientific research into the Earth's climate and potential climate change. Since November 2002, ExxonMobil has been a large sponsor of the GCEP, the Global Climate & Energy Project which was launched at Stanford University.[35] Characteristic of this project is the collaboration between scientists and large companies. The objective of the project is to research alternative sources of energy and

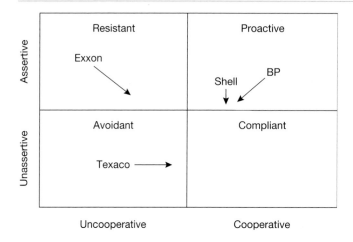

Figure 18.4 Responses to climate change by oil multinationals

Source: Levy and Kolk (2002: 289 figure 1)

Note: Positions as of 1998: arrows indicate subsequent movement.

the reduction of greenhouse gas emissions. Having donated US$100 million to develop more efficient technologies that reduce harmful emissions, it seems that ExxonMobil would like to contribute to a healthier environment. However, due to bad experiences with investments in renewable technologies in the past[36] the company will not pursue it. With respect to environmental research, ExxonMobil claims that it is a leading private sector donator. The company funds climate research programmes at top institutions such as the Massachusetts Institute of Technology, Carnegie-Mellon University, Bermuda Biological Station Research, Stanford Energy Modelling Forum and the International Energy Agency Greenhouse Gas Research and Development Program.

- ExxonMobil has been publishing a Corporate Citizenship Report since 2002 (see also Chapter 10). In the report, ExxonMobil expresses its belief that good corporate citizenship means helping to meet the world's growing demand for energy in an economically, environmentally and socially responsible manner.
- CEO Lee Raymond has said that the company will support mandatory reporting on emissions as an essential precondition to policies designed to reduce the impact of global warming. This statement was made in February 2003 after complaints from investors and consumers.[37] At the shareholders' meeting of 29 May 2003, 21 per cent of ExxonMobil's shareholders supported a motion that requires ExxonMobil to publish a report to communicate its views on alternative energy sources.

ExxonMobil almost has a trademark 'no-apologies' attitude which can be described as one of buffering. Nevertheless, the company seems to have become less vociferous in its opposition to emission controls in the political arena (Levy and Kolk, 2002: 297). The fact that major protest actions were still being staged against the company in December 2004 is an indication that the conflict is far from over. Apart from sponsoring the GCEP, ExxonMobil has shown little real disciplining of its conduct in response to the international criticism its stance on climate change has evoked. ExxonMobil's approach to the confrontation with Greenpeace is a typical example of the American CSR regime, in which the concrete CSR practice follows litigation. In October 2004, Greenpeace signed a court agreement that prevents its supporters from staging protests against ExxonMobil anywhere in the US for a duration of seven years. Breaches will bring the automic risk of fines and imprisonment to Greenpeace activists. Greenpeace agreed to the settlement in part to avoid an indefinite ban. According to Greenpeace, the case coincides with actions by the US government that such direct actions against companies are unacceptable in the present anti-terrorist climate (Van de Wateringen, 2005: 1; *FT*, 25 October 2004). This case is a good example of the moderate effect of the reputation mechanism.

OUTCOME

Whose interests were met?

The NGOs Greenpeace, FoEI and People & Planet have not (yet) succeeded in their goal. The NGOs intend to continue their campaign against ExxonMobil for as long as it refuses to change its stance.

ExxonMobil has not departed from its view that it is time to move beyond Kyoto and focus on technology research and development, economically sensible voluntary actions and an international approach that addresses the entire world and its population and not the fraction covered by Kyoto.[38]

> We do not believe Kyoto is the right approach. We fear it would impose dramatic economic costs in the developed world, while doing little to achieve its goal of addressing climate change since developing nations, which require most of the world's increased needs for energy to grow their economies, have no comparable commitments. Our investment criteria emphasize investment in areas where we have both relevant and leading-edge technology. Renewables, such as solar and wind power, do not meet either of these criteria. In our view, current renewable technologies do not offer near-term promise for profitable investment relative to attractive opportunities that we see in our core business. Therefore, we have chosen not to pursue investments in renewable energy options. We believe that companies interested in current renewable technologies should invest if they believe profit opportunities exist. However, we would note that other major energy companies have in the past year announced asset write-downs – amounting to a total of US$172 million – for investments in solar energy. This is a telling indicator of the merits of our approach.[39]

Issue resolved, case closed?

The issues surrounding ExxonMobil's position on climate change and the Kyoto treaty are far from resolved. ExxonMobil has become an icon of corporate *ir*responsibility and the focus of heated debates largely as a result of its stand on the Kyoto Protocol. ExxonMobil seems to have become the owner of the issue of climate change. An owner in denial, though. ExxonMobil became the main target of this campaign because of its repeated attempts to undermine the scientific consensus that has been reached on climate change and its active resistance to attempts to reduce carbon dioxide emissions. As the campaigners often state, the tiger seems to be 'deaf and in denial'. A report prepared by Friends of the Earth, titled 'Exxon's Climate Footprint' and presented on 29 January 2004, reveals that oil giant ExxonMobil and its predecessors' operations and products have generated between 4.7 per cent and 5.3 per cent of the carbon dioxide emissions produced in the past 120 years by humans across the globe.[40]

331

Lawyers in the US and UK are looking for ways to sue oil companies for the part they played in accelerating climate change much in the same way that tobacco companies have been sued for the damage their products have inflicted on consumers' health (e.g. lung cancer). Greenpeace regards ExxonMobil as the prime candidate for a lawsuit.[41] The deteriorating environmental performance of ExxonMobil is 'highly dangerous', according to the Climate Justice Programme, a group of NGOs and lawyers that support legal action against environmental polluters.[42]

ExxonMobil has been making an effort to communicate its views more effectively, including those on the environment which, some Exxon officials say, have been misinterpreted and misrepresented. The company has launched a communications campaign in an attempt to shift the focus from climate change to its plan for managing the environmental impact of fossil fuels. Despite what appears to be an attempt to reach out to stakeholders, Exxon has not departed from its controversial views. The company is still not willing to accept conclusive scientific proof of the existence of climate change, nor will it concede that CO_2 could be largely responsible.[43] In its most recent effort to put a check on protest actions, Exxon has secured a consent judgement against the Greenpeace group for entering the lobby and climbing on the roof of its Irving, Texas, headquarters. The ruling bans Greenpeace supporters from Exxon corporate property, filling stations and any event sponsored by the company or involving company officers throughout the US for the next seven years. The consent judgement, believed to be the first of its kind involving a US company and an activist group, prevents Greenpeace from staging protests on Exxon's property or filling stations, or at any event sponsored by the company or involving company officers.[44]

The aftermath

In January 2005, the European Union Greenhouse Gas Emission Trading Scheme (EU ETS) was launched as the largest multi-country, multi-sector greenhouse gas emission trading scheme in the world. The scheme is based on Directive 2003/87/EC, which came into force on 25 October 2003.[45] European governments have assigned rights to a certain amount of CO_2 emissions to 5,000 European corporations in order to reach the 2012 Kyoto target. Those that exceed their limit will have to buy credit from parties with a surplus. The EU has been a leading legislator on climate change and has taken a leadership role in international negotiations. NGOs have been urging the EU to remain in this role and to demonstrate the political will that exists to bring about change.[46] A voluntary initiative has also been launched in the US. In 2003, companies such as Ford, International Paper, DuPont and BP America set up the Chicago Climate Exchange, an emission trading system that is comparable to that of the EU (Lawrence et al., 2005: 221). Climate change, the Kyoto Protocol and the role of (international) business all form part of a complex global issue. Some scientists, business leaders and politicians are of the opinion that the Kyoto Protocol and its implications and rules are not the solution to the problem. In their view, Kyoto is an unworkable and inappropriate public policy response to an important, but complex issue. They argue that the implementation of the Kyoto Protocol would, in fact, do little to reduce greenhouse gas emissions while doing substantial economic harm to both developed and developing countries. Some academics, however, argue that European and Japanese companies will have a significant competitive advantage over US companies once they implement emission-controlling technologies and invest in renewable energy due to efficiency and market opportunities.[47] Others argue that US, Chinese and Indian companies will have an advantage over Europe and Japan given that they won't have to invest in measures to reduce emissions. International scepticism about the effectiveness of the protocol also remains since greenhouse gas emissions have increased dramatically since 1990, rendering the target of a reduction of more than 5 per cent an even greater challenge. In February 2005, the Kyoto Protocol came into effect in the wake of Russia's ratification of the treaty at the end of 2004.

A new question about the Kyoto Protocol was raised at the UN Climate Change Post-Kyoto Conference in Buenos Aires in December 2004: what is to follow after 2012? Several countries are reluctant to remain signatory to the treaty after 2012 if the US doesn't ratify it soon. Italy, for example, has called for ending the Kyoto Protocol in 2012, preferring voluntary agreements that would entice the US, China and India to tackle climate change.[48] Proceeding with the Kyoto Protocol in its present form would be meaningless without the participation of some of the world's biggest polluters. The first phase of the Protocol ends in 2012, after which it becomes unthinkable to go ahead without the US, China and India. Italy fears that European countries and their companies will eventually be forced to bear the burden of those who oppose the treaty. British Prime Minister Tony Blair, who has lead the group of eight (G8) nations in 2005 at Gleneagles, Scotland, has put climate change at the top of the agenda and hopes to bring the US back into the fold. The US is waiting for changes in the rules regarding participation of developing countries such as China, Brazil and India (responsible for around 40 per cent of total CO_2 emissions). The US government prefers a short-term solution to the long-term strategy of the Kyoto treaty. Will the US rethink its stance on the Kyoto Protocol now that it has isolated itself from the international community? If the US ratifies the treaty, the ExxonMobil Tiger will have to rise from its slumber and abide by the law. Only the future can tell what will happen. This International Business–Society challenge is to be continued.

Chapter 19

Lessons in reputation

CHAPTER CONTENTS

19.1 INTRODUCTION: VERIFYING THE REPUTATION CLAIM

It should be possible to establish the limits of social responsibility by means of the reputation mechanism. That is, in any event, one of the most important arguments of especially corporations and governments (Chapter 11). Can this claim be substantiated? In particular when a conflict flares up between an organization and critical stakeholders over corporate responsibilities, it can be ascertained whether the claim is founded. The reputation mechanism is supposed to have a corrective effect which manifests in demonstrable damage to consumer, capital and/or labour markets. Depending on the importance of each of these markets to the continuity of a company, the general reputation is supposed to play a very significant role. But does this effect apply to all firms equally?

This chapter draws together the concrete experiences of 18 major conflicts over the responsibilities of international companies. Five of the most telling cases since the beginning of the 1990s, were presented in the previous chapters. The website accompanying this book includes 13 additional cases (www.ib-sm.org). This chapter considers when, why and to what extent the reputation mechanism has had a *demonstrable*, *plausible* or *no* corrective effect in these 18 international conflicts (19.2). Correction is often accompanied by disciplining through codes of conduct, labelling and the like. Which disciplinary measures did companies take at the time or after the conflict (19.3)? Who emerged as the bargaining 'winners' of the issue-conflict: the entrepreneurs or the public interest organization and did it bring a solution to the societal issue closer to hand (19.4)?

19.2 CORRECTION IN PRACTICE

Stakeholder reactions to an issue on consumer, capital and labour markets signal that the reputation mechanism has been set in motion. Table 19.1 summarizes by case whether and to what extent there is evidence of demonstrable damage per market segment. The first conclusion in any case is that none of the companies was untouched by the reputation effect of the NGO campaigns. In more than two-thirds of the conflicts, demonstrable reputation damage was inflicted on at least one market segment. In the remaining conflicts reputation damage was plausible in at least one market segment.

Table 19.1 Reputation damage in CSR conflicts

Organization	Market reputation			Reputational damage
	Consumers	Capital	Labour	
C&A	o	–	–	Plausible
Schiphol Airport	–	oo	–	Demonstrable/slight
PepsiCo	ooo	o	n.a.	Demonstrable/very great
Heineken	o	oo	–	Demonstrable
Nike	o	oo	–	Demonstrable
Shell – Brent Spar	ooo	oo	oo	Demonstrable/very great
Shell – Nigeria	oo	oo	oo	Demonstrable/great
Adidas	o	oo	n.a.	Demonstrable
Cargill	o	–	–	Plausible/slight
GlaxoSmithKline	o	oo	n.a.	Demonstrable
IHC Caland	–	oo	–	Demonstrable/slight
ExxonMobil	o	o	o	Plausible
IKEA	o	–	–	Plausible
ABN Amro	o	oo	o	Demonstrable/great
Triumph	oo	–	o	Demonstrable
Nutreco	o	oo	o	Demonstrable/great
Unilever	o	–	o	Plausible
McDonald's	o	oo	–	Demonstrable/slight
ooo	2	0	0	
oo	2	11	2	
o	12	2	5	
–	2	5	8	
n.a.	0	0	3	

ooo = great and clearly demonstrable direct damage due to conflict.
oo = demonstrable damage.
o = plausible damage, but not clearly demonstrable.
– = neither clear, nor demonstrable direct damage due to conflict.
n.a. = non-available.

The corrective effect is the least demonstrable on the labour market. The relation between the labour market and reputation is less direct than it is on other markets. The corrective effect is stronger both on the consumer and capital markets, but the reputation effects on these markets are relatively unrelated to each other. Only in two strongly related cases did the company (Shell) experience demonstrable reputation damage *both* to their capital and consumer markets. In 11 of the cases a demonstrable effect was identified on capital markets while this applied to consumer markets in only four of the cases. In two cases, great damage to consumer markets was sustained. Capital markets, however, are also fickle. The reputation effect fades away quicker. In no instance did companies really suffer from a great reputation effect on the capital market.

Consumer market correction: indirect, via large stakeholders, lags long

In at least four cases, demonstrable evidence could be found that consumers and/or customers temporarily revoked their confidence in the company. The affair surrounding the intended sinking of the Brent Spar has cost Shell revenue losses of between 20 and 50 per cent in certain parts of Germany, while the 'Nigeria' affair cost Shell a prestigious sponsoring contract with the Royal Geographical Society in addition to petroleum contracts in Canada and the US. PepsiCo (faced with protests against its presence in Burma) lost contracts worth millions one after the other in the US and Canada, its restaurants were blockaded, and at a given moment revenues even declined by 85 per cent. On the same issue, lingerie manufacturer Triumph were threatened with the loss of consumer markets through boycotts organized by its trade organization and its largest customer (VendexKBB).

Twelve other companies have experienced plausible problems on consumer markets as a result of conflicts. Heineken suffered some reputation damage to important markets such as the Netherlands, the US and Denmark, while it lost a significant Asian market share due to its departure from Burma, which was immediately filled by competitors. Nutreco, confronted with an alleged presence of dioxine in its salmons, experienced great problems on its consumer markets due to the dioxin problem in general. Cargill experienced problems on its European consumer markets due to GM, but hardly any as a result of the conflict started by NGOs. Companies that were confronted with protests against the bad labour conditions in their international supply chains were affected differently. Nike had to watch as its revenues came under great pressure on the home market and also lost a few sponsoring contracts at important universities. It is difficult for consumers to reconcile toddlers' ballparks (IKEA), footballs (Adidas) and children's clothing (C&A) with the alleged use of child labour in countries of production.

Schiphol Airport and IHC Caland sustained no reputation damage to their consumer markets. The pressure of the environmental movement in the case of Schiphol was directed at the construction of a fifth runway and other environmental impacts and not at consumers. Consumers also do not have a commercial relationship with Schiphol, but with the airline companies. IHC Caland is a business-to-business company in the oil-rig industry and has a limited number of customers. That IHC maintained its position towards public opinion organizations actually strengthened its position on the consumer market where it was regarded as a reliable contracting partner. Both IHC and Schiphol operate in a market sector that is strongly influenced by government. Both companies could plead that their activities were supported by government in the sense that their actions were not prohibited.

Positioning of companies in the supply chain: b2b versus b2c

All organizations that suffered demonstrable reputation damage to consumer markets belong to the category of *corporate branders* (Chapter 11). For Shell, PepsiCo, ExxonMobil, Triumph,

McDonald's, Adidas and Nike there is no, or hardly any, distinction between the company name and product name. The reputation damage that was sustained had a direct impact on all products that are sold under the company logo. This effect is strengthened by the fact that all these companies operate in the b2c (*business-to-consumer*) segment. Corporate brand companies that operate in the b2b (*business-to-business*) segment, on the other hand, did not suffer any reputation damage on their consumer markets. Companies such as Unilever and GlaxoSmithKline that employ a unit branding strategy in the b2c market are also much less vulnerable to reputation damage to consumer markets. Consumers are not that quick to connect Magnum ice creams with a conflict over mercury thermometers involving Unilever, or GlaxoSmithKline toothpaste to HIV/Aids medicines and accompanying court cases. The icon value of the company is limited and with it the company is less susceptible to reputational damage to its consumer market as a whole. The same applies to Nutreco which only had the 'hard luck' that dioxin poisoning could occur in all segments of its differentiated food range.

Positioning and lifestyle

Within the corporate branding strategy, however, differences in reputational vulnerability can be observed between companies. Some companies attach great value to the image and the lifestyle they project through their branding. Twelve companies (PepsiCo, Nike, Triumph, IKEA, C&A, McDonald's, Heineken, Adidas and ABN Amro – and with a bit of goodwill, also Shell, ExxonMobil and GlaxoSmithKline) are known for advertising campaigns that are aimed at a lifestyle – complete with a philosophy of life and key target group. The more the reputation of the product is imbued with a specific lifestyle and matching image, the more vulnerable the company seems to reputation damage, and the quicker the company also resigns itself to the wishes of the public opinion organizations. Nike ('just do it') and PepsiCo ('the choice of a new generation') are the most extreme examples of this. Moreover, these companies are extremely vulnerable because they are heavily dependent on other players due to their distribution strategy.[1] In the analysed conflicts, Heineken and Adidas ran less of a risk of sustaining reputation damage because the lifestyle they propagate is less pronounced and, in this sense, they were less easy to tackle with media campaigns. All four companies started off with a buffering strategy with respect to NGOs; thus it was not caused by a difference in attitude during negotiations.

The reason why some companies are less vulnerable despite an image grounded in a lifestyle, is related to a shop formula and not individual products. Companies such as C&A, IKEA, ABN Amro and McDonald's, as distributors/distributive trades with their own 'shop' formula, appear to be less vulnerable to reputation damage to their consumer markets. Given that there are no influential primary stakeholders between the customer and company, the company itself can decide how to engage with a potential reputation problem on consumer markets. Companies that have no control over distribution will have to consult with their distributors at regular intervals.

Characteristic features of customers with a reputation of their own

In cases where demonstrable reputation damage was clearly sustained, the most influential stakeholders appeared to be both NGO and customer (with great purchasing power). These stakeholders do not only have their own reputation to uphold – according to their statutes – but also represent an important market segment. In the case of Nike and PepsiCo, large reputable universities such as Colgate, Harvard and Stanford exercised a great deal of influence. In the case of Triumph, the Norwegian Olympic Team withdrew its support and a knock-on effect threatened to spread to other Olympic organizations. In the case of Adidas, the relationship with international football unions (UEFA and FIFA) was at stake.

The relation is even more direct if the company is dependent on the reputation of distributors where a limited number of players dominate. Wholesaler VendexKBB forced the management of Triumph to reconsider by means of negative publicity campaigns in its own chain stores and the trade organization BodyFashion called the management of Triumph to account. The GMO dossier (Cargill) only really became important when a few large chain stores in England openly declared themselves against genetically modified soy in their food products. These influential stakeholders all fear sustaining reputation damage *themselves*.

Small clients: optimizing consumers or critical citizens?

In the minds (perception) of the individual consumer, reputation is especially important where food safety is concerned. Also in the case of lifestyle products – where the customer must pay significantly more for the reputation and the image of the company – the perception of individual consumers is important. If the image aims at a lower market segment, reputation effects on consumer markets decline sharply. Reputation effects in consumer markets of chains such as C&A, IKEA or McDonald's can be described as indirect and moderate. If small customers in these cases consider the reputation of a company, it is often only a form of protest. Such protest, for instance in the form of cards and letters has, according to a few interviewed companies (e.g. IKEA and Triumph), hardly led to products and services being passed over. Words are not turned into deeds straight away. Visitors to IKEA, confronted with the protest action against the alleged use of child labour in its carpet and rug production, filled in many cards, but did not expressly ignore the carpets. Many inquiries as to the origin of the carpets have, however, been made in different branches. Customers of Triumph and VendexKBB have similarly neglected to turn words into deeds. Consumers who make purchasing decisions largely on the basis of price are less inclined to translate the role of critical citizen into purchasing habits. Other consumers do not have the choice to boycott a company due to their large dependence on the product, such as HIV/Aids medication.

'The' consumer market is a complex reputation factor. In general, consumer markets only rise in importance in cases where companies are sufficiently dependent upon them, or where the reputation in one national market can be related to other major markets. The spread-effect for Shell of its bad reputation on a lead market in Germany to other European countries, really made a difference. The spread-effect increases in cases of small institutional and stakeholder distance (Chapter 13). In other cases, the spread of consumer markets over many countries that represent different CSR regimes, weakened the reputation mechanism. The Shell Brent Spar case, for instance, also involved Exxon (the equal partner in the oil platform). But Exxon was left almost unaffected by the Brent Spar affairs because its domestic stakeholders were much less affected by the case in this 'far away' location. There are specific market segments and specific stakeholders that fulfil an important role in the correction of companies through great purchasing power or concern about their own reputations. The lagging effect of a bad reputation is also considerable on consumer markets. Large, significant customers do not forget that easily. As the distance between companies and the consumer market increases, companies become less sensitive to the reputation mechanism. This is the case with unit branding and b2b companies.

Capital market correction: direct, heavily fluctuating and fast receding effect

Demonstrable reputation damage was sustained on capital markets in the case of 11 CSR conflicts. Sometimes temporary and sometimes prolonged deviations arose with respect to individual company trends and with respect to the most important corresponding stock exchange indices (AEX/Euronext and/or Dow Jones). It remains, incidentally, exceptionally difficult to isolate reputation effects on capital markets.[2] Conclusions have to be drawn carefully. Where companies suffered a reputation effect only on their capital market (IHC and Schiphol), it appears not to have been a matter of manipulation. In practice, reputation damage only truly occurs in combination with the two other relations, the consumer market and the labour market. Reputation effects on an entire trade sector – as a result of a dioxin crisis or the HIV/Aids price and patent discussion – are often greater than with reference to a single, concrete issue. Even greater is the effect of profit warnings, take-over announcements, reorganizations and other issues that are directly related to the domain of the market.

In the majority of cases, the relation between the issue life cycle and the reaction on the stock market was quite direct: if a company is accused of socially *ir*responsible conduct, the share price declines; if it tries to address the criticism through disciplinary measures, the share price rises. With the acceptance of contracts in Burma, the share price of IHC Caland saw a 20 per cent decline in one month. The public accusations against Adidas in connection with forced labour in China brought about a ten per cent fall in share price. The shares of McDonald's fell four per cent the moment a lawsuit was announced in connection with the chips conflict and rose slightly after the company apologized. The BBC broadcast about the alleged presence of dioxin in salmon farming resulted in a 14 per cent decline of Nutreco's share price. Rectification by the BBC was accompanied by slight recovery of the share price. When Unilever decided to close its mercury factory, its share price rose by a few per cent. The decision of PepsiCo to withdraw from Burma resulted in stock market gains of 11 per cent. When Adidas' listing on the Dow Jones Sustainability Group Index was extended – two years after the conflict – the share price rose by three per cent. When Unilever announced that the mercury factory in India was to be shut down, its share price rose by a few per cent. The publication of the CSR report of sportswear manufacturer Nike was rewarded with stock market gains of four per cent and the announcement of PepsiCo's withdrawal from Burma resulted in a share price increase of 11 per cent.

Average share price fluctuations directly after publicity surrounding a conflict amount to five to ten per cent (DHV, 2002: 24). The decline in share price value as a result of negative publicity around an issue is generally greater than share price increases as a result of the company attitude. By that time, damage to reputation – even when the claim is unfounded – has already been done. Reputation damage on consumer markets sticks longer than on capital markets. When some public interest organizations called on consumers in 1996 to boycott Shell in response to Nigeria, this boycott seemed relatively inefficient, as some customers were still boycotting Shell due to its involvement in the South African apartheid regime – an issue that dates back to the 1970s. Investors, however, had forgotten about that issue a long time ago.

Large stakeholders with a vulnerable reputation of their own

Small investors influence reputation effects on the capital market more than on the consumer market. To a certain extent, 'the' capital market also functions as reputation factor. Large stakeholders, of course, do play an important role, but the market for small investors mitigates their influence. Investment withdrawals by relatively large capital providers leave their mark. In the case of Shell, the World Bank withdrew as financier. In the case of IHC Caland, long-term investors ABP, ING, ABN Amro and the government (export subsidy) changed tack and withdrew their investments. But because their financial involvement appeared small, the company was still able to ignore these measures. In the case of other companies, institutional investors played a significant role in the background in negotiations on disciplinary measures that ultimately limited the reputation damage to financial markets. Stakeholders on the capital market who *themselves* have reputations to uphold respond most visibly and have the most lasting effect on company policy.

Independence from capital markets

Companies in the market sector cannot readily position themselves as independent of their customers. On capital markets, companies do have this option. All international family-owned businesses (IKEA, C&A, Cargill and Triumph) that have managed to maintain their independence of capital markets have – by definition – never confronted reputation damage to the stock exchanges. Family businesses do, however, borrow money from banks and other financial institutions. Nevertheless, family businesses experience fewer problems with these capital providers at the time of conflict. First, these capital providers need not fear for their reputations because the transaction is not publicized. In the case of share ownership by banks, this is often the case. Second, the private capital of family businesses is usually so great that the relative importance of external capital providers – and their influence – will never be great. The four family businesses are the only companies that did not sustain any demonstrable reputation damage to capital markets as a result of a CSR conflict.

Repetition effect, different composition of shareholders?

In the cases surrounding IHC and Shell Nigeria something remarkable occurred. The negative effect ebbed away the more frequently the company was brought in connection with the matter. IHC twice accepted a commission in Burma. The share price reacted many times stronger to the first assignment (decline of 29 per cent in six weeks) than it did to the second. In the case of Shell in Nigeria, the share price responded positively to the defensive handling of the matter by management. It could be that a company such as Shell, having been in the news so often in such a short time – but also because of its eventual position in the earlier conflict surrounding the Brent Spar – had built up a *reservoir of goodwill*. A different line of reasoning is also possible. The first sharp decline in the share price could have been the result of more 'ethically sensitive' investors selling their shares. These could subsequently have been bought by less ethically inclined or principled investors. It is not uncommon for the shareholder composition to change during a conflict. Ethical shareholders can exercise their 'exit' option only once, thereafter this instrument is spent. As they get mixed up in controversial issues more often and for prolonged periods, a company could retain fewer principled investors. A remark by the CEO of IHC Caland illustrates this effect:

> Losing shakeholders is not a problem long as there are others that will fill their place. So long as we do not violate human rights, we will conclude such a contract relating to Burma/Myanmar once again. God knows why most of the oil and gas can be found in undemocratic countries.
>
> (*FD*, 27 May 2000)

IHC seemed unimpressed by the departure of shareholders such as ABP, ING and ABN Amro. Eventually IHC's board decided not to take on any more contracts with Burmese relations either directly or indirectly.

In the case of Heineken, Shell Brent Spar and ABN Amro, a repetition effect also occurred but this time with a stronger negative correction. Whereas investors first responded negatively to Heineken going through with the construction of a brewery in Burma, when the company announced its withdrawal from Burma, the punishment was even more manifest (drop in share price of about 10 per cent). When, after long deliberation period – in which a gradual rise in share value could be noted – Shell eventually announced that it would not sink the Brent Spar, the share price declined once again (by five per cent). When ABN Amro announced that it would, indeed, inform its suppliers and relations of its position on blood diamonds, the share price likewise fell. This repetition effect could point towards a second punishment by ethical investors who, in light of the fact that the company yielded to societal pressure, see it as an admission of involvement or guilt. This second response could also point towards a phenomenon mentioned earlier: namely that the composition of the investor population has changed, is less 'ethical' and therefore that it responds negatively to company leadership yielding to societal pressure.

In most cases, the drop in share value as a result of a repeated conflict proved of short duration. A changed composition of the investor population in any event renders the share price less sensitive to future CSR conflicts. The tobacco and weapons industries have a very long history of CSR conflicts, but still enjoy high returns on the stock exchange.

Labour market: very indirect and difficult to demonstrate

The least direct is the relation between a reputation conflict and the reaction on the labour market. In a few cases, including Shell Brent Spar, Shell Nigeria, ExxonMobil and Triumph, the company itself reported unrest among personnel. Here, the trade union movement plays an important role. As soon as they join a campaign as NGO, problems of loyalty arise among employees: trade union member, employee or critical consumer? In practice, it appears that the role of employee usually prevails. In individual cases, employees draw conclusions from the CSR conflict, but there is little indication that this is a collective effect.

Three types of companies can be distinguished:

1   *Hollow corporations*: have very few employees of their own and outsource a lot to dependent suppliers in far-off countries (Nike and Adidas). Direct employees are paid exceptionally well, and are not unionized which makes it relatively easy to attract new employees for core positions. The reputation effect therefore does not occur. In countries to which these companies outsource, the 'labour reserve army' is so big that people can easily be replaced. In the countries of production the reputation effect on the labour market is even smaller.

2   *Flexible distributors*: such as McDonald's, IKEA and C&A have heavily standardized working environments, a very small group of core employees around which many flexible – temporary – employees are grouped. All three companies oppose trade unions, but do propagate a family bond with direct employees. The reputation effect is clearly less effective in the case of flexible employees than in the case of permanent staff. Therefore, these companies have not suffered any notable reputation damage to the labour market.

3   *Vertically integrated companies*: manufacturing companies such as Shell, ExxonMobil, Unilever, GlaxoSmithKline, Nutreco, but also service providers such as ABN Amro, have a large part of their international value chain in-house and therefore manage 'human resources' differently. They are clearly more vulnerable to reputation damage. Bad working conditions can also be passed on to suppliers less easily. A significant group of employees can be discerned that cannot be managed via flexible contracts and who joined the company not for a job but a career. Trade unions are generally well represented. In many of these companies a demonstrable reputation effect on the labour market could be discerned or was plausible. For these companies, the reputation effect is of greater importance, especially with regard to potential employees.

Additional costly consequences

A soiled image costs a lot of time and money to polish. As well as damage to reputation capital, conflicts generate many other costs. A selection from the cases shows the variety of possible effects:

- a stop to export subsidies from the government (IHC, in 2000, 21 million euro);
- loss of a consumer market and with it market share (Heineken, PepsiCo and Triumph in Burma);
- repair and dismantling costs (Unilever, Shell Brent Spar and Shell Nigeria);
- divestment costs (Heineken, PepsiCo, Triumph and Shell Nigeria);
- shipping delays (Cargill);
- postponed investments (Schiphol);
- lower pricing (GlaxoSmithKline);
- government fines and possible legal costs (Schiphol, McDonald's and Shell Nigeria);
- destruction of property (McDonald's, Triumph and Shell Brent Spar);
- more chaotic shareholder meetings, for instance due to shareholder resolutions (most firms);
- poor reputation in parts of scientific community (ExxonMobil, GlaxoSmithKline).

19.3 DISCIPLINING AND SELF-REGULATION IN PRACTICE

Certainly in a conflict, societal groupings will demand clarification from companies. If the answer of the company is inadequate, there is the risk that the conflict will persist. Table 19.2 inventories the variety of significant self-regulation and disciplinary measures that companies have taken in the period during or shortly after the conflict, so as to ease the pressure and settle the conflict. Self-regulation, disciplining and standardization refer to a standard for conduct a company imposes on itself or measures it takes in areas where legislation is absent or insufficient (Hemphill, 1992). Sometimes, the conflict accelerates the implementation of measures that have already been planned; sometimes it is clear that measures are new.

In half of the cases there is evidence of significant disciplining. In one case (Cargill), there is no evidence of disciplining at all, in another case (IHC Caland), of a very moderate and defensive form of disciplining. In the case of Schiphol, ExxonMobil, Nike, Adidas and Shell Nigeria the companies largely continued doing what they used to do and there is only indirect evidence of any disciplining. The conflict, therefore, has not truly been settled through disciplining and the chances are great that stakeholders will return to the CSR issue at a given moment. In nine cases, there is evidence of significant disciplining as a result of the conflict. In six of the cases, there is evidence even of the ultimate form of disciplining, namely, the closing down of a factory or withdrawal from the intended activity: Heineken, PepsiCo and Triumph in Burma, Unilever in India, ABN Amro in Africa and Shell which called off its initial decision to sink the Brent Spar. In each case, it became clear that things could only take a turn for the worse. Unilever, however, was already planning on closing the factory; thus, in that case, the conflict served as accelerator and it is therefore a lesser form of disciplining.

In two-thirds of the cases, the conflict led to the development or refinement of a code of conduct. A considerable number of companies (about 40 per cent) saw the conflict as a reason to (re)formulate CSR policy and implement measures to enhance transparency towards stakeholders. Increasingly, companies are setting down and explicating norms and values with respect to societal, social and ecological issues in, for instance, a code of conduct or reports. Companies are creating websites for CSR issues and are adopting international reporting

Table 19.2 Demonstrable disciplining

Case	
C&A*	• Code of conduct since 1996 (revised in 1998) • Monitoring organization SOCAM since 1996 • Discontinued 80 contracts in 1997 and sent 800 letters of warning to suppliers and importers regarding compliance with C&A code • Since end 1999 contribution to career advice centre for former child labourers in India
Schiphol*	• Code of conduct implemented since 1993 • Schiphol fund to compensate for noise pollution • ISO-4001 certificate • Sustainability report according to GRI guidelines • Extensive information on environmental norms, noise nuisance and measurement and the issue surrounding the fifth runway
PepsiCo*	• Divestment in Burma
Heineken*	• Divestment in Burma • Code of conduct
Nike	• Code of conduct (refined a number of times, and more stringent than ILO guidelines) • Subscribes to CERES principles • Suppliers must also adopt code • Collaborating in research of Global Alliance on conditions in production facilities • More supervisors and special personnel department for monitoring • *Social Responsibility Report* with the assistance of GRI guidelines • Extensive communication on issues on website
Shell Brent Spar	• Decided not to sink Brent Spar • Revision of code of conduct (subscribes to ILO and OECD) • Termination of hundreds of contracts with suppliers due to non-compliance • Annual *Shell Report* including environmental issues with the help of GRI guidelines • Separate issue-debates websites • Appointment of Social Responsibility Committee to monitor top management • Development of Sustainable Development Management Framework (SDMF)
Shell Nigeria*	• Application for clemency to Nigerian government • Revision of security policy with the assistance of UN documents • Refinement of code of conduct of 1976 (SGBS) • Demand on suppliers to endorse code in writing • Reference to Universal Human Rights code of conduct • Conciliatory plan Ogoniland since May 1996 • Separate issue discussion websites • Establishment of local community – and environmental projects (125 million euros in 1997) • Annual *Shell Report* including development of Nigeria issue
Adidas*	• Code of conduct (*Standards of Engagement*) and stricter monitoring • Appointment of monitoring team consisting of 30 people • Termination of contract with suppliers due to lack of compliance with code • Support of local education project in Pakistan in collaboration with NGO • Social and Environmental reports since 2000
Cargill*	• The company continues to deliver mixed soybeans

Table 19.2 continued

Case	
GlaxoSmith Kline	• Set up of 'Facing the Challenges' (next to the 'Positive Action' programme) • Lower pricing medicines for various sub-Saharan African countries • Publication of CSR Report • Set up CSR Committee to focus on social activities and strategies • Allowing various local producers production licences for making patent-protected ARV products
IHC*	• Code of conduct (revised once, however no solution to issue) • Freezing of order portfolio Burma (no settlement)
ExxonMobil	• Increased sponsoring for research on efficient technologies that reduce harmful emissions • Supports mandatory reporting on emissions as an essential precondition to policies designed to reduce the impact of global warming • Publication of (reactive) corporate citizenship report; support for mandatory reporting on emissions
IKEA*	• Signing of agreement with ILO • Tightening of controls • Code of conduct including external verification and reference to UN Convention on the Rights of the Child (art. 32.1) • Requirement of suppliers to endorse code in writing • Annual reporting on performance • Education project in India in collaboration with Unicef (US$500,000) • Support to CREDA, a local NGO in India, in education project • Cooperating with WHO and Unicef on vaccination project in India • Communication on issues with consumers via IKEA guide (the 'why' pages)
ABN Amro*	• Participation in investigating report on own conduct • Code of conduct and development Business Principles • Closing down of unverifiable purchasing offices in Africa by supplier • Active participation in the Kimberley Process against illegal trade in diamonds • Endorsement of UN resolutions on the trade of diamonds • Participation in World Diamond Council (WDC) • Letter to banks requesting cooperation • Member World Business Council for Sustainable Development (WBCSD) • Resolution for international certification and monitoring system for regulating trade in rough diamonds • CSR report according to GRI guidelines
Triumph	• Divestment Burma • Social services for employees in Burma • NGOs invited to explain issue at General Meeting • Refinement of code of conduct taking ILO and Global Compact guidelines into account
Nutreco*	• Complete cooperation with BBC research on conditions on production • Heightened attention to tracing and food safety, including new tracing system • Appointment *Corporate Food Safety Director* • Award winning sustainability report in line with GRI guidelines • Participation in World Business Council for Sustainable Development (WBCSD) • Project launched entitled 'Aquaculture and Society 2005'. This project focuses on a more sustainable way of fish breeding in cooperation with diverse stakeholders

Table 19.2 continued

Case	
Unilever*	• Closing down mercury factory • Alternative jobs for employees • Guidelines drawn up for clean-up • Revision on code of conduct 2002 • Annual CSR report
McDonald's*	• Self-appointment investigation • Public apology • Revision of labelling policy, extensive information on ingredients on websites and in restaurants • A *Dietary Practice/Vegetarian Advisory Panel* has been set up for advice on guidelines and restrictions • McDonald's has, in the wake of a lawsuit, donated US$10 million to, among others, Hindu and vegetarian groupings that are active in charity and educational projects • *Social Responsibility Report* with the assistance of GRI guidelines

* These cases can be found and downloaded at www.ib-sm.org.

standards on a large scale. In this regard, the GRI reporting standard in particular is embraced, which further underlines the trend towards greater international standardization and coordination (Chapter 12). In one-third of the cases, an explicit promise was made to monitor or improve compliance with (self-) regulatory measures. However, few companies actually instituted external auditing. Increasingly, companies such as Adidas, IKEA, C&A, Shell and Nike also require suppliers to sign the code of conduct with the conclusion of a contract. Hollow and flexible companies such as Adidas, IKEA, Nike and C&A therefore also use codes of conduct as a means to external disciplining. What prevails – CSR or control – is far from clear (see van Tulder and Kolk, 2001).

19.4 LESSONS IN CORRECTION AND DISCIPLINING

Companies have essentially four types of CSR and ICR strategies at their disposal: inactive, reactive/defensive; active and pro/interactive. These strategies represent specific combinations of disciplinary and corrective measures. Figure 19.1 positions the 18 companies in the framework of Chapter 11 (Figure 11.3). In the event of significant reputation damage, no company can allow itself the luxury of refraining from developing any disciplining initiatives. Only if the reputation damage is nil (Cargill) or modest (IHC Caland, ExxonMobil, Schiphol), can a company persist in its inactive or reactive attitude towards CSR. With this approach, they come closest to the ideal image of Friedman's capitalist company that concerns itself exclusively with 'its own affairs'. Apart from that, Friedman also envisioned a very different ideal corporation in his theoretical models: that is, a company that experiences strong competition from other companies and which serves markets that consist of essentially rational consumers. Instead, we find two companies in the 'Friedman' category that are entangled in oligopolistic competition in the b2b market and that seldom see eye to eye with individual consumers.

Companies that have not experienced any reputation damage, but strictly disciplined themselves nonetheless and entered into dialogue with stakeholders in advance of the conflict, are few and far between in practice and could, in any event, not be found in Part III. The companies that faced the threat of sustaining significant reputation damage, but adopted a reactive

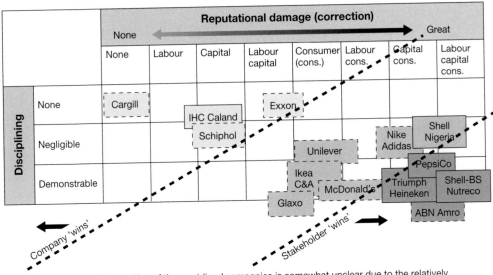

* The position of the semi-lined companies is somewhat unclear due to the relatively weak measurable indicators of reputational effects on the specific market.

Figure 19.1 Correction and disciplining: who wins?

and defensive stance (Nike, GlaxoSmithKline and Adidas), had to discipline themselves during the course of the conflict. Unilever and Schiphol have developed an active strategy. In the other cases, there is evidence of an interactive strategy, usually triggered by a (threatening) conflict with a public interest organization.

Winners and losers

Whose interests prevailed in settling the conflict? In four cases companies remained relatively insensitive to civil society campaigns. In the case of Cargill, IHC Caland, ExxonMobil and Schiphol Airport there is limited evidence of reputation damage, in particular on the consumer markets, which was accompanied by minor forms of disciplining. Three of the four winners are heavily oriented towards the b2b market. Cargill and IHC are operating exclusively on the b2b market. Schiphol, for the most part, operates as a b2b company. Disciplinary measures either have not, or have not clearly been, established. With respect to the call for withdrawal from Burma, only b2b company IHC refused to budge. In all cases, the company retained its policy and emerged as (virtual) winner from the struggle. As yet, public interest organizations have got the short end of the stick.

On the other hand, in at least six cases policy was modified to such an extent that the wishes of stakeholders on the CSR issue were largely complied with. This settled the issue. The reputation mechanism can be viewed as effective and the stakeholder emerges as (virtual) winner from the battle. This is always accompanied by demonstrable or likely reputation damage both to capital and consumer markets. Disciplining culminated in a divestment decision in four cases. The company leadership of Heineken, PepsiCo, Triumph and Shell (Brent Spar) were – for very diverse reasons – strongly opposed to this option and have therefore suffered clear defeat. ABN Amro has explicitly withdrawn from trade in 'conflict diamonds' even though it is not clear whether there was direct involvement or not. Nutreco came off worst, even when, at closer examination, it appeared that the accusation was false.

In eight cases, it is however significantly less clear whose interests prevailed. Unilever did, indeed, take the decision to close their mercury factory, but this decision had been taken long before and was only accelerated by the stakeholder campaign. In the case of Shell (Nigeria), stakeholder opinion indeed appears to have been important, but there is less evidence of disciplining and it is also not clear whether the matter has been resolved or not. Nike and Adidas conceded to the interests of stakeholders in part, especially due to the strong negative response on capital markets. Because they were not corrected in their consumer markets, the effect will probably remain minor. IKEA, C&A and McDonald's also present a mixed picture. In the analysis of Part III, it was noted that in these cases stakeholder interests were 'slightly' or 'partly' represented. In the case of McDonald's it was explicitly concluded that it was 'unclear' which interests were being represented. In all these cases, an unclear reputation effect (although classified as 'plausible') appears to have occurred on consumer markets. In this group of companies, no clear winners or losers emerge. It is also most likely that the issue will be appearing on the agenda again, certainly if the organizations have failed to take clear disciplinary measures – as in the case of Nike, Adidas, and Shell in Nigeria.

No significant relation has been identified between the nationality of companies, the susceptibility to reputation damage and the winner of the struggle. The same applies to the relation between being listed on the stock exchange and winning or losing a case. Both listed and unlisted companies can be found among the winners and losers. This confirms the assertion that reputation on capital markets is less relevant to winning or losing than it is in the case of consumer markets.

Negotiation dynamics

Does correcting lead to disciplining or does disciplining lead to correcting? The first scenario reflects the 'normal' reputation mechanism. There is a 'financial penalty' on lagging behind. The second scenario reflects the 'spectre' of Socially Responsible Corporations: by being at the forefront of self-regulation, the media and public interest groups readily address them on new issues. Their reputation is an easy target. Likewise, there is also a 'financial penalty' on being a frontrunner.

The distinction between a 'bridging' and 'buffering' attitude during the negotiation process can be useful in answering the above question of whether correcting leads to disciplining or vice versa. In Chapter 11, it was asserted that the choice for one of the two strategies depends on the strategic importance of the issue and the assessment of stakeholder legitimacy and power. A distinction can be drawn between a first and second reaction. Figure 19.2 categorizes companies by their attitude during the negotiation process. Companies that lag behind on CSR issues, or operate in an institutional context that prompts reactive behaviour, necessarily start off with a 'buffering' attitude. All US companies in the cases discussed, first adopted a buffering attitude. Companies that are truly at the forefront with respect to a CSR issue, or operate in a more cooperative bargaining context, such as the European companies, adopt a 'bridging' attitude as first reaction.

From buffering to . . .

. . . **buffering.** The reputation mechanism does not always work with b2b companies. This has already been concluded, but it is illustrated clearly once more by the attitude during negotiations. The two b2b companies were the only companies that could permit themselves a buffering attitude both in the first and second reaction, without it leading to any real damage. As yet, these companies have managed to safeguard their interests without dialogue. Schiphol,

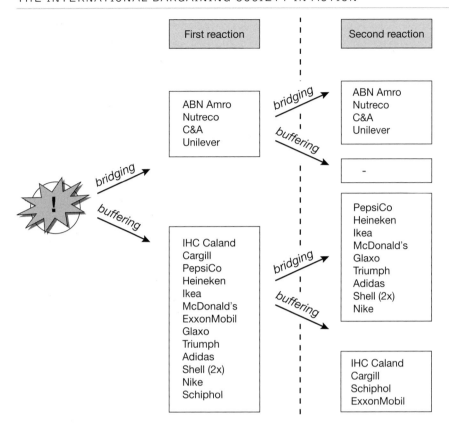

Figure 19.2 *Bridging and buffering in rounds of negotiation*

too, essentially maintained a buffering attitude towards the public interest groups that opposed its strategy. It will have succeeded if all legal means open to protesters are eventually eliminated via the judiciary. A persistent buffering strategy can especially be found with US companies.

. . . bridging. The companies that first employed buffering techniques and subsequently proceeded to bridging activities follow the classic pattern of first correction and threatening sanctions, after which disciplining leads to more positive stakeholder reactions. In all five cases of divestment in which stakeholders emerged as the unequivocal winner, a buffering–bridging trajectory was followed. After an initial dismissive attitude, there is thus no guarantee that a bridging attitude will actually be rewarded. In four cases, extensive reputation damage was inflicted also in the second instance (Shell Brent Spar and PepsiCo). In all cases, the organizations first denied the legitimacy of the complaints. PepsiCo and Shell stated that governments did not disapprove of their activities and/or that entrepreneurs should not adopt the role of legislator. Only once reputation damage had become very significant – in all cases especially on the consumer market – did 'bridging' initiatives take off. That was, in fact, too late and the damage already done.

Triumph and Heineken at first also dismissed the NGO campaigns, but they never put the legitimacy of these campaigns up for fundamental discussion. They adopted a more nuanced position – remaining in Burma was said to prevent worse things from happening – an argument which can even be founded ethically. When NGOs would not accept this argument, the companies complied. This succession of relatively nuanced and interactive steps led to far more understanding than in the previous four cases, as a result of which these cases followed Heineken and Triumph for a much shorter period. With their withdrawal from Burma, Heineken and Triumph rid themselves of a concrete stumbling block, while Shell and PepsiCo are still confronted with a more fundamental problem – namely, their relationship with governments in general.

The switch from a buffering to a bridging attitude has, in three companies (IKEA, Adidas and Nike), led to a milder attitude of public interest organizations and to one 'undecided' issue. In all cases, the issue concerns working conditions, which is more complex and is enacted on the profit/non-profit interface, which apparently gives cause for greater cooperation from public interest organizations, as they are also partly the 'issue-owner'.

From bridging to . . .

. . . **buffering.** No entrepreneur has really turned back from a bridging attitude at the beginning of a conflict. Reputation damage would most likely be insurmountable if an entrepreneur were to recoil into a more defensive attitude.

. . . **bridging.** Despite the fact that issues can be introduced by external stakeholders quite suddenly, ABN Amro,[3] Nutreco, C&A and Unilever, almost directly from the start of the conflict, tried to build bridges and entered into dialogue with stakeholders. Unilever and C&A were rewarded with not too much damage to their reputation.

The dialogue approach of both ABN Amro and Nutreco neatly represent the collaborative (neo-corporatist) CSR praxis in continental European countries, but could not avert significant reputation damage to both companies. Both cases (dioxin in fish, and war) represent classic crisis management issues and it is unavoidable that societal organizations will, in the first instance, correct companies via the reputation mechanism. In both cases, the bridging attitude adopted at the ouset of the conflict ensured that the conflict was brief and that it was eventually also settled relatively unproblematically. Nutreco could relatively easily obtain amendment in regard to the contested BBC documentary, especially since it cooperated in making the documentary right from the start.

Companies that adopt an open attitude from the outset and show the intention and willingness to settle the issue in joint consultation find themselves in the spotlight significantly less frequently, extensively and intensely. A closed and indifferent attitude intensifies a conflict. Stakeholders react to it immediately. The attitude that is adopted after the first allegations determines the atmosphere throughout the conflict.

Interface Management on the interface of profit/non-profit and public/private

Issues need to have an impact on the relationship between an entrepreneur as manufacturer and citizens as consumers; otherwise the reputation mechanism does not work. The analysed issue conflicts show, however, that issues on the profit/non-profit interface give rise to less significant conflicts than issues on the private/public interface. They also take longer to be settled effectively. The role of NGOs, in particular, could be responsible for this. NGOs that focus on public/private issues are generally *single-issue* NGOs. In the area of the environment Greenpeace and Friends of the Earth, for example, drive the reputation mechanism; in the area of human rights it is Amnesty International. NGOs fill the institutional vacuum that has presented itself in the relation between the market and the state, but their campaigns also aim

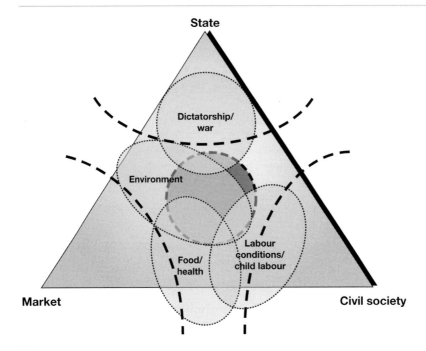

Figure 19.3 *Clustered issues on the interfaces*

to return responsibility either to government or companies. They, themselves, cannot resolve a dictatorship, make torture disappear or counteract environmental problems. On the interface of the state and the market, it therefore appears to be easier to simplify issues and to call the players in question to account on rather clear-cut roles. If negative consequences for consumers can be demonstrated, but the implications for their individual purchasing behaviour remain relatively limited, the effectiveness of the campaigns increases.

On the profit/non-profit interface, the issues are generally no less complex or less subject to over-simplification (child labour), but fewer single-issue NGOs operate here. The trade union movement, the Clean Clothes Campaign or FIFA cannot be classified simply as single-issue NGOs. In the conflict, responsibility can less readily be placed with governments and/or companies. Stakeholders are confronted with diverse roles – critical citizen, employer, calculating customer, family member, fellow human – which does make addressing an issue more complex. The issue loses its neutrality and the likelihood of settling it without complications declines strongly. The cases deal with four large clusters of issues: dictatorship/war (Burma, Nigeria), environment, food/health, and labour rights and working conditions. These clusters can be arranged on the public–private and profit–non-profit interfaces (Figure 19.3).

Strongest reputation effect: private/public interface

- *Dictatorship/war*: The Burma and Nigeria issues are most expressly enacted on the public/private interface. Most companies also invoke government responsibility in regard to this issue. If international organizations and national governments refrain from taking steps not only to condemn a dictatorial regime, but also to call an official boycott, why would companies take the lead? Most NGOs, however, assert that companies must shoulder their responsibilities specifically *because* governments do not or cannot respond adequately. The most important argument of NGOs in this is that the legitimate representatives of the population demand it. Of the four companies in the Burma case, there are three that met the demands of stakeholders. Only one b2b company appeared to be unmoved by civil society representatives (IHC). In the case of Shell in Nigeria the company eventually complied with the request of NGOs – on behalf of the Ogoni people – although it did not completely withdraw from Nigeria. The position in the international supply chain appeared to be more important than the issue. The ABN Amro case exhibited a similar dynamic.

■ *Environment*: Also in the four cases in the environmental cluster (Shell BS, Schiphol, ExxonMobil and Unilever), the position in the international supply chain determines the degree of sensitivity to the issue. The more recognizable a product, the more sensitive one is to reputation damage. This was the case least of all for Schiphol and most of all for Shell. Entrepreneurs employ the same arguments as in the other two clusters: they are behaving well when they are not doing anything wrong (reactive CSR argument), but stakeholders point out company responsibilities on behalf of individual consumers and petition for a more (pro)active strategy. The fonder the relationship between company and government – as in the case of Schiphol as undisputed transport hub of the Netherlands – the more difficult it is for an NGO to play parties off against each other, which hampers the effectiveness of the effort considerably. When representatives of local authorities joined NGOs in the Schiphol conflict, it appeared to have little effect – so long as central government refrained from changing its position. Through the tough attitude of Schiphol, its legitimacy remained intact. When representatives of central government supported the protest campaigns in the Shell Brent Spar case, it appeared to have great consequences for the legitimacy of Shell's approach in the conflict. Despite protest from various stakeholders of Exxon, it still remains one of the most profitable firms globally.

Weaker and more vague effect on reputation: profit/non-profit interface

■ *Food/health*: In the four cases in the food/health cluster (Cargill, Nutreco, GlaxoSmithKline and McDonald's), the position in the international supply chain also determines the manner in which the conflict with stakeholders is eventually settled. B2b company Cargill did not change tack, while distributor McDonald's and pharmacist GSK marginally did, and producer of end-products Nutreco, completely. The reactions of consumers/stakeholders are swift and strong, especially when food safety is at stake. Governments play an important role in overseeing food safety of end-products, where the most important conflict is essentially a matter of proper public/private alignment. Also here, companies essentially take the stand that the legislator has to ensure control of food safety and decide on ethical questions about technological advancements, such as GM. If semi-public supervisory bodies such as the Commodity Board or the Food Authority take no initiative, why should companies do so? In opposition to this, stakeholders draw attention to company responsibilities. The reputation mechanism works best when consumers are addressed exclusively as consumers (as in the case of Nutreco and McDonald's). In case of health issues, the working of the reputation mechanism is extremely complex and strongly contingent on the national CSR regime.

■ *Labour rights and working conditions*: In the four cases that concern working conditions and/or child care and child labour (Adidas, C&A, IKEA and Nike) the reputation effect was vaguer. All conflicts led to relatively undecided confrontations, although they did lead to the most explicit disciplining initiatives on the part of companies. It was mentioned earlier that in this cluster there is a connection between price strategy and sensitivity to the issue. The lower the price of the end-product, the less sensitive the company is to the issue. The companies that aim at a lower price segment are both hybrid (family) businesses. They are consequently less dependent on the capital market, but also operate on the profit/non-profit interface in other respects, which makes them less vulnerable to reputation damage. In this cluster, the link between legislation (or the absence thereof) and company responsibility is less pronounced. And the link with civil society responsibility too, is less clear.

Societal Interface Management on the interface of efficiency and ethics

The cases illustrate especially the confrontation between company strategies and accompanying efficiency requirements of 'the' market sector versus the ethical requirements formulated by NGOs on behalf of civil society. Hybrid organizations such as family businesses, in particular, are founded on different — and more explicitly ethical — aims, with the result that confrontations between NGOs and companies often generate surprising solutions. The Catholic orientation of C&A makes the company vulnerable to accusations of child labour. At the same time, it is easier for this company to integrate the new ethical issues into existing values and norms. Companies with less of a social 'vision' at their inception and operating in a less visible market sector, are less sensitive to an ethical appeal to the company. Companies with a lifestyle orientation and clear internal norms, for instance, regarding quality and recycling are more readily influenced by NGOs who can also more readily call them to account for inconsistent behaviour. The slogans of such companies provide the best fodder for efficiency/ethics interface dilemmas, the highlight of the 1990s being the confrontation between Nike's 'just do it' and NGOs' 'do it just' or 'just do just'.

In most cases, it seems that the conflicts barely changed the actual production or buying formulas. Conflicts do not (as yet) prompt companies to change their fundamental strategic choices with respect to the manner in which they position themselves in their supply chain and markets. This is also the most difficult challenge of Societal Interface Management. Here, the reputation instrument either does not, or only rarely, seem adequate. In this relation, ethical choices (for standardization, employee flexibility, contracts or not) are made that are not really up for discussion anywhere. In the event that the direct continuity of a company turns on ethical or unethical conduct, the continuity of the company usually seems to take precedence. That was the case with IHC Caland; due to the small number of customers and the nature of the market (b2b), the continuity of the company and its reputation with b2b customers were at stake. In terms of the Triple-E model, the company chose for efficiency above effectiveness.

The ethical outcome of many a reputation conflict tends towards the acceptance of unequivocal norms dictated by Western interests. In practice, it seems to lead to ethical imperialism rather than the acceptance of a 'moral free space' and the development of 'hypernorms'. Ethical relativism is usually punished by public interest organizations.

The progression of the concrete conflicts, in any event, shows that companies are not always exclusively oriented towards efficiency. They are increasingly testing their boundaries on the ethical interfaces. NGOs, on the other hand, are by no means always the most adequate representatives of ethics. That is because their set of instruments is relatively limited. NGOs can, for instance, sometimes mobilize the reputation mechanism too readily. There are at least three cases where NGO allegations were based in vague facts and unclear argumentation. This led to significant reputation damage to at least three companies. If we recall, the BBC had to rectify allegations with respect to the dioxin content of Nutreco salmon, but by then the market value of Nutreco had already declined significantly. In the case of the Brent Spar, Greenpeace eventually admittted that it dished up exaggerated numbers to the public.

The reputation mechanism acquires a momentum of its own and the reputation of the company is put in question in a dubious manner (van der Zwart, 2002). Once in a while this is strengthened by the arsenal and tactics that NGOs (have to) employ to activate the mechanism.

1 *Over-simplification and exaggeration*: NGOs use emotion and perception, consciously exclude finer nuances ('de-nuance'), simplify issues, omit the context or add other details (recontextualize). In this way, the 'attacked' organization and its vulnerable reputation end up in a contest where it is a matter of *proving you are right* rather than necessarily *being right*. The effective deployment of emotionally charged images via the Internet and TV supports this principle. The most effective is the so-called *attachment journalism*, where journalists are in such agreement with the aims of environmental and human rights organizations that they become an appendage to the NGO. Moreover, environmental organizations are accused of manipulating the numbers surrounding environmental issues (Lomborg, 2001), unnecessarily polarizing the debate as a result.[4] NGOs are most creative in their communication of simplified messages. Accusations against the child-friendly IKEA of using child labour hit the public hard, whether the allegations were true or not.

2 *Unambiguous interests and coalitions*: The NGOs that are most successful in using the reputation mechanism are single-issue movements. They represent a (seemingly) unambiguous interest and display scant responsibility for the way in which they go about pursuing their aims. NGOs are more effective in bringing their interests to the fore when they form coalitions with primary stakeholders in company spheres of influence: trade union FNV readily assists NGOs in influencing the labour market, and consumer organizations assist in reaching the consumer markets. In theoretical literature, this is referred to as the *indirect pathways of influence* (Frooman, 1999: 196). The deciding factor is the threat or pressure from other stakeholders, almost never the pressure of NGOs alone.

3 *Timing and targeting*: NGOs are most sucessful if their timing is good – which they control themselves. In this way the sit-in of the Brent Spar was planned for exactly three weeks prior to the North Sea conference and an important G-7 summit; the poster and card campaign against Nike and Adidas right before the World Cup and European Football Championships; the establishment of MOSOP in the UN year of Indigenous Peoples; and campaigns in front of the entrance to IKEA during the Saint Nicholas and Christmas rush. These are all publicity-sensitive moments. Through the acquisition of shares, NGOs get a turn to speak at shareholder meetings of listed companies. NGOs wait for political momentum, a big event or a shareholder meeting, but issue and event cannot always be linked effectively.

4 *Iconification*: In addition, it is important to take on a 'significant player'. NGOs, after all, are also strategic organizations. That, incidentally, does not alter the fact that small players are just as capable of unethical behaviour. In order to activate the reputation mechanism effectively, it is important to turn companies into icons of unacceptable social conduct. Issues are then associated with companies, which immediately puts a reputation in question. In this way, the companies that are chosen for the issue – such as Adidas, Nike, Shell, Schiphol, ExxonMobil and IKEA – figure as the epitome of the issues they are linked to. Thus NGOs mould issues into company-specific shapes. McDonald's, for instance, is often targeted as 'the' embodiment of globalization, 'the US and capitalism' and 'the meat industry'. The companies concerned are elevated to *issue owner* and threaten to become the plaything of public opinion. The connection can also be entirely at random. The Dutch Socialist Party conceded that they could just as easily have chosen a different furniture distributor, rather than IKEA, to bring the matter

to the public's attention. This tactic also leads to greater difficulty in addressing an issue where no iconification is possible. Examples are issues such as 'hunger' or diseases such as Aids, while companies could make a significant contribution to resolving complex issues such as these. NGOs are aware that change can be brought about quicker by placing pressure on, especially, 'national' companies, than by influencing (overseas) governments. Iconification also leads to international coordination problems with some NGOs. For instance, World Wildlife Fund (WWF) US set up a platform of companies willing to participate in the emission trading schemes introduced under the Kyoto treaty. However, because one of these companies was Nike, WWF Italy protested. In Italy, Nike is the icon of child labour.

5 *Digital pillory*: NGOs sucessfully utilize modern means of communication such as the Internet in their moral crusade against companies. They often make use of the Internet to organize international solidarity, coordinate demonstrations and disseminate calls for boycotts. By means of this relatively cheap network medium, information can be exchanged and a range of campaigns can be supported at a high speed. As such the Internet has become a scene of battle for social discontent. Many of the NGOs that specialize in identifying the 'villains' among companies are active on the Internet. In this way, the American 'CorpWatch' specializes in multinational companies and McSpotlight in McDonald's. The Free Burma Coalition (FBC) started as a purely Internet campaign organization. The reliability of information presented is difficult to verify. The same, for that matter, applies to company websites. Most websites have no editorial statute or supervisory body, as in the case of reputable newspapers. The quality of the information on some websites, however, is exceptionally high and the editors do everything in their power to make the information verifiable.

6 *No code of conduct*: A thorny subject for NGOs seems to be whether or not they possess a code of conduct themselves. When a code of conduct or a quality label is absent, the opposition has difficulty placing an NGO. Organizations such as Greenpeace refuse to adopt a code of conduct or anything else to regulate their behaviour. According to them, their members grant them a 'license to operate'. A lot remains to be said about it (cf. Chapter 3). NGOs that sustain damage to reputation often appear not to handle it very well and usually opt for a 'buffering' attitude. With this, it seems that NGOs are still in the 'Trust me' phase.

Whether NGOs can be accused of unethical behaviour in their use of such tactics is a complex question. The tactics have, nevertheless, appeared to be successful in the struggle over stakeholder perceptions. At this moment, regulating CSR via reputation calls for confrontation, and confrontation apparently calls for specific tactics to activate the reputation mechanism.

A solution nearer at hand?

In the event that a company gets the longest end of the stick in an issue conflict, the solution to the issue seems to remain farthest removed. In the area of genetic modification/manipulation, no company has withdrawn from further technological developments or undertaken initiatives for voluntary labelling of their own accord. Cargill, furthermore, has not taken any steps to refine its code of conduct. It appears difficult to address a technology issue through public discussion, not least because different CSR regimes around the world have come to different approaches to technology issues such as genetic modification. The same applies to longer-term public interest issues such as global warming in which governments have an important role to play. The position taken by ExxonMobil – in combination with the US government – is illustrative of this problem. The problem surrounding noise nuisance, pollution and expanding Schiphol's boundaries has not been solved. On the contrary, in 2005 the Netherlands was found to be one of the most polluted regions in Europe.

Victory by a public interest organization is not necessarily a step in the direction of resolving an issue. The signal of boycotting Burma from b2c companies that did withdraw was partly annulled by b2b companies that stayed on. In addition, dealing with the Burma issue via company withdrawals turned out to be doubly problematic, as other companies with different norms and value systems – less confronted with outspoken opinion groups in their home countries – filled the openings. In the case of IHC and Heineken, competitors from Asian countries were all set to take their place. The 2003 withdrawal of BAT from Burma highlighted the last British company present in the country and has also been due to continued pressure by the British government. But, in fact, it also meant the takeover by a Singapore investment company. The swap of Western by Asian companies – with their more inactive approach to CSR – contributes to a 'regionalization' and probably continuation of the regime. The latter development gave other companies – outspoken examples are TotalFinaElf (the French oil multinational) and Unocal (American oil multinational) an additional argument against withdrawal. Without international government coordination, the boycott instrument therefore seems to have little effect, or functions only in the very long term – as appeared to be the case in the boycott of the South African apartheid regime. In the meantime, however, many employees lose their jobs and their social well-being deteriorates in the short term. The three successive instances (PepsiCo, Heineken and Triumph) when opinion organizations managed to convince companies to withdraw from Burma, seemed to increase the effect of the boycott – also because some governments joined it. However, ten years after the first company withdrew the issue still has not been resolved. The same applies to Shell in Nigeria. For the local population, the issue is still just as topical.

None of the issues surrounding working conditions in countries of production on the profit/non-profit interface have truly been resolved, but individual companies have at least become active in setting up mostly small-scale community involvement initiatives in response to the issue in question. C&A, IKEA and Adidas, for instance, did not only refine their codes of conduct, they also launched education projects for children. Nike's raising of the minimum age of employment to above the international ILO guidelines in its very strict code of conduct does not seem particularly helpful in solving the problem of child labour. Work in combination with schooling for children would be a step in the right direction rather than dismissing children and propelling them into a life of prostitution and/or crime (cf. Kolk and van Tulder, 2002). Such an approach requires that the parties who are at loggerheads with each other over an issue be given the opportunity to come up with nuanced solutions.

In only three cases (Nutreco, Shell Brent Spar and Unilever – India), can it be asserted that the issue has been resolved. In the case of Nutreco, it was however a non-issue, which solved itself after rectification by the BBC. In the case of Unilever – or more specifically, Hindustan Lever – the solution was already in the making by the company itself. In the Shell Brent Spar affair, doubts remain about the imposed solution. Sinking the oil platform, according to many, would still have been the most responsible solution, since more safety and environmental risks were involved in the dismantling of the Brent Spar than would have been the case had it been sunk. The conflict has finally generated a more fundamental solution to all oil platforms, namely the drafting of an international accord. In most cases, solutions were not possible in cases where governments were not prepared to engage themselves as well.

With this, the harvest of 15 years' struggle is actually disenchantingly mixed. Few CSR issues have truly been resolved. There is much less to 'winning' a reputation conflict than many – including the media – think. Significant progress has however been made in the practical policy of individual companies who were put in the spotlight. Many companies moved from an inactive to an active or even relatively proactive stance on major CSR issues. One-third of the companies subscribed to the GRI guidelines and a few others have also agreed to the ILO guidelines or other international guidelines (such as the CERES principles) (cf. also Kolk, 2005b). Companies such as Shell, Nike, Unilever, PepsiCo and ABN Amro are currently regarded as forerunners in the field of ICR and have been included in sustainability investment indices such as the FTSE4Good, DSI4000 and the DJSGI. The conflicts have enhanced the transparency of the companies affected. Particularly Western companies actually respond to society's wish to 'prove it to me'.

19.5 CONCLUSION: ON THE EFFECTIVENESS OF REPUTATION

The use of the reputation instrument in the concrete struggle for CSR has generated a mixed and nuanced picture.

The corrective effect of the reputation mechanism is strong:

- in the case of lifestyle companies that aim for the higher market segment;
- on b2c markets;
- especially where consumer markets are concentrated in the home country;
- in the case of companies that do not have a privileged relation with the government – no strategic industry, mainport position or other reason for the (central) government to side with the company in conflicts;
- in the case of small institutional distance and high normative distance;
- in the case of company icons with clear 'ethical values';
- on capital markets for listed companies;
- on consumer markets especially indirectly via large stakeholders;
- on consumer markets: if the host market is not too important (Burma is a small market, therefore not too important an issue);
- in the case of issues on the public/private interface;
- in the event of very clear conflicting interests (simplified issues); it is easier to talk about whether or not to do business in Burma than whether or not to support GM;
- if the NGO is willing to formulate a negative interest;
- in the case of a developed issue (where the consequences are clearly measurable);
- in the case of previously damaged reputations (Nike still has a credibility problem);
- if an issue is important to a company (see icon, image, but also purchasing strategy);
- when an issue is raised for the first time;
- in countries where transparency and participation are regarded as important (liberal CSR regimes);
- in countries where significant societal conflicts are being thrashed out in overlapping spheres of influence;
- if newspapers/media can be interested;
- in companies that start out with a buffering attitude;
- in organizations heavily dependent on a few large stakeholders;
- if stakeholders cannot readily be exchanged;
- when these stakeholders have an (ethical) reputation of their own to uphold;
- if the NGO that raises the issue has a good reputation;
- if a 'domino-effect' threatens: other issues, other companies (oligopolistic competition), other countries.

Reputation mechanism has a *limited* or *no* corrective effect:

- on b2b markets;
- in the case of unit branding companies;
- on the labour market;
- in the case of companies with a privileged relation with government (Schiphol as transport hub, ExxonMobil, but also defence and other government departments);
- in the case of high institutional distance;
- in the case of image companies with low prices (and less clear-cut 'ethical values');
- in the case of specific issues on profit/non-profit boundary area;
- when there are no, or only weak, NGOs who want to support it;
- on capital markets in the case of family businesses (and other hybrid organizations);
- in cases where the company has spread activities over a large number of markets, which are relatively unrelated (large institutional distance);
- on consumer markets if the host market is very important (Burma for IHC Caland);
- in production locations that are not important or easily exchanged (there are many low-wage countries);
- in the case of technologies that people are far removed from (not GM, but certainly food safety);
- in the case of recurrent conflicts (issue fatigue);
- in the case of companies without previous reputation damage;
- when the issue is not that important to a company (no image, no dependence on international division of labour in the purchasing strategy);
- at the beginning of an issue's development (especially in the case of technologies that are difficult to explain and the impact of which is not clear to anyone);
- in countries where transparency and participation are regarded as less important;
- in countries where the overlapping spheres of influence are less dynamic (see Chapter 3);
- in the case of complex issues; issues management fall victim to the same problem that referendums have as decision-making mechanism – too simplistic, wrong/guiding questions, lacking legitimacy of organizers;
- when the NGO attempts to formulate a positive interest (WWF versus Greenpeace);
- when newspapers/media cannot be interested;
- in the case of organizations that have spread their dependencies over several stakeholders;
- if these stakeholders attach no value to their own reputation (which is, for instance, the case with small stakeholders such as consumers);
- in the event that stakeholders are easier to replace and the new generation of stakeholders is less principled (repetition effect);
- in the event that the NGO that highlights the case has not got a good reputation or few members (thus little legitimacy);
- in the event that a domino-effect is unlikely: for instance in the case of a very isolated issue, in a very competitive market (exemplary code of conduct absent) or in the case of companies that do not operate internationally.

The reputation mechanism has appeared to be more effective in correcting than disciplining companies. This does not detract from the fact that a great number of initiatives have followed under pressure from reputation corrections. The reputation mechanism does not function as 'what' – on markets and in the public opinion – but as 'who' – in the hands of concrete stakeholders, organized groups which, in interaction with government and companies, thrash out boundary conflicts. The reputation mechanism spares smaller players in societies where transparency is not an institutional virtue. The reputation mechanism and self-regulation also appear to lead to unpredictable outcomes. On sometimes illegitimate grounds companies are coerced, via (threatening) damage to their reputation, into disciplining without there being real cause for it. The reputation mechanism is blunt. As yet, it has barely led to effective solutions to ICR issues. Reputation probably only plays a role in the effective engagement with CSR and ICR issues if it is accompanied by a great number of other measures and probably also if the discussion on corporate responsibility takes place in another setting. Trying to bring about corporate responsibilities in practice via conflict, confrontation and control is perhaps less constructive than ICR via cooperation, dialogue and co-production. The concluding chapter delineates the preconditions and contours of an effective strategic stakeholder dialogue as ultimate form and challenge of Societal Interface Management.

Chapter 20

Towards a strategic stakeholder dialogue

With a contribution
by Muel Kaptein

CHAPTER CONTENTS

20.1 INTRODUCTION: ON THE REPUTATION TRAP AND THE LIMITS OF CONFRONTATION

Chapter 19 offered a sobering view on the effectiveness of issue conflicts in general and the reputation mechanism in particular. Despite countless codes of conduct, sustainability reports, new institutes and institutions, it is difficult to address societal issues effectively if relations remain fraught with tension. In the international arena the potential for confrontation increases, not least because rivalry extends beyond the firm to include also cultural and country rivalry. Confrontation triggers simplification and overly emotional statements. In this trend, the media play an important role. Comparative research in the UK shows that in 1974 the ratio of negative versus positive articles in newspapers was 3:1 and by 2001 it had shot up to 18:1 (Kamp, in ODE, March 2005: 3). The bargaining society in action seems to generate greater confrontation, greater rivalry between models and institutions coupled with a sharper distinction between 'right' and 'wrong'.

In the vast majority of cases, however, a clear distinction between right and wrong cannot be made. CSR and ICR issues – especially at the interface between market and civil society where most of the reputation conflicts arise – are an enormously complex, grey area. Companies, public interest organizations and governments can get caught up in the hostilities unleashed by the reputation mechanism – the reputation trap. Companies become overly defensive, being well aware that reputations are more easily lost than gained. NGOs become overly offensive, because their members expect a single-issue orientation that is best realized by adopting a watchdog role. Governments become overly passive for fear of reinforcing the perception of being bureaucratic, slow, legalistic and interventionist.

In 2004, a group of leading academics and practitioners in the field of CSR wrote that many people have become cynical about CSR initiatives 'as they're often used to promote an ideological agenda that gets big business and government off the hook for the state of the world. . . . [M]ajor NGOs are turning against CSR' (Shah *et al.*, 2004). They also maintained that it is 'time for CSR to grow up and address the systemic problems with globalization or fade away into irrelevance' (ibid.). The latter, however, is perhaps more an indication of the need to discuss matters differently in the bargaining society, than of the real state of affairs in the field of CSR. Chapter 8 already concluded that the notion of CSR 'fading away into irrelevance' is no option. Business strategy is all about operating at the interfaces of society, which gives sound reasons to state the business case for corporate responsibility, in particular, across borders.

The remaining chapters in Part II also showed that there is a range of approaches to CSR, many of which do not amount to a 'grown up' approach. National CSR regimes and inadequate international regulation are complicating factors that tend to reinforce a relatively inactive or reactive attitude towards corporate responsibility. But Part II also showed that, at the international level, multinationals have a bigger window of opportunity to shape their interfaces with society in a less defensive manner. Thus, the question that will be addressed in this final chapter is also the most future oriented and, perhaps, speculative in nature: 'How can MNEs develop a "grown up" version of corporate responsibility across borders (ICR) and escape the reputation trap?' The concrete analysis of the ins and outs of the societal debate since the beginning of the 1990s – as documented in Part III – allows us to demarcate this question further: 'How can companies, NGOs and governments use interactive cooperation and dialogue to reach a new and more effective (proactive) understanding of corporate responsibilities across borders?' It was concluded that bilateral talks stimulate negotiations in the form of dialogue (as opposed to confrontation) and the alignment of shared, but also conflicting interests.

This final chapter places the challenge of stakeholder engagement and dialogue within the analytical framework of the study as a whole (section 20.2) and examines recent experiences of stakeholder dialogue (section 20.3).[1] In the business world stakeholder dialogue is a relatively recent and still ill-researched development. Minimum requirements for (more) effective stakeholder dialogue are subsequently deduced from the experiences recounted (section 20.4). The greatest challenge of stakeholder dialogue is the active establishment of a *strategic* dialogue so as to deal with the international challenges of Societal Interface Management in a manner that is simultaneously pragmatic and idealistic. In the concluding section, the potential items on the agenda of this dialogue are touched on briefly, paving the way for a discussion of an international strategic stakeholder dialogue (section 20.5).

20.2 THE PRINCIPLE: RISE OF THE STAKEHOLDER DIALOGUE

Stakeholder dialogue made its first appearance in the mid-1990s as a specific form of stakeholder management. The dialogue was first initiated by more cooperatively inclined NGOs such as the WWF (for example in the context of the Marine Stewardship Council). Later, the stakeholder dialogue was embraced by individual companies such as the Body Shop, by business coalitions such as the WBCSD, and by international organizations such as the UN and the World Bank (see Chapter 12). On the one hand, the dialogue was a reaction of partnership-oriented NGOs (PONGOs) that could not identify with the *single-issue* approach of leading watchdog-oriented NGOs (WONGOs), and on the other hand it was an attempt by companies to do away with the conflict that had dominated CSR since the 1990s. Some companies realized that it would be unwise to wait for their reputations to come under threat before taking action. They understood the advantage of taking iniative themselves to introduce forms of disciplining in consultation with societal movements that would be viewed as adequately addressing corporate responsibility issues. In 2003, two-thirds of the largest international companies in the Netherlands stated that they were engaged in some form of structural dialogue with their stakeholders – up from 13 per cent in 1995 (van Tulder *et al.*, 2004). They also indicated that they expected that stakeholder dialogue would become even more important in the future.

Figure 20.1 depicts the road from confrontation to dialogue and from a defensive/reactive ICR strategy to a proactive ICR strategy within the correction/disciplining framework of Chapter 19. A proactive strategy is always interactive, but the important question is whether interaction should be based on confrontation, on dialogue, or on a combination of the two.

Towards greater stakeholder engagement

There are at least three reasons to opt for stakeholder involvement in policy design and implementation. First, a *pragmatic* argument: stakeholder participation increases the effectiveness of policies and strategies. By making stakeholders partners in the dilemmas the company is struggling with, mutual understanding can be achieved. In this regard, Heath (2001) uses the term *co-created meaning*. Furthermore, companies can ward off or minimize the damage of campaigns by critical stakeholders if they adopt a less confrontational stance (*buffering*) and exhibit a willingness to enter a dialogue and seek solutions in consultation with stakeholders (*bridging*). As it is impossible to satisfy the interests of each and every stakeholder, it is important that stakeholders are confident that the company will carefully consider their interests. An open dialogue can enhance or restore stakeholder confidence, remove tensions, relieve pressure (on company reputation) and offer opportunities to align expectations, ideas and opinions on issues such as child labour and genetic modification.

Second, a *moral* argument: stakeholder participation increases the legitimacy and democratic content of the strategies chosen. The most relevant issues are interface issues for which primary responsibility cannot be reduced to either governments, companies or civil society (Chapter 10). The stakeholder dialogue can focus on developing shared values, principles and interests.

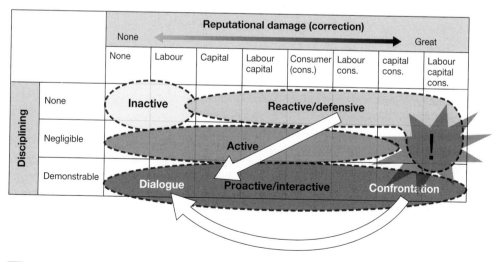

Figure 20.1 From confrontation to cooperation?

Third, a *content* argument: stakeholder participation can enhance the quality of the content of policies. Insights and arguments are presented that might not otherwise be heard in a technocratic environment. Stakeholder participation keeps 'groupthink' at bay – i.e. the unhealthy autistic group dynamics where group members strive too hard to conform to (perceived) group rules. The Brent Spar affair, for instance, has also been the result of the 'old chums' culture, which lulls director's inquisitiveness and make them all see things the same way (*The Economist*, 20 March 2004).

The 'business case' for greater stakeholder involvement, is therefore relatively straightforward (Kaptein and van Tulder, 2003) as it helps firms:

- to identify trends and future issues at an early stage and to prioritize these;
- to gain insight into stakeholders' views of the organization and current performance;
- to create an opportunity for the organization and stakeholders to gain a better understanding of each others' interests and dilemmas, and broaden support for the decisions the company eventually takes;
- to resolve specific tensions in the relationship with stakeholders;
- to gather suggestions and ideas for improving the company's social performance and for developing Key Peformance Indicators;
- to increase sensitivity towards stakeholder concerns and to develop a heightened sense of responsibility for social issues within the organization;
- to create greater trust in order to deal with problems more effectively;
- to avoid incidents that may receive wide public and media attention;
- to create a basis for joint projects, alliances and partnerships.

Being right does not imply being *put* in the right

The principle of stakeholder engagement is often far removed from the practice of stakeholder *dialogue*. In stakeholder dialogue, everything turns on the arguments that inform the weighing up of interests and the decisions that are made. As the cases of firm–NGO confrontation throughout Part III have shown, *being* right does not necessarily mean that stakeholders will *acknowledge* that the company is right. Through open and credible communication a company can, however, influence the perceptions and expectations of the public and possibly alter them. Scrupulously correct social conduct is impossible to achieve. Stakeholder interests must always be weighed against others. Policy, moreover, need not always be completely aligned with stakeholder demands as that would lead to losing sight of the financial bottom line. It is more convincing for a company to admit to actual and potential dilemmas in its interaction with society. Stakeholders will trust a company more if they are made partners in its dilemmas. Merely communicating with stakeholders through an annual report or other PR campaigns is no longer sufficient (Chapter 9).

The stakeholder dialogue is essentially an exchange of viewpoints on current concerns, a discussion of (future) interests and expectations, and the development of norms for the functioning of companies. Ultimately, a meaningful dialogue does not only enhance a company's sensitivity to its environment (Waddock and Smith, 2000), it also increases stakeholders' insight into the issues the company faces (Wheeler and Sillanpää, 1997). Stakeholder dialogue is acknowledged as 'a powerful catalyst for change. It promotes greater transparency, information sharing and inspires society to work together' (WBCSD, 2002: 1).

Reporting lends further structure to the stakeholder dialogue. Reporting offers an opportunity to verify whether all relevant perspectives have been engaged. It informs participating stakeholders of discussions with other stakeholders, and those stakeholders that are not taking part can be informed of the manner in which the company gives content to its responsibilities and, insofar as it is relevant, the manner in which their rights and interests are dealt with. It is especially in cases where reporting is accompanied by an invitation to respond (as Shell explicitly does with its *Tell Shell* strategy) that it can lead to greater involvement of stakeholders. In this sense, reporting strengthens the stakeholder dialogue and vice versa. By the beginning of the twenty-first century, 36 per cent of non-financial annual reports mentioned conducting a stakeholder dialogue (KPMG, 2002).

In many cases, companies had already been holding regular meetings with stakeholders such as employee representatives, government organizations, consumer organizations and the local community. By treating these talks as part of the stakeholder dialogue, the discussions became more structured and focused. In this respect, stakeholder dialogue need not be labour intensive or expensive. Through reporting, continuity is created in the stakeholder discussions, which is of value both to the company and stakeholders.

Stakeholder dialogue also creates an opportunity to develop shared *key performance indicators* (KPIs). Adequate KPIs are required for internal management and reporting. KPIs translate the ambitions and responsibilities contained in the code into measurable objectives for management and employees, as well as external stakeholders. The development of KPIs for sustainable business practice is still in its infancy. At present, a crystallized and balanced set of KPIs is still lacking. At this stage, it may even be desirable to refrain from seeking to establish a fixed set of norms of indicators. The societal issues that companies are being confronted with do not always lend themselves to the application of rigorous indicators and rules. Additionally, ideas and interpretations regarding sustainability are subject to continuous change. Moreover, the absence of such a set of KPIs stimulates companies to individually consult with stakeholders and reflect on what would demonstrate the sustainability of their company.

Table 20.1 Stakeholder debate versus dialogue

Stakeholder debate	Stakeholder dialogue
Competition with a single winner or only losers (either–or thinking; short-term oriented)	Cooperation where everyone could be a winner (and–and thinking; longer-term oriented)
Egocentric: the other is a threat or a means to personal end	Empathetic: the other party is seen as a possible ally and has inherent value
Putting yourself in a better light	Being yourself
Speaking while others must listen	Listening to others before speaking
Persuading	Convincing
Confrontational, combative and destructive, seeking out weaknesses and set on proving the other wrong while negating common aims and shared interest	Constructive, showing mutual understanding and respect so as to find shared aims from which to approach differences
A closed and defensive attitude because you have sole access to the truth	A vulnerable attitude: many truths exist and all parties are open to criticism about their performance in order to learn from one another
Taking and keeping	Giving and taking
Divide and rule	Share and serve
Separate/isolated responsibilities	Shared responsibilities

Source: Kaptein and Van Tulder, 2003

From debate to dialogue

A stakeholder dialogue shifts the relationship between company and stakeholders from confrontation and competition to consultation and cooperation. The call for 'prove it to me' has made way for one of 'involve me', 'join me' or 'engage me'. Table 20.1 depicts the characteristic differences between debating with stakeholders (in a conflict or confrontation) and engaging them in dialogue.

Ideally, a stakeholder dialogue is a structured, interactive and proactive process aimed at creating sustainable strategies. But, entering into a stakeholder dialogue is not a neutral exercise. By choosing for dialogue and taking their concerns and viewpoints seriously, a company expresses respect for stakeholders and demonstrates a willingness to learn (Kaptein and Wempe, 2002). Deliberately ignoring signals from society, making empty promises and displaying arrogant and autistic (inward-looking) behaviour are the foremost reasons for NGOs to let a company 'have it'.

20.3 EXPERIENCE WITH STAKEHOLDER DIALOGUE: FIVE CASES

Five brief examples of international companies that have engaged in a stakeholder dialogue show that strongly divergent forms of stakeholder dialogue exist with varying degrees of effectiveness.[2] Each case is based on a different position of departure within the disciplining/correction framework (Figure 20.1). The first four cases document relatively successful stakeholder dialogues (cf. Kaptein and van Tulder, 2003), whereas the last case was selected to illustrate the strategic limitations of stakeholder dialogue.

Case 1: a reactive stakeholder panel

In the late 1990s, an American chemical company initiated a stakeholder dialogue in Europe in response to harsh criticism on its environmental policy by the environmental movement. The company also met with opposition from its own employees regarding its environmentally unfriendly policies. As company management was rather dismayed at the unexpected criticism, they examined how they could go about learning more about stakeholder expectations and concerns about the environment. In addition to a reassessment of previously conducted reputation studies, trend analyses and scenario planning, it was decided to enter into a dialogue with stakeholders. This is not to say that the company did not previously communicate with its environment, but rather that it now adopted a more open and vulnerable position. The most critical (deduced by the fierceness of the response) and the largest (measured in terms of number of members) NGOs were invited for roundtable discussions, so-called *environmental workshops*. During these workshops, which were held in many countries by local subsidiaries, a large number of participants were invited to give their views on why, in their opinion, the company had failed, what was fundamentally wrong with the manner in which the organization managed its environmental impacts and what it could do to avoid such incidents in future. The workshops led to a reviewed environmental policy and a commitment to be more open towards stakeholders. In this regard, an annual sustainability report has been published ever since. NGO recognition and support for company policy has subsequently increased and the company is regularly cited in the media and by NGOs as a trendsetter.

Case 2: a reactive dialogue

A German financial services firm was unexpectedly confronted in the media with claims by pressure groups of allegedly granting loans for socially undesirable projects. To drive the message home, they made a public appeal to account holders to close their accounts. Even though the effect of this appeal was minimal, it did receive the necessary media attention. It was the media attention in particular that made the bank realize how powerless it was against such allegations. Although it had a clear and well-considered policy on the granting of credit, it was very difficult to communicate once the public debate had started. It seemed that appearances were against the firm and that made it an easy target for pressure groups. Because integrity and reliability makes or breaks the reputation of a bank, it decided to hold discussions with the pressure groups. The Public Affairs department received the activists at its offices on a number of occasions. The discussions resulted in a joint agreement in which the financial institution declared that it would take societal impacts into consideration in the evaluation of applications for substantial loans. At the same time, the pressure groups conceded that the bank was not primarily responsible for the manner in which loans are spent. It was also agreed that in the event of an alleged violation of the agreement, the parties would first talk to each other before involving the media. More than a year later, neither the pressure groups nor the financial institution has had any reason to arrange such a meeting.

Case 3: an active stakeholder dialogue

In the late 1990s, the main office of a European transport company held several meetings with environmental groups. This was triggered by the dissatisfaction these groups expressed over the quality of the company's annual environmental report. Given its sincere intentions, the company had difficulty understanding the criticism. The company thought it important to communicate this to its critics and to find out whether they had any useful suggestions for improving the report. The company made a conscious decision not to engage other stakeholders. The discussions with the environmental groups were not made public either as the company first wanted to establish what the discussions would yield. The environmental manager, who arranged the discussions himself, did not want to be too ambitious and overextend himself. A number of meetings were held with the respective environmental groups over a period of 18 months. It transpired that they did indeed have valuable suggestions to make for improving the environmental report. According to the environmental manager, support for the environmental policy among the environmental groups appeared to be growing during the consultation process. Unfortunately, the company neglected to verify this impression by asking the environmental groups themselves for their opinion on the discussions. The discussions were mentioned in the annual environmental report without otherwise going into the details of the results. In anticipation of the increasing use of annual sustainability reports by the business community, the environmental manager advised the Board of Directors to expand the environmental report to include an annual social report and, accordingly, extend the stakeholder dialogue to include the social discussion partners.

Case 4: a broad, proactive dialogue

In the spring of 2001, a European telecommunications company started a stakeholder dialogue upon the completion of its company code of conduct that had not yet been made public. The code of conduct formulates the responsibilities of the company towards its different stakeholders. The aim of the code was to rein in the tide of criticism stakeholders had expressed on the company's performance. The code defines the responsibilities and the ambitions the company strives to realize, also with regard to socially sensitive issues. The aim of the stakeholder dialogue was, in the first place, to inform stakeholders about the new code and the reasons for its introduction. The company also wanted to give stakeholders an opportunity to indicate whether, in their view, there was a discrepancy between the commitments expressed in the code and current practice. Should such a discrepancy exist, the company invited stakeholders to share their ideas and suggestions.

In this way, the company aimed to boost stakeholder support for the company as well as its performance levels. In preparation for the dialogue, a list was drawn up of all relevant stakeholders. An existing list of the Public Affairs department served as a basis for this. Subsequently, department managers, members of the Board of Directors and business unit managers were asked to make additions to this list. Likewise, media sources were consulted to identify stakeholders who had previously made critical remarks about the company. This finally produced a list of almost 100 stakeholder groups. Given that talks could not be held with all the groups in the short term, the list was divided into three categories: urgent stakeholders who had to be engaged within six months; less urgent stakeholders who could be invited for a second round of talks; even less important stakeholders who were informed of the code in writing and on whom the onus rested to make an appointment for a meeting.

It was agreed that the company would not only be represented by one Public Affairs official, but also at least one staff member from the department whose activities were associated with the stakeholder in question and preferably also the line manager. Such a delegation not only made clear to the stakeholders that the discussions were taken seriously, but it also stimulated more sensitivity to the expectations of stakeholders on the part of the staff members and line managers. In the end, Public Affairs 'only' fulfilled a facilitating role.

A meeting with top management was held to prepare for the dialogue. The 60 managers were invited to put themselves in stakeholders' shoes for one afternoon and critically examine the company. Then they had a discussion with the functionary who was actually going to hold the dialogue with the stakeholder concerned. This exercise allowed functionaries to prepare for the actual dialogue. The points of criticism that were gathered in the process were also later used to examine the accuracy of top management's view of the company and the extent to which stakeholders' views of the company diverged (perception gap) from theirs. Employees also received training in dialogue skills from the Public Affairs department.

In the first six months, individual discussions were held with 30 stakeholder groups. After an appointment was made by phone, the stakeholder was informed in writing of the rules of the dialogue. An important element in this concerned the confidentiality of the information exchanged. Confidential reports were made of the discussions and submitted for approval to the stakeholder in question. At the end of each session, the discussion was evaluated. Every six months, line management received a report on the outcome of the discussions. Problem areas and stakeholder suggestions in particular featured prominently in the reports. Some stakeholders were also invited to give their opinion in the staff magazine so that employees could gain insight into the interests of stakeholders. Most of the stakeholders experienced the discussion as positive and were optimistic about the follow-up. Management also generally regarded the discussions as valuable.

Case 5: a dialogue doomed to failure?

In 2002, a large English tobacco firm was the first in the industry to publish a social report. At the time of preparing the report, it attempted to start a stakeholder dialogue. From the company's perspective, however, the stakeholder dialogue did not appear to offer any solutions to the more fundamental dilemmas of the tobacco industry. This was confirmed by its initial experience with stakeholder dialogue, which proceeded with extreme difficulty. Stakeholders in the 14 countries that were discussed in its first social report were invited to participate in the dialogue. In the UK, 167 stakeholders were invited to attend the sessions that were to be led by independent senior clergymen – a decision meant to emphasize the objectivity and morality that was to permeate the process. Only 34 stakeholders accepted the invitation. Four of the 24 medical organizations that were invited, 2 of the 19 government or political representatives and 13 of the 32 representatives of business ethical organizations participated (*FT*, 4 July 2002). The societal groupings feared that their participation would be seen to legitimize the activities of the company while they were, in fact, fundamentally against the entire sector and only interested in discussing the complete termination of its activities. For the company leadership, that was two (strategic) bridges too many.

In all five cases, stakeholder discussions were conducted periodically. Mainly general management was involved, while hardly any monitoring of the quality of the dialogue took place. That a dialogue was being conducted was not always mentioned in the annual report – with the clear exception of the tobacco company – which indicates that stakeholder dialogue is still relatively weakly embedded in companies' general business strategy. A more (pro)active dialogue (Telecom and Transport) differs from a reactive (Chemical, Financial and Tobacco) dialogue in that discussions are more future oriented, an inventory is taken of the problem and not only general (central) management, but also other relevant employees are involved in the dialogue.

20.4 THE PROCESS: PRECONDITIONS OF AN EFFECTIVE STAKEHOLDER DIALOGUE

Stakeholder dialogue is not a panacea. Talks and negotiations cannot solve everything. That is, for instance, the strategic problem of the large tobacco firm above. In some cases, another course of action is required, such as government regulations, public pressure and private initiative. Stakeholder dialogues have a different function in different institutional settings. In the antagonistic (debate-oriented) setting of Anglo-Saxon CSR regimes, a stakeholder dialogue should overcome greater barriers – and thus should be organized differently – than in the more cooperative setting of most European countries. In the inactive setting of Asian countries and many developing countries, a stakeholder dialogue is more difficult to get started. But, because in these countries, institutions are still in a relative state of flux, new bargaining institutions are also easier to create.

Not everything needs to be discussed and all policies need not blindly be adjusted to meet the demands of the accusing parties. Many matters – in particular pertaining to the primary responsibilities of companies – will remain internal affairs. Furthermore, a stakeholder dialogue is not a substitute for meeting company responsibilities; a company remains responsible for its policies and conduct at all times. Stakeholders, on the other hand, have to accept that choices have to be made and that compromises are unavoidable. Stakeholder dialogue, therefore, does not imply that stakeholders should be involved in all decisions. Neither does it mean that each stakeholder expectation should be met. Even NGOs that acknowledge these limitations still voice considerable criticism on the actual practice of stakeholder dialogues. This experience influences their present and future attitude towards the potential of the stakeholder dialogue. This section considers this criticism in order to formulate the general preconditions for an effective stakeholder dialogue.

Criticism on the use of dialogues in practice

NGOs have criticized the notion of a stakeholder dialogue particularly for the manner in which it has been (mis)used in practice. First, companies have been accused of misrepresenting the facts to serve the interests of the company. This happens particularly when companies claim they are holding a 'dialogue' when in reality they are only 'sharing information'. A supermarket chain, for instance, that had given a group of 'stakeholders' (societal groups) a guided tour of a new branch a week before its official opening, claimed to have held a stakeholder dialogue. Second, dialogues have been used as a 'locking-in' exercise. In such a case, the 'dialogue' is used primarily as a means of making stakeholders 'accomplices' in the formulation of new policies without giving them a real say. The danger of 'hostage-taking' looms particularly large for many of the parternship-oriented NGOs (PONGOs). Third, criticism has been voiced on the selective inclusion of partners in the dialogue. If important stakeholders are left out of the dialogue because they have been too critical, it not only casts doubt on the company's intentions, but it also undermines the objective of the exercise which is to consider and learn from a variety of viewpoints and insights. Such selective inclusiveness ultimately functions as rubber stamp and can even perpetuate bad management practices. Fourth, NGOs have been critical of firms who use the dialogue primarily as a means to gather 'corporate intelligence'. Stakeholder concerns and criticism are heard with the aim of coming up with a timely strategy to counter potential stakeholder action.

If used inappropriately, the stakeholder dialogue will turn out to be yet another 'halo' concept. Or, as Rowell (2002) notes, it will primarily serve – and be interpreted by NGOs – as a 'divide and rule' tactic. This negative impression is to some extent corroborated by practice. It is interesting to note that 60 per cent of the meetings that managers of multinationals in the Netherlands decribe as a 'stakeholder dialogue' fail to meet the minimum requirements of a 'dialogue' (van Tulder *et al.*, 2004). Characteristic of these cases are the involvement of a very limited number of stakeholders and the fact that the dialogues are primarily operational and aimed at creating public support through the sharing of information (ibid.). So in practice there is a notable discrepancy between the alleged and actual motivations of managers in the use of 'stakeholder dialogue'.

This is a major reason why NGOs are still much less optimistic than managers about the potential of stakeholder dialogue as a means to address societal issues. It also explains why NGOs do not expect to abandon in the near future the primary role they are presently fulfilling. As shown in Chapter 7, this multifaceted role is primarily aimed at negotiation through confrontation (Table 7.2). In 2003, NGOs were still mostly fulfilling a protest role – as DONGOs/Orcas and WONGOs/Sharks – even though some of them were well aware that this role might prove limited in effectively addressing certain issues. This finding deviates slightly from other research claiming that NGOs are already moving away from their traditional Shark/Orca role towards the more interdependent 'Dolphin' role (SustainAbility and UN, 2003).[3]

Our own research conducted in 2003 showed that more than half of the NGOs included in the study still focused predominantly on their protest/confrontation role. No less than 80 per cent of the NGOs adopted more than one role – sometimes spread over the whole spectrum of possible relationships. This was particularly the case for NGOs with a long history and a large constituency. NGOs representing the interests of consumers (combining the role of watchdog with the role of competitor and shareholder) and workers (combining the role of partner, stakeholder, supervisor and watchdog) combine the largest number of roles. NGOs focusing on development cooperation (such as Oxfam) have been combining discussion and project partnership roles in their relationship vis-à-vis companies. A 'division of labour' has also been found among NGOs with some focusing on protests (e.g. the push strategy of Greenpeace) making it possible for others to engage in more constructive dialogues (e.g. the pull strategy of WWF). NGOs that attempted to combine both roles internally have confronted considerable coordination problems in the management of their campaigns, as well as legitimacy problems in relation to their members.

In the same research project, we asked leading INGOs what role(s) they expected to adopt in future ('five years from now' in the year 2009). Table 20.2 gives an overview of their answers.

Table 20.2 Anticipated NGO roles towards business for 2009

	Dependent NGO		Interdependent NGO			Independent NGO			
	Product oriented; realization			Process oriented; integration			Protest oriented; polarization		
	'Sea lions'		'Dolphins'		'Orcas'			'Sharks'		
	BONGO	PINGO	BINGO	SHANGO	STRONGO	BRONGO	SUNGO	DONGO	WONGO	DANGO
Nature, environment (N = 11)	0	6 (55%)	0	1 (9%)	3 (27%)	1 (9%)	3 (27%)	9 (82%)	6 (55%)	n.a.
Consumer interests (N = 7)	1 (14%)	1 (14%)	1 (14%)	3 (43%)	1 (14%)	1 (14%)	2 (29%)	6 (86%)	6 (86%)	n.a.
Human rights (N = 12)	0	8 (67%)	1 (8%)	0	2 (17%)	1 (8%)	1 (8%)	9 (75%)	4 (33%)	n.a.
Social-economic/ labour rights (N = 6)	0	2 (33%)	1 (17%)	1 (17%)	2 (33%)	1 (17%)	3 (50%)	4 (67%)	4 (67%)	n.a.
Social-economic/ general (N = 10)	0	2 (20%)	1 (10%)	0	1 (10%)	3 (30%)	3 (30%)	8 (80%)	5 (50%)	n.a.
Social-economic/ development (N = 10)	0	8 (80%)	0	1 (10%)	1 (10%)	2 (20%)	1 (10%)	10 (100%)	5 (50%)	n.a.

100%–80% = ▮   79%–60% = ▮   59%–30% = ▮   29%–10% = ▮   9%–1% = ▯

Source: Van Tulder et al., 2004: 101

By 2009, only marginal shifts in their chosen role vis-à-vis companies can be expected from NGOs. Almost half of all the NGOs anticipate that their role will not change at all, although they do anticipate that the intensity of their interaction with companies will increase. The importance of two roles is expected to increase slightly: partnerships (PONGOs) and strategic stakeholder dialogues (STRONGOs). NGOs are particularly interested in operational partnerships with firms. This illustrates their increasingly pragmatic orientation. The number of NGOs that considers (strategic) stakeholder dialogue an important tool of future interaction with firms increases slightly from one in eight to one in six. Labour rights NGOs and environmental NGOs, in particular, are pursuing stakeholder dialogue. But the majority of NGOs do not yet want to focus on a dialogue that involves relative interdependency.

Preconditions

If the negativity of the majority of NGOs towards stakeholder dialogue is indeed directly related to the questionable intentions of managers, their criticism is certainly warranted. It was, however, also found that the relatively poor praxis of dialogue can also be linked to a particularly weak conceptual understanding among managers of the meaning of dialogue in general and a stakeholder dialogue in particular (van Tulder et al., 2004). Reasons for this confusion are:

- *Conceptual*: concepts such as 'dialogue' are difficult and multifaceted, and managers are often not familiar with them: a real stakeholder dialogue, for instance, is an 'open dialogue' (Harris, 2002) which requires shared 'issue ownership', rather than a more limited dialogue where issue ownership is in the hands of the initiating party (the company). In all other instances such as information gathering, consultation and information sharing, 'dialogue' is a misnomer.
- *Complexity*: managers tend to underestimate the complexity of certain problems and therefore assume that less intensive forms of communication will suffice. Obviously, not every problem needs a dialogue, but where many parties are involved that believe that they are the 'issue owner', dialogue is necessary.
- *Initiative*: the initiative to hold a dialogue is often taken by stakeholders. In the event that stakeholders request a 'dialogue' and managers feel a different approach would be more suitable, the temptation to relabel existing practices as 'dialogue' is quite strong. Stakeholders, on the other hand, also regularly confuse dialogue with information sharing/gathering.
- *Selection*: different types of interaction can easily coexist and even replace one another. For instance, the gathering of information and preliminary testing of ideas during a round of consultation could easily be the first steps towards a dialogue. A consumer panel often forms part of a dialogue – but it does not replace it.

Conducting a stakeholder dialogue at the appropriate time and in the appropriate manner is not easy and depends on a range of factors. A stakeholder dialogue is only really effective if it is strategic and longer term-oriented. The *strategic* stakeholder dialogue displays the following features:[4]

1 Objectives

- *Sustainability*: The objective of a stakeholder dialogue is to generate better and more sustainable solutions to complex societal problems through the input of interested parties. While it aims to create pragmatic longer-term win–win solutions, the participants of a strategic stakeholder dialogue accept that this might imply short-term win–lose situations for some. All major parties participate in the dialogue process given that it seeks to prevent free-rider behaviour and foster a commitment to implement the formulated objectives. Major dilemmas that the parties face in the trade-off between efficiency and equity (Triple-E) are used as input to the dialogue and not as a part of the negotiations.

- *Vision on the dialogue*: A dialogue with stakeholders usually takes place over a given period of time. It is important that the company and stakeholders are aware of this. For a company, this means that it should have a clear vision of the stakeholder discussions as a whole. What is the underlying philosophy? What is the ultimate objective of the discussions? What criteria are employed in the selection of stakeholders for the dialogue, the manner in which and the frequency with which the discussions are held? The company guards against being too indiscriminate in this and seeks to find a balance between accepting invitations for discussions from stakeholders and, alternatively, inviting stakeholders for discussions.

2 Participants

- *Inclusiveness*: The stakeholder dialogue aims to integrate different views through the creation of a new viewpoint and common ground for all parties involved. Potential winners as well as potential losers are joined together in the dialogue.
- *Ownership*: Parties need to be commited to the discussion process at the highest levels in their organization. Issue engagement translates into issue ownership by the most important parties involved. A dialogue cannot be a one-off exercise. Several successive meetings create an opportunity to get to know each other better and foster commitment. According to the WBCSD (2002): 'Aim to build joint ownership for actions towards change to be taken following the dialogue.'
- *Legitimacy*: The dialogue brings together the most important stakeholders and aims to enhance trust through the mutual recognition of one another's expertise and legitimacy. A strategic stakeholder dialogue, therefore, does not consist only of meetings with NGOs, but also with suppliers, employees, shareholders and governments. The transparency of the dialogue process – along a set of rules – ensures the legitimacy of the outcome of the dialogue. The discussion partners refrain from acting independently of those they are representing. If they do, a situation may arise where one of the parties is called back or overruled and where the agreements that have been reached during the dialogue are not honoured. Nothing is more frustrating after a number of consecutive meetings than having to say that, on second thoughts, management or the Board cannot support the results. Just as trying, is if one of the participants is replaced by a successor who does not understand or respect the outcome of earlier meetings. Mutual trust also implies that the parties rely on one another to properly represent the interests and views of their constituents.

3 Procedures

- *Clear rules and benchmarks*: Strategic stakeholder dialogues seek to establish common standards as a means to measure progress and facilitate international coordination and implementation. The dialogue also aims to prevent information asymmetries from influencing the process. It is vital for instance that there is agreement on procedures for dealing with confidential information and the manner in which the parties involved report to their constituents and the media. A confidential discussion is dealt a fatal blow if sensitive information is made public prematurely or if another party is publicly discredited. In general, the likelihood of agreements being violated is proportional to the power imbalances between parties. When entering into a dialogue, both parties effectively place restrictions upon themselves.

■ *Learning*: The dialogue is usually based on the information the parties present about the actual situation. This results in a natural inclination to manipulate or present only those facts that fit one's agenda. It is therefore important that the facts presented are beyond any doubt, which is why an external party sometimes has to scrutinize the information in advance to assess its validity. It is also increasingly common for accountants to verify sustainability reports. But perhaps – given the problematic position of accountants – other verification institutions can be considered, unless accountants are also members of accreditation bodies such as the GRI. Participating parties must possess the skills to conduct a dialogue.

■ *Skills*: The characteristics of a dialogue, as summarized in Table 20.1, column 2, requires a wholly different repertoire and style of communication than that employed when taking part in a debate.

■ *Voices, not votes*: In a strategic stakeholder dialogue all interested parties are given sufficient opportunity to express their opinions. Every position is accepted as legitimate; the problem is separated from the people.

The more strategic a stakeholder dialogue becomes, the more the dialogue should adhere to the basic principles of effective negotiations as specified by Fisher and Ury (1981) in their influential study 'Getting to Yes'.[5] These principles have been widely acclaimed as an excellent means of avoiding the pitfalls of the manifold dilemmas encountered in a 'bargaining society'. Practical experience has shown that insufficient attention or inadequate responses to these preconditions can result in a situation where:

■ stakeholders feel ignored or abused;
■ the discussion becomes repetitive;
■ internal support for the discussions dwindles;
■ confidential information is abused;
■ consensus fails to be reached;
■ the dialogue is insufficiently strategic and proactive, which leads to new conflicts;
■ issues are not addressed appropriately, which leads to repeated (and more intense) confrontation;
■ the level of creativity with which issues are tackled is insufficient, which hampers an 'entrepreneurial' approach to issues.

There is no 'one best way' for conducting a strategic stakeholder dialogue (Zadek, 2001). It is co-determined by the degree of urgency of the issue, the legitimacy and power of stakeholders (Mitchell *et al.*, 1997), the nature of the issues at hand and the willingness of stakeholders to cooperate (Savage *et al.*, 1991). This also applies to the five cases of stakeholder dialogue discussed above (20.3). Many scholars tend to stress that 'trust' is the most important precondition for effective dialogues and societal change. However, issue conflicts arise precisely due to a lack of trust. So, do you talk because you trust each other, or do you trust each other because you talk? Trust is neither a necessary nor a sufficient condition for an effective stakeholder dialogue, just as conflict is neither an effective nor a sufficient condition for a company to acknowledge and meet its responsibilities. The ultimate challenge for an effective stakeholder dialogue, therefore, is to communicate with each other in spite of the absence of a mutual basis of trust and greatly diverging interests.

20.5 CONTENTS AND COMPONENTS OF A STRATEGIC STAKEHOLDER DIALOGUE

An effective dialogue is a stakeholder dialogue, but a stakeholder dialogue is only effective if it deals with strategic issues. An international stakeholder dialogue is only strategic, and also effective, if it adopts a proactive approach to engaging with international corporate responsibilities (see 'Towards a pragmatic-idealist approach to ICR', below) while keeping in mind the five most important challenges (see p. 376) of Societal Interface Management (Chapter 7). The final sections of this chapter and of this study reflect on the possible requirements for and components of such an approach.

Towards a pragmatic-idealist approach to ICR

The strategic analysis conducted in Part II identified four ICR approaches from the perspective of MNEs: inactive, reactive, active and proactive. Each approach embodies a distinct perspective on engaging with the international challenges of Societal Interface Management. Each of these corporate approaches can also be associated with specific international governance problems and ambitions. In international relations theory, it is thereby commonplace to distinguish between a 'realist' and an 'idealist' approach to problems of international governance. What does this imply for ICR strategies and the possible function of strategic stakeholder dialogues?

Realism

A *reactive approach to ICR* represents the 'realistic' approach to corporate responsibility issues and resonates strongly with reactive CSR regimes. It coincides with a liberal global trade and investment regime. Through efficiency-enhancing international trade, this regime is expected to generate greater prosperity for all (cf. Baghwati, 2004). Its international governance principles can be described as neo-liberalist (Gilpin, 2002). International realism legitimizes the active pursuit of (policy) competition between countries on the basis of self-interest. The setting for such endeavours is an international system of individual nation-states, which can be described as 'ordered anarchy'. Realist bargaining operates on the basis of majority rules and weighted voting. Another feature of this approach is the strong call for a 'level' playing field. The (neo-liberal) level playing field is based on the principles of a market economy, free trade and very limited regulation. These principles represent the lowest common denominator of what actors can agree upon to secure efficient global market constellations.

The realist approach presupposes that actors will not be able to reach agreement on any of the other values and goals. By treating all actors the same, the interests of weaker players in the international economy is easily violated since they are often too small or relatively powerless to use the level playing field to their advantage. It can be compared to a basketball match between giants and dwarfs – although the playing field is level, the competitive conditions remain decidedly unfair. The famous economist Paul Samuelson formulates this dilemma succinctly as: 'free trade as the protectionism of the strong'.

Idealism

The 'anti-globalization' movement can be viewed as exemplary of the *active (idealistic)* approach to ICR. It is often a direct response to the negative side of the realist regime. It aspires to the active pursuit of the highest possible human rights and labour standards. Idealism originally manifested in an appeal for 'transgovernmental governance' (Gilpin, 2002) that departs from the notion of interstate cooperation in pursuit of a common societal or community 'good'.

373

Idealist bargaining is characterized by persuasion and the principle of 'one country, one vote'. Idealism signifies a search for the highest possible denominator of what actors can agree upon. Idealist reasoning hopes to enourage a 'race to the top' in establishing ethical values. But an idealist approach to CSR issues also contains the risk of pursuing 'unrealistic' goals that will never materialize in practice due to major differences between the parties and the impossibility to decide upon anything on the basis of unanimity. Managers employing active ICR standards tend to focus primarily on their international integrity and other fiduciary duties. An international stakeholder dialogue on the basis of idealist principles requires a considerable degree of trust among all partners, which is probably only possible in cases where the actors are relatively equal in strength and size.

The idealism–realism dichotomy does not suffice to reveal all relevant dimensions of international governance problems and ICR strategies (Table 20.3). Two additions can be proposed to move beyond this simple dichotomy: pragmatism and pragmatic-idealism.

Pragmatism

An *inactive* approach to ICR is largely derived from international realism, but also takes the relative position of the national economy and/or core firms into account. Pragmatism comes into play especially when the rules of the game in the international arena have originally been set by others. An inactive approach to ICR is particularly adopted by latecomer firms and developing countries that experience the international rules of the game as 'unfair'. Pragmatism does not prevent countries and firms from participating in international dialogues and negotiations, but it does stimulate the selective implementation of rules that have been agreed upon. A pragmatic approach to ICR is particularly tempting for companies and countries that face serious development and competitiveness problems. Not taking these problems into account also creates serious social problems for the weaker countries and firms.

An inactive ICR approach embodies the risk of 'neo-*mercantilism*'.[6] Mercantilism was originally intended to keep prices for agricultural products as low as possible by discriminating against rural areas in favour of urban areas in Renaissance Europe (Cohen, 1998). Nowadays, mercantilism is a feature of international trade policy. The basic design of mercantilism is one of restricting imports and expanding exports. The mercantilist policies of the 1920s were associated with 'beggar-thy-neighbour' strategies that caused a global economic crisis. A less defensive version of mercantilist policies, are the so-called 'strategic trade' policies, in which countries try to use trade barriers and industry subsidies selectively 'in order to capture some of the profits of foreign firms' (Gerber, 2005: 97). Strategic trade policies are a response to the reality of imperfect competition across borders and increasing returns in the international marketplace (for instance on the basis of technological resources) (cf. Krugman, 1986). Strategic trade policy and neo-mercantilism, in practice, are also a response to the 'protectionism of the strong' embedded in realist strategies.

Pragmatic idealism

Finally, the ambition of a *proactive* ICR strategy is to interactively link home- and host-country norms and values through various interactions between home and host stakeholders. It combines the realist and idealist tradition in international relations and can be described as a 'pragmatic idealist' approach. Pragmatic (transgovernmental) governance networks and processes of consensus building seem particularly well suited to address international interface issues. The most elaborate transgovernmental governance networks at the moment are constructed in the form of regional integration agreements. Regional integration agreements provide a political,

Table 20.3 Four ICR approaches

	Inactive	Reactive	Active	Pro/interactive
	Indifferent corporate responsibility	International corporate responsiveness	International corporate responsibility	International community responsibility
	Pragmatism	Realism	Idealism	Pragmatic Idealism
Interaction principles	Debate		Dialogue	
	Global efficiency		Global equity	International effectiveness
	Participation	Weighted majority	Persuasion and unanimity	Consensus
International public–private interface	Limited international regulation; beggar thy neighbour; no common denominator	Active pursuit of policy competition; lowest common denominator: 'level playing field'	Search for new 'just' global public goods; prevent public 'bads'; highest possible denominator	Effective provision of 'public–private' goods; avoid policy competition through harmonization; 'fair playing field'
Governance principle	Neo-mercantilism	Neo-liberalism	Transgovernmentalism	Open regionalism?
Profit–non-profit interface	Race to the bottom is acceptable as long as it strengthens own comp. position	Active pursuit of race to the bottom in host countries	Global + multilateralism Defining a minimum threshold (bottom) that is just; active pursuit of 'race to the top'	Harmonizing standards for fair labour, environmental and human rights conditions
Prominent issues	(Core) growth regime issues	Primary responsibilities of host states and civil society	Fiduciary duties of company/managers	International interface issues
Leadership style	Transactional	Charismatic	Visionary and moral	Transformational

social and economic platform for strategic dialogues among the most important players in the region. The nature of those dialogues depends on the 'depth' and the 'breadth' of the regional integration initiative. If regional integration is only based on pragmatic considerations it can function as a stumbling block to globalization and strategic dialogues with important external stakeholders, particularly if neo-mercantilist policies are adopted. If regional integration is also based on idealistic considerations it can facilitate strategic interaction with outside stakeholders (such as firms from developing countries). This principle is implicit in the notion of 'Open regionalism' (Bergsten, 1997). In the international arena, proactive ICR seeks partnerships (public–private as well as profit–non-profit) in order to find pragmatic solutions to interface issues. *Benchmarks* and *best practices* can trigger or challenge the movement beyond the lowest-common-denominator solutions of realism, but without the risk of falling into the idealist trap – setting standards that are too high and winding up with an even lower common denominator. Only on the basis of multi-level and strategic stakeholder dialogues with a large number of (host/home) stakeholders can an appropriate proactive ICR strategy be developed.

Addressing five Societal Interface Management challenges

A proactive (pragmatic idealist) approach to ICR has the potential of reconciling the problems respectively associated with the pragmatist, realist and idealist approaches to international governance problems. But, the analysis in Part II also showed that the institutional require-ments for a proactive and pragmatic-idealist ICR strategy do not (yet) exist. Hardly any of national or international CSR regimes facilitate proactive ICR strategies. If multinational corpo-rations themselves were to take the initiative, what would such an ICR regime look like? Part I (Chapter 7) identified five Societal Interface Management challenges that need to be addressed. In terms of the international strategic stakeholder dialogue these challenges are: (1) the level and location of execution of strategic dialogues; (2) the trade-off in the public/private dialogue; (3) the trade-off in the profit/non-profit dialogue; (4) technological progress through stake-holder dialogues; (5) leadership roles in strategic stakeholder dialogues.

1 Local–national–international

At which societal level and in which arena should the dialogue be conducted? Chapter 5 revealed that companies concentrate most of their restructuring activities at the local and the regional levels. Some issues are, indeed, best addressed locally. Many environmental issues, for instance, concern negative externalities of production and distribution systems concentrated in the same locality. Customers and manufacturers live in the same neighbourhood and could address their problems quite adequately in a local-level dialogue. The enormous increase in the economic importance of so-called non-marketable good and services renders economies more 'local', making it possible to implement effective local solutions to local problems. The alternative globalization movement (cf. Korten, 1995) also emphasizes the local level in effectively dealing with numerous issues in the area of Societal Interface Management. This movement has gener-ated interesting ideas that are worth developing further.

On other matters, in the area of standardization, quality labels and codes of conduct, for example, the international level is indispensable. For the time being, international regions such as the EU, NAFTA, ASEAN and Mercosur seem to offer the best conditions for an effective dialogue on these issues. The adequate provision of global public goods can, in the short run, be served by (open) regionalism – provided it does not lapse into regional mercantilism. Within these regions, comparable approaches to ICR have been adopted, which creates better precon-ditions for an effective dialogue.

Globally, it seems of great importance that the exclusivity of *single-issue* organizations, on the side of entrepreneurs (market), the government (state) as well as civil society, is overcome. At the global level, the three first approaches to ICR (inactive, reactive, active) are also linked to rival economic systems (Asia, Anglo-Saxon and Europe respectively). For internationally operating firms, this rivalry and its associated uncertainty on the outlook of international institutions bears considerable risks (see Chapter 12). The formation of new coalitions between the three institutions of society will therefore have to be one of the first topics of discussion in a strategic stakeholder dialogue. One innovative way of addressing global issues is through the establishment of 'global issues networks' (Box 20.1).

2 Public/private

There is much hesitation among companies to call for legislation in certain areas or to have their self-regulatory activities verified by external parties. Public–private partnerships represent an important alternative in addressing more specifically matters that have been neglected. This, however, requires transparency and clear dialogue with citizens about the desirability of proposed projects. Improvements have to be made in line with the above-specified requirements for a stakeholder dialogue. Companies that adopt a proactive/interactive attitude and clearly communicate their thoughts with regard to collective goods will command more confidence from civil society than those who think exclusively in terms of private (marketable) goods and profit maximization. Governments, in turn, will be able to retreat to their core competencies.

In the past, international companies have actively used their powers in their dealings with cross-border governments. The prime challenge for international companies will be to define 'global' or 'regional' public goods and specify the extent to which they would like to contribute to that. This, for instance, would require them to define 'fair taxes' and 'fair competition',

---

BOX 20.1 GLOBAL ISSUES NETWORKS AS STRATEGIC STAKEHOLDER DIALOGUE

The idea of Global Issues Networks (GINs), initiated by J.F. Rischard in 2002 (and discussed in Chapter 9), explicitly addresses the most important problem of the international bargaining society, namely the lack of appropriate rules (institutions). In his elaboration on the manner in which the lacking institutions must be addressed, Rischard adopts a typically interactive international Societal Interface Management approach: he calls for setting up networks that are not hierarchically managed, but 'facilitated' by network managers. The participants of each issue network must represent the three spheres of the societal triangle more or less proportionally. Once the issue network is formed, approximately 2–3 years must be spent on the joint analysis of the problem and the generation of a possible solution after which for ten or more years the network is responsible for implementing the solutions. The number of participants increases drastically in this final phase. All participants conform to the rules of the game that have been established earlier or to an international standard. Rischard sees more use in a loose non-hierarchical network of pragmatists than in a centrally led hierarchically structured global nation attempting to address a given issue. He calls this 'network governance'. In this way, he skilfully steers the problem of internationally operating 'single-issue' players on a productive course. Could it work?

but also to formulate a view on how a 'race to the bottom' can be avoided. Whereas some firms will be tempted to deny the existence of such a race and thus adopt a *buffering* attitude, proactive MNEs will organize an international stakeholder dialogue on exactly this issue in an attempt to *bridge* conflicts of interest between governments, NGOs and firms.

In the preceding chapters we have seen that issues at the public–private interface generate the greatest reputational effects. Chapter 19 suggested that this can be due to the increasing willingness of single-issue NGOs to avail themselves of 'naming and shaming' tactics. It was also noted that these NGOs (human rights and environmental NGOs) are expecting to focus

---

BOX 20.2 CORE COMPANIES

The American comic hero Spider-man was inspired, but also confused by the statement 'With great power, comes great responsibility'. Spider-man's consecutive adventures not only turned around the exact implementation of this responsibility, but also on what exactly defined 'great power'. The same applies to the realm of International Business–Society Management. The power base of companies is primarily defined along the public–private and profit–non-profit interfaces in its relationship with governments and civil society. As Chapter 3 has indicated, comparing companies with countries – as many of the most critical company watchers tend to do – has its methodological deficiencies. In the (international) business literature a variety of concepts has been introduced to characterize and even measure the relative impact of companies on society. This includes sizable linkages and spill-over effects through the manifold network configurations managed by MNEs (Dunning, 1993). Rugman and D'Cruz (2000) introduced the concept of 'flagship firms', whereas Lorenzoni and Baden-Fuller (1995) use the concept of 'leader firms', to illustrate the power base of focal firms.

Most characterizations, however, tend to miss more subtle aspects of company power such as technological advantage, political involvement or horizontal/vertical positioning in supply chains (Muller, 2004: 165). Since 1995, the SCOPE team at Erasmus University has been developing and operationalizing the concept of 'core companies' as a proxy to measure the relative 'powers' of, in particular, Multinational Enterprises on Society (Ruigrok and van Tulder, 1995; van Tulder *et al.*, 2001). Key in this assessment is the positioning decisions made by companies in networks of (1) supply and demand (degree of vertical integration), (2) markets (degree of horizontal differentiation/diversification), (3) technologies (measured by R&D concentration ratios), and (4) societies (measured by degree of internationalization). Core companies generally share a comparatively large size; not necessarily because powers always require size, but because size mirrors the power accumulation of the past. The management of a core firm always has a vision of the position of the company in society and a relatively high degree of independence from other actors in the supply chain it operates, for instance, because it controls vital core technologies and other strategic competencies. Leading firms as regards codes of conduct and sustainable management practices can often be found in the group of core companies, not least because they are targeted by NGOs as 'icons' (see Chapter 19). This makes core companies also the most relevant 'agents of change' in International Business–Society Management. The approach chosen by core companies on their responsibilities has widespread effects on society. The exact documentation of the strategies of core companies, however, is only in its infancy. The future research effort at the Erasmus University therefore will focus in particular on the strategies of core companies around the world and the way these companies, in particular, can link their powers with appropriate responsibilities (www.ib-sm.org).

on either their watchdog or project partner roles in future. NGOs that operate at the public–private interface are characterized by a relatively strict division of roles where one group concentrates on confrontation and debate, and other groups on collaboration and dialogue. These NGOs will not suffer much from role conflicts. The bargaining environment for MNEs will therefore remain relatively antagonistic unless companies are able to convince the protest-oriented NGOs that they are addressing the problems they put on the agenda. Public–private issues should nevertheless encourage firms to pursue stakeholder dialogue more actively. The most important requirement for this dialogue is that it is strategic and explicitly aimed at sustainability. All major NGOs in this area are aimed at long-term issues. The fact that environmental and human rights NGOs have recently started to express an interest in strategic stakeholder dialogue presents a golden opportunity for firms (van Tulder *et al.*, 2004).

3 Profit/non-profit

Important innovations are taking place in the non-profit and voluntary sectors. More recognition for this both from governments and entrepreneurs can form the basis for conducting a more constructive and strategic dialogue. Social capital, stable working conditions, and good training and education are strategically invaluable for a well-functioning economy and competitive companies. Social capital in the form of 'created assets' such as R&D networks, high levels of education and stable governance structures, have become increasingly important in international location decisions. In addition, a revaluation of the labour movement as most relevant representative of civil society is also in order. When it comes to complex issues at the interface of market and civil society, not a single society can afford not to have adequately functioning organizations with sufficient resources, know-how, legitimacy and vision to conduct the dialogue on 'decent' wages and labour conditions.

As discussed in Chapter 19, NGOs operating at the profit/non-profit interface are often *multiple-issue* organizations, occupying a range of roles in their interaction with companies. The clearest examples are the labour movement and consumer interest organizations. In Europe, they combine the role of watchdog, shareholder, supervisor, partner and even of competitor. Among NGOs, trade unions seem most interested in engaging in strategic stakeholder dialogues with MNEs. But, because of its multiple roles, the actual dialogue will be more difficult to manage than the dialogue with single-issue NGOs at the public–private interface. At the same time, weaker reputation effects in labour markets as opposed to consumer or capital markets lower the urgency for MNEs to engage in proactive stakeholder dialogues. The longer tradition of confrontation at the profit/non-profit interface will make it more difficult to engage in a strategic stakeholder dialogue with NGOs. One of the challenges MNEs face particularly in their relationship with civil society representatives is to develop a credible *counterfactual argument* (see Chapter 13). What are the positive and negative spin-offs and spillover effects for local communities? An increasing number of companies refer in their sustainability reports to their direct and indirect contribution to employment, taxes or innovation in local communities. A major challenge will be to make these statements verifiable and comparable.

New social movements are materializing especially at the profit/non-profit interface. One part of this movement is adopting the role of 'competitor' (BINGO) for instance in the area of 'fair ware', 'fair trade' or 'fair food'. Strategic stakeholder dialogues between these competitors take the form of strategic alliances or joint-ventures. The experience with strategic alliances has not been very positive, though. This has been found in cases where the parties turned out to have conflicting aims. Another part of the new social movement focuses on development issues in particular. Most managers of development NGOs are increasingly open to pragmatic-idealist partnerships with firms. But they have to take care not to alienate their traditional constituencies. The members of these organizations joined them in the 1960s and 1970s – during the first phase of CSR – and are still very suspicious about the role of MNEs in developing countries. The challenge for firms is to develop these partnerships not only as a PR effort or as a market-entry strategy, but as a genuine collaborative effort. Strategic partnerships with development NGOs will only be successful and sustainable if this requirement is met.

4 Technology-society

The direction of technological progress is, arguably, the most strategic topic to organize a stakeholder dialogue on. Technological progress is an iterative process. Within companies, the interface between R&D, production and marketing departments often consists of Chinese walls. Whereas production and marketing are still to some extent capable of developing products in interaction with society and suppliers, R&D – certainly in large companies, due to the strategic character of the activity – takes place somewhat in isolation. If companies do collaborate, the outside world is shut out by closed strategic alliances or corporate venturing which often entails exclusive collaborations with external laboratories. In all cases, the interaction takes place especially in the technological area. Society is the most important stakeholder in technological advancement, but in practice it is barely involved in its development. The need for strategic stakeholder dialogues on technological advancements that are organized by companies, themselves, increases further with the growing 'privatization' and concentration of R&D expenditures in a limited number of core firms (Chapter 3).

The experience of Scandinavian countries shows that the involvement of specific stakeholder groups – for example, the elderly – in the development of specific products can lead to enormous market expansion for companies while simultaneously meeting the needs of a marginalized group in society. Technological progress is an area in which an informed government and open companies can discuss matters of principle at a much earlier stage. A strategic stakeholder dialogue can once again put flesh on the failed idea of a *Constructive Technology Assessment* of the early 1980s (led, for instance, by the Office of Technology Assessment in the US). In the past, several governments have attempted to involve (uninformed) citizens in major technology discussions, for instance on nuclear energy or on the introduction of biotechnology in food. But these efforts did not work in practice. Moreover, they tended to take the form of a 'debate', which is the wrong instrument and, as a result of which, it was never established to what extent a (strategic) dialogue could have delivered different results.

Citizens, however, can be more involved in the development of specific products. Innovation, as it happens, seldom consists only of technological development, but increasingly also of the adaptation and diffusion of relevant technologies in interaction with groups of stakeholders. By means of *issue advertising*, a company can start a dialogue on technological issues and make society partner in its dilemmas. An interesting example is the advertisements that appeared in a number of leading journals with respect to energy issues (see Box 20.3). The examples in the box illustrate that there are notable national and organizational differences in corporate issue advertising. An American firm such as ChevronTexaco stresses traditional technology – without reference to new technologies – global markets and growth possibilities. The Japanese company stresses its long-term aims and its adherence to standards in major host markets (with the additional clear marketing aim in suggesting the superiority of its technological solutions). The European company (Shell) shares its dilemmas with the public, specifies the trade-off between traditional (fossil fuels) and new technologies (solar power and the like) and invites the public to respond. The joint-venture between the state and two private companies (from the US and Europe), is most candid about the dilemmas confronted at the public–private interface and invites the public to participate in a dialogue.

BOX 20.3 ISSUE ADVERTISEMENT: FOUR WAYS TO DISCUSS FUTURE ENERGY PROBLEMS

'A license to operate in hydrogen energy?'

In 2002, the Nederlandse Aardolie Maatschappij (NAM) – a joint-venture of Shell, ExxonMobil and the Dutch government – launched a large-scale campaign involving the Dutch national newspapers, a separate website and round table discussions. Through the campaign, NAM challenged citizens to respond to the energy dilemma that companies cannot solve on their own and which concerns society as a whole. The NAM invited the general public to participate in a dialogue on the management of the country's future energy needs. By means of a separately established website, stakeholders could enter into dialogue with the company. Observations and opinions that were made or given were accessible to all users of the site. NAM was, among other things, curious about citizens' opinions about the development of energy technologies in the short and especially in the long term, the role of energy in society and issues such as the use of hydrogen energy. 'Should we (NAM and the rest of society) continue the exploration for new gas fields – in the Netherlands or preferably in other countries? Can we predict the consequences? Or should we focus more on alternative sources of energy? Do we already have the appropriate technology at our disposal to do so?' In reading the website and the advertisements in newspapers, it became clear that citizens are starting to become partners in issues of concern to the NAM and society as a whole.

'Aim: zero emissions'

In 2003/2004, Toyota, the Japanese car manufacturer, placed a series of advertisements in European newspapers (e.g. the *Financial Times*) in which it explicitly stated its aim to reduce emissions to zero in the near future in combination with its commercial ambition to sell fuel-efficient cars today. 'Reducing emissions to zero may seem a long way off. But this is our aim.' Toyota is a worldwide leader in the manufacturing and sale of hybrid cars which run on a rechargeable battery and petrol. Toyota boasts not only that its hybrid cars 'cut fuel consumption by almost 45 per cent, compared to a conventional petrol engine' but also that emissions 'are 80 per cent below the European standard for 2005'.

'The real price of oil'

In 2003, with a picture of the oil platform Brent Charlie in the North Sea at the top and a little motto at the bottom of the page ('Profits. Principles. Or both?'), Shell ran the following advertisement in *Business Week*:

> We're all involved in the oil business. Every time we start our cars, turn on our lights, cook a meal or heat our homes, we're relying on some form of fuel to make it happen. Up to now, it's inevitably been a fossil fuel, part of the carbon chain. And, just as inevitably, that will have to change. Long before we decide to stop using fossil fuels, costs will have already made the decision for us. Not just the monetary cost, but the human cost, the cultural cost, the environmental cost. We will, quite rightly, demand that our future energy is both sustainable and renewable. We will expect a lot from the likes of solar power, wind power, geothermal power and hydrogen fuel cells. And it will take time . . . we have to strike a balance . . . between the need to protect people's way of life and their environment and the need to provide them with affordable energy. . . . This is what Shell does every day, all over the world. This is why we need to hear from and listen to, everyone who has an interest in the world.

'Turning partnerships into energy'

In 2003, ChevronTexaco ran a number of advertisements (among others in the *Financial Times* and *The Economist*) under the heading: 'The world needs more energy and we're sharing ways to get it.' It read:

> Developing energy today requires the most advanced technology. Like the world's first floating spar platform that lets us simultaneously drill and produce in deep water. We're sharing innovations like that with our partners. And helping them build the skills to use them. Because meeting energy needs, while developing people and opportunity, is how we put strong partnerships together.

Another version of the same advertisement read:

> Developing energy together helps economies soar. . . . We're developing vast energy resources that once were locked far from global markets. . . . In the end, our partnerships deliver more than energy. They also deliver all the growth and promise that come with it.

In 2001–2002 the WBCSD was involved in about 25 international stakeholder dialogues. Some of the most important of these dialogues concerned innovation and technology. One example is the dialogue about an effective global intellectual property regime (IPR) that is aimed at aligning the interests of innovating companies with those of (poor) people. Whether current and future stakeholder dialogues organized by the WBCSD will generate new solutions to old dilemmas of Societal Interface Management, depends on the degree to which the WBCSD adheres to the preconditions of an effective stakeholder dialogue (which does not seem to be the case as yet).

5 Operational-visionary

Corporate vision and leadership are becoming increasingly 'in vogue'. Once the biggest scandals have faded away – only conceivable if the process is organized in the form of a strategic stakeholder dialogue – the more socially inspired themes can get the attention they deserve. If entrepreneurs want to concern themselves with the real CSR issues – and not only with those issues that society raises – proactive, transformational and international leadership is required. The extremely important role of visionary transformational CEOs in this process has become increasingly acknowledged (cf. Garten, 2002).

PRIORITIES

The themes proper to the 'domain of the market' are the logical first priority for entrepreneurs. No entrepreneur can afford the reputation of crook, fraud, money-grubber or speculator. Addressing these issues – such as 'fair' remuneration for CEOs – by organizing a strategic stakeholder dialogue has not really been attempted. The 'corporate governance' committees around the world have only come up with marginally adequate solutions, so the issue is bound to reappear with unpredictable effects on the reputation of the company and its CEO. There is still considerable room for proactive international leadership. A second priority is represented by issues at the public/private and profit/non-profit interfaces. In these areas, a great number of initiatives are already under way, but leaders could make coordination of, and reporting on, these activities the topic of a strategic stakeholder dialogue. A third priority concerns the themes for which the prime responsibility largely falls to government and civil society – such as individual freedom, democracy, sufficient clean air and prevention of war. Entrepreneurs can apply themselves to creating the preconditions for governments and other stakeholders to actually fulfil their responsibilities in these areas. At a minimum, this implies that initiatives are not obstructed and that leaders signal, for instance, the problems of *adverse selection* which hampers the effective spread of best-practice standards (Chapter 12).

GLOBALIZATION

One of the hottest generic issues that business leaders have been facing is 'globalization'. Leadership styles of CEOs can be judged from their attitude towards globalization in particular (Table 20.2). Large MNEs have been the prime shapers and (ideological) protagonists of globalization (cf. Sklair, 2001). For that reason, they are also targeted by critical NGOs that reproach them for the negative consequences of globalization. The way business leaders deal with globalization, therefore, influences the nature of the confrontation or dialogue between civil society and firms. Inactive business leaders only refer to the economic benefits of economic globalization and are primarily interested in the transactional side of internationalization processes. Reactive business leaders adopt more charismatic attributes and concentrate on shaping globalization to their own advantage. Normative leadership is found especially among CEOs that favour globalization for its social potential. Proactive business leaders try to form a balanced view of globalization that takes into account the costs and benefits, and the social and political dimensions of globalization. A balanced view requires a transformational leadership style, which in turn facilitates a strategic dialogue between company and stakeholders from government (politics) and civil society (social). The CEOs of the world's leading MNEs have been inclined to adopt transactional and charismatic leadership styles (Box 20.4). In a comment to the statements made by business leaders at the World Economic Forum in 2005, the *Financial Times* reproached business leaders for their particular 'poverty of ideas' on the real issues (in particular poverty and environmental degradation).

BOX 20.4 BUSINESS LEADERS ON 'GLOBALIZATION'

One way of establishing the strategic stance of business leaders on globalization is to analyse their written statements in their company's annual financial reports. It can be assumed that statements in a document with a clear legal status such as the financial report are more reliable than what can be found in a newspaper interview or public lecture. The messages of the CEOs of the *Fortune* Global 100 were examined for their views on economic, political and/or social globalization (Table 20.4). A total amount of 269 messages over four years (1990, 1995, 2000 and 2002) were analysed. The year 2000 represents the zenith of the 'globalization' movement, with 31.1 per cent of all instances where 'global(ization)' was referred to. Since then, the trend has gradually lost its appeal. The year 1995 represents the height of regionalism (43.7 per cent of all references made to regionalism) which seamlessly mirrors the formation of NAFTA and the enlargement of the EU in the same year. Over the whole period, most CEOs speak of economic globalization in favourable terms. Recently, CEOs have also started to pay attention to the advantages of social globalization particularly in response to the arguments and actions of the anti-globalization movement. Most statements of the CEOs, however, remain one-sided. In none of the annual reports do CEOs exhibit an awareness of the potentially negative impacts or dilemmas that accompany globalization. Only in the case of political globalization do arguments in favour and against globalization appear at the same time.

Table 20.4 CEO opinions on economic, political and social globalization (N = 269 annual reports on the basis of 42 keywords)

'Global' vision	1990	1995	2000	2002	Total	%
Pro economic (12/12)	20	52	83	54	209	64.5
Pro political (7/8)	3	8	6	11	28	8.6
Pro social (7/7)	15	18	16	21	70	21.6
Contra economic (0/5)	0	0	0	0	0	0
Contra political (3/6)	0	0	3	14	17	5.2
Contra social (0/4)	0	0	0	0	0	0
Total (29/42)	38	78	108	100	324	
%	11.7	24.1	33.3	30.9		

Source: SCOPE leadership research and Phoa (2005)

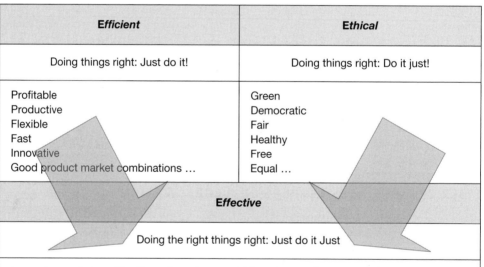

Efficient	Ethical
Doing things right: Just do it!	Doing things right: Do it just!
Profitable Productive Flexible Fast Innovative Good product market combinations ...	Green Democratic Fair Healthy Free Equal ...

Effective

Doing the right things right: Just do it Just

Improving market position through environmental investments; Improve market share through good labour conditions at suppliers; Innovation with justifiable patent protection; interactive innovation (products that fit real consumer preferences); high productivity through higher wages for employees; Innovative through employee diversity; Poverty as networking challenge: how to set up marketing, distribution and innovative networks in collaboration with local firms to structurally eradicate poverty

In short: **Sustainable sustainable competitive advantage (SSCA)**

Figure 20.2 The challenge of a sustainable sustainable competitive advantage

MBA EFFECT

A possible litmus test for the stakeholder dialogue is whether it can correct the so-called 'MBA effect'. Research conducted by the Aspen Institute among 2,000 MBA students in the US in 2001, shows that the norms and values of MBA students change during the course of their training: at the end of their studies they place lower value on customer needs and product quality than at the beginning, while they place higher value on shareholder value compared to stakeholder value (*Economist*, 27 July 2002). The MBA effect also relates to the 'hype character' of CSR and moral leadership. In 2002, Insead students in Europe 'introduced a graduate pledge in which they vowed to work only for ethical companies. Two years later the pledge was abandoned' (*Financial Times*, 25 April 2005). In the strategic stakeholder dialogue, managers, together with clients and other (societal) stakeholders, can join forces to redefine priorities so as to develop a more contemporary and sustainable vision of the role and position of the company in society. The strategic stakeholder dialogue thus operationalizes the ultimate objective that, according to management guru Michael Porter, every company should strive towards: 'sustainable competitive advantage'. In the context of this book this ambition is better described as creating a '*sustainable* sustainable competitive advantage'. Which entrepreneur would not aspire to effectiveness and to doing the right things right? In Figure 20.2 the challenge of a *sustainable* sustainable competitive advantage is summarized in a number of concrete management objectives.

20.6 EPILOGUE: THE PROCESS DETERMINES THE RESULT

An international strategic stakeholder dialogue can be the beginning of a new 'social contract' (Donaldson and Dunfee, 1999). In the history of humankind, the creation or adaptation of contracts has often been the subject of intense conflict – complete with revolutions and even wars. There is much reason to fear that the tug of war surrounding socially responsible or sustainable business practice will largely take the form of a debate. If that turns out to be the case, it would imply that the actors in this drama place more importance on being right than on pursuing what is right for society. In this chapter, an attempt was made to sketch the outlines of a procedure to move beyond this dilemma: a strategic dialogue with stakeholders that will eventually result in a new social contract. Such a contract, however, represents an *attitude* rather than a written agreement from which participants can derive a detailed set of rules.[7] Governments cannot disengage themselves from this dialogue. Although they may only be one of several players, it would not be desirable to assign them the role of 'secondary' stakeholder or referee. The contours of sustainable business practice, as yet, are too unclear to assume fixed rules of the game that governments (or other supervisors) can subsequently oversee.

It is impossible to set out the exact content of the dialogue between primary stakeholders with respect to societal interface challenges – this is precisely what should be the subject of discussion. The fairness of the outcome strongly depends on the correct structuring of the process. That process is called (international) Societal Interface Management. The academic discipline that documents this process is called 'International Business–Society Management' and its chief aim is to establish what determines the international success and failure of firms in interaction with society.

Notes

INTRODUCTION TO PART I

1 Since 1990, the UN Security Council has officially declared a threat to international peace and security 61 times, while this occurred only six times in the preceding 45 years (Simmons and de Jonge, 2001: 7).

2 UC Atlas of Global Inequality, http://ucatlas.ucsc.edu.

3 According to *Forbes* magazine, the three richest men in the world in 2004 were Bill Gates III (Microsoft, US$46.6 billion), Warren Buffet (investor, US$42.9 billion) and Karl Albrecht (Aldi supermarket chain, US$23 billion). http://www.forbes.com/maserati/billionaires2004.

1 RIVAL INSTITUTIONS: SOCIETY AS TRIANGULAR RELATIONSHIP

1 The definition of 'institutions' most often used is that given by institutional economist Douglas North (1991): 'Institutions . . . consist of formal rules, informal constraints – norms of behavior, conventions, and self-imposed codes of conduct – and their enforcement characteristics.'

2 For the sake of argument, designating the production of private goods to the 'market' and club goods to 'civil society' here has proceeded more schematically than reality would support. See also the discussion in section 1.2.

3 This statement, of course, must be qualified: parliament can always pose public questions and the auditor's office in most countries can carry out audits on its own initiative.

4 The group of leaders researched consisted of (1) all heads of state of countries with more than 300,000 inhabitants (N = 180), (2) the CEOs of the *Fortune* Global 100, (3) the leaders of the 20 most important NGOs such as Greenpeace, Amnesty International, Friends of the Earth.

5 The quick privatizations in the Central and Eastern European regions followed divergent strategies and had mixed results; Stiglitz (1999) and others have evaluated the distribution of ownership among employees (and why this failed), among the population (and what went wrong there) as well as the distribution over a few big institutional investors (and what failed there).

6 Ministry of Industry, Employment and Communication (2000) *Annual Report for Government-Owned Companies*, Stockholm.

7 Global Development Research Centre, www.gdrc.org, consulted March 2004.

8 According to the Swedish journal *Veckans Affärer*, Ikea founder Ingvar Kamprad surpassed Bill Gates in 2004 as richest man in the world with US$53 billion in capital. Ikea is a family-owned 'foundation'.

9 www.islamic-banking.com; consulted on 15 March 2004.

10 For statistical highlights on the modern cooperative housing movement see: http://web.uvic.ca/bcics/resarch/housing/statistics.html; from these data it can be seen that in Chile, for instance, over 20 per cent of low-rent housing is cooperative, Germany has over 800,000 housing cooperatives, New York City alone has 600,000 house units run as cooperatives, whereas Turkey has over 200,000 cooperative homes with 800,000 people.

11 see: www.eurocoopbanks.com (website European Association of Cooperative banks).

12 In 2003, students at Rome's Sapienza University paid up to 3,000 euros to pass their exams (*The Economist*, 24 January 2004). Officially, 25 per cent of Italian tertiary education funding comes from private sources, but this figure is probably too low. This is not surprising for a country with the largest 'informal' sector in Europe. In 2001/2002, the issue of 'grade inflation' popped up in the US and with Harvard University in particular; one professor even used two sets of grades: external/internal. External grades were considerably higher than the internal grades. The high tuition fees payed by students allegedly stimulates business schools to grant higher grades to stay on top of rankings and help students in their job applications (BBC News, 14 January 2002).

13 Hybrid organizations can also display streaks of great social *ir*responsibility. The international Mafia is an example of such a conscious hybrid (less tangible) organization that functions precisely at the edge of the various interfaces, exclusively with the interests of the family in mind. The objectives are laudable and many Mafiosi are deeply religious, with a strong sense of 'belonging' to the group. Superficial moral indignation at many of the principles of the Mafia will therefore not wash. But concern about the (often violent) methods that are used is all the more justified. The dividing line between (seemingly) socially/societally responsible and socially/societally irresponsible business practice can be slim and confusing.

2 RIVAL MODELS: INTERACTIONS WITHIN AND BETWEEN SOCIETIES

1 The 'threat' of punitive damages in court due to abuse of its monopoly position creates ever-increasing transaction costs for Microsoft. In 2003, Microsoft paid out more than US$2.6 billion in out-of-court settlements. An out-of-court settlement with AOL Time Warner – for unfair competition – for instance, cost the company US$750 million (*Vk*, 31 December 2003). A comparable out-of-court settlement with Sun Microsystems in March 2004 cost Microsoft US$1.6 billion (ibid., March 2004). The anti-trust fine imposed on Microsoft by the EC in 2004 – of more than US$600 million looks relatively small moneywise, but will have greater strategic consequences for the company. It is also the largest fine ever imposed on any company by the EC and has triggered debate in the US that the EC is abusing its regulatory powers in the economic rivalry with the US in high-tech areas such as software.

2 Since 2002, the Linux business model has progressed into a cooperative venture in which employees (programmers) of more than 20 large companies such as IBM, Intel and Hewlett-Packard along with thousands of individuals work together to improve the software. The software remains freely available to all-comers (*Business Week*, 31 January 2005).

3 Since 2001, Berners-Lee, as head of the World Wide Web Consortium based at MIT, is coordinating a global team to build a semantic web. This network will be able to handle the complex number of human languages which will lead to greater user-friendliness (*Business Week*, 4 April 2002).

4 *Business Week* (8 November 2004) featuring Berners-Lee in a series of 'great innovators' has a clear answer to the latter question: 'doing so might have made him – not Bill Gates – the world's richest person'. This is not that obvious, however. Patenting the WWW might have stalled the spread of the web, which in turn would have watered down his earning prospects considerably (it would probably also have lowered the spread of PCs and consequently limited Gates's earnings – which in turn would have made the Bill and Melinda Gates foundation less generous for addressing tropical diseases, see chapter 10).

5 The empirical validity of Hofstede's characterizations has been confirmed by an enormous number of studies; but they have also been strongly contested as too 'reductionist', a form of 'ex-post' reasoning, ascribing too much value to cultural characteristics, based only on one company's information (IBM) and the like. The masculinity/femininity dimension, in particular, has been under discussion for its analytical and conceptual usefulness. For this reason, we will refrain from using this dimension to elaborate on the characteristics of some of the successful models. Most other studies that have been equally well quoted primarily try to specify particular characteristics of Hofstede, come to more specific cultural clusters or make the link between national culture and corporate culture, not to rebut him; see in particular Trompenaars and Hampden Turner (1997). In the International Business literature, the discussion has focused on the issue of 'cultural distance' to explain particular management problems for firms that have to overcome greater or smaller cultural distances.

6 Other measures of openness are technology transfers (for which no reliable international comparative sources exist), migration, telephone conversations and remittances – personal financial transactions across borders. These measures are less useful for the present discussion.

7 Besides, many large countries (US, Japan, Brazil, China, India) in 1998 still had import shares below 15 per cent of GDP.

8 The measurement of outward FDI stock provides a minimum assessment of outward openness; many firms, after the initial investment, finance the expansion of their foreign activities out of 'reinvested earnings' that are not included in this FDI measurement. The ratio of new investment versus reinvested earnings can range from 1:1.5 to 1:9, depending on national accounting practices. See UNCTAD, 2003.

9 The criteria for calculating rankings include life expectancy, educational attainment and adjusted real income. Countries with a Human Development Index (HDI) of over 0.800 form part of the High Human Development group. Between 0.500 and 0.800, countries form part of the Medium Human Development group and below 0.500 they are part of the Low Human Development group.

10 Ireland can be mentioned as another success story: on the basis of very large inward FDI, it managed to change from one of Europe's poorest economies to relative wealth; Ireland's exports have the highest share of 'high-tech' within Europe (cf. UNCTAD, 2003 where Ireland and Singapore are compared). Ireland ranked seventeenth on the HDI list of 2003, thus occupying a substantially lower position than the three small European countries included in the text.

11 Which includes the so-called 'Rhineland model' (Albert, 1993); in this approach the model also includes most of the South and Central European countries that are generally not considered to belong to the Rhineland model.

3 RIVAL TRENDS: ADVANCING BUSINESS, TOWARDS GLOBALIZATION?

1 The SEPT model is increasingly being supplemented with an E for Ecology, but this factor is of a different order to the other four factors and comes across as somewhat of a fad.

2 There are many definitions of 'multinational' corporations (cf. Dunning, 1993). The UN started using the term 'transnationals' in the 1980s to circumvent the negative connotations attached to the notion 'multinational' corporation. Bartlett and Ghoshal (1989) use the concept 'transnational' corporation as a separate organizational form within the group of internationally operating companies. This study employs the most widely-used and relatively neutral meaning of the term 'multinational'; defined as a firm that operates facilities (assets) in more than one country. A firm that merely exports to (or imports from) other countries is a trading firm, not necessarily a multinational.

3 The average TNI of developing country MNCs was 45.7 per cent in 2001, and they held less than one-tenth in the absolute volume of foreign sales, employment and assets as compared to the largest multinationals from developed countries.

4 Following the logic of Chapter 2, one should therefore be able to discern between liberal, corporatist, business-statist, autocratic-religious and community-based multinationals. This would imply a new avenue of research: from country-of-origin to institution-of-origin effects.

5 The concept of global localization emerged from the debate in Japan. It has often been attributed to Sony's CEO Akiro Morita, and shows similarities to the 'local responsiveness' concept of Prahalad and Doz (1987) and the 'transnational corporation' concept of Bartlett and Ghoshal (1989). The glocalization concept originated in the discussion on answers to the barriers created by American and European authorities in response to the export successes of Japanese producers. See, for instance, The Japan Machinery Exporters' Association July 1989 document entitled 'Responding to the Need of Europeanization: Radical Measures' where the concept is also used.

6 Two examples: around 1995, ABN Amro Bank rephrased its ambition of becoming a 'global player' to becoming a 'network bank'; around 2001, Toyota officially denounced its ambition of manufacturing a 'world car'.

7 Worldwide, around 7,000 (visible) hedge funds have been identified, managing capital of US$500 billion. Hedge funds and derivatives are part of the 'speculative' capital wave. Derivatives are more specifically dubbed by Warren Buffet – the world's largest private investor – as 'financial weapons of mass destruction' for their detrimental effects. But opinions differ. Around 90 per cent of the world's 500 biggest companies use derivatives (*The Economist*, 24 January 2004).

8 The assessment of the nature of the present stage of technological development can be based on long-wave thinking. Since the industrial revolution five 'long waves' developed. These waves are also referred to as 'Kondratieffs' after the Russian economist who discovered more or less regular patterns of economic upswing and downswing. We have just passed the peak of the fifth Kondratieff that is expected to run until c.2015. The core or generic technologies that were conceived in the upswing of this

Kondratieff are information technology, biotechnology and new materials (van Tulder and Junne, 1988). Their further development is nowadays increasingly shouldered by private investments. Given the phase of the long economic wave this is not surprising: technology is, in many instances, more a question of (ongoing) development and diffusion than of fundamental research. Fundamental research that could trigger a sixth wave of economic growth is generally believed to be in areas such as nanotechnology and genomics.

4 RIVAL TRENDS: AN ADVANCING AND INCREASINGLY EMANCIPATED CIVIL SOCIETY?

1 Source: http://democracy.stanford.edu.

2 Shopping can even be an expression of patriotism: after September 11, President George W. Bush told Americans that it was their patriotic duty to go the malls and shop (Worldwatch Institute, 2003: xvii). Some claim that 'consumerism' as an individual mentality perhaps even more than 'capitalism' as an organizing principle of production, has won the ideological wars of the twentieth century.

3 The US, for instance, has no identifiable national inter-sectoral employers' body (see EIRO, 2002).

4 Related to this category are also those NGOs that rely on the government for additional funding for projects they carry out on behalf of civil society. These are largely local projects for the benefit of the local population. Such NGOs have been increasingly taking over part of what is traditionally regarded as government responsibilities while still retaining part of their independence. Belonging to this category are development aid organizations or 'co-financing' organizations. In many countries, they receive government funding to carry out projects in developing countries that are aimed directly at the local population, which cannot be realized through local governments. Oxfam is one of the biggest of these NGOs. In the 1990s, official development aid made available to INGOs dropped from US$2.4 billion in 1988 to US$1.7 billion, whereas private funding of these same NGOs more than doubled from US$4.5 to US$10.7 billion in the same period. This made development INGOs as source of development aid more important than governmental aid by OECD countries by the end of the 1990s (Clark, 2003; Kaldor et al., 2003: 12).

5 RIVAL TRENDS: A RECEDING STATE?

1 www.antislavery.org; consulted June 2005.

2 In the debate that arose over the course of 2001–02 about 'hasty privatizations' in the Netherlands, the director of finance and his deputy (W. Moerman and A. Betting) of the Ministry of Finance put forward the following interesting argument:

> Since 1975, the number of instances where the state participates in the economy have remained constant. In those days it was well over 40 and it is still the same. The composition of the portfolio has however changed drastically. Hoogovens, DSM, Postbank, Vredestein and many other healthy companies have partly or wholly been sold. But also DAF, Koninklijke Schelde and Fokker have been disposed of. New companies have been added to the portfolio: KPN, TPG, Tennet (nationalised last year) and PinkRoccade, for example. Not exactly a history of dogmatic privatisation. Many of the much discussed companies have not been privatised, but only made self-sufficient into a company. The shares are in the hands of the government. That applies particularly to the energy distributors and other utility companies. Since the beginning of the nineties, few large privatisations have taken place.
>
> (FD, 7 July 2002)

3 For a more detailed elaboration of this theme see the various chapters in Carillo et al., 2004.

4 The WTO has initiated a working group on assessing the relationship between trade and investment.

5 Source: WTO site; consulted 16 December 2001 (www.wto.org).

6 Figure 5.3 excludes around 14 more modest RIAs in the Caribbean, the Andes and Middle-America, the Middle East, West Africa and the Pacific.

7 Except for the bilateral free-trade agreement with Israel which is matched by equal deals with Mexico and Canada. The political motives of this agreement make it a very separate case. The US is also negotiating a bilateral agreement with Jordan and other states in the Middle East for comparable reasons.

6 MANAGING RIVALRY: THE INTERNATIONAL BARGAINING SOCIETY

1 Statement of Amy Domini, president of the New York-based Domini Assett Management Company (*FT*, 13 August 2003) and one of the most important benchmark providers for CSR (see Chapter 11).

2 Surfing around the web, one can for instance find the concept of 'bargaining society' applied to Uganda, Thailand or Hungary.

3 For an excellent overview of the main ideas of Nobel Prize laureates over the years, see McCarty, 2001 (who describes also the writings of many of the leading economists included in Box 6.1).

4 Institute for democracy and electoral assistance: http://www.idea.int/vt/index.cfm.

5 At the same time (in 1992) the general shareholder meeting at General Motors (GM) sent ripple shock waves around corporate America by effectively ousting the executive management of the firm. New US legislation on shareholder meetings in 1992 made monitoring by shareholders more adequate by allowing meetings between shareholders (Frentrop, 2002). Although the Business Round Table, a group of 200 CEOs of the largest US companies, disagreed with the new law, the SEC used the law to enforce shareholders' rights and better monitor management (Frentrop, 2002).

6 Quote from the principles, OECD (1998), no specific page.

7 CEOs in Japan and the UK serve the shortest periods in their appointments. The average in these two countries ranges from two to three years (*FD*, 25 September 2002).

8 The more unstable a political regime in a country is, the more business interests prevail. This has been the case in modern Italy, but also in the Central and Eastern European transition economies. In the 1989–2003 period, most of these countries witnessed on average a change of government every 1.5 years (*The Economist*, 13 March 2004; European Commission).

9 The classic case of the anti-globalization campaign against the WTO was its ruling against countries that tried to bar imports of dolphins as an inhibiting measure in the trade in fish.

10 Observers of the negotiations of the Doha trade round, have stated that precisely because of the success of the Brazilian growers, the willingness of many leading OECD countries to further liberate world trade deteriorated considerably.

7 MANAGING RIVALRY: THE CHALLENGE OF SOCIETAL INTERFACE MANAGEMENT

1 Host governments in developing countries might not even want to make use of the bargaining room they have. In particular, when attracting foreign firms, many governments have been helped by the first-entry firms themselves in creating the appropriate institutions. An example is Philips in China and Japan. In 1985, Philips set up the first joint venture in China (in Beijing). The legal department of the firm helped the Chinese government to draft a law regulating joint ventures and FDI. In 1954, the legal department of Philips did exactly the same in Japan (*Vk*, 10 April 2004).

2 This book concentrates on Business–Society Management issues. This section therefore further concentrates on illustrating the agencies that operate on the state–market interface. The problems of semi-public and/or semi-private supervision on the state–civil society interface (for instance, with social security agencies, educational and scientific institutes or health organizations) are comparable to those at the state–market interface, though.

3 The Federal Energy Regulatory Commission (FERC) in the US, for instance, had suddenly started to back away from liberalizing the retail electricity market. Following a number of controversial television broadcasts, the Federal Communications Commission (FCC) has started to re-regulate broadcasters (*The Economist*, 26 July 2003).

4 In 2003 US Congress tried to curb the powers of state financial regulators to impose structural reforms on banks and brokerages. The SEC chairman, William Donaldson, cautioned against the 'balkanization' of financial regulation (*FT*, 19 July 2003).

5 The effective regulation of credit rating agencies and hedge funds (*FT*, 27 January 2004) are particular topics of joint concern. Both organizations play an increasingly powerful role in international finance, whereby a few big credit rating agencies are increasingly considered a problem for effective regulation.

6 Serious research on disciplinary cases against members of specific professions, for that matter, is scarce. An examination of the functioning of the disciplinary tribunal of the Dutch Dental Association (Hubben

and Christian Dingelhoff 2002) comes to the conclusion that internal discipline is more effective than complaints submitted to an official legal disciplinary tribunal.

7 Nasdaq for instance oversees more than 5,000 listed companies. On average it initiates up to 400 insider trading investigations a year. It hands over 100–125 of those cases to the SEC or the US Department of Justice for further investigation and prosecution.

8 S. Sivakumar 'Insider trading – Following the SEC's lead', Business Line, Thursday, 26 April 2001; The Securities and Exchange Board of India had effective authorities for addressing insider trading since 1992. In the 1996–2000 period, SEBI took up 14 cases for investigation and completed investigations in six of these.

9 Thanks to inputs by Xavier van Leeuwen.

10 Media concentration in newspapers is particularly tangent in press agencies, where three press agencies (Reuters, AFP and AP) dominate the area; two of these agencies (AP Television and Reuters Television) are also leaders in televised news.

11 Article 19 (www.article19.org), Committee to Protect Journalists (www.cpj.org), FREE VOICE (www.freevoice.nl), Index on Censorship (www.indexonline.org), International Federation of Journalists (IFJ) (www.ifj.org), International Freedom of Expression Exchange (www.ifex.org), International Center for Journalists (www.icfj.org), International Press Institute (www.freemedia.at), Press Now (www.pressnow.org), Reporters Sans Frontières (www.rsf.org), World Association of Newspapers (www.wan-press.org), The World Free Press Institute (www.worldfreepress.org), World Press Freedom Committee (www.wpfc.org).

12 CNN set up a fact-checking department after two producers had made reports on the use of a poisonous gas during the Vietnam war, which turned out to be untrue. Star reporter Peter Arnett received a warning. The two producers were fired. At *The Cincinnatti Inquirer* a journalist was dismissed who claimed that banana producer Chiquita transported illegal narcotics on its boats. This also turned out to be false. The newspaper quickly started a fact-checking department.

13 The supervision on journalism during the Iraqi invasion was stronger than ever. American reporters were subject to military control and complied to supervision because the US government threatened to attack independent reporters. The bombardment of an independent British TV crew – with one fatality – showed the threat was a serious one.

14 The scientist Bruno Frey (2003) – having, himself, published many influential articles in many top journals – describes present-day publishing in scientific journals as an act of intellectual 'prostitution'.

15 This is the reason why some scientists are looking for different ways of publishing their results through the Internet, even when this implies a less 'prestigious' platform. This is called 'open access publishing' in which the author pays for the publication instead of the reader. This system has drawbacks as well, but is faster and circumvents the power of the big publishing houses. For more information see: Wellcome Trust (2003) *Economic Analysis of Scientific Research Publishing*; available online: www.wellcome.ac.uk.

16 Despite the fact the SEC is called the most powerful institute in the American free market economy, its authority is only as great as politics allows it to be (Seligman, 2003).

17 Fund managers in the US pay a fee for regulation of the financial services industry to the US Treasury. In the 1990s fee collections went from around US$0.2 billion to more than US$2.2 billion in 2000. On average less than half of this fee – also dubbed the 'SEC fee' – was appropriated by the Securities and Exchange Commission for the tasks officially dedicated to it. At the same time, the SEC had been complaining about understaffing and therefore more limited inspection capacity. After various accounting scandals, the funding for the SEC was increased from US$487 million in 2002 to US$716 million in 2003, but still only represented around half of the US$1.5 billion in fees (*FT*, 1 December 2003). Another example: since 1992, according to the 21st Century Intellectual Property Coalition, some US$650 million has been diverted from the patent office to unrelated programmes. The coalition represents a wide range of companies, including software, chemical, agricultural, paper and pharmaceutical firms, and trade groups, such as the Biotechnology Industry Organization, Aerospace Industries Association and Semiconductor Industry Association. 'America's innovators are prepared to pay out of their own pockets to improve the situation at the PTO, provided the money will go to the agency', the coalition said in a statement (www.ipo.org; consulted 25 June 2004).

18 With the exception of BINGOs and BONGOs, the acronyms for the respective NGO roles have been invented by one of us. Inspired by the proliferation of NGO acronyms we could not resist the temptation to put our acronym oar in.

19 The BINGO acronym is also used to refer to 'Big International NGOs'.

INTRODUCTION TO PART II

1 Friedman advanced his statement, essentially in theory and from neo-classical economic premises – departing from a hypothetical situation where the three societal spheres (market, state and civil society) are sharply delineated, interests and institutions do not clash, there is transparency in the market and perfect competition. The assertion by Friedman therefore remains interesting for the economic sciences, but not wholly adequate for entrepreneurs who have to implement concrete strategies in the short run and in the real world.

2 See, for instance, John Entine (1994) 'Shattered Image: Is The Body Shop Too Good to Be True?' *Business Ethics Magazine*. Entine, a journalist and American Enterprise Institute fellow, alleges that Roddick stole the concept of the Body Shop.

8 THE LOGIC: THE MULTIFACETED NOTION OF CORPORATE RESPONSIBILITY

1 The worldwide attention to CSR and/or sustainability management in the media increased four-fold in the period 2000–03. The international media-advisor Echo Research registered 5,324 major articles on the topic in this period (http://www.p-plus.nl).

2 www.iccwbo.org, consulted July 2004.

3 In the literature on corporate social performance (CSP) a range of concepts are employed to elaborate on the catch-all term 'corporate social responsibility'. This conceptual ambiguity contributes to the confusion on the terminology as regards processes and principles of CSR. Usually, they are separated from each other and categorized differently. But processes and principles (as well as the outcomes) of CSR are strongly interrelated. This prompted us to 'relabel' and 'reclassify' some of the concepts used in order to come to sharper distinctions for instance between various international CSR orientations (see the remainder of this chapter). In the corporate social performance model of Wood (1991), 'processes of social responsiveness' are separated from the 'principles of social responsibility'. 'Responsiveness' can, however, also be considered as a principle of CSP. The sharp distinction between 'processes' and 'principles' therefore obscures more than it reveals. When classifying the organizational attitudes linked to processes of 'corporate social responsiveness' Carroll (1979) and Wartick and Cochran (1985) – and many in their wake – use concepts like 'reactive', 'defensive', 'accommodative' and 'proactive'. Post (1979) was the first to introduce the distinction between 'reactive', 'proactive' and 'interactive'. These attributes are not linked to the principles of CSR or their outcomes and often overlap. In various other publications in the Business and Society literature, comparable inactive/reactive/proactive/interactive frameworks have been used. Originally introduced by Preston and Post (1975), Waddock (2002) and Lawrence *et al.* (2005) have further discussed and elaborated these categories. Mitnick (1995) suggests that firms historically may have passed through three alternative stances in their relationship with society: from corporate social responsibility (CSR1), via corporate social responsiveness (CSR2), to corporate social rectitude (CSR3). The distinctions used in Table 8.1 represent a slight reworking of these concepts in order to create a more concise framework that directly links principles and processes.

4 An excellent business example of this idea is Robert Eaton, the CEO of Chrysler, who declared that 'companies that focus on making money become more competitive, and that in turn means more economic growth, and more jobs, and all the other results that "stakeholders" care about' (quoted in Reich, 1998).

5 In the words of Anita Roddick (2000): 'inaction is no longer an option. If WE don't act, who will?'

6 US retailer Home Depot has even adopted this as its sales motto: 'Doing the right thing instead of just doing things right' (2003 Corporate Citizenship Report). Compare this to the strictly efficiency-oriented motto we found in one of the Chinese subcontractors to the toy industry: 'Do it right. Do it right now!'

7 This distinction departs from the distinction made by Peter Drucker, who states that 'efficiency is doing things right, effectiveness is doing the right things'. Rather than a digital approach, this book proposes to look at the dialectical trade-off between efficiency (thesis) and equity (anti-thesis), where the effectiveness question represents the search for a synthesis. Shell provides an excellent example of the latter ambition in an advertisement which reads as follows: 'Why Green is Good; a company which cares as much about how it makes money, as how much money it makes, will make money' (*FT*, 14 January 2004).

8 The 'guru guide' of the *Financial Times*, published in the summer of 2003, was a particularly helpful source in this overview.

9 www.efqm.org, visited August 2004.

9 THE OCCASION: ISSUES AND ISSUES MANAGEMENT

1 Some companies are refraining from making any special CSR statements so as to prevent stakeholders from interpreting their CSR strategy as yet another 'PR campaign'. Philips, the Dutch consumer electronics multinational, for instance, has developed a very explicit CSR strategy imposing relatively strict codes on its suppliers, but according to an official statement: 'Philips does not employ special campaigns on CSR. We regard sustainable management as integral part of our normal management praxis' (Email, *Vk*, 24 March 2004).

10 THE STAKES: FIRMS – PART OF THE PROBLEM OR PART OF THE SOLUTION?

1 More detailed discussions about the issues mentioned in this chapter are included in the 'issue dossiers' available on the website: www.ib-sm.org.

2 The WRM, an influential NGO dealing with deforestation, makes the following assessment:

> Although many NGOs believe that certification of wood and other forest products is a good idea, there are a number of doubts about whether the actual process is moving in the right direction. The issue has resulted in confrontations between environmental organizations in countries such as Brazil, where some NGOs are working hard to convince logging companies to move into Forest Stewardship Council (FSC) certification, while other NGOs accuse those same NGOs of thereby promoting further forest destruction. There is also great controversy regarding the convenience of certifying forestry operations in countries such as Indonesia – where local peoples' land rights are unrecognized by the government – and in Thailand, where most NGOs consider that there should be no certification because forests are already protected by an existing logging ban and that certification can undermine their efforts to protect forests.
>
> (wrm.org. consulted February 2005)

In 2005, the biggest market for illegal logging turned out to be China. Many forest product importers are not very enthusiastic about FSC certification, because it forces them to reveal their suppliers. This knowledge is a critical part of their competitive advantage vis-à-vis major customers. FSC certification helps to marginalize importers.

3 It is statistically difficult to establish a clear-cut relationship between absolute levels of GDP and health. Countries with comparable levels of GDP show variable levels of health and longevity.

4 From the pharmaceutical, food/beverages, mining, energy, automotive, consumer electronics and the financial services industries.

5 The minimum level needed to meet basic needs is called the 'poverty line'. The preconditions for satisfying basic needs vary across time and societies. Therefore, poverty lines vary in time and place, and each country uses a yardstick appropriate to its level of development, societal norms and values (World Bank, 2003; www.worldbank.org).

6 Internationally comparative data are difficult to find, due to large differences in definitions used. The EIRO (European Industrial Relations Observatory, online, www.eiro.eurofound.eu.int) estimated that 8 per cent of employees in the EU can be considered 'poor'. The highest levels of 'working poor' were registered in Germany and Italy, and the lowest in Denmark and Portugal.

7 The problem of illiteracy is not limited to developing countries only. According to UNDP figures the relative share of illiterate people in the US is 16.5 per cent, in the UK (15 per cent), Ireland (15 per cent) and France (12 per cent). The number of functional illiterates is often substantially higher: according to the National Adult Literacy Survey, 42 million adult Americans cannot read; 50 million can recognize so few printed words they are limited to a 4th or 5th grade reading level.

8 For instance, the Center for Corporate Citizenship at Boston College (Massachusetts, US) which is a membership-based research organization like so many other colleges in the US. The around 300

members represent the biggest and most international ('global') companies in the US. The center defines the essence of corporate citizenship along three core principles: minimizing harm, maximizing benefit, and being accountable and responsive to stakeholders. The center has a very operational mission definition: 'to help [their member companies] define, plan and operationalize their corporate citizenship. Our goal is to help business leverage its social, economic and human assets to ensure both its success and a more just and sustainable world.'

9 For example, the International Centre for Corporate Social Responsibility (ICCSR) at Nottingham University Business School (UK). The ICCSR was founded in 2002 following a £3.8 million endowment from British American Tobacco (BAT). That the centre is solely sponsored by a company that is so clearly implicated in major public health issues is, of course, rather awkward. The partners signed a clear memorandum of understanding containing a number of provisions that guarantee the independence of the centre. The centre conducts research on a large number of basic social/public interest/non-profit issues.

11 THE MECHANISM: REPUTATION AND CORRECTION

1 Full quote: 'Reputation, reputation, reputation! Oh, I have lost my reputation! I have lost the immortal part of myself, and what remains is bestial' (William Shakespeare *Othello. ACT II Scene 3*).

2 See also http://www.reputations.org, www.reputationinstitute.com and www.harrisinteractive.com/pop_up/rq.

3 http://www.ftse4good.com, consulted on 6 January 2002.

4 http://www.trouw.com, consulted on 23 November 2001.

12 THE CONTEXT: RIVAL CSR AND ICR REGIMES

1 Some early conventions such as the Universal Declaration of Human Rights (1948) acknowledge corporate entities by referring to 'non-state actors' (Abrahams, 2004: 12).

2 Short descriptions of other regimes – including 'indigenous CSR' and 'hybrid CSR regimes' – can be found on the website for this book.

3 World Bank, Governance Research indicators, www.worldbank.org.

4 The UK could become another example. Some groups of southern stakeholders are attempting to use UK Company Law to file claims of negligence and failure to respect basic labour rights against a number of British mining companies (Abrahams, 2004: 35).

5 In the course of the 1990s, a number of selective purchasing laws were enacted by state and local governments, specifically to prevent governments from dealing with companies doing business in Burma.

6 In contrast to authors in other countries, the tendency in the US is often to address the short-term profitability and the competitive advantage dimension of adopting particular ICR strategies. Donaldson (1989), for instance, goes to considerable length to stress that anti-corruption policies can result in a 'competitive advantage' for MNEs that adopt them.

7 Directly: in 2001 the Canada Business Corporation Act was amended to expand the power of shareholders to enact resolutions on ethical issues in the shareholders' meeting (McKague, 2003). Indirectly: in 2000 the UK government required pension funds to disclose how they take account of social environmental and ethical factors in their investment decisions. Although fund managers are not required to adopt any particular policy (Fox et al., 2002), it is nevertheless reported that the share of SRI in British pension funds has increased substantially since then.

8 Other Anglo-Saxon countries such as the UK (19 per cent), Canada (3.2 per cent) and Australia (appr. 5 per cent) are world leaders in SRI as a percentage of total market capital (IFC, 2003).

9 In Chapter 11, other telling differences of the SRI funds between continental Europe and the Anglo-Saxon countries were illuminated that support the above analysis. See also: www.sricompass.org.

10 South Korea: uses a 'best practice' system in which companies that practise prevention-oriented environmental management receive the certificate 'environment-friendly'. The system is voluntary. Taiwan employs an 'eco-labelling' (GreenMark) scheme for its procurement practices (Fox et al., 2002).

11 Examples include: UNAIDS and Coca Cola, work together on coordinating AIDS education, prevention and treatment; UNDP and Cisco Networking collaborate on delivering e-learning to LLDCs; UNICEF

and ILO have allied with sporting goods manufacturers against child labour; World Bank partnership with GAP and Nike on improving working conditions of workers in developing countries.

12 Representatives of Global Compact do not agree with this point of criticism. It notes (in personal communication with the authors) that the best industry and company codes can still be quite narrow in focus and not address broader issues such as human rights and anti-corruption. The GC tries to encourage firms to 'grow' into these new issues. In 2005, around 2,000 companies are signatories of the Global Compact. Many of them are based in developing countries, which renders the Global Compact the largest CSR initiative in the world.

13 Labels around the world include a large number of ambiguous qualifications, for instance: biological ('bio') in a label is often not defined; 'light' is not specified by the UK Food standards agency, 'low fat' is not specified anywhere; on the other hand, all food sold as 'organic' in Europe must be produced according to European laws on organic production.

14 The *Key mark*, introduced by CEN in the mid-1990s to coordinate quality marks, is not well established yet.

15 The certification of Chiquita bananas by the Rainforest Alliance (RA) is another example of the problem encountered by labels across regime borders. Of the Chiquita bananas sold in Europe, 90 per cent are certified by the Rainforest Alliance, but the typical RA logo of a green frog will not be found on the bananas in European shops. For various reasons – partly related to European quota policy for bananas – the company chose to distribute the bananas only with the company's logo. Chiquita bananas in Europe thus lie on the shelves next to 'fair trade' or 'Ok' bananas, and consumers electing to purchase 'fair bananas' will simply overlook Chiquita bananas.

16 For instance, half of the German DAX companies that also had a US stock market listing considered withdrawal by November 2004 due to mounting regulatory costs in the US (*FT*, 19 November 2004). Major companies, particularly from the UK, France and Japan, expressed their willingness to delist from the US stock exchanges. Firms that are strongly dependent on American financiers and customers (such as BT or Daimler-Chrysler) realized that this would probably not be a feasible option.

17 The preference among groups of leading national companies for particular reporting strategies seems to suggest a distinct national CSR regime: Japanese companies such as Toyota, Suzuki, Subaru or Komatsu publish an Environmental & Social Report; UK companies such as Royal Mail Group plc, Shell, Amersham plc, Corus, Royal Mail, Rio Tinto produce an HSE report; and in 2002, 45 per cent of the companies in the Global *Fortune* Top 250 published an environmental, social or sustainability report (KPMG, 2002). Sustainability reports were initially published particularly in Scandinavia, the UK and the US.

13 THE PROCESS: ICR AS MANAGING DISTANCE

1 In 2005, for example, the Economist Intelligence Unit country-risk ratings of emerging markets, indicated that Iraq and Zimbabwe were the riskiest countries (above 80 per cent maximum risk), whereas Chile, Hong Kong and Singapore were the least risky (around or below 20 per cent maximum risk) (*Economist*, 26 February 2005).

2 The right to (1) freedom of physical movement; (2) ownership of property; (3) freedom from torture; (4) a fair trial; (5) non-discriminatory treatment; (6) physical security; (7) freedom of speech and association; (8) minimal education; (9) political participation and (10) the right to subsistence.

3 In the Global Corruption Report 2004, Transparency International notes that in the past corrupt government leaders were supported by Western state donors. For various reasons, presidents Suharto of Indonesia, Marcos of the Philippines and Mobutu of Zaire, together, accumulated around US$50 billion – more than the total annual amount of Western development aid. Corrupt leaders continue to exist. But governments as sources of financial support for corrupt leaders have been replaced with companies, according to Transparency International. The arms and oil sectors figure prominently in the provision of funding for corrupt officials.

4 There exists an International Development Ethics Association (IDEA), www.development-ethics.org.

5 The idiosyncratic motivation of Japanese MNEs makes it risky to apply these insights to more established MNEs from Europe or North America. Recent research on the internationalization of Japanese manufacturing firms (Delios and Henisz, 2003) shows for instance that incorporating *policy uncertainty* yields better results in establishing an optimal investment sequence. The reception of firms in the host

economy by local stakeholders (competitors, policy makers, suppliers and customers) proves influential in the success of particular entry strategies. It can be expected that this will probably also apply to other Asian multinationals who share market seeking as prime motive for internationalization and are all confronted with considerable institutional distance – although this distance from the US is smaller than from Europe (see Chapter 12).

INTRODUCTION TO PART III

1 Nagelschmidt, in Heath and Nelson, 1986: 212.

14 DO IT JUST – THE NIKE CASE

1 http://www.nike.com/nikebiz/nikebiz.jhtml?page=3&item=facts, consulted on 20 May 2005.

2 CorpWatch was known as Transnational Resource & Action Centre (TRAC) in 1997. www.corpwatch.org/article.php?list=type&type=108, consulted December 2004.

3 www.corpwatch.org/issues/sweatshops, consulted on 21 September 2001.

4 www.caa.org.au/campaigns/nike, consulted on 22 July 2002.

5 www.caa.org.au/campaign/nike/reports/machines/response.html, consulted on 12 June 2002.

6 www.mallenbaker.net/csr/CSRfiles/nike.html, consulted on 25 May 2005.

7 www.theglobalalliance.org, consulted on 22 July 2002.

8 www.behindthelabel.org, consulted on 12 June 2002.

9 The Alliance has existed for 5 years and ended December 2004.

10 'Indonesian Nike workers allege sexual harassment', FT, 22 February 2001.

11 Press release, Nike 27 June 2002, the fiscal year ended 31 May for Nike.

12 Press release, Nike 28 June 2001.

13 Press release, Nike 20 September 2001.

14 Press release, Nike 20 December 2001.

15 www.globalreporting.org, consulted on 2 May 2005.

16 All reports are downloadable at www.nike.com/nikebiz, consulted on 20 May 2005.

17 Murphy and Mathews (2001), 'Nike and global labour practices', case study prepared for the New Academy of Business, Business Innovation Network for Social Responsible Business. New Academy of Business, Bristol, UK.

18 Press Release, Nike, 12 May 2005. See also www.fairlabor.org.

19 www.oxfam.org.au/campaigns/nike, consulted on 15 October 2001.

20 www.caa.org.au/campaigns/nike/reports/machines, consulted on 8 March 2002.

21 www.csreurope.org/news/_page1990.aspx, consulted on 13 November 2004.

22 www.mallenbaker.net/csr/nl/54.html#anchor899, consulted on 14 March 2005.

23 To be downloaded at www.nike.com/nikebiz/nikebiz.jhtml?page=29.

24 www.globalreporting.org/organisations/details.asp?Organisation_pk=8711 , consulted on 2 May 2005.

15 THE OCEAN AS RUBBISH DUMP? – THE SHELL BRENT SPAR CASE

1 www.greenpeace.nl/about/greenpeace-nederland, consulted on 18 May 2005.

2 'Greenpeace occupies oil platform', FD, 2 May 1995.

3 www.greenpeace.org, consulted on 15 December 2001.

4 'Dumping oil tank could set an example for others', Vk, 3 June 1995.

5 'Blockade Shell Headquarters by Greenpeace', FD, 24 May 1995.

6 'Dumping-battle lasts four months', Het Parool, 21 June 1995.

7 'Kohl attacks Shell over rig dumping', FT, 16 June 1995.

8 'Also boycott of Shell pumps in The Netherlands due to dumping', Het Parool, 14 June 1995.

9 'Swamped by sea of public anger', *FT*, 22 June 1995. This statement has also been confirmed by Mr Tim van Kooten, Issues manager of Shell Netherlands.

10 'London threatens Shell with retaliation', *FD*, 22 June 1995.

11 'Shell yields: Brent Spar not to be dumped in ocean', *FD*, 21 June 1995.

12 'Shell cornered by growing opposition against dumping platform', *Trouw*, 15 June 1995.

13 'Shell persists in dumping despite growing protest', *FD*, 20 June 1995.

14 'A black day', *Trouw*, 27 June 1995.

15 'The battle for Brent Spar', *FD*, 22 February 2000.

16 'Shell receives apologies by Greenpeace', *FD*, 6 September 1995.

17 'Research confirms Shell was right about the content of Brent Spar', *FD*, 19 October 1995.

18 'Shell and the action group', *Vk*, 4 January 1996.

19 'Shell pleads for code', *NRC Handelsblad*, 5 January 1996.

20 http://europa.eu.int/scadplus/leg/nl/lvb, consulted on 3 October 2001.

21 'Shell sees profit in having a good name', *Vk*, 14 September 2002.

22 'Shell on the rocks', *The Economist*, Vol. 335, Nr. 7920, pp. 57–58.

23 www.sustainability-index.com/htmle/data/djsi_world.html, consulted on 3 November 2001.

16 PROVOCATIVE BRAS FROM BURMA – THE TRIUMPH INTERNATIONAL CASE

1 Cases to be downloaded from www.ib-sm.org.

2 http://www.cleanclothes.ch/d/firmen.htm, consulted on 17 November 2003.

3 http://www.burmacampaign.org.uk/reports/boycott_triumph.htm, consulted on 17 November 2003.

4 'Bras burnt in protest', *FD*, 20 January 2001.

5 www.aftenposten.no/english/sports/article248880.ece, consulted on 31 January 2004.

6 www.burmacampaign.org.uk/pressreleases/sanctions_briefing.html, consulted on 5 June 2003.

7 http://www.cleanclothes.org/companies/triumph.htm, consulted on 5 June 2003.

8 'Triumph leaves Burma', *Algemeen Dagblad*, 10 January 2002.

9 www.triumph-international.com, consulted on 16 August 2002.

10 http://www.triumph.com/index.php, consulted on 3 November 2004.

11 The code can be downloaded in various languages from www.triumph-international.com.

12 http://www.burmacampaign.org.uk/reports/boycott_triumph.htm, consulted on 3 November 2004.

13 'Burmese promise threatens to mislead the outside world, again', *FD*, 10 May 2001.

14 http://www.burmacampaign.org.uk/aboutburma/briefhistory.html, consulted on 11 November 2004.

15 http://www.burmacampaign.org.uk/reports/boycott_triumph.htm, consulted on 11 November 2004. See also www.irrawaddy.org/news/2003/june43.html.

16 http://www.cfob.org/Media_Statements/Media_Statements.shtml (Canadian Friends of Burma), consulted on 25 November 2004.

17 http://www.burmacampaign.org.uk/aboutburma.html, consulted on 4 December 2004.

18 'Call for boycott "wrong" travel agencies', *Vk*, 10 April 2002.

19 Statements made in their code of conduct, Zurzach, 12 December 2001.

17 'DO MORE, FEEL BETTER, LIVE LONGER, BUT ONLY IF YOU CAN AFFORD IT?' – THE GLAXOSMITHKLINE CASE

1 www.gsk.com/about/about.htm, consulted on 6 January 2004.

2 Based on pharmacy markets in the US, Canada, Germany, Italy, France, Spain, UK, Brazil, Mexico, Argentina, Australia, New Zealand, Japan (IMS Health, 2002).

3 'Still no end to the slowdown', *FT*, 30 April 2002.

4 'Drugs firms out of the dock', BBC News Online, 29 February 2001.

5 Oxfam, Briefing paper on GlaxoSmithKline: Dare to lead, Public health and company wealth, 2001.

6 'Major pension fund presses Glaxo for cheaper AIDS drugs', *Business Report*, 17 April 2002.

7 Pharmaceutical Shareowners Group (2004) *The Public Health Crisis in Emerging Markets*, September 2004.

8 Stancich, R. (2004) 'Pharmaceutical firms must do more to reduce ethical risk, says shareholder', *Ethicalcorp.com* (21 September 2004) http://www.ethicalcorp.com/content.asp?ContentID=2799, consulted on 8 October 2004.

9 Only 10 per cent of R&D expenditure is spent on research into 90 per cent of the world's diseases. (Global Forum for Health Research, 2004).

10 The *Sunday Times* 100 Best Companies to work for, 2002.

11 'Paying for AIDS', *Newsweek*, 18 March 2001.

12 GlaxoSmithKline, Global Community Partnership; about positive action, 2002.

13 'Glaxo to further cut price of AIDS drug used in Africa', *Wall Street Journal*, 28 April 2003.

14 www.businessfightsaids.org, consulted on 18 January 2005.

18 A CHANGING CLIMATE FOR A SLEEPING TIGER? – THE EXXONMOBIL CASE

1 http://www.exxonmobil.com/Corporate/About/History/Corp_A_H_XOMToday.asp, consulted 2 December 2004.

2 See e.g. www.dontbuyexxonmobil.org; www.exxonsecrets.org (this website is the first chapter of a larger Greenpeace project providing a research database of information on the corporate-funded anti-environmental movement); www.greenpeace.org; www.foei.org; http://www.peopleandplanet.org; www.campaignexxonmobil.org; and even www.mcspotlight.org/beyond/companies/exxon.html.

3 This means that companies are able to achieve reduction in emission in cooperation with other companies or governments, either by trading emission credits or by a partnership in an offset project once the Protocol has been ratified (Kolk and Pinske, 2004: 311).

4 www.worldenergy.org/wec-geis/publications/default/archives/tech_papers/other_tech_papers/WECco2rpt97app.asp#table1, consulted on 1 December 2004.

5 www.reuters.co.uk/newsArticle.jhtml?type=worldNews&storyID=639086, consulted on 18 December 2004.

6 Remarks by ExxonMobil CEO Lee Raymond. Exxon Mobil, 7th Annual Asia Oil & Gas Conference, Kuala Lumpur, Malaysia, 10 June 2002. http://www2.exxonmobil.com/corporate/Newsroom/Spchs Intvws/Corp_NR_SpchIntrvw_KLSpeech_100602.asp.

7 ExxonMobil advertisement 'Moving past Kyoto . . .', http://www2.exxonmobil.com/Files/Corporate/170401.pdf.

8 http://www2.exxonmobil.com/Files/Corporate/170401_1.pdf, consulted on 1 December 2003.

9 www.globalclimate.org, consulted on 20 December 2004.

10 Greenpeace (2002) 'Denial and deception', http://www.stopesso.com/pdf/exxon_denial.pdf.

11 There are StopEsso/ExxonMobil Campaign offices (and related anti-ExxonMobil websites) in Canada, France, Germany, Luxembourg, the US and the UK. Besides this Campaign network, various other campaigns against ExxonMobil can be found: Stop ExxonMobil Alliance (US, started in 2002), Campaign ExxonMobil (ExxonMobil shareholders dedicated to ensuring the company takes responsibility for its role in the problem of global warming and commits to developing clean renewable energy), PressurePoint (US group targeting ExxonMobil for using its corporate power to influence government policy on climate change, human rights and environmental protection) and Citizens for Legitimate Government (US group focusing on the link between ExxonMobil's funding of US president George W. Bush's election campaign and its corporate influence over the Bush administration).

12 www.dontbuyexxonmobil.org, consulted on 5 May 2004.

13 www.foei.org, consulted on 5 May 2004.

14 For further information, download the briefing document 'The Case against Exxon'. Also see the report 'Decade of Dirty Tricks', Greenpeace's latest report on Exxon's alleged attempts to sabotage the Kyoto Protocol, on www.dontbuyexxonmobil.org and also see www.exxonsecrets.org.

15 www.ethicalcorp.com (article by Lisa Roner published on 19 July 2004).

16 See ExxonMobil's 'Standards of business conduct' (2004), at www2.exxonmobil.com/AP-English/About/SG_VP_Principles.asp, consulted on 5 December 2004.

17 www.publicintegrity.org/about/about.aspx.

18 www.exxonmobileurope.com/Corporate/Newsroom/SpchsIntvws/Corp_NR_SpchIntrvw_AnnualMeeting_010530.asp, consulted on 28 November 2004.

19 www.imperialoil.com/Canada-English/HomePage.asp, consulted on 3 November 2004. (Imperial Oil is the Canadian subsidiary of ExxonMobil.)

20 www.corpwatch.org, consulted on 4 April 2003.

21 www.fortune.com/fortune/mostadmired/subs/2003/allstars/0,16202,,00.html.

22 www.pwc.com, consulted on 3 November 2004.

23 'Change of Climate', *Ethical Corporation Magazine*, November 2004, pp. 17–18.

24 Report Deutsche Bank: www.greenpeace.org/multimedia/download/1/135843/0/deutschebank.pdf, consulted on 13 October 2003.

25 Business Respect – CSR Dispatches No. 56, 18 May 2003, www.mallenbaker.net/csr/nl/56.html#anchor 942, consulted on 8 July 2004.

26 www.ceres.org/news/news_item.php?nid=66 (speech by Sean Harrigan of California Public Employees' Retirement System (CalPERS) CERES Conference Boston, MA, 15 April 2004).

27 www.claros.co.uk, consulted on 27 October 2004.

28 www.campaignexxonmobil.org, consulted on 27 October 2004.

29 www.csrwire.com, published on 13 May 2004 by CERES.

30 http://www.prweek.com/home/message.cfm, consulted on 19 December 2004.

31 www.dontbuyexxonmobil.org/posting/1065533869, consulted on 8 December 2004.

32 www.dontbuyexxonmobil.org/posting/1081775227, consulted on 8 December 2004.

33 *Fortune Magazine*, yearly first edition, 1997–2004, also see www.fortune.com.

34 http://www.ethicalcorp.com. 'Is ExxonMobil beginning to mellow?' published on 22 November 2004 by Ethical Corporation Newsdesk.

35 GCEP: http://?gcep.stanford.edu/ (also General Electric is involved as a sponsor).

36 Supposedly ExxonMobil has lost around US$500 million on investments in synthetic fuels, solar power, nuclear energy, office systems and efficient electric motors.

37 www.mallenbaker.net/csr/nl/50.html#anchor840 (23 February 2003 'Exxon Mobil CEO supports mandatory CO_2 emissions reporting').

38 www.exxonmobil.com/Corporate/Newsroom/Newsreleases/corp_xom_nr_100701_6.asp, consulted on 3 November 2004.

39 www.exxonmobil.com/corporate/Newsroom/Publications/eTrendsSite/chapter5.asp, February 2004, consulted on 25 December 2004.

40 The report can be downloaded at www.foei.org/media/2004/0129.html.

41 www.ode.nl/news.php?nID=370, consulted on 13 December 2004.

42 http://www.endevil.com/blacklist.html, consulted on 9 December 2004.

43 www.texasobserver.org, article by Jake Bernstein, 23 April 2004: 'Tiger Tussle'.

44 www.ethicalcorp.com/content.asp?ContentID=3040, published on 27 October 2004 by Lisa Roner.

45 More details on this can be found on http://europa.eu.int/comm/environment/climat/emission.htm.

46 www.foei.org/climate/kyoto.html, consulted on 19 January 2005.

47 www.wnf.nl, consulted on 23 November 2004.

48 http://www.reuters.co.uk/newsArticle.jhtml?type=worldNews&storyID=639086 (15 December 2004).

19 LESSONS IN REPUTATION

1 The paradox, for these players, seems to be the source of their success – a corporate branding strategy by means of which they could pressurize the distributive trade to accept lower margins – has now become

the source of their problem: greater recognizability among end consumers strengthens the power of the supply chain, but also increases vulnerability to reputation damage. Vulnerability increases because the distributors are less inclined to protect the interests of the brand of their suppliers and could even use the CSR argument to strengthen their negotiating position slightly. This could be called the '*Intel inside*' dilemma of CSR.

2 So-called 'event-studies' have, however, been conducted on the effect of the riots during the WTO convention in Seattle on the share prices of large MNEs.

3 ABN Amro, for example, started with bridging due to previous experiences in a conflict surrounding financing mining projects.

4 Other parties in the public discussion make use of similar tactics. In this way, the first tactic (simplification and exaggeration) is for instance a direct translation of the editing formula of the most influential weekly magazine in the world, *The Economist*: 'First simplify, then exaggerate'. *The Economist* generally opposes the claims made by NGOs.

20 TOWARDS A STRATEGIC STAKEHOLDER DIALOGUE

1 Throughout this chapter the results of a 2004 research project on the use of stakeholder dialogue in the Netherlands will be used to illustrate the status and the future of the stakeholder dialogue (cf. van Tulder *et al.*, 2004). The research included (1) a representative questionnaire sent to largest 100 home and host multinationals located in the country with a response rate of 51 per cent; and (2) structured interviews with 56 leading NGOs of which 98 per cent were international. In many respects the Netherlands can be seen as a leading laboratory for the implementation of stakeholder dialogues. The country also has a long tradition of continuous (tripartite) bargaining between NGOs, government and business, so the institutional setting is most conducive to stakeholder dialogue.

2 The names of the companies that these cases pertain to are omitted as the dialogue in some cases is still under way and, as a result, only limited information can be published.

3 The main reason for this discrepancy is probably due to the fact that our research (van Tulder *et al.*, 2004) categorized NGO roles in much greater detail, making more specific – not necessarily different – conclusions possible. Another explanation for the differences in the results can be attributed to a different methodology used (questionnaires versus structured interviews), and not necessarily to the selection of NGOs included in the study.

4 This listing combines features for successful stakeholder dialogues as identified by: Zadek, 2001; Kaptein and Wempe, 2002; Hemmati, 2002; Kaptein and van Tulder, 2003; van Tulder *et al.*, 2004.

5 The basic principles of Fisher and Ury (1981) are: (1) separate the people from the problem; be hard on the problem, soft on the people; (2) focus on interests, not positions; realize that each side has multiple interests; for a wide solution reconcile interests; (3) generate a variety of possibilities before deciding what to do; invent options for mutual gain; try to broaden your options; change the scope for a proposed agreement; (4) insist that the result be based on some objective standard; frame each issue as a joint search for objective criteria.

6 Gilpin (2002) considers the scenario of 'new medievalism' which represents the end of the nation-state, the rise of multinational corporations, NGOs and international organizations – a state of affairs that, in his view, could lead to international chaos. We considered this scenario in Chapter 5 and found that, although the importance of nation-state might be declining, it would be inaccurate to suggest its demise in the foreseeable future. Rather, new constellations of states are appearing, which is perhaps more aptly described by the term 'neo-mercantilism'.

7 In a speech at the World Economic Forum in Davos, Lord Browne, the CEO of British Petroleum, stated that: 'businesses and stakeholder groups are turning to negotiation in order to arrive at a tangible social contract.' He referred to it as 'a bargain of mutuality' (February 2005).

Bibliography

Aaronson, S. and Reeves, J. (2002) 'The European response to public demands for global corporate responsibility', paper presented for the National Policy Association (US).

Abowd, J. and Kaplan, D. (1999) 'Executive compensation: six questions that need answering', *Journal of Economic Perspectives*, Fall 1999.

Abrahams, D. (2004) *Regulating Corporations. A resource guide*, Geneva: United Nations Research Institute for Social Development.

Ackerman, R.W. and Bauer, R.A. (1976) *Corporate Social Responsiveness: the modern dilemma*, Reston, VA: Reston Publishing.

Ackoff, R.L. (1999) *Re-creating the Corporation: a design of organizations for the 21st century*, New York: Oxford University Press.

Aghion, P. and Howitt, P. (1997) *Endogenous Growth Theory*, Cambridge, MA: MIT Press.

Agle, B., Mitchell, R. and Sonnenfeld, J. (1999) 'Who matters to CEOs? An investigation of stakeholders' attributes and salience, and CEO values', *Academy of Management Journal*, Vol. 42, No. 5: 507.

Agmon, T. (2003) 'Who gets what: the MNE, the national state and the distributional effects of globalization', *Journal of International Business Studies*, 34: 416–427.

Albert, M. (1993) *Capitalism vs Capitalism: how America's obsession with individual achievement and short-term profit has led it to the brink of collapse*, New York: Four Walls Eight Windows.

Alesina, A., Roubini, N. with Cohen, G. (1997) *Political Cycles and the Macroeconomy*, Cambridge, MA: MIT Press.

Alsop, R. (2001) 'Harris Interactive Survey indicates fragility of corporate reputations', *The Wall Street Journal*, 7 February.

—— (2004) *The 18 Immutable Laws of Corporate Communication*, London: Kogan Page Ltd.

Ambrosini, V., Johnson, G. and Scholes, K. (1998) *Exploring Techniques of Analysis and Evaluation in Strategic Management*, Harlow: Prentice Hall.

Ammenberg, J. (2003) 'Do standardised environmental management systems lead to reduced environmental impacts?', PhD thesis, Linkoping University.

Anderson, P.H. and Sorensen, H.B. (1999) 'Reputational information: its role in interfirm collaboration', *Corporate Reputation Review*, Vol. 2, No. 3: 215–230.

Anderson, R. and Reeb, D. (2003) 'Founding-family ownership and firm performance: evidence from the S&P 500', *Journal of Finance*, Vol. 58, No. 3: 1301–1327.

Andriof, J. and Marsden, C. (1999) 'Corporate citizenship: what is it and how to assess it?', *Personalführung*, Vol. 8: 34–41.

—— and McIntosh, M. (eds) (2001) *Perspectives on Corporate Citizenship*, Sheffield: Greenleaf Publishing.

——, Waddock, S., Husted, B. and Sutherland Rahman, S. (2003) *Unfolding Stakeholder Thinking 1: theory, responsibility and engagement*, Sheffield: Greenleaf Publishing.

BIBLIOGRAPHY

Anheier, H. and Katz, H. (2003) 'Mapping global civil society', in: M.Kaldor, H. Anheier and M. Glasius (eds), *Global Civil Society 2003*, London: London School of Economics, pp. 241–258.

——, Glasius, M. and Kaldor, M. (2001) *Global Civil Society Yearbook*, London: London School of Economics.

Ansoff, H.I. (1975) 'Managing strategic surprise by response to weak signals', *California Management Review*, Vol. 18, No. 2: 21–23.

—— (1980) 'Strategic issue management', *Strategic Management Journal*, Vol. 1: 131–148.

Appeldoorn, F. (2004) *Prospects of Change in the Corporate Governance Landscape*, MA Thesis, Erasmus University Rotterdam.

Appelman, M., Gorter, J., Lijesen, M., Onderstal, S. and Venniker, R. (2003) 'Equal rules or equal opportunities? Demystifying level playing field', Central Planning Bureau Document, No. 34, The Hague.

Arbix, G. and Zilbovicius, M. (1999) 'Local adjustment to globalization: a comparative study of foreign investment in two regions of Brazil, Greater ABC and greater Porto Alegre', SEED.

Atkinson, G. (1999) 'Developing global institutions: lessons to be learned from regional integration experiences', *Journal of Economic Issues*, June 1999.

Backer, L. (2001) 'The mediated transparent society', *Corporate Reputation Review*, Vol. 4, No. 3: 235–251.

Baghwati, J. (2004) *In Defense of Globalization*, Oxford: Oxford University Press.

Bailes, A. and Frommelt, I. (2004) *Business and Security: public private sector relationships in a new security environment*, Stockholm International Peace Research Institute.

Barber, B.R. (1995) *Jihad versus McWorld. How globalism and tribalism are reshaping the world*, New York: Times Books.

Barich, H. and Kotler, P. (1991) 'A framework for marketing image management', *Sloan Management Review*, Vol. 32: 94–104.

Barney, J. (1986) 'Strategic factor markets: expectations, luck and business strategy', *Management Science*, Vol. 32, No. 10: 99–120.

—— (1991) 'Firm resources and sustained competitive advantage', *Journal of Management*, Vol. 17: 99–120.

Baron, D. (2002) *Business and its Environment*, 4th edn (International Edition), Upper Saddle River, NJ: Pearson Education.

Barro, R. (1999) 'Inequality, growth and investment', NBER Working Paper 7038.

Bartlett, C. and Ghoshal, S. (1989) *Managing Across Borders: the transnational solution*, London: Century Business.

—— and —— (1997) *The Individualised Corporation*, London: Random House.

——, —— and Birkinshaw, J. (2003) *Transnational Management. Text, cases, and readings in Cross-Border Management*, 4th edn, New York: McGraw Hill.

Basu, K. (2001) 'On the goals of development', in: G.M. Meier and J.E. Stiglitz (eds), *Frontiers of Development Economics. The Future in Perspective*, Washington/New York: World Bank/OUP, pp. 61–86.

Beatty, R.P. and Ritter, J.R. (1986) 'Investment banking, reputation and the underpricing of initial public offerings', *Journal of Financial Economics*, Vol. 15, No. 1: 213–232.

Bebchuk, L. and Fried, J. (2004) *Pay without Performance. The unfulfilled promise of executive compensation*, Cambridge, MA: Harvard University Press.

Bennis, W. (1989) *On Becoming a Leader*, Reading, MA: Addison-Wesley.

Bergsten, F. (1997) 'Open regionalism', Working Paper 97–3, *Institute for International Economics*.

Berman, D., Binet, L., Bonnevie, L., Hakokongas, L., Meybaum, J., Moon, S., Smith, D. and Warpinski, A. (2001) *Recherche Médicale en Panne pour les Maladies des Plus Pauvres*, October, Médecins Sans Frontières.

Berman, E. (2004) 'Hams, Taliban and the Jewish underground: an economist's view of radical religious militia', NBER Working paper 10004; available online: http://www.nber.org/papers/1004

Beugelsdijk, S. and van Schaik, A. (2001) 'Social capital and regional economic growth', CentEr Discussion Paper, 102.

Blumentritt, T. (2003) 'Foreign subsidiaries' government affairs activities. The influence of managers and resources', *Business & Society*, Vol. 42, No. 2: 202–233.

Borensztein, E., De Gregorio, J. and Lee, J.-W. (1998) 'How does FDI affect economic growth', *Journal of International Economics*, Vol. 45: 115–135.

Boulding, K.E. (1981) *A Preface to Grants Economics*, New York: Praeger.

Bourguignon, F. and Morrisson, C. (1999) 'The size distribution of income among world citizens: 1820–1990', World Bank, mimeo.

Bowie, N.E. and Vaaler, P. (1999) 'Some arguments for universal moral standards', in: G. Enderle (ed.), *International Business Ethics. Challenges and approaches*. Notre Dame and London: University of Notre Dame Press, pp. 160–173.

Boyer, R. and Saillard, Y. (eds) (2002) *Regulation Theory: the state of the art*, London and New York: Routledge.

Braithwaite, J. and Drahos, P. (2000) *Global Business Regulation*, Cambridge: Cambridge University Press.

Bray, J. (2004) 'International business attitudes towards corruption', in: Transparency International, *Global Corruption Report 2004*, London: TI, pp. 316–318.

Bromley, D.B. (1993) *Reputation, Image and Impression Management*, Chichester: John Wiley & Sons.

Brooks, I., Weatherston, J. and Wilkinson, G. (2004) *The International Business Environment*, New York: Financial Times/Prentice Hall.

Brouthers, K. and Brouthers, L. (2000) 'Acquisition or greenfield start-up? Institutional, cultural and transaction cost influences', *Strategic Management Journal*, Vol. 21, No. 1: 89–97.

Brown, J.K. (1979) 'This business of Issues: coping with the company's environments', Conference Board, New York.

Brown, T.J. and Dacin, P.A. (1997) 'The company and the product: corporate associations and consumer product responses', *Journal of Marketing*, Vol. 61, No. 1: 68–84.

Brundtland, G.H. (1987) *Our Common Future*, Oxford: Oxford University Press.

Buckley, P. and Casson, M. (1991) *The Future of the Multinational Enterprise*, Basingstoke/London: MacMillan.

Buller, P.F. and McEvoy, G.M. (1999) 'Creating and sustaining ethical capability in the multi-national corporation', *Journal of World Business*, Vol. 34: 326–343.

Business in the Environment (2001) 'Investing in the future', Research report, 24 May 2001.

Cadbury, Sir A. (1992) 'Report of the Committee of the financial aspects of corporate governance', London: The Committee and Gee.

Cairncross, F. (1997, 2000) *The Death of Distance: how the communications revolution will change our lives*, London: Orion Business Books (completely updated in 2000 and published by Harvard Business School Press).

Cameron, D. (1978) 'The expansion of the public economy: a comparative analysis', *American Political Science Review*, LXXII (4): 1243–1261.

Capon, C. (2004) *Understanding Organisational Context; inside & outside organisations*, New York: Financial Times/Prentice Hall.

Caporaso, J. and Levine, D. (1992) *Theories of Political Economy*, Cambridge: Cambridge University Press.

Carillo, J., Lung, Y. and van Tulder, R. (eds) (2004) *Cars, Carriers of Regionalism*, London: Palgrave-MacMillan.

Carkovic, M. and Levine, R. (2000) 'Does FDI accelerate economic growth?', University of Minnesota, Working Paper.

Carley, M. (2002) 'Industrial relations in the EU, Japan and USA, 2001', *European Industrial Relations Observatory Online*, http://www.eiro.eurofound.eu.int.

Carr, D., Markusen, J. and Maskus, K. (1998) 'Estimating the knowledge-capital model of the multinational enterprise', *NBER Working Paper Series*, no. 6773.

Carroll, A. (1979) 'A three dimensional conceptual model of corporate performance', *Academy of Management Review*, Vol. 4: 497–505.

—— (1999) 'Corporate social responsibility', *Business & Society*, Vol. 38, No. 3: 268–295.

Carter, S.M. and Deephouse, D.L. (1999) 'Tough talk and soothing speech: managing reputation for being tough and for being good', *Corporate Reputation Review*, Vol. 4, No. 2: 308–332.

—— and Dukerich, J.M. (1998) 'Responses to changes in corporate reputation', *Corporate Reputation Review*, Vol. 1, No. 3: 250–270.

Casado, F. (2000) 'Social standards: measuring and reporting corporate social performance', *Corporate Reputation Review*, Vol. 3, No. 2: 145–163.

Castells, M. (1996) *The Rise of Network Society*, 3 vols, Oxford: Blackwell.

Caves, R.E. (1980) 'Industrial organization, corporate strategy and structure', *Journal of Economic Literature*, Vol. 18: 64–92.

—— (1996) *Multinational Enterprise and Economic Analysis*, Cambridge: Cambridge University Press.

—— and Porter, M.E. (1977) 'From entry barrier to mobility barriers', *Quarterly Journal of Economics*, Vol. 91: 421–434.

Cawson, A., Morgan, K., Webber, D., Holmes, P. and Stevens, A. (1990) *Hostile Brothers: competition and closure in the European electronics industry*, Oxford: Clarendon Press.

CCCB (2004) *State of Corporate Citizenship Survey*, Boston, MA: The Center for Corporate Citizenship.

Charmes, J. (2000) 'Informal sector, poverty, and gender: a review of empirical evidence', Paper commissioned for World Development Report 2000/2001. Washington, DC: World Bank.

Chase, W.H. (1982) 'Issues management conference, a special report', *Corporate Public Issues and Their Management*, No. 7, December.

Christian Aid (2004) *Behind the Mask: the real face of corporate social responsibility*, www.christianaid.org.uk.

Clark, J. (2003) *Worlds Apart: civil society and the battle for ethical globalization*, London: Earthscan/Kumarian.

Clarkson, M.B.E. (1995) 'A stakeholder framework for analyzing and evaluating corporate social performance', *Academy of Management Review*, Vol. 20, No. 1: 92–117.

Coase, R.H. (1988) *The Firm, the Market and the Law*, Chicago, IL: The University of Chicago Press.

Cogan, D.G. (2003) *Corporate Governance and Climate Change: Making the connection*, A CERES Sustainable Governance Project Report and prepared by the Investor Responsibility Research Center.

Cohen, D. (1998) *The Wealth of the World and the Poverty of Nations*, Cambridge, MA: MIT Press.

Commission of the European Communities (2001) *Green Paper: Promoting a European framework for Corporate Social Responsibility*, Brussels: CEC, Directorate General for Employment and Social Affairs.

Connor, T. (2004) 'Time to scale up cooperation? Trade unions, NGOs, and the international anti-sweatshop movement', *Development in Practice*, Vol. 14, Nos. 1 and 2.

Conti, T. (1993) *Building Total Quality*, London: Chapman & Hall.

Contractor, F., Kundu, S. and Hsu, C.-C. (2003) 'A three-stage theory of international expansion: the link between multinationality and performance in the service sector', *Journal of International Business Studies*, Vol. 34, No. 1: 5–18.

Coriat, B., Dumoulin, J., Flori, Y.-A., Barnett, T., Souteyrand, Y. and Moatti, J.-P. (2003) 'Patents, generic drugs and the markets for antiretrovirals' in: ANRS (ed.), *Economics of Aids and Access to HIV/AIDS Care in Developing Countries, Issues and Challenges* http://www.iaen.org/papers/anrs.php (consulted on 18 October 2004).

Cox, R. (1987) *Production, Power and World Order: social forces in the making of history*, New York: Columbia University Press.

CPB (1997) *Challenging Neighbours: rethinking German and Dutch economic institutions*, Berlin/Heidelberg/New York.

Creyer, E.H. and Ross, W.T. (1997) 'The influence of firm behavior on purchase intention: do consumers really care about business ethics?', *Journal of Consumer Marketing*, Vol. 14, No. 6: 421–432.

Dankbaar, B. and van Tulder, R. (1999) *The Construction of an Open Standard. Process and implications of specifying the Manufacturing Automation Protocol (MAP)*, The Hague: Netherlands Organization for Technology Assessment.

Davids, M. (1990) 'The champion of corporate social responsibility', *Business and Society Review*, Vol. 74: 40–43.

Davidson, B. (1993) *Black Man's Burden: Africa and the curse of the nation-state*, New York: Three Rivers Press.

Davis, K. (1973) 'The case for and against business assumptions of social responsibilities', *Academy of Management Review*, Vol. 20, No. 1: 92–117.

Daviss, B. (1999) 'Profits from principles, five forces redefining business', *The Futurist*, March.

Deephouse, D.L. (2000) 'Media reputation as a strategic resource: an integration of mass communication and resource-based theories', *Journal of Management*, Vol. 26, No. 6: 1091–1112.

de Grauwe, P. and Camerman, F. (2003) 'Are multinationals really bigger than nations?', *World Economics*, Vol. 4, No. 2: 23–37.

Dehn, G. and Calland, R. (eds) (2004) *Whistleblowing Around the World: law, culture and practice*, Tokai: Blue Weaver Marketing.

Delios, A. and Henisz, W. (2003) 'Policy uncertainty and the sequence of entry by Japanese firms, 1980–1998', *Journal of International Business Studies*, Vol. 34: 227–241.

Demoustier, D. (2001) *L'économie Sociale et Solidaire s'associer pour Entreprendre Autrement*, Coll. Alternatives Economiques, Paris: Édition La Découverte.

Dent, C. (1997) *The New European Economy*, London: Routledge.

Derber, C. (1998) *Corporation Nation. How corporations are taking over our lives and what we can do about it*, New York: St Martin's Griffin.

De Soto, H. (2000) *The Mystery of Capital. Why capitalism triumphs in the West and fails everywhere else*, New York: Basic Books.

De Wit, B. and Meyer, R. (2003) *Strategy. Process, content, context. An international perspective*, 3rd edition, London: Thomson Business Press.

DHV (2002) 'Alles van waarde wordt uit conflict geboren', Press report by DHV, research in cooperation with Rotterdam School of Management, June.

Dicken, P. (2003) *Global Shift: reshaping the global economic map in the 21st century*, 4th edn, London: Sage Publications; New York: Guilford Press.

DiMaggio, P. and Powell, W.W. (1983) 'The iron cage revisited: institutional isomorphism and collective rationality in organizational fields', *American Sociological Review*, Vol. 48: 147–160.

Disdier, A.-C. and Head, K. (2004) 'The puzzling persistence of the distance effect on bilateral trade', *Centro Studi Luca D'Agliano*, Development Studies Working Papers, No. 186, October.

Doh, J. and Teegen, H. (eds) (2003) *Globalization and NGOs. Transforming business, government, and society*, Westport, CT: Praeger.

—— and Guay, T. (2004) 'NGOs and international corporate responsibility: how nongovernmental organizations influence international labor and environmental standards', in: Hooker, J. and Madsen, P. (eds), *International Corporate Responsibility: exploring the issues*, International Management Series: Vol. 3, Pittsburg, KS: Carnegie Mellon University Press.

Donaldson, T. (1989) *The Ethics of International Business*, The Ruffin Series in Business Ethics, New York/Oxford: Oxford University Press.

—— (1996) 'Values in tension: ethics away from home', *Harvard Business Review*, September/October.

—— and Dunfee, T. (1999) *Ties that Bind: a social contract approach to business ethics*, Boston, MA: Harvard Business School Press.

Dowling, G.R. (2001) *Creating Corporate Reputation*, New York: Oxford University Press.

——, Hart, S. and Young, B. (2000) 'Do corporate global environmental standards create or destroy market value?', *Management Science*, Vol. 46 No. 8: 1059–1074.

Drucker, P. (1994) *Post-capitalist Society*, New York: Harper Business.

—— (1999) *Management Challenges for the 21st Century*, Oxford: Butterworth Heinemann.

Dunning, J. (1993) *Multinational Enterprises and the Global Economy*, Wokingham: Addison-Wesley.

—— (2001) *Global Capitalism at Bay?*, London: Routledge.

—— (ed.) (2003) *Making Globalization Good*, Oxford: Oxford University Press.

Dutton, J.E., Dukerich, J.M. and Harquail, C.V. (1994) 'Organizational images and member identification', *Administrative Science Quarterly*, Vol. 39: 239–263.

405

Easson, A. (2001) 'Tax incentives for foreign direct investment part I: recent trends and countertrends', *Bulletin for International Fiscal Documentation*, July.

Easterly, W. (2002) *The Elusive Quest for Growth; economists' adventures and misadventures in the tropics*. Cambridge, MA: The MIT press Documentation.

Edelman, M. (1964) *The Symbolic Uses of Politics*, Urbana, IL: University of Illinois Press.

Edelman, R. (2002) 'Rebuilding public trust through accountability and responsibility', Ethical Corporation conference, New York.

Eden, L. and Rodriguez, P. (2004) 'How weak are the signals? International price indices and multinational enterprises', *Journal of International Business Studies*, Vol. 35: 61–74.

—— and Yu, T. (2001) 'What do you have to declare? Transfer price manipulation in US merchandise imports', Paper presented *at Academy of International Business Annual Meeting*, Sydney, Australia, November 16–20.

Edwards, M. and John Gaventa (eds) (2001) *Global Citizen Action*, Boulder, CO: Lynne Riener.

Eigen, P. (2003) *Das Netz der Korruption* (The Network of Corruption), Frankfurt: Campus Verlag.

EIM (2001) *Family Business in the Dutch SME sector*, research by EIM by H.E. Hulshoff and H.W. Stigter, 6 March 2001.

EIRO (2002) online at www.eiro.eurofound.eu.int

Elkington, J. (1999) *Cannibals with Forks, the Triple Bottom Line of the 21st Century Business*, Oxford: Capstone Publishing.

—— and Fennell, S. (1998) 'Shark, sealion or dolphin?' *Tomorrow*, Vol. VIII, No. 41, July–August.

——, Kuszewski, J. and Zollinger, P. (2001) 'Elephants in the Boardroom', *Tomorrow, Global Sustainable Business*, June, Vol. 11, No. 3: 78.

Ellen, P.S, Mohr, L.A. and Webb, D.J. (2000) 'Charitable programs and the retailer: do they mix?', *Journal of Retailing*, Vol. 76, No. 3: 393–406.

Enderle, G. (2000) 'Whose ethos for public goods in the global economy? An exploration in International Business ethics', *Business Ethics Quarterly*, Vol. 10: 131–144.

Ernst & Young (1999) 'Transfer pricing 1999 global survey: practices, perceptions and trends in 1919 countries for 2000 and beyond', Amsterdam.

Esping-Andersen, G. (1990) *The Three Worlds of Welfare Capitalism*, Princeton, NJ: Princeton University Press.

Esposito, J. (2004) *Islam. The straight path*, Revised third edn, Oxford: Oxford University Press.

Ethier, W. (1998) 'Regionalism in a multilateral world', *The Journal of Political Economy*, December.

Etzioni, A. (1988) *The Moral Dimension: towards a new economics*, New York: The Free Press.

EU (2001) *EU Green Paper*, publication of the EC concerning Corporate Social Responsibility (Green Paper consultation), 18 July 2001.

Ewing, R.P. (1980) 'Evaluating issues management', *Public Relations Journal*, June, Vol. 36: 14–16.

Eyestone, R. (1978) *From Social Issues to Public Policy*, New York: Wiley & Sons.

Fama, E.F. (1980) 'Agency problems and the theory of the firm', *Journal of Political Economy*, Vol. 88, No. 2: 288–307.

FAO (2001) 'The state of food insecurity in the world', Rome: FAO.

Farrell, D. (2002) 'The hidden dangers of the Informal Economy', *McKinsey Quarterly*, No. 3.

Fisher, R. and Ury, W. (1981) *Getting to YES: negotiating agreement without giving*, Boston: Houghton Mifflin.

Flanagan, W. and Whiteman, G. (2005) 'AIDS is not a business – a study in global corporate responsibility: securing access to low-cost HIV medications', Amsterdam: Proceedings second Carnegie Bosch Institute conference on International Corporate Responsibility.

Fombrun, C. (1996) *Reputation: realizing value from the corporate image*, Boston, MA: Harvard Business School Press.

—— and Gardberg, N. (2000) 'Who's tops in corporate reputation', *Corporate Reputation Review*, Vol. 3, No. 1: 13–17.

—— and Rindova, V. (2000) 'The road to transparency: reputation management at Royal Dutch/Shell', in: M. Schultz, M.J. Hatch and M.H. Larsen (eds), *The Expressive Organization*, Oxford: Oxford University Press, pp. 77–96.

—— and Shanley, M. (1990) 'What's in the name. Reputation building and corporate strategy', *Academy of Management Journal*, Vol. 33, No. 2: 233–258.

—— and van Riel, C. (1997) 'The reputational landscape', *Corporate Reputation Review*, Vol. 1, No. 1: 5–13.

—— and —— (2004) *Fame and Fortune. How successful companies build winning reputations*, New York: *Financial Times*/Prentice Hall.

——, Naomi, A. and Sever, J.M. (2000) 'The reputation quotient: a multi-stakeholder measure of corporate reputation', *The Journal of Brand Management*, Vol. 7, No. 4: 241–255.

Food and Agricultural Organisation (2003) *The State of Food Insecurity in the World*, Rome: FAO.

Fortanier, F. (2004) 'The impact of Foreign Direct Investment on sustainable development: reviewing the evidence', in: J. Cramer *et al.* (eds), *Investing in Developing Countries. The future role of FDI*, The Hague: Stichting Maatschappij en Onderneming (SMO), pp. 23–35.

—— and van Tulder, R. (2006, forthcoming) *Networking for Development*, London & New York: Routledge.

——, Muller, A. and van Tulder, R. (2005) 'Internationalisation and performance: exploring the role of organizational structure', Paper presented at the *Academy of Management Annual Meeting 2005*, 5–10 August, Honolulu, Hawaii, US.

Fox, T., Ward, H. and Howard, B. (2002) *Public Sector Roles in Strengthening Corporate Social Responsibility: a baseline study*, Washington, DC: The World Bank.

Frank, R. (2003) *What Price the Moral High Ground? Ethical dilemmas in competitive environments*, Princeton, NJ: Princeton University Press.

Frederick, W.C., Post, J.E. and Davis, K. (1992) *Business and Society: corporate strategy, public policy and ethics*, New York: McGraw-Hill.

Freedom House (2003) *The World's Most Repressive Regimes 2003*, Washington, DC: Freedom House.

Freeman, C. (1992) *The Economics of Hope: essays on technical change, economic growth and the environment*, New York: Pinter Publishers.

Freeman, R.E. (1984) *Strategic Management: a stakeholder approach*, Boston, MA: Pitman Press.

—— and Gilbert, D.R. Jr (1987) 'Managing stakeholder relationships', in: S.P. Sethi and C.M. Falbe (eds), *Business and Society: dimensions of conflict and cooperation*, Lexington, KY: D.C. Heath, pp. 397–422.

Frentrop, P. (2002) 'Ondernemingen en hun aandeelhouders sinds de VOC, Corporate Governance 1602–2002', Prometheus: Amsterdam.

Frey, B. (2003) 'Publishing as prostitution. Choosing between one's own ideas and academic failure', *Working Paper Series*, No. 117, Zurich: Institutute for Empirical Research in Economics.

Friedman, M. (1962) *Capitalism and Freedom*, Chicago, IL: University of Chicago Press.

Frooman, J. (1999) 'Stakeholder influence strategies', *Academy of Management Review*, Vol. 24, No. 2: 191–205.

Fukuyama, F. (1992) *The End of History and the Last Man*, New York: The Free Press.

—— (2002) *Our Posthuman Future: consequences of the biotechnology revolution*, New York: Farrar, Straus, and Giroux.

Gafoor, A. (1995) *Interest-free Commercial Banking*, Groningen: Apptec Publications.

Garbett, T.F. (1988) *How to Build a Corporation's Identity and Project its Image*, Massachusetts: Lexington.

Garten, J.E. (2002) *The Politics of Fortune, a New Agenda for Business Leaders*, Boston, MA: Harvard Business School Publishing.

Gerber, J. (2005) *International Economics*, 3rd edition, New York: Pearson Addison Wesley.

Getz, K. (2004) 'The social responsibilities of business in weakened civil societies', in: Hooker, J. and Madsen, P. (eds), *International Corporate Responsibility: exploring the issues*, International Management Series: Volume 3, Pittsburg: Carnegie Mellon University Press, pp. 17–43.

Geus, A. de (1997) *The Living Company: habits for survival in a turbulent environment*, London: Nicholas Brealey.

Ghauri, P. and Usunier, J. (2003) *International Business Negotiations*, 2nd edition, Oxford: Pergamon.

Ghemawat, P. (2003) 'Semiglobalization and International Business Strategy', *Journal of International Business Studies*, Vol. 34, No. 2: 138–152.

Giddens, A. (1995) *The Consequences of Modernity*, Oxford: Polity Press.

Gilpin, R. (2002) *The Challenge of Global Capitalism: the world economy in the 21st century*, Princeton, NJ: Princeton University Press.

Gladwin, T.N. and Walter, I. (1980) *Multinationals Under Fire. Lessons in the management of conflict*, New York: John Wiley & Sons.

Gleckman, H. and Krut, R. (1997) 'Neither International nor Standard. The limits of ISO 14001 as an instrument of global corporate environmental management', in: C. Sheldon (ed.) *ISO 14001 and Beyond, Environmental Management Systems in the Real World*, Sheffield: Greenleaf Publishing.

Globerman, S. and Shapiro, D. (2003) 'Governance infrastructure and US foreign direct investment', *Journal of International Business Studies*, Vol. 34, No. 1: 19–39.

Glyn, A. and Miliband, D. (eds) (1994) *Paying for Inequality. The economic cost of social injustice*, London: IPPR/Rivers Oram Press.

Gomes-Casseres, B. (1990) 'Firm ownership preferences and host government restrictions: an integrated approach', *Journal of International Business Studies*, Vol. 21, No. 1: 1–22.

Gómez-Meija, L. and Palich, L. (1997) 'Cultural diversity and the performance of multinational firms', *Journal of International Business Studies*, second quarter: 309–335.

Googins, B. and Rochlin, S. (2000) 'Creating the partnership society: understanding the rhetoric and reality of cross-sectoral partnerships', *Business and Society Review*, Vol. 105, No. 1: 127–144.

Graus, W., Voogd, M. and Langeraar, J.-W. (2004) *Ranking Power*, Report Commissioned by the European office of the WWF for its 'powerswitch campaign'.

Gray, J. (1998) *False Dawn: the delusions of global capitalism*, New York: The New Press.

Gray, R. (2001) 'Thirty years of social accounting, reporting and auditing: what (if anything) have we learnt?' *Business Ethics: A European Review*, Vol. 10, No. 1: 9–15.

Gregory, J.R. (1991) *Marketing Corporate Image: the company as your #1 product*, Lincolnwood, IL: NTC Business Books.

GRI (2002) *Sustainable Reporting Guidelines 2002*, 3rd revised version, Global Reporting Initiative, Boston/Amsterdam.

Gropp, R. and Kostial, K. (2000) 'The disappearing tax base: is foreign direct investment eroding corporate income taxes?', *Working Paper Series*, No. 31, European Central Bank.

Grunig, J.E. (ed.) (1992) *Excellence in Public Relations and Communications Management*, Hillsdale, NJ: Lawrence Erlbaum Associates.

Gutiérrez, R. and Audra, J. (2004) 'Effects of corporate social responsibility in Latin American communities: a comparison of experiences', paper for second Carnegie Bosch Institute conference on International Corporate Responsibility, Amsterdam: June 2004.

Habermas, J. (1990) *Moral Consciousness and Communicative Action*, Cambridge, MA: MIT Press.

Habib, M. and Zurawicki, L. (2002) 'Corruption and foreign direct investment', *Journal of International Business Studies*, Vol. 33, No. 2: 291–307.

Hall, R. (1992) 'The strategic analysis of intangible resources', *Strategic Management Journal*, Vol. 13: 135–144.

Haller, T., Blöchlinger, A., John, M., Marthaler, E. and Ziegler, S. (2000) *Fossile Resoursen, Erdölkonzerne und Indigene Völker*, Infostudie 12, Giessen: Focus Verlag.

Handy, C. (1989) *The Age of Unreason*, London: Business Books.

—— (1994) *The Empty Raincoat*, London: Hutchinson.

Harris, R. (2002) 'Best practice in stakeholder dialogue #1', *ECNewsdesk*, 10 April.

Harrison, P. (2004) 'Corporate social responsibility: an information strategy', paper for second Carnegie Bosch Institute conference on International Corporate Responsibility, Amsterdam: June 2004.

Hart, J. (1992) *Rival Capitalists: international competitiveness in the United States, Japan, and Western Europe*, Ithaca, NY: Cornell University Press.

Hart, S.L. and Sharma, S. (2004) 'Engaging fringe stakeholders for competitive imagination', *Academy of Management Executive*, Vol. 18, No. 1: 7–18.

Harzing, A. (2003) 'The role of culture in entry mode studies: from negligence to myopia?', *Advances in International Management*, Vol. 15: 75–127.

—— and Sorge, A. (2003) 'The relative impact of country of origin and universal contingencies on internationalization strategies and corporate control in mulitnational enterprises: worldwide and European perspectives', *Organization Studies*, Vol. 24, No. 1: 187–214.

Heath, R.L. (ed.) (2001) *The Handbook of Public Relations*, Thousand Oaks, CA: Sage Publications.

—— and Nelson, R.A. (1986) *Issues Management; corporate public policymaking in an information society*, Beverly Hills, CA: Sage Publications.

Hedström, P. (1986) 'The evolution of the bargaining society: politico-economic dependencies in Sweden', *European Sociological Review*, Vol. 2, No. 1, May.

Hemmati, M. with contributions from Dodds, F., Enayati, J. and McHarry, J. (2002) *Multi-stakeholder Processes for Governance and Sustainability. Beyond deadlock and conflict*. London: Earthscan Publications Ltd.

Hemphill, T.A. (1992) 'Self-regulating industry behavior: antitrust limitations and Trade Association Code of Conduct', *Journal of Business Ethics*, No. 11: 915–920.

Hertz, N. (2002) *The Silent Takeover, Global Capitalism and the Death of Democracy*, London: Arrow.

Heugens, P. (2001) 'Strategic issues management: implications for corporate performance', PhD thesis ERIM Rotterdam School of Management, No. 7.

Hilton, S. and Gibbons, G. (2002) *Good Business*, New York: Texere.

Hilts, P. (2003) *Protecting America's Health. The FDA, business and one hundred years of regulation*, New York: Knopf.

Hofstede, G. (1991) *Cultures and Organizations: software of the mind*, Maidenhead: McGraw-Hill.

Hooker, J. and Madsen, P. (eds) (2004) *International Corporate Responsibility: exploring the issues*, International Management Series: Volume 3, Pittsburg: Carnegie Mellon University Press.

Houlder, V. (2000) 'The Kyoto Protocol. Vital talks loom at The Hague. Energy and Utilities Review 5', *Financial Times*, 29 September.

Howard, K., Ighodoro, M., Roberts, R. and Turner, J. (1998) 'Ethical social and environmental accountability', Institute of Social and Ethical Accountability and the Chartered Institute of Management Accountants.

Hubben, J. and Christaans-Dingelhoff, I. (2002) *De Tandarts in de Tuchtrechtspraak 1994–2001*, The Hague: SDU.

Hufbauer, G., Schott, J. and Elliot, K. (1990) *Economic Sanctions Reconsidered*, 2nd edn, Washington, DC: Institute for International Economics.

Huntington, S. (1993) 'The clash of civilisations?', *Foreign Affairs*, Vol. 72, No. 3.

—— (2004) *Who Are We? The challenges to America's national identity*, New York: Simon & Schuster.

Hupe, P. and Meijs, L. (2000) *Hybrid Governance. The impact of the nonprofit sector in the Netherlands*, The Hague: Social and Cultural Planning Office, working document, No. 65.

Hupperts, P. (2004) 'Corporate social responsibility in the South: the other context', *Corporate Social Responsibility* (C005) April.

Hymer, S. (1976) *The International Operations of National Firms: a study of Direct Foreign Investment*, Cambridge, MA: MIT Press (PhD thesis from 1960) Harmondsworth: Penguin.

IMS (2002) *HIV – A Growing Market Dominated By A Few Players*. Website IMS Health. http://www.imshealth.com/ims/portal/front/articleC/0,2777,6025_40147825_19622,00.html.

Ingram, P. and Clay, K. (2000) 'The choice-within; constraints new institutionalism and implications for sociology', *Annual Review of Sociology*, August, Vol. 26: 525–546.

Intermediair (2002) *Image-research 2002, the Strongest Brands Among Employers*, translated from Dutch, VNU Business Publications.

409

International Finance Corporation (2003) *Towards Sustainable and Responsible Investment in Emerging Markets*, Washington, DC: IFC/World Bank.

International Labour Organization (ILO) (2001) *World Employment Report 2001*, Geneva: ILO.

—— (2003) *Global Employment Trends 2003*, Geneva: ILO.

—— (2004) *Global Employment Trends for Youth 2004*, Geneva: ILO.

International Metalworkers' Federation (IMF) 'Global works councils', undated internal document.

International Red Cross/Red Crescent (2000) *Annual Disaster Report*, Geneva.

Jeffcott, B. and Yanz, L. (1999) *Voluntary Codes of Conduct: do they strengthen or undermine government regulation and worker organizing?* Maquila Solidarity Network.

Johansen, L. (1979) 'The bargaining society and the inefficiency of bargaining', *Kyklos*, Vol. 32, No. 3: 497–522.

Johanson, J. and Vahlne, J.-E. (1977) 'The internationalization process of the firm', *Journal of International Business Studies*, Vol. 8, No. 1: 23–32.

Johns Hopkins Center for Civil Society Studies (1999) *Global Civil Society – dimensions of the non-profit sector*, Baltimore, MD: Johns Hopkins.

Johns Hopkins University (1997) *Global Civil Society At-a-Glance*, Washington, DC: Institute for Policy Studies.

Johnson, J. (1983) 'Issues management: what are the issues?', *Business Quarterly*, Vol. 48, No. 3: 22–31.

Jones, B.L. and Chase, W.H. (1979) 'Managing public policy issues', *Public Relations Review*, Vol. 5, No. 2: 2–23.

Jones, G. (1996) *The Evolution of International Business*, London: Routledge.

—— and Lundan, S. (2001) 'The "Commonwealth Effect" and the process of internationalisation', *The World Economy*, Vol. 24, No. 1: 99–118.

——, —— and Burke, S.B. (1997) 'Commonwealth trade and investment study'. Commissioned by the Commonwealth Secretariat and Hanson Cooke Publishing Ltd. University of Reading.

——, Jones, B.H. and Little, P. (2000) 'Reputation as reservoir: buffering against loss in times of economic crisis', *Corporate Reputation Review*, Vol. 3, No. 1: 21–29.

Jong, H.W. de (ed.) (1988) *The Structure of the European Industry*, 2nd revised edition, Dordrecht: Kluwer.

Jordan, G. (2001) *Shell, Greenpeace and the Brent Spar*, Basingstoke: Palgrave.

Juran, J. (1988) *Juran on Planning for Quality*, New York: The Free Press/Macmillan.

Kaldor, M., Anheier, H. and Glasius, M. (2003) *Global Civil Society 2003*, London: London School of Economics.

Kamp, J. (2003) *Because People Matter: towards an economy for everyone*, Paraview Special Editions.

Kaplan, R. and Norton, D. (1996) *The Balanced Scorecard*, Boston, MA: Harvard Business School Press.

Kaptein, M. (2004) 'Business codes of multinational firms: what do they say?', *Journal of Business Ethics*, Vol. 50, No. 1: 13–31.

—— and van Tulder, R. (2003) 'Toward effective stakeholder dialogue', *Business and Society Review*, Vol. 108, No. 2: 201–222.

—— and Wempe, J. (1999) *Sustainability Management: balancing and integrating economic, social and environmental responsibility*, management report, No. 51.

—— and —— (2002) *The Balanced Company, a Theory of Corporate Integrity*, New York: Oxford University Press.

Karliner, J. (1997) *The Corporate Planet. Ecology and politics in the age of globalization*, San Francisco, CA: Sierra Club Books.

Karpoff, J.M. (2002) 'Why reputation counts more than regulation', *European Business Forum*, Spring 2002, Vol. 9: 78–79.

—— and Lott, J.R. Jr (1993) 'The reputational penalty firms bear from committing criminal fraud', *Journal of Law and Economics*, Vol. 36, No. 36: 757–802.

Katzenstein, P. (ed.) (1978) *Between Power and Plenty: foreign economic policies of advanced industrial states*, Madison, WI: University of Wisconsin Press.

—— (1985) *Small States in World Markets: industrial policy in Europe*, Ithaca, NY and London: Cornell University Press.

Keillor, B. and Tomas Hult, G. (2004) 'Predictors of firm-level political behaviour in the global business environment: an investigation of specific activities employed by US firms', *International Business Review*, Vol. 13: 309–329.

Keller, K.L. (1993) 'Conceptualizing, measuring and managing customer-based brand equity', *Journal of Marketing*, Vol. 57: 1–22.

—— and Aaker, D.A. (1998) 'The impact of corporate marketing on a company's brand extensions', *Corporate Reputation Review*, Vol. 1, No. 4: 356–378.

King, A. and Lenox, M. (2000) 'Industry self-regulation without sanctions: the chemical industry's Responsible Care program', *Academy of Management Journal*, Vol. 43, No. 4: 698–716.

Klein, N. (2000) *No Logo*, London: Flamingo.

Kobeissi, N. (2004) 'Foreign investment in the MENA region: analyzing non traditional determinants', paper presented for Carnegie Bosch Institute Second Conference on *International Corporate Responsibility*, June: University of Amsterdam.

Kogut, B. and Singh, H. (1988) 'The effect of national culture on the choice of entry mode', *Journal of International Business Studies*, Vol. 19, No. 3: 411–432.

—— and Zander, U. (1993) 'Knowledge of the firm and the evolutionary theory of the multinational corporation', *Journal of International Business Studies*, fourth quarter: 625–645.

Kolk, A. (2000) *Economics of Environmental Management*, Harlow: *Financial Times*.

—— (2003) 'Trends in sustainability reporting in the Fortune Global 250', *Business Strategy and the Environment*, Vol. 12, No. 5: 279–291.

—— (2005a) 'Environmental reporting by multinationals from the Triad: convergence or divergence?' *Management International Review*, Vol. 45, No. 1: 145–166.

—— (2005b) 'More than words. An analysis of sustainability reports', *New Academy Review*, Vol. 3, No. 3: 59–75.

—— and Levy, D. (2001) 'Winds of change: corporate strategy, climate change and oil multinationals', *European Management Journal*, Vol. 5: 501–509.

—— and —— (2004) 'Multinationals, environment and global competition; research in global strategic management', in: S. Lundan (ed.) *Research in Global Strategic Management, Volume 9*, Elsevier, pp. 171–193.

—— and Pinske, J. (2004) 'Market strategies for climate change', *European Management Journal*, Vol. 22, No. 3: 304–314.

—— and —— (2005) 'Business responses to climate change: identifying emergent strategies', *California Management Review*, Vol. 47, No. 3: 1–15.

—— and van Tulder, R. (2002) *International Codes of Conduct. Trends, sectors, issues and effectiveness*, Rotterdam/Amsterdam: SCOPE.

—— and —— (2004a) 'Internationalization and environmental reporting: the green face of the world's leading multinationals', in: S. Lundan (ed.), *Multinationals, Environment and Global Competition*, Elsevier: Research in Global Strategic Management, Volume 9: 95–117.

—— and —— (2004b) 'Ethics in International Business; multinational approaches to child labour', *Journal of World Business*, Vol. 39: 49–60.

—— and —— (2005) 'Setting new global rules? Multinationals and codes of conduct', *Transnational Corporation* (forthcoming).

——, —— and Welters, C. (1999) 'International codes of conduct and corporate social responsibility', *Transnational Corporations*, Vol. 8, No. 1: 143–180.

Korten, D. (1995) *When Corporations Rule the World*, West Hartford, CT: Kumarian Press.

——, Perlas, N. and Shiva, V. (2002) 'Global civil society: the path ahead', Global Civil Society Forum, online on: http://www.pcdf.org/civilsociety/default.htm, consulted 2 May 2005.

Kostova, T. and Zaheer, S. (1999) 'Organizational legitimacy under conditions of complexity: the case of the multinational enterprise', *Academy of Management Review*, Vol. 24, No. 1: 64–81.

Kotter, J. (1990) *A Force for Change: how leadership differs from management*, New York: The Free Press.

Kottler, P. (2000) *Marketing Management*, Englewood Cliffs, NJ: Prentice-Hall.

Kovach, J. and Rosenstiel, T. (2001) *The Elements of Journalism: what newspeople should know and the public should expect*, New York: The Crown Publishing Group.

KPMG and Universiteit of Amsterdam (2002) *KPMG International Survey of Corporate Sustainability Reporting 2002*, De Meern: KPMG.

Krasner, S. (1978) *Defending the National Interest*, Princeton, NJ: Princeton University Press.

Kreps, D.M. and Wilson, R. (1982) 'Reputation and imperfect information', *Journal of Economic Theory*, Vol. 27, No. 2: 253–279.

Kruck, C., Borchers, J. and Weingart, P. (1999) 'Climate research and climate politics in Germany: assets and hazards of consensus-based risk management', in: C. Miller and P. Edwards (eds), *Changing the Atmosphere: science and the politics of global warming*, Cambridge, MA: MIT Press.

Krugman, P. (ed.) (1986) *Strategic Trade Policy and the New International Economics*, Cambridge, MA: MIT Press.

—— (1997) *Pop Internationalism*, Cambridge, MA: MIT Press.

Kumar, R., Lamb, W. and Wokutch, R. (2002) 'The end of South African sanctions, institutional ownership, and the stock price performance of boycotted firms', *Business & Society*, Vol. 41, No. 2: 133–165.

Kydland, F. and Prescott, E. (1977) 'Rules rather than discretion: the inconsistency of optimal plans', *Journal of Political Economy*, Vol. 85, No. 3: 473–492.

Lawrence, A., Weber, A.T. and Post, J.E. (2005) *Business and Society; stakeholders, ethics, public policy*, 11th edn, New York: McGraw-Hill.

Legge, K. (1995) *Human Resource Management, Rhetorics and Realities*, London: MacMillan Business.

Lenox, M.J. and Nash, J. (2003) 'Industry self-regulation and adverse selection: a comparison across trade association programs', *Business Strategy and the Environment*, Vol. 12, No. 6: 343–356.

Levitt, T. (1983) 'The globalization of markets', *Harvard Business Review*, May/June: 92–102.

Levy, D. and Kolk, A. (2002) 'Strategic responses to global climate change: conflicting pressures on multinationals in the oil industry', *Business and Politics*, Vol. 4, No. 3: 275–300.

Lewin, A. and Volberda, H. (eds) (2003) *The Co-evolution Advantage: Mobilizing the Self-renewing Organization*, Armonk, NY: M.E. Sharpe.

Liang, G. (2004) *Does China need Competition Policy?*, Rotterdam: Erasmus University, ERIM PhD Series Research in Management, No. 47.

Liddell, H., Verschure, B. and Vrolijk, M. (2004) 'Access denied: reputation effects of limiting access to ARV drugs', research project Master Business–Society Management, RSM Erasmus University. The complete report can be downloaded at www.ib-sm.org.

Lieberman, G.F. (1983) *3,500 Good Quotes for Speakers*, New York: Doubleday.

Lilli, W. (1983) 'Perzeption, Kognition, Image', in: M. Irle and W. Bussman (eds), *Handbuch der Psychologie*, Vol. 12, No. 1.

Linder, S. and Vaillancourt Rosenau, P. (2000) 'Mapping the terrain of the public–private policy partnership', in: P. Vaillancourt Rosenau (ed.), *Public–Private Policy Partnerships*, Cambridge, MA: MIT Press, pp. 1–18.

Little, P.L. and Little, B.L. (2000) 'Do perceptions of corporate social responsibility contribute to explaining differences in corporate price-earnings ratios?', *Corporate Reputation Review*, Vol. 3, No. 2: 137–142.

Litz, R. (1996) 'A resource-based view of the socially responsible firm: stakeholder interdependence, ethical awareness, and issue responsiveness as strategic assets', *Journal of Business Ethics*, Vol. 15: 1355–1363.

Lodgson, J. and Wood, D. (2002) 'Business citizenship: from domestic to global level of analysis', *Business Ethics Quarterly*, Vol. 12, No. 2: 155–188.

—— and —— (2004) 'Implementing global business citizenship: multilevel motivations and an initial research agenda', in: Hooker, J. and Madsen, P. (eds), *International Corporate Responsibility: exploring the issues*, International Management Series: Vol. 3, Pittsburg: Carnegie Mellon University Press, pp. 423–446.

Logan, D., Roy, D. and Regelbrugge, L. (1997) *Global Corporate Citizenship – rationale and strategies*, Washington, DC: The Hitachi Foundation.

Lomborg, B. (2001) *The Skeptical Environmentalist*, Cambridge: Cambridge University Press.

Lopez, H. (2004) 'Pro-poor growth: a review of what we know (and what we don't)', *World Bank papers*, PRMPR, draft September.

Lorenzoni, G. and Baden-Fuller, C. (1995) 'Creating a strategic center to manage a web of partners, *California Management Review*, Vol. 37. No. 3: 146.

Louche, C. (2003) 'Mirror, Mirror on the wall . . .', *European Business Forum*, 15, Autumn: 52–56.

Lu, J. and Beamish, P. (2004) 'International diversification and firm performance: the S-curve hypothesis', *Academy of Management Journal*, Vol. 47, No. 4: 598–609.

Lubbers, E. (2003) *Battling Big Business, Countering Greenwash, Front Groups and Other Forms of Corporate Deception*, Monroe, ME: Common Courage Press.

Lull, J. and Hinerman, S. (eds) (1997) *Media Scandals: morality and desire in the popular marketplace*, London: Polity.

Maathuis, Onno (1999) 'Corporate branding: the value of the corporate brand to customers and managers', PhD thesis at Erasmus University Rotterdam.

McCarty, M.H. (2001) *The Nobel Laureates; how the world's greatest economic minds shaped modern thought*, New York: McGraw-Hill.

McCombs, M.E. and Shaw, D.I. (1972) 'The agenda setting function of the mass media', *Public Opinion Quarterly*, Vol. 36: 176–187.

McEwen, T. (2001) *Managing Values and Beliefs in Organisations*, New York: Financial Times/Prentice Hall.

McGuire, J.B., Sundgren, A. and Schneeweis, T. (1988) 'Corporate social responsibility and firm financial performance', *Academy of Management Journal*, Vol. 31: 854–872.

——, Dow, S. and Kamal, A. (2003) 'CEO incentives and corporate social performance', *Journal of Business Ethics*, Vol. 45, No. 4.

McKague, K. (2003) *Compendium of Ethics Codes and Instruments of Corporate Responsibility*, Canada: York University Toronto.

McKelvey, M. (2002) 'Managing co-evolutionary dynamics', *18th EGOS Colloquium*, Subtheme 11: Adaptation, Selection and long-lived organizations, 4–6 July, Barcelona.

McKendall, M., DeMarr, B. and Jones-Rikkers, C. (2002) 'Ethical compliance programs and corporate illegality: testing the assumptions of the corporate sentencing guidelines', *Journal of Business Ethics*, Vol. 37, No. 4: 367–384.

McMillan, G.S. and Joshi, M.P. (1997) 'Sustainable competitive advantage and firm performance: the role of intangible resources', *Corporate Reputation Review*, Vol. 1: 81–85.

McWilliams, A. (2001) 'Corporate social responsibility, a theory of the firm perspective', *Academy of Management Review*, Vol. 1: 117–127.

—— and Siegel, D. (2000) 'Corporate social responsibility and financial performance: correlation or misspecification?', *Strategic Management Journal*, Vol. 21: 603–609.

Mahon, J.F. and Waddock, S.A. (1992) 'Strategic issues management: an integration of issue life cycle perspectives', *Business & Society*, Vol. 31: 19–32.

Maignan, I. and Ralston, D. (2002) 'Corporate social responsibility in Europe and the U.S.: insights from business' self representations', *Journal of International Business Studies*, Vol. 33, No. 3: 497–514.

Malanczuk, P. (1997) *Akehurst's Modern Introduction to International Law*, 7th revised edn, London and New York: Routledge.

Margolis, J. and Walsh, J. (2001) *People and Profits? The search for a link between a company's social and financial performance*, Mahwah, NJ: Lawrence Erlbaum Associates.

Matten, D. and Crane, A. (2005) 'Corporate citizenship: toward an extended theoretical conceptualization', *Academy of Management Review*, Vol. 30, No. 1: 166–179.

Mauser, A. (2001) *The Greening of Business*, Delft: Eburon.

Meadows, D., Randers, J. and Meadows, D. (2004) *Limits to Growth: the 30-year update*, Chelsea: Green Publishing.

——, Meadows, D.L., Randers, J. and Behrens, W. III (1972) *The Limits to Growth: a report for the Club of Rome's project on the predicament of mankind*, New York: Potomac Associates.

Megginson, W. and Netter, J. (2001) 'From state to market: a survey of empirical studies on privatization', *Journal of Economic Literature*, XXXIX (June): 321–389.

Meier, G. and Stiglitz, J. (eds) (2001) *Frontiers of Development Economics*, Washington, DC: World Bank and Oxford University Press.

Meijs, L. and Bridges Karr, L. (2004) 'Managing volunteers in different settings: membership and programme management', in: R. A. Stebbins and M. Grahem (eds), *Volunteering as Leisure/Leisure as Volunteering*, Oxford: CABI, pp. 177–193.

—— and van der Voort, J. (2004) 'Corporate volunteering: from charity to profit–non profit partnerships', *Australian Journal on Volunteering*, Vol. 9, No. 1: 21–31.

Metcalfe, L. and Metcalfe, D. (2002) 'Tools for good governance: an assessment of multiparty negotiation analysis', mimeo.

Meyer, K. (2004) 'Perspective on multinational enterprises in emerging economies', *Journal of International Business Studies*, Vol. 35: 259–276.

Meznar, M.B. and Nigh, D. (1995) 'Buffer or Bridge? Environmental and organizational determinants of public affairs in American firms', *Academy of Management Journal*, Vol. 38, No. 4: 975–996.

Michael, B. (2004) 'Strategic options for multi-national corporate programmes in international corporate social responsibility', paper presented at Carnegie Bosch Institute *Second Conference on International Corporate Responsibility*, June: University of Amsterdam.

Micklethwait, J. and Wooldridge, A. (2003) *A Short History of a Revolutionary Idea*, Weidenfeld & Nicholson.

Milgrom, P. and Roberts, J. (1982) 'Predation, reputation and entry deterrence', *Journal of Economic Theory*, Vol. 27, No. 2: 280–312.

Mintzberg, H. (1973) *The Nature of Managerial Work*, New York: Harper & Row.

—— (2001) *Getting Past Smith and Marx: Toward a Balanced Society*, electronic pamphlet.

Mitchel, L.E. (2001) *Corporate Irresponsibility, America's Newest Export*, New Haven, CT: Yale University Press.

Mitchell, R.K., Agle, B.R. and Wood, D. (1997) 'Toward a theory of stakeholder identification and salience', *Academy of Management Review*, Vol. 22: 853–886.

Mitnick, B.M. (1995) 'Systematics and CSR: the theory and processes of normative referencing', *Business & Society*, Vol. 34, No. 1: 5–33.

Mitroff, I. and Anagnos, G. (2001) *Managing Crises before They Happen*, New York: Amacom.

Mol, M. (2001) *Outsourcing, Supplier-Relations and Internationalisation: global source strategy as a Chinese puzzle*, ERIM PhD Series in Management, No. 10.

—— and van Tulder, R. (2002) 'Solution in search of a problem: global sourcing', *European Business Forum*, Issue 9, Spring: 56–60.

Monks, R. and Minow, N. (2001) *Corporate Governance*, 2nd edn, Oxford: Blackwell Publishers.

Moore, R.H. (1979) 'Research by Conference Board sheds light on problems of semantics, issue identification and classification', *Public Relations Journal*, Vol. 35, November: 43–46.

Moran, T. (ed.) (1998) *Managing International Political Risk*, Malden, MA: Blackwell.

Morisset, J. and Prinia, N. (2001) 'How tax policy and incentives affect foreign direct investment' in Foriegn Investment Advisory Service, *Using Tax Incentives to Compete for Foreign Investment: are they worth the costs?*, FIAS Occasional Paper 15.

Morrison, J. (2002) *The International Business Environment. Diversity and the global economy*, Basingstoke: Palgrave Macmillan.

Moss Kanter, R. (1985) *The Change Masters*, Simon & Schuster.

Mulder, A. (2004) *Government Dilemmas in the Private Provision of Public Goods*, ERIM PhD Series in Management, No. 45.

—— and van Tulder, R. (2004) 'Public–private partnership: beneficial to whom?', *European Business Forum*, Issue 18, Summer: 24–26.

Muldoon, J. (2003) *The Architecture of Global Governances: an introduction to the study of international organizations*, Boulder, CO: Westview Press.

Muller, A. (2004) *The Rise of Regionalism. Core company strategies under the second wave of integration*, ERIM PhD Series in Management, No. 38.

——, Frans, D. and van Tulder, R. (2004) *The Development Squeeze: income loss to Less Developed Countries (LDCs) as a result of tax incentives and transfer price manipulation*, Report to the Dutch Ministry of Development Cooperation, The Hague.

Murphy and Matthews (2001) 'Nike and global labour practices', case study prepared for the New Academy of Business, Business Innovation Network for Social Responsible Business. Bristol: New Academy of Business.

Mytelka, L. (2000) 'Location tournaments for FDI: inward investment into Europe in a global world', in: N. Hood and S. Young (eds), *The Globalization of Multinational Enterprise Activity and Economic Development*, London: MacMillan Press Ltd, pp. 278–294.

Nelson, R. (1996) *The Sources of Economic Growth*, Cambridge, MA: Harvard University Press.

Nestle, M. (2002) *Food Politics: how the food industry influences nutrition and health*, Berkeley, CA: University of California Press.

Nike (2001, 2004) (Corporate) Social Responsibility Reports.

North, D (1991) 'Institutions', *Journal of Economic Perspectives*, Vol. 5: 97–112.

Nye, J. (2002) *The Paradox of American Power: why the world's only superpower can't go it alone*, New York: Oxford University Press.

OECD (1997) *Eco-labelling: actual effects of selected programmes*, OECD/GD (97) 105.

—— (1998) *Principles of Corporate Governance*, Paris: OECD.

—— (1999) *Building Public Trust: Ethics measures in OECD countries*, Public Management Policy Brief, Paris: OECD.

—— (2001) *The Well-being of Nations; the role of human and social capital*, Paris: OECD.

—— (2002) *Recent privatisation trends in OECD countries*, Paris: OECD.

—— (2004) *OECD Guidelines for Multinational Enterprises: specific instances considered by national contact points to date*, Paris: OECD.

—— (2005) *Going for Growth: economic policy reforms in OECD countries*, Paris: OECD.

O'Grady, S. and Lane, H. (1996) 'The psychic distance paradox', *Journal of International Business Studies*, second quarter: 309–333.

O'Higgens, E. (2002) 'Crisis management: be prepared', *European Business Forum*, Vol. 9, Spring: 75–77.

Olson, M. (1971) *The Logic of Collective Action: public goods and the theory of groups*, Cambridge, MA: Harvard University Press.

Oman, C.P. (2000) 'Policy competition for foreign direct investment', OECD Development Centre.

Orlitzky, M., Schmidt, F. and Rynes, S. (2003) 'Corporate social responsibility and financial performance: a meta analysis', *Organization Studies*, Vol. 24, No. 3: 403–441.

Osborne, S. (ed.) (2000), *Public–Private Partnerships: theory and practice in international perspective*, London: Routledge, pp. 293–310.

O'Sullivan, M. (2001) *Corporate Governance, Innovation, and Economic Performance in the EU*, synthesis report, Fontainebleau: INSEAD.

Otten, R., Bauer, R. and Koedijk, K. (2002) 'International evidence on ethical mutual fund performance and investment style', LIFE Working Paper, No. 02.59.

Oxelheim, L. and Ghauri, P. (eds) (2004) *European Union and the Race for Foreign Direct Investment in Europe*, Oxford: Pergamon.

Oxfam (2000) *Tax Havens*, Oxfam Policy Paper – 6/00.

—— (2004) *The Rural Poverty Trap: Why agricultural trade rules need to change and what UNCTAD XI could do about it*, Oxfam Briefing Paper, No. 59.

Padmanabhan, P. and Cho, K. (1999) 'Decision-specific experience in foreign ownership and establishment strategies: evidence from Japanese firms', *Journal of International Business Studies*, Vol. 30, No. 1: 15–44.

Park, J. (2004) 'Socially responsible investing: steering the global financial market toward a new ethical architecture?', paper for second Carnegie Bosch Institute conference on International Corporate Responsibility, Amsterdam: June 2004.

415

Patterson, B. (1993) 'Crisis impact on reputation management?', *Public Relations Journal*, Vol. 49, No. 11: 46–47.

Pearce, J. and Robinson, R. (2000) 'Cultivating Guanxi as a foreign investor strategy', *Business Horizons*, Vol. 43, No. 1: 31–44.

Pearson, C.H. and Clair, J.A. (1998) 'Reframing crisis management', *Academy of Management Review*, Vol. 23, No. 1: 59–76.

Peck, S.I. and Ruigrok, W. (2000) 'Hiding behind the flag? Prospects for change in German Corporate Governance', *European Management Journal*, Vol. 18, No. 4: 420–429.

Peng, Mike (2004) 'Identifying the big question in International Business research', *Journal of International Business Studies*, Vol. 35: 99–108.

Peteraf, M.A. (1993) 'The cornerstones of competitive advantage', *Strategic Management Journal*, Vol. 14: 179–191.

Petrella, R. (1999) *Le Manifeste de L'Eau. Pour un contract mondial*. Editions Labor.

Phoa, L. (2005) 'Fora for future. Business leaders shaping global visions', Rotterdam School of Management, masters thesis.

Pierik, R. and Houwerzijl, M. (2004) 'Western policies towards child labor abroad', Tilburg University, unpublished paper.

Piore, M. and Sabel, C. (1984) *The Second Industrial Divide: possibilities for prosperity*, New York: Basic Books.

Pollitt, C. (2003) *The Essential Public Manager*, Maidenhead: Open University Press.

Porter, M. (1986) 'Competition in global industries, a conceptual framework', in: M. Porter (ed.), *Competing in Global Industries*, Boston, MA: Harvard Business School Press.

—— (1990) *The Competitive Advantage of Nations*, New York: The Free Press.

—— (2003) 'CSR – a religion with too many priests', *European Business Forum*, Issue 15, Autumn.

—— and Kramer (2002) 'The competitive advantage of corporate philanthropy', *Harvard Business Review*, December.

—— and van der Linde, C. (1995) 'Green and competitive: ending the stalemate', *Harvard Business Review*, September–October: 120–134.

Post, J. (1976) *Corporate Behaviour and Social Change*, Reston, VA: Reston Publishing Co.

—— (1979) 'The corporation in the public policy process – a view toward the 1980s', *Sloan Management Review*, Vol. 21: 45–52.

—— and Berman, S. (2001) 'Global corporate citizenship in a dot.com world', in: J. Andriof and M. McIntosh, *Perspectives on Corporate Citizenship*, Sheffield: Greenleaf Publishing, pp. 66–82.

Post, J., Lawrence, A. and Weber, J. (2002) *Business and Society; Corporate Strategy, Public Policy, Ethics*, International Edition, Boston, MA: McGraw Hill.

Poulantzas, N. (1978) *L'Etat, le Pouvoir Le Socialisme*, Paris: Presses Universitaires de France.

Prahalad, C.K. (2004) *The Fortune at the Bottom of the Pyramid. Eradicating poverty through profits*, Wharton, PA: Wharton School Publishing.

—— and Doz, Y. (1987) *The Multinational Mission. Balancing local demands and global vision*, New York: The Free Press.

—— and Hart, S. (2002) 'The fortune at the bottom of the pyramid', *Harvard Business Review*, September.

Prakash, Aseem (2002) 'Responsible care: an assessment', *Business & Society*, Vol. 39, No. 2: 183–209.

Preston, L.E. and Post, J.E. (1975) *Private Management and Public Policy*, Englewood Cliffs, NJ: Prentice Hall.

Pride, W.M. and Ferrell, O.C. (1997) *Marketing: Concepts and Strategies*, Boston, MA: Houghton Mifflin.

Putnam, R. (1995) 'Bowling alone: America's declining social capital', *Journal of Democracy*, Vol. 6: 65–78.

—— (2000) *Bowling Alone: the collapse and survival of American community*, New York: Simon & Schuster.

Rajan, R. and Zingales, L. (2003) *Saving Capitalism from the Capitalists*, New York: Crown Business.

Rani Parker, A. (2003) 'Prospects for NGO collaboration with multinational enterprises', in: J. Doh and H. Teegen (eds), *Globalization and NGOs. Transforming business, government, and society*, Westport, CT: Praeger, pp. 81–105.

Reed, D. (2002) 'Employing normative stakeholder theory in developing countries. A critical theory perspective', *Business & Society*, Vol. 41, No. 2: 166–207.

Reich, Robert (1998) 'The new meaning of Corporate Social Responsibility', *California Management Review*, Vol. 40, No. 2: 8–17.

Reich, M. (2000) 'The global drugs gap', *Science*, Vol. 287: 1979–1981.

Renner, M. (2002) *The Anatomy of Resource Wars*, Washington, DC: Worldwatch Institute Paper, No. 162.

Ricart, J., Enright, M., Ghemawat, P., Hart, S. and Khana, T. (2004) 'New frontiers in international strategy', *Journal of International Business Studies*, Vol. 35: 519–534.

Ries, A. (1997) *Focus*, London: HarperCollins Business.

Rischard, J.-F. (2002) *High Noon, 20 Global Issues, 20 Years to Solve Them*, New York: Basic Books.

Ritzer, George (1993) *The McDonaldisation of Society*, Thousand Oaks, CA: Pine Forge Press.

Robbins, S.P. (2000) *Essentials of Organizational Behavior*, Englewood Cliffs, NJ: Prentice Hall.

Roberts, P.W. and Dowling, G. (1997) 'The value of a firm's corporate reputation: how reputation helps attain and sustain superior performance', *Corporate Reputation Review*, Vol. 1, No. 1: 72–76.

Roddick, A. (2000) *Business as Unusual*, London: Thorsons.

Rodrik, D. (1999) *The New Global Economy and Developing Countries: making openness work*, Washington, DC: Overseas Development Council.

Rose-Ackerman, S. (1999) *Corruption and Good Government: causes, consequences and strategies for reform*, Cambridge: Cambridge University Press.

Rotman, D. (1997) 'Global warming: chemical producers feel the heat', *Chemical Week*, Vol. 159, No. 4: 25–29.

Rowell, A. (2002) 'Dialogue: divide and rule', in: E. Lubbers (ed.), *Battling Big Business: countering greenwash, infiltration and other forms of corporate bullying*, Foxhole: Green Books, pp. 33–44.

Rowley, T.J. (1997) 'Moving beyond dyadic ties: a network theory of stakeholder influences', *Academy of Management Review*, Vol. 22, No. 4: 887–910.

—— and Berman, S. (2000) 'A brand new brand of corporate social performance', *Business & Society*, Vol. 39: 397–418.

Rugman, A.M. (2002) *The End of Globalization*, London: Random House.

—— and D'Cruz, J. (2000) *Multinationals as Flagship Firms: regional business networks*, Oxford: Oxford University Press.

—— and Hodgetts, R. (2002) *International Business*, 3rd edn, *Financial Times*/Prentice Hall.

—— and Verbeke, A. (2004) 'Perspective: a perspective on regional and global strategies of multinational enterprises', *Journal of International Business Studies*, Vol. 35: 3–18.

—— and —— (1998) 'Corporate strategies and environmental regulations: an organizing framework', *Strategic Management Journal*, Vol. 19: 363–375.

Ruigrok, W. and Wagner, H. (2003) 'Internationalization and performance: an organizational learning perspective', *Management International Review*, Vol. 43, No. 1: 63–83.

—— and van Tulder, R. (1995) *The Logic of International Restructuring*, London: Routledge.

Saiia, D., Carroll, A. and Buchholtz, A. (2003) 'Philanthropy as strategy. When corporate charity "begins at home"', *Business & Society*, Vol. 42, No. 2: 169–201.

Salomon, L., Sokolowski, W. and Anheier, H. (2000) 'Social Origins of Civil Society: An Overview', Working Papers of the Johns Hopkins Comparative Nonprofit Sector Project, December.

Sampson, A. (2004) *Who Runs This Place? The anatomy of Britain in the 21st Century*, London: John Murray.

Sassen, S. (2001) *The Global City: New York London Tokyo*, Princeton, NJ: Princeton University Press.

Savage, G., Nix, T., Whitehead, C. and Blair, J. (1991) 'Strategies for assessing and managing organizational stakeholders', *The Executive*, Vol. 5, No. 2: 61–75.

417

Saxton, K.M. (1998) 'Where do reputations come from?', *Corporate Reputation Review*, Vol. 1, No. 4: 393–399.

Schneider, F. (2002) *Global Survey on the Size and Importance of the Informal Sector*, World Bank: Rapid Reponse Unit (RRU).

Schneider, S. and Barsoux, J.-L. (1997) *Managing Across Cultures*, London: Prentice-Hall.

Schoonman, E. (1995) *Issuesmanagement*, Zaventem: Samson. Only available in Dutch.

Schultz, M., Hatch, M.J. and Holten Larsen, M. (eds) (2000) *The Expressive Organization. Linking identity, reputation and the corporate brand*, Oxford: Oxford University Press.

Schumacher, E.F. (1973) *Small is Beautiful*, London: Blond & Briggs Ltd.

Schuyt, T. (2002) 'A second Golden Era?' (Dutch article, translated), *ESB*, 21 June, pp. 496–498.

Schwartz, P. and Gibb, B. (1999) *When Good Companies Do Bad Things*, New York: Wiley & Sons.

Scott, A. (ed.) (1997) *The Limits of Globalization*, London: Routledge.

Scott, S.G. and Lane, V.R. (2000) 'A stakeholder approach to organizational identity', *Academy of Management Review*, Vol. 25, No. 1: 43–62.

Scott, W.R. (1987) *Organizational, Rational, Natural and Open Systems*, London: Prentice Hall.

Seligman, J. (2003) *The Transformation of Wall Street: a history of the Securities and Exchange Commission and modern corporate finance*, 3rd edn, New York: Aspen.

Sen, A. (1999) *Development as Freedom*, Oxford: Oxford University Press.

Sen, S. and Bhattacharya, C. (2001) 'Does doing good always lead to doing better? Consumer reactions to corporate social responsibility', *Journal of Marketing Research*, Vol. 38, No. 2: 225–243.

SER (Social Economic Council) (2000) *Advies: De Winst van Waarden*, No. 11, Den Haag. English version: see SER 2001.

SER (2001) *Corporate Social Responsibility. A Dutch approach*, Assen: Royal Van Gorcum.

Servan-Schreiber, J.-J. (1967) *Le Defi American*, Paris: Denoël.

Sethi, S.P. (1975) 'Dimensions of corporate social performance', *California Management Review*, Spring: 58–64.

—— (2002) *Setting Global Standards: guidelines for creating codes of conduct in multinational corporations*, New York: Wiley.

Shah, R., Murphy, D. and McIntosh, M. (eds) (2004) *Something to Believe In. Creating trust and hope in organisations: stories of transparency, accountability and governance*, Sheffield: Greenleaf publishing.

Shapiro, C. (1983) 'Premiums for high quality products as returns to reputations', *Quarterly Journal of Economics*, No. 98: 659–679.

Shapiro, S.P. (1987) 'Social control of impersonal trust', *American Journal of Sociology*, Vol. 93: 623–658.

Sharfman, M.P., Shaft, T.M. and Tihanyi, L. (2004) 'A model of the global and institutional antecedents of high-level corporate environmental performance', *Business & Society*, Vol. 43, No. 1: 6–36.

Shell (1997) *Statement of General Business Principles*.

—— (2001) *The Shell Report: People, planet & profits*.

Simerly, R.L. (2003) 'An empirical examination of the relationship between management and corporate social performance', *International Journal of Management*, Vol. 20, No. 3: 353.

Simmons, P.J. and de Jonge Oudraat, C. (eds) (2001) *Managing Global Issues: lessons learned*, Carnegie Endowment for International Peace, Washington, DC.

Slinger and Deakin (1999) in Shell International (2001) *A Better Way to do Business – external affairs in the 21st century: the response*, The Hague.

Sklair, L. (2001) *The Transnational Capitalist Class*, Oxford: Blackwell.

Slager, A. (2004) *Banking Across Borders*, Rotterdam: ERIM PhD Series in Management no. 41.

Slangen, A. (2005) 'Studies on the determinants of foreign entry mode choices and performance', PhD Dissertation, Tilburg University.

Smith, R. and Walter, I. (2001) *Rating Agencies: is there an agency issue?*, New York: Stern School of Business.

Snow, C.P. and Collini, S. (1993) *The Two Cultures*, Cambridge: Cambridge University Press.

Social Investment Forum (2003) *2003 Report on Socially Responsible Investing Trends in the United States*, Washington, DC: SIF.

Spar, D. and Yoffie, D. (1999) 'Multinational enterprises and the prospect for justice', *Journal of International Affairs*, Vol. 52: 557–581.

Spero, J. and Hart, J. (2003) *The Politics of International Economic Relations*, 6th edn, Wadsworth: Thomson.

Srivastava, R.K., McInish, T.H., Wood, R. and Capraro, A.J. (1997) 'The value of corporate reputation: evidence from the equity markets', *Corporate Reputation Review*, Vol. 1, No. 1: 62–68.

Stanwick, P. and Stanwick, S. (1998) 'The determinants of corporate social performance: an empirical examination', *American Business Review*, Vol. 16, No. 1: 86–93.

Statman, M. (2000) 'Social responsible mutual funds', *Financial Analysts Journal*, Vol. 56, May/June.

Steiner, G.A. and Steiner, J.F. (2000) *Business, Government and Society*, 9th edn, New York: McGrawHill.

Stiglitz, J. (1989) 'Imperfect information in the product market', in: R. Schmalensee and R. Willig, *Handbook of Industrial Organization*, Amsterdam: Noord-Holland Press, pp. 769–847.

—— (1999) 'Wither Reform? Ten years after the transition', *World Bank Annual Bank Conference on Development Economics*, Washington, DC: The World Bank.

—— and Wallsten, S. (2000) 'Public–private technology partnerships: promises and pitfalls', in: P. Vaillencourt Rosenau (ed.), *Public–Private Policy Partnerships*, Cambridge, MA: MIT Press.

Stigson, B. (2002) *WBCSD Sector Projects*, Geneva, Switzerland: WBCSD.

Stopford, J. and Strange, S. with Henley, J. (1991) *Rival States, Rival Firms: Competition for world market shares*, Cambridge: Cambridge University Press.

Sturdivant, F.D., Ginter, J.L. and Sawyer, A.G. (1985) 'Managers' conservatism and corporate performance', *Strategic Management Journal*, Vol. 6, No. 1: 17–38.

Su, C. and Littlefield, J. (2001) 'Entering Guanxi: a business ethical dilemma in mainland China', *Journal of Business Ethics*, Vol. 33: 199–210.

SustainAbility (2000) *The First International Benchmark Survey of Corporate Sustainability Reporting 2000*. www.sustreport.org/business/report/trends.html.

—— (2004) *Gearing Up: from corporate responsibility to good governance and scalable solutions*, London/New York, in consultation with The UN Global Compact Office.

—— and United Nations (2003) *The 21st Century NGO: in the market for change*, London.

Swanson, D. (1995) 'Addressing a theoretical problem by reorienting the corporate social performance model', *Academy of Management Review*, Vol. 20, No. 1: 43–64.

Swift, A. and Perry, A. (2001) *Vanishing Footprints. Nomadic people speak*, Oxford: New Internationalist Publications Ltd.

Tansey Martens, L. and Kelleher, A. (2004) 'A global perspective on whistleblowing', *International Business Ethics Review*, Vol. 7, No. 2.

Tanzi, V. (2000) 'Globalization, technological developments, and the work of fiscal termites', IMF Working Paper WP/00/181.

Tapscott, D. and Ticoll, D. (2003) *The Naked Corporation. How the age of transparency will revolutionize business*, New York: Free Press.

Teegen, H. (2003) 'Business–Government–NGO bargaining in international multilateral clean development mechanism projects in the wake of Kyoto', in: J. Doh and H. Teegen (eds), *Globalization and NGOs. Transforming business, government, and society*, Westport, CT: Praeger, pp. 107–127.

——, Doh, J. and Vachani, S. (2004) 'The importance of nongovernmental organizations (NGOs) in global governance and value creation: an International Business research agenda', *Journal of International Business Studies*, Vol. 35: 463–483.

The Economist (2004) 'Living dangerously; a survey of risk', 24 January 2004.

The Environment Council (1999) *Guidelines for Stakeholder Dialogue: a joint venture*, London: The Environment Council, p. 25.

't Hoen, E.F.M. (2003) 'TRIPS, pharmaceutical patents and access to essential medicines: Seattle, Daha and beyond' in: ANRS (ed.) *Economics of AIDS and Access to HIV/AIDS Care in Developing Countries, Issues and Challenges*, available online at www.iaen.org/papers/anrs.php, consulted 18 October 2004.

419

Thomas, A.S. and Simerly, R.L. (1994) 'The chief executive officer and corporate social performance: an interdisciplinary examination', *Journal of Business Ethics*, Vol. 13, No. 12: 959.

Tieleman, H.J., van Luijk, H.J., van Noort, W.J. and van Riemsdijk, M.J. (1996) *Conflicten tussen actiegroepen and ondernemingen*, Stichting Maatschappij and Onderneming, Hooiberg, Epe.

Tomei, M. (1998) 'Indigenous peoples and oil development: reconciling conflicting interests', ILO sectoral activities working paper, Geneva: ILO.

Topouzis, S. and van Wijk, J. (2003) 'Using weapons as ploughshares: patenting strategies and corporate ethics in anti-AIDS drug markets', unpublished working paper.

Transparency International (2004) *Global Corruption Report 2004*, London: TI.

Trompenaars, F. and Hampden-Turner, C. (1997) *Riding the Waves of Culture: understanding cultural diversity in business*, London: Nicholas Brealey Publishing.

UIA (ed.) (2001) *Yearbook of International Organizations 2000/2001: guide to global civil society networks*, Munich: Union of International Associations (http://www.uia.org/uiapubs/pubyear.htm).

UNAIDS (2003) *AIDS epidemic Update*, Geneva: Joint United Nations Programme on HIV/AIDS.

—— and WHO (2004) '2004 report on the global AIDS epidemic' available online at www.unaids.org/bangkok2004/GAR2004_pdf/UNAIDSGlobalReport2004_en.pdf, consulted 18 October 2004.

UNCTAD (1997) *World Investment Report 1997: transnational corporations, market structure and competition policy*, Geneva and New York: UNCTAD.

—— (2000a) *Model Law on Competition; draft commentaries to possible elements of a model law or laws*, New York and Geneva: United Nations.

—— (2000b) *Tax Incentives and Foreign Direct Investment: a global survey United Nations*, New York and Geneva.

—— (2000c) *World Investment Report 2000*, New York and Geneva: United Nations.

—— (2001) *World Investment Report 2001. Promoting linkages*, Geneva: UNCTAD.

—— (2002) *The Least Developed Countries Report 2002. Escaping the poverty trap*, Geneva and New York: UNCTAD.

—— (2003) *World Investment Report. FDI policies for development: national and international perspectives*, New York and Geneva: United Nations.

UNDP (1999) *World Development Report 1999*, New York.

—— (2002) *Human Development Report 2002*, New York.

Unicef (2004) *The State of the World's Children 2005*, Unicef.

Vachani, S. (1990) 'Distinguishing between related and unrelated international geographic diversification: a comprehensive measure of global diversification', *Journal of International Business Studies*, second quarter: 307–322.

Vaillencourt Rosenau, P. (ed.) (2000) *Public–Private Policy Partnerships*, Cambridge, MA: MIT Press.

van de Wateringen, S. (2005) 'The greening of black gold', PhD Thesis, University of Amsterdam.

van den Berghe, D. (2003) *Working Across Borders: multinational enterprises and the internationalisation of employment*, ERIM PhD Series in Management, No. 29.

van den Bosch, F. and van Riel, C. (1998) 'Bridging and buffering as environmental strategies of firms', *Business Strategy and Environment*, Vol. 7: 24–31.

van der Heijden, K. (1996) *Scenarios: the art of strategic conversation*, Chichester: Wiley.

van der Zwart, A. (2002) *Reputationmechanism in Motion: effective concerning CSR-related issues?*, MA thesis, Rotterdam School of Management. Available only in Dutch at www.alexvanderzwart.nl.

van Ginneken, J. (1999) *Breinbevingen, Snell Omslagen in Opinie and Communicatie*, Amsterdam: Boom.

van Lindenberg, P.-W. (2003) 'The future of the global compact', MA thesis, Rotterdam School of Management.

van Luijk, H. and Schilder, A. (1997), *Patronen van verantwoordelijkheid (Patterns of Responsibility)*, Schoonhoven: Academic Service.

van Oosterhout, H. (2005) 'Corporate citizenship; an idea whose time has not yet come', *Academy of Management Review* (forthcoming).

van Raamsdonk, R. (2004) 'Benchmarking corporate governance', MA thesis, Rotterdam School of Management.

van Riel, C. (1995) *Principles of Corporate Communication*, Harlow: Prentice Hall.

—— (1997) *Identiteit and Imago*, tweede ed., Academic Service, Schoonhoven.

—— (ed.) (2000) *Strategic Corporate Communications, selection of articles*, Alphen a/d Rijn: Samson.

—— (ed.) (2001) *Corporate Communication: Het managen van reputatie*, Dordrecht: Kluwer.

van Riemsdijk, M.J. (1994) 'Action or dialogue (Actie of dialoog. Over de betrekkingen tussen maatschappij and onderneming)', Dissertation Twente University.

Van Rijsbergen, B. (2004) 'Fighting the HIV/AIDS crisis: the corporate approach', Rotterdam School of Management: MA Thesis.

van Tulder, R. (1996) *Skill Sheets*, Amsterdam: Elsevier.

—— (ed.) (1999) *Redrawing Organizational Boundaries*, Sviib Congres, Rotterdam.

—— (2002a) 'The power of core companies', *European Business Forum*, No. 10, Summer: 9–11.

—— (2004b) 'Peripheral regionalism: the consequences of integrating Central and Eastern Europe in the European automobile space', in: J. Carillo *et al.* (eds), *Cars, Carriers of Regionalism*, London: Palgrave-MacMillan, pp. 75–91.

—— (2004c) 'The risk of go-it-alone: the Japanese car industry – from boom to bust?', in: J. Carillo *et al.* (eds) (2004) *Cars, Carriers of Regionalism*, London: Palgrave-MacMillan, pp. 205–218.

—— and Audet, D. (2004) 'The faster lane of regionalism', in: J. Carillo *et al.* (eds), *Cars, Carriers of Regionalism*, London: Palgrave-MacMillan, pp. 23–42.

—— and Junne, G. (1988) *European Multinationals and Core Technologies*, Chichester: John Wiley & Sons.

—— and Kolk, A. (2001) 'Multinationality and corporate ethics: codes of conduct in the sporting goods industry', *Journal of International Business Studies*, Vol. 32, No. 2: 267–283.

—— and van der Zwart, A. (2003) *Reputaties op het Spel. Maatschappelijk verantwoord ondernemen in een onderhandelingssamenleving* (*Reputations at stake, bargaining in a negotation society*), Utrecht: Het Spectrum.

—— and Ruigrok, W. (1997) 'The nature of institutional change: managing rival dependencies', in: Ash Amin and Jerzy Hausner (eds), *Beyond Market and Hierarchy. Interactive governance and social complexity*, Cheltenham: Edward Elgar, pp. 129–159.

——, Kaptein, M., van Mil, E. and Schilpzand, R. (2004) *Strategische Stakeholderdialoog: opkomst, succesfactoren, toekomst*, Erasmus University Rotterdam, Schuttelaar & Partners.

——, van den Berghe, D. and Muller, A. (2001) *Erasmus (S)coreboard of Core Companies*, Rotterdam School of Management.

van Wijk, J. (2002) 'Dealing with piracy. Intellectual asset management in music and software', *European Management Journal*, Vol. 20, No. 6: 689–698.

Vernon, Ray (1966) 'International investment and international trade in the product life cycle', *Quarterly Journal of Economics*, Vol. 80 (May): 190–207.

—— (1971) *Sovereignty at Bay: the international spread of U.S. enterprises*, New York: Basic Books.

—— (1977) *Storm over the Multinationals. The real issues*, Cambridge, MA: Harvard University Press.

—— (1998) *In the Hurricane's Eye. The troubled prospects of multinational enterprises*, Cambridge, MA: Harvard University Press.

Veser, M. (2004) 'The influence of culture on stakeholder management: social policy implementation in multinational corporations', *Business & Society*, Vol. 43, No. 4: 426–436.

Visser, J. (2002) 'Why fewer workers join unions in Europe: a social custom explanation of membership trends', *British Journal of Industrial Relations*, Vol. 40, No. 3: 403–430.

Vives, A. (2004) *The Role of Multilateral Development Institutions in Fostering Corporate Social Responsibility*, mimeo, Inter-American Development Bank.

Volberda, H. and Lewin, A. (2003) 'Co-evolutionary dynamics within and between firms: from evolution to co-evolution', *Journal of Management Studies*, Vol. 40, No. 8: 2111–2136.

Waddock, S. (2002) *Leading Corporate Citizens: visions, values, and value added*, New York: McGraw-Hill.

—— and Smith, N. (2000) 'Corporate responsibility audits: doing well by doing good', *Sloan Management Review*, Winter: 75–83.

421

Wadell, S. (2000) 'New institutions for the practice of corporate citizenship: historical, intersectoral, and developmental perspectives', *Business and Society Review*, Vol. 105, No. 1: 107–126.

Wall, S. and Rees, B. (2001) *Introduction to International Business*, New York: *Financial Times*/Prentice Hall.

Wallerstein, M. and Golden, M. (1997) 'The fragmentation of the bargaining society: changes in the centralization of wage-setting in the Nordic countries, 1950–1992', *Comparative Political Studies*, Vol. 30: 699–731.

Wartick, S. and Cochran, P.L. (1985) 'The evolution of the corporate social performance model', *Academy of Management Review*, Vol. 10, No. 4: 758–769.

—— and Mahon, J. (1994) 'Towards a substantive definition of the corporate issue construct: a review and synthesis of the literature', *Business & Society*, Vol. 33, No. 3: 293–311.

—— and Wood, D. (1999) *International Business and Society*, Oxford: Blackwell Publishers.

Watson, S. and Weaver, G. (2003) 'How internationalization affects corporate ethics: formal structures and informal management behavior', *Journal of International Management*, Vol. 9, No. 4: 75–93.

Weber, M. (1947) *The Theory of Social and Economic Organization*, New York: Free Press.

Weigelt, K. and Camerer, C. (1988) 'Reputation and corporate strategy: a review of recent theory and applications', *Strategic Management Journal*, Vol. 9: 443–454.

Weiss, J.W. (1998) *Business Ethics, a Stakeholders and Issues Management Approach*, Texas: Dryden Press.

Wells, L. (1998a) 'God and fair competition: does the foreign direct investor face still other risks in emerging markets?', in: T. Moran (ed.), *Managing International Political Risk*, Malden, MA: Blackwell, pp. 15–43.

—— (1998b) 'Multinationals and the developing countries', *Journal of International Business Studies*, Vol. 29, No. 1: 101–114.

Werner, K. and Weiss, H. (2002) *Black Book on Brand Companies*, English version not yet available, German version (new version) Das Neue Schwarzbuch Markenfirmen, Deuticke Verlag, 2003.

Westdijk, B. (2003) *Poor Business: the impact of multinational corporations on poverty*, MA thesis, Rotterdam School of Management.

Whawell, P. (1998) 'The ethics of pressure groups', *Business Ethics*, Vol. 7, No. 3: 178–181.

Wheeler, D. and Silanpää, M. (1997) *The Stakeholder Corporation: a blueprint for maximizing stakeholder value*, London: Pitman Publishing.

Whetten, D., Cameron, K. and Woods, M. (2000) *Developing Management Skills for Europe*, London: Prentice Hall.

Whiteman, G. and Cooper, W.H. (2000) 'Ecological embeddedness', *Academy of Management Journal*, Vol. 43, No. 6: 1265–1282.

—— and Mamen, K. (2002) 'Examining justice and conflict between mining companies and indigenous peoples: Cerro Colorado and the Ngäbe-Buglé', *Journal of Business and Management*, Vol. 8, No. 3: 293–310.

Whitley, R. (1998) 'Internationalization and varieties of capitalism: the limited effects of cross-national coordination of economic activities on the nature of business systems', *Review of International Political Economy*, Vol. 5, No. 3, 445–481.

—— (1999) *Divergent Capitalism: the social structuring and change of business systerms*, Oxford: Oxford University Press.

WHO, UNICEF, UNAIDS, MFS (2002) *Sources and Prices of Selected Drugs and Diagnostics for People Living with HIV/AIDS* – May, Geneva: WHO.

—— (2003) *Sources and Prices of Selected Drugs and Diagnostics for People Living with HIV/AIDS* – June, Geneva: WHO.

—— (2004) *Sources and Prices of Selected Drugs and Diagnostics for People Living with HIV/AIDS* – June, Geneva: WHO.

Williams, R.J. and Barrett, J.D. (2000) 'Corporate philanthropy, criminal activity and firm reputation', *Journal of Business Ethics*, Vol. 26: 341–350.

Williamson, O. (1975) *Markets and Hierarchies*, New York: The Free Press.

Wilson, E. (1975) *Sociobiology*, Cambridge, MA: Harvard University Press.

Windsor, D. (2004) 'Global corporate social responsibility: international regimes and the constellation of corruption, poverty and violence', in: J. Hooker and P. Madsen (eds), *International Corporate Responsibility: exploring the issues*, International Management Series: Volume 3, Pittsburg: Carnegie Mellon University Press, pp. 43–67.

Wood, D.J. (1991) 'Corporate social performance revisited', *Academy of Management Review*, Vol. 16, No. 4: 691–718.

—— and Jones, E. (1995) 'Stakeholder mismatch: a theoretical problem in empirical research on corporate social performance', *International Journal of Organizational analysis*, Vol. 3, No. 3: 229–267.

Wootliff, J. and Deri, C. (2001) 'NGOs: the new super brands', *Corporate Reputation Review*, Vol. 4, No. 2: 157–164.

World Bank (1997) *World Development Report 1997: the state in a changing world*, Oxford: Oxford University Press.

—— (2001) *Trade Blocks*, Oxford: Oxford University Press, The World Bank.

—— (2002a) *World Development Report 2002: building institutions for markets*, New York: Oxford University Press.

—— (2002b) *A Revised Forest Strategy for the World Bank Group*, October, Washington.

—— (2003) *Race to the Top: attracting and enabling global sustainable business*, Washington, DC: The World Bank, International Finance Corporation.

—— (2004) *Doing Business in 2004: understanding regulation*, New York: Oxford University Press.

World Business Council for Sustainable Development (2002) *Stakeholder Dialogue: The WBCSD's approach to engagement*, Switzerland.

World Commission on Forests and Sustainable Development (1999) *Our Forests, Our Future*, Cambridge: Cambridge University Press.

World Resource Institute, United Nations Environment Programme and World Business Council for Sustainable Development (2002) *Tomorrow's Markets: global trends and their implications for business*.

World Trade Organisation (2000) *Mapping of Regional Trade Agreements*, WT/REG/W/41.

Worldwatch Institute (2003) *State of the World. Special focus: the consumer society*, New York & London: W.W. Norton & Company.

Wortel, E.M. (2004) *Business Ethics in Conflict Areas. The Congo case*, The Hague: SMO publication.

Wright Mills, C. (1959) *The Sociological Imagination*, New York: Oxford University Press.

Wynfrey, F. (2004) 'The corporate form and corporate responsibility in the international context', in: J. Hooker, and P. Madsen, (eds), *International Corporate Responsibility: exploring the issues*, International Management Series: Volume 3, Pittsburg: Carnegie Mellon University Press, pp. 85–101.

Yergin, D. (1991) *The Prize. The epic quest for oil, money and power*, New York: Simon & Schuster Inc.

Yin, J., McGee, R. and Doowon, L. (2001) 'WTO trade disputes and its future development: an empirical analysis', paper submitted to Association of International Business, Sydney.

Zadek, S. (2001) *The Civil Corporation*, London: Earthscan.

—— (2003) 'In defense of non-profit accountability', *Ethical Corporation*, 19 September.

Zenisek, T.J. (1979) 'Corporate social responsibility: a conceptualization based on organizational literature', *Academy of Management Review*, Vol. 4, No. 3: 359–368.

Zwetsloot, G. (1999) *Naar een Inherent Veiligere, Gezandere en Schonere Productie*, Oration: Erasmus University Rotterdam.

Zyglidopoulos, S. and Phillips, N. (1999) 'Responding to reputational crises: a stakeholder perspective', *Corporate Reputation Review*, Vol. 2, No. 4: 333–338.

Index

Page numbers given in **bold** type indicate major coverage of organizations involved in the cases in Part III of the book.

427

431